Child Safety, Welfare and Well-being

Sibnath Deb
Editor

Child Safety, Welfare and Well-being

Issues and Challenges

Springer

Editor
Sibnath Deb
Department of Applied Psychology
Pondicherry University
Puducherry, Pondicherry
India

ISBN 978-81-322-2424-2 ISBN 978-81-322-2425-9 (eBook)
DOI 10.1007/978-81-322-2425-9

Library of Congress Control Number: 2015942752

Springer New Delhi Heidelberg New York Dordrecht London

Printed on acid-free paper

Springer (India) Pvt. Ltd. is part of Springer Science+Business Media (www.springer.com)

Foreword

Sometimes I despair when I hear influential people, such as politicians, business, or community leaders say: "Our children are our most precious resource." Why do I despair? Because very often, nothing happens. Some seem to think that by making this statement, a statement we all agree with, their responsibility to children has been met. They have uttered a socially acceptable phrase and they then move on to a new topic.

I hasten to add that there are others in positions of influence who do take children's rights seriously. I applaud such people. They are the group that says children are important and do something about it.

In 2013 I met many people of this category at a remarkable conference organized by Prof. Sibnath Deb in Pondicherry, India. It was remarkable because of the diversity of speakers and attendees, who all learned from each other.

We often tend to confine ourselves to our own areas of specialty, be it psychology, education, therapy, medicine, or sociology, to name a few. But children in need do not recognize these distinctions. Their rights cross all of these arbitrary boundaries.

This volume will broaden your interest beyond your own area. It is about child protection and the rights of children in their broadest aspects. It is about the right of children to be free from abuse, neglect and exploitation, their right to education, their right to food and shelter, their right to be loved, their right to enjoy childhood, and their right to be heard.

We have come a long way in recognizing the rights of children, but there is a long way to go. One way to make progress is to look beyond our own area of interest. There is so much more we can learn from others, not just others interested in child rights, but other organizations that have had success in reducing problems. Their insights and techniques can sometimes be usefully applied to child protection and children's rights.

One example is the patient safety movement where major improvements have been achieved by: clear communication; fixing problems in the system, rather than blaming the individual; accurate data collection; a scientific understanding of the underlying causes of error; seeing problems as opportunities to learn and improve;

listening to and respecting the views of patients and encouraging effective teamwork. Such initiatives sound simple, but they could influence those of us who are concerned about protecting children and ensuring their rights are met.

Another example is the new discoveries in science, particularly molecular genetics, that will be increasingly useful to our field: a better understanding of why the early childhood years are so important; an understanding of how our childhood experiences can influence the way our genes function, leading to specific treatments and new pharmaceuticals that can be tailored for an individual's genetic make-up.

But the accumulation of new insights and new knowledge will be of little use unless we use those insights and that knowledge to help children. So the next time someone in a position of influence or authority says "Children are our most precious resource," it is our job as child advocates to hold them accountable and to say "There is a lot that can be done," to ask "What are you going to do about it?" and more importantly, to say "How can I help?"

Kim Oates
Emeritus Professor, University of Sydney
Australia

Preface and Acknowledgments

Children are the future of a nation. And the development of children at the physical, mental, psychological, emotional, intellectual, or moral level is contingent upon the fulfillment of certain basic conditions such as adequate nutrition, medical care, quality education, a happy home, a safe environment, and the loving care or attention of elderly people. It is only then that we can expect children to blossom into good citizens and to contribute to society. In this sense, child safety, welfare, and well-being are of prime importance for a nation. In developed countries, issues related to children receive considerable attention, not only in terms of theory, but also in terms of practice. Research, legislations, and programs about children are generally followed by their effective implementations. The case is not so with the developing nations where legislations, policies, and programs about children are dismally few; and those taken up often go unimplemented or poorly implemented. It is documented that an incredibly large number of children across the world are not safe. Their welfare and well-being are left at the mercy or whim of the respective authority.

Child abuse and neglect are alarmingly on the rise throughout the globe. They come in various forms and guises, and pose various risks to the victims. Documented evidence shows the terrible consequences of this evil on their physical, psychological, and social health. They often suffer from low self-esteem and emotional instability, resulting in their erratic personality, social maladjustment, poor academic performance, and sometimes in their proneness to self-inflicted physical injury. Studies show that many intervention programs were found to be beneficial in helping the victims out of their problems. Few researches on child welfare and safety have been carried out in the developing countries. The problem of child abuse and neglect is a lot more complex in India than in many developing countries because of its huge children population, its enormous socio-economic diversity, as well as its varied cultural beliefs and practices concerning child rearing. The federal government should do more for the child protection issue and act as such. This issue has so far been given little importance, as proven by poor budget allocation.

The general aim of this document is to present the emerging features and measures of child safety, welfare, and their overall well-being. It thus intends to share the emerging issues with policy-makers, researchers, academics, and professionals working at a grass-root level for creating awareness about child rights and for their implementation. Experienced professionals and academics from developed and developing countries contributed chapters to this document on a wide range of issues. A number of new issues are covered in this book, which were not addressed by the previous competitive literature. The issues covered fall under four broad parts as follows:

Part I: Nature and Extent of Child Abuse and Neglect

This part is comprises seven chapters focusing on the nature of child abuse and neglect in different contexts, for example, child sexual abuse in trusted relationships, cyberbullying, conflict and its psychosocial consequences, problems of corporal punishment, and male circumcision (Chaps. 2–8). In Chap. 2, Kim Oates traces how various developments of understanding child protection have taken place in the past 50 years after the publication of the Battered Child Syndrome article by Kempe and his colleagues in 1962, and discusses changes in our perspective to see abuse as a children's rights issue. Rebecca P. Ang highlights an emerging issue in Chap. 3 and describes how children and adolescents get attracted to the virtual world and indulge in the high risk behavior of cyberbullying. In Chap. 4, Sibnath Deb and Mrinalkanti Ray present the nature and extent of child abuse and neglect in India, its impact, the risk factors involved, and finally discuss the poor implementation of appropriate legislations. Practice of corporal punishment in Pakistan and related legislations are the focus of Chap. 5 by George W. Holden and Rose Ashraf. In Chap. 6, Roopesh B.N. explains the impact of child sexual abuse in general and considers the children who experience the same problem from a trusted relationship and their responses to the assault. Waheeda Khan, in Chap. 7, holds out the disastrous effects of the Kashmir conflict on the lives of innocent children and calls for the need for immediate attention of the government to resolve this conflict. In Chap. 8, Ester I.J. Erlings speaks about the variations in legislations of different countries about the ritual of male circumcision, raises concern for the protection of child rights in terms of physical integrity, and suggests the reforms of legislations.

Part II: Child Rights and Its Practice

There are three chapters in this part (Chaps. 9–11), which emphasize the rights of children with respect to nutrition, health, and education. They treat in detail the nuances of different national and international legislations. In Chap. 9,

Bernadette J. Madrid and Dian Traisci-Marandola outline the sorry state of health of mothers and children even 15 years after the inauguration of the Millennium Development Goals. Inaccessibility to primary education and privation of basic nutrition are other issues addressed in this chapter, finally arguing for basic minimal facilities for all children, such as nutrition, education, and health care. Jagannath Pati, in Chap. 10, deals with the subject of right to information versus right to confidentiality with respect to child adoption and discusses issues and concerns in case of root search of adopted children and the challenges involved in adoption. In Chap. 11, Vimla Veeraraghavan underscores the importance of the Right to Education Act, 2009, for ensuring compulsory education for all children up to class VIII as a legal right and explains the role of teachers in imparting quality education to bring out the talents of the children.

Part III: Rights of Vulnerable Children

The specialty of this part consists in the presentation of issues and perspectives of some categories of vulnerable children, for example, the rights of children with disability, children diagnosed with HIV/AIDS, the problems of children working as child laborers or in precarious circumstances like disaster and adoption. There are seven chapters in this part (Chaps. 12–18). In Chap. 12, Seema Sahay, Archana Verma, Suhas Shewale, and Murugesan Periyasamy emphasize the need for protection of rights of children affected by HIV/AIDS and recommend child's rights to preventive health care, education, and life. In Chap. 13, Nilanjana Sanyal throws light on the challenges that arise after the adoption of a child, raises her concerns for vulnerabilities of adopted children to abuse and neglect, and appeals to adopted parents to be resilient enough to bring up adopted children well. N.K Chadda and Vandona Gambhir Chopra, in Chap. 14, examine the status of child labor in India, decrying the denial of basic rights of working children regarding survival, development, and participation. They warn us of the adverse effects of working condition on child health. In Chap. 15, Prerna Sharma critically discusses the rights of children with disability and the violation of their rights, also pointing out the barriers encountered in ensuring their rights. Chitra Shah, a social activist working with disabled children, recounts her firsthand experience, in Chap. 16, with regard to the status of disabled children, the stigma attached to disability, and emphasizes the need for community-based intervention program to prevent the abandonment of children with special needs. In Chap. 17, Subhasis Bhadra brings to our notice the challenges faced by children in the wake of natural disasters like Tsunami and suggests a range of psychosocial measures based on his working experience with the survivors. In Chap. 18, Neela Dabir, K. Anuradha, and Raji Satyamurthy write about the benefits of innovative and cost-effective approaches for the education of marginalized children who are mostly deprived of basic primary education in India. The action research was implemented by two nongovernment organizations (NGOs)—Rainbow Homes (schools for street girls) and Door Step Schools (coeducational schools for the children of underprivileged families) in Kolkata, Hyderabad, and Delhi.

Part IV: Protective Measures

This part contains eight chapters that describe field-based experiences of the researchers on the protection of child rights in different circumstances, for example, child custody cases, mandatory reporting, sexual abuse, and preventive measures (Chaps. 19–26). Jenny Gray, in Chap. 19, emphasizes the need for setting up an effective system for child protection by the State government following multidisciplinary approaches. In Chap. 20, Stefanie Platt, Juhayna Ajami, Nicole Kluemper, Robert Geffner, Morgan Shaw, and Alexandra Assalley argue for the adoption of appropriate evaluative measures for assessing allegations about child abuse in custody cases and discuss challenges in the investigation process of allegations. Child abuse and neglect differ in nature from case to case, a point addressed by Ben Mathews in Chap. 21. In his view, legal and policy response should be based on the gravity and nature of abuse and needs. In Chap. 22, Sue Foley, Jenny Rose, and Liana Lowenstein explain the needs for recognition of the views of children and the importance of listening to them. Lucia C.A. Williams and Sabrina M. D'Affonseca, in Chap. 23, agree with the latest legal provisions in Brazil concerning child sexual abuse and discuss the crucial role of the media in bringing to light the incidences of sexual abuse. In Chap. 24, Bharti Ali provides a pen picture of the deprivation of 20 % children from their basic rights to name and nationality. She states that unless child protection becomes an indicator for national development, the problem will persist or will get worse. In Chap. 25, Lina Acca Mathew speaks in favor of a multidisciplinary approach for protection of children from sexual abuse in India. According to her, the NGOs and CBOs need to engage with the issue in order to ensure effective pre-trial and trial procedure in the interest of the child. Finally, in Chap. 26, Mala Bhandari vigorously defends the protection of child rights at the grass-root level, pins down the missing links in local institutions, and offers suggestions for improving the situation.

Although this document covers a wide range of issues related to child safety and welfare, it is very important to do further research on those issues about which we do not have much evidence. Evidence would help us to understand better the issues and to adopt corrective measures. The issues which call for particular attention of the researchers include:

- Evaluation of various government social welfare measures like Integrated Child Development Scheme (ICDS), Integrated Child Protection Scheme (ICPS), and Panchayati Raj Institutions for child protection, in addition to various vocational trainings and rehabilitation programs for street children, trafficked children, and child laborers.

- Follow-up study on girl child marriage and child trafficking in order to understand the kind of adversities they experience.
- Challenges in the recovery of trafficked children and integrating them into mainstream society.
- Benefits and challenges of disadvantaged children under institutional care and their mental health.
- Knowledge and perception of the community about corporal punishment, sexual abuse of children, and its impact.
- Challenges in implementing child welfare-related legislations like Protection of Children from *Sexual Offences Act, 2012*, Right to Education Act 2009, *Juvenile Justice* (*Care and Protection* of Children) Amendment Act, 2006, The *Prohibition of Child Marriage Act, 2006,* The Child Labor (Prohibition and Regulation) Amendment Bill, 2012 and their benefits.

Some of the core issues related to safety, welfare, and well-being of disadvantaged children like children engaged in domestic work, street children, trafficked children, juvenile delinquents held in observation homes, and children living with single parent are left out of this document. Another volume is necessary to address these issues.

It is hoped that this book will prove useful for psychology, law, social sciences (sociology, anthropology, education, and women studies, for example), and medical sciences (nursing, community medicine, psychiatry, pediatric, forensic medicine, for example). It is also hoped that the book will be greatly useful to NGOs, policy makers, researchers, and law enforcement agencies working with children.

The editor is grateful to all resource persons for their contributions to a good cause. The editor is also grateful to Dr. Mrinalkanti Ray, Sagar Bhattacharyya, Sujata Ghosh, Anjali Gireesan, and Pooja Sathyanarayanan for their professional support in bringing out the document. The editor has chosen to refrain from making stylistic or linguistic changes in the various articles so as to retain their individualistic flavor. Efforts have been made to check the facts and thus to produce an unbiased document. Yet, if there occur any factual or typographical errors, or errors in the citation of references, these are sincerely regretted.

Sibnath Deb

Contents

Part IV Protective Measures

Editor and Contributors

About the Editor

Prof. Sibnath Deb Ph.D., D.Sc. Department of Applied Psychology, Pondicherry University (A Central University), Puducherry, India and Adjunct Professor, School of Public Health and Social Work, Queensland University of Technology, Brisbane, Australia has 26 years of teaching and research experience. Currently he is coordinator of UGC SAP project. In 1994, Prof. Deb did an intensive course on 'Qualitative Research' from the University of Western Australia, Australia. During April 2009–August 2009, Prof. Deb visited the School of Public Health, Queensland University of Technology, Brisbane, Australia as Visiting Faculty. Prof. Deb has produced ten Ph.D.'s and successfully coordinated more than 50 large-scale qualitative and quantitative studies in addition to publishing more than 100 research papers, writing eight books and editing four. Prof. Deb is on the editorial board of the '*Journal of Interpersonal Violence*', published by the University of Washington, USA and consulting editor of a number of journals. During 2004–2008, he served the International Society for Prevention of Child Abuse and Neglect (ISPCAN) as Councilor Member. In 2009, Prof. Deb received '*Endeavor Executive Award*' from the Australian Government. His current areas of research interest include child protection, students' mental health, adolescent reproductive health, and HIV/AIDS.

Contributors

Dr. Juhayna Ajami Psy.D graduated from The George Washington University in Washington, DC in June 2013 with a doctoral degree in Clinical Psychology. Dr. Ajami completed practicum experiences centered on providing individual therapy to adults and adolescents involved with the legal system, as well as completing neuropsychological assessments for inpatient committed adults, court-ordered psycho-educational assessments for juveniles, psychological evaluations to help determine eligibility for disability, and psychological and neuropsychological assessments for asylum seekers and survivors of torture. Dr. Ajami joined IVAT and the forensic consulting team at FVSAI in July 2013, functioning as a postdoctoral fellow and case manager in forensic and clinical psychology. Dr. Ajami is also an Assistant Editor for the following journals: *Journal of Child Custody; Journal of Child Sexual Abuse; Journal of Aggression; Maltreatment, & Trauma; Journal of Family Violence; and the Journal of Child & Adolescent Trauma.*

Bharti Ali is Co-Director of HAQ—A Centre for Child Rights based in New Delhi. She has been working as child right activist for the past 20 years and is actively involved in court cases related to child trafficking and child sexual abuse. She has delivered invited lectures in several national and international conferences and seminars on child protection.

Dr. Rebecca P. Ang Associate Professor, Psychological Studies Academic Group, National Institute of Education, Nanyang Technological University, Singapore, has long research and teaching experience. After completion of Master of Communication Studies from the Nanyang Technological University, Singapore in 1996, Dr. Rebecca did Ph.D. from the Texas A&M University, USA in 2000. Dr. Rebecca is a Registered Psychologist of the Singapore Psychological Society and Nationally Certified School Psychologist (NCSP), USA. Internationally Dr. Rebecca P. Ang is known for her significant contribution to the field of students' mental health, especially on academic stress and anxiety of students. She has published more than 90 research papers in referred journals, written 5 books, and 11 book chapters in addition to producing a number of Ph.D.'s successfully. For significant contribution to the academic and research field, Dr. Rebecca has received five awards like (i) International Council of Psychologists Seisoh Sukemune/Bruce Bain Early Career Research Award 2006. This award was given in recognition of outstanding early career contributions to scholarly endeavors addressing psychological issues of multinational significance, (ii) NTU Research Outcome Award and Recognition (ROAR) 2006. This award was given in recognition of research productivity and impact, (iii) *School Psychology Review* Outstanding Article of the Year Award 2002.

K. Anuradha Executive Director, Rainbow Homes, Rainbow Foundation India, Hyderabad, is the driving force behind the campaign to bring street-children into the fold of mainstream Education. She is instrumental in advocating Urban Deprived Children (UDC) for residential care for children who entered education late but failed to complete it in the mandated 8 yrs. She inspired 21 partners across 7 states to join the endeavor. After leaving a government job as school teacher, Anuradha devoted her time to spreading values like justice, peace, secularism, and democracy; campaigned for gender justice in Mahila Samakhya; worked with the UNDP for poverty alleviation, justice for victims of violence with Action Aid; engaged with Safai Karmachari Andolan for eradicating manual scavenging—as its national core team member since 2004; she initiated the Caring Citizens' Collective (CCC) to reach out to families in despair. She is the person behind the Campaign for Citizens' Shelters (CFCS) for homeless.

Rose Ashraf is a graduate student in clinical psychology in the Department of Psychology at Southern Methodist University. She received her BS in psychology from The University of Texas at Dallas. While obtaining her undergraduate degree, Ashraf worked with Dr. Marion Underwood studying adolescents' relationships with their peers. As a student at The University of Texas at Dallas, Ashraf received several awards including the Buhrmester Research Award, Santrock Travel Award, Dean's Scholar Award, and the Mary McDermott Cook Outstanding Student Award. Currently, Ashraf is pursuing her interests in parent–child relationship under the direction of Dr. George Holden. Specifically, her interests include various parenting practices, the immediate and long-term impact on children, and children's perspectives of these behaviors. Ashraf's thesis involves an examination of verbal negatives (e.g., yelling, threats, verbal hostility) directed at children by their parents based on audio-recordings in the home.

Alexandra Assalley B.A. is completing her doctorate (Psy.D) in Clinical Forensic Psychology at the Chicago School of Professional Psychology—Los Angeles campus. She earned her Bachelor of Arts degree in Political Science, with a minor in Economics from DePaul University in Chicago, Illinois. Currently, Ms. Assalley is completing her pre-doctoral internship as part of the clinical and forensic team at IVAT and FVSAI.

Dr. Subhasis Bhadra MSW, M.Phil, Ph.D. Assistant Professor and Head of the Department of Social Work, Gautam Buddha University, Greater NOIDA, Uttar Pradesh, India, began his career working with those affected by the Gujarat earthquake (2001) and subsequently worked in areas affected by riots (Gujarat, 2002), Tsunamis (Southern India and Southeast Asia, 2004), earthquakes (Kashmir, 2005), terrorist attacks (Mumbai serial Train Blast, 2006), Japanese Tsunami (2011) creating and implementing psychosocial programs with organizations, like Care India, American Red Cross, Oxfam India, Action Aid, International Medical Corps. e-mail: bhadrasubhasis@gmail.com.

Dr. Mala Bhandari Ph.D. in Sociology from University of Delhi has keen interest in academic and action research in socially relevant issues, especially those concerning child protection, gender, and development. She has been a Consultant to various international organizations such as Save the Children, U.K. and International Labor Organization for their projects on Child Labor and Child Protection. She has conducted several empirical research studies and action projects in the fields of gender, child labor, and formal school system. She is life member of The Indian Society of Labor Economics, Indian Sociological Society, and Civil Society Network in South Asia and Child Rights in Practice Network, University of Victoria, British Columbia. She is an Executive Member of the All India Women's Education Fund Association. Dr. Bhandari has been a visiting faculty at School of Gender and Development Studies, IGNOU where apart from teaching the M.A. Gender Studies (Face to Face course) students, she has developed the course/content material for M.A. (Long Distance) course in Gender and Development. She is also associated with IMI, New Delhi and IMS, Noida. e-mail: mail@sadrag.org.

Prof. N.K. Chadha a Professor of Psychology at University of Delhi and presently the HOD of the Department of Psychology, is a Ph.D. from Delhi University and a Post-Doctorate from University of Virginia, USA. He is also the President of two prestigious organizations dedicated to the better future of psychological prospects in India: (i) India Career Development Association (ICDA), and (ii) Indian Association of Positive Psychology (IAPP). Professor Chadha has been teaching in the University of Delhi since 1982. He has taught courses in research methodology, Organizational behavior social gerontology, and applied social psychology. Prof. Chadha is a prolific researcher and a foremost thought leader of our times. He has contributed in several areas like psychometrics, organizational behavior, social psychology, and aging to name a few. He is the author of 22 books and more than 100 research articles in National and International Journals of repute. Widely acclaimed as a global authority in the area of psychometrics, Prof. Chadha is also the author of several psychometric scales widely used today. He has been conducting many ongoing research projects with foreign universities. He has been awarded many national and international awards and honors.

Dr. Vandana Gambhir Chopra an Assistant Professor of Psychology in one of the leading colleges of University of Delhi and an alumnus of Nehru Homoeopathic Medical College and Hospital, one of the premier and reputed homeopathic colleges of India. A gold medalist from University of Delhi, she started her professional career as a physician and is currently working as Assistant Professor of Psychology at Keshav Mahavidyalaya, DU. Her field of involvement in psychology research work span across psychometric testing, organizational behavior, personality psychology, social psychology, competency mapping, positive psychology, consumer behavior, and geriatrics mental health. In her spare time, she likes to read books on spirituality, exploring dimensions of the human mind.

Dr. Sabrina Mazo D'Affonseca is Postdoctoral Researcher at the *Universidade Federal de São Carlos* (Federal University of São Carlos), UFSCar, in Brazil, conducting a national research on Special Education. She is associated researcher of LAPREV (The Laboratory of Analysis and Prevention of Violence) supervising research in domestic violence, especially in mother–child interaction. Dr. Sabrina Mazo D'Affonseca has a Ph.D. in Psychology from the University of São Carlos, Brazil, an M.A. in Special Education also from the University of São Carlos, Brazil, and a B.A. Degree from the University of São Carlos, Brazil. She made an internship in the Department of Psychology at Southern Methodist University (SMU), in Dallas (2011–12) with Professor George W. Holden. She is author of eight papers in peer reviewed scientific journals and wrote 6 chapters of books. She was professor at University of São Carlos for 4 years and at *Centro Universitário Central Paulista—Unicep* (Central University Center Paulista) for 2 years, teaching graduate courses. She has made presentations at national and international conferences.

Prof. Neela Dabir is a trained social worker, educator, and researcher with more than 30 years of experience. Her areas of interest include violence again women and vulnerable children. Currently, she is Deputy Director, Tata Institute of Social Sciences, Mumbai. Prior to that she worked as the Registrar of TISS and Chairperson for Center for Equity for Women, Children and Families and as Chairperson for International Students Office, TISS. She has published a number of articles in national and international journals in addition to writing two books, viz., *Women in Distress,* 2000 (Rawat

Publications, Jaipur) and *From Street to Hope: Faith Based and Secular Programs in Los Angeles, Mumbai and Nairobi for Street Living Children, 2011.* Sage: Delhi. Prof. Dabir has written following three manuals and monograph: 1. SAARATHI—Training Manual for frontline workers in child development agencies 2. Juvenile Justice Pack—A set of seven booklets for all the stakeholders in the JJ System for the children in conflict with the law—coauthored with Ms. Mohua Nigudkar. 3. Innovative Programs servicing Homeless and Street-Living Children across the World, Urban Initiatives, L.A. USA, 2005. Coauthors—Dr. Kristin Ferguson, Dr. Donna Spruijt-Metz, Dr. Grace Dyrness, Dr. Donald Miller, Dr. Karl Dortzbach.

Prof. Lúcia Cavalcanti de Albuquerque Williams is a senior Faculty in the Department of Psychology at the *Universidade Federal de São Carlos* (Federal University of São Carlos), UFSCar, in Brazil, where she coordinates LAPREV (The Laboratory of Analysis and Prevention of Violence), doing research, teaching, and community outreach efforts in addressing and preventing violence, particularly family and school violence. She is the author of 14 books and over 80 papers in peer reviewed scientific journals. She has received many awards, such as her work as considered "Exemplary Practices in the Perspective of Gender and Ethnicity in Health" by the Pan American Health Organization, PAHO/WHO, and Third Prize in Prevention of Child Abuse by the Women's World Summit Foundation (WWSF), in Geneva, both in 2009. She was a visiting professor twice in Argentina, teaching graduate courses at University of Mar Del Plata (2010), and National University of Cordoba (2012). She has several international research partnerships, such as with the American Psychological Association (APA) for validation in Brazil of the ACT parental training program, the University of California at Davis for a mutual research project on Parental Alienation, and the Children's Hospital at Westmead/Sydney, Australia for validating to Brazil Shaken Baby Syndrome prevention materials. She was twice the Vice-President of the Brazilian Psychological Association (2009–2013).

Esther I.J. Erlings is a Ph.D. Fellow in The Chinese University of Hong Kong. She has presented research papers in several national and international conferences. Her areas of research interest are child protection and legal issues related to protection of child rights. e-mail: e.erlings@yahoo.com.

Sue Foley BSOC.STUD, MSW, MA (Childhood studies), MED. Cert IV TAA clinical social worker and tele-psychiatry coordinator, the Department of Psychological Medicine, The Children's Hospital at Westmead, NSW. Australia. Sue Foley is a senior clinical social worker and educator who has worked with abuse and neglect issues for over 40 years. She is passionate about the rights of children and about a string clinical and safety focus in working to understand how to meet the developmental, relational, and health needs of children affected by abuse and neglect of all kinds. She is currently engaged in trauma focused mental health clinical work and clinician education, as well as undertaking forensic family assessments. She is currently a member of the council of the International Society for the Prevention of Child Abuse and Neglect (ISPCAN) and has been involved with this organization for over 30 years. Her interest in sharing practice examples arises with a commitment to education and learning as an essential component of social justice, empowerment, and addressing disadvantage of all kinds.

Prof. Robert Geffner is a licensed psychologist and the President and Founder of a nonprofit international resource and training center (the Family Violence & Sexual Assault Institute in Texas and now in California), the Founding President of the Institute on Violence, Abuse and Trauma at Alliant International University. He is also a Distinguished Research Professor of Psychology at Alliant International University in San Diego, and editor of five professional journals (including the *Journal of Child Sexual Abuse, Journal of Family Violence,* the *Journal of Child & Adolescent Trauma,* and the *Journal of Child Custody*). He has a Diplomate in Clinical Neuropsychology from the American Board of Professional Neuropsychology, and is Board Certified in Couple and Family Psychology from the American Board of Professional Psychology. Dr. Geffner is currently Co-chair of the National Partnership to End Interpersonal Violence Across the Lifespan (NPEIV) and president of the American Academy of Couple & Family Psychology.

Jenny Gray is a trained social worker in New Zealand and has worked in child welfare settings there and in the UK. She joined the British Government in 1990 and has held a number of roles, including working on the development of methodologies to inspect children's services and developing policies, including on assessment, and related materials to support their national implementation. Her current responsibility is to provide professional advice on child protection in the Department for Education. She has lead responsibility for a number of policy areas including reviewing child deaths. Jenny has been a member of ISPCAN since 1992 and the Council since 2004. Since joining ISPCAN she has been involved in the Working Group on Child Maltreatment Data. Jenny chaired the External Relations and Consultancy Committee during 2008–2010, edited the LINK for six years and *World Perspectives* in 2010. She has been a member of the Organizing Committee for a number of ISPCAN conferences and congresses and will assume the Presidency of ISPCAN in September 2012.

Prof. George W. Holden is Professor of Psychology at Southern Methodist University in Dallas, TX. Holden's research interests are in the area of social development, with a focus on parent–child relationships. His work, into the determinants of parental behavior, parental social cognition, and the causes and consequences of family violence, has been supported by grants from the National Institute of Child Health and Human Development, National Institutes of Justice, Department of Health and Human Services, the Guggenheim Foundation, the Hogg Foundation for Mental Health, and most recently, the U.S. State Department. He is the author of numerous scientific articles and chapters, as well as two books. *Parenting: A Dynamic Perspective* (2010) and *Parents and the Dynamics of Child Rearing* (1997). In addition, he co-edited *Children Exposed to Marital Violence* (1998) and the *Handbook of Family Measurement Techniques* (2001). Holden is a fellow of the American Psychological Society and a member of the Society for Research in Child Development, the American Professional Society on the Abuse of Children, and the Society for Research in Human Development, where he served as president. He has been or is on the editorial boards of *Child Development, Developmental Psychology, Journal of Emotional Abuse, Journal of Family Psychology*, and *Parenting: Science and Practice.*

Prof. Waheeda Khan is former Head in the Department of Psychology and presently Hony. Director of the University Counseling & Guidance Centre, Jamia Millia Islamia (A Central University), Delhi, India. She has more than 23 years of teaching, research, and administrative experience. She has supervised/supervising 27 doctoral students and published more than 50 research papers. Her research areas are related to environment, terrorism/violence, counseling, mental health, stress, emotion and coping in adolescents, youth, and women. She has been awarded JRF/SRF and Post-Doctoral Research Associate awards by the Government of India and Fellowship of the Year award by NESA. She has been the recipient of ARTS program twice, which is organized by International Union of Psychological Sciences. She has been recently appointed Adjunct Faculty, Co-guide and member of Ph.D. Advisory Committee, Texila American University (Distance & Online Program), Georgetown, South America. e-mail: profwkhan@gmail.com; wkhan@jmi.ac.in.

Dr. Nicole S. Kluemper graduated from Alliant International University, San Diego in August 2013 with a doctoral degree in Clinical Psychology. Dr. Kluemper joined IVAT and the forensic team at FVSAI in October 2013, functioning as a postdoctoral fellow in forensic and clinical psychology. Previously, Dr. Kluemper graduated from Capella University with a Master of Arts in General Psychology. During her practical, Dr. Kluemper co-led multiple groups for adult survivors of childhood abuse, and was trained on multiple evidence based practices including Parent Child Interaction Therapy (PCIT), Trauma Focused Cognitive Behavioral Therapy (TF-CBT), and Prolonged Exposure (PE). Dr. Kluemper's dissertation research involved trauma, dissociation, and suggestibility as they relate to reported trauma experiences. Dr. Kluemper has presented at conferences around the country on the topic of ethics and psychological research.

Liana Lowenstein MSW, RSW, CPT-S Child Psychotherapist in Private Practice, Toronto, Canada. Liana Lowenstein is a Registered Clinical Social Worker and a Certified Play Therapist-Supervisor who has been working with children and their families since 1988. Liana is known as a dynamic speaker and presents trainings across North America and abroad. Her recent speaking engagements include South Africa, Israel, England, and New Zealand. Liana provides clinical supervision to mental health practitioners, runs a play-therapy internship program, and consults to several mental health agencies. As the founder of Champion Press, Liana has authored and published numerous books, including the highly acclaimed Paper Dolls and Paper Airplanes: Therapeutic Exercises for Sexually Traumatized Children (with Crisci & Lay 1997), Creative Interventions for Troubled Children & Youth (1999), Creative Interventions for Children of Divorce (2006), and Creative Interventions for Bereaved Children (2006). She is the editor of Assessment and Treatment Activities for Children, Adolescents, and Families (Volumes One through Three) and Creative Family Therapy Techniques. Her recently launched Cory series will include volumes that help children cope with issues of divorce, sexual abuse, and domestic violence.

Dr. Bernadette J. Madrid M.D., FPPS is the Director of the Child Protection Unit of the University of the Philippines Manila—Philippine General Hospital. She is a

Clinical Associate Professor of Paediatrics at the UP College of Medicine. She is also the Executive Director of the Child Protection Unit Network, an NGO that supports the training of Child Protection Professionals and the development of Child Protection Units in the Philippines. She has been awarded as one of the Outstanding Women in the Nation's Service in 2001 for her work in child protection and one of the five Most Outstanding Philippine Doctors for 2004. Dr. Madrid is actively involved in the integration of child abuse prevention in the undergraduate and graduate medical curriculum. Dr. Madrid has published several articles on domestic violence and child abuse and neglect (CAN). She has chaired previous regional consultations by the World Health Organization on the WHO World report on Violence and Health and the Health Sector Response to Sexual Violence. She was a member of the Executive Council of the International Society for the Prevention of Child Abuse and Neglect and Chair of the Asian Forum.

Prof. Ben Mathews Ph.D., LLB, BA is Director of Research in the School of Law at Queensland University of Technology in Brisbane, Australia. Dr. Mathews conducts interdisciplinary research at the forefront of international scholarship in child abuse and neglect, public policy and law. Dr. Mathews has published over 50 scholarly works on children and the law, with a key focus on mandatory reporting law, theory and practice, and civil claims for child abuse. He has an international reputation, holds Adjunct positions at two overseas institutions, and is a member of the editorial board of the leading journal in the child abuse field. He is now co-editing a major new book on mandatory reporting laws, which will be published in 2014. In recent years Dr. Mathews has undertaken major studies of the law, theory and practice of mandatory reporting laws. Dr. Mathews has been involved in the two largest empirical studies of mandatory reporting in Australia: a study of Queensland nurses' reporting of all types of child abuse and neglect; and leadership of a three year Australian Research Council-funded study of teachers reporting child sexual abuse in Queensland, New South Wales and Western Australia. Results of the ARC study led to: significant reform of Queensland legislation (2012 amendments to the *Education (General Provisions) Act 2006*); improvements to reporting policies and teacher training (in Queensland and Western Australia, and elsewhere); and delivery of innovative teacher training methods.

Lina Acca Mathew Assistant Professor, Government Law College, Ernakulam (Former Name-His Highness Maharajas Law College), Kerala has been carrying out her doctoral research on child sexual abuse related legislations. She has a special interest for protection of children from sexual abuse. She has attended several national and international conferences on child abuse and neglect and presented papers.

Emeritus Professor R. Kim Oates M.D., D.Sc., MHP, FRACP, FRCP, FAFPHM, FRACMA, DCH is a pediatrician who trained in the Sydney, London and Boston. Most of his professional work has been associated with the Royal Alexandra Hospital for Children (now The Children's Hospital at Westmead) and the University of Sydney, Australia. He has a long-standing interest in child development, child behavior, and the problems of child abuse, neglect and advocacy on behalf of children. In 2000 he received the Kempe award from the USA for 'Outstanding contributions to the community on behalf of children', the first time this has been awarded outside the USA. He has been on the Council of the International Society for the Prevention of Child Abuse and Neglect (ISPCAN) for two periods, each of 12 years, including 2 years as President and 6 years as treasurer. He has written 13 books and has over 300 publications. He is currently Emeritus Professor of Pediatrics at the University of Sydney and Director of undergraduate Quality and Safety at the Clinical Excellence Commission where he has a focus on teaching about how errors in hospital can be reduced.

Dr. Jagannath Pati is an India-based rehabilitation specialist with over 25 years' experience working across national and international platforms. Dr. Pati has substantive experience working in multicultural environments with diverse population groups, with experience spanning on-ground field work and communications research and policy issues related to children in need of care and protection. Dr. Pati has extensive experience with central government and autonomous bodies and has demonstrated competence in initiating and maintaining close, cross-cultural partnerships at the national, state and regional level of stakeholders including children homes, non-government organizations and civil societies. He has been actively involved in capacity building and promoting national resource mobilization in India particularly for service providers of children in need of care and protection. Dr. Pati is a Senior Fulbright Awardee and has published a number of books and volume of literature on development issues. He has contributed several papers in national and international conferences.

Murugesan Periyasamy is a postgraduate in Social Work with medical and psychiatric specialization from Madurai Institute of Social Sciences, Madurai Kamaraj University, Tamil Nadu. He was working as a Medical Social Worker since 1998 at National Institute for Research in Tuberculosis (NIRT). Presently he is working as a Scientist "B" in the Division of Socio Behavioral Research at National AIDS Research institute, Pune. He was involved as counselor in various clinical trial studies on Tuberculosis and HIV/AIDS. His work involved detailed sociological assessment of TB and HIV/AIDS patients to decide suitability prior to the enrolment in to Randomized Controlled clinical trials. He is also involved in various socio behavioral research studies in both National Institute for Research in Tuberculosis (NIRT) Chennai and in National AIDS Research Institute (NARI), Pune. He has published 6 peer reviewed article in international and national journal. He is the Principal Investigator for a research project titled "Determinants of loss to follow-up in free ART program in selected sites in Maharashtra, India" and Co- Investigator for other five research projects of NARI &NIRT.

Dr. Stefanie Platt Psy.D graduated from Alliant International University in San Francisco in 2012 with a doctoral degree in Clinical Psychology with an emphasis in Forensic Psychology. Previously, Dr. Platt graduated from Pepperdine University with a Master of Arts in Clinical Psychology in 2007. Dr. Platt was selected and trained in Forensic Psychology under South Africa's Investigative Psychology Unit. While working on her graduate degree, Dr. Platt court-ordered assessments for families involved with Child Protective Services. Dr. Platt joined IVAT and the forensic consulting team at FVSAI in July 2012 and has continued with the agency working as the Training Director and a Forensic Psychologist since September, 2013. Currently, Dr. Platt serves as the Clinical Director for the Professional Clinical and Forensic Services Department at IVAT. Dr. Platt is on the editorial board for the *Journal of Child Custody* and works as an Assistant Editor for the following journals: *Journal of Child Sexual Abuse; Journal of Aggression; Maltreatment, & Trauma; Journal of Family Violence; and the Journal of Child & Adolescent Trauma*. Additionally, Dr. Platt is an adjunct Professor at Alliant International University.

Dr. Mrinalkanti Ray a child right activist received a Master's degree in English Literature from the University of Calcutta and an M.Phil. degree in English Literature from Rabindra Bharati University in the City of Calcutta. Later he earned a Ph.D. degree in English Literature from the University of Laval (Université Laval), Canada. The subject of his doctoral dissertation is William Wordsworth, exploring his debt to the French Enlightenment and original reworking of French Enlightenment ideas. Dr. Ray wrote this dissertation under the joint supervision of Dr. Kathryn Ready (now an Associate Professor in the Department of English at the University of Winnipeg) and Dr. Thierry Belleguic (a full professor in the Department of Literatures at the Université Laval). He completed the *Diplôme supérieur* in French at the *Alliance Française de Calcutta*. Among his areas of research interest are eighteenth-century and British Romantic literature. Dr. Ray has presented papers at several conferences, including one at the University of Oxford. He has taught several undergraduate courses of English Literature at the Université Laval. At the moment, he is employed in writing articles while on the job market for a faculty position in North America.

Dr. B.N. Roopesh is Assistant Professor in Clinical Psychology, National Institute of Mental Health and Neurosciences (NIMHANS), Bangalore, India. After obtaining Ph.D. from the NIMHANS, he did Post-Doctoral Research in the Downstate Medical Center, New York, USA. He has published 14 research papers and presented papers in 16 conferences. Till date he has completed six research projects successfully.

Jenny Rose MMH (Child & Adol), BSW, BA (Welf), Dip Bus, Cert IV TAA, the Department of Social Work, The Children's Hospital at Westmead, NSW. Australia. Jenny Rose is a senior Social Worker who has been working with children and families for over 20 years. She currently works at the Children's Hospital at Westmead in Sydney, Australia where she enjoys working with vulnerable families from a range of cultural backgrounds. She is interested in using a range of child-friendly, creative strategies to help children make sense of events that happen in their lives. Jenny is also the Social Work Student Educator and has great success in applying playful strategies to adult education.

Dr. Seema Sahay is an anthropologist, completed her Master's and Doctorate from Department of Anthropology, University of Delhi (Delhi). Currently, she is working as Scientist at National AIDS Research Institute, Pune (India). Dr. Sahay has successfully led clinic- and field-based qualitative, quantitative and descriptive epidemiological research studies. She has completed over 15 national and international collaborative projects as Principal Investigator and Co-investigator. Major areas of her research are HIV prevention, care and support, mental health, pediatric and adolescent HIV/AIDS, and clinical trials. Currently, she is leading studies on new prevention technologies, pediatric and adolescents HIV/AIDS, mental health and HIV prevention and care in rural India. Her other academic affiliations are: Faculty for Ph.D., Department of Anthropology, University of Pune (Pune); Faculty for Ph.D. in Health science, Symbiosis International University (Pune); Faculty for MPH program at KLE University (Belgaum). She is member of Ethics Committee at National Institute of Virology (Pune) and Bharti Hospital and Medical College, Bharti Vidyapeeth (Pune). She is in the Editorial Board of several peer reviewed journals. She has published over 42 papers in national and international journals and has authored book chapters and coauthored a book.

Prof. Nilanjana Sanyal Department of Psychology, University of Calcutta has 30 years of work experience as teacher, psychoanalyst and psychotherapist. Prof. Sanyal has imparted training in counseling in various governmental institutions and NGOs, both nationally and internationally. She has to her credit a number of national and international publications and is also a columnist in different national dailies and magazines. She has edited a book and is a co-author of a Test Manual. She has 19 book chapters to her credit till date. Her research interests include personality and clinical psychology, interpersonal relationships, and psychodynamic psychotherapy. She is a Co-Researcher for the creation of registered assessment methodologies, namely, the Fairy Tale Test (FTT) with Dr. Carina Coulacouglou, University of Athens, Greece, and State Trait Anxiety Inventory—2 Children and Adolescents (STAXI—2 C/A) with Dr. Thomas Bruner and Dr. Charles D. Spielberger, University of South Florida, Tampa, U.S.A. She is a Gold Medalist of Calcutta University. She received Jubilee Merit Prize and Jawaharlal Nehru Award from Government of India along with the Subhashini Basu Memorial Prize from Indian Psychoanalytic Society for excellence of a research paper. She is the recipient of Bharat Jyoti Award, 2012 for meritorious achievement and life time contribution to social works, and Prof. Maya Deb Memorial Award from Asiatic Society, Kolkata, 2012 apart from other awards.

Ms. Raji Satyamurthy is the Program Director for Every Child Counts (ECC)—Citizens' Campaign at Door Step School, a Non-Government Organization (NGO) that works towards the literacy of educationally marginalized children in India. With a Masters in Computer Science and an overall experience of nearly two and a half decades, she has been consulting with Door Step School since September 2010, helping to set up structures for new programs including developing the methodology, processes and measures of impact. She jointly wrote and published a working paper on the ECC Citizens' Campaign, an innovative program for universal elementary education, for Tata Institute of Social Sciences (TISS), Mumbai. Her current work is on developing partnerships for expanding the ECC program and developing grass-root level programs addressing barriers to universal enrolment and literacy for migrant communities.

Chitra Shah Director of Satya Special School, Puducherry—a Centre for Children with Special Needs has been working with disabled children for the last 20 years. She has a special interest in delivering services to the children with special needs at the community level in addition to delivering institution-based support services. Under her dynamic leadership a group of multidisciplinary professionals are able to deliver quality services to the children with special needs which really made the differences in an isolated Union Territory like Puducherry.

Dr. Prerna Sharma is presently an Assistant Professor in the Department of Social Work, SNDT Women's University, Mumbai, since 2007. She has also worked with Tata Institute of Social Sciences as a lecturer for four years prior to that from 2002, when she moved from social work practice in field to education. She has worked with several organizations like the United Nations High Commissioner for Refugees, Spastics Society of India, Mumbai (now known as ADAPT) and SHARE, a community based organization working to empower women by building leadership and social action skills in them. Dr. Sharma is a member of board of trustees, SHARE and member of the Advisory Board of Sanskar India Foundation in Mumbai. She has presented papers in national and international conferences and published articles in journals. Dr. Sharma successfully completed international training program linking Development and Human Rights conducted by Dignity International. Her work and research interests lie in the areas of child rights, disability and inclusion, human rights and the concerns and issues of senior citizens.

Morgan Shaw M.A is a completing her doctorate (Psy.D.) in Clinical Forensic Psychology at the California School of Forensic Studies at Alliant International University. She earned her Master of Arts degree at this same university in 2012. Prior to that, Ms. Shaw earned her Bachelor of Arts degree in Psychology from the University of California, at Santa Barbara. Currently, Ms. Shaw is part of the clinical and forensic team at IVAT and FVSAI where she will become the post-doctoral fellow.

Suhas Shewale has completed her Master of Public Health from University of Pune. Her research in the initial years of her career focused on testing community-based interventions to improve maternal and child health and nutrition in the most marginalized communities of eastern India. She is currently working at National AIDS Research Institute for a project addressing JE/AES prevention and control through community based strategies. She has a background in research particularly in developing and implementing monitoring-evaluation methodologies for community based programs. She has experience of field-based research with skills in research design, developing evaluation tools, developing mobile phone based application as tool for study evaluation, development IEC materials for interventions, developing training programs for data collectors and growth monitors and data analysis.

Dian Traisci-Marandola APRN, MSN, MPH is a pediatric nurse practitioner and public health specialist who have focused on developing public health programs and health systems for underserved, underinsured children. Ms. Marandola established

Public Health Associates after 9/11 to consult with local public health departments on the development and field testing of public health emergency response plans including opening points of distribution. She is an advocate for integrating the unique needs of children and special needs populations in disaster planning and response. When the aftermath of Hurricanes Katrina and Rita unfolded, Ms. Marandola participated as a volunteer in disaster primary care activities in New Orleans as a clinician and strike team assessor with Operation Assist a collaborative effort between the Children's' Heath Fund and Columbia University's National Center of Disaster Preparedness (NCDP). This experience afforded a first-hand lesson that in the aftermath of a traumatic event, reliable measures of local recovery are essential for planners and policymakers. Ms. Marandola holds master's degrees in public health and in nursing from Columbia University. She is currently a doctoral student in nursing practice at Rush University, College of Nursing, with a focus on health system transformation.

Prof. Vimala Veeraraghavan Ph.D. (Psychology) from Delhi University. She has 40 years of teaching, administrative and research experience in the field social sciences, which includes psychology, educational psychology, clinical psychology, mental health, forensic psychology and related subjects in central universities like Delhi University and Jawaharlal Nehru University, Indira Gandhi National Open University, and the only private university Amity University. She has received several awards for her academic achievements. Important positions held include (i) Emeritus Professor, Psychology, Indira Gandhi National Open University, New Delhi; (ii) Professor of Psychology and Director General, Amity Institute of Behavioural Health and Allied Sciences, Amity University Uttar Pradesh; (iii) Served as Professor and Head, Department of Applied Psychology University of Delhi South Campus, New Delhi and (iv) Professor and Head, Dept. of Psychology, Delhi University. She has been a Visiting professor to Thammasat University, Bangkok, Thailand. She served as an expert consultant to various national level bodies in government and private organizations. e-mail: vveera2000@gmail.com.

Archana Verma an anthropologist by training, has completed Masters in Anthropology from Department of Anthropology, University of Delhi, Delhi. She has initiated her research career in care & support in the field of HIV/AIDS. She has been working at National AIDS Research Institute since three years in the Division Social-Behavioral Research. Currently she is pursuing doctorate on 'Mental health of perinatally infected adolescents with HIV'. She is working in a multi-centric study on "community willingness to accept the new HIV prevention technologies" sponsored by ICMR in the capacity of Senior Investigator. She is also coordinating a community-based study on Pediatric HIV/ AIDS and disclosure. Her research skills are conducting community based studies, conducting studies using qualitative and quantitative research techniques, and data analysis of descriptive epidemiological studies. Her areas of work are field-based studies like pediatric and adolescents HIV/AIDS, mental health of adolescents, and new prevention technologies for HIV in India.

Chapter 1
Introduction—Child Safety, Welfare, and Well-Being: Need of the Hour

Sibnath Deb

Introduction

Biological parents or immediate caregivers are generally responsible for the safety and protection of children. If biological parents or immediate caregivers fail in their duties, the concerned local government is then obligated to take care of children, as per the verdict of the United Nations Convention on the Rights of the Child (1989). That being said, to ensure the safety and protection of child rights is everybody's responsibility, and this responsibility has been recognized by the international community in 1989 through the United Nations Convention on the Rights of the Child (CRC). Violence against children in any form constitutes a violation of the basic rights of children. During childhood, young people deserve unconditional love from their parents, as well as all the necessities for proper physical, mental, and social development (Deb 2010). A fundamental assumption of the United Nation Convention is that family should be the natural environment for the growth and well being of all its members, particularly its children. Yet, very regrettably, it is in the family where child abuse occurs most often.

S. Deb (✉)
Department of Applied Psychology, Pondicherry University, Puducherry, India
e-mail: sibnath23@gmail.com

S. Deb (ed.), *Child Safety, Welfare and Well-being*,
DOI 10.1007/978-81-322-2425-9_1

Phenomenon of Child Safety, Welfare and Well-Being in Different Social Strata

A large number of children irrespective of age, gender, caste, religion, and socio-economic background are not safe in today's society, whether at home or in educational institution or in the community (Pinheiro 2006; WHO 2010; Deb and Mukherjee 2011; Deb and Walsh 2012). They are treated as minor and unimportant by elderly people. Although children constitute a substantial percentage of global population, they form a minority in matters of legal protection, government policy, and benefits as citizens. Almost always, they find themselves at the mercy of their immediate caregivers for their safety and welfare (Deb 2009). As in other Asian countries, violation of child rights is quite common in India owing to the insensitivity of the communities to child rights (Chou et al. 2010; Chiang et al. 2012; Nguyen et al. 2010). Although reliable national and international-level data are not available, there exist data based on regional studies, which indicate that the problem is serious and deep-rooted (The Report of MWCD, GOI 2007; Deb and Modak 2010; Deb and Walsh 2012).

Similarities are observed in the developing countries regarding child safety and welfare issues. Violence against children in Asian countries is directly linked to socio-economic and demographic variables of a given society. Developing countries can generally be divided into three groups in terms of income, namely, low, middle, and high income groups. Each group has its own set of beliefs and practices when it comes to parenting. The nature of child abuse and neglect varies in keeping with different socio-economic strata. In low-income families, child abuse and neglect result from illiteracy and poverty (Deb 2009). The highest rates of school dropout, petty crimes, juvenile delinquency (Deb and Mitra 2001), and child mortality and morbidity are found among the children of lower social strata. These children become vulnerable to sexual abuse, exploitation, and trafficking (Deb 2005; Deb et al. 2005). The gender discrimination is caused by multiple social and cultural factors. Girl children are considered as burdens to the family and are discriminated against with respect to nutrition, education, and medical care. Issues of girl child marriage and adolescent pregnancy are recurrent in this class of society, putting at risk the lives of both the mother and the child (Deb 2009). Since parents of low-income families remain busy earning wages for their livelihood, they can hardly look after the child's safety and well-being. Poor income is one of the main causes of family disturbances which children witness. As a result, they tend to become emotionally disturbed. Family disturbances and lack of supervision for studies lead to high number of school dropouts, lowering the literacy rate, and increasing the crime rate.

There are many similarities in child rearing practices and disciplining methods of the people of upper and middle-income groups. Issues of abuse relate mostly to the parenting styles and unrealistic expectations of the parents regarding the child's education and career (Deb and Chatterjee 2008). Parents psychologically put pressure on children and do not hesitate to inflict corporal punishment in the hope of better academic performance, which often leads to depression and anxiety among the children (Deb 2004).

Many studies reported the detrimental effects of child abuse and neglect on their physical and mental health (Pinheiro 2006; WHO 2010; Deb and Madrid 2014). UNICEF (2009) *Multiple Indicator Cluster Surveys* covering 37 low-income countries revealed that almost 86 % of children aged 2–14 years suffered both physical and psychological aggression.

International Efforts for Child Safety and Prevention of Child Abuse

Considering the gravity of the problem, the United Nations (UN) declared November 19 as the World Day for Prevention of Child Abuse and Violence against Children. The UN thus seeks to raise awareness about children's rights so that they are treated with love and respect. Certainly, it is a laudable move, as it contributed to increase awareness among the common people about child rights. As a result of the efforts of different international and professional organizations like UNICEF, SCF, Oak Foundation, ECPAT, OXPAM, ILO, Plan International, ISPCAN and research works of academics, direct activities in the field by the social activists and community-based organizations, new legislations, policies, and programs are being drafted and enforced to ensure the safety of the children worldwide.

Recognizing children's rights to safety and protection from all forms of physical and mental violence, as many as 37 countries have already put a ban on corporal punishment in all venues. This project is monitored by the Global Initiative to End all Corporal Punishment of Children (www.endcorporalpunishment.org). It is salutary that more and more developing countries are bringing in legislations to entirely ban corporal punishments.

Latest Efforts by the Government of India for Child Safety and for Their Welfare

The Government of India (GOI) acceded to the UN Convention on the Rights of the Child on December 11, 1992. It reflects the commitment of the government to address the issue of child abuse and neglect. In an attempt to fight this problem, the "Ministry of Women and Child Development" has been set up with independent charges. Furthermore, the GOI has recently taken up a number of legal and social measures for child safety and protection of their Rights, which include the Protection of Children from Sexual Offences Act, 2012 (POCSO Act 2012), The Rights of Children to Free and Compulsory Education Act 2009, The National Commission for Protection of Child Rights Act 2005, Integrated Child Protection Scheme (ICPS), and so on.

Section 3 (VI) of the Rules under the Juvenile Justice (Care and Protection of Children) Act 2000 (56 of 2000), amended by the Amendment Act 33 of 2006, talks about the "Principle of Safety" in the following manner:

> (a) At all stages, from the initial contact till such time he remains in contact with the care and protection system, and thereafter, the juvenile or child or juvenile in conflict with law shall not be subjected to any harm, abuse, neglect, maltreatment, corporal punishment or solitary or otherwise any confinement in jails and extreme care shall be taken to avoid any harm to the sensitivity of the juvenile or the child.
> (b) The state has a greater responsibility for ensuring safety of every child in its care and protection, without resorting to restrictive measures and processes in the name of care and protection.

Gradually a good number of educational institutions in the developing countries are trying to come up with a Child Protection Policy and form Child Protection Team with a representative from teachers, guardians, psychologists, and students. At the same time, some NGO's have adapted Child Protection Policy for rendering effective services to children. It is relevant to mention here that, from 2003 to 2007, a series of multidisciplinary training programs was organized on child protection in India by the editor of the book. These programs were organized as part of the International Society for Prevention of Child Abuse and Neglect's (ISPCAN) regular training program. These training programs were funded by the OAK foundation, Switzerland, and attended by police officers, doctors, NGO personnel, judges from the Juvenile and Family courts and personnel from the Observation Homes. These programs were aimed at making them aware about the seriousness of the issues, legislations, policies, and programs related to child safety. In the programs, it was discussed how to respond to the problems as professionals by deploying their characteristic skills in identification and remedy.

Need for Reporting of Abuse

The first step in prevention of any form of violence against children is to bring the issue to light through reporting. Reporting of any offence is very important as it could help to render justice to the victim and to punish the perpetrators. In addition, it would help to understand the nature and magnitude of the problem, and to plan need-based intervention program. Unfortunately the reporting of child sexual abuse is very low across the world both in urban and rural areas for many reasons, such as humiliation, disclosure of identity, social stigma, lack of trust on the system and social support, laxity of juvenile justice system, lack of knowledge about legal procedures, apprehension of further victimization, and so on (Deb and Modak 2010; Deb and Mukherjee 2011). And to speak of giving corporal punishment, it is as tardy as the legal system and it is hardly pronounced. Traditionally, psychological abuse is not recognized as an abusive activity against children in the developing countries. Of course, defining psychological abuse and assessment of the same is difficult. Scolding children for minor mistakes and unrealistic expectations of parents is perceived to be their rights in developing countries like India. This issue requires more attention from the academics and other professionals for defining the boundary of psychological abuse.

Need for New Legislations for Prevention of Child Sexual Abuse and Child Trafficking

There have been a number of incidents in the recent past where children were raped and then killed in order to suppress the evidence. This sort of heinous crimes necessitates strict legislations. Similarly, it is imperative to amend existing laws in consideration of the present scenario of child sexual abuse and child trafficking (Deb 2014). With regard to mandatory reporting of child sexual abuse, the United States, Canada, and Australia have made effective legislations specifying the category of social agents and professions for mandatory reporting. The Trafficking Act of Ghana (2005) for mandatory reporting of child trafficking is a good example in this context.

Need for Systematic Development of Documentation System, Monitoring, Research, and Evaluation of Existing Program

Compared to developed countries, most of the developing countries have very poor or little documentation systems. Without proper documentation, it is difficult to assess any situation and to design need-based intervention program. In India, there is no system of assessment and documentation of child abuse and neglect cases in the hospitals, both in government and non-government sectors. Policy makers have to be aware of the great importance of documenting child abuse and neglect in hospitals. It is very important that the hospitals send the data every month to the Central Documentation System. For the assessment of child sexual abuse and intentional physical injury, there should be a uniform procedure. In default of a uniform policy, doctors follow different procedures in different set-ups as the situations demand.

Research on different issues related to child abuse such as cyberbullying, child custody issues, child trafficking, and efficacy of community-based and institutions-based intervention programs are required for generating more evidence. Developing countries still need population-based data for understanding the magnitude of the problem and taking corrective measures. In some developing countries like India, policies are not made on the basis of systematically generated evidence.

Monitoring and evaluation are also essential when it comes to checking the quality of implementation of any program and its effectiveness, for example, how mid-day meal is benefiting the target groups, what the perception of the parents of the beneficiaries of mid-day meals has about their quality, what about the effectiveness of childline, and so on. In developing countries, monitoring and evaluation is not given adequate importance probably because of the drawbacks inherent in the system.

Prevention

Prevention of child abuse and neglect and ensuring their safety is possible through education, awareness, advocacy, and effective implementation of child rights legislations and programs. As with other countries, the Government of India has contrived various legislations and policies for protection of child rights as mentioned earlier. For effective implementation of the legalizations and programs, political will is needed for the allocation of more funds. More funds are required for the infrastructure development for the construction and renovation of children/observation homes. The conditions of children/observation homes in different states under the Social Welfare Department are in a sorry state with poor infrastructure for accommodating a large number of children. Safety of the children in the Observation Homes should be ensured in addition to making arrangement of skill building training program and counseling facilities by trained counselors. The performance of the Observation Homes should also be monitored periodically by experienced professionals for ensuring the safety and well-being of the disadvantaged and victimized children.

For generation of resources and fund, corporate sectors could be approached by the local government as part of their social responsibility. Arguably, there cannot a better investment of resources than for the welfare and well-being of the children.

Media should be utilized for the spread of information about socio-legal measures for child protection among community members. Awareness of social measures will encourage needy people to come forward to avail themselves of the facilities, while awareness about legal measures will serve to discourage the perpetrators from committing offences against children. Likewise, awareness about legal measures will encourage victim to report the crime and to seek justice.

Prioritization of the issue of the protection of child rights in the national agenda will bring about change in the national policy. In addition, there is a need for improvement of documentation system and for encouraging people to report child abuse (whether physical or sexual) and child trafficking to the respective agencies for protection and justice.

Strengthening the System with Trained Human Resources

There is an urgent need to recruit Child Protection Officers in every district as per the Integrated Child Protection Scheme (ICPS 2015) and also to recruit female Juvenile Officer in every police station (or at least one female Juvenile Officer for 2/3 police stations) as mentioned in the Juvenile Justice (Care and Protection) Act (2000) (amended in 2006). Simultaneously, arrangement of periodic training programs for the law enforcement agencies, Child Protection Officers, NGO personnel and authorities of educational institutions will help them to manage or to implement better the social and legal measures.

Intervention: Assessment and Treatment

Evidence-based intervention program should be adopted for redressing psychological trauma of sexually abused and trafficked children. There is also a need to develop school-based intervention program for the children to address some of the issues which torment them, such as academic stress, corporal punishment, sexual abuse, and discrimination based on caste and intellectual ability. School-based intervention programs are needed for life skill development, as well as for sensitizing the students about issues like good touch and bad touch which will help them to deal with unwanted situations more effectively. Very few schools in India have intervention program on any of these issues on a regular basis. Sometimes they organize a workshop or seminar when the school authority receives a circular from the education department. However, some of the NGOs are doing commendable jobs in the educational institute in India and other developing countries in sensitizing the students about sexual abuse issues and about the way to deal with them. From the first-hand experience of the editor, school-based intervention program on adolescent reproductive and sexual health is beneficial in providing them with correct knowledge and information about the issue and thus in making them psychologically stronger to cope with various challenging issues in everyday life.

The first step of intervention program is assessment of the nature of abuse experienced by a child after doing the reporting, followed by mental state examination for need-based psychological support services. Unfortunately, very few educational institutions in India have such facilities. The goal of the clinical assessment is to determine the child's and the caregiver's overall functioning, adaptation, and level of symptomalogy. To begin, a thorough assessment of the family's strength and problems should be ascertained, including the problems that need to be addressed at the parental, child, family, and social systems levels. Procedures for assessments are interviews, paper-and-pencil measures, or structured observations with the child, siblings, and caregivers.

Periodic school-based sensitization programs for the teachers and parents about child rights are indispensable for changing their mindset about the issue and about the friendly disciplining methods. These two social agents who are primarily responsible for the growth and development of the child often lack adequate knowledge; they have wrong perceptions about child rights as revealed by an Indian study (Deb and Mathews 2012).

It is worth mentioning here three evidence-based intervention programs: Abuse-Focused Cognitive Behavioural Therapy (AF-CBT), Parent-Child Interaction

Therapy (PCIT), and Trauma focused cognitive behavioral therapy (TF-CBT). They all were found to be beneficial to victimized children and to their family members.

AF-CBT targets individual child's and parent's characteristics related to the abusive experience, as well as the family context in which coercion or aggression exists. PCIT is a treatment approach originally developed to treat children ages 2–7 with serious behavioral problem. PCIT utilizes live coaching and focuses on improving the behaviors of both the parent and the child. Parents learn to model positive behaviors and are trained to act as "agents of change" for their children's behavioral or emotional difficulties.

TF-CBT is an evidence-based treatment approach that addresses the negative effects of sexual abuse and other traumatic events by combining elements drawn from cognitive, behavioral, and family therapies.

In addition to legal measures, there is a need to bring all the perpetrators indulging in severe child abuse and neglect under the mental health intervention program to change their attitude and behavior toward children. Although this is a difficult task but this approach will save thousands of children from abuse and maltreatment. Abusing children in different forms is nothing but also an indication of an impulsive and hostile behavior of elderly people and in case of sexual abuse it is a sign of perversion. This type of behavior of elderly people requires psychological and even in some cases psychiatric intervention. Increasing rate of mental health problems is another issue which concerns the public health and other professionals since mental health problem has a direct link with child abuse and neglect (Deb 2010). Parents with mental health problem often fail to provide quality care to their children and these children become the victim of neglect and maltreatment. Therefore, it is very important for close family members to seek mental health support services for the person who is suffering from minor or major mental health problems before or after marriage instead of keeping the information secret. There is also a myth among general population in India that a person's mental health problems will be solved automatically after marriage. This wrong notion affects the life partner and the next generation adversely. This issue requires debate and discussion for bringing appropriate legislation and policies to protect the rights of innocent people.

Child neglect is a very common phenomenon in the developing countries like India, Bangladesh, Pakistan, Nepal, Mayanmar, and so on. About one-fourth of the families in India live below the poverty line and they are unable to provide adequate nutrition, medical care, and education to their children. Respective local government also fails to provide the basic facilities to these poor children, although it was instructed in the UNCRC (1989). Officially there might be some programs, but the benefits of the programs do not reach these poor children. There is no effective mechanism for monitoring the implementation of the programs.

However, in the developed countries intervention program for some forms of neglect has indicated promising results that include home visitation as a primary approach. In the developing countries it is a big challenge to implement similar program because of lack of resources and population size.

Challenges

Despite a range of socio-legal measures, children in society experience neglect, abuse, and maltreatment. For ensuring their safety, welfare, and well-being, federal and provincial governments should work in concert with each other, review the present legislations and policies and programs, and come up with comprehensive policies for addressing challenges, which are almost similar across the developing countries. These challenges include: (i) ensuring primary education for all the children as mentioned in The Rights of Children to Free and Compulsory Education Act (2009) (India); (ii) the implementation of school-based intervention programs across the country, both in rural and urban areas, for sensitizing the parents and teachers about child rights and negative consequences of corporal punishment; (iii) ensuring nutrition and safe drinking water for all the children through mid-day meal program and Integrated Child Development Scheme (ICDS); (iv) rehabilitation of thousands and thousands of children living on the street through NGOs; (v) eradication of child labor and child marriage and ensuring their socio-economic rehabilitation; (vi) the prevention of child trafficking for commercial sexual abuse and ensuring rehabilitation of trafficked children after recovery and connecting them with the family members; (vii) addressing gender discrimination, social stigma, cultural belief and practices with regard to education, nutrition, health care, HIV/AIDS, disability through culturally sensitive programs using electronic media and involving community-based organizations; (viii) ensuring that the orphan and destitute children as well as children from poor families are adopted by genuine adopters following proper procedures for their better future; (ix) the prevention of child pornography and cyberbullying through effective legislations; (x) prevention of marriage of elderly people with major mental health problem.

Immediate Need of the Hour

The formation of the State Commission for Protection of Child Rights in all the states in India should speed up, since the State Commission has a greater role to play in every state in the implementation of the legislations and social welfare programs for the children. The State Commission also plays a pivotal role in developing better the coordination among the government and the NGOs.

Counseling facilities by trained psychologists for students in the educational institutions should be arranged. The government should also have a policy for the recruitment of trained counselors.

Community-based intervention program should be strengthened with help from the NGOs to house a large number of orphan and destitute children with basic facilities.

It is important to look into some of the core issues like rapid population growth, poverty, illiteracy, unemployment, and primary health issues at the national program of the Government of India, which are directly linked with child abuse and neglect. Otherwise, whatever efforts are being made, they may not have desired results (Deb 2009).

References

Bonner, B. L. (2013). Advances in Mental Health Intervention. In Deb et al. (Eds.), *Student's Mental Health* (pp.163–183). New Delhi: Akansha Publishing House.

Chiang, W. L., Huang, Y. T., Feng, J. Y., & Lu, T. H. (2012). Incidence of hospitalization due to child maltreatment in Taiwan, 1996–2007: A nationwide population–based study. *Child Abuse and Neglect, 36*(2), 135–141. doi:10.1016/j.chiabu.2011.09.013, http://www.ncbi.nlm.nih.gov/pubmed?term=Chiang%20WL%5BAuthor%5D&cauthor=true&cauthor_uid=22405478, http://www.ncbi.nlm.nih.gov/pubmed?term=Huang%20YT%5BAuthor%5D&cauthor=true&cauthor_uid=22405478, http://www.ncbi.nlm.nih.gov/pubmed?term=Feng%20YT%5BAuthor%5D&cauthor=true&cauthor_uid=22405478, http://www.ncbi.nlm.nih.gov/pubmed?term=Lu%20TH%5BAuthor%5D&cauthor=true&cauthor_uid=22405478.

Chou, C. Y., Su, Y. J., Wu, H. M., & Chen, S. H. (2010). Child physical abuse and the related PTSD in Taiwan: The role of Chinese cultural background and victims' subjective reactions. *Child Abuse and Neglect, 35*(1), 58–68. doi:10.1016/j.chiabu.2010.08.005, http://www.ncbi.nlm.nih.gov/pubmed?term=Chou%20CY%5BAuthor%5D&cauthor=true&cauthor_uid=21334068, http://www.ncbi.nlm.nih.gov/pubmed?term=Su%20YJ%5BAuthor%5D&cauthor=true&cauthor_uid=21334068, http://www.ncbi.nlm.nih.gov/pubmed?term=Wu%20HM%5BAuthor%5D&cauthor=true&cauthor_uid=21334068, http://www.ncbi.nlm.nih.gov/pubmed?term=Chen%20SH%5BAuthor%5D&cauthor=true&cauthor_uid=21334068.

Deb, S. (2009). Child protection: Scenario in India. *International Journal of Child Health and Human Development*, 2(3), 339–348.

Deb, S., & Chatterjee, P. (2008). *Styles of parenting adolescents: The Indian scenario*. New Delhi: Akansha Publ House.

Deb, S., & Mitra, K. (2001). Deviance among disadvantaged children in Kolkata and reasons thereof. *Indian J Criminol Criminalistics, 22*(1), 41–53.

Deb, S. (2004). *Corporal punishment of children at home and in the school: A comparative study of attitude, perception and practice of parents and teachers*. Paper presented in the 15th International Congress on Child Abuse and Neglect, held during Sept. 19–22, 2004 in Brisbane, Australia.

Deb, S. (2010). Child protection: Scenario in India. *International Journal of Child Health and Human Development, 2*(3), 339–348.

Deb, S., & Modak, S. (2010). Prevalence of violence against children in families in Tripura and its relationship with socio-economic, cultural and other factors. *Journal of Injury and Violence Research, 2*(1), 5–18. doi:10.5249/jivr.v2i1.31.

Deb, S. (2005). Child trafficking in South Asia: Dimensions, roots, facets and interventions. *Social Change, 35*(2), 143–155. doi:10.1177/004908570503500211.

Deb, S., Srivastava, N., Chatterjee, P., & Chakraborty, T. (2005). Processes of child trafficking in West Bengal: A qualitative study. *Social Change, 35*(2), 112–123. doi:10.1177/004908570503500208.

Deb, S., & Mukherjee, A. (2011). Background and adjustment capacity of sexually abused girls and their perceptions of intervention. *Child Abuse Review, 20*, 213–230. doi:10.1002/car.1153.

Deb, S., & Walsh, K. (2012). Impact of physical, psychological, and sexual violence on social adjustment of school children in India. *School Psychology International, 33*(4), 391–415. doi:10.1177/0143034311425225.

Deb, S., & Mathews, B. (2012). Children's rights in India: parents' and teachers' attitudes, knowledge and perception. *International Journal of Children's Rights, 20*, 1–24. doi:10.1163/157181811X616022.

Deb, S. & Madrid, B. (2014). Burden of child abuse and neglect with special reference to socio-legal measures: a comparative picture of India, Philippines and Japan (Vol. 2, pp.77–106). In Conte Jon (ed.), *Child Abuse and Neglect Worldwide*, California: PRAEGER.

Deb, S. (2014). Legislation concerning reporting of child sexual abuse and child trafficking in India: A closer look. In Mathews Ben & Bross C. Donald (Eds.), *Mandatory reporting laws and the identification of severe child abuse and neglect*. Australia: Springer.

Nguyen, H. T., Dunne, M. P., & Le, A. V. (2010). Multiple types of child maltreatment and adolescent mental health in Viet Nam. *Bulletin of the World Health Organization, 88*(1), 22–30. doi:10.2471/BLT.08.060061.

Pinheiro, P. S. (2006). *World report on violence against children*. Geneva, Switzerland: United Nations Secretary-General's Study on Violence against Children.

Report on Child Abuse and Neglect. (2007). New Delhi: Min Women Child Dev, Government of India.

The Rights of Children to Free and Compulsory Education Act (2009).

The Integrated Child Protection Scheme (ICPS) (2015). A centrally sponsored scheme of government of india—Civil society partnership with the ministry of women & child development, Government of India.

The Juvenile Justice (Care and Protection of Children) Act (2000). (amended in 2006, India).

The Rules of the Juvenile Justice (Care and Protection of Children) Act (2000) (amended in 2006, India).

The Commissions for the Protection of the Child Rights Act (2005).

The Protection of Children from Sexual Offences Act (2012).

The Trafficking Act of Ghana (2005).

The U.N. Convention on the Rights of the Child (CRC) (1989).

UNICEF. (2009). *Progress for children: a report card on child protection: Innocenti Report Card Number 8*. New York: UNICEF Division of Communication.

World Bank Annual Report. (2010). https://www.google.co.in/url?saℑt&rctℑj&qℑ&esrcℑ←s&sourceℑweb&cdℑ2&cadℑrja&uactℑ8&vedℑ0CCgQFjAB&urlℑhttp%3A%2F%2Fsiteresources.worldbank.org%2FEXTANNREP2010%2FResources%2FWorldBank-AnnualReport2010.pdf&eiℑq_OwU-XsO4OQuATklILAAQ&usgℑAFQjCNEQtk9RRIodpxEODx9Rmxfw-GJeEUQ&sig2ℑeKTTTD0z1s0HfjHP5e6uIA&bvmℑbv.69837884,d.c2E.

Part I
Nature and Extent of Child Abuse and Neglect

Chapter 2
Fifty Years of Child Abuse: Milestones, Misconceptions, and Moving On

Kim Oates

Introduction

It is helpful to look back on the past in child protection and to see how far we have come in a relatively short time. It is only 50 years since Henry Kemp and colleagues coined the phrase "The Battered Child Syndrome" (Kemp et al. 1962). Looking back at achievements as well as errors can be helpful on those occasions when we become despondent and feel that we are making little progress in child protection. We can look back and see just how far we have come as well as looking forward to see how much still we have to do.

Child abuse is a spectrum which covers neglect, failure to thrive, physical abuse, sexual abuse, and emotional abuse. These different aspects of child abuse have similarities as well as differences with some children experiencing several types of abuse. It can be difficult to interpret research studies that group each type of abuse together, treating them as if they are the same thing in the analysis and then drawing conclusions. This is something we need to be aware of when reading the research literature in this area.

Child abuse is important not just because of the immediate effects on the child, which are bad enough in themselves, but also because in many of these children there are long-lasting effects which impair their ability to function effectively in their adult lives and in their role as parents.

K. Oates (✉)
Sydney Medical School, University of Sydney, Sydney, NSW 2006, Australia
e-mail: kim.oates@sydney.edu.au

S. Deb (ed.), *Child Safety, Welfare and Well-being*,
DOI 10.1007/978-81-322-2425-9_2

Milestones

My own background is medical, so some of these key milestones may seem to have a medical bias. Others may have a somewhat different list.

While there had been some early description of child abuse as far back as the 1880s, by West in London and Tardieu in Paris, the modern era is generally regarded as starting in 1946 when Caffey, an American radiologist, described multiple fractures in the long bones of children who also had chronic subdural hematoma (Caffey 1946). If you read Caffey's paper today, the diagnosis of child abuse seems obvious. These children had subdural hematomas, retinal hemorrhages, and multiple fractures. Yet Caffey could give no clear explanation in this paper. He described the features of abuse, and often gets the credit for being one of the first to describe it, but he did not really recognize it as such. In 1946, society and the professional groups were not yet ready to hear this type of information.

It was not until 9 year later that Woolley and Evans talked about the significance of these injuries and the fact that they although they resembled accidental trauma, they were really inflicted by the parents (Woolley and Evans 1955). The connection suddenly became clear.

Henry Kempe had been concerned about child abuse since the 1950s but could get little interest from his colleagues. He got his chance when he became Chair of the 1961 Program Committee of the American Academy of Pediatrics and used his position to organize a session on "The Battered Child", a phrase he coined.

The next year the classic paper "The Battered Child Syndrome" (Kempe et al. 1962) was published in the Journal of the American Medical Association. It was the turning point in the recognition of the extent of the problem.

In a survey to find the 10 most influential papers published on child abuse (Oates and Cohn-Donelly 1997) the paper by Kempe and colleagues was the clear winner.

By 1972, Caffey was much clearer about abuse, this time publishing a landmark paper on the shaking of babies titled "On the theory and practice of shaking infants" in the American Journal of Diseases of Children (Caffey 1972). He was not the first to describe the damage caused by shaking, but this paper popularized the notion. We learnt that what pediatricians used to call the "spontaneous subdural hematoma of infancy" was not that spontaneous after all and that it was usually caused by inflicted trauma.

Another advance occurred in 1972 when we learnt about Munchausen Syndrome by Proxy in a paper from the UK (Meadow 1977). When we read this paper we realized that we too had seen similar cases. It alerted us to a further dimension of abuse which had been right before our eyes, but often missed.

In 1978 Kempe's paper "Sexual abuse, another hidden pediatric problem" was published (Kempe 1978). It was not the first paper on child sexual abuse, but it was probably the most important. This was because of Kempe's stature in the field. By 1978, Kemp was so well known in this field that when he spoke or wrote he could not be ignored. This was the paper that brought child sexual abuse out of the closet.

Then in 1978 we were reminded about the importance of emotional abuse. "The elusive crime of emotional abuse" (Garbarino 1978) paper brought a variety of concepts about emotional abuse into a clear framework which greatly improved our understanding in this area.

We now know so much more about child abuse. We understand the importance of the ecological model: we know that child abuse can involve more than just the child and the family. It can involve the extended family, the community in which the child and family live, and the values of the society in which that community exists.

Misconceptions

There have also been misconceptions, mistakes wehave made in getting to where we are now but that have helped us to learn.

Once the misconceptions of the past was when we have insisted that "children never lie". Is this true? In the 1970s and 1980s we confused the fact that children can give accurate stories of their abuse with the assertion that children never lie. Anyone who has had anything to do with a child knows that they do not always speak with what we would regard as the truth. They make up stories and can happily garnish the truth to avoid getting into trouble. This is not surprising as adults do this as well.

However, this insistence in court that children "never" lie about anything did not add credibility to our cause when we were asked to give evidence in court. However, it is true that that child rarely lie about abuse.

False accusations of child sexual abuse do occur, but the incidence is less than 2 % (Oates et al. 2000). However, the research findings about the reliability of children are inconsistent with views of the general public. Yarmey and Jones (1983) found that when members of the public were asked how an 8-year old child would respond to questions by police in court, less than 50 % believed that the child could give an accurate account. This is at odds with the research evidence about the reliability of children's memories.

One of the most robust findings of memory research is that children from as young as 6 years of age are just as accurate as adults in recalling events and are no more suggestible than adults (Goodman et al. 2001; Davis 1998). Children do make good witnesses. They rarely make up stories of abuse. But the blanket assertion that "children never lie" dented our credibility.

Another past mistake was to be dogmatic about the diameter of the hymen in cases of child sexual abuse. This view probably led wrongful diagnosis in some cases.

The basis for this view was a paper by Cantwell (1983), stating that a hymen opening greater than 4 mm was indicative of sexual abuse. However, we know a lot more now. The correct data about the hymen is that there is a wide normal variation in shape and size. It depends on the age of the child, the position in which the child is examined, and the method used for examination (Finkel 2009). There is a wide range of normal. The vaginal or hymen diameter cannot be relied on as the sole diagnostic criteria of penetration. Another pitfall was the view that mandatory reporting was a panacea which would help to solve many of our problems. But is it a help or hindrance? Some countries who do not have mandatory reporting want it. Others who do have it want to abandon it. Although over 60 countries have some form of mandatory reporting, there is no real consensus (Dubowitz 2012).

There are clearly some benefits of mandatory reporting: It provides a clear statement that government takes child abuse seriously. It raises public awareness. It encourages early identification which may prevent further abuse and death. It provides a database so that the size of the problem can be measured and monitored. It results in services being provided and its introduction is often accompanied by public and professional training and education.

There can also be disadvantages of mandatory reporting: It may not distinguish between serious and less serious reports. It can be discriminatory as poor and more vulnerable groups are more likely to be those reported. Many cases cannot be substantiated. The large numbers being reported result in child protection services becoming overloaded. There is a danger that with so many resources goes into investigating reported cases that there are few resources left for adequate meaningful intervention on the scale required another early misconception was that domestic violence and child abuse were unrelated. We now know that domestic violence and child maltreatment have a 30–60 % overlap (Jaffe et al. 2012). This is useful knowledge as when we are see domestic violence we also need to consider the question as to whether there is concurrent child abuse.

A further misconception is that sexual abuse is thought to be an isolated crime in otherwise law-abiding people. This may be so in many cases, but certainly not all. A review of police and court records of 180 child sexual abuse offenders 10 years after initial offence found that 60 % had a criminal conviction for offences other than sexual abuse, including violence and robbery (Parkinson et al. 2004). So while some abusers may be otherwise normal, we need to be aware that others offend in many other ways as well, with sexual abuse being just part of a broad spectrum of their criminal behavior.

There was a time when it was believed that alcohol was not a significant factor in precipitating or facilitating abuse. However, the current evidence is that alcohol can be an influencing factor in 77 % of child maltreatment cases (Meredith and Price-Robertson 2011).

Domestic violence, other criminal activity, and alcohol abuse are just three examples of our reluctance to look at the bigger picture in the early years of child protection work.

Another pitfall has been to blame individuals when it is the system that needs fixing. Child protection systems are complex. They involve a variety of staff and procedures. Lessons from the mining and aircraft industries have shown that up to 80 % of errors are due to problems in the system. The message is clear. We need to build safer systems to protect children and to support people who work in the area, not to discipline individual staff members when things go wrong.

Where We Are at Present

Is the incidence of child abuse falling? It seems to be in the USA. Finkelhor and Jones (2006) have shown that neglect, physical abuse, sexual abuse, and juvenile homicide have all fallen significantly in recent years. Neglect has not fallen by as much, but the other three have fallen sharply.

What is the reason for this fall? Finkelhor has suggested several possibilities: perhaps increased public awareness; more prevention programs, and the use of pharmacotherapy, particularly anti-depressants are some of the possibilities. He also speculates that it may also be due to incarceration, where in the United States long prison sentences for abuse are common, so that perhaps many of the offenders are not able to offend again.

But is it really falling? A study by Gilbert, and colleagues (2012) showed no consistent evidence for a decrease in all forms of child maltreatment in Sweden, England, New Zealand, and Western Australia. However, this information is difficult to interpret as child abuse rates vary considerably between countries. What the paper did point out was that the lower level of child maltreatment in Sweden compared with USA was consistent with lower rates of child poverty between the two countries and with Swedish government policies which provide high levels of universal support for parenting.

The detection and management of child abuse and neglect is expensive. In Australia, where I am based, the cost of child abuse and neglect to our society was between $10.7 and $30.1 billion in 2007 for a country of only 22 million people.

On a global level, a study for the World Health Organization on the global impact of disease found that child sexual abuse contributed to between 4 and 5 % of the total burden of disease in men and 7–8 % of the burden of disease in females (Andrews 2004). This study also found that for some disorders, the percentage attributed to child sexual abuse is even higher, particularly panic disorders, suicide attempts, and post traumatic stress disorder.

We now recognize that childhood abuse and neglect have long-term consequences in many areas of life, but it is only relatively recently that we have been able to understand the reason.

Felitti et al. (1989) looked at the relationship between adverse childhood experiences and adult mental and physical health in a cohort of over 13,000 adults. They used 8–10 categories of adverse childhood experiences (ACE), including abuse and neglect and found that a third had an ACE score of zero, (no adverse childhood experiences), but 16 % had four adverse childhood experiences and 10 % had five or more adverse childhood experiences.

When these researchers looked at the relationship between physical and mental health problems and adverse childhood experiences they found a linear relation between the number of adverse childhood experiences and a range of health problems. The more adverse childhood experiences, the greater the likelihood of suicide attempts, being prescribed anti-depressants, having memory gaps for large periods of their childhood, being smokers, alcoholics, intravenous drug users, being promiscuous, and more likely to have teenage pregnancy. Even physical problems such liver disease and coronary artery disease were more likely with a greater number of adverse childhood experiences. The experiences of childhood can be long-lasting. They are not like footprints in the sand, where the effects disappear fairly quickly. The experiences of childhood are like footprints in cement explaining why early childhood is so important.

Moving on: The Possibilities

What about the possibilities? A recent paper showed that adolescents who have a history of abuse have reduced gray matter and the location of gray matter reduction depends on the type of abuse (Edminston et al. 2011). Future advances in understanding brain function are going to tell us much more about abuse and this knowledge may one day be able to lead to more effective, targeted treatments.

Can child abuse change the way our genes function? Does our genetic make-up protect some of us and make others of us more vulnerable? Binder et al. (2009) looked at the FKBP5 gene and abuse. These researchers studied 762 adults and looked at two things. The first was whether they had been abused as children. 70 % had not been abused as children and 30 % had been abused. The second thing they looked at was whether the FKBP5 gene had a normal expression (was functioning normally) or a low expression.

They found that adults who had a low expression of the gene and who had also been abused as children had doubled the incidence of post traumatic stress disorder. It seems that here is a gene which may give some protection against the adverse effects of child abuse because, when it is not well-expressed, the adverse effects of childhood abuse may be more likely to appear. There is much to learn in this exciting area.

A similar finding appeared in Nature Neuroscience (McGowan et al. 2009). This was about the NR3C1 gene, thought to modulate stress. The researchers analyzed 36 brains. Twelve of the brains were from people who had suicide but where there was no history of abuse. Twelve were from people who had committed suicide and where there was also a history of abuse and 12 were from people who had died accidently. It was found that in those who had suicide and who also had a history of abuse, there was less expression of the gene.

What might findings like these mean? They suggest that childhood abuse seems to reduce the ability of some genes to be expressed (to function fully), an example of how life events may alter our biology, by altering how our genes are expressed.

In practical terms, with genetic advances proceeding so rapidly, it may become possible to detect these genes through genetic testing, so that in people with low levels of expression of these genes there might be the opportunity to improve their environment or to provide help to them early on. It may even be possible at same stage to deliver genetic therapy, to boost the expression of particular genes to protect against abuse, or to counteract the adverse effects of abuse.

Drugs may be able to be designed to treat people with particular genetic profiles and these will also undoubtedly have a role in the prevention and treatment of abuse. The possibilities are very exciting.

What Other Disciplines Can Teach Us

We can also learn much from other disciplines. In Australia there has been a 35 % reduction in motor traffic deaths over the last 8 years even though there are many more cars on the road now. The reason for this success has been due to a combination of legislation, surveillance, safer roads, and safer cars as well as public education about road safety.

It is a similar story with coronary artery disease, with an 85 % reduction in deaths over the last 30 years. This is a spectacular success story, even though life is more stressful now than 30 years ago. It occurred because of a combination of public education (less smoking, better diet, and exercise), much more effective emergency treatment and ongoing medical support.

The lessons for child protection from these good results in reducing road deaths and deaths from heart disease are that a combined approach is needed, a combination of legislation, public education, reducing risk factors, early intervention, and better treatment. The success also occurred because governments and the public realized that these were serious problems and that something needed to be done.

The child protection field can also learn from the quality and safety movement. The airlines and mining industries have reduced error markedly and saved lives by a combination of; simplifying systems; having a skilled and knowledgeable work force; providing a supportive working environment; having reasonable work schedules for staff; seeing errors as opportunities for improving the system rather than blaming the individual; having clear guidelines for performance appraisal, having a culture where errors are reported without fear of retribution and robust systems to collect data on errors with a view to improving the systems.

The health industry, which learnt from the mining and aircraft industries now knows the value of clear, unambiguous communication, using "time out" to ensure the whole team understands what is about to be done, clear handover at the end of shifts and learning from error.

It took the health industry 20 years to start to catch up with the airline and mining industries in developing safer systems and blame free reporting. How long will it take the child protection system to catch up and produce safer systems to protect children?

So the future holds some very exciting possibilities: in genetics, in psychopharmacology, in learning from successes in other areas such as reducing traffic accidents and heart disease and in designing safer systems.

A Future Challenge

One of the next big challenges for us is to make the future safe from corporal punishment for the next generation of children. If we really take a stand, right now, we may be able to protect the current generation of children. This is an international issue.

The argument against corporal punishment becomes side-tracked when people disagree by saying "Children need discipline." Of course they need discipline. But hitting is just one form of discipline and research shows it to be one of the least effective. And it can have adverse longer term consequences for later mental health problems and in increasing the likelihood of aggressive behavior (Gerschoff 2002; Simons and Wurtele 2010; Taylor et al. 2010).

Why do parents hit their children? Because we learnt most of our parenting skills when we were children, from the way our parents treated us. Hitting children is intergenerational. But we now know that this teaches children that violence is an acceptable way to resolve conflict.

It is the experience of many parents that physical punishment does work. But we now know that the change in behavior is often short lived and what the child really learns is to avoid the behavior in front of the adult.

Hitting a child contravenes the United Nations Convention on the Rights of the Child (UNCRC). Article 19 of the Convention (United Nations 1989) states that: … Children are to be protected from all forms of physical violence while in the care of their parents…"

Continuing international concern about violence toward children resulted in the UN Secretary General commissioning a report on violence against children in which stated (United Nations 2006) … No violence against children is justifiable… This study marks the end of adults' justification of violence against children, whether accepted as traditional or disguised as discipline…"

The rights of children in this area are now recognized by legislation against corporal punishment of children existing in 46 countries as of June 2015. The momentum to prevent children being hit in any way is growing. But legislation alone is not enough. It needs to be combined with major investment in helping parents to learn about more effective, less harmful methods of discipline which are known to work, complemented by government policies which support parenting.

The future is preventing child abuse has much to offer. We have come a long way in the last 50 years in understanding child abuse, initially as something seen mainly as an individual family problem, later expanded to an ecological view involving the broader community and society and now acknowledged in many countries to be a key issue in the protection of children's rights.

In 2011 in New Delhi, at an ISPCAN conference, a declaration was made, the Delhi Declaration (Seth and van Niekerk 2011). A declaration which aimed to make the Asia Pacific area a safer place for children by declaring a commitment and pledging a resolve to stand against the neglect and abuse of children and to strive for achievement of child rights and the building of a caring community for every child, free of violence and discrimination. It is our challenge to implement this.

References

Andrews, G. (2004). Comparative quantification of health risk, global and regional burden of disorders attributable to selected major risk factors. In: Ezzati et al. (Eds), Chapter 23 in global health risk, WHO, Geneva

Binder, E. B., Bradley, R. G., Liu, W., Epstein, M. P., Deveau, T. C., Mercer, K. B et al. (2008). Association of FKBP5 polymorphisms and childhood abuse with risk of posttraumatic stress disorder symptoms in adults, *JAMA*, 299, 1–1510. doi:10.1001/jama.299.11.1291

Caffey, J. (1946). Multiple fractures in the long bones of infants suffering from subdural hematoma. *American Journal of Roentgenology, 56*, 163–173.

Caffey, J. (1972). On the theory and practice of shaking infants. *Amer. J. Dis. Child., 124*, 161–169. doi:10.1001/archpedi.1972.02110140011001.

Cantwell, H. (1983). Vaginal inspection as it relates to child sexual abuse in girls under thirteen. *Child Abuse and Neglect, 7*, 171–176. doi:10.1016/0145-2134(83)90069-8.

Davis, S. (1998). Social and scientific influences on the study of children's suggestibility: A historical perspective. *Child Maltreatment, 3*, 186–194. doi:10.1177/1077559598003002011.

Dubowitz, H. (Ed.). (2012). *World perspectives on child abuse, international society for prevention of child abuse and neglect*. USA: Denver Co.

Edmiston, E. E., Wang, F., Mazure, C. M., Guiney, J., Sinha, R., Mayes, L. C., & Blumberg, H. P. (2011). Corticostriatal–limbic gray matter morphology in adolescents with self-reported exposure to childhood maltreatment. *Archives of Pediatrics and Adolescent Medicine, 165*, 1069–1077.

Felitti, V. J., Anda, R. F., Nordenberg, D., Williamson, D. F., Spitz, A. M., Edwards, V., & Marks, J. S. (1998). The relationship of adult health status to childhood abuse and household dysfunction. *American Journal of Preventive Medicine, 14*(4), 245–258.

Finkel, M. (2009). Medical evaluation of child sexual abuse, *American Academy of Pediatrics*, 2009 Evanston, p. 63

Finkelhor, D., & Jones, L. (2006). Why have child maltreatment and child victimization declined? *Journal of Social Issues, 62*, 685–716. doi:10.1111/j.1540-4560.2006.00483.x.

Garbarino, J. (1978). The elusive crime of emotional abuse. *Child Abuse and Neglect, 2*, 89–99. doi:10.1016/0145-2134(78)90011-X.

Gershoff, E. T. (2002). Corporal punishment by parents and associated child behavior experiences: A meta-analytic and theoretical review. *Psychological Bulletin, 128*, 539–579. doi:10.1037//0033-2909.128.4.539.

Gilbert, R., Fluke, J., O'Donnell, M., Gonzalez-Izquierdo, A., Brownell, M., Gulliver, P., & Sidebotham, P. (2012). Child maltreatment: variation in trends and policies in six developed countries. *Lancet, 379*, 758–772. doi:10.1111/j.1365-2214.2012.01375_4.x.

Goodman, G. S., Bottoms, B. L., Rudy, L., Davis, S. L., & Schwartz-Kenney, B. M. (2001). Effect of past abuse experiences on children's eyewitness memory. *Law and Human Behavior, 25*, 269–298.

Jaffe, P. G., Campbell, M., Hamilton, L. H., & Juodis, M. (2012). Children in danger of domestic homicide. *Child Abuse and Neglect, 36*(1), 71–74.

Kempe, C. H., Silverman, F. N., Steele, B. F., Droegemueller, W., & Silver, H. K. (1962). The battered child syndrome. *JAMA, 1962*(181), 17–24.

Kempe, C. H. (1978). Sexual abuse, another hidden problem. *Pediatrics, 62*, 382–389.

McGowan, P. O., Sasaki, A., D'Alessio, A. C., Dymov, S., Labonté, B., Szyf, M., & Meaney, M. J. (2009). Epigenetic regulation of the glucocorticoid receptor in human brain associates with childhood abuse. *Nature Neuroscience, 12*(3), 342–348.

Meadow, R. (1977). Munchausen syndrome by proxy: The hinterland of child abuse. *Lancet, 2*, 343–345.

Meredith, V., & Price-Robertson, R. (2011). *(20110*. Australian Institute for Family Studies: Alcohol misuse and child maltreatment.

Oates, R. K., Jones, D. P. H., Denson, D., Sirotnak, A., Gary, N., & Krugman, D. (2000). Erroneous concerns about child sexual abuse. *Child Abuse and Neglect, 24*, 140–157. doi:10.1016/S0145-2134(99)00108-8.

Oates, R. K., & Cohn-Donnelly, A. (1997). Influential papers in child abuse. *Child Abuse and Neglect, 21*, 319–326. doi:10.1016/S0145-2134(96)00169-X.

Parkinson, P., Shrimpton, S., Oates, R. K., Swanston, H., & O'Toole, B. (2004). Non-sex offences committed by child molesters. *International Journal of Offender Therapy and Comparative Criminology, 48*, 28–39. doi:10.1177/0306624X03257246.

Seth, R., & van Niekerk, J. (2012). *Delhi declaration, E10 green park main*. India: New Delhi.

Simons, D. A., & Wurtele, S. K. (2010). Relationships between parents' use of corporal punishment and their children's endorsement of spanking and hitting other children. *Child Abuse and Neglect, 34*(9), 639–646. doi:10.1016/j.chiabu.2010.01.012.

Taylor, C. A., Mangarella, J. A., Lee, S. J., & Rice, J. C. (2010). Mothers' spanking of 3 year old children and subsequent risk of children's aggressive behavior. *Pediatrics, 125*, 1057–1065. doi:10.1542/peds.2009-2678).

United Nations. (1989). *Convention on the rights of the child*. Geneva, Switzerland: High Commissioner for Human Rights.

United Nations. (2006). *World report on violence against children*. Geneva, Switzerland: United Nations Publishing Services.

Woolley, P. V., & Evans, W. A. (1955). Significance of skeletal lesions in infants resembling those of traumatic origin. *Journal of the American Medical Association, 158*, 539–543. doi:10.1001/jama.1955.02960070015005.

Yarmey, A. D., & Jones, H. P. (1983). Is the psychology of eyewitness identification a matter of common sense? In S. M. A. Lloyd-Bostock & B. R. Clifford (Eds.), *1983, Evaluating eyewitness evidence* (pp. 13–40). Chichester: Wiley.

Chapter 3
Cyberbullying: Its Prevention and Intervention Strategies

Rebecca P. Ang

Introduction

With the advent of the Internet and other electronic technologies, bullying has taken on a new form. The transmutation of bullying has surfaced from the physical to the virtual; the Internet has become a new arena for social interactions, permitting children and adolescents to say and do things with some anonymity and limited oversight by adult monitors. Cyberbullying has been defined as the use of electronic communication technology as a means to deliberately threaten, harm, embarrass, or socially exclude another (e.g., Patchin and Hinduja 2006). Other researchers such as Law et al. (2012) also suggested that bullying whether it is traditional face-to-face bullying or cyberbullying should include the component of a power differential between bully and victim.

Kowalski and Limber (2007) examined cyberbullying among 3,767 middle school students in United States. They found that 11 % had been victims of cyberbullying, 7 % had been cyberbullies/cyber-victims, and 4 % had been cyberbullies at least once over the past couple of months. In a separate study, Spriggs et al.(2007) used a nationally representative sample of 6–10th graders from the United States, and found that parental communication, social isolation, and classmate relationships were similarly related to bullying across racial/ethnic groups. Cyberbullying is recognized to be a global phenomenon cutting across cultural groups and contexts (Ang et al. 2014; Ang et al. 2011; Li et al. 2012). It should be noted though that in some Asian counties such as Japan for example, the reported prevalence rate could be an underestimate due to possible under-reporting or translation issues (Aoyama et al. 2012).

R.P. Ang (✉)
National Institute of Education, Nanyang Technological University, Singapore, Singapore
e-mail: rebecca.ang@nie.edu.sg

S. Deb (ed.), *Child Safety, Welfare and Well-being*,
DOI 10.1007/978-81-322-2425-9_3

Bullying in cyberspace has extensive and potentially severe consequences such as school refusal, depressive symptoms, and suicide (Raskauskas and Stoltz 2007). In part, cyberbullying has been facilitated by the speed with which children and adolescents are using the Internet and social networking sites. According to the Pew Internet and American Life Project research, 66 % of Internet users are social networking site users (Rainie et al. 2012). This rate is even higher among adolescent Internet users between the ages of 12 and 17 (80 %), which suggests that having a presence on a SNS is almost synonymous with being online for adolescents (Lenhart et al. 2011). The rise in the number of children and adolescents online may also suggest an increase in the number of children and adolescents at risk for engaging in unhealthy, dangerous, and aggressive online social interactions even though a majority of children and adolescents report positive online experiences (Finkelhor et al. 2000; Ybarra and Mitchell 2004). Taken together, it is timely and important to review child and parent variables associated with cyberbullying, and to examine prevention and intervention strategies aimed at protecting vulnerable young people online.

Child and Parent Variables Associated with Cyberbullying

Internet Use

In a large, nationally representative survey of adolescents who use the Internet regularly, Ybarra and Mitchell (2004) found that specific usage characteristics were related to online harassment. Three of these characteristics will be highlighted here. First, adolescents who used the Internet most often for chat rooms were 3.5 times more likely than adolescents who used the Internet most often for all other activities (except email or Instant Messaging) to harass or cyberbully others online. Second, 54 % of online harassers rated themselves as an Internet expert versus 6 % who rated themselves as novices, compared to 29 % of non-harassers who rated themselves as an Internet expert versus 25 % who rated themselves as novices. Third, self-rated importance of the Internet was associated with a two-fold increase in the odds of reporting Internet harassment behavior. These associations remained statistically significant even after controlling for all other significant factors.

In related research, in a sample of 780 adolescent Facebook users from Singapore, Liu et al. (2013) found privacy concern to directly and significantly decrease adolescents' risky disclosure of personally identifiable information. Put differently, adolescents who were less concerned about the security of their online personal information tended to disclose more personally identifiable information on Facebook. Many types of content that Facebook users generate meet the definition of personally identifiable information such as one's full name, date of birth, home address, mobile phone numbers, and personal photographic images (especially face and other distinguishing characteristics). Generally, individuals who have a greater willingness to disclose personal information online have a higher possibility of cybervictimization and a higher possibility of engaging in other potentially risky behaviors such as meeting people face to face who were first encountered online (Lenhart et al. 2011; Liau et al. 2005; Mesch 2009). Collectively, these results suggest that children and adolescents, who find themselves online frequently, especially if they actively engage in social networking and are not concerned about personal privacy, are particularly vulnerable.

Psychosocial Difficulties

Children and adolescents who face various types of psychosocial problems and difficulties are also vulnerable online. In Ybarra and Mitchell's (2004) study, they found that indications of psychosocial challenge were associated with significantly elevated odds of harassing others online. For example, 32 % of online harassers compared to 10 % of non-harassers reported frequent substance use and that represented a four-fold increase in odds of Internet aggression against others. Also, 6 % of online harassers versus 1 % of non-harassers reported physical or sexual victimization by an adult in the previous year. Additionally, adolescent-reported delinquency, depressive symptomotology, and receiving a failing grade at school were also related to elevated odds of harassing others online.

Psychosocial difficulties have also been linked to excessive and problematic Internet use. As reviewed earlier, Internet use has robust links with cyberbullying and harassment. Problematic Internet use can be specific or generalized in nature (Davis 2001); specific problematic Internet use is the excessive or overuse of specific Internet functions such as gambling or viewing sexual material, and generalized problematic Internet use covers multidimensional overuse of the Internet resulting in negative consequences for the individual. Both theoretical and empirical studies have linked psychopathological, psychosocial difficulties such anxiety, depression, loneliness, and shyness with problematic Internet usage (Caplan 2002; Davis 2001; Kraut et al. 1998; Morahan-Martin and Schumacher 2000).

Proactive Aggression

The proactive-reactive aggression distinction was first introduced by Dodge and Coie (1987), and this typology focuses on the function as opposed to the form of aggressive behavior. Proactive aggression is defined as instrumental aggressive behavior that occurs without apparent provocation or instigation, and is motivated by anticipated rewards and outcomes resulting from aggressive acts. In contrast, reactive aggression is defined as a hostile, impulsive and angry response that functions as retaliation to a real or perceived threat, provocation or frustration. Similarly, there is a large body of literature on violence that refers to instrumental and hostile/expressive manifestations of aggression (Anderson and Bushman 2002; Hickey 2003), and they are distinguished by the expected goals and motivations of the perpetrator. Instrumental aggression is thought of as a premeditated means of obtaining a particular goal, while hostile/expressive aggression is thought of as unplanned, thoughtless, and primarily perpetrated in reaction to anger-inducing situation. Taken together, it is important to note that reactive/hostile/expressive aggression is performed in response to external social stimuli that are perceived to be aversive and proactive/instrumental aggression is motivated by internal desires and goals (e.g., domination) that are perceived to be attractive.

Previous research has shown differential correlates for both proactive and reactive aggression (e.g., Seah and Ang 2008). In particular, there is sufficient empirical evidence to posit a link between proactive aggression and traditional face-to-face bullying (e.g., Dodge and Coie 1987; Dodge et al. 1997; Hubbard et al. 2001; Salmivalli et al. 1996). More recently, there has also been emerging empirical evidence showing the association between proactive aggression and cyberbullying. For example, in a large sample of 1431 school-going adolescents (682 boys and 726 girls) from 12 to 17 years of age from Spain, Calvete et al. (2010) examined cyberbullying in relation to other indicators of aggressive behavior such as proactive, reactive, direct, and indirect behaviors as well as the justification of violence. The authors used multiple regression analysis and this model tested explained 13 % of the variance in cyberbullying behavior. Of the various indicators of aggressive behavior, Calvete et al. found that proactive aggression and belief justifying violence were the only two correlates associated with cyberbullying.

In a study using a cross-cultural sample of adolescents from the United States and Singapore, Ang et al. (2014) found that both proactive and reactive aggression were correlated with cyberbullying across cultures, and that percentages of adolescents involved in cyberbullying across the two countries were relatively comparable. These rates of 17.9 and 16.4 % for United States and Singapore, respectively, fell within the range of prevalence rates obtained across multiple studies as reported by Calvete et al. (2010). Of note were the findings indicating that nationality did not moderate the relationship between proactive aggression and cyberbullying, and between reactive aggression and cyberbullying. As expected, Ang et al. found proactive aggression to be positively associated with cyberbullying, after controlling for reactive aggression, in both the United States and Singapore samples, and the combined sample. Conversely, as expected, the relation between reactive aggression and cyberbullying was not found to be statistically significant after controlling for proactive aggression across the United States, Singapore and combined samples. This means that while proactive aggression could uniquely contribute additional variance in predicting the scores in cyberbullying across both US and Singapore adolescents, reactive aggression could not.

Normative Beliefs About Aggression

Normative beliefs are individuals' own cognitions about the acceptability or unacceptability of a behavior and serve to regulate actions by prescribing the range of permitted and prohibited behaviors and these beliefs are expected to be universal across cultures (Huesmann and Guerra 1997). Individuals who endorse normative beliefs about aggression view bullying and use of aggressive behavior as acceptable. The dearth of social and contextual cues available in cyberspace might lead to an activation of these normative beliefs supportive of aggression in adolescents, particularly those with narcissistic traits such as exploitativeness which are closely aligned to correlates of proactive aggression such as lack of empathy and a blatant disregard for others (e.g., Werner et al. 2010). Anonymity on the Internet can operate to reduce self-awareness resulting in deindividuation, and a deindividuated person has a weakened ability to regulate his or her behavior and a lower likelihood of caring about what others think of his or her behavior (Zimbardo 1970). McKenna and Bargh's (2000) review suggests that scholars are in agreement that higher levels of interpersonal misunderstandings and aggression are more likely to occur in computer-mediated interactions compared to face-to-face interactions.

Williams and Guerra (2007) found that adolescents' normative beliefs endorsing aggression are associated with all forms of bullying including cyberbullying. With specific reference to cyberbullying, the authors found that an increase in one unit of the normative beliefs about aggression scale led to a 24 % increase in odds of cyberbullying (Williams and Guerra 2007). Similarly, in a longitudinal study involving middle school adolescents, Werner et al. (2010) found that greater acceptance and approval of both overt and relational aggression were associated with increases in cyberbullying. Additionally, this association has empirical support cross-culturally. Ang et al. (2011) investigated the role of normative beliefs about aggression in relation to cyberbullying across two adolescent samples—one from Singapore and another from Malaysia. Ang et al.'s findings demonstrated that normative beliefs about aggression partially mediated the relationship between narcissistic exploitativeness and cyberbullying in both Singapore and Malaysia adolescent samples. Normative beliefs about aggression have been shown to be one mechanism of action by which narcissistic exploitativeness could exert its influence on cyberbullying. These findings extend previous work (e.g., Williams and Guerra 2007) and show that such beliefs can be the mechanism of action in both offline and online contexts.

Contextual cues serve regulatory functions, and reduced contextual cues in online social interactions could lead to deregulated online behavior (Kiesler et al. 1984). For narcissistic individuals with a tendency for exploitativeness in particular, the anonymity of the Internet could exacerbate their sense of disregard for others and their belief that aggression is acceptable and justifiable (Rigby and Slee 1991). Especially in a cyber context where cues are absent or ambiguous, when these children and adolescents are confronted with a potentially conflictual social situation, these beliefs about legitimacy of aggression are likely to be activated. Gradually, more empirical evidence is emerging that normative beliefs of aggression not only act as a mediator facilitating bullying behavior in traditional contexts but these findings can similarly be extended to online contexts, across cultures.

Parent–Child Relationship

Several aspects of poor parent–child relationships have been shown by research to be closely related to cyberbullying and harassment. Ybarra and Mitchell's (2004) work showed that 44 % of online harassers reported having a very poor emotional bond with their caregivers versus only 16 % who reported a strong emotional bond. Conversely, 19 % of non-harassers reported having a very poor emotional bond with their caregivers compared to 32 % who reported a strong emotional bond. Infrequent caregiver monitoring was also associated with an 84 % increase in the odds of reporting Internet harassment behavior. What appears to be particularly noteworthy about these findings is that despite adjusting for significant personal characteristics and all other aspects of the caregiver–child relationship, a poor emotional bond remained significantly related to online harassment and an adolescent with a poor emotional bond with his/her caregiver was still more than two times as likely to engage in online harassment compared with an adolescent with a strong emotional bond with his/her caregiver. Additionally, poor caregiver monitoring was associated with more than 50 % increased likelihood of harassing others online.

Related research has also shown that parents' knowledge and awareness of children's and adolescents' online activities have been associated with lower levels of problematic Internet use among adolescents in the United States (Sun et al. 2005), China (Huang et al. 2010), Italy (Milani et al. 2009), South Korea (Park et al. 2008), and Singapore (Liau et al. 2008). In line with previous research, Ang et al. (2012) found that parents who were perceived to have greater knowledge and awareness of adolescents' online activities had adolescents who reported a lower level of problematic Internet usage, and conversely, lower perceived parental knowledge and awareness was associated with higher levels of problematic Internet usage. Ang et al. extended previous research by demonstrating that perceived parental knowledge and awareness acted not just as a main effect but as a moderator to modify the already empirically established link between loneliness and generalized problematic Internet use in an adolescent sample. Therefore, collectively, these research findings suggest that parental knowledge of their children's and adolescents' online activities, and having a communicative and open parent–child relationship is important in contributing to children's and adolescents' positive adjustment in the use of the Internet across various domains.

Research studies in the social media domain also report consistent and similar results providing further support that a poor parent–child relationship is a risk factor for cyberbullying. Parents have consistently been identified to be the major source of social influence with respect to children's media consumption (Buijzen and Valkenburg 2005; Carlson et al. 1992; Moscardelli and Divine 2007). Researchers defined the strategies parents use to supervise children's media use or help children interpret media content as parental mediation (Warren 2001). In the Internet era, two main types of parental mediation have been found: active mediation and restrictive mediation. In active mediation, parents discuss with children the positive and negative aspects of Internet content, and teach children how to protect themselves from uncomfortable experiences online. In restrictive mediation, parents also use restrictions to limit children's Internet use, for instance, they limit the number of hours the child can surf the Internet, or prohibit the viewing of certain websites (Miyazaki et al. 2009).

Generally, parental mediation has been described as one of the most effective methods to protect children from negative media influence (Buijzen and Valkenburg 2005; Livingstone et al. 2011). In Liu et al. (2013) study, the authors found that active mediation decreases adolescents' disclosure of personal information both directly and indirectly by increasing privacy concern, while restrictive mediation only indirectly decreases such disclosure through privacy concern. Therefore, adolescents whose parents discuss the consequences of engaging in risky Internet behaviors and teach them methods to protect themselves may perform much better in protecting their personal information compared to adolescents whose parents mainly utilize rule setting to limit their Internet behaviors without explanation. That said, it is important to underscore the fact that these results do not completely negate the use of restrictive mediation strategies; while active mediation is more helpful, both types of mediation can be used effectively and appropriately to protect children and adolescents. These results are consistent with findings in a majority of previous studies (Fujioka and Austin 2002; Nathanson 1999; Shin et al. 2009; Youn 2008).

Prevention and Intervention Strategies

In order to better protect vulnerable children and adolescents online, it is important to review prevention and intervention strategies with specific reference to cyberbullying and online harassment. These strategies should target and address specific child and adolescent issues and variables. Additionally, parent-related and parent–child relationship variables should also be specifically targeted and addressed because there must be a recognition that parents continue to play a crucial and critical role in the lives of children and adolescents. Ultimately, prevention and intervention strategies need to be multi-pronged and multi-systemic in order for them to be effective.

Empathy Training and Changing Beliefs Supporting Aggression

Empathy training and education should be included in cyberbullying prevention and intervention programs. Such training has been successful in reducing offline aggressive, bullying behavior (e.g., Bjorkqvist et al. 2000). The effect sizes vary across studies but on average, the magnitude is of a small to medium range (Derzon et al. 1999; Ttofi et al. 2008). For example, children and adolescents could be taught to view issues and grievances from the victim's perspective, and to learn to vicariously experience the emotions of the victim as opposed to engaging in typical responses of victim blaming (Chibbaro 2007). Generalizing these empathy skills from an offline to an online context with reduced social-contextual cues is a big challenge. Therefore, it is important in the context of providing empathy training and education, to personalize the serious and real consequences of cyberbullying (e.g., suicide), sending the message that if these consequences can happen to a fellow peer, it could happen to anyone including themselves.

Previous research have also shown that proactive aggressive children and adolescents, and those having normative beliefs of aggression view aggression as a legitimate response; they construe cyberbullying as an acceptable way to attain instrumental goals, expecting positive outcomes from their actions (e.g., Dodge et al. 1997; Hubbard et al. 2001; Werner et al. 2010). Prevention and intervention programs need to target changing of mindsets. Changing mindsets about the acceptability of aggression is not easy, but research has shown that such beliefs and cognitions can be modified (Guerra and Slaby 1990). In such programs, children and adolescents learn that cyberbullying is not a legitimate response, and that such actions hurt the victims and victims do not deserve to be hurt.

Guidelines Governing Internet Behavior

Shea (1994) recommended promoting Netiquette, a set of rules and guidelines for Internet etiquette. Especially in a cyber context where cues are absent or ambiguous, when children and adolescents are confronted with a potentially conflictual social situation, beliefs about legitimacy of aggression are likely to be activated resulting in deregulated online behavior (Kiesler et al. 1984). Since disinhibition in computer-mediated communication is governed by norms, Shea (1994) then recommended that one way of reducing the incidence of disinhibited online behavior is to attempt to change those norms. Netiquette should encompass changing beliefs about the acceptability of cyberbullying; children and adolescents should be explicitly taught that such beliefs supporting the use of aggression are not acceptable and not justifiable. Thus, Netiquette has the potential to reduce antisocial disinhibited behavior both by explicit prohibition and by establishing more appropriate prosocial norms in online communities.

When researchers consider guidelines for Internet behavior or any other aspect of prevention and intervention, it is not only interesting but crucial to understand the issue of culture in the context of cyberbullying as opposed to an offline context. Various studies reviewed have shown cross-cultural similarity with respect to different aspects related to cyberbullying. For example, relatively similar cyberbullying rates across countries have been reported (Calvete et al. 2010), similar relationship patterns between proactive aggression and cyberbullying across United States and Singapore samples have been found (Ang et al. 2014), and similar trends across the United States, Italy, China, South Korea, and Singapore with respect to parents' knowledge of their children's online activities in relation to problematic Internet use have been documented (Huang et al. 2010; Liau et al. 2008; Milani et al. 2009; Park et al. 2008; Sun et al. 2005).

Cinnirella and Green's (2007) innovative study could provide some insight. Using an experimental design, Cinnirella and Green studied the effects of communication type (face-to-face and computer-mediated communication) and culture (participants from individualist versus collectivist cultures) on social conformity. The authors found an interaction between communication type and culture in which cultural differences were shown only in the face-to-face condition and absent from the computer-mediated condition. Therefore, Cinnirella and Green's experimental findings suggest that cultural differences in social behavior may indeed be negated or operate differently when communication is computer-mediated. Taken together, though inconclusive, it may be possible that the nature of the Internet might be to flatten certain cross-cultural differences.

Develop Positive Parent–Child Relationships Early

The need to establish and develop positive parent–child relationships cannot be overemphasized. This is central to all prevention and intervention strategies targeted at parents. Ybarra and Mitchell's (2004) research remind us of the importance of a positive and strong parent–child emotional bond; a positive and healthy parent–child relationship can help to reduce the likelihood of cyberbullying. Additionally, poor caregiver monitoring is also implicated in increased odds of being an Internet harasser (Ybarra and Mitchell 2004). These results and implications are consistent with social media research findings that parental mediation strategies are crucial in helping children and adolescents recognize the risks and consequences of personal information disclosure along with learning methods of protecting personal information and making discerning choices about what information they can reveal (Liu et al. 2013; Salaway et al. 2008).

Not only it is important to establish and develop a positive parent–child emotional bond, it is critical to establish this as early as possible. In Ang et al. (2012) study, she and her colleagues found that parents who had knowledge about their adolescents' online activities and parents who did not were more differentiated at low levels of adolescent-reported loneliness than at high levels of adolescent-reported loneliness. At low levels of loneliness, parents who were reported to be aware of their adolescents' online activities had adolescents who indicated a much lower level of problematic Internet use. In comparison, parents who were reported to be unaware of their adolescents' online activities had adolescents who indicated a much higher level of problematic Internet use. In contrast, at high levels of loneliness, both groups of parents were associated with adolescents who reported similarly high levels of problematic Internet use. What this means is that in a non-clinical, school-going sample of adolescents, these results suggest that parents' perceived knowledge and awareness of their adolescents' online activities are likely to be associated with a lower level of problematic Internet use if this occurs at low levels of loneliness. These results have implications for prevention and early intervention work. This implies that for the parent–adolescent interaction to be effective, it may be best to cultivate a positive relationship early and to intervene at an earlier stage where loneliness has not reached a higher, more maladaptive level. Therefore, establishing and cultivating a positive parent–child relationship early has numerous advantages and goes a long way in helping with protecting vulnerable children and adolescents in the online environment.

Adopting a Multi-systemic Approach

While targeting child-related and parent-related variables are important, cyberbullying prevention and intervention efforts are incomplete without simultaneously addressing multiple dimensions of the child and adolescent environment including family, peers, school and community (Espelage and Swearer 2004). In the school setting for example, all parties are encouraged to work cooperatively to identify, resolve and prevent cyberbullying incidents from happening. Such efforts could include system-level, classroom and community interventions, as well as individual interventions with children/adolescents, peers, and parents.

Given how quickly technology is advancing, many parents do not have sufficient knowledge to educate their children on how to protect their online security. Schools as a social agent that is tightly linked to children and adolescents as well as their parents may be the best platform to provide supports to parents. O'Neill, Livingstone, & McLaughlin (2011) suggested that schools could organize workshops for parents on digital literacy and safety skills. Additionally if industry could concurrently play their part in self-regulation, this could work hand in hand with parents' supervision, and it will make children's online security issues much easier to handle and manage. Therefore, if policy makers could urge the Internet Service Providers for example, to make their privacy settings and reporting mechanisms more user-friendly and explicit, that could go some way in assisting cyberbullying prevention (O'Neill et al. 2011). Taken together, adopting a multi-systemic approach when considering cyberbullying prevention and intervention would likely result in the most effective outcomes.

Conclusion and Recommendations

Cyberbullying is a global phenomenon and a universal concern. With the anonymity provided by the Internet and the reduced social and contextual cues available in cyberspace, children and adolescents tend to become less conscious of what others may think of his or her behavior resulting in a higher chance of interpersonal conflict. Children and adolescents also tend to engage in more high risk behaviors online. Child variables associated with cyberbullying were reviewed and these include Internet usage patterns and characteristics, psychosocial difficulties and challenges, proactive aggression features and normative beliefs about the acceptability of aggression. Likewise, parent–child relationship variables such as a poor emotional bond, a lack of knowledge about the child/adolescent's online activities, and a lack of adequate parental monitoring and parental mediation have been reviewed to be related to cyberbullying. Based on these variables reviewed, strategies targeting both child/adolescent issues, parent-related, and parent–child relationship variables were highlighted as suitable targets for prevention and intervention work. Specifically, there is a need for empathy training and to modify the belief that aggression is a legitimate and acceptable response. Where possible, it would be helpful to establish appropriate prosocial norms in online communities. As parents play a very important role in the lives of children and adolescents, it is crucial to nurture and develop a positive parent–child emotional bond and to establish that as early as it is feasibly possible. Finally, for prevention and intervention strategies to be effective, it should be multi-pronged and should encompass multiple systems such as the family, the peers, the school and the community.

References

Anderson, C. A., & Bushman, B. J. (2002). Human aggression. *Annual Review of Psychology, 53*, 27–51. doi:10.1146/annurev.psych.53.100901.135231.

Ang, R. P., Chong, W. H., Chye, S., & Huan, V. S. (2012). Loneliness and generalized problematic Internet use: Parents' perceived knowledge of adolescents' online activities as a moderator. *Computers in Human Behavior, 28*, 1342–1347. doi:10.1016/j.chb.2012.02.019.

Ang, R. P., Huan, V. S., & Florell, D. (2014). Understanding the relationship between proactive and reactive aggression, and cyberbullying across US and Singapore adolescent samples. *Journal of Interpersonal Violence, 29*, 237–254. doi:10.1177/0886260513505149.

Ang, R. P., Tan, K. A., & Mansor, A. B. (2011). Normative beliefs about aggression as a mediator of narcissistic exploitativeness and cyber-bullying. *Journal of Interpersonal Violence, 26*, 2619–2634. doi:10.1177/0886260510388286.

Aoyama, I., Utsumi, S., & Hasegawa, M. (2012). Cyberbullying in Japan: Cases, government reports, adolescent relational aggression, and parental monitoring roles. In Q. Li, D. Cross, & P. K. Smith (Eds.), *Cyberbullying in the global playground: Research from international perspectives* (pp. 183–201). Hoboken, NJ: Wiley-Blackwell.

Bjorkqvist, K., Osterman, K., & Kaukiainen, A. (2000). Social intelligence—empathy=aggression? *Aggression and Violent Behavior, 5*, 191–200. doi:10.1016/S1359-1789(98)00029-9.

Buijzen, M., & Valkenburg, P. M. (2005). Parental mediation of undesired advertising effects. *Journal of Broadcasting and Electronic Media, 49*, 153–165. doi:10.1207/s15506878jobem4902_1.

Calvete, E., Orue, I., Estevez, A., Villardon, L., & Padilla, P. (2010). Cyberbullying in adolescents: Modalities and aggressors' profile. *Computers in Human Behavior, 26*, 1128–1135. doi:10.1016/j.chb.2010.03.017.

Caplan, S. E. (2002). Problematic Internet use and psychosocial well-being: Development of a theory-based cognitive-behavioral measurement instrument. *Computers in Human Behavior, 18*, 553–575. doi:10.1016/S0747-5632(02)00004-3.

Carlson, L., Grossbart, S., & Stuenkel, J. K. (1992). The role of parental socialization types on differential family communication patterns regarding consumption. *Journal of Consumer Psychology, 1*, 31–52. doi:10.1016/S1057-7408(08)80044-7.

Chibbaro, J. S. (2007). School counselors and the cyberbully: Interventions and implications. *Professional School Counseling, 11*, 65–67. doi:10.5330/PSC.n.2010-11.65.

Cinnirella, M., & Green, B. (2007, February 25). Does cyber-conformity vary cross-culturally? Exploring the effect of culture and communication medium on social conformity. *Computers in Human Behavior. 23*. doi:10.1016/j.chb.2006.02.009.

Davis, R. A. (2001). A cognitive-behavioral model of pathological Internet use. *Computers in Human Behavior, 17*, 187–195. doi:10.1016/S0747-5632(00)00041-8.

Derzon, J. H., Wilson, S. J., & Cunningham, C. A. (1999). *The effectiveness of school-based interventions for preventing and reducing violence*. Nashville, TN: Vanderbilt Institute of Public Policy Studies.

Dodge, K. A., & Coie, J. D. (1987). Social-information-processing factors in reactive and proactive aggression in children's peer groups. *Journal of Personal and Social Psychology, 53*, 1146–1158. doi:10.1037/0022-3514.53.6.1146.

Dodge, K. A., Lochman, J. E., Harnish, J. D., Bates, J. E., & Pettit, G. S. (1997). Reactive and proactive aggression in school children and psychiatrically impaired chronically assaultive youth. *Journal of Abnormal Psychology, 106*, 37–51. doi:10.1037/0021-843X.106.1.37.

Espelage, D. L., & Swearer, S. (Eds.). (2004). *Bullying in American schools*. Mahwah, NJ: Lawrence Erlbaum.

Finkelhor, D., Mitchell, K., & Wolak, J. (2000). *Online victimization: A report on the nation's youth*. Retrieved from Crimes against Children Research Center: http://www.unh.edu/ccrc/NJOV_info_page.htm.

Fujioka, Y., & Austin, E. W. (2002). The relationship of family communication patterns to parental mediation styles. *Communication Research, 29*, 642–666. doi:10.1177/009365002237830.

Guerra, N. G., & Slaby, R. G. (1990). Cognitive mediators of aggression in adolescent offenders II. *Intervention. Developmental Psychology, 26*, 269–277. doi:10.1037//0012-1649.26.2.269.

Hickey, E. W. (Ed.). (2003). *Encyclopedia of murder and violent crime*. Thousand Oaks, CA: Sage.

Huang, X., Zhang, H., Li, M., Wang, J., Zhang, Y., & Tao, R. (2010). Mental health, personality, and parental rearing styles of adolescents with Internet Addiction Disorder. *Cyberpsychology, Behavior, and Social Networking, 13*, 401–406. doi:10.1089/cyber.2009.0222.

Hubbard, J. A., Dodge, K. A., Cillessen, A. H. N., Coie, J. D., & Schwartz, D. (2001). The dyadic nature of social information processing in boys' reactive and proactive aggression. *Journal of Personality and Social Psychology, 80*, 268–280. doi:10.1037//0022-3514.80.2.268.

Huesmann, L. R., & Guerra, N. G. (1997). Children's normative beliefs about aggression and aggressive behavior. *Journal of Personality and Social Psychology, 72*, 408–419. doi:10.1037/0022-3514.72.2.408.

Kiesler, S., Siegel, J., & McGuire, T. W. (1984). Social psychological aspects of computer mediated communications. *American Psychologist, 39*, 1123–1134. doi:10.1037/0003-066X.39.10.1123.

Kowalski, R. M., & Limber, S. P. (2007). Electronic bullying among middle school students. *Journal of Adolescent Health, 41*, S22–S30. doi:10.1016/j.jadohealth.2007.08.017.

Kraut, R., Patterson, M., Lundmark, V., Kiesler, S., Mukopadhyay, T., & Scherlis, W. (1998). Internet paradox: A social technology that reduces social involvement and psychological well-being? *American Psychologist, 53*, 1017–1031. doi:10.1037/0003-066X.53.9.1017.

Law, D. M., Shapka, J. D., Domene, J. F., & Gagne, M. H. (2012). Are cyberbullies really bullies? An investigation of reactive and proactive online aggression. *Computers in Human Behavior, 28*, 664–672. doi:10.1016/j.chb.2011.11.013.

Lenhart, A., Madden, M., Smith, A., Purcell, K., Zickuhr, K., & Rainie, L. (2011). *Teens, kindness and cruelty on social network sites: How American teens navigate the new world of "digital citizenship"*. Retrieved from Pew Internet and American Life Project: http://www.pewinternet.org/~/media//Files/Reports/2011/PIP_Teens_Kindness_Cruelty_SNS_Report_Nov_2011_FINAL_110711.pdf.

Li, Q., Cross, D., & Smith, P. K. (Eds.). (2012). *Cyberbullying in the global playground: Research from international perspectives*. Hoboken, NJ: Wiley-Blackwell.

Liau, A. K., Khoo, A., & Ang, P. H. (2005). Factors influencing adolescents engagement in risky Internet behavior. *Cyberpsychology and Behavior, 8*, 513–520. doi:10.1089/cpb.2005.8.513.

Liau, A. K., Khoo, A., & Ang, P. H. (2008). Parental awareness and monitoring of adolescent Internet use. *Current Psychology, 27*, 217–233. doi:10.1007/s12144-008-9038-6.

Liu, C., Ang, R. P., & Lwin, M. O. (2013). Cognitive, personality, and social factors associated with adolescents' online personal information disclosure. *Journal of Adolescence, 36*, 629–638. doi:10.1016/j.adolescence.2013.03.016.

Livingstone, S., Haddon, L., & Görzig, A. (2011). *EU kids online*. Retrieved from London School of Economics and Political Science: http://www2.lse.ac.uk/media@lse/research/EUKidsOnline/EUKidsII%20%282009-11%29/EUKidsOnlineIIReports/Final%20report.pdf.

McKenna, K. Y. A., & Bargh, J. A. (2000). Plan 9 from cyberspace: The implications of the Internet for personality and social psychology. *Personality and Social Psychology Review, 4*, 57–75. doi:10.1207/S15327957PSPR0401_6.

Mesch, G. S. (2009). Parental mediation, online activities, and cyberbullying. *Cyberpsychology and Behavior, 12*, 387–393. doi:10.1089/cpb.2009.0068.

Milani, L., Osualdella, D., & Di Blasio, P. (2009). Quality of interpersonal relationships and problematic Internet use in adolescence. *Cyberpsychology and Behavior, 12*, 681–684. doi:10.1089/cpb.2009.0071.

Miyazaki, A., Stanaland, A. J., & Lwin, M. O. (2009). Self-regulatory safeguards and the online privacy of preteen children: implications for the advertising industry. *Journal of Advertising, 38*, 79–91.

Morahan-Martin, J., & Schumacher, P. (2000). Incidence and correlates of pathological Internet use among college students. *Computers in Human Behavior, 16*, 13–29. doi:10.1016/S0747-5632(99)00049-7.

Moscardelli, D. M., & Divine, R. (2007). Adolescents' concern for privacy when using the Internet: an empirical analysis of predictors and relationships with privacy-protecting behaviors. *Family and Consumer Sciences Research Journal, 35*, 232–252. doi:10.1177/1077727X06296622.

Nathanson, A. I. (1999). Identifying and explaining the relationship between parental mediation and children's aggression. *Communication Research, 26*, 124–143. doi:10.1177/009365099026002002.

O'Neill, B., Livingstone, S., & McLaughlin, S. (2011). Final recommendations for policy, methodology and research. Retrieved from LSE Media and Communications: http://www2.lse.ac.uk/media@lse/research/EUKidsOnline/D7.pdf.

Park, S. K., Kim, J. Y., & Cho, C. B. (2008). Prevalence of Internet addiction and correlations with family factors among South Korean adolescents. *Adolescence, 43*, 895–909.

Patchin, J. W., & Hinduja, S. (2006). Bullies move beyond the schoolyard: A preliminary look at cyberbullying. *Youth Violence and Juvenile Justice, 4*, 148–169. doi:10.1177/1541204006286288.

Rainie, L., Lenhart, A., & Smith, A. (2012). *The tone of life on social networking sites*. Retrieved from Pew Internet and American Life Project: http://www.pewinternet.org/~/media//Files/Reports/2012/Pew_Social%20networking%20climate%202.9.12.pdf.

Raskauskas, J., & Stoltz, A. D. (2007). Involvement in traditional and electronic bullying among adolescents. *Developmental Psychology, 43*, 564–575. doi:10.1037/0012-1649.43.3.564.

Rigby, K., & Slee, P. T. (1991). Bullying among Australian school children: Reported behavior and attitudes toward victims. *Journal of Social Psychology, 131*, 615–627. doi:10.1080/00224545.1991.9924646.

Salaway, G., Caruso, J. B., Nelson, M. R., & Ellison, N. B. (2008). The ECAR study of undergraduate students and information technology. Retrieved from the EDUCAUSE: http://net.educause.edu/ir/library/pdf/ERS0808/RS/ERS0808w.pdf.

Salaway, G., Caruso, J. B., Nelson, M. R., & Ellison, N. B. (2008). The ECAR study of undergraduate students and information technology. Retrieved from the EDUCAUSE: http://net.educause.edu/ir/library/pdf/ERS0808/RS/ERS0808w.pdf.

Seah, S. L., & Ang, R. P. (2008). Differential correlates of reactive and proactive aggression in Asian adolescents: Relations to narcissism, anxiety, schizotypal traits, and peer relations. *Aggressive Behavior, 34*, 553–562. doi:10.1002/ab.20269.

Shea, V. (1994). *Netiquette*. San Francisco, CA: Albion Books. Retrieved from http://www.albion.com/netiquette/book/index.html.

Shin, W., Schriner, M., & Cho, S. (2009, May). *Teen online privacy and POS (Parent Over Shoulder): Effects of parental mediation on online teen disclose of personal information*. Paper session presented at the meeting of International Communication Association, Chicago, IL.

Spriggs, A. L., Iannotti, R. J., Nansel, T. R., & Haynie, D. L. (2007). Adolescent bullying involvement and perceived family, peer and school relations: Commonalities and differences across race/ethnicity. *Journal of Adolescent Health, 41*, 283–293. doi:10.1016/j.jadohealth.2007.04.009.

Sun, P., Unger, J. B., Palmer, P. H., Gallaher, P., Chou, C. P., Baezconde-Garbanati, L., & Anderson, J. C. (2005). Internet accessibility and usage among urban adolescents in Southern California: Implications for web-based health research. *Cyberpsychology and Behavior, 8*, 441–453. doi:10.1089/cpb.2005.8.441.

Ttofi, M. M., Farrington, D. P., & Baldry, A. C. (2008). *Effectiveness of programs to reduce school bullying: A systematic review*. Stockholm, Sweden: Swedish Council of Crime Prevention.

Warren, R. (2001). In words and deeds: parental involvement and mediation of children's television viewing. *Journal of Family Communication, 1*, 211–231. doi:10.1207/S15327698JFC0104_01.

Werner, N. E., Bumpus, M. F., & Rock, D. (2010). Involvement in Internet aggression during early adolescence. *Journal of Youth and Adolescence, 39*, 609–619. doi:10.1007/s10964-009-9419-7.

Williams, K. R., & Guerra, N. G. (2007). Prevalence and predictors of Internet bullying. *Journal of Adolescent Health, 41*, S14–S21. doi:10.1016/j.jadohealth.2007.08.018.

Ybarra, M. L., & Mitchell, K. J. (2004). Online aggressor/targets, aggressors, and targets: A comparison of associated youth characteristics. *Journal of Child Psychology and Psychiatry, 45*, 1308–1316. doi:10.1111/j.1469-7610.2004.00328.x.

Youn, S. (2008). Parental influence and teens' attitude toward online privacy concern. *Journal of Consumer Affairs, 42*, 362–384. doi:10.1111/j.1745-6606.2008.00113.x.

Zimbardo, P. (1970). The human choice: Individuation, reason, and order versus deindividuation, impulse, and chaos. In W. J. Arnold & D. Levine (Eds.), *Nebraska symposium on motivation* (Vol. 17, pp. 237–307). Lincoln, NE: University of Nebraska Press.

Chapter 4
Child Abuse and Neglect in India, Risk Factors, and Protective Measures

Sibnath Deb and Mrinalkanti Ray

Introduction

One of the evils that cripple India and hinder her growth is child abuse. Figuring as she does among the nations with the largest child populations, India could amply take advantage of this human resource if it is provided with basic facilities and support services. Otherwise, this resource would threaten to be a considerable national burden. India is extraordinarily rich in cultural diversity, suggesting that every culture has its typical beliefs and practices about child-raising. Not that all these measures are beneficial or always beneficial; some of them prove detrimental and even destructive at times. For normal physical, psychological, and social development, children require basic facilities like nutrition, education, entertainment, security, medical care, and parental love. They can consequently arrive at their full potentials and flower into ideal citizens. With a population of over 1.23 billion, India has achieved a literacy rate of 74.04 %. About 70 % of her people live in rural areas, as compared to 30 % that live in urban areas (Census of India 2011). Even 65 years after independence, poverty is widespread, mostly in the rural regions. Like anywhere else in the world, it is poverty which is the root cause of child abuse and neglect in India. According to the 2010 World Bank Report, 32.7 % of people in India live below the international poverty line of US$1.25 a day, while 68.7 % subsist on less than US$2 a day (PPP). Similarly, the

S. Deb (✉)
Department of Applied Psychology, Pondicherry University, Puducherry, India
e-mail: sibnath23@gmail.com

M. Ray
Child Rights Activist, University of Laval, Quebec City, Canada

S. Deb (ed.), *Child Safety, Welfare and Well-being*,
DOI 10.1007/978-81-322-2425-9_4

2010 United Nations Development Programme estimated that 29.8 % of Indians live below the country's national poverty line (Mandal 2010). The children of these families are easy preys of human trafficking and sexual abuse (Census of India 2011). Children make up about 44.4 % of the total population regardless of their socio-economic background, and one in every two children is deprived of primary education, adequate nutrition, and medical care (Indian National Family Health Survey 2005–2006). Girls of especially rural areas are grossly discriminated against with respect to education, nutrition, and health care, the reason being that they, unlike boys, are regarded as burdens of the family (Deb 2006).

Corporal Punishment, Psychological and Sexual Abuse, and Neglect

Child abuse and neglect is a major social problem of India (Deb 2006). Public health professionals are justified in giving a special importance to this issue (Theodore et al. 2000). But the solution to the problem sounds difficult especially for the lack of documentation system, because without documentation, it is hard to conceive of the magnitude of the problem and to plan out intervention program. Reliable data about child abuse that comes in such forms as sexual exploitation and corporal punishment could be garnered by trained personnel of hospitals, police stations, and educational institutions. Several cases of sordid child sexual abuse were brought to light by the media, allowing the public and the policy-makers alike to perceive the gravity of the problem and to contemplate new legislations. Let us now take a glance at the findings of some local studies available to us. Leaving aside its methodological limitations, the Study of the Ministry of Women and Child Development, Government of India, on child abuse covering 13 states provides a glimpse of the nature of the problem. According to this study, children in the age group of 5–12 years have experienced the worst of abuses. Boys are as much at risk of being abused as girls and the abusers are generally those placed in position of trust and authority (MWCD Report on Child Abuse and Neglect 2007). When protectors turn into perpetrators or predators, the assumption that home the safest place for a child simply dwindles into a myth (Virani 2000). The negative image of the protectors pushes the children to choose bad companions and unhealthy lifestyles. Consequences of this problem are many, but one consequence that towers over all the rest is the ailing health of these children. "The Child is father of the Man," proclaims the English poet William Wordsworth in the epigraph of his celebrated poem "The Immortality Ode." If it is so, a dysfunctional childhood predicts a dysfunctional adulthood, which implies that the health of an individual is of paramount importance.

According to the 2012 Report of the Indian National Commission for Protection of Child Rights based on the survey of 2009–2010 covering seven states of India, 99.7 % of the children reported one or more types of punishment.

As many as 81.2 % children were subjected to outward rejection when told that they were incapable of learning. Three-forth (75 %) children testified that they used to be caned and 69 % children testified that they were slapped in the cheek (Report of the National Commission for Protection of Child Rights 2012). It is relevant to mention here that Section 17(*l*) of the Rights of Children to Free and Compulsory Education Act, 2009, ruled against physical punishment or mental harassment to students in schools. In a Kolkata-based study, 52.4, 25.1, and 12.7 % adolescents reported about psychological, physical, and sexual abuse (Bhattacharya 2011). According to a study in Tripura, India, about 20.9, 21.9, and 18.1 % of children suffered psychological, physical, and sexual violence respectively (Deb and Modak 2010). Speaking of corporal punishment, 33.3 % of male and 40 % of female teachers confessed that they were in the habit of physically punishing students, as the Kolkata-based study reveals. And those who are unaccustomed to exercising physical punishment did not bother to speak against this practice, apparently because they saw nothing wrong with it, or because they did not wish to offend or alienate their abusive colleagues. Findings also revealed that 60 % of male teachers and 53.4 % of female teachers used to be physically punished in their childhood (Deb and Adak 2006). One recent incident as reported by a local newspaper proves that the practice of child sacrifice out of superstitious beliefs is still prevalent in India. In January 2011, a 5-year-old Dalit girl child named Rajalakshmi, the daughter of a poor agricultural laborer, was decapitated in the midst of pomp and ceremony in the belief that the sprinkling of the victim's blood on a construction site is propitious for its success. This barbaric crime was perpetrated in a village in Madurai district of the state of Tamil Nadu. Surprisingly enough, a member of an active political party masterminded it (DMK Functionary 2012; Helpless Dalit Girl 2012).

A study that covered a group of 120 migrant child laborers working in households, tea stalls, garages, and shops in South Kolkata has shown that an overwhelming number of children got abused (Deb 2005a, b). A study of 35 trafficked children and young women found that trafficking is usually done with offers of false marriages and jobs, or through abduction and sale (Deb et al. 2005). In another study, the authors (Chatterjee et al. 2006) observed that six of 41 trafficked children contracted HIV/AIDS.

Child marriage was legally banned in India as early as 1929. Today, even 85 years after independence, this outrageous custom prevails in many regions of India. Nearly 45 % of women in India are married off before they reach 18 years of age, a fact corroborated by a joint Indo-American study in the Lancet. The report adds that more than 40 % of the world's child marriages take place in India (Eighty Years 2009). The states which are in the forefront of girl child marriages are Rajasthan, Bihar, Uttar Pradesh (UP), Chattisgarh, and Madhya Pradesh. Customs reign over reason and common sense in these states. In the rural areas of Rajasthan, the situation is worse, as exemplified by the assault of enraged villagers of Jhalawar District on 12 government officials when the latter attempted to thwart the child marriage of about 42 couples. Later, these villagers stormed into the Churiliya Police check-post and did incalculable damage to it (Villagers Attack 2012).

Another bane of India is malnutrition which particularly affects her child population. According to the National Family Health Survey–3 (2006), more than 56 % of the teenage girls in India are anemic with a hemoglobin count of less than the standard 12 g/dL. The incarceration of child-domestic-servants is a common occurrence while their masters go out on travels. In 2012 in New Delhi, a family allegedly practicing medical profession locked up their 13-year-old maidservant in the house without foods or provisions before setting out for a vacation in Thailand (Doctors in the Dock 2012).

Child sexual abuse is as rampant in India as ever. By way of example, we may refer to the two cases that happened in Uttar Pradesh in May (2012) and to one case that happened in the Coimbatore district of Tamil Nadu on June 11, 2013. The Coimbatore case is particularly disturbing, for it happened in a children's home run by a church, where one or two men managed to infiltrate and raped two little girls, aged 10 and 11, at knifepoint, and then fled. A more shocking case is, however, the brutal gang rape and murder of two cousin sisters, aged 14 and 15, in Badaun, UP. Their abductors snatched them as they went out of home in the evening into the fields to answer nature's call (as they had no toilets at home). Their corpses were spotted hanging from a mango tree the next day. Those entrusted with maintaining law and order are occasionally found to be negligent about their duties. A compelling proof is the refusal of the local police to file the case when reported by the distraught parents of the missing girls. The cops did so only hours later when faced with angry villagers crowding the compound of the police station. A week later, a similar crime was repeated in Sitapur. A minor girl stepped out of her house to relieve herself in the fields and fell on the clutch of six hyenas of men. Her body was later discovered suspended from a tree (NDTV 2014).

Child trafficking for commercial sexual exploitation is on the rise in India, and the hub of this notorious trade is West Bengal or, more precisely, Kolkata (Sanlaap 2003; Sen 2005). The trade operates by way of recruitment, transport, and transfer of children picked through abduction, deception, or force. Since girls for commercial sex are in great demand in other countries, the trade has become increasingly transnational (International Labor Organization 2005; UNICEF 2005). Cases were that children simply disappeared overnight, at an average rate of one in every 8 min, according to the National Crime Records Bureau (Ministry of Home Affairs, Government of India 2010).

Reported Cases of Child Rape and Abduction in India

Apart from abuse, children suffer other forms of criminal offences like murder, trafficking, kidnapping, and infanticide. To date, there is no separate classification of offences against children in India. The offences committed against children or the crimes in which they are victims are usually labeled as Crime against Children. Indian penal code and the various protective and preventive "Special and Local Laws" specifically mention the offences wherein children are the victims. The age of child varies as per definition given in the concerned Acts and Sections, but the age of child has been specified to be below 18 years as per the Juvenile Justice Act 2000.

The cases in which children get victimized and abused fall into two broad Section (i) Crimes committed against Children are punishable under Indian Penal Code (1860) (IPC) and (ii) Crimes committed against Children are punishable under Special and Local Laws (SLL).

A total of 5,484 cases of child rape were reported in the country during 2010, compared to 5,368 cases in 2009. This means an increase of 2.2 % child rape during the year.

A total of 10,670 cases of abduction of children were reported during the year, as compared to 8,945 cases in the previous year. This means that there is a significant increase of 19.3 % abduction. And yet, the reporting of child sexual abuse and trafficking is incredibly low (Crime in India Report 2010).

Report of Child Abuse and Neglect Cases in India

Compared to the industrialized countries of the West, the reporting of child sexual abuse and of corporal punishment is done tardily in India, as two recent local studies demonstrate (Mukherjee 2006; Modak 2009). Csorba et al. (2006) tell us that cases of sexual abuse are rarely reported across the geographical boundaries for a variety of reasons, such as the fear of social stigma, the perceived harassment, the reluctance of parents or their disbelief, and of course the threats from the perpetrators. According to a study in Kolkata, only 1.7 % of sexually abused cases were reported to the police (Deb and Mukherjee 2011). And according to another study in Agartala (Tripura), 15.5 % of sexually abused cases were reported (Modak 2009). A primary reason why reporting is rarely done is that the victims do not wish to incur the grudge of the perpetrators. If the cases are reported to the police, the victims or their families run the risk of being pursued by the perpetrators for retaliation. Another reason is the fear of social stigma which many victims cannot afford to bear with (Mukherjee 2006). There also lies the problem of shortage of professionals to administer psychological and medical services to sexually abused children. As a result, the majority of the children get to live with the grim experience of sexual abuse for the rest of their lives, and this materially impacts on their personalities, their interpersonal relationships, and their career developments (Deb and Sen 2005).

Risk Factors to Child Abuse

Risk factors for child abuse vary in accordance with the type of abuse, socio-economic background, and demographic characteristics of the nation in question. But underlying the variables of risk factors are some common denominators, such as poverty, gender, parental educational background, parental mental health and substance dependence, family and social environment. Doctors from their first-hand clinical experiences indicated that there are numerous caregiver risk factors which put children at risk of emotional abuse (Glasser et al. 2001). Caregiver risk factors include the mental health difficulties of the caregivers, their alcohol or drug abuse, parental conflict or domestic violence, and caregiver childhood maltreatment (often responsible for discontinuities of caregiving to their own children). The child risk factors are usually identified as follows:

(i) **Child Related Factors**

- **Birth History of a Child**
  Premature birth, birth anomalies, low-birth weight, and exposure to toxins can act as risk factors for children, in that they are likely to predispose children to neglect and abuse (Cederbaum et al. 2013). Child's temperament is another important factor. If children are difficult or slow to warm up, or if they have aggressive temperament or behavioral problem or attention deficit problem, they are at risk of abuse. Similarly, childhood trauma and negative childhood experiences not only impair their early development, but also render them vulnerable in later stages. Vulnerable are also those children who are neglected or who hang out with anti-social peer group. The same is true of those who get into wrong companionship, and later try sex and drugs out of curiosity or for making money.
- **Age and Gender of the Child**
  Risk factor depends on age as well. Children of younger age are evidently at high risk of abuse—the younger the age, the higher the risk. The abuse of children between birth and 3 years of age has been reported to be at its worst. The risk diminishes as the age advances. Children during infancy and early childhood stage requiring close supervision are prone to certain forms of maltreatment such as Battered child Syndrome and physical neglect (Kempe et al. 1962). Boys and girls are equally at risk of abuse. To put it in short, a child's vulnerability to abuse is proportionate to his (her) age, as well as to his (her) physical, mental, emotional, or social development.
- **Girl Child**
  Generally speaking, the health or the living condition of a girl child is far from agreeable. The reason is traced back to the age-old prejudice that male child is superior to female child. The 2011 Census has shown that there is a significant decline in female population of India (Ministry of Statistics and Programmed Implementation 2012). Each phase of life of a female is blighted by gender discrimination which results in an unbalanced ratio between male and female population (Fikree and Pasha 2004). An unwanted girl child is systematically eliminated through abortion. And those who are lucky to escape infanticide often find themselves extremely neglected. This is another reason for a higher girl-child mortality rate (George 1997). Chances of her dying between her first and fifth birthday are 40 % higher than those of a boy (Filmer et al. 2004). It is worth noting that India has world's largest gender survival gap (Save the Children 2008).

- **Vulnerable Children are at Risk**
While a vast number of children are predictably vulnerable in India, most vulnerable are those who are orphaned or living outside of parental care or born into poor families. And greatly vulnerable are those discriminated as sex workers or the children of sex workers, street children, children with disabilities, children of lower castes and, of course, children of the Dalits (the so-called untouchables). They all are at risk of falling victims to abuse and neglect by care-givers and society alike.
- **Children with Physical, Cognitive, and Emotional Disabilities**
Children with physical, cognitive, and emotional disabilities are more likely to be maltreated than children without disabilities (Sobsey 1992). The maltreatment may even become repeated. It is because the abusers know that they can get away with it, since these children do not have the ability to understand that abusive treatment is inappropriate and unacceptable. It is also because the abusers know that such children are unable to escape or to defend themselves. Children with intellectual disability or those having chronic illnesses are at high risk of maltreatment (Jaudes and Mackey-Bilaver 2008). Such children become very dependant and are generally considered as burdens even by their parents. If children are stolid or unresponsive to affection, or if they live apart from their parents on account of frequent hospitalizations, chances of poor care and further abuse are high.
Vulnerable to abuse and neglect are also the children who are affected with HIV. They may be affected with this deadly virus directly, meaning that they live with it. They may be affected with it indirectly, meaning that they live with a family member who has it. Similarly vulnerable are the children who are orphaned following the death of their parent(s) from AIDS or AIDS-related diseases. Children living in institutional lodgings or with extended family members are also vulnerable to neglect with respect to care and support.
- **Child Laborers and Domestic Assistants**
Children are employed as child laborers in numerous sectors such as domestic chores, agriculture, construction works, factories, and roadside business, to name a few. These children are often exploited and maltreated not just physically or psychologically, but also sexually (Bajpai 2003). As anticipated, some of them sustain injuries, some are left with permanent disabilities, some meet death, and some get infected with HIV/AIDS (MWCD Report on Child Abuse and Neglect 2007). Their basic needs of food, health, and education are scarcely attended to.
- **Street Children**
A large number of children live on the street either with their parents or on their own. Child begging on the street is a common scene in Indian cities. According to UNICEF (1986), Street children fall into three categories: (a) “children at risk,” those who live in families but work on the streets to supplement the family income; (b) “children on the street,” those who have some family support but work on the streets; and (c) “children of the street,”

those who live and work on the streets without any family support. Since these children live on the street, they become more vulnerable to all forms of abuse, exploitation, and maltreatment (Mathur et al. 2009).

- **Orphans and Children in Institutional Care**
  It is customary to put disadvantaged or orphaned children in institutional care for their safety and well-being. Paradoxically enough, the seemingly safe havens usually turn out to be veritable hells. The kind of environment in which these institutions are wrapped up is favorable to different kinds of corruptions and malpractices. In other words, these institutions present high risks, since the environment itself is risky (Keeshin and Campbell 2011). Children living in different institutions are at risk of emotional, physical, and sexual abuse by inmates, peers, care givers, and others in default of any viable system to protect them. Despite the dreadful nature of tyranny and humiliation endured, there is no escape, for the abuses go unreported all the same. To make matters worse, they come to be known as problem children and are compelled to live at the mercy of the authorities of the institution. All this plunges them into the depths of despair.
- **Sex Tourism**
  Sex tourism is another serious problem in some parts of India. Sex tourists indulge in sex and abuse children of both sexes. A prominent example of Indian sex tourism is Goa (ECPAT 2009). Children (even from well-to-do families) are brought in through pimps or mediators who make hefty profits which come not only from the supply of children to clients, but also from the sale of children. These children are either kidnapped or by making false promise they are indulged in sex tourism (Bandopadhyay 2012). They are sexually abused, very often repeatedly. Sooner or later, they end up being prostitutes.
- **Cultural Beliefs and Misconceptions as Risk Factors**
  Colostrums are believed to be beneficial to a new-born child for increasing their immune capacity. Unfortunately, a large number of Indian mothers, especially those from rural areas, abstain from providing colostrums to their new-born children, apprehending that it is injurious to children's health, just because it looks dirty. Their children are left vulnerable as a result. There is a misconception among semi-literate or illiterate people in rural India that a person with HIV/AIDS will be cured from that disease if they have sexual intercourse with a minor girl. Driven by this notion, many adults sexually abuse innocent girl children and transmit the disease to them.
  Indeed, child prostitution has assumed such a proportion that it has taken root in cultural belief, as exemplified in the consignment of female children as *devadasis* (temple prostitutes). Fear of diseases, curses, and superstitious beliefs induce parents to consign their daughters to the goddess.
  Child marriage is a cultural practice in some communities in India (Raj et al. 2009). Girl children married off to adult men are vulnerable to different health-related problems including sexually transmitted diseases (ICRW 2007). Gender discrimination with respect to nutrition and education is a very common phenomenon in rural India.

(ii) **Family-related Factors**

Specific life situations of some families, such as single parenting, domestic violence, and stressful life, augment the possibility of maltreatment.

- **Family Size, Family Income, and Family Dynamics**

  Both the parents are indispensable for the proper upbringing of children. Children living with single parents, or living with a large or joint family, are much more at risk of physical and sexual abuse or neglect than children living with biological parents (Stith et al. 2009; Weissman et al. 2003). Poor economic condition of the family also accounts for child neglect and maltreatment. Finally, the family functioning, communication, and conflict resolution methods, all play determining roles in the development of children (Whitaker et al. 2008).

- **Family Violence**

  Research indicates that the families in which spouse abuse takes place, child maltreatment also occurs there (Rumm et al. 2000). They themselves become victims of physical or emotional abuse, and are neglected by parents due to disturbed family environment. Their witnessing of parental violence takes a heavy toll on their mental and emotional life. Elder and partner violence also contributes to child abuse (Stith et al. 2009).

- **Stressful Life Events in the Family**

  Stress of adult or elderly people plays a negative role in a family as far as the the well-being of children is concerned. Evidence indicates a connection of physical abuse with stressful life events, parenting stress, and emotional distress. Evidence also demonstrates that neglectful families report more day-to-day stress than non-neglectful families (Stith et al. 2009). Losing a job, physical illness, marital problems like divorce (Weissman et al. 2003), or interpersonal relationship problems among family members may trigger negative emotions like hostility, anxiety, or depression which may aggravate family conflict, maltreatment, and bad childhood experiences (Dong et al. 2004).

(iii) **Parental Factors**

A number of parents-related factors are responsible for child abuse and neglect. As per the United Nations Convention on the Rights of Child, it is parents' responsibility to ensure basic facilities for child development. If parents fail to provide the same, it is the nation's responsibility to look after a child by providing him or her with basic facilities and a roof.

- **Personality and Mental Health of Parents**

  Research shows that no specific characteristic or personality trait can be associated with maltreating parents or caregivers. But they were invariably found to have low self-esteem, poor impulse control, aggressive tendency, depressive mood, anxiety problem, and anti-social behavior. Parents with dominating and hostile personality, with major mental health problems, and with very high expectations of their children tend to abuse them more than their counterparts (Hien et al. 2010; Cancian et al. 2010; Fleming et al. 1997; Waller and Swisher 2006; Wallio 2009).

- **History of Childhood Abuse**
  Research shows that abused parents are particularly abusive (Afifi et al. 2011). Research also shows that about one-third of all individuals who have been maltreated as children are likely to subject their children to maltreatment, thus keeping in motion the cycle of abuse (Dixon et al. 2007). It is also likely that children who either experience maltreatment or witness violence between their parents or caregivers learn violent behavior and also learn to justify that behavior.
- **Substance Abuse and Violent Behaviors**
  Parents who are dependent on substance are unable to provide quality care and supervision to their children and therefore these children. Having thus experienced neglect, such children gradually become dependent on peer group members (Waller and Swisher 2006). As a result, their education gets affected. Alcoholic father and absence of female caregiver increase the risk of children to be abused within the family (Carter and Myers 2007; Fleming et al. 1997).
- **Child Rearing Practices**
  Lack of knowledge about child rearing practices and absence of elderly people (grandparents, for example) in a family is often a contributing factor in child maltreatment. Poor parenting skills, unrealistic expectations of the children, and inappropriate punishment are also identified as forms of child abuse (Scannapieco and Connell-Carrick 2005; Stith et al. 2009).
- **Adolescents as Parents**
  Children of young parents are at high risk of neglect because of their inexperience and lack of mental maturity (Rumm et al. 2000). Several studies of physical abuse have demonstrated that teenage mothers with low levels of education tend to do child abuse more than older mothers (Afifi 2007; Sidebotham and Heron 2006).

(iv) **Community and Environmental Factors**
Child safety in the community is a big challenge, since people with different backgrounds and mentalities live in the same community or neighborhood. A family is highly susceptible to its community and neighborhood, for the simple reason that there are constant interactions between them. In any community, people with poor economic background and low social network experience discrimination, social isolation, and different challenges (Carter and Myers 2007). Evidence clearly indicates that poor economic conditions and mental health problems of parents have high correlation with child maltreatment (Cancian et al. 2010; Carter and Myers 2007). Children living in underdeveloped and hostile environment with low social support and especially those who are out of school are at high risk of neglect and all types of abuse (Wikström and Loeber 2000; Drake and Pandey 1996; Zolotor and Runyan 2006).

Effects of Child Abuse and Neglect

Abuse and neglect jeopardize the development of brain, not to speak of its harmful effect on mental, social, and physical health and career development of a child (Deb and Walsh 2012; Kendall-Tackett 2002). Physical or sexual abuse often predisposes a child to an increased risk of depression, borderline personality disorder (BPD), post-traumatic stress disorder (PTSD), and other psychiatric disorders. Depression is ubiquitous in abused survivors (Briere and Elliot 1994; Gladstone et al. 1999; Zuravin and Fontanella 1999). Abused children often suffer from lifelong psychological consequences like low self-esteem and relationship difficulties which are detrimental to health. A stable and strong social support is predictive of sound health (Deb and Mukherjee 2011).

Juvenile delinquents are steadily on the rise in India. Studies show that most of them are actually victims of abuse, neglect, family violence, social discrimination, and prolonged deprivation from basic care and support facilities. As a result, they get involved in anti-social activities knowingly or unknowingly under the influence of peer group members, and are termed juvenile delinquents as per Juvenile Justice Act (JJ Act) (2000). Over 33,000 juveniles, mostly in the age group from 16 to 18 years, were arrested for crimes like rape and murder across the country in 2011, the highest being in the last decade (Juvenile Delinquency 2013). The news of the Delhi gang rape that occurred on December 16, 2012, caught international attention. The National Crime Records Bureau (NCRB) study reveals that the number of juveniles raping girls and women in the state has shot up in the last 3 years (Mishra 2013). Psychiatrists and women rights activists claim that easy access to pornography and rapidly changing food habits are primarily responsible for the dramatic rise in rape cases (Mishra 2013).

Legislative Measures for Protection of Child Rights in India

India is a signatory to the United Nations Convention on the Rights of the Child (1989), which is a significant development. It means that the Government of India endorses all the rights as outlined in the UN Convention on the Rights of the Child. Now, it is the obligation of government to ensure its implementation through appropriate legislations and social policies or programmers. It is encouraging that the government has already adopted a number of legislations and social measures in this direction.

The latest initiative the government has taken is to bring new legislations. As such, The Protection of Children from Sexual Offences Act 2012 (POCSO Act 2012) was passed by the Indian Parliament, which mandated the reporting of offences against children without specifying the category of person or profession. For example, Section 19 of POCSO Act, 2012 defines the reporting of offences in the following manner:

> Any person (including the child), who has apprehension that an offence under this Act is likely to be committed or has knowledge that such an offence has been committed, he shall provide such information to (a) the Special Juvenile Police Unit; or (b) the local police.

The Section 19 has given sufficient importance to proper recording of complaint, and insists that the recording be checked by the informant in order to avoid errors or discrepancy.

Furthermore, the Section 19 has mandated the Special Juvenile Police Unit or local police to make immediate arrangements for care and protection of the child informant for a safe shelter within 24 h and to report the matter to the Child Welfare Committee and/or the Special Court within 24 h.

The POCSO Act, 2012, also mandated the media, studio, and photographic profession-related persons to report sexual exploitation of the child to the police. For example, Section 20 of POCSO Act, 2012, states the obligation of media and photographic facilities to report cases, as we see below:

> Any personnel of the media or hotel or lodge or hospital or club or studio or photographic facilities, by whatever name called, irrespective of the number of persons employed therein, shall, on coming across any material or object which is sexually exploitative of the child (including pornographic, sexually related or making obscene representation of a child or children) through the use of any medium, shall provide such information to the Special Juvenile Police Unit, or to the local police, as the case may be.

Section 21 of POCSO Act, 2012, clearly states the punishment for failure to report or record a case. As per sub-Section (2) of Section 19, a person shall be punished with imprisonment of either description which may extend to 6 months or with fine or with both.

The Rights of Children to Free and Compulsory Education Act 2009 was passed by the Indian Parliament for ensuring free and compulsory education to all children from the age of 6–14 years. At the same time, this Act prohibits physical punishment and mental harassment of children in schools. As per the Section 17(I) of the Rights of Children to Free and Compulsory Education Act, 2009,

> "No child shall be subjected to physical punishment or mental harassment." Section 17(2) states that "Whoever contravenes the provisions of sub-Section (I) shall be liable to disciplinary action under the service rules applicable to such person."

In this Act also, there is no provision for mandatory reporting of corporal punishment to the appropriate authority.

The Commissions for Protection of Child Rights Act, 2005, ensures the establishment of the State Commission for Protection of Child Rights in every state, and in due course child protection officers will be appointed in every district of the country. The National Commission for Protection of Child Rights has been established in 2006 and all the states and the Union Territories are in the process of setting up State Commissions for Protection of Child Rights. The objective of these National and State Commissions is to guarantee the proper enforcement of children's rights and the effective implementation of laws and programmers relating to children. Despite the legislation, the State Commission for Protection of Child Rights is yet to be formed in many states. The singularity of this Act is its coverage of a wide range of issues relating to Child Protection. To give an example, every district should appoint a Child Protection Officer to closely monitor and work with grass-root level organizations.

The juvenile Justice (Care and Protection of Children) Act (2000) (amended in 2006, India) is primarily aimed at consolidating the law relating to juveniles in conflict with the law and to children in need of protection by addressing their problems, that is, by catering to their respective needs and by adopting a child-friendly approach within the limits of jurisdiction. With that aim in view, various institutions were established for offering services to the troubled juveniles and the endangered children for their eventual rehabilitation. Two committees (namely, the Juvenile Justice Board and Child Welfare Committee) are also supposed to be formed in each district or for a group of districts in order to facilitate the task. This Act also dictates the recruitment of a female juvenile officer for every police station or for every two/three police stations as feasible, for this would encourage a female victim of sexual assault to visit the police station for reporting the case. So far, very few police stations have put this recommendation into effect.

In addition, the legal measures taken for addressing different types of abuse and neglect include: (i) The Child Marriage Restraint Act (1929); (ii) The Prohibition of Child Marriage Act (2006) (January 10, 2007); (iii) The Child Labor (Prohibition and Regulation) Act (1986); The Immoral Traffic (Prevention) Act (1956); and The Indian Penal Code (1860).

Numerous other statutes that promote commitments to child health, prevent gender discrimination, and ensure safety are: (i) The Infant Milk Substitutes, Feeding Bottles and Infant Foods (Regulation of Production, Supply and Distribution) Act (1992) (56); (ii) The Pre-conception and Pre-natal Diagnostic Technique (Prohibition of Sex Selection) Act (1994) (57); (iii) The Persons with Disabilities (Equal Opportunities, Protection of Rights and Full Participation) Act (1995) (58); (iv) The Guardian and Wards Act (1890) (59); and (v) The Young Persons (Harmful Publications) Act (1956) (60).

Some of the constitutional provisions for protection of child rights are: (i) offering free and compulsory education for children aged 6–14 years (Article 21A); (ii) prohibiting human trafficking and bonded labor (Article 23); prohibiting child labor (Article 24); offering early childhood care and education for children until they complete the age of 6 years (Article 45), and so on. Though provisions are there in the Indian Constitution for the protection of children, they unfortunately lack in specificity and consequently give rise to ambiguities in interpretation. Hence it is difficult to implement them in the practical world.

Social Welfare Measures for Children

Apart from the constitutional provisions, legislative measures, and policies, there are different social welfare programmers and schemes intended to promote the welfare of children. Since health, nutrition, and education are all interrelated and inter-dependent, the following policies, for example, are in the right direction as far as the welfare of children is concerned.

- **Integrated Child Development Scheme (ICDS):**
  This scheme was initiated in 1975 with the aim of facilitating early childhood development comprising education and a good health. It is one of the effective

measures employed to ensure nutrition to the underprivileged and impoverished children of society (Kapil 2002). It has its shortcomings, but with certain modifications, it promises to be more effective (Kapil 2002; Kapil and Pradhan 2000). First-hand experience of the author about the evaluation of ICDS programmers in different states indicates that the success of this program is owing to the Anganwadi workers. A dynamic Anganwadi worker is capable of mobilizing his community for running the center efficiently. However, it is to be noted that in another block the center failed to mobilize or motivate the community people despite the same support facilities which are provided by the government.

- **Integrated Child Protection Scheme (ICPS):**
  This scheme was initiated with the aim of governing all the child protection legislations and policies. As such, it is a comprehensive scheme, and it seeks to make sure that the best interests of the children are taken care of.
  Among other social welfare schemes are Rajiv Gandhi National Creche Scheme for the Children of Working Mothers, Rajiv Gandhi Scheme for Empowerment of Adolescent Girls (RGSEAG) or SABLA, Mid-Day Meal (MDM), and Total Sanitation Campaign (TSC). The benefits of the schemes are mixed. In some states, these programmers are successfully implemented while in some others it was partially successful in achieving long-term objectives. It is imperative to create awareness of the schemes among the target groups through block development office and/or Panchyat. Periodic monitoring and evaluation should be carried out to optimize the benefits to the beneficiaries. It is worthwhile to mention that special girl child scheme named "Kanyashree Package" of Government of West Bengal for prevention of forced girl child marriage and child trafficking has been recognized by the Department of International Development (DFID), the United Kingdom, and the UNICEF. The scheme was launched in October 2013 with a view to awarding an annual scholarship of Rs 500 to girls between 12 and 18 years of age to continue with their studies, provided they are unmarried. A one-time grant of Rs 25,000 is also made to the girl, when she turns 18, to pursue higher studies. According to the Chief of Field Office, UNICEF, West Bengal, there has been visible changes at the ground level with regard to enrolment of girl students and child marriage (Singh 2014). Similar or need-based innovative social schemes should be undertaken by all the states for child protection by taking into account the point of sustainability.

Conclusion

Evidence demonstrates the nature and extent of child abuse and neglect in India, and the risk factors involved in it. A number of legal and social measures have been adopted by the Government of India for the safety and welfare of children, but the problem lies with their implementation. It rests with the state government to implement any socio-legal measures adopted by the federal government. Some states implement the schemes quite efficiently while others, regrettably, do not attach much importance to them. More funds for child protection should be allocated and the issue should be given top priority in the agenda of the government, for children are the most precious assets of a nation. The United Nations declared "World Day for Prevention of Child Abuse and Violence against Children, November 19" for raising awareness among the people about this issue with the celebration of the day. It is certainly a commendable step in terms of the child-friendly environment. Finally, we all have to bear in mind that child protection is the sacred responsibility of every conscientious citizen.

Recommendations

1. Ensuring nutrition, education, basic health care facilities, and safety for all the children through community and institution-based approach; in this regard, local health officials should take help from the Panchayat (the village council) and school authorities. Corporate sectors should come forward with support as part of corporate social responsibility.
2. Creating awareness about child rights among people of all sections of the society.
3. Ensuring effective and timely intervention of government policies and programs for the needy children and periodic monitoring and evaluation of the same.
4. Involvement of community members for effective implementation of government policies and programs like Right to Free and Compulsory Education Act 2009, midday meal program, Integrated Child Development Scheme (ICDS), Integrated Child Protection Scheme (ICPS) and so on.
5. Given the seriousness of child sexual abuse and child trafficking for commercial sexual exploitation, there is an urgent need to amend existing legislation or bring new legislation for mandatory reporting of these two types of child abuse (Deb 2014). As for the notification of child trafficking, Panchayat Members (elected by the villagers), village health workers, and of course parents should step up to report the incident to local police, child protection officer, and/or child welfare committee members, since they have close contact with the village people. For sexual abuse cases, people/professionals like parents, doctors, nurses, teachers, and personnel from the Non-Government Organizations (NGO) should be mandated for reporting. It is also necessary to state clearly about the range of activities which should be considered as sexual abuse as defined by the international legislation and/or the World Health Organization (WHO). In Indian societies, sexual intercourse with a minor is usually considered as sexual abuse, but such acts as stimulation, showing pornographic picture, touching private parts of a child, and so on are not generally recognized as sexual abuse and ignored.

References

Afifi, M. (2007). Gender differences in mental health. *Singapore Medical Journal, 48*(5), 385.

Afifi, T. O., Mather, A., Boman, J., Fleisher, W., Enns, M. W., MacMillan, H., & Sareen, J. (2011). Childhood adversity and personality disorders: Results from a nationally representative population-based study. *Journal of Psychiatric Research, 45*(6), 814–822. doi:10.1016/j.jpsychires.2010.11.008.

Bandyopadhyay, R. (2012). Child-sex tourism, HIV/AIDS, and social justice in India. *Peace Review, 24*(2), 143–146. doi:10.1080/10402659.2012.677320.

Bajpai, A. (2003). *Child rights in India: Law, policy, and practice*. Oxford, USA: Oxford University Press. doi:10.1093/acprof:oso/9780195670820.001.0001.

Bhattacharyya, B. (2011). *A Study on perceived home environment, adjustment, anxiety, self-concept and self-confidence of the adolescents*, Unpublished Doctoral Thesis, Calcutta University.

Briere, J. N., & Elliot, D. M. (1994). Immediate and long-term impacts of child sexual abuse. *The Future of Children, 4*, 54–69.

Cancian, M., Slack, K. S., & Yang, M. Y. (2010). *The effect of family income on risk of child maltreatment*. Madison, WI: Institute for Research on Poverty, University of Wisconsin-Madison.

Carter, V., & Myers, M. R. (2007). Exploring the risks of substantiated physical neglect related to poverty and parental characteristics: A national sample. *Children and Youth Services Review, 29*(1), 110–121. doi:10.1016/j.childyouth.2006.08.002.

Cederbaum, J. A., Putnam-Hornstein, E., King, B., Gilbert, K., & Needell, B. (2013). Infant birth weight and maltreatment of adolescent mothers. *American Journal of Preventive Medicine, 45*(2), 197–201. doi:10.1016/j.amepre.2013.03.016.

Census of India. (2011). *Office of the registrar general*. New Delhi, India: Ministry of Home Affairs, Government of India. 2001.

Chatterjee, P., Chakraborty, T., Srivastava, N., & Deb, S. (2006). Short and long-term problems faced by the trafficked children: A qualitative study. *Social Science International, 22*(1), 167–182.

Csorba, R., Lampe, L., Borsos, A., Balla, L., Poka, R., & Olah, E. (2006). Female child sexual abuse within the family in a Hungarian Country. *Gynecol Obstet Invest*, *2*, 61(4), 188–193.

Crime in India Report. (2010). Ministry of Home Affairs, Government of India.

Deb, S. (2006). *Children in agony: A sourcebook*. New Delhi: Concept Publishing Company.

Deb, S., & Walsh, K. (2012). Impact of physical, psychological, and sexual violence on social adjustment of school children in India. *School Psychology International, 33*(4), 391–415. doi:10.1177/0143034311425225.

Deb, S., & Mukherjee, A. (2011). Background and adjustment capacity of sexually abused girls and their perceptions of intervention. *Child Abuse Review, 20*, 213–230. doi:10.1002/car.1153.

Deb, S., & Modak, S. (2010). Prevalence of violence against children in families in Tripura and its relationship with socio-economic, cultural and other factors. *Journal of Injury and Violence Research, 2*(1), 5–18. doi:10.5249/jivr.v2i1.31.

Deb, S. (2005a). Child abuse and neglect in a metropolitan city: A qualitative study of migrant child labor in South Kolkata. *Social Change, 35*(3), 56–67. doi:10.1177/004908570503500304.

Deb, S., Srivastava, N., Chatterjee, P., & Chakraborty, T. (2005). Processes of child trafficking in West Bengal: A qualitative study. *Social Change, 35*(2), 112–123. doi:10.1177/004908570503500208.

Deb, S., & Sen, P. (2005, November 16–18). *A study on psychological trauma of young trafficked women*. Presented in the 6th Asian Conference on Child Abuse and Neglect held in Singapore during.

Deb, S. (2014). Legislation concerning reporting of child sexual abuse and child trafficking in India: A closer look. In Mathews Ben & Bross C. Donald (Eds.), *Mandatory reporting laws and the identification of severe child abuse and neglect*. Australia: Springer.

Deb, S., & Adak, M. (2006). Corporal punishment of children: Attitude, practice and perception of parents. *Social Science International, 22*(2), 3–13.

Deb, S. (2005b). Child trafficking in South Asia: Dimensions, roots, facets and interventions. *Social Change, 35*(2), 143–155. doi:10.1177/004908570503500211.

Dixon, L., Hamilton-Giachritsis, C., Browne, K., & Ostapuik, E. (2007). The co-occurrence of child and intimate partner maltreatment in the family: Characteristics of the violent perpetrators. *Journal of Family Violence, 22*(8),675–689.

DMK functionary held for child sacrifice. (2012, April 29). *The Hindu*, (p. 1). Chennai, India.

Doctors in the dock. (2012, April 5). *The Hindu*, (p. 12). Chennai, India.

Dong, M., Anda, R. F., Felitti, V. J., Williamson, D. F., Dube, S. R., Brown, D. W., & Giles, W. H. (2004). Childhood residential mobility and multiple health risks during adolescence and adulthood: the hidden role of adverse childhood experiences. *Archives of Pediatrics and Adolescent Medicine, 159*(12), 1104–1110.

Drake, B., & Pandey, S. (1996). Understanding the relationship between neighborhood poverty and specific types of child maltreatment. *Child Abuse and Neglect, 20*(11), 1003–1018.

ECPAT. (2009, March 8–10). Offenders beware: Child sex tourism case studies: Analyses of child sex tourism cases in preparation of the international expert meeting on combating child sex tourism Berlin.

Eighty years after it has been banned, 45 % of the girls are still married off before. (2009, March 9). *Times of India* (p. 11). Kolkata, India.

Fikree, F. F., & Pasha, O. (2004). Role of gender in health disparity: The South Asian context. *BMJ: British Medical Journal, 328*(7443), 823. doi:10.1136/bmj.328.7443.823.

Filmer, D., King, E.M., & Pritchett, L. (2004). *Gender disparity in South Asia: Comparisons between and within countries*. Retrieved February 27, 2004, from www.worldbank.org/html/dec/Publications/Workpapers/WPS1800series/wps1867/wps1867.pdf. (World Bank policy research working paper No 1867).

Fleming, J., Mullen, P., & Bammer, G. (1997). A study of potential risk factors for sexual abuse in childhood. *Child Abuse and Neglect, 21*(1), 49–58.

George, S. M. (1997). Female infanticide in Tamil Nadu, India: From recognition back to denial? *Reproductive Health Matters, 5*(10), 124–132. doi:10.1016/S0968-8080(97)90093-8.

Glasser, M., Kolvin, I., Campbell, D., Glasser, A., Leitch, I., & Farrelly, S. (2001). Cycle of child sexual abuse: Links between being a victim and becoming a perpetrator. *The British Journal of Psychiatry, 179*(6), 482–494. doi:10.1192/bjp.179.6.482.

Gladstone, G., Parker, G., Wilhelm, K., & Mitchell, P. (1999). Characteristics of depressed patients who report childhood sexual abuse. *American Journal of Psychiatry, 156*, 431–437.

Helpless dalit girl child a victim of superstition. (2012, April 29). *The Hindu* (p. 4). Chennai, India.

Hien, D., Cohen, L. R., Caldeira, N. A., Flom, P., & Wasserman, G. (2010). Depression and anger as risk factors underlying the relationship between maternal substance involvement and child abuse potential. *Child Abuse and Neglect, 34*(2), 105–113. doi:10.1016/j.chiabu.2009.05.006.

Indian National Family Health Survey. (2005–2006). http://www.rchiips.org/nfhs/factsheet.shtml.

International Labor Organization. (2005). *A global alliance against forced labor*. Geneva, Switzerland: Author. Retrieved March 8, 2010, from http://www.ilo.org/wcmsp5/groups/public/—ed_norm/—declaration/documents/publication/wcms_081882.pdf.

ICRW. (2007, August 12). *Methods, tools and measurement: Latest findings from the field*. Paper presented at the How to Reduce the Stigma of AIDS, Toronto, ON, Canada.

Jaudes, P. K., & Mackey-Bilaver, L. (2008). Do chronic conditions increase young children's risk of being maltreated? *Child Abuse and Neglect, 32*(7), 671–681. doi:10.1016/j.chiabu.2007.08.007.

Juvenile delinquency on rise, 33,887 minors arrested in 2011. (2013, January 13). *The Indian Express*. New Delhi. www.archive.indianexpress.com/news/juvenile-delinquency-on-rise-33887-mi.

Kapil, U. (2002). Integrated Child Development Services (ICDS) scheme: A program for holistic development of children in India. *The Indian Journal of Pediatrics, 69*(7), 597–601. doi:10.1007/BF02722688.

Kapil, U., & Pradhan, R. (2000). Integrated Child Development Services Scheme (ICDS) in India: Its activities, present status and future strategy to reduce malnutrition. *Journal of the Indian Medical Association, 98*(9), 559–566.

Kempe, C. H., Denver, M., Silverman, F., Cincinnati, M., Steele, B., & Droegemueller, M. et al. (1962). The battered child syndrome. *Journal of the American Medical Association*, 181(7), 17–24; Republished in *Journal of the American Medical Association*, (1984) *251*(22); Reprinted in *Child Abuse and Neglect*, (1985) *9*(2), 143–154.

Keeshin, B. R., & Campbell, K. (2011). Screening homeless youth for histories of abuse: Prevalence, enduring effects, and interest in treatment. *Child Abuse and Neglect, 35*(6), 401–407. doi:10.1016/j.chiabu.2011.01.015.

Kendall-Tackett, K. (2002). The health effects of childhood abuse: four pathways by which abuse can influence health. *Child Abuse and Neglect, 26*(6), 715–729. doi:10.1016/S0145-2134(02)00343-5.

Mandal, J. (2010). *Poverty reduction*. http://www.undp.org.in/whatwedo/poverty_reduction.

Mathur, M., Rathore, P., & Mathur, M. (2009). Incidence, type and intensity of abuse in street children in India. *Child Abuse and Neglect, 33*, 907–913. doi:10.1016/j.chiabu.2009.01.003.

Ministry of Statistics and Programmed Implementation. (2012). *Children in India, 2012 a statistical appraisal*, Government of India.

Mishra, A. K. N. (2013, July 18). *Juvenile delinquency on the rise*. Chennai: The Times of India.

Mukherjee, A. (2006). *A study on the impact of sexual abuse on mental disposition of girl children*. An Unpublished Doctoral Dissertation. Kolkata, India: University of Calcutta.

Modak, S. (2009). Violence against children in Tripura and its impact. *Doctoral Dissertation*. Calcutta, India: Calcutta University.

NDTV (2014, June 03, 22:22 IST). *Girl allegedly killed, hanged from tree in Uttar Pradesh Again*. www.ndtv.com/article/india/girlallegedkilled.

Raj, A., Saggurti, N., Balaiah, D., & Silverman, J. G. (2009). Prevalence of child marriage and its effect on fertility and fertility-control outcomes of young women in India: a cross-sectional, observational study. *The Lancet, 373*(9678), 1883–1889. doi:10.1016/S0140-6736(09)60246-4.

Report of the National Commission for Protection of Child Rights. (2012).

Report on Child Abuse and Neglect. New Delhi: Min Women Child Dev. (2007).

Rumm, P. D., Cummings, P., Krauss, M. R., Bell, M. A., & Rivara, F. P. (2000). Identified spouse abuse as a risk factor for child abuse. *Child Abuse and Neglect, 24*(11), 1375–1381. doi:10.1016/S0145-2134(00)00192-7.

Sanlaap. (2003). *Red alert: Combat commercial sexual exploitation of children*. Kolkata, India: Author.

Save the Children. '*State of the World's Mothers 2008: Closing the gender gap for children under 5*'.

Sen, S. (2005). *Trafficking in women and children in India*. New Delhi, India: National Human Rights Commission.

Scannapieco, M., & Connell-Carrick, K. (2005). *Understanding child maltreatment: An ecological and developmental perspective*. Oxford, USA: Oxford University Press.

Sidebotham, P., & Heron, J. (2006). Child maltreatment in the "children of the nineties": A cohort study of risk factors. *Child Abuse and Neglect, 30*(5), 497–522. doi:10.1016/j.chiabu.2005.11.005.

Singh, S. S. (2014, June 22). *Global pat for Bengal's girl child scheme* (p. 9). Chennai: The Hindu.

Sobsey, D. (1992). *Violence and abuse in the lives of people with disabilities: The end of silent acceptance?*. Baltimore, MD: Paul H Brookes Publishing Co.

Stith, S. M., Liu, T., Davies, L. C., Boykin, E. L., Alder, M. C., Harris, J. M., & Dees, J. E. M. E. G. (2009). Risk factors in child maltreatment: A meta-analytic review of the literature. *Aggression and Violent Behavior, 14*(1), 13–29. doi:10.1016/j.avb.2006.03.006.

Theodore, A. D., Chang, J. J., Runyan, D. K., Hunter, W. M., Bangdiwala, S. I., & Agans, R. (2000). Epidemiologic features of the physical and sexual maltreatment of children in the Carolinas. *Pediatrics, 115*(3), e331–e337. doi:10.1542/peds.2004-1033.

The National Crime Records Bureau. (2010). *Accidental deaths and suicides in India: 2000*. Delhi, India: Ministry of Home Affairs, Government of India.
The U.N. Convention on the Rights of the Child 1989 (CRC).
The Protection of Children from Sexual Offences Act, 2012.
The Juvenile Justice (Care and Protection of Children) Act, 2000 (amended in 2006, India).
The Child Marriage Restraint Act, 1929.
The Prohibition of Child Marriage Act, 2006 (2007, January 10).
The Child Labour (Prohibition and Regulation) Act, 1986.
The Immoral Traffic (Prevention) Act, 1956.
The Indian Penal Code, 1860.
The Infant Milk Substitutes, Feeding Bottles and Infant Foods (Regulation of Production, Supply and Distribution) Act, 1992.
The Pre-Conception and Pre-natal Diagnostic Technique (Prohibition of Sex Selection) Act, 1994.
The Persons with Disabilities (Equal Opportunities, Protection of Rights and Full Participation) Act, 1995.
The Guardian and Wards Act, 1890.
The Young Persons (Harmful Publications) Act, 1956.
UNICEF. (1986). *Children in especially difficult circumstances: Supporting annex, exploitation of working and street children*. New York: United Nations Children's Fund.
UNICEF. (2005). *Multiple indicator cluster surveys (MICS)*. New York, NY: Strategic, Information Section, Division of Policy and Planning.
Villagers attack Rajasthan Officials. (2012, April 23). *The Hindu* (p. 3). Chennai, India.
Virani, P. (2000). *Bitter chocolate: Child sexual abuse in India*. Penguin Books India.
Wallio, S. C. (2009). *Caregiver physical health and protective factors against child abuse and neglect*. Unpublished Thesis.
Waller, M. R., & Swisher, R. (2006). Fathers' risk factors in fragile families: Implications for healthy relationships and father involvement. *Social Problems, 53*(3), 392–420. doi:10.1525/sp.2006.53.3.392.
Weissman, A. M., Jogerst, G. J., & Dawson, J. D. (2003). Community characteristics associated with child abuse in Iowa. *Child Abuse and Neglect, 27*(10), 1145–1159.
Whitaker, D. J., Le, B., Karl Hanson, R., Baker, C. K., McMahon, P. M., Ryan, G., et al. (2008). Risk factors for the perpetration of child sexual abuse: A review and meta-analysis. *Child Abuse and Neglect, 32*(5), 529–548. doi:10.1016/j.chiabu.2007.08.005.
Wikström, P. O. H., & Loeber, R. (2000). Do disadvantaged neighborhoods cause well-adjusted children to become adolescent delinquents? A study of male juvenile serious offending, individual risk and protective factors, and neighborhood context. *Criminology, 38*(4), 1109–1142. doi:10.1111/j.1745-9125.2000.tb01416.x.
Zolotor, A. J., & Runyan, D. K. (2006). Social capital, family violence, and neglect. *Pediatrics, 117*(6), 1124–1131. doi:10.1542/peds.2005-1913.
Zuravin, S. J., & Fontanella, C. (1999). The relationship between child sexual abuse and major depression among low-income women: A function of growing up experiences? *Child Maltreatment, 4*, 3–12. doi:10.1177/1077559599004001001.

Chapter 5
Children's Right to Safety: The Problem of Corporal Punishment in Pakistan

George W. Holden and Rose Ashraf

Introduction

Children have the right to safety and protection from assaults, battery, and violence. However, in most countries around the world, children are routinely hit by adults. All too often, children are physically injured or emotionally scarred. Who are the perpetrators of these assaults? None other than the two categories of adults entrusted to promote the children's healthy development: parents and teachers. Children are hit and assaulted under the guise of discipline. These attacks by adults are described under the euphemistic language of "spanked," "smacked," "slapped," or a dozen other similar terms, including the more general term, "corporal punishment" (CP).

There are many causes of this commonly practiced approach to child-rearing discipline. We cite just three. Violence and aggression were central to the survival of hunter-gatherer societies and it is reasonable to assume that violent childrearing practices were common among prehistoric ancestors (Glover 1999). Second, certain branches of Christianity have promoted harsh physical punishment of children (Greven 1991; Heimlich 2011). The Book of Proverbs in the Old Testament continues to be cited as justification for hitting children (e.g., Pearl and Pearl 1994). A third etiological source is parent–child conflict. Parents frequently engage in minor conflicts with their children and an all too common solution for parents, whether angry or not, is to use physical might to enforce their wishes (e.g., Dix 1991; Holden et al. 2014b).

G.W. Holden (✉) · R. Ashraf
Southern Methodist University, Dallas, TX, USA
e-mail: gholden@mail.smu.edu

S. Deb (ed.), *Child Safety, Welfare and Well-being*,
DOI 10.1007/978-81-322-2425-9_5

Corporal punishment is a demeaning and humiliating punishment that is potentially injurious. Thus, it is an assault on a child's dignity (Newell 2011). It is also a clear violation of the child's right to safety. The United Nations adopted the Convention on the Rights of the Child (CRC) in 1989. This document is the single most widely ratified human rights treaty (Britto and Ulkuer 2012). Only two countries have not ratified it: Somalia, and the United States. Among the 45 articles, one (Article 19) states: "States Parties shall take all appropriate legislative, administrative, social and educational measures to protect the child from *all forms of physical* or mental *violence*, injury or abuse, neglect or negligent treatment, maltreatment or exploitation, including sexual abuse, while in the care of parent(s), legal guardian(s), or any other person who has the care of the child" (italics added). The article has subsequently and repeatedly been explicated to recognize CP as a form of physical violence (Bitensky 2010). As children's rights advocates note, children should enjoy the same right that adults have: the right not to be hit—by anyone (Newell 2011).

Recognition of children's right to safety and protection from all forms of physical and mental violence has led 46 countries to prohibit CP in all venues, as monitored by the Global Initiative to End all Corporal Punishment of Children (www.endcorporalpunishment.org). Other countries are making progress in approaching the passage of prohibitions (Durrant and Smith 2011). For example in the early summer of 2014, the Brazilian Senate passed a ban on CP. The bill was signed by President Dilma Rousseff into law on June 27, 2014. We next consider some of the reasons, in addition to its violation of a child's rights, that CP is widely regarded as a problematic behavior.

The Problem of Corporal Punishment

Corporal punishment of children is a problematic behavior for many reasons. First, it does not promote good behavior—its intended goal—but rather can result in unintended negative consequences. In her groundbreaking meta-analysis, Gershoff (2002) found that CP was linked to one positive outcome (i.e., immediate child compliance), but was significantly associated with multiple undesirable child or family variables. For example, children punished with CP are more likely to engage in aggression, have mental health problems (e.g., anxiety, depression), and experience poorer quality of parent–child relations than children who are not hit. More recent empirical studies have continued to find that CP use is correlated with a variety of negative consequences, including decreased cognitive performance (Gershoff 2013), although a recent meta-analysis (Ferguson 2013) did not find as strong negative effects as Gershoff did. The most serious unintended consequence is physical child abuse. Parents who rely on CP are more at risk for physical child abuse (Zolotor et al. 2011).

A second problem with CP is that it is not effective at promoting good behavior. Ironically, the single most common reason why parents use CP is because they believe it as an effective disciplinary technique to promote good behavior (Ateah and Durrant 2005). In fact, mothers' positive attitudes toward CP when their child is an infant predict frequency of use 4 years later (Vittrup et al. 2006). In one way, CP does work: parents observe their children immediately stop engaging in the undesired behavior after a spanking. However, they fail to recognize that hitting does not promote good behavior for very long. In an observational study, 73 % of children who received CP were "misbehaving again" within 10 minutes (Holden et al. 2014b). So, in line with theoretical accounts of the ineffectiveness of punishment in parents (Domjan 2015), CP has not been found to be an effective disciplinary technique.

A third type of problem with CP is that it contributes to a "culture of violence" (Straus 1996). Where there is CP, there is more aggression and heterotypic continuity of the aggressive behavior. The violent acts may take on different manifestations as the child grows (e.g., bullying, dating violence, marital violence, approval of violence, harsh discipline, and child maltreatment) but the aggression continues (Straus et al. 2014). Countries that have more violent crimes are also countries where CP is widely practiced (Barry 2007).

The Prevalence of CP Around the World

There are an increasing number of journal publications that document the international extent of the problem. As these cross-cultural studies have repeatedly found, in many countries, a majority of children are spanked, slapped, and hit. For example, one investigation used the Multiple Indicator Cluster Survey, a nationally representative study of households from 24 low and middle-income countries, to assess child-rearing violence. Based on reports from more than 30,000 caregivers, the majority of informants (63 %) revealed that they or some other caregiver in the household had used physical violence on their child in the past month (Lansford and Deater-Deckard 2012).

To give an idea of the range of countries that have been assessed, we summarize, in Table 5.1, a sampling of the available data that have been published in international journals. The data come from a total of 12 countries and the Pacific Islands (e.g., Samoa, Tonga, & Cook Islands). The data indicate that CP is widely practiced on children and youth in homes and schools. There is one exception: Sweden. Corporal punishment has been banned there since 1979. In many of the other countries, more than 2/3 of the children regularly receive some form of CP.

That sampling of countries includes at least one nation from all five major regions of the world (Africa, North America, South America, Asia, and Europe). Still there are countries in sub-regions that, to date, have not received adequate attention in international journals with regard to CP. For example, there are few published reports about the extent of CP in South Asia. Next we will summarize what information we have found about CP in one country from that region, Pakistan.

Table 5.1 Examples of the extent of corporal punishment use by parents and teachers around the world

Country	Informant & type of CP	Frequency of use & individuals	Author(s)
Chile ($N = 919$)	Adolescent reports of CP (infrequent or more)	19.3 % of mothers 9.5 % of fathers	Ma, Han, Grogan-Kaylor Delva and Castillo 2012
China ($n = 241$)	Parental reports of spank/slap/hit of 7–10 year olds	60 % of boys hit 48 % of girls hit	Lansford et al. 2010
Columbia ($n = 108$)	Parental reports of spank/slap/hit of 7–10 year olds	63 % of boys hit 68 % of girls hit	Lansford et al. 2010
Egypt ($N = 2170$)	10–15 year-olds' reports of hitting/punching beating/whipping by parents	49 % of parents	Youssef et al. 1998a
Egypt ($N = 2170$)	10–15 year-old's reports of slapping/beating/whipping by teachers	82.3 % teachers	Youssef et al. 1998b
Italy ($n = 203$)	Parental reports of spank/slap/hit of 7–10 year-olds	66 % of boys hit 61 % of girls hit	Lansford et al. 2010
Jordan ($n = 114$)	Parental reports of spank/slap/hit of 7–10 year olds	80 % of boys hit 66 % of girls hit	Lansford et al. 2010
Kenya ($n = 100$)	Parental reports of spank/slap/hit of 7–10 year-olds	97 % of boys hit 82 % of girls hit	Lansford et al. 2010
Pacific Islands ($N = 1376$)	Parental reports of spank (at least fortnightly) of 2 year-olds	34.5 % of mothers 55 % of fathers	Schluter et al. 2007
Philippines ($n = 120$)	Parental reports of spank/slap/hit of 7–10 year-olds	77 % of boys hit 71 % of girls hit	Lansford et al. 2010
Sweden ($n = 101$)	Parental reports of spank/slap/hit of 7–10 year-olds	6 % of boys hit 9 % of girls hit	Lansford et al. 2010
Tanzania ($N = 409$)	6–15 year-olds' reports of hit with object by parents	83 % of boys hit 81 % of girls hit	Hecker et al. 2013
Tanzania ($N = 409$)	6–15 year-olds' report of spanked/slapped/pinched by teachers	98 % of boys hit 91 % of girls hit	Hecker et al. 2013
Thailand ($n = 120$)	Parental reports of spank/slap/hit of 7–10 year-olds	72 % of boys hit 58 % of girls hit	Lansford et al. 2010
United States ($n = 310$)	Parental reports of spank/slap/hit of 7–10 year-olds	36 % of boys hit 38 % of girls hit	Lansford et al. 2010

Corporal Punishment in Pakistan

South Asia is composed of Pakistan, India, Bangladesh, and Sri Lanka, as core countries along with Nepal, Bhutan, Maldives, and sometimes Afghanistan and Myanmar. There are studies in international journals that report on CP in India (e.g., Runyan et al. 2010) but, to our knowledge, none from Pakistan or the other seven countries of South Asia.

Why focus on Pakistan? The issue of corporal punishment in Pakistan is of interest for multiple reasons. First, the population of Pakistan, of more than 196 million people, makes it the 6th most populous nation (CIA 2014). The fertility rate of four children per woman means that it has the highest population growth rate in the region after Afghanistan (Kugelman and Hathaway 2011). However, the issue of CP in the country has received little research attention and, from our investigation, no reviews.

Pakistan is a unique country in several ways. First, although its history dates back to almost 2,500 B.C., the country as it is known today is relatively new. The Islamic Republic of Pakistan was formed in 1947. Prior to that, it was a part of British India. In 1906 the All India Muslim League was formed to protect Muslim interests. The League became popular in the 1930s under the leadership of Muhammad Ali Jinnah, and established the Lahore Resolution. Under this resolution, the League demanded that independent states be formed east and west of British India with a constitution modeled on Islamic ideology. Pakistan's independence from India is largely attributed to the All India Muslim League, which aimed to create an independent state in order to protect the interests of Muslims.

The history of the country's founding leads to its second unique feature: it is a deeply religious country. The state religion is Islam and 96.4 % of the population is made up of Muslims. Sunni Muslims comprise 85–90 % of the population and Shias make up 10–15 % (CIA 2014). The remaining population includes other Muslim sects, Hindus, and Christians.

Despite its religious homogeneity, it is an ethnically diverse country. Almost 45 % of the population is Punjabi (44.7 %) but there are also Pashtun (15.4 %), Sindhi (14 %), and other ethnic groups. More than 10 languages are spoken in the country in addition to the national language of Urdu. This ethnic diversity calls for caution in making generalizations about Pakistanis (CIA 2014). Most citizens live in one of four provinces: Punjab, Sindh, Khyber Pakhtunkhwa, and Balochistan but about 7 % of Pakistanis live in four territories (Federally Administrated tribal areas, Kashmire, Gilgit-Baltistan, & Islamabad Capital).

The topic of CP of Pakistani children periodically appears in the news outlets. For example, a newspaper article (Iqbal 2012) reported that a 15 year-old boy died from his injuries a few days after being beaten with a stick by his teacher in a small town in Punjab. The boy had previously complained to his father that his teacher frequently beat students. School CP was in the news at least seven other times during that year. Reports described child injuries and, in two cases, deaths resulting from suicides following threats of or experiencing CP according to Pakistan's Society for the Protection of the Rights of the Child (Society for the Protection of the Rights of the Child 2012).

Given Pakistan's Islamic faith, where does Islam stand with regard to CP? Although CP is not mentioned in the Qu'ran, parenting and the transactional role of parents and children is clear in the *Hadith*, or the teachings of the Prophet Muhammad. Parents are held responsible for raising their children to be Godly and moral beings and will ultimately be judged on if they have adequately fulfilled this responsibility. Although the *Hadith* discusses the importance of being affectionate and kind toward children, it also discusses the use of CP:

> *Order your sons to pray when they are seven, and spank them if they do not pray when they are ten.* (Sabig 1978 cited by Obeid 1988)

In essence, parents are encouraged to use loving methods to teach their children, but when a strong punishment is called for, it is permissible to use CP. Note too that the age of child is clearly stated. Spanking a child younger than 10 years is not prescribed.

We next review the extent to which CP is used in Pakistani schools and homes. Due to the limited number of published studies, the data come from several types of sources including a book, journal articles, and reports from non-governmental organizations (NGOs).

CP in Pakistani Schools

Currently, there are no national statistics available concerning the prevalence of CP in Pakistani schools. In response to this data void, three non-governmental organizations have collected information in specific regions of Pakistan. Plan International surveyed teachers in the second largest province in Pakistan, Punjab. They found that 89 % of the public and private school administrators sampled reported they used CP.

A much more comprehensive approach was taken by Save the Children, UNICEF, and the Khyber Paktunkhwa provincial government, who teamed up to study school CP in three districts of the region (Global Initiative to End All Corporal Punishment of Children 2012). Surveys were given to 3,528 children aged 6–14 years, 1,231 parents, and 486 teachers from public (government) and religious schools. Every child reported having received CP at least once. The most common punishments reported were smacking, hitting with an object (e.g., shoe, brick, iron rod, knife), hair-pulling, ear-twisting, and being placed in painful (and humiliating) positions.

Another NGO took a different approach. They surveyed 600 school heads and 630 parents from various schools in the Khyber Paktunkhwa province (formerly called the North-West Frontier Province) (Coalition on Child Rights with UNICEF 1998). The majority of headmasters (57 %) said that CP was necessary for a variety of reasons. The most common rationales given were that it was necessary for maintaining discipline (68.7 %), facilitating learning (55.1 %), and building character (50.7 %). The educators reported 63 incidents of injury as a result of physical punishment, including falling unconscious, and severe injuries to the face and eyes.

Interviews with parents revealed that most parents (78 %) knew the punishments were occurring in the schools and 64 % reported being aware that their children were the recipients. Of the parents surveyed, 40 % agreed that the CP was appropriate, 27 % believed it was inappropriate but necessary, and the remaining

30 % believed it was inappropriate. A total of 74 parents reported injuries to their children due to CP, ranging from fractures to permanent neurological damage (Profanter 2007).

In addition to surveys concerning the prevalence of CP, we located one empirical investigation that examined the impact of CP in schools on students' academic performance and personality development (Naz et al. 2011). A sample of 10–16 year-old youth was interviewed to assess reports of CP in schools. Three groups of 120 students were then compared: those who reported receiving no CP, mild CP (slapped or hit on the hand or leg, pushed or pulled), and severe CP (hit on head, beat with a stick, ear or hair pulling). The researchers found that the experience of CP in the classroom adversely affected academic performance. Students who experienced mild or severe CP were more likely to miss classes, to dropout, and generally to have poorer academic performance than students who did not experience any CP.

The study also found that experiencing physical punishment was correlated with negative psychological effects. Students in the mild and severe CP groups were more likely to report depression, lower self-esteem, pessimism, and apprehension. When interviewed about their emotions, the students who had received mild or severe CP groups reported feeling hostile and vengeful of society, hatred, and frustration significantly more than the other students (Naz et al. 2011).

CP in Pakistani Homes

Compared with school CP, there are even fewer studies available documenting the prevalence of CP in Pakistani homes. There is a paucity of empirical literature on the issue. For example, although Hyder and Malik (2007) discussed violence against children broadly in their review, they do not explicitly address the issue of corporal punishment.

We located only two studies that provide information about the use of CP by parents. The largest dataset was a survey of 4,200 school children aged 5–16 years living in KPK Province (NCCR, 2001). The survey found that parents reportedly used multiple forms of CP. All of the children and youth revealed that they were physically punished at home. The most commonly reported punishments were being slapped on the face (54 %), slapped on the back (29 %), hit with a stick (16.6 %), kicked (12.3 %), having hair pulled (11 %), hit with another object (2 %), and being shaken (1.1 %). According to the children, their offenses included: being naughty (47 % boys, 41 % girls), school problems (22 % boys, 25 % girls), playing (18 % boys, 25 % girls), disobeying adults (37 % boys, 16 % girls), making noise (12 % boys, 12 % girls), and forgetting an important task (8 % boys, 4 % girls).

An investigation into parental attitudes about CP backs up the children's reports. A survey by the Society for the Protection of the Rights of the Child (2012) revealed that 76 % of parents supported CP and considered it a necessary tool in correcting behavior. Similarly, 67.4 % of 640 parents interviewed believed that CP was either "right," or "wrong but unavoidable." Similarly, Malik (2010) refers to an unpublished report indicating that fathers believe physical punishment is necessary for disciplining children.

Profanter (2007) also interviewed children. When asked if they believe CP is acceptable, 54.1 % of children said it was not okay and approximately 70 % of the children reported they would not physically punish their children when they became parents. Interestingly, many students cited Islamic virtues as reasons they would not hit their own children (e.g., respecting others is obligatory, treating children with love and kindness). Given the high rate of parental use of CP, not surprisingly 92.9 % of children reported that they were afraid of their parents (Profanter 2007).

Cultural Considerations

Pakistani parenting values are strongly influenced by several prominent cultural beliefs such as the importance of patriarchal orientations and child obedience. Those beliefs directly contribute to practicing harsh, physical discipline (Maker et al. 2005; Malik 2010; Stewart et al. 1999). The first study to indicate this was a focus group investigation about parent education in Pakistan (Brieland and Brieland 1957), published 10 years after the country was founded. In those discussions, discipline was one of seven topics a group of mothers from Peshawar wanted to discuss. "Several" mothers reported that they used spanking regularly as a discipline method but also commented that it did not improve their children's behavior.

Linguistically, the Urdu term used to describe parent–child relationships, *tarbiat*, is associated with a connotation of training and supervision. Pakistani parents are likely to view child training—and correcting misbehavior—as an important aspect of their parenting role. A study of more than 300 Pakistani youth by Stewart et al. (2000) suggests that like in Confucian cultures, the concept of "training" guides Pakistani parents in their child-rearing behaviors, especially with daughters.

A central value of many Islamic societies is *izzat*, the concept of honor. This cherished family value can be damaged by the misbehavior of one's children. Eliciting proper child behavior through disciplining children is regarded as a parenting imperative. In addition, conformity and respect for parents are widely shared values in Islamic/Pakistani culture. Consequently, each of these cultural constructs may contribute to a greater desire for immediate obedience, parental control, and the desire to use CP.

Evidence for the importance of disciplining children was found in a study of British Pakistani mothers who were compared with British White mothers (Ali and Frederickson 2011). Although there was no difference in the reported frequency of using CP, the authors found that the Pakistani mothers were more likely to report following through with discipline with boys as well as "reminding" their children about discipline.

Cultural differences are also reflected in the lexicon associated with discipline. In English, there are words like "spanking," "slapping," and "smacking" to describe the act of CP; however, the actual behaviors associated with these words may vary across families. There are no equivalent words in Urdu for these general terms. Instead, the Urdu language uses quite direct and specific terms to describe physical punishment (e.g., *thappar* is slapping on the face, *danda* is hitting with a stick, *jhoota* is hitting with a shoe). Unlike English, which utilizes different words when a child is hit (e.g., spank, smack, paddle) versus when an adult is hit (e.g., hit, assault, battery), Urdu uses the same terms across the lifespan. Urdu speakers use *maar* to describe CP, which directly translates to "hitting." Similarly, *maar peet* and *peetna* both mean "beating" and are commonly used to describe more severe physical punishments.

Do Pakistanis and South Asians in general hold more punitive attitudes in childrearing than others? This question was studied by Maiter et al. (2004) with a group of parents who had emigrated from South Asia and moved to Canada. Seven of the 29 participants were from Pakistan. When reacting to four vignettes about the use of CP, most parents (90 %) perceived the described actions as inappropriate "to some extent" or to "a large extent." The authors concluded that South Asian parents are not significantly more supportive of punitive punishment than other populations.

Pakistani Parents in the West

South Asian values about parenting emphasize obedience, quickly maturing into adulthood, and stringent expectations, potentially leading to conflict and harsh treatment (Maker et al. 2005). Studies of South Asian parents in western countries indicate that these parents are likely to have experienced CP as children, and are likely to endorse CP use when disciplining their own children. Irfan and Cowburn (2004) found that 75 % of British Pakistanis (aged 16–25) reported having experienced CP during childhood, with being slapped as the most common, followed by being punched (50 %), and spanked (42 %). Siblings were the perpetrators 35 % of the time, followed by mothers (33 %), and fathers (19 %). Of this subgroup, 72 % accepted it as an appropriate method of discipline (Irfan and Cowburn 2004). Comparable results were found by Maker et al. (2005): 73 % of South Asian American women reported having experienced at least one type of physical abuse and this experience predicted the acceptance of physical abuse as a parental right. In contrast, a comparison of British Pakistani and White mothers found that the British Pakistani mothers were more likely to follow through on discipline with their sons, but there was not a difference between the two groups on their self-reported use of physical punishment (Ali and Frederickson 2011). Similarly, South Asian parents living in Canada for 12 years did not differ from other populations on their attitude toward CP (Maiter et al. 2004). It appears that South Asian parents tend to endorse CP, even while living abroad, but this endorsement may dissipate once they become more acculturated. Further research is needed to confirm this hypothesis.

Legal Status of CP in Pakistan

We next consider what the legal status of CP in Pakistan is. Corporal punishment conflicts with the *Convention on the Rights of the Child*, adopted by the United Nations General Assembly in 1989. Although Pakistan ratified the CRC in 1990, it cannot be invoked into court until legislation is passed that would enforce it.

Perhaps prompted to action by the media attention and children's rights, there have been periodic legislative efforts made to ban corporal punishment in schools. Legal reform efforts are discussed in further detail below.

There are three types of laws that pertain to the use of CP in Pakistan: federal, provincial, and Shariah.

Federal Law

Under current Pakistani law, CP of children is legal. Article 89 of the Penal Code states:

> 89. Act done in good faith for benefit of child or insane person, by or by consent of guardian: Nothing which is *done in good faith for the benefit of a person under 12 years of age*, or of unsound mind, or by consent, either expressed or implied, of the guardian or other person having lawful charge of that person, is an offence by reason of any harm which it may cause, or be intended by the doer to cause or be known by the doer to be likely to cause to that person: Provided First: That this exception shall not extend to the intentional causing of death, or to the attempting to cause death; Secondly: That this exception shall not extend to the doing of anything which the person doing it knows to be likely to cause death, for any purpose other than the preventing of death or grievous hurt; or the curing of any grievous disease or infirmity; Thirdly: That this exception shall not extend to the voluntary causing of grievous hurt, or to the attempting to cause grievous hurt, unless it be for the purpose of preventing death or grievous hurt, or the curing of any grievous disease or infirmity; Fourthly: That this exception shall not extend to the abetment of any offence, to the committing of which offence it would not extend.

Pakistan Penal Code Act XLV of 1860 (Italics Added)

The Penal Code contains multiple sections that allow CP of children and confer significant discretion on parents or guardians. The phrase "*done in good faith for the benefit of a person under twelve*" is key. This clause confers a considerable discretion to the parent or guardian. Both phrases "*in good faith*" and "*for the benefit*" allow for a punitive act to be rationalized and defensible in court. With this language, children lose their right to physical safety.

Other provisions of the code grant further discretion to punishers. The phrase "*other person is having lawful charge of that person*" allows any person in charge of a child, not just a legal guardian, to employ CP. The combination of this phrase with the provision that consent may be implied rather than explicit adds considerable ambiguity. For example, could a parent leaving their child in the care of another adult constitute implied consent for punitive discipline?

In addition to granting full discretion to parents, teachers, and other persons with legal charge of children, this article provides virtually no protection for children. What protection it provides is in its few exceptions: it does not include *intentionally* causing death, *intentionally* attempting to cause death, or *intentionally* causing grievous harm. However, even the severest cases of CP, resulting in child fatalities, may be excused by the alleged intention. If a person does not intend to cause harm, or is unaware of the harm that their actions may cause, the behavior is not considered unlawful.

An obvious limitation of the Penal Code is that it contains no mention of punishment of children older than 12 years of age. Overall, the ambiguity and broad application of this law can provide a convenient justification for CP in home, school, and alternative care settings. It can also provide a cover for physical child abuse. Even if a parent or teacher violated this law, it is unclear whether complaints to police would be investigated and the law enforced. We were unable to discover any information about complaints, investigations, or enforcement of the law.

Provincial Laws

Currently, laws in three of Pakistan's four provinces mention corporal punishment of children. In Punjab, the most populous province, the Destitute and Neglected Children Act 2007-Amendment: Article 35 of the Act, provides an allowance for the guardian (i.e., person with lawful control or custody) to inflict physical punishment on a child as long as there is "sufficient reason."

However, in the other two provinces, some statutory restraints are imposed. In the province of Sindh, the Right of Children to Free & Compulsory Education Act 2013 makes CP unlawful in government schools for children aged 5–16. Prior to this, the Children Act of 1955 allowed for the use of physical punishment "for a proper reason." In Khyber Pakhtunkhwa, the Child Protection and Welfare Act 2010 bans CP in the home and other settings. However, this act fails to ban CP completely, because the prohibition is only within the context of Sect. 89 of the Penal Code; it does not overwrite Sect. 89 of the Penal Code.

To compensate for that loophole, in 2012 a Grievances Redressal Mechanism was established in order to address complaints related to CP in school settings. The goal of this system was to ensure thorough investigation of reported cases in both public and private schools. Additionally, the 2010 act was expanded in 2012 to include other areas under provincial control. The revised act now indicates that CP, as well as other forms of violence against children, is punishable by imprisonment and fines.

Children living in the sparsely inhabited Federally Administrated Tribal Areas, an area bordering Afghanistan that comprises just 2.3 % of the Pakistani population, have the greatest legal protection from teacher violence. In 2012, the Free and Compulsory Education Bill was passed, which prohibits teachers in both government and private schools from administering CP. However, that area is commonly described as "lawless" as there is no evidence that the statute is enforced.

Shariah Law

Shariah law adds an additional layer of complexity to the legal status of CP in Pakistan. Although CP is not mentioned in the *Qur'an*, CP is mentioned in the *Hadith* (Obeid 1988). Specifically, in the narrations by Dawud: "The Prophet said: Order your children to pray at the age of seven, and beat them [lightly] if they do not do so by the age of ten." It is with this *Hadith*, and the Islamic construct of parents training children to be upstanding and religiously active adults, that many Muslims interpret the use of CP to be encouraged by their belief system. However, there is no mention of CP in the most valued text, the *Qur'an*, and there exist sayings in the *Hadith* that speak against abuse and cruelty. For example, according to Bukhari and Muslim, Muhammad said "abusing a Muslim is a sin, and killing him is disbelief." Thus, there is some ambiguity regarding the use of CP.

Federal or provincial laws do not apply to *hadd* offenses. *Hadd* offenses are those that have predetermined punishments in Islamic law (i.e., theft, fornication, adultery, consumption of alcohol, or other intoxicants). These offenses continue to be punished by CP, including whipping, and apply to children from the onset of puberty. Thus, 9.4 year-old girls and 11.4 year-old boys, the average age of puberty found in one study in Peshawar, may be subject to CP under Shariah law.

Another type of CP allowed under the Pakistani Penal Code is the penalty of *qisas*. *Qisas* is a punishment causing similar pain at the same location of the perpetrator as he or she caused to the victim; it also has its roots in Islamic law. The Penal Code prohibits *qisas* for minors. However, a minor is defined as a male under 18 years old; females can be subjected to the punishment at any age.

Recent Efforts at Legal Reform

It is difficult to elicit support for stricter prohibitions against the practice when CP is a sanctioned punishment in the penal system. Although Article 12 of Juvenile Justice System Ordinance 2000 bans children from receiving CP while in police custody, this provision is commonly interpreted to mean that CP cannot be given as a sentence of the court (Global Initiative to End All Corporal Punishment of Children 2012). In other words, while the article outlaws police officers from using CP, in practice this prohibition is only applied when the juvenile is in official custody and being charged. If, for instance, the juvenile is brought in for questioning, CP may be utilized. Furthermore, this ordinance is not recognized in all Pakistani courts.

Nevertheless, over the past few years there have been multiple efforts to ban CP, both provincially and federally. Three examples will be cited. In Balochistan, the Prohibition of Corporal Punishment Bill of 2011 was submitted to the provincial congress (Provincial Assembly). The bill called for an outright ban CP in all settings, but was not passed. In Punjab, an amendment under consideration in 2012 called for a complete ban on CP with punishments of up to six months in prison and/or a fine of Rs. 1,000,000 (more than $10,000). This proposed amendment did not progress to the point where it was voted on.

Most recently, a bill was introduced into the National Assembly in 2013 to ban CP in schools and other educational institutions. The bill was expressly intended to override Article 89 of the Penal Code, and thereby eliminate any justification for CP. The bill spelled out a punishment for those who use CP of a fine of up to 50,000 Pakistani rupees (~ $500.00) and imprisonment for up to a year. The bill was unanimously passed by the National Assembly in March 2013, but was not passed by the Senate. Therefore President Asif Ali Zardari did not have the opportunity to sign the bill into law during the 2013 National Assembly.

Recommendations

It is clear that corporal punishment of children is a significant problem in Pakistan, like most countries. Consequently, the children of Pakistan are not being protected and their rights, as identified in the CRC, are being violated. Based on that observation, we can propose three types of recommendations with the goal of reducing and then ending the CP of Pakistani children.

First, we consider the legal recourse. As a start, the CRC, ratified by Pakistan in 1990, needs to be adhered to. Laws need to be passed in all provinces and at the federal level to protect children from CP. In those provinces with recent CP laws, further work needs to be done in educating parents, teachers, and law enforcement so the prohibitions are upheld. Additionally, the process of filing and reviewing CP complaints using the Grievances Redressal Mechanism in should be simplified and standardized to ensure it will be utilized and effective.

Along with the passage of new legislation, a public health educational campaign is needed. Such a campaign can inform the public as well as train healthcare providers, school administrators, and parents about the potential consequences of CP. A parallel campaign is needed to educate and promote the use of non-violent management approaches for parents and teachers. There are many books and curriculums available for schools that provide "positive discipline" techniques (e.g., Durrant 2013; Kersey and Masterson 2012; Nelsen 2006). Parents need to be informed about alternatives and educated as to why this approach is beneficial for them and their children. Given Pakistan is a deeply religious country, it will be important to involve imams in this effort to use non-violent approaches to childrearing and education.

Our third recommendation involves research. To further understand the issue of CP in Pakistan and arrive at sound recommendations for addressing the problem, there is a considerable need for empirical research. Without carefully documenting the prevalence and correlates of CP in Pakistan, as well as the key determinants of the behavior, it will be difficult to develop appropriate and well-targeted efforts at intervention and prevention. Thus, an initial effort would be to systematically document the prevalence of the problem in the schools and homes. Another important area to investigate is how best to modify Pakistani attitudes and behavior regarding CP. For example, to what extent is can attitude change occur simply by providing information about the problems linked to CP (e.g., Holden et al. 2014a)?

Conclusion

The available evidence indicates that CP continues to be widely used both in Pakistani schools and homes. Despite its wide acceptance, it is a problematic behavior because of its ineffectiveness in promoting good behavior, its unintended consequences, and its infringement on the right to safety and protection of children. The fact that there have been several recent legislative efforts to ban the practice in Pakistan is promising. Those efforts indicate that there are many Pakistanis who are committed to ending the practice of CP and promoting the safety, physical integrity, and respect of the rights of children.

References

Ali, S., & Frederickson, N. (2011). The parenting dimensions of British Pakistani and White mothers of primary school children. *Infant and Child Development, 20*, 313–329. doi:10.1002/icd.696.

Ateah, C. A., & Durrant, J. E. (2005). Maternal use of physical punishment in response to child misbehavior: Implications for child abuse prevention. *Child Abuse and Neglect, 29*, 169–185. doi:10.1016/j.chiabu.2004.10.010.

Barry, H. (2007). Corporal punishment and other formative experiences associated with violent crimes. *Journal of Psychohistory, 35*, 71–82.

Bitensky, S. H. (2010). The mother of all human rights: The child's right to be free of corporal punishment as hard international law. *Ohio Northern University Law Review, 36*(3), 701–720.

Brieland, D., & Brieland, C. G. (1957). A parent education project in Pakistan. *Marriage and Family Living, 19*, 348–351. doi:10.2307/347801.

Britto, P. R., & Ulkuer, N. (2012). Child development in developing countries: Child rights and policy implications. *Child Development, 83*, 92–103. doi:10.1111/j.1467-8624.2011.01672.x.

CIA. (2014). The world factbook. Retrieved 2/18/2014 from http://www.cia.gov/library/publications/the-world-factbook/index.html.

Dix, T. (1991). The affective organization of parenting: Adaptive and maladaptive processes. *Psychological Bulletin, 110*, 3–25. doi:10.1037/0033-2909.110.1.3.

Domjan, M. (2015). *The principles of learning and behavior* (7th ed.). Stanford, CT: Cengage Learning.

Durrant, J. E. (2013). *Positive discipline in everyday parenting* (3rd ed.). Stockholm, Sweden: Save the Children Sweden.

Durrant, J. E., & Smith, A. B. (Eds.). (2011). *Global pathways to abolishing physical punishment*. New York: Routledge.

Ferguson, C. J. (2013). Spanking, corporal punishment and negative long-term outcomes: A meta-analytic review of longitudinal studies. *Clinical Psychology Review, 33*, 196–208.

Gershoff, E. T. (2002). Corporal punishment by parents and associated child behaviors and experiences: A meta-analytic and theoretical review. *Psychological Bulletin, 128*, 539–579. doi:10.1037/0033-2909.128.4.539.

Gershoff, E. T. (2013). Spanking and child development: We know enough now to stop hitting our children. *Child Development Perspectives, 7*, 1–5.

Global Initiative to End All Corporal Punishment of Children. (2012, July). The nature and extent of corporal punishment- prevalence and attitudinal research in South Asia. Retrieved 2013, from End Corporal Punishment: http://www.endcorporalpunishment.org/pages/pdfs/prevalence/SouthAsia.pdf.

Glover, J. (1999). *Humanity: A moral history of the twentieth century*. New Haven, CT: Yale University Press.

Greven, P. J. (1991). *Spare the child: The religious roots of punishment and the psychological impact of physical abuse*. New York: Alfred A. Knopf.

Heimlich, J. (2011). *Breaking their will: Shedding light on religious child maltreatment*. Amherst, NY: Prometheus Books.

Holden, G. W., Brown, A. S., Baldwin, A. S., & Croft Caderao, K. (2014a). Research findings can change attitudes about corporal punishment. *Child Abuse and Neglect, 38*, 902–908. doi:10.1016/j.chiabu.2013.10.013.

Holden, G. W., Williamson, P. A., & Holland, G. W. O. (2014b). Eavesdropping on the family: A pilot investigation of corporal punishment in the home. *Journal of Family Psychology, 28*, 401–406.

Hyder, A. A., & Malik, F. A. (2007). Violence against children: A challenge for public health in Pakistan. *Journal of Health, Population and Nutrition, 25*, 168–178.

Irfan, S., & Cowburn, M. (2004). Disciplining, chastisement and physical child abuse: Perceptions and attitudes of the British Pakistani community. *Journal of Muslim Affairs, 24*, 89–98. doi:10.1080/1360200042000212151.

Iqbal, A. (2012, December 10). *Teacher beats student to death*. Retrieved from DAWN News: beta.dawn.com/news/770233/teacher-beats-student-to-death-2.

Kersey, K., & Masterson, M. (2012). *101 principles of positive guidance with young children: Creating responsive teachers*. New York: Pearson Professional Development.

Kugelman, M., & Hathaway, R. (2011). Reaping the divident: Overcoming Pakistan's demographic challenges *Woodrow Wilson International Center for Scholars*. Washington, DC.

Lansford, J. E., & Deater-Deckard, K. (2012). Childrearing discipline and violence in developing countries. *Child Development, 83*, 62–75. doi:10.1111/j.1467-8624.2011.01676.x.

Maker, A. H., Shah, P. V., & Agha, Z. (2005). Child physical abuse: Prevalence, characteristics, predictors, and beliefs about parent-child violence in South Asian, Middle Eastern, East Asian, and Latina women in the United States. *Journal of Interpersonal Violence, 20*, 1406–1428. doi:10.1177/0886260505278713.

Malik, F. (2010). Determinants of child abuse in Pakistani families: Parental acceptance-rejection and demographic variables. *International Journal of Business and Social Science, 1*, 67–80.

Maiter, S., Alaggia, R., & Trocmé, N. (2004). Perceptions of child maltreatment by parents from the Indian subcontinent: Challenging myths about culturally based abusive parenting practices. *Child Maltreatment, 9*, 309–324. doi:10.1177/1077559504266800.

Naz, A., Khan, W., Daraz, U., Hussain, M., & Khan, Q. (2011). The impacts of corporal punishment on students' academic performance/career and personality development up-to secondary level education in Khyber Pakhtunkhwa Pakistan. *International Journal of Business and Social Science, 2*, 130–140.

NCCR (2001). Violence against children in the family and in schools. Submission by NGS Coalition on Child Rights Pakistan to the CRC Day of General Discussion, 28 September, 2001. NGOs Coalition on Child Rights/UNICEF.

Nelsen, J. (2006). *Positive discipline*. New York: Ballantine Books.

Newell, P. (2011). The human rights imperative to eliminate physical punishment. In J. E. Durrant & A. B. Smith (Eds.), *Global pathways to abolishing physical punishment: Realizing children's rights* (pp. 7–26). New York: Routledge.

NGO Coalition on Child Rights with UNICEF. (1998). *Corporal punishment in primary schools of North West Frontier Province Pakistan.*

Obeid, R. A. (1988). An Islamic theory of human development. In R. M. Thomas (Ed.), *Oriental theories of human development: Scriptural and popular beliefs from Hinduism, Buddhism, Confucianism, Shinto, and Islam* (pp. 155–174). New York: Peter Lang.

Pakistan Penal Code Act XLV. (1860).

Pearl, M., & Pearl, D. (1994). *To train up a child*. Pleasantville, TN: No Greater Joy Ministries.

Profanter, A. (2007). *Che Charta Dab Dey, Halta Abad Dey: A Pushto saying meaning Where there is physical punishment, there is order and respect*. New York: Peter Lang.

Runyan, D. K., Shankar, V., Hassan, F., Hunter, W. M., Jain, D., Paula, C. S.,... Bordin. I. A. (2010). International variations in harsh child discipline. *Pediatrics, 126*, e701-e711. doi: 10.1542/peds.2008-2374.

Society for the Protection of the Rights of the Child. (2012). Violence against children: Corporal punishment. In *The State of Pakistan's Children* (pp. 158–165). http://www.sparcpk.org/.

Stewart, S. M., Bond, M. H., Zaman, R., Mcbride-Chang, C., Rao, N., Ho, L. M., & Fielding, R. (1999). Functional parenting in Pakistan. *International Journal of Behavioral Development, 23*, 747–770.

Stewart, S. M., Bond, M. H., Ho, L. M., Zaman, R. M., Dar, R., & Anwar, M. (2000). Perceptions of parents and adolescent outcomes in Pakistan. *British Journal of Developmental Psychology, 18*, 335–352.

Straus, M. A. (1996). Spanking and the making of a violent society. *Pediatrics, 98*, 837–842.

Straus, M. A., Douglas, E. M., & Medeiros, R. A. (2014). *Primordial violence: Spanking and its relation to psychological development, violence, and crime*. New York: Routledge Thomas.

Vittrup, B., Holden, G. W., & Buck, J. (2006). Attitudes predict the use of physical punishment: A prospective study of the emergence of disciplinary practices. *Pediatrics, 117*, 2055–2064. doi:10.1542/peds.2005-220.

Zolotor, A. J., Theodore, A. D., Runyan, D. K., Chang, J. J., & Laskey, A. L. (2011). Corporal punishment and physical abuse: population-based trends for three-to-11-year-old children in the United States. *Child Abuse Review, 20*, 57–66.

irritability, and anger outbursts. Depending on the severity, it can also lead to other problems such sleep disturbance, bed wetting, decline in academic performance, and school dropout. It can also lead to increased sexual interest and inappropriate sexual behavior. The long-term effect of the sexual abuse, are usually seen in young adult or adulthood where the person experiences difficulties with self-esteem, trust issues, interpersonal relationship, and sexual functions. In a study of high school students in Goa, India, Patel and Andrew (2001) found that one-third of the children surveyed had experienced some form of sexual abuse, and these individuals had significantly poorer academic performance, poorer mental and physical health, greater substance abuse, poorer parental relationships and higher rates of consensual sexual behaviors than their non-abused counterparts.

Adults, who were sexually abused as children develop depression, become dependent on alcohol and drug abuse and sometimes end up being re-victimized. Few of those who were abused as children, themselves become perpetrators when they become adults.

It is also seen that, few children do not experience any symptom after the sexual abuse. These children are generally considered to be afraid or in denial of their emotions as a way of coping with the stress of the abuse. However, research shows that this is not true in a substantial number of cases (Clancy 2009; Loftus and Ketcham 1994).

One of the worst negative effects of sexual abuse of children is adjustment problem in later life, as reported by a number of researchers (Deb and Walsh 2012). For example, Swanston et al. (2003) explored the psychological adjustment of 103 sexually abused children (mean age = 19.1) in Sydney after 9 years of reporting of sexual abuse to Child Protection Units in two children's hospitals in Sydney and compared the same to non-abused young people of similar age and gender. Findings revealed that the sexually abused young people performed more poorly than non-abused young people on psychometric tests of depression, self-esteem, anxiety, and despair. The longer the duration of abuse, the greater was the likelihood of negative effects in the form of emotional and behavioral trauma and school problems. Ray and Jackson (1997) found that family characteristics especially family environment was significantly related to sexually abused children's current social and psychological adjustment. In a Kolkata-based study Deb and Mukherjee (2011) made an attempt to understand the adjustment capacity and depression of sexually abused girls in the age group 13–18 years in Kolkata, India. The study also attempted to understand how the sexually abused girls perceived the psychological interventions, i.e. individual and group counseling, which they had received. Findings disclosed that 69.2 % of sexually abused girls suffered from moderate or severe depression compared with 27.5 % of non-sexually abused girls. The study also found that 20.8 and 60.1 % of sexually abused girls had poor levels of social and emotional adjustment, respectively, compared with 4.17 and 32.5 % of non-sexually. Overall the perception of more than two-thirds of the sexually abused girls of the rehabilitation homes they lived in was found to be positive. Furthermore, the girls who reported that they gained considerably from counseling had a better adjustment capacity compared to those who reported they did not benefit from counseling.

Belief in Trauma

It is a general belief among many people who are in the field of child sexual abuse that, child sexual abuse is a traumatic experience for the child. According to this view, every sexual child abuse induces traumatic feelings in the child. Trauma generally refers to extreme consequences and is usually equated with shock and a great deal of suffering, most often associated with situations such as some calamity, extreme violence, murder, rape, and the like. If a person has undergone trauma she will experience symptoms such as fearfulness, depression, sadness, anxiety, sleeplessness, and get repeated thoughts of the traumatic experience. As mentioned earlier, majority of the children who are sexually abused, especially by a trusted person, do not report the abuse and do not show symptoms of trauma. Adherents of the trauma experience believe that if the child is not experiencing the symptoms of the trauma, then that child has repressed the memories of the abuse. They argue that child sexual abuse is so traumatic to the child that the child unconsciously represses and/or suppress the whole experience as a process of the ego to cope up with the traumatic experience. This repression and/or suppression are considered to be one of the reasons why many children do not report sexual abuse and/or feel any negative effects of the abuse. It is generally believed that the repression of these memories in childhood will have adverse consequences during adulthood.

The believers of the traumatic experience model of child sexual abuse do not draw much of a distinction between the types of abuse. For them all types of abuses are the same, and all types of abuse result in traumatic experiences either immediately or later in adulthood. However, they might believe that a more severe form of sexual abuse as well as abuse by somebody in a close relation causes more traumas. On the other hand, the believers of the traumatic experience model do not take into the account the circumstances wherein a particular child did not oppose the abuse, due to some reason, and due to which the child might end up feeling guilty for being party to the abuse later in life. Furthermore, cognitive psychological studies that have looked into the phenomenon of repressed memory of child sexual abuse cast doubts about the repressed memory phenomenon (Loftus and Ketcham 1994; Whittier 2011).

Trauma or Confusion

One of the main reasons for the belief that child sexual abuse results in traumatic experience is that child sexual abuse is viewed from an adult centric point of view. That is, the adult projects her/his views, opinions, and beliefs about the experience of child sexual abuse onto the child. For adults, sexual abuse is a traumatic experience, and this feeling is projected onto the child, and believe and expect (rather involuntarily) that the child also might be experiencing the abuse as traumatic (Clancy 2009).

Adults have clear boundaries with respect to, their personal and intimate space. They have definite conceptualizations regarding their body, and that it belongs to them. They have control over, who can broach their personal and intimate space and who cannot and how much; what are another person's personal space and private body; what is sex and related issues, what can be considered as abuse and what is not. Children's knowledge and awareness varies in all the above aspects. They may not know about personal space, who can breach them and who cannot and how much. Usually young children have either poor understanding or have only a vague knowledge about sex. Furthermore, they may not know about what is sexual abuse, even though they might know that something is not alright. In addition, if the perpetrator concocts a story around the abuse (for example, that the abuse act is a forgiveness ritual for a mistake done by the child), as it usually happens with young children, it will be difficult for the child to perceive the act as sexual abuse.

A related issue deals with the aspect of cognitive development. Cognitive functions in young children that are necessary to understand what is good and what is not, are not fully developed. This is especially true about sex and sexual abuse. This is compounded by society's restrictions and limitations on talking or discussing about sex with young children. In this scenario, unless the sexual abuse involves force, violence or is done by someone outside the trusting relationship, it would be difficult for the young child to perceive it as not good.

The following example emphasizes the cognitive development factors. A child's uncle creeps to the child's bed during night, talks to the child affectionately, abuses the child and gives chocolates and gifts after that. But the same uncle talks less and avoids the child during the day time (Virani 2000). Here, the child is confused as to 'who is my real uncle?' is it the one that the child sees in the night or the one the child encounters during day time.

Other factors that influence the perception of abuse are the upbringing of the child by the parents. Many parents insist that the child is to follow what is said without questioning; parents often times do not provide reasons for why they want the child to behave in a particular way, and many times parents say 'do as I say but not as I do'. In this environment, if abuse happens, the child might believe that the adults have the right to do whatever they want to the child, and that the child should just accept it. In addition, there are parents who punish (for e.g., spanking) the child for even small mistakes and sometimes even without knowing the cause of the child's behavior. Again in this scenario, a child might develop less attachment with as well as fear of the punishing parent, both of which are not conducive to reporting the abuse.

One of the cognitive development factors of childhood is that of egocentric thoughts, where for a child, the world revolves around itself. Given this and certain child rearing practices of the parents, the child tends to believe that it is s/he who is responsible for the abuse and not the abuser and takes the blame on herself/himself with self statements such as "I might have done something wrong" and "I deserve this, or else why would he do this for me." Not reporting the abuse after it has happened for the first or first few times, further increases the chance of confusion that the child undergoes. Such as, 'I kept quiet for first few times, is there a problem with me?'; "I did not report it to anyone after it happened, so will others think I encouraged it because I did not report?"

Conclusion and Recommendations

A majority of children are fairly resilient. They usually outgrow various adverse experiences that have occurred in childhood. This applies even more too non-sexual, abusive experiences. One of the factors that influence the resilience of the child to any adverse experience is how the parents and surroundings react to the same. For the psychologist treating the child who has been sexually abused, the child's wellbeing and mental health is far more important than legal issues related to the perpetrator. Therefore, primarily a good treatment plan is to make the child function as normally as possible and help to cope up with the abuse and to prevent further adverse effects of the sexual abuse, such as secondary victimization. If the clinician believes that all child sexual abuse results in trauma and tries to treat it as such, even when the child does not report any trauma feelings, real healing cannot take place. Given this, clinicians should be sensitive about what actually is experienced by the child and work towards the wellbeing of the child.

A number of steps are suggested for addressing this sensitive issue:

(i) There is a need to extend unconditional mental health support to the victim and their family members by professional psychologists or counselor. Continuous/periodic supportive counseling services to be provided to the victim and other family members.
(ii) Ensuring safety of the child, as in a number of cases where either biological father or close family members are involved in the crime so the child must be shifted to a safe custody. Otherwise, morale of the child and career will be badly affected.
(iii) There is a need to report each and every case of child sexual abuse to the competent authority for justice and safety.
(iv) Perpetrators should be sensitized about the negative effect of the act and they should be counseled instead of keeping them left out from the intervention strategies.
(v) Not to stigmatize the child and allowing the child to resume all daily activities.
(vi) There is an urgent need to amend or bring legislation for mandatory reporting of child sexual abuse incidents to the police as suggested by Deb (2015). Doctors, family members mainly parents, nurses, and teachers should be mandated for reporting of any child sexual abuse case to the police.

References

Clancy, S. A. (2009). *The trauma myth*. New York: Basic Books.

Csorba, R., Lampe, L., Borsos, A., Balla, L., Poka, R., & Olah, E. (2006). Female child sexual abuse within the family in a Hungarian country. *Gynecologic and Obstetric Investigation, 61*(4), 188–193.

Deb, S., & Mukherjee, A. (2011). Background and adjustment capacity of sexually abused girls and their perceptions of intervention. *Child Abuse Review, 20*, 213–230. doi:10.1002/car.1153.

Deb, S., & Mukherjee, A. (2009). *Impact of sexual abuse on mental health of children*. New Delhi: Concept Publishing Company.

Deb, S. & Sen, P. (2005). A study on psychological trauma of young trafficked women. Presented in the 6th Asian Conference on Child Abuse and Neglect held in Singapore during Nov. 16–18, 2005.

Deb, S., & Walsh, K. (2012). Impact of physical, psychological, and sexual violence on social adjustment of school children in India. *School Psychology International, 33*(4), 391–415. doi:10.1177/0143034311425225.

Deb, S. (2015). Legislation concerning reporting of child sexual abuse and child trafficking in India: A closer look. In Mathews Ben & Bross C. Donald (Eds.), *Mandatory Reporting Laws and the Identification of Severe Child Abuse and Neglect*. Australia: Springer.

Deb, S., & Madrid, B. (2014). Burden of child abuse and neglect with special reference to socio-legal measures: A comparative picture of India, Philippines and Japan (77-106). In Conte Jon (Ed.), *Child Abuse and Neglect: Worldwide*. California: US, PRAEGER.

Gilbert, R., Widom, C. S., Browne, K., Fergusson, D., Webb, E., & Janson, S. (2009). Child maltreatment 1: Burden and consequences of child maltreatment in high-income countries. *The Lancet, 373*, 68–81. doi:10.1016/S0140-6736(08)61706-7.

Gorey, K. M., & Leslie, D. R. (1997). The prevalence of child sexual abuse: integrative review adjustment for potential response and measurement biases. *Child Abuse and Neglect, 21*(4), 391–398. doi:10.1016/S0145-2134(96)00180-9.

Loftus, E., & Ketcham, K. (1994). *The myth of repressed memory: False memories and allegations of sexual abuse*. New York: St. Martin's Griffin.

Modak, S. (2009). *Violence against children in Tripura and its impact. Dissertation*. Calcutta: Calcutta University.

Mukherjee, A. (2006). *A study on the impact of sexual abuse on mental disposition of girl children. Unpublished Doctoral Thesis*. Kolkata, India: University of Calcutta.

Patel, V., & Andrew, G. (2001). Gender, sexual abuse and risk behaviors in adolescents: A cross-sectional survey in schools in Goa. *National Medical Journal of India, 14*, 263–267.

Pereda, N., Guilera, G., Forns, M., & Gomez-Benito, J. (2009). The prevalence of child sexual abuse in community and student samples: a meta-analysis. *Clinical Psychology Review, 29*(4), 328–338. doi:10.1016/j.cpr.2009.02.007.

Putnam, F. W. (2003). Ten-year research updates review: Child sexual abuse. *Journal of the American Academy of Child and Adolescent Psychiatry, 42*(3), 269–278. doi:10.1097/00004583-200303000-00006.

Ray, K. C., & Jackson, J. L. (1997). Family environment and childhood sexual victimization. A test of the buffering hypothesis. *Journal of Interpersonal Violence, 12*(1), 3–17. doi:10.1177/088626097012001001.

Swanston, H. Y., Plunkett, A. M., O'Toole, B. I., Shrimpton, S., Parkinson, P. N., & Oates, R. K. (2003). Nine years after child sexual abuse. *Child Abuse and Neglect, 27*(8), 967–984. doi:10.1016/S0145-2134(03)00143-1.

Virani, P. (2000). *Bitter chocolate: Child sexual abuse in India*. New Delhi: Penguin Books.

Whittier, N. (2011). *The politics of child sexual abuse*. New York: Oxford University Press.

World Health Organization. (2002). *World report on violence and health*. Geneva: World Health Organization, Office of Publications.

Chapter 7
Conflict in Kashmir: Psychosocial Consequences on Children

Waheeda Khan

Introduction

Violence, abuse, neglect of children is common; they are abused and neglected by their parents or other caregivers everywhere in the world. But true extent of such things is not easy to measure as it is less reported, varies from place to place and is context specific. Relation is also observed between conflict and worse condition of such children. As with violence against intimate partners, child abuse includes physical, sexual, and psychological abuse, as well as neglect. Probably the broadest assessment of this statement is the data on physical violence compiled by the Innocent Research Centre for the UN Secretary-General's Study on Violence against Children (2006), which led to an estimate of between 500 million and 1.5 billion children experiencing violence annually. Reliable data on non-fatal child abuse is scarce, but studies from various countries suggest that children below the age of 15 years are frequently victims of abuse or neglect. In most places, boys are the victims of beatings and physical punishment more often than girls, while girls are at higher risk of infanticide, sexual abuse, neglect, and being forced into prostitution. Children who face abuse and neglect appear to be associated with increased rates of mood disorders and anxiety problems. The strongest association was with Post Traumatic Stress Disorder (PTSD) and Obsessive Compulsive Disorder (OCD). Depression and withdrawal symptoms were common among children as young as of 3 year old, who experienced emotional, physical, and environmental neglect (Dubowitz et al. 2002). Other psychological and emotional conditions associated with abuse and neglect include panic disorder, dissociative disorders,

W. Khan (✉)
Department of Psychology, Jamia Millia Islamia, New Delhi 110025, India
e-mail: profwkhan@gmail.com

S. Deb (ed.), *Child Safety, Welfare and Well-being*,
DOI 10.1007/978-81-322-2425-9_7

Attention Deficit Hyperactivity Disorder (ADHD), depression, anger, PTSD, and reactive attachment disorder (Teicher 2000).

The condition of children is worsening in states of armed conflict and Kashmir is no exception. The impact of conflict in Kashmir is such that the exposure to actual armed conflict is limited but, the detrimental effects are in terms of repression, loss of security, income and service access, disrupted schooling, displacement, military harassment and other forms are visible in the lives of children and their families (Wessells 1998). Since the initiation of armed conflict in Kashmir, it has undergone many transformations at the micro and macro levels, with major implications for women and children. The impact has major consequences on the survival, development, mental health and overall well being of children and adolescents (Khan and Ghilzai 2002). The major problems that children are suffering from armed conflict in Kashmir are presented under the following headings:

Social Disruption

Some of the environmental threats to children commonly associated with conflict include displacement from homeland, family dispersal, separation and discord, destitution, loss of service access and social interaction, and the presence of military personnel. Usually a number of military camps are found to be located near schools in Kashmir which create a threatening atmosphere for students and teachers alike, particularly for females who fear sexual harassment etc. Often the disruption occurs in Kashmir during the times of combat and children somehow manage to leave their village and remain in their relative's place till the situation improves.

Civil and Political Violations

The close presence of large numbers of security personnel often leads to human rights abuse, and much more than this, it entails the militarization of society, the strain of life under constant vigilance, restriction of movement, frequent harassment, and intimidation. Check-points, surveillance operations, interrogations, search operations in homes and places of work, restrictions on the press and activists all undermine normal interaction and community life in many conflict regions (Machel 2001).

In Kashmir also, civilians resent frequent searches and intimidation by the security forces. They feel angry about arbitrary change in laws by the military personnel and their counter-insurgency operations. Such happenings create a sense of mistrust, insecurity, and helplessness in the lives of common people and their children. A study conducted by Jong et al. (2008) in Kashmir showed that almost half of the respondents (48.1 %) mentioned that they felt safe only occasionally or never, and they had to suffer crackdowns, frisking by security forces, round-up raids, damage to property, burning of houses, mistreatment, humiliation, and threats. It was found that nearly one in ten people (9.4 %) lost one or more members of their nuclear family because of violence. Almost 11.6 % interviewees mentioned that they had been victims of sexual violence since 1989. People dealt with stress by isolating themselves (22.3 %) or becoming aggressive (16 %). In another study, Jong et al. (2008) reported frequent direct confrontations with violence since the start of conflict, including exposure to crossfire (85.7 %), round up raids (82.7 %), the witnessing of torture (66.9 %), rape (13.3 %), and self-experience of forced labor (33.7 %), arrests/kidnapping (16.9 %), torture (12.9 %), and sexual violence (11.6 %). Males reported more confrontations with violence than females.

Transformation in Roles and Responsibilities

When families undergo times of deprivation and material loss, it is not surprising that they may turn to their children as an economic resource. This is true in many places but particularly so in a conflict ridden situation when regular breadwinners are absent, killed, or injured. The likelihood of hazardous work increases in conflict because of the reduction in normal economic opportunities and the prevailing climate of lawlessness and impunity. It will also depend on local cultural factors which, for example, may create few obstacles to the employment of boys but ensure that girls are largely prevented from pursuing any public economic activity. In Kashmir as well, the sons are encouraged to migrate for work. The Hanji community is increasingly relied on the earning capacity of their children in carpet weaving. Some families have become so indebted that they have committed their children in bonded labor to the owners of carpet factories. During conflict, children who have lost their father or the prime bread earner and they are left to run the households with younger siblings or simply left to fend for themselves on the streets of larger towns. Conflict increases the pressures on the young to work, possibly at the expense of their schooling. It also leads to under-nourishment and malnutrition; inability of parents to pay for the basic necessities of school education, such as uniform and writing materials; and more often than not leads to the child's withdrawal from religious, social, and cultural events.

The survey done by Dabla (1999) revealed that 84.7 % of such child respondents lived with their mothers, 4 % with their uncle, 9 % with mother's father, and 2 % with their father's father. These children faced problems like economic hardships, psychological setback, denial of love and affection, and apathy by relatives and friends. Total dropouts among child respondents were 57 % during 1989–1999; 27 % at primary level, 48 % at middle level, and 25 % at the matric and above level. Children who were not going to school were engaged in domestic work (3.7 %), handicrafts (37.8 %), automobile workshops (3.7 %), non-governmental service (3.7 %), and business houses (3.65 %). These child workers felt that they got lesser wages and were exploited regularly.

Vulnerability to Children

Many conflicts are now being fought with a combination of high-tech hardware and traditional weaponry. The variety of combat activities enabled by this mix of weaponry leads to the injury and death of child civilians in a wide range of situations. Some of the most common are as follows:

(a) **Bystander Injury**
The sudden outbreak of gun battles between opposed forces may cause injury to children caught up in crossfire. This is a particular problem in Kashmir due to the fact, already noted, that many army checkpoints and camps, which are obvious target of militant attacks, are situated very close to schools.

(b) **Bombing and Shelling**
The increasingly sophisticated weaponry involved in the launching of shells and bombs which are both dropped and planted usually in markets pose an unavoidable threat to children and their families. Not only are the numbers of casualties from a single incident often great, the unpredictable nature of such activities contribute to an atmosphere of fear and anxiety.

(c) **In Combat**
In Afghanistan and Sri Lanka, particularly children are reported to have been killed in direct military action. The age of these combatants does not appear to discourage either their superiors or their enemies from treating them just as any other soldiers. Same is the case of Kashmir where young boys are taken along with military personnel who use them as a shield while searching houses. Even if there is no combat, still the psychological torture of that time period is more than evident.

Loss of Parents

Orphanages seeking to accommodate children who have lost the care of their families due to conflict have become commonplace in Kashmir. It is reported that Kashmir has 33,000 conflict widows and only 8.7 % remarried and it has also created conditions where children are abused by step parents. Residing in orphanages, children are exposed to new risks, incidences of orphan children being abused and beaten for petty reasons in Kashmir are often reported. UK-based child rights organization, Save the Children, has revealed that the estimated population of orphans in Jammu and Kashmir is 2,14,000 and 37 % of them were orphaned due to the armed conflict (Kumar 2012). The report titled "Orphaned in Kashmir—The State of Orphans in Jammu and Kashmir" based on a study conducted in six districts of the state revealed that 37 % of the orphans lost one or both parents due to the conflict while 55 % were orphaned due to the natural death of parents and remaining 8 % due to other reasons.

The proportion of children orphaned due to conflict is highest in Anantnag district of south Kashmir. The largest number of children orphaned due to conflict was in Anantnag, (56 %), followed by Ganderbal (48 %), Baramulla (33 %), and Rajouri (31 %); but number of orphans is higher in the Valley than Jammu region. The study revealed that 5 % of the orphans were either physically abused or intimidated, such as having guns pointed at them, threatened by armed actors, accused of providing support to the fighting sides, physically assaulted and hurt, used as bait to capture their parents or as human shields during the conflict. "Among the orphans attending schools, a large number said that the main distraction in school was that they had worries about their families (28 %), noise of explosions during conflict (19 %), and intimidating presence of troops (13 %)," the report adds. As per the survey, one-third of the orphans had faced emotional stress during the conflict, "while 38 % felt despair and skepticism about the future, 32 % said that their anxiety was triggered by sudden loud noises or seeing battle uniforms". The child rights group has made number of recommendations for overall betterment of orphans in the state like formulation of child protection policy, setting up of child protection committees and so on.

Education of Children

It is a widely accepted fact that schooling is vital for children's social and cognitive development. In the conflict situation of Kashmir, regular school attendance and formal education entails considerable risks for students. One major effect of the violence reported was fear among children (24.6 %). School related problems also scored high, such as being unable to attend school was 15.5 % (Jong et al. 2006). Frequent 'Hadtal' on different conflict related issues have deteriorated the quality of education. This 'Hadtal' can go for months together, thus having strong negative repercussions on the young generations of Kashmir. In previous few years, Kashmir experienced long-term 'Hadtal' which could go for 4–6 months on different conflict related issues like Amaranth cave, Nelofar, and Asiya case and some other killings. Students were later examined for half portion of their syallabi, which was assumed to be a way out in such situation but actually damaging their future. Children learnt new ways of ventilating by showing aggression and were given due reinforcement for the same, although this does not lead to any positive growth in them. Madhosh (1999) in his study revealed that strife in the violence torn valley liquidated the educational system, tore the age old socio-cultural fabric, and stress had a telling effect on the biophysical, psychological, and social health of children. Exposure to violent conflict had a large and statistically significant negative effect on the enrolment of girls and they are less likely to complete their mandatory schooling.

Aggression/Stone Pelting

The on-going turmoil has taken a paradigm shift when people, especially children, started expressing aggression by pelting stones and bearing its negative consequences. They throw stones on armed personnel at small distances in which they too are beaten and injured. Khan et al. (2012) studied different types of eye injuries between June–September 2010. Most of the victims (75 %) were young boys between 16–26 years with a mean age of 20.95, 95 % of cases were males. The main cause of injury was stones (48.3 %) and pellets (30 %) besides rubber bullets, sling shots, and tear gas shells.

Most of the stone pelters are school and college going students. When any one among them is injured or killed, it further fumigates the entire peer circle and escalates the tension. Some of the stone pelters are arrested after which they are tortured. On 18 march 2011, 5255 persons, including 799 students, were arrested across the state for allegedly resorting to 'stone pelting' during summer unrest. Different reasons have been given by different parties for stone pelting which actually represent their own political interests. However, Margoob (2010) a well known psychiatrist of the valley commented that recent developments of defying law and order could also be a manifestation of the ever-increasing indescribable levels of frustration and anger among this 'trauma generation', who have hardly seen a minute of complete peace or tranquility in their lives.

Loss of Childhood

Childhood is known for freedom, fun and playing different games and Kashmir before armed conflict was no exception. Children used to stay out late in the evening and play different games. The charm would add more during the holy month of Ramazan in which children, especially girls could sing songs till late evening and this was part of the Kashmiri culture. But now the situation is totally different. Children are involved more in indoor games and have lost all those fun filling opportunities. They are more tense and stressed and have lost the real childhood.

Mental Health

Armed conflict in Kashmir has high impact on mental health of children. Empirical studies on children in an armed conflict showed the determinant effects on children's mental health and wellbeing. The psychiatric literature shows that conflict situation increases disorder prevalence (Hoge 2004). Some of the commonly found mental health problems in the valley are described below:

(a) **Post Traumatic Stress Disorder**
Millions of children are exposed to traumatic experiences each year. A significant number of these traumatized children develop a clinical syndrome with significant emotional, behavioral, cognitive, social, and physical symptoms called PTSD (Perry and Azad 1999). Kashmir being a conflict zone is not free from it, about 30–50 % showed PTSD. A study conducted by Margoob (1995) on children in Kashmir reported that of 103 children 37 showed symptoms of PTSD. In another study on orphan children, PTSD was found commonest psychiatric problem (40.62 %) followed by MDD (25 %) and conversion disorder (12.5 %) as reported by Margoob et al. (2006). Exposure to political hardships not only increases children's psychological symptoms but also make their psychological coping modes ineffective in mitigating this relationship (Punamiki and Suleiman 1990). A study by Dabla (2001) reported that most crucial problems the children faced after the death of their father is economic hardship. Yousuf and Margoob (2006) conducted a study on 100 cases of PTSD in children, in the age range of 03–16 years, in Govt. Psychiatric Diseases Hospital, Srinagar. The most common traumatic event experienced was witnessing the killing of a close relative (49 %), followed by witnessing the arrest and torture of a close relative (15 %). The commonest symptoms were somatic complaints followed by convulsion symptoms.

(b) **General Anxiety and Depression**
Kashmiri children are found to have general anxiety symptoms more apart from other problems. The continuous threat and unpredictability due to armed conflict has given rise to such problems. Children are always apprehensive and insecure about themselves and their family and this could be the core reason behind the anxiety problems they are afflicted with. Many children are reported as being phobic of army personnel. Depression is another problem which has been seen rising in the past two decades in the valley. Amin and Khan (2009) reported that due to continuing conflict in Kashmir during the last 18 years there has been a phenomenal increase in psychiatric morbidity. They revealed that the prevalence of depression is 55.7 % and the highest prevalence rate of 66.7 % was observed in 15–25 year old age group. Depression is much higher in rural areas (84.7 %) as compared to urban areas (15.3 %).

(c) **Dissociative Disorders**
Dissociative disorders which were quite common in the Freudian times can now be seen in abundance among Kashmiri children. The well known fact is that these disorders have some stressor as a cause and thus stands true for Kashmiri children as well. The effect of armed conflict in the form of repression of desires, threats, suppression, humiliation, and insecurity is part of culture now and could easily lead to such consequences. At times it is associated to parenting which too is somehow affected by the present situation. Most of the school teachers are now unable to handle such emerging problem among young students.

(d) **Feelings of Insecurity/Suppression**
The feeling of insecurity is common among people of Kashmir and children. When a child arrives home late from school, the anxious reaction of parents clearly indicates the deep rooted insecurity which is a result of armed conflict. Children do not feel free to move as parents keep on telling them about harmful consequences. This insecurity is found more among girls than boys (Raina and Bhan 2013). Women in general have suffered from sexual molestation and a number of rape cases by armed personals. This information makes girl children more insecure. It restricts their normal movements and they are usually accompanied by elders. They are not able to come out of this aura and feel suppressed. A study done by Jong et al. (2008) revealed that Kashmiri women are among the worst sufferers of sexual violence in the world. Interestingly, the figure is much higher than that of Sierra Leone, Sri Lanka and Chechnya. Rape is not incidental to conflict. It can occur on a random and uncontrolled basis due to the general disruption of social boundaries and the license granted to soldiers and militants.

Rebellious Nature

The generation gap between parents and young generation has widened due to present volatile scenario. Young generation do not see parents as their role models when it comes to political issues; rather blame them for not doing anything about it. So they start experimenting with their own aggressive methods to express their suppressed feelings and would go against any authority. Margoob (2010), a well known psychiatrist of the valley reported that since the young brain is yet to fully develop psychological mechanisms, children/adolescents are much more vulnerable to emotional actions and reactions. When they assume that they are getting pushed against the wall they get dominated by their emotions and stop caring for the consequences. Youngsters identify with the group rather than with their individual identities and can accordingly get heavily involved in activities that essentially had been nonexistent in the society earlier.

Psychological trauma may become evident in disturbed and antisocial behavior, such as family conflict and aggression toward others. This situation is often exacerbated by the availability of weapons and by people becoming habituated to violence after long exposure to conflict. The impact of conflicts on mental health is, however, extremely complex and unpredictable. It is influenced by a host of factors such as the nature of the conflict, the kind of trauma and distress experienced, the cultural context, and the resources that individuals and communities bring to bear on their situation (Summerfield 1991). According to the findings from the recent literature on traumatized children, childhood trauma not only has the capacity to cause short-term symptoms but it can also affect a child's overall personality development, interpersonal functioning, self-esteem, and coping ability throughout their lifespan (Arroyo and Eth 1985). Of greater concern is that generations of children who are growing up with chronic violence in their lives, may reach adulthood with the perception that violence is an acceptable means of resolving ethnic, religious, or political differences.

Conclusion

Armed conflict in Kashmiri has very negative impact on all inhabitants of the valley but most serious effects are seen on children. It has engrossed their whole life and hampers their overall development, be it physical or psychological. It has led to loss of their values and has been affected by structural changes in the society. Children have lost the feeling of security even while being with their family and perceive themselves as helpless. Conflict has filled their tender hearts with anger and frustration and they have lost their peace of mind. Health, which is mostly valuable for a child is crippled by armed conflict and children suffer from psychological problems of PTSD, anxiety, depression etc. It has taken away from them the happy period of childhood and left them stressed with a number of adult responsibilities. Some are left in orphanages as they have lost their caretakers at the time when they need them most. Armed conflict is leaving its long-term effect by compromising education of children which is most important for the future development of society.

Recommendations

The issue under discussion is very grave in nature and need rigorous efforts to curb at different levels; however some of the helpful recommendations following Reddy and Reddy (2003) and others are given below:

- In conflict time army/security personnel's camps should not be established near schools.
- Clinical psychologists/Counselors should be appointed in every school.
- School buses to be used for security of children while travelling.
- Condition of orphanages to be made better.
- Education should be given a priority and should not get disturbed by hurdles etc.
- Education should focus on imbibing values and religious teachings without misinterpreting in wrong ways; parents should be provided psycho-education.
- Right parenting and modeling for children should be focused and exposure to negative impact of media should be minimized.
- Security personnel should not be allowed to demonstrate violence in public.

- An interdisciplinary approach including Psychologists should be followed in forming the policies/preventive/rehabilitative measures in dealing with impact of violence on children.
- Information should be shared across national and international authorities to promote effective response to all problems of children affected by armed conflict.
- Government and NGOs must make efforts to reconstruct the economy of the affected families by providing income—generating assets.
- The UNICEF and other NGOs working for rehabilitation of affected children in war/conflict should guarantee the rights of children as enshrined in the Convention of Rights of the Child and as per law of land.
- Public education awareness campaigns on the dangers of drug abuse, child abuse/neglect, mental/physical health aspects, nutrition, child care, education, and gender sensitization etc. should be organized by the state and centre.

Acknowledgement The academic input given by Mr. Mohd Altaf (Research Scholar, Department of Psychology, Jamia Millia Islamia (New Delhi) is gratefully acknowledged.

References

Amin, S., & Khan, A. W. (2009). Life in conflict: Characteristics of depression in Kashmir. *International Journal of Health Sciences, 3*(2), 213–223.

Arroyo, W., & Eth, S. (1985). *Children traumatized by central American warfare. Post-traumatic stress disorders in children*. Washington, DC: APA Press.

Dabla, B. A. (1999). *Impact of conflict situation on women and children in Kashmir: Report of the research project*. Srinagar: Kashmir University, Department of Sociology.

Dabla, B. A. (2001). Orphans in the orphans' valley: Need for the help network. *New Hope, 2*(1).

Dubowitz, H., Papas, M. A., Black, M. M., & Starr, A. H. (2002). Child neglect: Outcomes in high risk urban preschoolers. *Pediatrics, 109*, 1100–1107. doi:10.1542/peds.109.6.1100.

Hoge, M. (2004). Combat duty in Iraq and Afghanistan: Mental health problems, and barriers to care. *New England Journal of Medicine, 351*(1), 13–22. doi:10.1056/NEJMoa040603.

Jong, K. D., Ford, N., Kam, S., Lokuge, K., Fromm, S., Galen, R. V., & Kleber, R. (2008). Conflict in the Indian Kashmir valley I: Exposure to violence. *Conflict and Health, 2*(10), 1–7. doi:10.1186/1752-1505-2-11.

Jong, K. D., Kam, S. V., Fromm, S., Galen, R. V., Kemmere, T., Weerd et al. (2006). Kashmir, violence and health: A quantitative assessment on violence, the psychosocial and general health status of the Kashmiri population. Retrieved from http://www.artsenzondergrenzen.nl/pdf/kashmirfinalversion221106.pdf.

Khan, W., & Ghilzai, S. (2002). Impact of terrorism on mental health and coping strategy of adolescents and adults in Kashmir. *Journal of Personality and Clinical Studies, 18*, 33–41.

Khan, S., Maqbool, A., Abdulla, N., & Ken, M. Q. (2012). Pattern of ocular injuries in stone palters in Kashmir valley. *Saudi Journal of Ophthalmology, 26*(3), 327–330. doi:10.1016/j.sjopt.2012.04.004.

Kumar, R. (2012, May). Children of conflict, they need a helping hand. Retrieved from http://www.greaterkashmir.com/news/2012/May/26/children-of-conflict-7.asp.

Machel, G. (2001). *The impact of armed conflict on children*. Cape Town: David Philip.

Madhosh, A. G. (1999). *The present turmoil and plight of children in Kashmir*. Srinagar: Kashmir University, Faculty of Education.

Margoob, M. (2010, Aug 4). It's the manifestation of anger among Kashmir's trauma generation. Retrieved from: http://articles.timesofindia.indiatimes.comarticles.timesofindia.

Margoob, M. (1995). Depressive disorders in Kashmir. *JK-Practitioner, 2*(1), 22–23.

Margoob, M. A., Rather, Y. H., Khan, A. Y., Singh, G. P., Malik, Y. A., Firdosi, M. M., & Ahmed, S. (2006). Psychiatric disorders among children living in orphanages experience from Kashmir. *JK Practitioner, 13*(11), 53–55.

Perry, B. D., & Azad, I. (1999). Post traumatic stress disorder in children and adolescents. *Current Opinions in Pediatrics, 11*(4), 310–316.

Punamiki, R. L., & Suleiman, R. (1990). Predictors and effectiveness of coping with political violence among Palestinian children. *British Journal of Social Psychology, 29*(1), 67–77. doi:10.1111/j.2044-8309.1990.tb00887.x.

Raina, S., & Bhan, K. S. (2013). A study of security-insecurity feelings among adolescents in relation to sex, family system and ordinal position. *International Journal of Educational Planning and Administration, 3*(1), 51–60.

Reddy, G. N., & Reddy, S. N. (2003). *Managing childhood problems: Support, strategies and interventions*. New Delhi: Kanishka Publishers.

Summerfield, D. (1991). The psychosocial effects of conflict in the third world. *Development in Practice, 1*, 59–173.

Teicher, M. D. (2000). Wounds that time won't heal: The neurobiology of child abuse. Cerebrum: The dana forum on brain. *Science, 2*(4), 50–67.

United Nations Secretary General Study (2006). Violence against children. Retrieved from http://www.unviolencestudy.org/.

Wessells, M. G. (1998). The changing nature of armed conflict and its implication for children: The Graca Machel/U. N. Study. *Peace and Conflict: Journal of Peace Psychology, 4*(4), 321–334. doi:10.1207/s15327949pac0404_2.

Yousuf, A., & Margoob, M. A. (2006). Pediatric PTSD: Clinical presentation, traumatic events and socio-demographic variables—experience from a chronic conflict situation. *JK-Practitioner, 13*(11), 40–44.

Chapter 8
The Law and Practices of Ritual Male Circumcision: Time for Review

Esther I.J. Erlings

Introduction

"When correctly performed, ritual male circumcision (RMC) has no long-lasting harmful effect" (Schiratzki 2011). Pronounced in 2011, this statement seems rather outdated in the light of present-day evidence to the contrary (see below). More to the point is Marshall (2009) who argues that "circumcisions are usually performed in a spirit of benevolence and with attempts to mitigate pain and suffering and to promote post-procedure healing". The question is whether benevolence and sincerity of belief of the parents is sufficient to justify RMC (Brigman 1984–1985). Some recent developments, especially in the courts, have indicated that perhaps it is not. This paper discusses the situation in three countries where circumcision is completely unregulated (England), regulated, or even facilitated (The Netherlands), or questioned per se (Germany). The discussion then turns to international law, which seems to favor regulation and medicalization, before arguments are made on how regulation is an inefficient approach to circumcision as it may solve problems relating to physical pain, but it cannot deal with arguments on psychological well-being and autonomy.

Nota bene, this article is concerned with RMC on minors who are too young to consent (or withhold consent) to the procedure; it does not deal with the circumcision of legally competent adolescents, or adults.

E.I.J. Erlings (✉)
The Chinese University of Hong Kong, Hong Kong, China
e-mail: e.erlings@yahoo.com

S. Deb (ed.), *Child Safety, Welfare and Well-being*,
DOI 10.1007/978-81-322-2425-9_8

Ritual Male Circumcision (RMC): The Practice and Its Origins

RMC refers to an intervention whereby the foreskin (prepuce) is removed from the penis for non-therapeutic reasons. The amount of skin removed depends on techniques used, and convictions as to what constitutes a genuine circumcision (Pollack 2008).

RMC should be distinguished from therapeutic circumcision, which is circumcision as a cure for a medical condition, or routine circumcision, which is performed for the perceived benefits it will accord to the child. It deserves mention that none of these health benefits have been definitely proven to result from circumcisions (Both 2004; Dave et al. 2003; Hill and Denniston 2003; Snyder 2008; Koninklijke Nederlandsche Maatschappij tot bevordering der Geneeskunst KNMG 2010).

Circumcision pre-dates most religions, including Judaism and Islam; there is evidence that it has been undertaken for about four millennia (Johnson 1993), if not longer (Marshall 2009). Circumcision has nevertheless become a defining manifestation of Judaism, where it is deemed to represent the Covenant of God with man (Leviticus 12:4) and Islam, which considers circumcision to be part of the *Sunnah*, the teachings of the Prophet Muhammad. Circumcision is not mentioned in the Holy Qur'an (Marshall 2009).

Judaism requires the circumcision to be carried out on the eighth day after birth, under Islam there is no agreement on the right moment (Baum 1999), which may be just after birth, up to early adolescence (Schmitz 2001). Under both religions, circumcision is seen as a rite of initiation; the child becomes a full member of the religious community. This is why, although other manifestations may no longer take place, parents do still insist on having their sons circumcised (KNMG 2010).

RMC Under Domestic Law and Practice

England

Unlike medical circumcisions, RMC's in England are not subject to any medical or even basic hygiene requirements.[1] This situation has led to the practice of the so-called "kitchen table circumcisions" whereby a boy is circumcised at the home

[1]Although the courts have expressed a preference for circumcisions performed in a medical context, rather than traditional context. In AT v FS&Anor, the court ordered that it would be in the best interests of the child to receive his circumcision in hospital. *AT v FS&Anor* 2011 WL 5105519, per Hedley J at [26].

of the parents, often on the kitchen table, without anesthetics, or any sanitary precautions (Pringer and Brereton 1991). However, this practice is not illegal. An additional worrying development is the advent of "circumcision camps" whereby a number of boys are circumcised at the same time by a religious circumciser. Hygiene conditions at these camps can be genuinely appalling. Paranthaman et al. (2010) describe a circumcision camp that took place in Oxford, and at which 32 RMC's were performed[2]:

> [C]ircumcisions were carried out in a library with book shelves, tables, fabric covered chairs, internal and external doors, stone surround window frames and carpet flooring. The room was in a poor state of décor. There were no hand-washing facilities inside the library and the nearest hand-washing facilities were either in the toilet along the corridor or in the kitchen. […] four packs of instruments were used over the course of 3 days. It was difficult to obtain reliable information on where and how decontamination of instruments took place, although it was clear that full infection control precautions were not implemented.

Of the 29 boys where follow-up information was available, 13 had developed complications and six required hospital admission due to the seriousness of their complications (Paranthaman et al. 2010). This compares to a general 1.5–6 % (higher for children over 12 (Weiss et al. 2010))[3] complication rate in a hospital setting (Weiss et al. 2010; Madden and Boddy 1991). What is particularly noticeable about this case is that, although *disciplinary* action was taken against the circumciser who was a registered doctor, apparently no *legal* action was taken against him or the parents (Paranthaman et al. 2010). The parents, who were under a legal obligation to exercise parental responsibility in the interest of their children,[4] faced no consequences whatsoever for having them circumcised under deplorable and dangerous circumstances.

Certainly, the General Medical Council (GMC) obliges doctors who perform RMC's to ensure that they have the skills and experience to perform the procedure, that they use appropriate means and maintain hygienic conditions (GMC 2008), but this is not a requirement for the performance of RMC by non-doctors. The same goes for the British Medical Association (BMA) guidance on medical conditions, and the best interests (which should be paramount) and views (which should be sought) of the child (BMA 2006). In this respect, it becomes especially problematic that the National Health Service does not cover RMC's, although medical indications can be given for minor problems that would not normally require circumcision (Dalton 2008), as this makes parents more likely to seek non-medical circumcisions to which the guidelines do not apply.

[2]The circumcisions were in fact performed by a registered doctor, albeit one who had received his training and very limited practice abroad. The circumstances of the camp were however exemplary of circumcision camps not performed by medical practitioners.

[3]Dalton argues that "To be brutally frank, infant circumcision is 'safer' because infants do not report complications." (Barkham 2012).

[4]Also in matters of religion. *Gillick v West Norfolk & Wisbech Area Health Authority* [1985] UKHL 7.

Circumcision in England is not only legal; it is also fully within parental power. As Wall J held in *Re J*[5]:

> [W]here two parents, jointly exercising parental responsibility for a male child, because he to be ritually circumcised in accordance with the tenets of their religion, that exercise of parental responsibility is lawful. [at 692]

The situation is rather different in the separated family. Wall J, while submitting that a case could be conceivable in which it would be in the interests of a child to be circumcised against the wishes of an opposing parent, found in *Re J* that this was not so *in casu*. Of importance to his decision was the child's lifestyle and upbringing, the potential strengthening, or weakening of family ties, the risks, pain, and stress the operation would cause and the attitude of the child's primary care giver. Interestingly, the judgment did not refer to the autonomy of the child. This *lacuna* was remedied by *Re S*.[6] In that case the parents belonged to two different religions and the mother wanted her son to be circumcised in the face of opposition from the father. The court held that it would be in the son's interest to be raised in both the religion of his mother and father, but that he should not be circumcised, because "it should be for the son to make his own informed decision when he [will be] Gillick competent."[7]

England thus applies a very liberal regime to RMC, which may be sought by parents under almost every circumstance, despite parental obligations to exercise parental responsibility in the interests of their child. Only when parents are divorced is attention paid to the impact of the procedure, the rights and (religious) autonomy of the child: in these cases, the wellbeing, rights, and autonomy of the minor outweigh the rights of parents as is clear from the cases discussed in this section.

The Netherlands

The Dutch State focuses on the regulation, rather than desirability, of RMC (Smith 1998). Circumcisions can only be performed by doctors in public hospitals, or in private (circumcision) clinics, or by a *mohel*, who has received the necessary (subsidized) education to do so (Schmitz 2001). Circumcision by a traditional circumciser is illegal (Schmitz 2001). A particular feature of the Dutch circumcision landscape is the existence of specialized circumcision clinics that cater in large part to the Muslim population. These clinics allow for rituals surrounding the circumcision (as long as they do not hinder the surgeon during the procedure),

---

[5]*Re J* [1999] 2 F.L.R. 678.

[6]*Re S (Children) (Specific Issue Order: Religion: Circumcision)* [2004] EWHC 1282 (Fam); [2005] 1 F.L.R. 236; [2004] Fam. Law 869. Confirmed on Appeal *S (Children)* [2004] EWCACiv 1257; 2004 WL 2652660.

[7]Gillick competency refers to the competence of minors to take informed decisions. *S (Children)* [2004] EWCACiv 1257; 2004 WL 2652660, per Thorpe LJ, at 6.

while at the same time offering a clean medical environment with qualified and specialized doctors and surgeons (Besnijdenis Centrum Nederland 2012). In 2005 the government decided to no longer cover RMC under the national health insurance (Ministerie van Volksgezondheid, Welzijn en Sport 2005), and as a result circumcision clinics have proven a valuable alternative to the less personal and more expensive procedures in public hospitals (Trouw 2005).

The strict requirements governing the procedure are nevertheless coupled with a very liberal stand on RMC *ansich*. Religious freedom, specifically including the right of parents to raise their children in their religion, is one of the core values of Dutch society and the government is prone to regulate and accommodate, as opposed to banning religious practices.[8] In 2010 the Dutch Medical Association (KNMG) adopted the official position that RMC should be discouraged and eventually prohibited (KNMG 2010); however, the government indicated that this was only the opinion of a Dutch organization and not the Dutch State (Tweede Kamer 2011). The KNMG had argued that there was no sufficient evidence for RMC to have (preventive) health benefits, that an unjustifiable discrimination had come into existence as female circumcision was outlawed in all its forms (even forms comparable to, or less severe than RMC) while male circumcision was not, and that parental rights to freedom of religion could not outweigh the child's own rights to freedom of religion (including the right to change religion) and physical integrity (KNMG 2010). The government in response held succinctly:

> A prohibition would limit the freedom of religion. The government may only do so by means of legal regulation, when a legitimate aim is present and there is proportionality between the protected interest and the limitation. This is the case for female circumcision. […] The circumcision of boys–when the procedure is correctly performed-does not, however, lead to negative effects on physical and mental functioning. On this basis there is no ground for a prohibition. (Tweede Kamer 2011)

The responsible minister did emphasize the fact that RMC is a medical procedure, which, under Dutch law, means that children up from the age of 12 need to co-consent to the procedure and children above 16 may take their own decisions (Articles 447(1), 450(2) and 465(1) Wet op de Geneeskundige Behandelingsovereenkomst). This should lead to a certain respect for the autonomy of older children.

The reaction of the Council for Public Health and Care Services, like the government, focused on the comparison between male and female circumcision, which it felt was out of place, and merely mentioned that it disagreed with the KNMG placing physical integrity above religious interests (Raadvoor Volksgezondheid en Zorg 2010). No reactions by the government, or governmental agencies, have followed the German polemic.

The differing opinions regarding RMC have placed judges in a difficult situation, although they appear to side with the government. In a 2007 case, the highest

[8]The Dutch government for example regulated the wearing of headscarves in schools (Ministerie van Onderwijs, Cultuur en Wetenschap 2003) and is in the process of adopting regulation concerning the ritual slaughter of animals (Rijksoverheid 2012).

administrative court avoided having to consider whether RMC was a violation of the prohibition of inhuman, cruel, or degrading treatment,[9] yet, in another case that same year, a family law judge prevented the circumcision of a child in care mainly because the reasons given by the mother were *not* religious in nature.[10] A different situation arises when parents are separated and one of the parents is opposed to the circumcision. In 2002, the appeals court of 's-Hertogenbosch concluded that if parents could not agree on the circumcision of their child, it should not be carried out as it was an "irreversible physical interference without any medical necessity." It held that:

> even though circumcision at the age of 5 is usual, Islam does not prescribe it. The circumcision may take place at a later point in time when the child is itself capable of making the decision.[11]

Other than on comparisons with female circumcision, the judgment focused on the rights and autonomy of the child, including physical integrity. This has been the same in a very recent case, which is still under review.[12] In that case a father, who did not have formal parental responsibility or custody, had his children circumcised whilst they were staying with him—criminal charges were laid against him for assault and battery. No definite judgment has yet been delivered, but the Advocate General at the Supreme Court found that, while RMC could potentially be consented to by parents holding parental responsibility as a part of the religious upbringing of their children, it was likely that the father in this case was guilty of assault and battery, especially given the violation of physical integrity and pain RMC undeniably caused.[13]

Although there is opposition to RMC from the medical profession (as well as from some members of the general public (Schmitz 2001)), the standpoint of the Dutch State remains that parental rights weigh heavier than the rights of the child, unless parents are divorced, at which point a child's rights and autonomy do take priority. In an intact family, the government contends itself with the idea that regulation in order to avoid unnecessary harm is sufficient to safeguard children's rights.

Germany

In the summer of 2012, Germany experienced an uproar that spread over the world, when a court in Cologne ruled that RMC was an unjustifiable violation of the rights of the child (Hans 2012; Eddy 2012). *In casu*,[14] a doctor was prosecuted

[9]23 Mei 2007, Raad van State, Afdeling Bestuursrechtspraak, zaak 200701063/1, *LJN*BA6061 §2.2.

[10]31 Juli 2007, Rechtbank Zutphen, zaak 83927 JE RK 07-110, *LJN* BB0833.

[11]26 November 2002, Gerechtshof 's-Hertogenbosch, zaak R200200450, *LJN*: AF2955 §4.4.

[12]05 Juli 2011, Hoge Raad, zaak 09/04431, *NJB* 2011, 1494.

[13]05 Juli 2011, Hoge Raad, zaak 09/04431, *NJB* 2011, 1494, Conclusie Nr. 09/04431.

[14]Dr. K, Landgericht Köln, 07.05.2012, Wa. 151 Ns 169/11.

after complications following a circumcision required the child, who was hemorrhaging, to be taken to hospital. Both parents had consented to the procedure and the doctor had given appropriate aftercare. Therefore, the decision mainly focused on the legality of circumcision itself. The court held:

> [T]he right of parents to determine the religious upbringing of their children does not have priority when balanced against the child's right to physical integrity and self-determination, so that their consent to circumcision goes against the best interests of the child. [at III]

The court considered that circumcision was a substantial and irreparable alteration of the child's body, which additionally interfered with the right of the child to later on decide on his own religion. The court further held that it would not be an unreasonable limitation of parental rights in upbringing, when parents would have to wait until their child would be old enough to decide for himself whether he wished to wear the mark of their religion, or not.

Reactions to the judgment varied considerably: the association for pediatric surgeons welcomed the decision (Deutsche Gesellschaftfür Kinderchirurgie 2012), as did a large part of the general public. Those fighting for children's rights seized the opportunity and immediately after the Cologne ruling a Rabbi was prosecuted for circumcising boys as a non-medical practitioner (to be dismissed later on): doctors were subsequently advised to place a (temporary) stop on ritual circumcisions (Ewing 2012). The German Medical Association was less positive about the ruling: it feared that the practice would go underground if declared illegal (Graumann 2012). Religious organizations for their part strongly condemned the ruling and the president of the Central Council of Jews even doubted whether life for Jews in Germany would still be possible (Grumman 2012).

Rarely has a country seen such a swift reaction of politicians to a social question. The German chancellor assured the public that Germany would still allow RMC's, afraid that the judgment would make the country "laughing stock" in Europe (DPA 2012). The city of Berlin announced that, under certain conditions, RMC would be lawful in Berlin (DPA 2012) and the Bundestag ordered the government to draft legislation specifically allowing RMC to take place under specified circumstances (Deutscher Bundestag 2012a). Within weeks a bill was introduced allowing for medicalized RMC's to be performed based on the sole consent of parents. Circumcisions could only be performed by a competent doctor, or, within the first 6 months, by a representative of a religion "having received such education as to have reached a competence similar to that of a doctor" (meaning that an educated *mohel* could perform the procedure) (Deutscher Bundestag 2012b). The proposal seemed to build on a 2006 case that came before the courts in Düsseldorf, where a 77 year old man had performed circumcisions on several boys, many of whom developed complications. Although the man had been appointed as a circumciser in Turkey, this, the court ruled, did not alter the fact that he was carrying the procedure out as a non-doctor and under bad hygienic circumstances and was therefore convicted (Günter Jerouschek 2008; Hans 2012b). Parental consent to the circumcisions was not questioned.

The bill engendered its fair share of critique, although, surprisingly, not from the religious communities (Neukirch 2012). The German Medical Association argued that the bill was flawed because it allowed for circumcisions to be performed by non-doctors (Bundesärtzekammer 2012). The pediatric surgeons remained opposed to RMC on non-consenting minors *tout court* (Deutsche Gesellschaftfür Kinderchirurgie 2012) as was the left-wing opposition which put forward a series of amendments to the proposed law (Deutscher Bundestag 2012c). The amendments envisaged a prohibition to perform RMC's on boys below the age of 14; so that children could take the decision themselves when sufficiently mature (ANP 2012). The critique turned out to be of no avail: just before the end-of-year recess, the German government by vast majority adopted the new law in its original form.[15]

The audacious ruling of the court in Cologne opened a broad discussion and even prompted legislative action. What is interesting is that it is not the first ruling of its kind; in 2007, a Frankfurt court had ruled that circumcision violated the child's right to self-determination, physical integrity, and fundamental personal rights, including the right to choose his own religion.[16] The Cologne ruling was virtually identical to this previous decision with the exception that in the 2007 case, the parents were divorced and the mother, who held custody, was opposed to circumcision. It is at least questionable that the arguments, which had gone unnoticed in the case of divorced parents, should cause such a stir when applied to a child in an intact family. Especially since in all cases the best interests of the child should prevail and it seems hard to justify that the rights to physical integrity, self-determination, and religion are only in the interests of a child of divorced parents.

RMC Under International Law

The Council of Europe

Following several reports in which the Council of Europe's (CoE) Committee on Equal Opportunities for Women and Men (Zapfl-Helbing 2004) and Venice Commission (2008) told states not to unduly restrict RMC as this was "clearly a manifestation of religion protected by international instruments" (Venice Commission 2008), the European Court of Human Rights held in 2010 that:

> [T]he rites and rituals of many religions may harm believers' well-being, such as […] circumcision practiced on Jewish or Muslim male babies.[17]

---

[15]Gesetz über den Umfang der Personensorge bei einder Beschneidung des männlichen Kindes vom 20. Dezember 2012. *Bundesgesetzblatt* Jahrgang 2012 Teil I Nr. 61, Bonn 27. Dezember 2012, p. 2749.

[16]OLG Frankfurt 4. Zivilsenat, 21.08.2007, 4 W 12/07, in particular at [19].

[17]*Case of Jehovah's Witnesses of Moscow and others v. Russia*, European Court of Human Rights, application 302/02, with judgment of 10 June 2010 § 144.

In its judgment, the Court deemed the practice "contentious". In the wake of the German circumcision affair, the CoE's Parliamentary Assembly took an even stronger stand and adopted a recommendation and resolution on the physical integrity of children (Parliamentary Assembly 2013a, b). The latter claims that RMC is a:

> [Category] of violation of the physical integrity of children, which supporters of the procedures tend to present as beneficial to the children themselves despite clear evidence to the contrary.

Although the resolution and accompanying report do not call for the outright prohibition of RMC, but for its regulation, the resolution garnered much critique and a counter-motion seeking to clarify that the Parliamentary Assembly supported the right of parents to have their children circumcised. That counter-motion was nevertheless not adopted and it is thus safe to say that although the CoE still tolerates RMC, it is not favorably looked upon.

The United Nations

The main United Nations (UN) treaty concerned with children's rights is the Convention on the Rights of the Child (CRC). Its monitoring body, the Committee on the Rights of the Child (CmRC) has dealt with RMC on several occasions, although it has not (yet) outright condemned RMC. However, whereas in the past the CmRC merely expressed concern about the health of children undergoing circumcision in unsafe or unhygienic conditions (CmRC 2000; CmRC 2001) in 2013 it placed circumcision itself under the heading of "harmful practices" (CmRC 2013). Indeed, the implementation handbook of the CRC invites review of practices including "all forms of […] circumcision" (Hofvander 2008). Two Special Rapporteurs on the UN Declaration on the Elimination of All Forms of Intolerance and Discrimination Based on Religion and Belief have on the other hand proposed that under UN law, RMC is permissible as an aspect of *parents'* right to freedom of religion (Vidal d'Aleida Ribeiro 1986). RMC is moreover likely to form part of ceremonial acts or rituals associated with certain stages of life as protected by Article 18(1) of the International Covenant on Civil and Political Rights (ICCPR) according to 4 of General Comment 22 (Human Rights Committee 1993).

The World Health Organization (WHO) as a specialized UN agency and UNAIDS have more explicitly addressed the question of male circumcision. The UNAIDS guidance report on "Safe, Voluntary, Informed Male Circumcision" devotes several paragraphs to the circumcision of minors unable to consent. The guiding principle should be the best interests of the child, but after having been given all relevant information (including on risks involved in the procedure) parents are free to decide in favor of circumcision (UNAIDS 2008). Unlike a 2007 report which encouraged circumcision of neonates as the procedure is less complicated and risky than in elder boys or men (World Health Organisation, London School of Hygiene, Tropical Medicine & UNAIDS 2007), the current report thus states:

> Parents considering circumcision of an infant boy should be provided with all the facts so they can determine the best interests of the child. In these cases, determining the best interests of the child should include diverse factors–the positive and negative health, religious, cultural and social benefits. Because the HIV-related benefits of circumcision only arise in the context of sexual activity, and because male circumcision is an irreversible procedure, parents may consider that the child should be given the option to decide for himself when he has the capacity to do so (UNAIDS 2008).

This quote could be taken as a step to open the way for a limitation, or even final prohibition, of RMC on incompetent minors. Nevertheless, a year later the WHO published a report specifically dealing with "Traditional Male Circumcision" (WHO 2009) and while this report did place emphasis on accompanying RMC with education on reproductive health (something only possible in the case of elder children), it did not consider as problematic that in some countries young children would undergo circumcision upon the decision of a parent, or other family member. Quite to the contrary: the report recommends that children be circumcised at younger age, meaning before adolescence, to ensure that they are already circumcised before starting sexual activity and, perhaps even more worrying, the report suggests that women can "secretly" take their boys to hospital at a "younger age" for a medical circumcision allowing for safety while fulfilling the traditional circumcision requirement (WHO 2009). Such secret circumcisions would hardly address the problems arising from competing interests in the case of RMC's.

Like many national governments, the international organizations primarily emphasize safety in the circumcision procedure, rather than physical integrity, autonomy and self-determination rights of children. This stands in strong opposition to the road taken by courts in cases of divorce. The latter seem to be more willing to be informed by what research and the literature have suggested with regard to circumcision.

The Child's Well-Being and Autonomy

The Physical Well-Being of the Child and Later Adult

The physical well-being of the child appears to be the main concern of governments and international organizations; their focus evolves primarily around the provision of safe circumcisions that cause children as little pain as possible. Equally, researchers have, and still do, place great emphasis on the attack upon the physical wellbeing of children, primarily by describing the possible, and often horrible, complications which could arise following a circumcision (Williams and Kaila 1993; Richards 1996; Snyder 2008). For overviews see Boyle et al. (2002) and Weiss et al. (2010). The child is forced to undergo "actual bodily harm" to a degree that some have classified as child abuse (Richards 1996). Bridgman (1984–1985) explains that male circumcision *is* a form of child abuse, because it is an:

> intervention that is not medically warranted, has no psychological benefits, is painful because performed without anesthesia, leaves a wound, carries a significant risk of surgical complications and deforms the penis.

The emphasis on the medical-physical aspects of circumcision can be explained by three factors.

Firstly, it cannot be denied that a form of harm is done to children. It is now accepted that infants can feel pain and that they do feel pain during and after a circumcision (Boyle et al. 2002; Snyder 2008; Marshall 2009). Moreover, the physical alteration caused by circumcision undeniably touches upon the physical integrity of the child. Seeing that the pain and invasion on physical integrity are real, and given the risks involved in circumcision procedures, the argument made is that circumcision is hard to justify, because the same harm would not be permitted in other contexts, despite the sincere beliefs of parents.

The second reason for the reliance on physical integrity arguments is that both national and international law offer clear provisions protecting the right to physical integrity and the avoidance of harm. National provisions on assault and battery could possibly apply, as well as specific laws on mutilation. On the international level, the ECHR offers Articles 3 (the right not to be subjected to inhuman and degrading treatment) and Article 8 (the right to privacy, which has been interpreted as including physical integrity, especially with regard to consent in the medical context), in addition to Article 20(1) of the European Convention on Human Rights and Bioethics (prohibition of non-therapeutic tissue removal from those who cannot consent) (Hill and Denniston 2003; Fortin 2009). Circumcision is equally considered to be contrary with the ICCPR articles on torture and inhuman and degrading treatment (Article 7), the security of the person (Article 9) and the special protection to which children are entitled (Article 24) (Svoboda 1997; Bhimji 2000; Doctors Opposing Circumcision 2008). Under the CRC, an argument is made to consider RMC as a traditional practice prejudicial to the health of a child (Article 24), in addition to declaring the practice a violation of the right not to be subjected to violence when in the care of parents (Article 19), the right not to be subjected to inhuman or degrading treatment (Article 37) and even the right to life, as circumcision may lead to death as a result of complications (Article 6) (Hodgkin and Newell 1998; Smith 1998; Bhimji 2000; Doctors Opposing Circumcision 2008).

The third reason for the prevalence given to physical integrity arguments is that it allows for an argument against circumcision based on religious grounds. Both Jewish and Muslim writers (Rothenburg 1991; Braver Moss 1991; Mahdawi 1990; Pollack 2008) and organizations (e.g. Muslims against the Circumcision of Children, Jews against Circumcision, or The Israeli Association against Genital Mutilation) have questioned circumcision on the basis that it runs contrary with fundamental religious precepts, rather than being in accordance with them. Pollack (2008), a Jewish author and educator writes:

> Circumcision may be an ancient rite, but it is wrong. It is wrong in terms of Jewish values, for it violates the most fundamental Jewish principles of sanctifying life.

Muslims against the Circumcision of Children quotes from the Qur'an:

> Allah is the One who made the Earth a habitat for you, and the sky as a structure, and He has designed you, and has perfected your design (Qur'an 40, p. 64).

Both the Jewish and Muslim faiths consider life and health to be sacred and prohibit the intentional hurting of living beings (Smit 1998; Braver Moss 1991; Pollack 2008; Pont 2008). As a result, adherents of both faiths have accepted that RMC violates the rights of children and have found replacing rites of initiation.

While the argument on the physical well-being of the child could thus well lead to the questioning of RMC per se, it has often led to a regulation of the practice; grounded in the idea that lexicalization of RMC would at least greatly reduce the harm and pain involved. However, this approach is insufficient, because the main problems with circumcision may actually lay in areas less tangible than physical harm.

The Psychological Well-Being of the Child and Later Adult

After the establishment that infants do feel pain and that circumcision is therefore physically harmful, attention began to be paid to the psychological effects of circumcision. Often, these accounts were, and are, linked to the pain connected with RMC. Cansever (1965), in a seminal article on religious circumcision of children aged 4–6, noted that the painful experience of circumcision led to a weakening of ego, feeling of helplessness, less efficient functioning, anxiety, and aggressive behavior. As a defence mechanism, children either acted unsocial zed, or withdrew and isolated themselves (Cansever 1965). Somewhat the same has been concluded in respect of neonates subjected to circumcision, albeit with the addition that the traumatic experience and change in behavior negatively affected attachment to parents (Dixon et al. 1984; Laibow 1991). Dixon et al. (1984) conclude:

> Neonatal circumcision is a procedure that is experienced adversely by the infant to the extent that it disrupts the course of behavioral recovery that is expected following birth.

Not only does the reaction to the pain of circumcision cause psychological problems, the very experience of circumcision can make infants and children feel "anxious, fearful, and vengeful" (Chamberlain 2008).

In addition to more immediate psychological effects, psychological distress at later age has equally been described. A minority of men feels mutilated by the procedure and some will even seek reconstructive surgery to overcome this feeling (Schultheiss et al. 1998).

Of increasing importance, however, is the research on circumcision and Post Traumatic Stress Disorder (PTSD). Boyle et al. give an extensive overview of the literature in this field and concluded that, although the research in this area suffers from sampling issues, high percentages of PTSD have been found following routine, religious and cultural circumcisions, either medical, or traditional (Boyle et al. 2002). Therefore, it is not only the procedure, but also the very fact of being circumcised that causes psychological problems. On this account, circumcision itself becomes questionable under Article 19 of the CRC, which prohibits mental violence to be inflicted upon children in parental care (Hodgkin and Newell 1998) and Article 5 of the UN Declaration, which demands that States eliminate traditional practices which are injurious to children (Brems 2006).

Autonomy and Self-determination of the Child

After years of discussion on the physical and mental (very much in that order) health issues resulting from circumcision, the era of the rights of the child has slowly caused a move toward a different discussion of RMC. In the past, the prime question used to be whether the parents' freedom of religion and the need to provide a child with a primary culture and education justified the causing of harm through circumcision (Baum 1999; Freeman 1999), which could then to a great extent be limited through regulation. Nowadays, attention is equally being paid to the autonomy and self-determination of the child, and, indeed, the child's own right to freedom of religion.

Baum (1999) has submitted that autonomy is not violated by circumcision on non-consenting minors, because the majority of men consent in retrospect, and with modern surgical techniques, circumcision is no longer irreversible. Yet, the claim that many men consent in retrospect (Baum does not offer any evidence for his statement), does not mean that autonomy has not been impaired. Moreover, the very fact that man actually goes through a painful procedure to restore the foreskin (Schulteiss et al. 1998) is rather a contra-indication for circumcision at younger age, especially when they refer to having been circumcised "due to *their* [parental] religious beliefs" (Hardy 2012, emphasis mine). Consequently, most authors have claimed that the circumcision of minors unable to consent does violate a child's rights and autonomy. RMC, they argue, violates the child's right to freedom of religion under international law protected by Articles 18 ICCPR, 14 CRC and 9 ECHR (Svoboda 1997; Bihmji 2000; DOC 2008; Fortin 2009; Gilbert 2007), or respect for the child's person under Article 16 CRC (Svoboda 1997). Moreover, the CRC obliges adults to let children participate in decisions that affect them according to their age and maturity (Article 12); including health decisions (Hodgkin and Newell 1998). The autonomy interests that a child has, and its moral right to an open future (Feinberg 1980), could potentially bar the legitimacy of circumcision (Gilbert 2007; Fox and Thomson 2008; Schiratzki 2011), which leaves a permanent mark, as if a religion was stamped on a child.

Of great importance with regard to the autonomy argument are the recent court cases dealing with divorced parents or children in care. In all these cases, national judges, while having initially focused on the health implications for children (as in *Re J*) have now all argued that RMC goes against the autonomy interests of minors (*Re S*, Dutch cases and German cases). The religion of a parent has not been taken to be enough reason to impose a circumcision. While parents were found to be free to *educate* their children, circumcision had to wait until the boy would be old enough to choose a religion and decide on the intervention himself. Courts have taken children to be subjects with rights, rather than objects of parental concern: an approach consistent with human rights and the best interests of the child. Schiratzki (2011) notes:

> Is a child who partakes in a religious tradition a subject, or could the child being regarded as a representative of "others", the object of parental manifestation of religion? The view of the child as an "other" is an interpretation hard to reconcile with the raising awareness of children's autonomy.

On the other hand, the same author doubts that human rights law would currently support autonomy arguments on the basis of self-determination or religion. While the CRC and ECHR do grant autonomy rights to children under the abovementioned articles, "both instruments underline parental rights in relation to children's right[s]" (Schiratzki 2011; Marshall 2009).

The Way Forward

Fox and Thomson (2008) have argued against the qualification of RMC as child abuse. I share that opinion, dependant on how the circumcision is performed: kitchen table circumcisions would in my opinion constitute abuse, while medical zed circumcisions would not necessarily. To classify circumcision as abuse would put various mechanisms into motion against otherwise loving parents and it would rule out any possibility of regulation, insofar that would be desirable. Instead, RMC could be classified as a harmful practice that States should seek to eliminate.

Many states and international organizations have chosen to regulate and medicalize, rather than prohibit, circumcision. The WHO has, in the context of female circumcision, been fiercely opposed to medicalization because "body mutilation cannot be condoned by health services personnel" (WHO 1996). The same could be argued for cases of RMC. However, regulated medicalization of a practice gives a clear signal to the population that the practice is an intervention that is not self-evident, or even harmful. Moreover, it provides a forum for education on the harms and risks of RMC and existing initiation alternatives. In societies where RMC is prevalent, medicalization may be a first step toward a change in practice.[18] Yet, medicalization should only be a first step on the road to the abolishment of RMC performed on minors unable to consent since it does little for the

[18] For example in South-Africa where large parts of the male population are circumcised. The South-African government instituted a licensing regime with strict requirements for the performance of circumcisions (Marshall 2009).

psychological harms RMC causes and nothing at all for the impact on the child's autonomy and self-determination. Eventually the approach as adopted by the courts in divorce cases should be followed and circumcision should be postponed until the child is able to decide on the procedure himself. The argument that the pain, risks and encroachment upon rights and autonomy justify a limitation of parental rights (if parents have a right to submit their child to circumcision at all) is valid. It is therefore inconsistent that States and International Organizations refuse to acknowledge it in regard to children who do not come before the courts. States have an obligation to protect the best interests of children where parents do not, and it is time that governments protect these interests, whether the child concerned has divorced parents, or lives in an intact family.

Conclusion

Over the last years, the circumcision debate has moved from a focus on physical health, via psychological health to questions of autonomy. This shift is equally observable in the laws and, even more, in the judgments of different States in the world. Having arrived at the conclusion that RMC is an unjustified encroachment upon the autonomy and self-determination, physically, mentally as well as morally, of a non-competent child, it is now time to work toward its postponement until the child is able to make its own informed decision. Although as an initial step medicalization could help to raise awareness about the risks and harms of circumcision (while ensuring safety in the meantime), this solution is not helpful to combat adverse effects on the child's psyche or autonomy. Genuine respect for the person a young boy is and will be requires leaving the circumcision decision to him, when he is old enough to make it.

References

ANP. (2012). Opposite Duitsland: Besnijdenis pas vanaf 14 jaar. *Reformatorisch Dagblad*. Retrieved December 18, 2012, from http://www.refdag.nl/nieuws/buitenland/oppositie_duitsland_besnijdenis_pas_vanaf_14_jaar_1_693436.

Barkham, P. (2012). *Circumcision: the cruellest cut? The Guardian*. Retrieved, December 18, 2012, from http://www.guardian.co.uk/world/2012/aug/28/circumcision-the-cruellest-cut

Baum, S. (1999). Religious circumcision: Free from interference? In A. Jones & N. De Marco (Eds.), *University college London jurisprudence review, 1999*. London: University College London.

Besnijdenis Centrum Nederland. (2012). Culturele beleving, informative voor patienten. *Besnijdenis Centrum Nederlan*. Retrieved December 18, 2012, from http://www.besnijdeniscentrum.nl/index.php.

Bhimji, A. (2000). Infant male circumcision: A violation of the Canadian charter of rights and freedoms. *Health Care Law (Toronto), 1*, 1–33.

Boyle, G. J., Goldman, R., Smith, J. S., & Fernandez, E. (2002). Male circumcision: Pain, trauma and psychosexual squeal. *Journal of Health Psychology, 7*, 329–343. doi:10.1177/135910530200700310.

Braver Moss, L. (1991).*The Jewish roots of anti-circumcision arguments*. Paper Presented at the Second International Symposium on Circumcision, 30 April-3 May 1991, San Francisco, California. Retrieved December 18, 2012, from http://www.nocirc.org/symposia/second/moss.html.

Brems, E. (2006). *Article 14: The right to freedom of thought, conscience and religion*. Leiden; Boston: Martinus Nijhoff Publishers.

Brigman, W. E. (1984–1985). Circumcision as child abuse: The legal and constitutional issues. *Journal of Family law*, 23, 3, 337–351.

British Medical Association (2006). *The law and ethics of male circumcision. Guidance for doctors*. BMA: London

Both, N. (2004). The law and ethics of male circumcision: Guidance for doctors. *Journal of Medical Ethics, 30*, 259–263. doi:10.1136/jme.2004.008540.

Bundesärtzekammer, (2012). *Stellungnahme der Bundesärtzekammer zum Entwurf eines Gesetzes über den Umfang der Personensorge bei einder Beschneidung des männlichen Kindes*. Berlin: Bundesärtzekammer.

Cansever, G. (1965). Psychological effects of circumcision. *British Journal of Medical Psychology, 38*, 321–331. doi:10.1111/j.2044-8341.1965.tb01314.x.

Chamberlain, D. B. (2008). Delusional psychologies of circumcision and civilization. In: G. C. Denniston, F. Mansfield Hodges, M. F. Milos (Eds.), *Circumcision and human rights*. Dordrecht: Springer Netherlands.

Committee on the Rights of the Child. (2000). Concluding observations of the Committee on the Rights of the Child. *South Africa*. UN Doc. CRC/C/15/Add.122.

Committee on the Rights of the Child. (2001). Concluding observations of the committee on the rights of the child. *Lesotho*. UN Doc. CRC/C/15/Add.147.

Committee on the Rights of the Child. (2013). Concluding observations of the committee on the rights of the child. *Israel*. UN Doc. CRC/C/ISR/CO/2-4

Dalton, J. (2008). Conservative management of foreskin conditions. In: G. C. Denniston, F. Mansfield Hodges, M. F. Milos (Eds.), *Circumcision and human rights*. Dordrecht: Springer Netherlands.

Dave, S. S., Johnson, A. M., Fenton, K. A., Mercer, C. H., Erens, B., & Wellings, K. (2003). Male circumcision in Britain: Findings from a national probability sample. *Sexual Transmissible Infections, 79*, 499.

Deutscher Bundestag. (2012a). 17. Wahlperiod, 19.07.2012, *Bundestagsdrucksache* 17/10331.

Deutscher Bundestag. (2012b). 17. Wahlperiod, 05.11.2012, *Bundesdrucksache* 17/11295.

Deutscher Bundestag. (2012c). *Beschneidung, EU-Gipfel, Studiengebühren, Wahlrecht*. Retrieved December 18, 2012, from http://www.bundestag.de/dokumente/textarchiv/2012/41954763_kw50_vorschau/index.html.

Deutsche Gesellschaft für Kinderchirurgie. (2012) (2012b), Pressemitteilung October 2012, Beschneidung und Kinderrechten nicht bagatellisieren, Kinderchirurgen positionieren sich zu Gesetzentwurf. *Deutsche Gesellschaft für Kinderchirurgie*. Retrieved December 18, 2012, from http://www.dgkic.de/index.php/presse/204-pressemitteilung-oktober-2012.

Dixon, S., Snyder, J., Holve, R., & Bromberger, P. (1984). Behavioral effects of circumcision with and without anesthesia. *Journal of Developmental and Behavioral Pediatrics, 5*, 246–250.

Doctors Opposing Circumcision. (2008). *Doctors opposing circumcision human rights report: International human rights law and the circumcision of children*. Retrieved December 18, 2012, from http://www.doctorsopposingcircumcision.org/info/info-humanrights2006.html#n14.

DPA, AFP, Reuters. (2012). Berlin allows circumcision. *Deutsche Welle*. Retrieved December 18, 2012, from http://www.dw.de/berlin-allows-circumcision/a-16222070.

Eddy, M. (2012). In Germany, ruling over circumcision sows anxiety and confusion. *New York Times*. Retrieved December 18, 2012, from http://www.nytimes.com/2012/07/14/world/europe/in-germany-ruling-over-circumcision-sows-anxiety-and-confusion.html.

European Commission for Democracy through Law (Venice Commission) and OSCE/ODIHR Advisory Council on Freedom of Religion and Belief. (2008). *Joined opinion on freedom of conscience and religious organizations in the republic of Kyrgyzstan*. Opinion 496/2008. Council of Europe, Document CDL-AD 032.

Ewing, J. (2012). Some religious leaders see a threat as Europe grows more secular. *New York Times*. Retrieved December 18, 2012, from http://www.nytimes.com/2012/09/20/world/europe/circumcision-debate-in-europe-reflects-deeper-tensions.html?pagewanted=all&_r=0.

Feinberg, J. (1980) The child's right to an open future. In: A. Aiken, & H. LaFollette (Eds.), *Whose child? Children's rights, parental authority and state power*. Totowa, New Jersey: Littlefield, Adams & CO

Fortin, J. (2009). *Children's rights and the developing law*. Cambridge, New York: Cambridge University Press.

Fox, M. & Thomson, M. (2008). Reconsidering 'best interests'. Male circumcision and the rights of the child. In: G. C. Denniston, F. Mansfield Hodges, M. F. Milos (Eds.), *Circumcision and human rights*. Dordrecht: Springer Netherlands.

Freeman, M. D. A. (1999). A child's right to circumcision. *BJU International, 83, Suppl. 1*, 74–78. doi:10.1046/j.1464-410x.1999.0830s1074.x.

General Medical Council. (2008). *Personal beliefs and medical practice–guidance for doctors*. Retrieved December 18, 2012, from http://www.gmc-uk.org/guidance/ethical_guidance/personal_beliefs.asp#Footnote6.

Gilbert, H. (2007). Time to reconsider the lawfulness of ritual male circumcision. *European Human Rights Law Review, 3*, 279–294.

Graumann, D. (2012). Spiegel staff, circumcision debate has Berlin searching for answers. *Der Spiegel online international*. Retrieved December 18, 2012, from http://www.spiegel.de/international/germany/circumcision-debate-has-german-government-scrambling-for-a-law-a-846144.html.

Günter Jerouschek, J. (2008). Beschneidung und das deutsche Recht. Historische, medizinische, psychologische und juristische Aspekte. *Neue Zeitschrift für Strafrecht, 6*, 313–319.

Hans, B. (2012) (2012a). Beschneidung aus religiösen Gründen ist strafbar. *Der Spiegel*. Retrieved December 18, 2012, from http://www.spiegel.de/panorama/justiz/religioes-motivierte–beschneidung–von–jungen-ist-laut-gericht-strafbar-a-841084.html.

Hans, B. (2012, June 27) (2012b). Muslims and Jews outraged by circumcision ruling. *Der Spiegel online international*. Retrieved December 18, 2012, from http://www.spiegel.de/international/germany/religious-communities-debate-court-s-circumcision-ruling-a-841276.html.

Hardy, P. (2012). Comment. Circumcision and foreskin restoration hit the mainstream media in Australia. *Intactivists of Australasia*. Retrieved December 18, 2012, from http://intactivistsofaustralasia.wordpress.com/2012/10/02/circumcision-and-foreskin-restoration-hit-the-mainstream-media-in-australia/.

Hill, G., & Denniston, G. C. (2003) HIV and circumcision: New factors to consider. *Sexual Transmissible Infections, 79*, 495–496. doi:10.1136/sti.79.6.495.

Hodgkin, R., & Newell, P. (1998). *Implementation handbook for the convention on the rights of the child*. New York: UNICEF.

Hofvander, Y. (2008). Circumcision in European countries. review of the possible annual number of laws and regulations and of economic aspects. In: G. C. Denniston, F. Mansfield Hodges & M. F. Milos (Eds.), *Circumcision and human rights*. Dordrecht: Springer Netherlands.

Human Rights Committee. (1993). *General comment no. 22: The right to freedom of thought, conscience and religion (art. 18)*. UN Doc CCPR/C/21/Rev.1/Add.4.

Johnson, J. (1993). A history of the Jews. Phoenix Press. In: Baum, S. (1999). Religious circumcision: free from interference? In: A. Jones & N. De Marco (Eds.), *University College London Jurisprudence Review 1999*. London: University College London.

Koninklijke Nederlandsche Maatschappij tot bevordering der Geneeskunst (KNMG). (2010). *Niet-therapeutische circumcise bij minderjarige jongens. KNMG Standpunt, 2010*. Utrecht: KNMG.

Laibow, R. (1991). *Circumcision and its relationship to attachment impairment*. Paper presented at the Second International Symposium on Circumcision. San Francisco, CA. May 1991. In: Pollack, M. (2008). Circumcision: If it isn't ethical, can it be spiritual? In: G. C. Denniston, H. Mansfield, & M. F. Milos (Eds.), *Circumcision and human rights*. Dordrecht: Springer Netherlands..

Madden, P., & Boddy, S. A. (1991). Should religious circumcisions be performed on the NHS. *BMJ: British Medical Journal, 302*(6767), 47.

Mahdawi, M. K. A. (1990). Al-Bayan bil-Qur'an, 2 Volumes, Vol. 1. Casablanca: Al-dar al-gamahiriyyah, Misratahand Dar al-afaq al-gadidah. In: Aldeeb Abu-Sahlieh, S.A. (1994). To Mutilate in the Name of Jehovah or Allah, *Medicine and Law*, 13(7–8), 575–622.

Marshall, W. (2009). *Non-therapeutic male circumcision. Issues paper no. 14*. Hobart: Tasmania Law Reform Institute.

Ministerie van Onderwijs, Cultuur en Wetenschap (2003). Leidraad Kleding op scholen

Ministerie van Volksgezondheid, Welzijn en Sport. (2005). *Brief naar aanleiding van kamervragen over jongensbesnijdenis uit het ziekenfondspakket*. Kamerstuk DBO-CB-U-2561084, 11 Maart 2005.

Neukirch, R. (2012). Berlin presents draft law allowing circumcision. *Der Spiegel Online International*. Retrievd December 18, 2012, from http://www.spiegel.de/international/germany/germany-justice-ministry-presents-draft-law-to-allow-circumcision-a-857982.html.

Paranthaman, K., Bagaria, J., & O'Moore, E. (2010). The need for commissioning circumcision services for non-therapeutic in the NHS: Lessons from an incident investigation. *Oxford Journal of Public Health, 33*(2), 280–283. doi:10.1093/pubmed/fdq053.

Parliamentary Assembly of the Council of Europe (2013a). Recommendation 2023 (2013) Children's right to physical integrity

Parliamentary Assembly of the Council of Europe (2013b). Resolution 1952 (2013) Children's right to physical integrity

Pollack, M. (2008). Circumcision: If it isn't ethical, can it be spiritual? In: G. C. Denniston, H. Mansfield, & M. F. Milos (Eds.), *Circumcision and human rights*. Dordrecht: Springer Netherlands.

Pont, B. (2008). *Droit et Religion*–Course Université Paul Cézanne. *Aix-Marseille, III*, 2008–2009.

Pringer, M. D., & Brereton, R. J. (1991). Should religious circumcisions be performed on the NHS? *British Medical Journal, 302*, 292.

Raad voor Volksgezonheid en Zorg. (2010). De ene besnijdenis is de andere niet. Reactie op KNMG stand punt jongensbesnijdenis. *Raad voor Volksgezonheid en Zorg*. Retrieved 18 December, 2012, from http://rvz.net/nieuws/bericht/de-ene-besnijdenis-is-de-andere-niet-reactie-op-knmg-standpunt-jongensbesnijdenis.

Richards, D. (1996). Male circumcision: Medical or ritual? *Journal of Law and Medicine, 3*(4), 371–376.

Rijksoverheid, Regels ritueel slachten naar Tweede Kamer. Nieuwsbericht 01-11-2012. Rijksoverheid. Retrieved 18 December, 2012, from http://www.rijksoverheid.nl/nieuws/2012/11/01/regels-ritueel-slachten-naar-tweede-kamer.html

Rothenburg, M. (1991). Ending *circumcision in the Jewish community*? Paper Presented at the Second International Symposium on Circumcision, 30 April-3 May 1991, San Francisco, California. Retrieved December, 18, 2012, from http://www.nocirc.org/symposia/second/rothenberg.html.

Schiratzki, J. (2011). Banning God's Law in the name of the holy body—the nordic position on ritual male circumcision. *The Family in Law, 5*, 35–53.

Schmitz, R. F. (2001). *Rituele besnijdenis van jongens in Nederland*. Utrecht: DrukkerijZuidam & Uithof, B.V.

Schultheiss, D., Truss, M. C., Stief, C. G., & Jonas, U. (1998). Uncircumcision: A historical review of preputial restoration. *Plastic and Reconstructive Surgery, 101*(7), 1990–1998.

Smith, J. (1998). Male circumcision and the rights of the child. In: M. Bulterman, A. Hendriks & J. Smith (Eds.), *To Baehr in our minds: Essays in human rights from the heart of the Netherlands* (SIM Special No. 21). Utrecht: Netherlands Institute of Human Rights (SIM), University of Utrecht.

Snyder, J. L. (2008). The normal, natural penis and the effects of circumcision. In: G. C. Denniston, F. Mansfield Hodges & M. F. Milos (Eds.), *Circumcision and human rights*. Dordrecht: Springer Netherlands.

Svoboda, J. S. (1997). Routine infant male circumcision: Examining the human rights and constitutional issues. In G. C. Denniston & M. F. Milos (Eds.), *Sexual mutilations: A human tragedy*. New York: Plenum Press.

Trouw, Redactie religie en filosofie. (2005). Besnijdenisklinieken opened in rap tempo vestigingen. *Trouw.* Retrieved December 18, 2012, from http://www.trouw.nl/tr/nl/4324/Nieuws/archief/article/detail/1724139/2005/08/02/Besnijdenisklinieken-openen-in-rap-tempo-vestigingen.dhtml.

Tweede Kamer der Staten General. (2011). *Vragen van het lid Wiegman-van Meppelen Scheppink.* Vergaderjaar 2011–2012. Aanhangsel van de Handelingen. Ah-tk-20112012-406.

UNAIDS. (2008). *Safe, voluntary, informed male circumcision and comprehensive HIV prevention programming. Guidance for decision-makers on human rights, ethical and legal considerations*. Geneva: UNAIDS.

Vidal d'AleidaRibeiro, A. (1986). *Implementation of the declaration on the elimination of all forms of intolerance and of discrimination based on religion or belief.* UN Doc. E/CN.4/1987/35.

Weiss, H. A., Larke, N., Halperin, D., & Schenker, I. (2010). Complications of circumcision in male neonates, infants and children: A systematic review. *BMC Urology, 10*, 2–14. doi:10.1186/1471-2490-10-2.

Williams, N., & Kapila, L. (1993). Complications of circumcision. *British Journal of Surgery, 80*, 1231–1236. doi:10.1002/bjs.1800801005.

World Health Organization (Ed.) (1996). *Female genital mutilation: Information kit*. Geneva: Department of Women's Health, Health Systems and Community Health.

World Health Organization, London School of Hygiene & Tropical Medicine and UNAIDS. (2007). *Male circumcision: Global trends and determinants of prevalence, safety and acceptability*. Geneva: World Health Organization.

World Health Organization. (2009). *Traditional male circumcision among young people*. Geneva: World Health Organization.

Zapfl-Helbing, R. (2004). *The involvement of men, especially young men, in reproductive health*. Report of the Committee on Equal Opportunities for Women and Men. Council of Europe, doc. 10207.

Part II
Child Rights and Its Practice

Chapter 9
Child's Right to Health, Education, and Freedom from Hunger

Bernadette J. Madrid and Dian Traisci-Marandola

> *The enjoyment of the highest attainable standard of health is one of the fundamental rights of every human being.*
>
> World Health Organization Constitution

Introduction

The world's 7 billionth baby—Danica Galura—was born in the Philippines on October 31, 2011. Danica was born prematurely to parents who live in poverty. She was born into a world where children are not "enjoying" the highest standard of health in the least *and* the most developed countries. Dr. Eric Tayag of the Philippines' Department of Health noted that the birth came with a warning, "Seven billion is a number we should think about deeply," he said. "We should really focus on the question of whether there will be food, clean water, shelter, education, and a decent life for every child."

Every disadvantaged child bears witness to a moral offence: the failure to secure their right to survive, thrive, and participate in society. Hundreds of millions of the world's poorest children live in urban slums, the indicator of abject poverty in the cities. These children lack access to basic services and they are vulnerable to dangers ranging from violence and exploitation to injuries, illness and death resulting from living in crowded settlements atop hazardous rubbish dumps or alongside

B.J. Madrid (✉)
Child Protection Unit, Philippine General Hospital, University of the Philippines Manila, Metro Manila, Philippines
e-mail: madridbernie@gmail.com

D. Traisci-Marandola
Division College of Nursing, Organization Rush University, Chicago, Illinois, USA
e-mail: dianmarandola@gmail.com

S. Deb (ed.), *Child Safety, Welfare and Well-being*,
DOI 10.1007/978-81-322-2425-9_9

railroad tracks. UNICEF and their partners demonstrate that scarcity and dispossession afflict the most marginalized children and families disproportionately. Children who live in slums are least likely to attend school (UNICEF 2012).

The purpose of this chapter is to review the status of health, nutrition, and education needs of vulnerable children. An exploration of the structure, processes, and outcomes around enhancing the determinants of health will be presented. Program and policy recommendations rooted in collaboration across sectors will be made that will require the transformative energy of all members of society to accelerate change on behalf of children. It is predicted that the 8 billionth babies will be born in 2025. Leaders are empowered to escalate the relevance of their knowledge of best practices, of the research and statistics to solve the problems faced by children. This chapter challenges the reader to aggressively intervene to make the right-to-health a reality before the 8 billionth babies is born.

The UN Committee on Economic, Social and Cultural Rights, which monitors compliance with the International Covenant on Economic, Social and Cultural Rights, adopted a General Comment on the Right to Health in 2000. General Comment no. 14 states that the right to health extends not only to timely and appropriate health care but also to the underlying determinants of health. According to the General Comment, the right to health contains four elements which are embraced by the primary care approach (Fig. 9.1):

- **Availability**: A sufficient quantity of functioning public health and health care facilities, goods and services, as well as programmers.
- **Accessibility**: Health facilities, goods, and services accessible to everyone. Accessibility has four overlapping dimensions:
  - Non-discrimination
  - Physical accessibility
  - Economical accessibility (affordability)
  - Information accessibility.

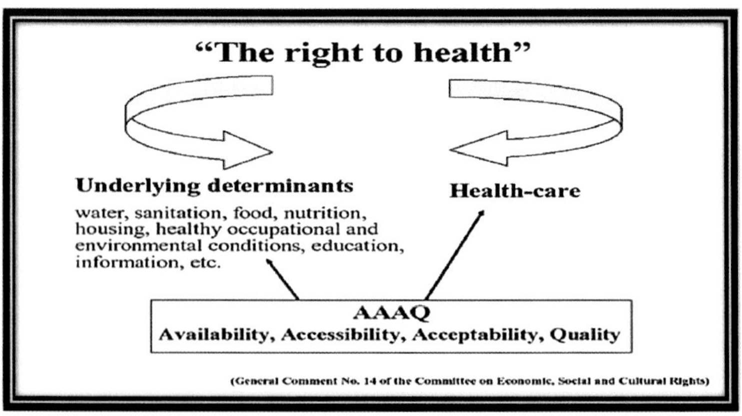

Fig. 9.1 Underlying determinants of child health care

- **Acceptability**: All health facilities, goods, and services must be respectful of medical ethics and culturally appropriate as well as sensitive to gender and life-cycle requirements.
- **Quality**: Health facilities, goods and services must be scientifically and medically appropriate and of good quality.

Health Behaviors	• Diet & access to nutritious food and clean water • Physical Activity • Smoking • Use of alcohol and drugs • Exposure to environmental toxins: lead, 2nd hand smoke
Clinical Care: prevention works *(Palfrey, 2006, p. 186)*	• **Newborns**: Screenings, immunizations, nutritional assessment, developmental assessment and intervention, anticipatory guidance with focus on sleep, nutrition, relationship building • **Early Childhood:** Immunizations, developmental assessment, anticipatory guidance with focus on safety and nutrition • **School Age**: Anticipatory guidance on safe bike riding & helmet safety, prevention of violence & abuse • **Adolescence**: Promoting healthy behaviors with smoking, alcohol and drug use prevention violence prevention. • **Mental Health**: Children need access to the continuum of developmental, behavioral and mental health assessment & intervention. • **Oral Health**: Children need access to oral health care across their growth and development
Access	• Children living in poverty have less access to clinical care, less access to transportation, less access to nutritious foods, less access to education. • Lack of Sanitation leads to illnesses greatly exacerbated during flooding • Children need to be read to: "Reach Out and Read" reaches the child through effectively teaching the parent to start lifelong learning in the home. • Children need to eat food rich with micro-nutrients. • Lack of iron in a child's diet leads to iron deficiency anemia which in turn impacts the development of the brain
Social Determinants ***Catlin, B., Jovaag, A., Remington, P., & Williams Van Dijk, J. (2014).)***	• Universal Primary Education • Books for reading throughout childhood • Books for children who are visually impaired • Employment • Income • Family and Social Support • Community Safety

Chart 9.1 Indicators and determinants of health

	• Environment – Anti -Climate Change Behaviors • Freedom from violence • Freedom from unsafe environment
Programs	Public – private partnerships to eradicate extreme hunger, abject poverty, promote development, sustainable environments
Policies	• Governmental: global, regional, country, provincial and local • Laws: local & national • Child Protection Policies • Universal Educational Policies • Universal Human Rights Instruments: UN Conventions and treaties (United Nations Human Rights, n.d., p. 1).

Chart 9.1 (continued)

Determinants of Health

The need to address health inequities through an approach that goes beyond the health sector was first addressed in the Alma-Ata Declaration of 1978, followed by the Ottawa Charter for Health Promotion in 1986. Since then, there has been a global movement to investigate and act upon the determinants of health, *the causes of the causes*, of health inequities. The World Health Organization (WHO) Commission on the Social Determinants of Health (CSDH) concluded in 2008 that the social conditions in which an individual is born, grows, lives, works, and ages are the single most important determinants of health status (Marmot et al. 2013, p. 379).

Health has its roots in a number of fundamental clinical and public health principles; many have little to do with the actual provision of health care. Health disadvantage involves inadequate health care, lack of access to nutritious foods, unhealthy behaviors and adverse exposure to the social determinants of health. These determinants include lack of access to education, poor economic and social conditions, compromised environmental factors, as well as ineffective, inefficient public policies and values that shape health (Institute of Medicine 2013a, b, p. 1) (Chart 9.1).

Child Friendly Communities

The underlying social determinants around health contribute to the overall well-being of children across the spectrum. There are stark differences between the least healthy and healthiest places to grow up in terms of health behaviors, access to health care, social and economic factors and the environment.

The healthiest places have better access to healthy foods, parks, exercise facilities, and ensure that children have enough to eat. Children have access to primary, oral and mental health care; Immunizations are up to date. Children have access to education beyond primary grades. Children are embraced within their families and the communities where they live (Dreher and Skemp 2011).

The least healthy places have higher rates of pediatric morbidity and mortality, of smoking, obesity, physical inactivity, teen births, and sexually transmitted infections. The least healthy places have higher unemployment, more children living in poverty, higher violent crime, more deaths due to injuries, and more people without enough social support. The least healthy places have more homeless children, households that are overcrowded, homes that lack adequate facilities to cook, clean, or bathe (Catlin et al. 2014, p. 2). Children go to bed hungry at night.

Need for Data

Data attest to the reality that the current determinants of health do not assure that the rights of children are maintained, in a timely, efficient, or equitable way. As a global society we lack the answer to the public health question: "what is the optimal balance of investments (e.g., dollars, time, people, policies) in the multiple determinants of health over the life course that will maximize overall health outcomes and minimize health inequities at the population level?" (Kindig 2014, p. 1).

This lack of insight has slowed down our ability to assure children's rights. Lack of data often becomes an excuse for not acting on the volumes of information and best approaches that we do know. Developed in the early 1990s by UNICEF and conducted by national authorities, Multiple Indicator Cluster Surveys (MICS) are the largest source of statistical information on children. The surveys have been designed to provide a manageable framework with which to aggregate data and monitor progress toward global goals ("MICS" 2014, p. 1).

Community Based Monitoring Systems—CBMS

CBMS promotes the concept of mobilizing and developing the capability of communities for data generation and utilization. CBMS offers a methodology for bottom-up budgeting, disaster risk reduction and management, local governance, vulnerability mapping, program design and targeting, and impact monitoring while building safe, resilient and proactive communities. CBMS are effective approach used in the Philippines; this systematic approach represents an organized way of collecting information at the local level for use of local government units, national government agencies, non-government organizations and civil society. CBMS provides local statistics or benchmark information for evidence-based policymaking. The CBMS has several features: (1) it is locally based; (2) taps local personnel as monitors; and (3) has a core set of indicators (Community Based Monitoring System 2014).

Problems of Inequity

The issue of rising income inequity is one of global concern. Health researchers have shown low-income countries contribute 56 % of global disease burden, but account for only 2 % of global expenditure on health. The World Vision report, *The Killer Gap: A Global Index of Health Inequality for Children* (2013) ranked 176 countries according to the size of the gap between those who have greatest access to good health and those who have the most barriers using the four indicators of life expectancy, personal cost of using health services, adolescent fertility rate and coverage of health services. The index shows that while the greatest gaps exist in the poorest and most fragile contexts and countries, material wealth alone does not guarantee equity. Although a child may have insurance does not mean that this child has access to health care services (Starfield and Shi 2004, p. 3).

Classic examples of ranking and inequity include the United States and Singapore who are no. 46 and no. 57, respectively, of 176 while Cuba is no. 9. Children who fall through the cracks in the health system are those who suffer several deprivations at the same time such as being poor, being an ethnic minority, being unregistered at birth, suffering a disability, being orphaned, or being trafficked. Relying on averages in terms of data may mask inequity, for example only eight countries have achieved MDG 4 "reduce child deaths by two-thirds by 2015". Bangladesh and Peru are two of these eight countries but they are low in the Global Health Gap Index with Bangladesh at no. 128 and Peru at No. 98.

Among the many causes of the gap are: poverty, lack of equal investment in the early years of life, policies and practices that have prioritized urban growth over rural communities, unequal employment, lack of social security, high out-of-pocket health care spending, lack of investment in national health workforces and gender disparities. In addition, there is great inequity within most countries. Economist Joseph Stiglitz argues, "We are paying a price in terms of our politics and society—inequity is undermining our basic values." Some policymakers seek to understand how to bridge this gap (Blaya 2014, p. 1).

Need for Resource Development

Universal protection systems should identify measurable outcomes, not merely be used as a temporary component of a national crisis response. It has been shown, time and again, that economic policies considered in isolation from their social consequences can have major impact on nutrition, health and education which in turn adversely affects long-term economic growth, setting off a vicious cycle. The increased levels of poverty, hunger and unemployment due to global crisis will continue to impact billions for years to come (Liebert 2011). Reforms are needed to achieve universal health coverage for the poorest and hardest to reach communities. Emerging trends in the fiscal, social and political environment need to be integrated into a given system's strategic planning.

"A new Global Investment Framework for Women's and Children's Health demonstrates how investment in women's and children's health will secure high health, social, and economic returns. This global framework calls for strengthening of health systems and six investment packages for maternal and newborn health, child health, immunization, family planning, HIV/AIDS, and malaria, followed by simulation modeling to estimate the health and socio-economic returns of these investments.

Continuing historical trends of coverage increases is not sufficient. Accelerated investments are needed to bring health benefits to the majority of women and children. Increasing health expenditure by five dollars per person per year up to 2035 in 74 high-burden countries could yield up to nine times that value in economic and social benefits. These returns include greater gross domestic product (GDP) growth through improved productivity, and prevention of the needless deaths of 147 million children, 32 million stillbirths, and 5 million women by 2035. These gains could be achieved by an additional investment of $30 billion per year, equivalent to a two percent increase above current spending (Global Investment Framework for Women's and Children's Health 2013).

Convention on the Rights of the Child-Protection, Provision, and Participation

In 1990, 193 countries began working under the United Nation's guidelines entitled "The Convention on the Rights of the Child which provides a framework of rights to which every child is entitled (Stahlhofer 2013, p. 21). The basic principle of the rights of the child is that society has an obligation to meet the essential needs of children and to provide assistance for the development of the child's personality, talents, and abilities.

The Convention on the Rights of the Child provides a frame work with *articles* for improving children's lives around the world. It covers both individual child health and public health practices and provides a unique, child-centered approach. The articles are grouped into protection, provision, and participation outlining specific rights to compulsory education with attention to drop-out prevention at all ages along with access to health services and nutrition (Waterston and Goldhagen 2007, p. 176). The indivisibility and interdependence of children's rights means that all the other rights contribute to the realization of the right to health and health care and vice versa (Fig. 9.2).

When a State ratifies the Convention on the rights of the child, the obligations under the Convention become legally binding. The Convention on the Rights of the Child ties into the Declaration of the Rights of the Child from 1959 that the "child by reason of his physical and mental immaturity, needs special Safeguards and care, including appropriate legal protection before and after birth" ("Declaration," 1959, p. 1). The CRC continues to note that the child should grow up in a family environment, in an atmosphere of happiness; love and understanding in order to be prepared to live an individual live in society ("Convention," 1990, p. 1) (Chart 9.2).

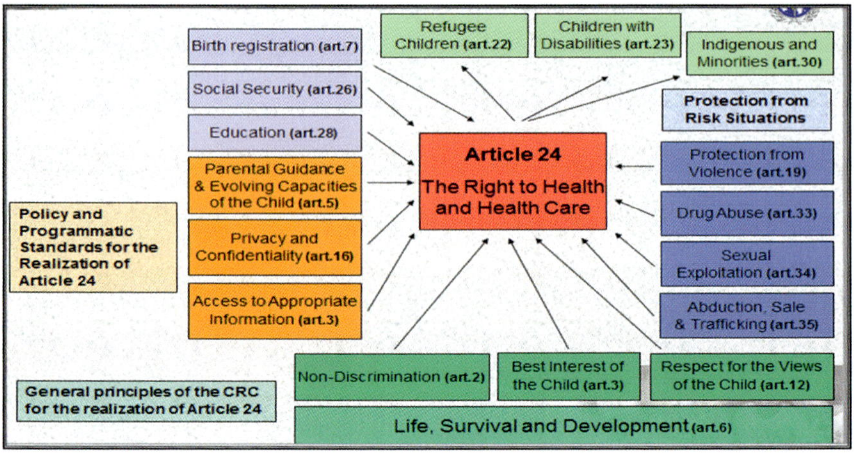

Fig. 9.2 Stahlhofer, M., World Health Organization, 2013

Signs of moving in a positive direction	• When the MDGs were first implemented 30,000 children less than 5 years of age were dying every day; today 18,000 children are lost to disease, poor nutrition and poverty. • Access to clean water, safe food and adequate sanitation can reduce the risk of childhood mortality by as much as 50%. • Progress is being made on many fronts – albeit unevenly • More children in primary grades; tendencies to drop out before high school begins • Vitamin A supplementation has been occurring in the Western Pacific Region for decades; Foods fortified with vitamin A are available in Malaysia and the Philippines with some progress in the Democratic People's Republic of Korea, Indonesia, Thailand and Vietnam.
Signs of moving in the wrong direction	• Low-income countries contribute **56% of global disease burden**, but account for only **2% of global expenditure on health.** • Poverty indicators are moving upwards • In 2012, 2.9 million newborn babies died within 28 days - two out of every five child deaths. Of these, 1 million babies died on their first – and only – day of life. • Policy does not exist guaranteeing a community health worker to be at the mothers side during delivery • Lack of attention to human rights such as harmful traditional practices, slavery, torture and inhuman, degrading treatment, and violence against children can have serious physical and mental health consequences. • Under nutrition accounts for 1/3 of deaths of children under five • water and food related illnesses are a major cause of ill health and malnutrition

Chart 9.2 Rights of the child to health, nutrition and education

Millennium Development Goals

The Convention on the Rights of the Child did not accomplish accelerated change and improvement for children living in poverty. The United Nations launched eight Millennium Development Goals (MGDs) to alleviate abject poverty by 2015. The MDGs were designed to eradicate extreme poverty, one of the main challenges of our time and a major concern of the international community. The MDGs require the combined efforts of all, governments, civil society, and the private sector to establish more effective partnerships to achieve impact and change.

The Millennium Development Goals reflect a time bound target with interrelated and reinforcing benchmarks to measure progress. These eight goals target: (1) hunger and poverty, (2) primary education, (3) gender equality and empower women, (4) reduce child mortality, (5) improve maternal health, (6) combat HIV/AIDS, malaria, and other diseases, (7) ensure environmental sustainability, and (8) develop a global partnership for development. The MDGs are human rights based— "the rights of each person on the planet earth to health, education, shelter, and security."

The MDGs represent a blueprint agreed to by countries and the world's leading development institutions, all by the target date of 2015. The MDGs have galvanized unprecedented efforts to meet the needs of the poorest in the world. The UN is also working with governments, civil society, and other partners to build on the momentum generated by the MDGs and carry on with an ambitious post-2015 development agenda. From these sites, explore the efforts of the UN and its partners for building a better world (http://www.unicef.org and http://www.girlsrights.org).

All the UN agencies come together under the UNDG (UN Development Group) and ECHA (Executive Committee on Humanitarian Affairs) to share methodologies and approaches in this regard where in the past few years WHO is actively engaged in operational zing a human rights-approach to public health (WHO 2002). At its current success rate, it is reported that the MDGs will not be realized until 2025, 10 years after its original goal.

Report: The Experiences and Status on MDGs 1, 2, and 4

DG 1: Eradicate Hunger—A Child's Right to Nutrients, Safe Water, and Safe Food

Nutrition is a cross-cutting theme to achieve any of the MDGs (Save the Children 2012, p. 4).

Under nutrition is the largely preventable cause of over a third—3.5 million—of all child deaths and can be seen as stunting, severe wasting, and intrauterine growth restriction. Under nutrition will have caused irreversible damage for future development toward adulthood. Eighty percent of the world's stunted children live in just 20 countries (http://www.partnersinhealth.org).

Malnutrition and disease work in a deadly cycle. In 2013, the prevalence of underweight children aged 0–5 years increased from 24.6 to 26.2 % accounting for about 3.35 million children. A malnourished child is more likely to suffer from disease, and the more they suffer from disease the more likely they are to be malnourished and the downhill spiral continues (Save the Children 2012, p. 24).

Clean Water and Food Safety

The Western Pacific Rim has made great strides in improving access to clean water and sanitation. Evidence shows that water and food related illnesses continue to be a major cause of ill health and malnutrition which results in lost lives and lost productivity among poor households. Water and food related hazards are the main cause of diarrhea which is the second leading cause of child mortality. Access to clean water, safe food, and adequate sanitation can reduce the risk of childhood mortality by as much as 50 % (WHO 2009, p. 40).

Incredibly, four-fifths of undernourished children live in just 20 countries across four regions—Africa, Asia, Western Pacific, and the Middle East. These are the priority nations for action; in order of population size include India, Indonesia, Pakistan, Bangladesh, Vietnam, Philippines, Egypt, South Africa, Sudan, and Nepal (Maternal and Infant Under Nutrition 2008, p. 179).

Interventions

In 2008, the Lancet medical journal identified a package of 13 direct interventions—such as vitamin A and zinc supplements, iodized salt, and the promotion of healthy behavior, including hand washing, exclusive breastfeeding and complementary, nutritional feeding practices—that were proven to have an impact on the nutrition and health of children and mothers. This cost-effective and affordable package could prevent the deaths of almost 2 million children under five and a substantial amount of illness if it was delivered to children in the 36 countries that are home to ninety percent of the world's malnourished children (Maternal and Infant Under nutrition 2008).

Vitamin A

Vitamin A deficiency is a major contributor to the mortality of children under five. MIC Surveys suggest that children living in poor, rural areas—those likely to be at greatest risk—may be disproportionately missed by Vitamin A programs. Reports show the need to accelerate and sustain the gains for Vitamin A programming as a central component to achieve the MDG child survival goal.

In its series on child survival, Lancet lists Vitamin A supplementation in two doses among the key interventions achievable on the large scale. It is recognized as one of the most cost-effective interventions for improving child survival (Edejer 2005). Vitamin A supplementation has sparked the innovative delivery of multiple interventions through child health survival packages (UNICEF 2007, p. 33). Vitamin A supplementation has been occurring in the Western Pacific Region for decades; Foods fortified with vitamin A are available in Malaysia and the Philippines with some progress in the Democratic People's Republic of Korea, Indonesia, Thailand, and Vietnam (UNICEF 2007, p. 10).

Recommendations

Innovative private—public partnerships are essential to accelerate positive nutrition outcomes include:

- Development of a national action plan which integrates health and nutrition,
- Draw clear lines of responsibility, accountability, and leadership on nutrition within the country so that all ministries and stakeholders know the role they play
- Connect health, trade and agriculture, environment and finance, plus others together (Save the Children 2012, p. 92)

MDG 2: Achieve Universal Primary Education—A Child's Right to Education

The healthiest of places have a comprehensive educational program for children from preschool to post-secondary education (Gakidou et al. 2010). Children begin to read at an early age and have books at home. Learning is a priority.

Less supportive communities provide for minimal education. Children in the poorest households and children in rural areas are least likely to attend primary school as they are used to help parents farm or are put to work in low paying jobs at an early age. World-wide, 84 % of primary school aged children attend school, but only half attend high school (UNESCO 2000a). Most countries have reached gender parity in primary education; Gender disparities become more evident as children approach adolescence (UNICEF 2011a, b, p. 14).

The World Education Forum—held in Dakar, Senegal during April, 2000—was a most important event for universal primary education. The Dakar Forum reinforced *The Education for* All movement as a global commitment to provide quality basic education for all children, youth and adults, pledging to universalize primary education and massively reduce illiteracy by 2015.

The Dakar Forum identified six key education goals which provide structure to meet the learning needs of all children, youth, and adults by 2015. They have not been achieved and continue to be valid today (UNESCO 2000b).

- **Goal 1**: Expanding and improving comprehensive early childhood care and education, especially for the most vulnerable and disadvantaged children.
- **Goal 2**: Ensuring that by 2015 all children, particularly girls, children in difficult circumstances and those belonging to ethnic minorities, have access to, and complete, free and compulsory primary education of good quality.
- **Goal 3**: Ensuring that the learning needs of all young people and adults are met through equitable access to appropriate learning and life-skills programs.
- **Goal 4**: Achieving a 50 % improvement in levels of adult literacy, especially for women, and equitable access to basic and continuing education for all adults.
- **Goal 5**: Eliminating gender disparities in primary and secondary education, and achieving gender equality in education by 2015, with a focus on ensuring girls' full and equal access to and achievement in basic education of good quality.
- **Goal 6**: Improving all aspects of the quality of education and ensuring excellence of all so that recognized and measurable learning outcomes are achieved by all, especially in literacy, numeracy, and essential life skills.

MDG 4: Reduce Child Mortality—The Child's Right to Health

Overview: Child mortality is a key indicator not only of child health and nutrition but also of the implementation of child survival interventions and more broadly of the effectiveness of social and economic development (Gakidou et al. 2010). These data are updated annually by the United Nations Group for Child Mortality Estimation (ICME) which is comprised of World Bank, World Health Organization, UN Department of Economic and Social Affairs, UN Children's Fund (United Nations 2013). Globally, the four major killers of children under the age of five are pneumonia (18 %), diarrheal disease (15 %), pre-term birth complications (12 %), and birth asphyxia (9 %). Under nutrition is an underlying cause in more than a third of under-five deaths (United Nations 2013).

Newborns

The statistics around childbirth for both the infant and the mother demonstrate a failure of the system designed to provide them health care. In 2012, 2.9 million newborn babies died within 28 days—two of every five child deaths. Of these, 1 million babies died on their first—and only—day of life. Unless we urgently start to tackle deaths among newborn babies, there is a real danger that progress in reducing child deaths will stall, and we will fail in our ambition to be the generation that can end all preventable child deaths. But, as *Ending Newborn Deaths* reveals, the crisis is even bigger than originally considered. In 2012 there were 1.2 million stillbirths where the heart stopped beating during labor (Wright et al. 2014).

In the Philippines, despite reductions in national under-five and infant mortality rates, the neonatal mortality rate has remained constant at the level of approximately 18 deaths per 1000 from the 1990s to 2007. A focus on health interventions by trained staff at well-functioning facilities and supported by a strong referral system help reduce mortality (Kraft et al. 2013). Most of the interventions to save newborns use low-cost products but these need to be scaled up for universal access. Kangaroo mother care and exclusive breastfeeding which have no cost would save more babies (Madrid 2014, Chap. 3).

Fairer distribution of essential health services in 47 key countries could prevent the deaths of 950,000 newborns—reducing newborn mortality in these countries by 38 % (Wright et al. 2014). To end all preventable newborn deaths and stillbirths during labor, policy needs to articulate provisions for universal access to properly trained and equipped health workers at birth. This chapter sets out that reforms are critical to achieve universal health coverage and access to care for the poorest and hardest-to-reach communities.

Early Childhood Development

Early childhood is critical for laying the foundation for physical health, cognitive development, socio-emotional development and behavior. This is the time of the most rapid development of the brain in the child's life. Parenting experiences, adequate nutrition, exposure to stressors and environmental toxins, psychosocial stimulation and access to health care will determine current and future health. The Consultative Group on Early Childhood Care and Development's Task Force for the Post-2015 Development Agenda (2012) posit that Early Childhood Development (ECD) is key to gender equality and empowerment, better health and education outcomes, improved skills, abilities and productivity, narrow the income, ethnic, and geographic inequality gaps, provide timely intervention for persons with disabilities, and is a cost effective strategy for eliminating disadvantage (Consultative Group on Early Childhood Care and Development Taskforce 2012).

Early intervention programs for marginalized and disadvantaged children have demonstrated remarkable results with respect to improving the outcomes for children and families to the level of their more-advantaged peers (Engle et al. 2011). According to Heckman et al. (2010), every dollar invested in high-quality early childhood program produces a 7–10 % per annum return on investment (Heckman et al. 2010). Supportive services early in life can change the trajectory of development making it possible for disadvantaged children to catch up. The earlier the intervention the better it is for the child. Since risk factors tend to occur together, integrated interventions have been shown to be more effective in the reduction of multiple risks. For example combining nutrition, responsive child feeding and child stimulation interventions have been shown to work in addressing stunting which is associated with lack of stimulation (Engle et al. 2011).

Adolescents

Among the multitude, not all adolescents enjoy access to quality education, health care, protection, and participation. Accidents account for over a third of their deaths either from road injuries or acts of organized or random violence (UNICEF 2011a, b, p. 3) Adolescence is a critical period where it is possible to break the vicious cycles of intergenerational poverty, poor health and nutrition, gender discrimination, and violence. This is the best time to catch up with nutrition and micronutrient deficiencies such as iron and foliate before pregnancy occurs. Often teens fly under the radar at a time when they are at risk for exploitation, homelessness due to disenfranchisement from parents, poverty, teen pregnancy, and dropping out of school to work. Exposure and use of alcohol, tobacco, and drugs escalates during adolescence.

In the Philippines twenty-two percent (22 %) of the Philippine population is between 10 and 19 years old. In order to achieve Millennium Development Goals (MDGs) 4 (reduce child mortality), 5 (improve maternal health) and 6 (combat HIV/AIDS, malaria and other diseases), it is essential to address adolescents' health (MDG 2014). For a child to be born well, this is where it starts. Many adolescents in developing countries are poorly nourished, have poor education and become pregnant at a young age. In the Philippines, 52 % of child sexual abuse cases seen at the Child Protection Units nationwide are from the 13–19 age groups (Madrid 2009).

Pregnancy among Filipino girls under the age of 20 years increased by 65 % over a 10-year period, from 2000 to 2010, despite a reverse trend in teen marriages, which is on the decline, according to the Philippine National Statistics Office (NSO). The Philippine 2011 Family Health Survey showed that while childbirth is slowly decreasing among women in the older age groups, it is increasing among girls 15–19 years old, from 39 per 1,000 live births in 2006 to 54 in 2011, across all regions in the Philippines. The Philippine Food and Nutrition Research Institute Report (2011) describe that three of every 10 pregnant women who are under 20 are at risk of their health worsening due to malnutrition. These teen mothers may manifest many risky health behaviors such as smoking, drinking, poor prenatal care, and abortion (Madrid 2014).

Girls and the Girl Child

In the Western Pacific Region, poverty often wears a woman's face in line with an estimated 70 % of the world's poor being women. Indicators of human poverty, including health indicators often reflect severe gender based disparities. In this way, gender inequality is a significant determinant of health outcomes in the Region, with women and girls often at an extraordinary disadvantage (WHO 2009, p. VI).

The Millennium Development Goals (MDGs) attempted to achieve gender equality. However, the MDGs failed to include a comprehensive goal toward the empowerment of girls and are all too far from being achieved. Therefore, post-2015 the UN must re-evaluate methods for undertaking gender equality. The girls of the 58th session of 2014's Commission on the Status of Women demanded that in the next development agenda the UN incorporate girls as participants—politically, socially, and economically. A stand-alone goal for girls requires sufficient consideration as well as a dedicated effort that includes realistic and achievable targets and indicators to ensure success. Three key areas that must be put into action are education, poverty and violence. These girl advocates noted that these issues along with the consistent inclusion of girls will lead to girls' empowerment and an ultimate worldwide respect for the girl child (WGG—UN Commission on Status of Women 2014, p. 1).

In too many parts of the world, girls experience "apartheid of gender". Beginning from birth, their fundamental rights are denied and violated. The low value placed on girls- subjects them to exclusion, exploitation, and violence. Lack of access to education and adequate health care, sexual abuse, female genital cutting, trafficking, and too early child bearing are some obstacles that impede their full development and deprive millions of girls of the opportunity to play a productive and equal role in their societies. Today, the scourge of HIV/AIDS disproportionately affects girls in many parts of the world with increasingly destructive effects on their societies (Rehabilitation International 2014). In situations of armed conflict girls are frequent and deliberate targets of systematic rape, abduction, and murder. Even in some refugee camps and public health emergency shelters where they have sought protection, girls are too often exploited (WGG—Girls Fact Sheet 2014a, b).

Girls continue to be locked out of school and locked into inequality. The cultural and societal obstacles that girls face are huge. Barriers to quality education include poverty, poor quality education, child labor, child trafficking, HIV/AIDS, remote geographic location, inadequate infrastructure, discrimination, mother's lack of education, civil conflict, natural disasters, and violence (WGG—Education 2014).

Children with Differing Abilities

Anthony Lake, Executive director of UNICEF notes that for far too many children with disabilities, the opportunity to contribute as equal participants in society and enriching the life of the communities does not exist. Far too often, children with disabilities are among the last in line for resources and services especially where these are scarce to begin with. Far too regularly children with disabilities are objects simply of pity or worse, discrimination and abuse (UNICEF 2013, p. iii). Evidence shows that there is a highest incidence of disability among population stricken by poverty. The World Bank estimates that 20 % of the world's poorest people are disabled, and tend to be regarded in their own communities as the most disadvantaged and least likely to access health, adequate nutrition, and education (UNICEF—The State of the World's Children 2013).

On December 13, 2006 the Convention on the Rights of Persons with Disabilities (CRPD) was adopted at the United Nations. The CRPD makes a clear link between disability rights and human rights.

Maternal Influences

The health and nutrition of the mother before and during pregnancy affects fetal and early post-natal life and determine structure, function, and adaptive capacities of key organ systems (WPHNA 2011). A *Save-The-Children* report sets out an agenda to tackle a crisis around birth. Save the Children, UNICEF, and the Global Health Nursing & Midwife On-line Forum advocate for a properly skilled midwife or other trained health worker during delivery to save newborn lives, mother's lives and prevent stillbirths during labor. However, access to these services is deeply unequal; in 2012, 40 million women—the poorest and most marginalized—gave birth without a trained health worker present (Wright et al. 2014, p. 47).

Children whose mothers did not have adequate prenatal care also had significantly fewer well-child visits, and were significantly less likely to have adequate immunizations, even after controlling for income, health insurance coverage, bearing of a child, and access to health care among others (Kogan et al. 1998). Maternal depression affects the physical, psychological, and behavioral health and development of children at all ages. Depression occurring during pregnancy has been shown to lead to preterm labor Li et al. (2009). being small for gestational age (U.S. Department of Health and Human Services, Office of Women's Health 2009) and alters the fetus immune and stress response system (Diego et al. 2009; Mattes et al. 2009); Oberlander et al. 2008). A meta-analysis on maternal depression and early childhood growth in developing countries also showed that the children of depressed mothers were at an increased risk of both underweight and stunting: the combined OR was approximately 1.4 (Surkan et al. 2011).

The systematic analysis of the effect of educational attainment of mothers on child mortality by Gakidou et al. (2010) showed that of the 8.2 million fewer deaths in children younger than 5 years between 1970 and 2009, 4.2 million (51.2 %) could be attributed to increased educational attainment in women of reproductive age. This contribution of maternal education is far greater than increasing income. Even a few years of schooling is advantageous for child survival. Analyses of states that achieved high life-expectancies despite low-income levels revealed a common characteristic: sustained political commitment to equitable access to primary schooling and health care for both genders (Cleland 2010).

Moving Forward

Beyond 2015: A Global Development Agenda

As this chapter notes, MDGs have been a catalyst for more children realizing their rights. However, qualitative and quantitative reports expose that much needs to be done beyond the MDG closing date of 2015. "The outcome document of the 2010 High-level Plenary Meeting of the General Assembly on the MDGs requested the Secretary-General to initiate thinking on a post-2015 development agenda and include recommendations in his annual report on efforts to accelerate MDG progress. The outcome of the Rio+20 Conference on Sustainable Development initiated an inclusive intergovernmental process to prepare a set of sustainable development goals (SDGs). There is broad agreement on the need for close linkages between the two processes to arrive at one global development agenda for the post-2015 period, with sustainable development at its center" (MDGs: Post 2015, 2014).

Establish a Culture of Quality

Quality is a key organizational dimension in a culture of collaboration, continuous improvement, accountability, analytics, transparency, systems of care, and workforce development. Enablers of quality include categories such as technology, education of those who interact with children, finance, dimensions that contribute to child's health and the quest to always improve performance (Berwick 2001) (Chart 9.3).

Based on concepts developed at the Institute of Healthcare Improvement, the priority areas for improvement of quality are actually considered as primary drivers of quality. These drivers include population health metrics and information technology, evidenced—based practices, research and evaluation, systems thinking, sustainability and stewardship, policy and workforce training and education. The six priority areas reflect the complex interactive nature of the public health system as lack of quality in one area can potentially negatively impact quality in another. They function interactively as system-level drivers that have an impact across the entire public health system, and synergistically integrate strategies to advance improvements in quality and population health outcomes. The aim of accomplishing these priorities seeks to influence public health agendas and outcomes, globally. The aims are multidimensional as they include population centered, equitable, effective, efficient, proactive, health promoting, risk reducing, vigilant, and transparent programing (Institute for Healthcare Improvement 2014).

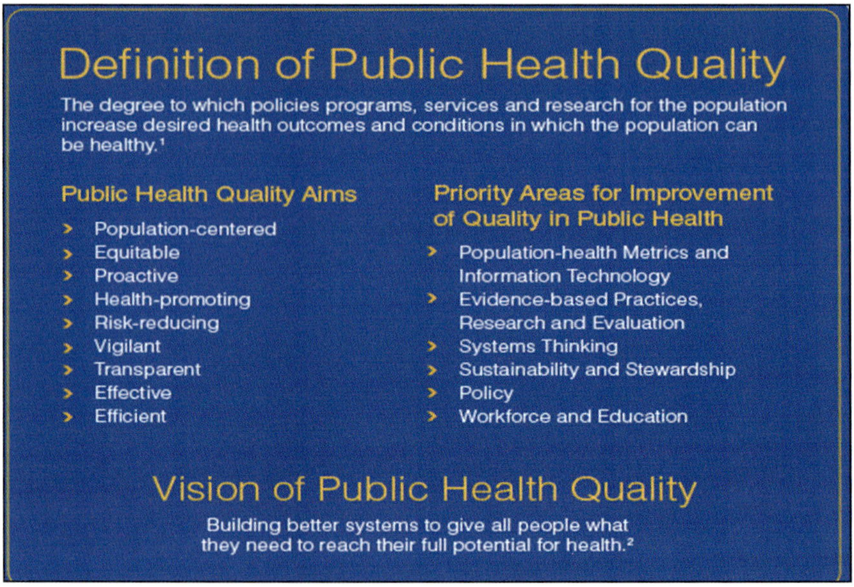

Chart 9.3 Definition of public health quality

Health Information Technology—Enabling Quality Solutions

Population Health Metrics and Information Technology

This section looks at how information technology (IT) reduces or deepens inequalities. IT may improve methods and analytical capacity to collect, evaluate, and disseminate data that can be translated into actionable information and outcomes in population health the local, state, and national level. IT facilitates the improvement of data collection for population subgroups which represents a core value of public health. The informed use of health care quality data can serve as a catalyst to bridge population-based public health programs as a strategy to improve population health, eliminate health inequities, and bridge gaps between health care, public health and the social determinants of health (PAHO) (http://www.paho.org).

Analytic support as represented in Fig. 9.3 will be the bridge that supports the collection and interpretation of measured data and indicators that represent opportunities for improvement.

Data analytics supports the use of data derived from emerging information and communications technologies (ICT). ICT may defy the financial, geographical, and logistical barriers that exist in creating a context for ongoing interaction, easy access to information, and collaborative learning. A variety of ICT support the development and maintenance of relationships that overcome geographical

Fig. 9.3 Analytic support

distance and time constraints, increase transparency, and enable better community outreach and participation (Bacigalupe 2014). See this link for resources and strategies to achieving meaningful use maximizing use of health care IT: http://www.healthit.gov/providers-professionals/resource-center.

A successful IT solution is available on a 24 h a day basis, 7 days a week and this solution is built on the following global considerations yet implemented with resources and support available at the local level:

1. Recruitment, education, and retention of clinicians in a "rural/limited resource" setting,
2. Development of education content, technologies, and tools that work in "limited resource" settings,
3. Adoption of health IT that not only drives operational workflow, but also enables clinicians to have access to external resources for additional information and education, and external consultation/telemedicine (Dockter 2014, p. 1).

One Voice: Working Together—Achieving MDG No. 8

The goal for all stakeholders is to speak with a unified voice so as to champion policies and systems that advance a child's human rights. Cultivation of global partnerships for development satisfies MDG No. 8 while enabling the achievement of all other MDGs. The answers may be lacking as to the optimal balance of allocation of resources to address the multiple determinants of health over a child's life course. However through collaboration, overall outcomes will be maximized while inequities at the population level will be minimized (CDC 2013). As commonalities within organizational missions are identified, stakeholders will more effectively develop partnerships while influencing policy and systems that impact the outcomes for child health, nutrition and education.

Potential partners are stakeholders from a number of venues: global, regional and country wide government agencies, healthcare providers, non-governmental community organizations, business leaders, policymakers, and the public. In seeking to achieve large-scale, systemic changes, several initiatives have recognized the important role of key individuals—leaders, champions, catalysts, and policy entrepreneurs—in the development of beneficial policy changes. Level of change does not necessarily correspond to levels of formal power, visibility, ambition, or technical knowledge; transformation requires diverse attributes of all individuals who may substantially contribute to policy advances that improve the lives of all children.

Recommendations

Eradication of extreme poverty supported by sustainable development presents complex challenges. This chapter reports on the extraordinarily difficult lives faced by children and support the following vital recommendations:

- Assure that a child's rights to health, comprehensive access to fortified diets, safe water and food are placed as a priority in developing innovative, transformational public health solutions, processes and outcome measures for children
  - Identify clear lines of responsibility, accountability and leadership when administering these public health programs
  - Establish that improvement of social determinants of health are a priority on national agendas
  - Support the implementation of the Social Protection Floor Initiative (United Nations 2011)
- Assure that early childhood development promotes an equitable start to a healthy life and is an essential foundation to achieve learning for all
- Establish that educational priorities must include primary and secondary programs to promote literacy.
- Assure that all women have access to properly trained health care attendants at birth
- Establish vitamin A fortification and administration programs

Next Steps—Where There Is a Will, There Is a Way

"Political will is attitude. It is what a group of people wants and cares about. Political will is the energy that fuels movement and change. For political will to be harnessed, there has to be clarity of purpose and fundamental agreement among the general populace that they are willing to change. There can be no shilly-shallying. That is where the child health dilemma is stuck. Political will around children's issues have never galvanized" (Palfrey 2006, p. 209).

As the Millennium Development Goals come to conclusion, there is much to be done as child advocates assure a child's right to health, education and nutritious, safe food and clean water. As we prepare for sustainable development beyond 2015 and eradication of poverty, we are challenged to work across interprofessional boundaries to build new, effective, efficient partnerships to reduce the morbidity and mortality of children. Human rights principles should be a basis for addressing inequities in child health to succeed in developing children who are fit, fed and ready to learn (Stahlhofer 2013, p. 1).

Global citizenship is generating energy for change. All stakeholders coming together for children will be a formidable force for innovation and transformation. The *World We Want* is a platform created by the United Nations and civil society to amplify people's voices in the process of building a global agenda for sustainable development. Please refer to http://www.worldwewant2015.org for additional information and to express your priorities for sustainable development activities.

The MDGs are drawing to conclusion with major gaps waiting to be filled. As the post 2015 agenda integrates three core dimensions of sustainable development—the social, the economic and the environmental—the central message must be that *sustainable development starts with safe, healthy, and well-educated children* (Millennium Development Goals—Post 2015, 2014, p. 1; UNICEF—Every Child Counts 2014; UNICEF—Post 2015; Agenda 2014). Time is running out on achieving sustainable development and eradication of poverty if we are going to make a difference before the 8 billionth baby is born.

References

Bacigalupe, G. (2014, March 31). Improving equity through health information technology in the US and internationally [discussion group comment]. http://www.ghdonline.org/health-it-equity/discussion/improving-equity-through-health-it-in-the-us-and-i/.

Berwick, D. (2001). *Institute of medicine report: Crossing the quality chasm: A new health system for the 21st century [policy brief]*. Institute of Medicine. http://www.IOM.org.

Blaya, J. (2014, March 26). Improving equity through health IT in the US and internationally [GHD-online Improving health care delivery through global collaboration comment]. Retrieved from ghdonline@globalhealthdelivery.org.

Catlin, B., Jovaag, A., Remington, P., & Williams Van Dijk, J. (2014). *County health rankings: Key findings*. http://www.countyhealthrankings.org.

Center for Disease Control and Prevention (2013). *The public health approach to violence prevention*. http://nij.gov/journals/273/Pages/violence-prevention.aspx.

Cleland, J. (2010). The benefits of educating women. *The Lancet, 376*(9745), 933–934.

Community Based Monitoring System. (2014). *Partnership for economic policy*. http://www.pep-net.org/about-cbms.

Consultative Group on Early Childhood Care and Development Taskforce for the Post-2015 Development Agenda (2012). *Key to equality: Early childhood development*. Retrieved April 3, 2014, from http://www.worldwewant2015.org/node/291323.

Convention on the Rights of the Child. (1990). http://www.ohchr.org/EN/professionalinterest/pages/crc.aspx.

Declaration of the Rights of the Child (1959). http://www.declarationontherightsofthechild.

Diego, M. A., Field, T., Hernandez-Reif, M., Schanberg, S., Kuhn, C., & Gonzalez-Quintero, V. H. (2009). Prenatal depression restricts fetal growth. *Early Human Development, 85*, 65–70. doi:10.1016/j.earlhumdev.2008.07.002.

Dockter, I. (2014, April 4). Improving equity through health IT in the US and internationally [health-it-equity@ghdonline.org comment]. https://www.ghdonline.org/health-it-equity/discussion/improving-equity-through-health-it-in-the-us-and-i/#reply-11965.

Dreher, M., & Skemp, L. (2011). *In healthy places, healthy people: A handbook for culturally informed community nursing practice* (2nd ed.). Indianapolis, IN: Sigma Theta Tau International.

Edejer, T. T. (2005). Cost effectiveness analysis of strategies for child health in developing countries. *British Medical Journal, 331*, 1177–1182. doi:10.1136/bmj.38652.550278.7C.

Engle, P., Fernald, L., Alderman, H., Behrman, J., Ogara, C., Yousafzai, A., … The Global Child Development Steering Group. (2011). The Global Development Steering group, strategies for reducing inequalities and improving developmental outcomes for young children in low-income and middle-income countries. *The Lancet, 378*(9799), 1339–1353. doi:10.1016/S0140-6736(11)60889-1.

Every Child Counts: The State of the World's Children 2014 in Numbers. (2014). P.4. http://www.unicef.org/sowc2014/numbers.

Gakidou, E., Cowling, K., Lozano, R., & Murray, C. (2010). Increased educational attainment and its effect on child mortality in 175 countries between 1970 and 2009: A systematic analysis. *Lancet, 376*, 959–974.

Global Investment Framework for Women's and Children's Health Study Group. (2013, November 19). Advancing social and economic development by investing in women's and children's health: A new global investment framework. *The Lancet, 1*. http://dx.doi.org/10.1016/S0140-6736(13)62231-x.

Heckman, J. J., Moon, S. H., Pinto, R., Savelyev, P. A., & Yavitz, A. (2010). The rate of return to the High Scope Perry Preschool Program. *Journal of Public Economics, 94*(1), 114–128.

Institute for Healthcare Improvement. (2014). http://www.ihi.org/Topics/QualityCostValue/Pages/Overview.aspx.

IOM. (2013a). *U.S. health in international perspective: Shorter lives, poorer health*. http://www.iom.edu/intlmortalityrates.

IOM. (2013b). *World migration report 2013—Migrant well-being and development*. Geneva 19, Switzerland. Retrieved June 23, 2014, from http://www.iom.int/cms/wmr2013.

Kindig, D. A. (2014). Retrieved June 25, 2013, from http://rwjscholars.pophealth.wisc.edu/bios/dkindig.htm.

Kogan, M., Alexander, G., Jack, B., & Allen, M. (1998). The association between adequacy of prenatal care utilization and subsequent pediatric care utilization in the United States. *Pediatrics, 102*, 25–30. doi:10.1016/j.jpubeco.2009.11.001.

Kraft, A. D., Nguyen, K. H., Jimenez-Soto, E., & Hodge, A. (2013). Stagnant neonatal mortality and persistent health inequality in middle-income countries: A case study of the Philippines. *PLoS ONE, 8*(1), e53696. doi:10.1371/journal.pone.0053696. Epub 2013 Jan 7.

Li, D., Liu, L., & Odouli, R. (2009). Presence of depressive symptoms during early pregnancy and the risk of preterm delivery: A prospective cohort study. *Human Reproduction, 24*(1), 146–153. doi:10.1093/humrep/den342.

Liebert, N. (2011). *No social justice without social protection—What can international development do to make the social protection floor initiative work? [Issue brief]*. New York, NY: Friedrich - Ebert - Stiftung.

Madrid, B. (2009). *Building support for the primary prevention of child maltreatment*. http://www.who.int/…/violence/5th_milestones_meeting/bernadette_madrid.pptx.

Madrid, B. (2014). Environmental influences. In X. Navarro, A. Bauzon, J. Aquilar, & O. Malanyaon (Eds.), *Fundamentals of pediatrics: competency-based*. Quezon City, Philippines: C&E Publishing Inc.

Marmot, M., Filho, A., Vega, J., Solar, O., & Fortune, K. (2013). Action on social determinants of health in the Americas [Letter to the editor]. *Pan American Journal of Public Health, 34*(6), 379.

Maternal and Child Under Nutrition: An Urgent Opportunity [series]. (2008, January 18). *The Lancet, 371*(9608), 179. http://dx.doi.org/10.1016/S0140-6736(07)61869-8.

Mattes, E., McCarthy, S., Gong, G., van Eekelen, J. A., Dunstan, J., & Foster, J. (2009). Maternal mood scores in mid-pregnancy are related to aspects of neonatal immune function. *Brain, Behavior, and Immunity, 23*, 380–388. doi:10.1016/j.bbi.2008.12.004.

MDG Sub-national Report—Philippines 2014. (2014). http://www.ph.undp.org/content/philippines/en/home/presscenter/pressreleases/2014/03/24/mdgs-subnational-reports-launched/.

MICS. (2014). Retrieved June 25, 2013, from http://www.childinfo.org/mics.html.

Millennium Development Goals and Post 2015 Development Agenda [report]. (2014). http://www.un.org/en/ecosoc/about/mdg.shtml.

Oberlander, T. F., Weinberg, J., Papsdorf, M., Grunau, R., Misri, S., & Devlin, A. M. (2008). Prenatal exposure to maternal depression, neonatal methylation of human glucocorticoid receptor gene (NR3C1) and infant cortisol stress responses. *Epigenetics, 3*, 97–106.

Palfrey, J. (2006). Professional advocacy. In *Child health in America: Making a difference through advocacy* (ed.) (pp. 186–187). Baltimore, Maryland: The Johns Hopkins University Press.

Philippine Food and Nutrition Research Institute Report. (2011). http://www.fnri.dost.gov.ph/images/stories/Fnri%20Files/Annual_Report_2011/annual%20report%202011%20hq%20final.pdf.

Rehabilitation International. (2014). *Advancing the rights and inclusion of persons with disabilities worldwide—Convention on the rights of persons with disabilities*. http://www.riglobal.org/resource-center/convention-on-the-rights-of-persons-with-disabilities/what-is-the-the-crpd/.

Save the Children. (2012). *A life free from hunger* [report]. Retrieved from Save the Children: http://www.savethechildren.org/atf/cf/%7B9def2ebe-10ae-432c-9bd0-df91d2eba74a%7D/A%20LIFE%20FREE%20FROM%20HUNGER%20-%20TACKLING%20CHILD%20MALNUTRITION.PDF.

Stahlhofer, M. (2013). The right to health and the CRC—linkage between health and human right. *World Health Organization*. http://www.who.int/mediacentre/multimedia/podcasts/2009/child_rights_20091120/en/.

Starfield, B., & Shi, L. (2004). The medical home, access to care, and insurance: A review of evidence. *Pediatrics, 113*(5), 1493–1498.

Surkan, P., Kennedy, C., Hurley, K., & Black, M., (2011). Maternal depression and early childhood growth in developing countries: systematic review and meta-analysis. *World Health Organization Bulletin*. Retrieved May 26, 2011, from http://www.ncbi.nlm.nih.gov/pmc/articles/PMC3150769/. doi:10.2471/BLT.11.088187.

The State of the World's Children, Executive Summary, Children with Disabilities. (2013). http://www.unicef.org/sowc2013.

UNESCO. (2000a). *Dakar framework for action—Education for all: meeting our collective commitment* [report]. Retrieved June 24, 2012, from http://www.unesco.org/education/efa/wef_2000/.

UNESCO. (2000b). *Education Report*. http://www.unesco.org/education/efa/wef_2000.

UNICEF. (2007). *Vitamin a supplementation-A decade of progress*. New York. Retrieved June 23, 2013, from http://www.unicef.org/publications/index_39363.html.

UNICEF. (2011a). *Boys and girls in the life cycle—Sex disaggregated data on the selection of well-being indicators, from early childhood to young adulthood*. UNICEF: Division of Policy and Practice.

UNICEF. (2011b). *The state of the world's children, 2011 executive summary, Adolescence—The age of opportunity*. NY: UNICEF. Retrieved June 23, 2012, from http://www.unicef.org/publications/index_57468.html.

UNICEF. (2012). *The state of the world's children—children in an urban world—2012*. Retrieved June 24, 2013, from http://www.unicef.org/sowc2012.

UNICEF. (2013). *The state of the world's children—children with disabilities—2013*. Retrieved June 24, 2013, from http://www.unicef.org/sowc201.

UNICEF. (2015). *Post 2015 Agenda*. http://www.unicef.org/2015

United Nations. (2011). *The global social crisis-report on the world social situation*. United Nations, New York: United Nations Publications.

United Nations—Commission on Status of Women: Girls Section. (2014). Girls statement on the status of girls and MDGs for the 58th UN Commission on the status of women. http://www.girlsrights.org.

Child Protection Unit: Global Campaign for Violence Prevention. (n.d.). http://www.childprotection.org.ph/.

United Nations. (2013). *Levels and trends in child mortality—Report 2013*. Report from World Bank, World Health Organization, UN Department of Economic and Social Affairs, UN Children's Fund. http://reliefweb.int/report/world/levels-trends-child-mortality-report-2013.

United Nations Human Rights. (n.d.). Retrieved June 26, 2013, from http://www.un.org/en/rights/.

United Nations. (2014). *World we want initiative*. http://www.worldwewant2015.org.

U.S. Department of Health and Human Services, Office of Women's Health. (2009). *Depression during and after pregnancy fact sheet*. Retrieved February 13, 2013, from http://www.womenshealth.gov/publications/our-publications/fact-sheet/depression-pregnancy.html.

Waterston, T., & Goldhagen, J. (2007). Why children's rights are central to international child health. *Archive of Disease of Childhood, 92*(2), 176–180. doi:10.1136/adc.2006.098228.

WHO. (2002). http://www.wpro.who.int.

WHO. (2009). *Integrating poverty and gender into health programs: module on water, sanitation and food* [source book for health professionals]. Geneva, Switzerland: WHO Press.

Working Group on Girls, Girls: Fact sheet. (2014a). Retrieve June 24, 2014, from http://www.grilsrights.org.

Working Group on Girls, Education Fact Sheet. (2014b). Retrieve June 24, 2014, from http://www.grilsrights.org.

World Public Health Nutrition Association. (2011). The time to prevent disease begins before conception, *DOHaD Position Paper*. http://www.wphna.org/htdocs/2011_apr_wn4_un_summit.htm.

World Vision (2013). *The killer gap: A global index of health inequality for children*. Retrieved April 3, 2014, from http://www.worldvision.ca/ABOUTUS/Media-Centre/Documents/KillerGapreport.pdf.

Wright, S., Mathieson, K., Brearley, L., Jacobs, S., Holly, L., & Wickremasinghe, R., (2014). *Ending newborn deaths—A save the children report.* http://www.savethechildren.org.uk/sites/default/files/images/Ending_Newborn_Deaths2.pdf.

Chapter 10
Adoption: Right to Information Versus Right to Confidentiality

Jagannath Pati

Introduction: Children's Identity

Many people think of the issues that take place before and during an adoption, but fail to recognize that it is important to anticipate and understand the issues that may arise after you have brought a child into your family. Adoption is an emotional experience. It is also a physical, biological, and psychological experience. Existing literature reveals that adoptees may begin experiencing the desire to seek information during adolescence but most do not begin an active search until adulthood.

A person's right to know her biological or genetic origins raises some of the hardest legal and ethical issues that we have had to face in the last decade or so. This question arises not only in the case of adopted children, but also in cases of abandoned or displaced children those conceived by artificial insemination or born out of wedlock. It opens up, in the words of [leading international human rights lawyer] Geraldine van Beuren, "a whole Pandora's Box—the principle of the best interests of the child and her right to know very often conflicts with other competing rights such as the mother's right to privacy and autonomy and the rights of the adoptive parents." (http://www.thehindu.com/opinion/op-ed/a-difficult-road-to-her-roots/article4562334.ece).

Identity is one of the seven lifelong core issues in adoption. Connecting with cultural roots is crucial for a child's identity development.

J. Pati (✉)
Central Adoption Resource Authority, Ministry of Women and Child Development, Goverment of India, New Delhi, India
e-mail: jpati.in@gmail.com

S. Deb (ed.), *Child Safety, Welfare and Well-being*,
DOI 10.1007/978-81-322-2425-9_10

Adoption is a social, emotional, and legal process through which children not being raised by their birth parents become full, permanent, and legal members of another family. As such, adoption involves the rights of three distinct “triad members”: the birth parents, the child, and the adoptive parents. Adoption is also a lifelong process. Ethical issues change over time as children who were adopted become adults and may choose to claim their right to know their genetic and historical identity. It is imperative that professionals working within adoption act ethically to ensure the rights of all the involved parties at all points in the process. In this section, find resources to help guide the professional’s ethical practice in all phases of adoption (https://www.childwelfare.gov/adoption/adopt_ethics).

Adoption carries developmental opportunities and risks. Many adoptees have remarkably good outcomes, but some subgroups have difficulties. Generally, infant, international, and trans-racial adoptions may complicate adoptees’ identity formation. Those placed after infancy may have developmental delays, attachment disturbances, and post-traumatic stress disorder. Useful interventions include preventive counseling to foster attachment, post-adoption supports, focused groups for parents and adoptees, and psychotherapy (Nickman et al. 2005).

One of the most difficult, but normative, tasks faced by adoptive parents is talking with their child about adoption (Brodzinsky et al. 1992). Parental anxiety is usually tied to their uncertainty about how the child will react to this information and whether parent–child ties will be weakened. In addition, enquiring about the child’s adoption story will offer the clinician an opportunity to reinforce the thought of the adoptive parents to realize that their child is having a “whole life” that began, with a biological mother and father, as all lives do (Lifton 1994; Nickman 1985).

Every human being cares about his/her family roots in order to acquire a personal identity as a sound basis for an optimal development. The desire to know about one’s roots generally sets in during adolescence, or sometimes, even later. Adoption brings a radical change to the life of a child. It is therefore justified only in the cases where it serves the best interest of the child and provides him with genuine shelter. Adoption in a foreign country should only be an option when and if there is no viable alternative in the child’s country of origin (http://www.ssiss.ch/en).

Positive identity development during adolescence, in general, is a complex process and may pose additional challenges for adolescents adopted from a different culture. Adoptive identity mediated the influence of racial socialization on psychological well-being, and ethnic affirmation mediated the influence of ethnic socialization on adoptees’ well-being. It is important to provide supportive counseling services for adoptees who are exploring their adoptive identity (Mohanty 2013).

The right to know one’s origins is guaranteed both by International Convention on the Rights of the Child and by the Hague Convention. The Hague Convention in particular, states that Countries of Origin of the children must guarantee access to their adoption files and therefore should keep all the relevant information concerning them. Hague Convention also lays down that the competent authorities shall ensure access for children to the relevant information with appropriate counsel. Whatever their origin (institution, foster family) or their age upon arrival might be, all adoptees need to build their own adoptive identity, understand what it means to be adopted and the circumstances which caused their adoption to happen. All needs encountered by adoptees in relation to their adoption status will require answers from their adoptive parents. On the other hand, adoptive parents frequently need help in order to understand their children's behavior concerning adoption, as well as certain guidelines as to what would be the best way to address it.

Krueger et al. (1997) explain that adopted persons naturally engage in an existential quest for truth about their heritage, which can remain as a psychological longing or result in an active search. If adopted persons were not motivated to search, the adoption process would be simplified without loss and yearning for biological roots (Freundlich 2000). To explain this need, Krueger et al. (1997) describe it as "a quest for authenticity, meaningfulness, and a sense of being, freedom, and belonging." For an existential perspective, the quest for one's worth, parents and origins is part of the quest for authenticity, meaningfulness, being, and freedom. Most researching adoptees are women, and they generally seek their mothers (Moran 1994). Adoptive men, in contrast, tend to seek their birth fathers (Pacheco and Eme 1993).

Children need some knowledge of their heritage to foster self-esteem later on in life. Long-term studies have shown that children whose heritage was celebrated in their adoptive families by and large grew up to be healthy, self-respecting adults (afabc website).

There have been a lot of debates on the adoptive child's search for his "Identity" and "Roots"—with its social, emotional, and legal implications in national and international forums. In the Indian socio-cultural context, this issue takes on a unique dimension. The right of the adoptee to search for his/her roots and identity is diametrically opposite to the birth mother's right to secrecy and confidentiality of her identity. The "search" has serious repercussions on the emotional well-being of all the three integral corners of the adoption triad, i.e. the adoptee, the birth parent, and the adoptive parents.

The concept of "children's identity" tends to focus on the child's immediate family, but it is increasingly recognized that children have a remarkable capacity to embrace multiple relationships, speak several languages fluently and enjoy a complex, multicultural world. From the secure foundation of an established family environment, children can enjoy complex and subtle relationships with other adults and with a range of cultures, to a much larger degree than may be recognized. Thus, the children's best interests and sense of identity may be sustained without having to deny the knowledge of their origins, for example, after reception into State care, through "secret" adoptions or anonymous egg/sperm donations and so forth (Rachel and Peter 2002).

Name, nationality, and family are only some elements of identity. Other aspects of identity include:

- The child's personal history since birth—where he or she lived, who looked after him or her, why crucial decisions were taken, etc?
- The child's race, culture, religion, and language. An "unlawful" interference in this aspect of identity could include:
  - The suppression of minority languages in the education system, state information, and the media;
  - State persecution or proscription of the practice of a religion;
  - Failure to give adopted, fostered or institutionally placed children the opportunity to enjoy their ethnic, cultural, linguistic, or religious heritage.

A person's right to know one's biological parents is well-entrenched in law, in most of the civilized countries around the world. Typically, the visiting adoptees look for information on their life prior to adoption to fill the void experienced in their lives. If handled well, to their satisfaction, it can lead to closure of this sensitive issue and they can move on with their lives. However, this must be done, keeping in mind the birth parent's right to confidentiality as this is the commitment given to them at the time of relinquishment of their child, especially in the case of unwed mothers who desire anonymity because of the strong stigma attached to unwed parenthood. This is a very sensitive issue to be handled, keeping in mind the social taboos in the country of origin. Professional social workers of the adoption agency are equipped with techniques to handle such situations and not the activists having international connections generating funds for the purpose.

International adoptions present unique challenges in securing accurate and truthful background information and history on individual children. Differences in culture, language, terminology, and the competence of medical resources, all profoundly affect this process. The access to information and the quality and reliability of information varies widely from country to country. In countries where programs are well-established and sophisticated, child information can be very complete and available. This information is routinely updated by orphanages, institutions or hospitals that are all under the authority of appointed government ministries. The range of cooperation on the part of these authorities, however, is often irregular and inconsistent (http://www.holtintl.org/ethics.shtml).

It has been observed that rarely a biological mother goes back to the adoption agency to reclaim her surrendered child within the stipulated period. While searching for his/her birth parent, a child is sure to experience many difficult emotions. Fear, guilt, anger, anxiety, exhilaration—all may play a part. It has also been noticed that in most cases, foreign adoptive parents do help their adopted children gather more information about their biological parent and their country of origin. The right of the adoptee to search for his or her roots and identity is diametrically opposite to the birth mother's right to secrecy and confidentiality of her identity. The "search" has serious repercussions on the emotional well-being of all the three integral corners of the adoption triad, i.e. the adoptee, the birth parent, and the adoptive parents.

The child's best welfare and interest should be of paramount consideration in all questions relating to his/her adoption. Searching for birth family relatives is a sensitive and emotional process. The intent to search may be allowed only upon the personal request made by the adult adoptee or adopter. Minors who are interested to search for their biological parent may be represented by their adoptive parents. The request must be made in writing to the particular foreign adoption agency, which processed their case, in association with the local adoption agency. The adoptive parents should respect the adopted child's right to enjoy the reciprocal rights and obligations arising from the relationship of parents and child.

The adoptee's rights and those of his/her biological parents, on the one hand, as well as those of his/her adoptive parents on the other, can sometimes lead to conflict. It then becomes a matter of seeking solutions that respect the needs and rights of all concerned parties and with those of the child as a priority. Searching of roots may be treated as a natural emotional response. The contact between the child placed in adoption and its biological mother is a distant reality in India, as the biological mother hardly resides in the place/address given in the surrender deed due to social stigma. Getting to know more about the social background of the biological mother may be quite meaningful in the sense that it may yield positive results in terms of improved self-concept, self-esteem, and ability to relate to others. Thus the professional social worker can play a meaningful role through counseling and helping older adoptees in their search missions.

For some, the interest in searching is a matter of intense curiosity. They seek a sense of connection to someone of similar genetic makeup. They want to know if their birth relatives look like they do, speak as they do, or demonstrate similar gestures or body language. They want to know if they share similar characteristics, such as a dry sense of humor, athletic or musical abilities, or an outgoing personality. For others, searching is important for their emotional development. Some adoptees have a desire to know and understand why their birthparents made an adoption plan for them. They want to know if their birth parents ever regretted their decision or missed them. Birthparents, on the other hand, wish to tell their birth children the reasons and circumstances for giving them up for adoption. Birthparents also wonder if the adoptive parents treated their child well, and if the child has been happy.

The adoptee has the basic rights and needs to search for his/her origin and identity, hence, he/she should not be denied the opportunity to search and to know his/her roots. All agencies and authorities involved in the process should ensure the observance of confidentiality in matters related to the adoption. While non-identifying information e.g., medical records, circumstances which lead to the adoption of the child (but not necessarily divulging the identity of concerned individual etc) may be made available to both adoptive parents/s and birth parents and the adoptee under 18 years old, identifying information e.g., names, address, personal background etc. can be shared only between and among the adult adoptee, adoptive parents and his/her birth parents and only of they give their written consent (Rachel and Peter 2002).

There is no research about the number of adoptees searching for their birth parents. While searching for the birth parent, a child is sure to experience many difficult emotions. Counseling in this area helps the adoptee to cope with his adoptive status. While some adoptees that are quite comfortable with this knowledge, there are some who feel a sense of being "incomplete", like the oft-quoted "missing link" or the "missing piece of the jigsaw" situation. The issue that often lurks in the mind of the adopted child is, "Why was I given up? Did my parents not love me and want me?" Counseling the adopted child and the adoptive parents with this issue helps to resolve many unarticulated problems. The whole question of "who is a parent?" is reflected upon and children feel comfortable with the fact that parenting is far more than the biological process of birth.

Experience has shown that there is no co-relation between children who have a need to "search" for their biological "Roots" and their level of adjustment or security in their adoptive homes. Therefore, the belief that children who are happy and well-adjusted do not have a need to search and vice versa is not necessarily true. The psychological need to know one's roots or identity is found to be the most important reason as to why adoptees want to know about their biological parents.

Guiding Principles/Policies

Laxmi Kant Pandey versus Union of India case of 1982

The Honorable Supreme Court of India has given the direction that it may not be desirable to give information to the child about its biological parents whilst the child is young as this might have the effect of encouraging his/her curiosity to meet its biological parents. But if after attaining the age of maturity, the child wants to know about his/her biological parents, it should not raise any serious objection. The child is not likely to be easily affected by such information at this stage and in such a case, the foreign adoptive parents may in exercise of their discretion, furnish such information to the child if they so think fit.

Guidelines Governing the Adoption of Children (2011)

Adoption guidelines formulated by CARA and notified by the Government of India also affirm that confidentiality is required to be maintained regarding the child's origin. If the right of a biological unwed mother, her confidentiality, is not maintained, most would prefer to abandon their child. This would mean putting the life of the infant in jeopardy, rather than legally relinquishing and ensuring its rehabilitation. In most cases, the biological mother moves on with her life and starts life afresh, after relinquishing her child. It would cause an upheaval in her already settled life, if such information is divulged. Thus, her fundamental right to life and privacy needs to be protected.

Para 52 of the Guidelines Governing the Adoption of Children (2011)

(1) The right of the child to obtain information about his or her origin derives from the right to know his or her biological parents as provided for in Article 7(1) of the UN Convention on the Rights of the Child.
(2) The adoption agencies shall, therefore, facilitate root search by the adopted child, if the child desires to know his or her history but in doing so, the age and maturity of the child shall be taken into consideration.
(3) The child's rights must also be balanced against the right of birth parents not to have their identity disclosed to the child.
(4) The right of adopted child should not infringe on the biological parents' right to privacy.
(5) If the biological parent(s) have at the time of surrendering the child expressed their willingness, in writing, to be contacted by the child when he or she grows up, then all relevant information including identity and address of the parents shall be disclosed to the child, but if the biological parent(s) have specifically requested anonymity, then only reasons and circumstances under which the surrender was effected can be disclosed.
(6) There may be situations where the biological parent(s) leave some articles etc. with the child during surrender process and such articles must be, to the extent possible, preserved by the adoption agency, to be handed over to the child when he or she comes for root search.
(7) A root search by a third party shall not be permitted and the concerned agencies or authorities shall not make public any information relating to biological parent(s), adoptive parents or adopted child.

As per Para 86(n) of the CARA Guidelines, the adoption agency shall facilitate root search by the adoptive child, if the child desires to know his or her history; especially information relating to his or her biological mother, father, and siblings. However, in doing so, the age and maturity of the child would be considered. In case of unwed mother or other parents not willing to be contacted, Specialized Adoption Agency (Recognized Indian Placement Agency) shall not pass on the information regarding the biological mother to the child or the adoptive parents.

United Nations Convention on Rights of the Child (UNCRC 1989)

Relevant Articles:

Article 2: All rights to be recognized for each child in jurisdiction without discrimination on any ground.
Article 3(1): Best interests of the child to be of primary consideration in all actions concerning children.

Article 7: Birth registration, right to name and nationality and to know and be cared for by parents
Article 8: This article of the Convention on the Rights of the Child concerns the children's rights to identity and their rights to have such identity preserved or, where necessary, re-established by the State. Although article 8 only describes three aspects of identity—nationality, name, and family relations—other articles, such as article 2 (non-discrimination), article 16 (protection from arbitrary interference in privacy, family, and home) and article 30 (right to enjoy culture, religion, and language), should render unlawful most forms of interference in children's identity. Article 20 also provides that children deprived of their family environment should where possible have continuity of upbringing, particularly with regard to their ethnic, cultural, and linguistic background (Rachel and Peter 2002).
Article 12: Respect for the child's views in all matters affecting the child; opportunity to be heard in any judicial or administrative proceedings affecting the child.

Convention on Protection of Children and Cooperation in Respect of Inter-Country Adoption—1993

Article 16 (2): It shall transmit to the Central Authority of the receiving State its report on the child, proof that the necessary consents have been obtained and the reasons for its determination on the placement, taking care not to reveal the identity of the mother and the father if, in the State of origin, these identities may not be disclosed.

Article 30: (1) The competent authorities of a Contracting State shall ensure that information held by them concerning the child's origin, in particular, information concerning the identity of his or her parents, as well as the medical history, is preserved. (2) They shall ensure that the child or his or her representative has access to such information, under appropriate guidance, in so far as is permitted by the law of that State.

Article 30 of the Convention imposes on Contracting States an obligation to preserve any information they have about the child and his or her origins. There is also an obligation to ensure the child has access to that information under certain conditions. Article 30 should be read in conjunction with Article 16, because the information referred to is required for the preparation of the report on the child that the Central Authority of the State of origin is to transmit to the Receiving State. Therefore, as a practical matter, it may be beneficial for States to include the retention of records as a duty of the same office that prepares the report on the child. States may also want to clearly determine, and include within their laws, the length of time that records should be kept. The child's right must be balanced against the right of birth parents not to have their identity disclosed to the child who is relinquished for adoption. For example, in some countries, an unmarried mother who had consented to the adoption might be later harmed by the disclosure of her past. Therefore, Article 30 does sanction some restrictions to the right of the child to have information, as access is only "in so far as is permitted by the law of that State." Furthermore, States of Origin are permitted to withhold identifying information from the report on the child in accordance with Article 16(2).

While Article 30 acknowledges the right of the child to discover his or her origins under certain circumstances, it is necessary to limit the possibility of misuse of personal data, which is disclosed during the adoption process. Consequently, the Convention establishes minimum safeguards by prescribing that the information on the child and the prospective adoptive parents should only be used for the purposes for which it was gathered or transmitted. These obligations and safeguards are also given emphasis through the requirements of Article 9(a) that Central Authorities shall take all appropriate measures to "collect, preserve and exchange information about the situation of the child and the prospective adoptive parents, so far as is necessary to complete the adoption".

Article 30(1) of the Hague Convention on Inter-country Adoption stipulates that competent authorities of a Contracting State shall ensure that information held by them concerning the child's origin, in particular, information concerning the identity of his or her parents, as well as the medical history, is preserved. (2) They shall ensure that the child or his or her representative has access to such information, under appropriate guidance, in so far as is permitted by the law of that State.

REPORT AND CONCLUSIONS OF THE SECOND SPECIAL COMMISSION ON THE PRACTICAL OPERATION OF THE HAGUE CONVENTION OF 29 MAY 1993 ON PROTECTION OF CHILDREN AND CO-OPERATION IN RESPECT OF INTERCOUNTRY ADOPTION (17–23 September 2005)

Para 109: Many experts stated that personal information had to be retained in the files in order for the adopted children to have future access to the information on their origins. Currently, more and more adopted children were looking for information on their origins. In the same manner, more and more biological parents sought information on the whereabouts of their adopted children. It was said that the gathering of as much information as possible was important to guarantee the best interests of the child as adoption is a lifelong experience and every piece of information could be important for the adoptee. Countries of origin should be encouraged to collect information about birth parents, such as a photograph, or a gift to present to their children, for the future benefit of the adoptee. As more and more adoptees search for their biological families, it is important to have long-term policies and procedures for the preservation of information.

Para 110: Not all States had the same notion of confidentiality. It was agreed that a child had a right to information on his /her own background. The right of the child to obtain information about his or her origins derives from the right to know his or her parents as provided for in Article 7(1) of the UN Convention on the Rights of the Child. But the right of adopted children to information did not have to infringe the biological parents' right to privacy. Information would not be made public, but only supplied to the adopted child. Furthermore, factual information, such as age, health, and social circumstances, could be given without disclosing the names of the parents. In many countries, the disclosure of information is based on the mutual consent by the adult adopted child and the biological parents.

Para 111: However, it was stated that the child's right must be balanced against the right of birth parents not to have their identity disclosed to the child who is relinquished for adoption. For example, in some countries an unmarried mother who had consented to the adoption might be later harmed by the disclosure of her past. Therefore, Article 30 does sanction some restrictions to the right of the child to have information, as access is only "in so far as is permitted by the law of that State." Furthermore, States of Origin are permitted to withhold identifying information from the report on the child in accordance with Article 16(2).

UNICEF's Position

Adoptees should be able to access basic information on their birth parents (which, moreover, can be of great importance in regard to health issues) that does not enable the latter to be identified. This information would normally be contained in the report on the child prepared prior to the authorization of the adoption. Such access must be accompanied by appropriate counseling and guidance. The obvious implication of this is that adequate records be preserved for a long period (at least 50 years, according to the 2008 European Convention on the Adoption of Children which is yet to enter into force).

To the extent that both parties freely consent to identification and that this is deemed to be in conformity with the interests of all concerned, UNICEF encourages the establishment of procedures that will enable this to happen under appropriate conditions. UNICEF does not believe, that such initiatives can be justified by reference to CRC Article 7 (right to know one's parents), given the nature of adoption, its consequences in terms of family ties, and the fact that the child's parents are therefore those who adopted him or her (UNICEF Guidance Note on Inter-country Adoption in the CEE/CIS Region, Sept. 2009).

Understanding the Surrendering Process

It is important to understand the surrendering process of a child before the Child Welfare Committee, a competent authority for children in need of care and protection and is located at the district level in each State in the country. In India, abandoned and surrendered children are placed in adoption following due process of law. First of all, a child has to be adoptable and for such process the involvement of CWC is mandatory. A reconsideration period of 60 days is given to the surrendering mother/parents during which they can reclaim the child, if not the child can be declared legally free for adoption. As per adoption guidelines (2011), the Specialized Adoption Agency or the CWC shall ensure that a copy of the

Surrender Deed is retained by the surrendering parents or legal guardian, as the case may be, for reconsideration of their decision to surrender the child.

In case of abandoned children, there is hardly any scope to reach their roots.

Para 14. Procedure in case of Surrendered Children.

(1) A child may be surrendered in case:

(i) The child is born as a consequence of non-consensual relationship;
(ii) The child is born of an unwed mother or out of wedlock;
(iii) One of the biological parents of the child is dead and the living parent is incapacitated or unfit to take care;
(iv) The parents of the child are compelled to relinquish him or her due to physical, emotional, and social factors beyond their control.
(v) In all cases of surrendering the child, the admission procedure as laid down in sub paragraph 11 (2), (3), (4) and (5) shall be followed.

(2) In case the child is surrendered through the Specialized Adoption Agency, the procedure will be as follows:-

(i) The Specialized Adoption Agency shall produce the child to be surrendered along with the surrendering parent(s) before the Child Welfare Committee within 24 h of receiving such child, excluding the time taken for the journey.
(ii) On directions of the Child Welfare Committee, the Specialized Adoption Agency may continue to keep the child in its temporary care until his or her restoration or rehabilitation.
(iii) In case of a single mother, unwilling to appear before the Child Welfare Committee, one member of the Child Welfare Committee, preferably female, may meet the mother separately.
(iv) In case of biological parents surrendering a child, this process shall be before a two member Child Welfare Committee.
(v) In case the Committee is not sitting, the child may be produced before the single member of the Committee as per the provisions contained in subsection (2) of Section 30.

(3) The information to be submitted to the Child Welfare Committee by the Specialized Adoption Agency, among other details, shall contain the following namely:-

(a) The details of the biological mother and father, including:-

(i) the social and psychological background;
(ii) the proof of address and identity;
(iii) known medical history of both biological parents and,
(iv) details of close relatives, if available.

(b) The details of the child being surrendered, including:–

    (i) social and psychological background;
    (ii) details of sibling(s), if any;
    (iii) known medical history;
    (iv) date and place of birth along with birth certificate, if available.

(Source: Guidelines Governing the Adoption of Children-2011)

Para 15. While completing the surrender process.

(1) In case the parents or one of parents approaches a Specialized Adoption Agency for surrendering the child, the agency shall make all efforts, including counseling, to prevent surrender of such child.
(2) Efforts shall also be made by the Child Welfare Committee for exploring the possibilities of parents retaining the child by counseling of the parents and explaining the consequences of surrender.
(3) If the parents are still unwilling to retain the child, such a child shall be kept initially in the custody of the SAA.
(4) If the surrender is inevitable, a deed of surrender as provided in Schedule-II shall be executed and signed by the person or persons surrendering the child and two other witnesses in the presence of the Child Welfare Committee.
(5) If a child born out of wedlock is surrendered, both parents should sign the surrender document and in case one of them is dead, proof of death in support thereof is to be furnished.
(6) Where the death certificate is not available, a certificate from local Panchayat or Municipal authority should be produced.
(7) When a child is born to a married couple but is surrendered by one biological parent and the whereabouts of the other parent is not known, the child shall be treated as abandoned and further procedures shall be followed accordingly.
(8) In case of a child born out of wedlock, only the mother herself can surrender the child and if she is a minor, the signature of an accompanying close relative will be obtained on the surrender document.
(9) If the surrender is affected by any person other than the biological parent(s), the child shall be treated as abandoned and the same procedure shall be followed as that for an abandoned child.
(10) The Specialized Adoption Agency shall facilitate the surrender process before the Child Welfare Committee.
(11) The Specialized Adoption Agency and the Child Welfare Committee shall ensure that the surrendering parents or the legal guardian is made aware that they can reconsider the surrender and reclaim the surrendered child only within a period of 60 days from the date of such surrender.

(12) In all cases of surrender, confidentiality shall be maintained by the authorities and agencies involved in the process.
(13) The Specialized Adoption Agency or the CWC shall ensure that a copy of the Surrender Deed is retained by the surrendering parents or legal guardian, as the case may be, for reconsideration of their decision to surrender the child.
(14) The Committee shall declare the surrendered child legally free for adoption after the expiry of a reconsideration period of 60 days.

Para 16. Declaration of a child legally free for adoption by the Child Welfare Committee:

(1) If all efforts for tracing the parents of an orphan or an abandoned child placed with a Specialized Adoption Agency on a temporary basis, have failed, and, in case of surrendered children, if the reclaim period of 60 days is over, the particular agency shall approach the Child Welfare Committee for declaring the child legally free for adoption.

(Source: Guidelines Governing the Adoption of Children-2011)

Feedback from Recognized Adoption Agencies in India

1. More and more adoptees are visiting Adoption Agencies from where adopted to know about their birth background.
2. Typically, the visiting adoptees are looking for information on their life prior to adoption to fill the void experienced in their lives. If handled well to their satisfaction, it can lead to closure of this sensitive beginning of their lives. However, this must be done, keeping in mind the birth parent's right to confidentiality as this is the commitment given to them at the time of relinquishment of their child, especially in the case of unwed mothers, who desire anonymity because of the strong stigma attached to unwed parenthood.
3. The social implication of "uprooting" the birth parent's family life (which includes children born subsequently through marriage) needs to be considered seriously in the Indian context.
4. Some adoptees manifest a compelling need to know the name and address of the birth parents, or even meet them. This can only be done after taking permission of the birth family and implies contacting the birth family before disclosing any information. This should only be done by the adoption agency which was responsible for the relinquishment and subsequent adoption.
5. If the biological parents are traced, their desire to meet or not to meet their relinquished child must be respected. However, if it is possible to bring the parents and the relinquished adoptee together, it should be done discreetly and sensitively in the agency from where the adoptee was placed. This is to be

done only by a senior and experienced social worker of the concerned adoption agency that placed the child in adoption.

6. The information should be conveyed in person and not via correspondence or email. This means the adoptee should visit the particular adoption agency from where adopted.
7. As far as possible, relevant information can only be given to the adoptee if he or she is an adult, 18 years of age and above. When background information is sought by adoptees even before they are 18 years, in such cases, counseling by a professional social worker is highly recommended, keeping in view the sensitivity of such information. As far as possible, the adoptee must be accompanied by his/her adoptive parents and only non-identifying information can be given.
8. Third party searches undertaken by adoptees or foreign adoption agencies need to be discouraged.
9. It is a personal issue between the adopted child and the Indian agency, and the records maintained are confidential.

Third Party Search

Several ethical issues are involved in third party root search. CARA guidelines affirm that confidentiality is required to be maintained as regards the child's origin is concerned.

Relinquishment is valid when it is done before the CWC, an independent body and also called competent authority, in case of children in need of care and protection as per the Juvenile Justice Act. Thus, there can be no question of playing fraud with the biological mother. This is a confidential document and as per the Hon'ble Supreme Court's order in L. K. Pandey versus Union of India, confidentiality has to be maintained during the adoption process.

Older Adoptees Must Know

1. Children or adults in inter-country adoption face unique challenges in locating birth parents. Each country has its own laws governing information access. In addition, there is great variation in record-keeping practices across countries and cultures, and in many cases, searchers will find that no information was ever recorded, that records were misplaced, or cultural practices placed little emphasis on accurate record-keeping.
2. In case of an abandoned child, one has remote chance of finding one's biological mother. In case of surrender by unwed mother, there is very less chance also to be reunited with the biological mother as the unwed mother mostly gives a false address or does not stick to the address given at the time of surrender.

3. In India, we have hardly come across cases of root search in domestic adoptions. In cases of inter-country adoptions, the child-placing agency is the best beginning point for an international search. The foreign accredited agency or the central authority should be able to share the name and location of the Indian adoption agency, perhaps, the names of caregivers, attorneys, or others involved in the placement or adoption. The agency, or its counterpart abroad, may be able to provide specific information on names, dates, and places. They also may be able to offer some medical history, biographical information on parents, and circumstances regarding the adoption.
4. One must remember that one has been surrendered or abandoned by his/her biological mother for a better life, respectable in all sense. Therefore, a child is welcome to find relevant information of his/her social background but it should not lead to a tragic end. Unlike western culture, here in India, if biological mother's family comes to know that she had a child before her marriage, she might invite the wrath of her husband and in laws. Therefore, a child is strongly advised to have the help of the particular adoption agency in India while he/she got adopted. It is advised not to take the help of third person and keep away from media or press who may not put child's situation correctly.
5. There are two points of view regarding what should be done in such a situation. Particularly in India, the adoptive parents usually wish to keep the matter as secret. At present, many agencies promote the view that when the child grows up, information may be given regarding the birth mother's social background, circumstances and reasons for surrender etc. However, the identity of the mother is not revealed for protecting all t concerned in the adoption triad. Adoption agencies in India have a sealed and confidential record system. There is no access to the relinquishment document and it remains a property of the Court.
6. It has been observed that rarely a biological mother (unwed mother) turns back to an adoption agency to reclaim her surrendered child within the stipulated period. While searching for the birthparent, a child is sure to experience a plethora of difficult emotions, including fear, guilt, anger, anxiety, and exhilaration. It has also been noticed that in most of the cases, particularly foreign adoptive parents do help their adoptive children to gather more information about their biological parent and their country of origin. Older adoptees must be aware of the fact that third party search would be dangerous and it may lead to utter frustration.
7. Counseling in this area helps the adoptee to cope with his or her adoptive status. There are some adoptees who are quite comfortable with this knowledge and there are some who feel a sense of 'void'. Counseling the adopted child and the adoptive parents of this issued aims helps to resolve many unarticulated problems.

It is not easy for a mother to let her child go. She may not be well-educated but the act of relinquishing the child shows that she has respect for human life.

Conclusion

Freedom of information, including the right to access information held by public bodies, has long been recognized not only as crucial to democracy, accountability, and effective participation, but also as a fundamental human right, protected under international and constitutional law.

It is widely accepted among adoption professionals today that parental preparation, education, and support is crucial for the stability of an adoption and for the long-term emotional well-being of all family members. Every adoption is meant to be permanent and last forever, as children need permanency in order to thrive as they mature into adulthood. Most of the adopted children have benefited while there are few cases of adjustment issues. This also happens with biological family, so also in domestic adoptions. At present, many agencies promote the view that when the child grows up, information may be given regarding the birth mother's social background, circumstances, and reasons for surrender, etc. However, the identity of the mother is not revealed for protecting all concerned in the adoption triad.

In some of the cases in the recent past, we have seen the apex Court, Bombay High and Karnataka High Court have not supported the root search cases and have ordered that information regarding the biological parents of the Petitioner cannot be divulged on account of the confidentiality agreement, which is binding on the recognized adoption agency. It can lead to a feeling of further abandonment.

The recognized adoption agencies should provide independent advice, counseling, and support to anyone approaching for background search of his/her adoption. The Child Welfare Committee (CWC) is the competent authority which is involved at the pre-adoption stage, is required to handle the issue very sensitively and should refer the matter to the particular adoption agency, in case approached by an older adoptee. Furthermore, the Committee should not disclose any information without professional assistance.

Efforts to contact the biological mothers/parents may create a fear in the minds of the biological parents, especially the unwed mothers, who may out of fear of their identity being revealed, abandon the children, and dump them in garbage bins rather than relinquish them to adoption agencies.

References

Brodzinsky, D. M., Schechter, M. D., & Henig, R. (1992). *Being adopted: The lifelong search for self*. Toronto: Anchor Books, Doubleday.

Freundlich, M. (2000). *Adoption and ethics: The market forces in adoption* (Vol. 2). Washington, DC: Child Welfare League of America.

Guidelines Governing the Adoption of Children. (2011) http://www.adoptionindia.nic.in.

Hague Convention on Inter-country Adoption. (1993) (http://www.hcch.net/index_en.php?act=conventions.text&cid=69).

Krueger, M., Jago, J. & Hanna, F. J. (1997). Why adopted persons search: An existential treatment perspective. *Journal of Counseling and Development*, 75. Retrieved December 2, 2006, from the Psychology and Behavioral Sciences Collection database.
Pandey, L. K. vs. Union of India case of 1982, Supreme Court of India website.
Letter to CARA from Maharastra based adoption agencies on root search. (2010).
Lifton, B. J. (1994). *Journey of the adopted self: A quest for wholeness*. New York: Basic Books.
Mohanty, J. (2013). Ethnic and racial socialization and self-esteem of Asian adoptees: The mediating role of multiple identities. *Journal of Adolescence, 36*(1), 161–170. doi:10.1016/j.adolescence.2012.10.003.
Moran, R. A. (1994). Stages of emotion: An adult adoptee's post reunion perspective. *Child Welfare Journal, 73*, 249–260.
Nickman, S. L., Rosenfeld, A. A., Fine, P., MacIntyre, J. C., Pilowsky, D. J., Howe, R. A., & Sveda, S. A. (2005). Children in adoptive families: Overview and update. *Journal of the American Academy of Child and Adolescent Psychiatry, 44*(10), 987–995. doi:10.1097/01.chi.0000174463.60987.69.
Nickman, S. L. (1985). Losses in adoption: The need for dialogue. *Journal of the American Psychoanalytic Study of the Child, 40*, 365–398.
Pacheco, F., & Eme, R. (1993). An outcome study of the reunion between adoptees and biological parents. *Child Welfare, 72*, 53–64.
Rachel, H. & Peter, N. (2002). Implementation handbook for the convention on the rights of the child. UNICEF, USA (http://www.holtintl.org/ethics.shtml).
Report and Conclusions of the Second Special Commission on the Practical Operation of the Hague Convention of 29 May 1993 on protection of children and co-operation in respect of intercountry adoption (17–23 September 2005).
The Case for Transracial Adoption (afabcwebsite).
United Nations Convention on Rights of the Child. (UNCRC 1989).
UNICEF guidance note on inter-country adoption in the CEE/CIS region. September 2009.

Chapter 11
Dropouts to Learners: The Challenge of the Right to Education Act 2009

Vimala Veeraraghavan

Introduction

It is perhaps too early to assess the actual impact on the ground of the RTE Act. Although the Act came into effect in April, 2010, the rules have been promulgated only last year in most states and implementation process is on. However one can attempt to assess the impact at policy and program levels as well as the expected impact at the ground level in the coming years. Also one can look at the research data on dropouts and make suggestions for effective implementation of the RTE Act and the achievement of its objectives of providing quality education to all children without exception.

The RTE Act has been superimposed on Sarva Shiksha Abhiyan, the flagship program of central and state government for attaining the goal of universal elementary education. The program has been in implementation for more than a decade and doubtless has had a good impact on enrollment. What the RTE Act seeks is to introduce right-based approach so that every child's right can be enforced through legal means with a grievance redressal procedure and an appeal to National and State Commission of Children for Protection of Rights. It also makes it legally obligatory on the part of various authorities of the government, state and local levels, to provide requisite number of schools and appoint teachers according to norms, ensure that the teachers are sufficiently qualified, provide defined minimum physical facilities in all the schools, simplify admission procedures, and ensure the transaction of curriculum on desired lines. It also gives important voice to parents and local community in the management of the school.

V. Veeraraghavan (✉)
Department of Psychology, Indira Gandhi National Open University, New Delhi, India
e-mail: vveera2000@gmail.com

S. Deb (ed.), *Child Safety, Welfare and Well-being*,
DOI 10.1007/978-81-322-2425-9_11

In particular, the RTE Act pays special attention to the quality of education provided in the school. In fact, according to a distinguished educationist, Section 29 of the RTE Act is the heart and soul of the Act. This section stipulates that the curriculum for elementary education will take into account the following:

(a) Conformity with the values enshrined in the Constitution
(b) All round development of the child
(c) Building up of the child's knowledge, potentiality, and talent
(d) Development of physical and mental abilities to the fullest extent
(e) Learning through activities, discovery, and exploration in a child friendly and child centered manner
(f) Medium of instruction, shall as far as practical be in the child's mother tongue
(g) Making the child free of fear, trauma, and anxiety and helping the child to express views freely
(h) Comprehensive and continuous evaluation of the child' understanding of knowledge and his or her ability to apply the same.

The above provisions should be read with rules prescribing that the teacher shall maintain a file containing a pupil cumulative record for every child which shall be the basis for awarding the certificate for completion of elementary education.

The requirement that the teacher shall maintain a cumulative record for every child arises also from the stipulation in Section 30 of the Act that no child shall be required to pass any Board examination till completion of elementary education and that every child completing the elementary education shall be awarded a certificate.

The RTE Act therefore places a great responsibility on the teachers and has very high expectations from them. To facilitate the performance of their duties the Act provides for the appointment of specific number of teachers in accordance with prescribed student-teacher ratio, filling up of all vacancies in teacher positions within stipulated time, prescribing of minimum qualifications and teacher eligibility tests for appointment of teachers, and training programs of pre-service and in-service and provision of various academic support services. The rules also require teacher participation in curriculum formulation, development of syllabi, training modules, and text book development. The Act prescribes inter alia that the teacher shall be regular and punctual, conduct and complete curriculum within the specified time, assess the learning ability of each child and supplement additional instructions if required, and hold regular meetings with parents and appraise them about regularity and progressive learning and other relevant information about the child.

Attention has been drawn to the above provision to show that if the RTE Act has to succeed in its objectives much greater attention is required to training of teachers particularly to improve their ability to adopt flexible teaching learning method, evaluation and assessment to meet with the greater diversity among student population, the high expectation of the Act and the responsibility imposed on them. The Teacher Eligibility Test as now in force is intended to ensure that teachers have sufficient subject matter competence. But what is needed is not only subject matter competence but a great deal of ability in transacting the curriculum in the classroom and in working with the parents and the community to ensure that the individual student's needs are met adequately.

It calls for a sea change in the perspectives and practices of teaching. To quote from a recent document of the Ministry of HRD on Framework for implementation of the RTE Act, (Sarva Shiksha Abhiyan 2009), in-service training for teachers should be provided every year so as to enable them to continuously upgrade their knowledge and teaching skills and work toward a shift in their understanding the practices of teaching and learning in the following manner:

From	To
Teacher directed, fixed designs	Learner centric flexible processes
Learner receptivity	Learner agency, participation in learning
Knowledge as "given", fixed	Knowledge as constructed, evolving
Learning as an individual act	Learning as a collaborative, social process
Disciplinary focus	Multidisciplinary educational focus
Assessment judgmental, mainly through competitive tests for ranking through narrow measures of achievement leading to trauma and anxiety	Assessment for learning, self assessment to enhance motivation, through continuous non threatening processes, to record progress over time

(*Source* National Curriculum Framework 2005, p. 110)

Let us now take up the school dropout scenario in India and see how the RTE can deal with the same.

The Phenomenon of Dropouts

The difficulty in estimating the number of dropouts is also clear from a recent report of NUEPA (2012a) on Education for All. The Report cites the following figures:

1. Census figures of 2001 estimated out of school children at 32 million or 28 % of the age group 6–14 years in that year.
2. SRI IMRB Report of 2005 (an independent survey) estimated the number at 13.5 million or 6.94 % (4.34 % in urban areas and 7.8 % in rural areas).
3. SRI IMRB Report of 2009 estimated the number 8.1 million in 2009, that is, 4.2 % of the children in the age group 6–14 years.
4. National Sample Survey (66th round) (2009–2010) estimated the non attending children at 14.25 million children.

NUEPA report concludes that although estimates of out of school children in the age group 6–14 years, using different sources of data provide varying figures, all the estimates do indicate that the number of out of school children in India has declined substantially during the last few years. Moreover this decline in the percentage of school children is across gender and all social categories. For girls it has decreased from 7.9 % in 2005 to 4.6 % in 2009. For SC population it has decreased from 8.1 % in 2005 to 5.9 % in 2009. The decrease is more noticeable in rural areas where the percentage of school children dropped from 7.1 % in 2005 to 4.4 % in 2009.

The definition of non-attending children in NSS survey refers to non-attendance during a particular period which is different from enrollment data in official figures.

NUEPA's report Education For All (2012a) gives a overall dropout rate for classes 1–8 at 42.7 % in 2007–2008 (43.7 % for boys and 41.3 % for girls). It also indicates that the retention rate at the primary level (Class 5) has increased from 53 % in 2001 to 74 % in 2009.

The retention rate up to class V estimated by NUEPA through its annual DISE 2011 document shows a retention rate of approximately 75 % up to class V. The retention rate shows the number of children surviving up to class V out of a given cohort. The terms out of school children may include dropouts as well as irregularly attending children. Not all children who fail to reach class V would be dropouts as some may continue to attend lower classes which in future will decline due to non-detention policy.

Whatever the definition and method of statistical compilation the fact remains that a substantial number of children fail to achieve the learning goals set for universal elementary education up to class V and class VIII, as was pointed out in Pratham study given below.

Recent Research Evidence on Dropouts

Traditionally the reason for non-attendance and dropout of children have been attributed to (i) physical accessibility of schools (ii) lack of facilities in schools, (iii) transport arrangements, (iv) absence of teachers, (v) absence of facilities at school, (vi) poverty and socio economic conditions of children leading to employment of children as income earners in various occupations, (vii) social factors based on caste and gender, (viii) lack of education particularly among mothers, (ix) poor teaching and learning in the schools, and (x) inappropriate teacher behavior.

Despite the economic and social progress over the last few decades the above causes are still very much in operation as can be seen from some of the recent research studies and programs. A brief summary of conclusions of these studies is given below.

A study in Delhi by Sajjad et al. (2012), suggests the reasons for dropout as under:

(i) Abysmal quality of education (22 %)
(ii) Poverty in households (34 %)
(iii) Helping in household chore (25 %), and
(iv) Supplementing family income (18 %).

The study suggests conditional cash transfer program as in Mexico and Brazil where cash support is extended to poor families, conditional on children attending schools and going to clinic for check up. Although the study recognizes such a program, it may be difficult to implement in a populated country like India.

In its annual status of education report ASER rural (2009) released in the year 2010, Pratham, the well-known NGO tried to get reliable estimates of the status of children schooling and basic learning (reading, writing and math ability) at district levels. The survey recorded the household and village characteristics, education of fathers as well. The analysis was based on 29 districts covering children 3–16 years of age. Children aged 5–16 years were assessed on reading tasks, arithmetic tasks, English tasks etc. The report observed that amongst children in the age group of 6–14 years, the dropout had come down from 4.3 % in 2008 to 4 % in 2009. Of school girls had dropped from 7.2 % in 2008 to 6.8 % in 2009. Over 50 % of 12 year olds are enrolled in schools. Only 25 % of all rural children in standard V could read simple sentences. Of these over 80 % could understand the meaning of the sentences. By standard VIII, 60 % of all children could read a simple sentence. In all the North Eastern states, except Tripura, Goa, Himachal Pradesh, and Kerala, more than 80 % of children in standard VIII, could not read simple sentences fluently but they could understand the meaning.

It was found that the percentage of children taking paid tuition increased in every class in both private and government schools. The incidence of tuition in Bihar and Orissa was high. This very large numbers of government school children taking tuition (more than 33 % in class I to 50 % in standard VIII) is indeed significant. Water was available in 75 % government primary schools, usable toilet were found in over 50 % government schools. In standard 1–2 more than 70 % children could read letters of words except in Tamil Nadu (62 %) and UP (68 %). In standard 3–5 more than 50 % children could read the level 1 set or more, except UP and Jammu & Kashmir. In other words, the Pratham study highlights the inadequate learning attainment in language and maths. However, using another methodology of assessment the NCERT has been able to give a more positive report on the attainment of language and maths abilities in children.

Uma (2011) in a study on reasons for the rising school dropout rates in rural India has stated on the basis of a study that 50 % of children who join class I dropout by class VIII. With each successive class students quit in large numbers. By class V every third kid has dropped and by class VIII, every second kid dropped out of school. The net enrollment ratio for classes 6–8 was reported as 54 %, that is only 54 % of all children in this age group were enrolled. This meant that 44 million children in this age group did not go to school. For classes 1–5 the net enrollment was 97 % leaving out 4 million children.

In a study conducted by her drawn on 154 rural girl students, she found the following reasons for children dropping out of the school:

(1) Child not interested in studies
(2) Parents not interested in studies
(3) Financial constraints

(4) Unable to cope
(5) To work for wage/salary
(6) Participation in other economic activities
(7) Attend to domestic duties
(8) Facility for study does not exist in the nearby town.

The main reason for dropping out in her study was found to be financial difficulties for both boys and girls. About 31 % boys and 13 % girls also reported that they were just not interested in further studies. Twenty-eight percent (28 %) girls said that their families and relatives did not approve of their further continuation of their studies. Parents wish to discontinue children's education was cited as the most important reason (29 % for all age groups). About two-fifth (42 %) of girls were pulled out of school by their parents so that the girls could look after their siblings (53 %). For boys the reason given was to help in family occupation (57 %) and the perception that education will not be helpful in future (42 %). The research study concludes that there is a great need for literacy drive amongst parents, vocational training for skills for income generation, and continuing education. It also emphasizes the need for greater awareness of gender justice and women's empowerment, if Right to education is not to remain as a mere paper exercise.

Another study on school dropout in rural setting, Govindaraju and Venkatesan (2010), have cited census figures to show that while 96 % of children enrolled in primary school by age of 10, 40 % would have dropped out. While some 3 crore children do not go to school, 8.5 crore children are dropouts. The reasons for dropping out may be failure in academics, non-availability of schools, and inaccessibility of schools, pushing out due to teachers, behavior/school environment and financial problems. Based on the study they have classified the reasons for dropout under the following categories (i) child centered, (ii) parents centered, (iii) teacher centered, and (iv) environment centered and have analyzed the reasons under these four categories. Neglect, poor or lack of interest in teachers, fear of teachers, misbehavior by teachers, irregular classes, poor teaching, overtly strict discipline, discrimination, cruelty or punishment meted out by teachers, absence of teachers, lack of female teachers are listed under teacher centric causes.

Poor interest or neglect, over freedom and affection of parents, giving up parental responsibilities, denial of school for female children, gambling, alcoholism and other vices, death of a parent, parent discord, and illiteracy are among the parent centric causes.

Transient or prolonged illness, accidents, disabilities, handicapped child, early menarche or marriage of the child, age of the child, disinterest in studies, distraction in play or games, inferiority feelings, problem behaviors in child, poor academic performance, preference to go for work and earn money, fear of punishment by teachers, love affairs, perception that there are no job opportunities after studying, pride and ego are among the child centric factors.

Caste factors, poverty in family, tradition, change of school, or medium of instruction, influence by television or mass media, drought or famine in the village, tribal life, frequent shifts or migration of family, poor home background, distance from school, poor school maintenance, absence of toilet facilities in school, intimidating system of examination, are among the environment centric reasons.

The authors conclusion is that the empirical evidence suggests three major clusters viz., parent, teacher student with significant differences in relation to gender, occupation and educational status of teachers, the SES and education of parents and gender of the dropout students themselves.

Another program in Samashtipur by SDPP (2012) analyses an intervention program organized in consultation with the Bihar government in 13 blocks of Samashtipur district. The intervention includes an early warning system (to check student absenteeism) and recreation and enrichment activities to make the school more attractive. This includes life skills, arts, crafts, sports and games, storytelling and engaging teachers and volunteers in the above. The program also proposes to measure the following outcomes: (i) school dropouts, (ii) engagement in school, (iii) progression in school, and (iv) the student, teacher and parent attitude.

The report of status and trends by NUEPA (2012b) emphasizes that the RTI Act requires the government and the local authorities to ensure that the child belonging to the weaker sections, disadvantaged groups etc. are not discriminated against and prevented from pursuing and completing elementary education on any ground. The approaches to ensure inclusion of all children in elementary education include special initiative for enhancing educational access for disadvantaged and weaker sections of the community. It also states that area intensive and target group initiatives including assessment of educational status of specific social and cultural groups, alternative schooling opportunity for special group such as out of school children and support, community based innovative and experimental projects by voluntary agencies are important aspects of the initiative to bridge gender and social gap in education. It also emphasizes the importance of early childhood care and education and meeting the learning needs of young people and adolescents generally improving the levels of adult literacy to achieve the objectives of UEE. It has several recommendations for bridging gender gap and promoting gender equality as well as for improving educational quality and student learning.

In this chapter, efforts have been made to pay special attention on the following two issues:

Prevention of Dropouts and Needs of Inclusive Schools

RTE has stipulated that all children should be admitted to schools without screening which means children with poor academic performance will also be admitted which indicates the need for inclusive education and inclusive schools. The term 'inclusive schools' refers to one that encourages every child, irrespective of its socio-economic background, gender or academic ability, achieve its fullest potential through diverse teaching and learning styles appropriate to children (Doran 2011). Many of the classroom practices and procedure including assessment method and relationship between children and parents may need to be modified to achieve the above goals of inclusion. While children with high abilities should always be encouraged, attention should also be given equally to the poor performing children so that the causes of poor performance are understood and the children are assisted to overcome their learning difficulty. Some of these difficulties may arise due to early upbringing or socialization or the lack of it and will need cognitive, emotional, and behavioral interventions. Some of these children may have special need and the teachers should identify these special needs and assist in provision for education of the same.

For all these, the school or the local cluster of schools should be able to provide for aptitude, interest and personality tests as an aid to learning. This will help all children and not the only poor performing children. In a recent paper Ricconuini et al. (2012), stated that Cognitive Behavior Intervention (CBI) can be taught in a series of 10 or more classes. It can be taught to students by general and special education teachers, school psychologists or behavior specialists in one-to-one, small group or large group instructional format. Although the specific cognitive and behavioral component may vary, a variety of instructional techniques can be used including mentoring by teacher and peer modeling, role play, and behavioral rehearsal. A decade ago, in another study on guided learning Dash and Khan (2001) demonstrated the impact of guided learning on cognitive performance of children. They concluded that school instruction should capitalize on the potential development level of students using dynamic assessment methods.

A common instructional theme in using CBI to reduce aggression and dropout was that the students were exclusively taught strategy and appropriate behavior response by the teacher. The instructional design teachers included multiple models, frequent opportunities for guided practice, plenty of corrective feedback, positive reinforcement, independent practice, and specific generalization strategies. Additionally it would be helpful if teachers monitor students' progress by observing and recoding student behavior across various settings. When students do not make progress, teachers provide additional model, feedback, and opportunities to practice.

Motivational Climate of Schools

In view of the high expectations in school from the teachers the Act specifically prohibits deployment use of teachers for non educational purposes except for decennial population census, disaster relief duty or duties relating to elections to local authority, state legislature and parliament. Since there are many elections, teachers perhaps must be exempted from election duties as well. Also teachers are involved in supervising construction and other similar non-academic works which needs to be prohibited. The intention is that teachers should have sufficient time to discharge the responsibilities expected of them. The training arrangements are also intended to help them in this regard. But little attention seems to have been paid in raising their motivational and leadership levels in schools. Professionals in Psychology, Management, and Education who have worked on organizational and institutional climate have to be involved in raising the motivational climate and in teacher training programs. This involvement has to be at the level of the schools, clusters of schools, at the block, and district level, state and national levels. Without raising the school's climate, motivational level and commitment of teachers, it would be impossible to make a success of the RET Act implementation. This commitment and motivation can come only through a person oriented organizational approach. To quote from a recent report in Ireland, "to create a positive student behavior schools must develop in a consistent and sustained way the person oriented dimension of their organization. They must display high level of emotional intelligence, that is, the ability to empathize, to motivate, to build supportive alliances, to persist and to show warmth and acceptance."

Again to quote further from the report, "The teachers and other adults in the schools have to influence student behavior through their thinking, their actions and their feeling. There should be an effective leadership of the school and in the larger school it means distributive leadership which means wide involvement of staff in a range of school processes and their empowerment for the purpose. Recent research on school leadership points out that successful leaders set directions, develop people and redesign their organizations and in the process also actively involve all the staff members. This means they develop shared vision and group goals, set high performance expectations, provide individual support and intellectual and emotional stimulation, set examples and promote collaborative and participative relations with parents and community."

The leadership practices in schools that have above average enrollment of challenging students are specifically referred to in the Irish report (DES Publication 2006). These are

(i) Constantly managing tensions and problems relating to particular circumstances and context of the schools
(ii) Coping on a daily basis with unpredictability and conflict while retaining the core values of the school.
(iii) Personal and professional values that place human needs before organizational needs, that is, to be people oriented.
(iv) Sharing decision making with others through staff empowerment.
(v) To see their jobs not as desk job but as people centered enterprise.

The leaders of the school are especially aware of the importance of building positive relations with students, teachers and parents. They do this through a process of trust and empowerment and engaging other students and parents in dealing with decision making.

The link between teachers' learning and behavior is fundamental to all good practice. The teachers play a pivotal role in fostering classrooms that are conducive to quality teaching and learning. Where there is good teaching and learning, behavior difficulties would be considerably reduced especially if teaching and learning is tailored to the capacity and interest of the students. Apart from the pedagogic skills, the teachers should develop the capacity to build positive and mutually respectful relation with students and others. The pastoral care function of the teachers and the school is as important as the academic function and when conflicts occur either with teachers or with parents or students, the adults concerned do not insist on their 'pound of flesh'. Schools should be centers of reconciliation and not places for power struggle or for holding out, or to triumph over some other person especially over a vulnerable student.

For children and young people with emotional and behavioral difficulty, inclusion means

(i) Maximizing their access to and engagement with social and educational setting appropriate to their needs and aspirations
(ii) Providing environment where they experience a personal sense of security
(iii) Respect and being valued
(iv) Supportive relationship
(v) Sharing their life with positive adult role models
(vi) Clear, humane, and flexible boundary settings
(vii) Successful achievement boosting their self-esteem
(viii) Opportunities to obtain academic and vocational qualifications
(ix) Chance to develop and exercise personal responsibility

Raising Motivational Level of Students

If RTE Act has to succeed, the school has to aim at improving the motivation level of the students. If the motivation of students for learning improves it should have the beneficial impact on the motivation of the teachers as well. Many studies have been made on the issue of motivation for learning and psychologists make a distinction between intrinsic and extrinsic motivation (Mukunda 2009). The more intrinsic the motivation is (that is something from within rises for accomplishing certain goal); greater will be the impact or achievement in learning.

Evolutionary psychologists believe that for certain kinds of knowledge there is this intrinsic motivation arising from the Rights of Children, no matter from which socio-economic or family background the student comes from. However, for other kinds of knowledge which are essential to acquire from the school there has to be a certain measure of extrinsic motivation, that is a system of reward and punishment which in the school context would mean non-physical penalties of various kinds and also appropriate praise rewards and recognition. In a recent book (Mukunda 2009) on ('What did you ask at school today—A handbook of child learning', 2009), it is stated that "there are many possible reasons for the lack of intrinsic motivation among school children: emotional or physical insecurity and ill health, evolutionary constraints, a lack of perceived control over the learning process, the misuse of reward, irrelevant of material and difficult level of work, the classroom environment and most importantly teacher behavior and student beliefs." She cites Maslow's hierarchy of needs to say that only when the needs at the base of the pyramid are met the child will be motivated to learn. "If the child is hungry and anxious or unloved he will not be intrinsically motivated to achieve competence in the school. When a child goes through an emotionally shaky patch (family or peer related) school performance suffers immediately. A teacher who wants learning to happen has no alternative but to involve himself with the student's emotional life."

The main objective of the teacher and of the school in its various practices is to encourage the intrinsic motivation of the students and use praise and reward system and occasional punishment system as well to ensure that classrooms and schools function in an orderly manner and children are motivated to learn and observe the codes of behavior which is a powerful way of inculcating the democratic and humane values inherent in our Constitution.

Teacher Training

In-service and pre-service training program for teachers presently seem to give little attention to capacity building for teachers in these vital areas. Moreover the extreme diversity in the student's background has to be managed by the new paradigm of teaching learning processes with great flexibility and with links to career and vocational skills. All this requires effective use of principles of interpersonal as well as educational psychology. The syllabus of teacher training institutes must incorporate materials on testing for aptitude, interest and personality and their application under varying local circumstances and contexts. Psychological assessment and counseling based thereon could also help reduce non-attendance and dropouts. The in service training programs must incorporate sufficient knowledge both theoretical and applied in psychological tests and assessment and counseling. Even at the level of recruitment of teachers it is necessary to provide for aptitude test before they are appointed, as teaching is one profession which requires a certain measure of commitment to children and interest in educational activities, without which the teachers will be unsuccessful despite their subject knowledge. The teachers must be proficient in identification of learning difficulty, in assessment and evaluation, in behavior guidance, enhancing motivation of children as well as interacting with parents and community.

Parental and Community Involvement

Section 21 of the Act provides that the government schools and aided schools should constitute a school management committee consisting of elected representatives of local authority, parents or guardians of children and teachers. Three fourths of this committee is to consist of the parents or guardians. This does not mean that the school principal and the school work under the control of the parent as the government and aided schools are working under designated authority of the government. The main purpose of the school management committee is to prepare and recommend school development plan and monitor the working of the school. The principal and teachers of the school should develop positive and cooperative relation with the school management committee and use it as a source of strength for the school in achieving its objectives and resolving many day to day problems. Since some of the parents of the poor and marginalized sections of the society may not be able to be in touch with the school, some volunteers, NGOs and representatives of the school managing committee could act as a bridge in order to ascertain the difficulties of the children who are not attending school regularly and those who have other problems. The school management committee and NGOs can be of assistance in providing special training program particularly in regard to vocational and life skills.

In conclusion, India is a vast country and we would be dealing with approximately 200 million children across classes 1–8. They are distributed across rural and urban areas with vastly different economic, social and geographical situations. The policy prescription should provide for sufficient flexibility and delegation of authority to decide on academic and other practices most conducive to getting the best results of quality education for every single child and developing its potential. The RTE Act seeks to make the common citizen and every one aware of the Rights of Children and provide for the enforcement of these rights through monitoring redressal of grievances and appeal to National Commission for Protection of Rights. It seeks to ensure while there is flexibility in the delivery of education according to local requirements and needs, sufficient resources are provided to ensure adequate basic facilities, sufficient number of teachers and ensure that there is universal acceptance of basic approach to quality education and one that is child friendly and promote the growth of children and give meaning to their life and also enable them to make a living.

It recognizes that life and vocational skills are important and children should learn both within the school and community but at the same time the Rights of children to their childhood should not be deprived by forcing them into child labor especially in prohibited activities. It is also the responsibility of the school that along with academic reform envisaged in the RTE Act there are also sufficient opportunities for children to develop their vocational and work skills and life skills in general according to the emerging opportunity. It is the special responsibility of the school to provide for the development of these skills in school in a guided manner whether in family occupation or otherwise so that at the end of elementary education, children may choose their career in appropriate manner.

The biggest impact of RTE Act may come, if effectually implemented through the enforcement of provisions for grievance redressal and monitoring especially as Section 31 of the Act clearly states that NCPCR (National Commission for Protection of Child's Rights) and their state counterparts are responsible for monitoring the Rights of the Child. According to the Ministry of HRD's document framework for implementation of RTE Act for implementation, the NCPCR will have to look at children's rights in two domains, (i) children out of school, and (ii) children in school, and monitor every aspect of the Act including the reservation of 25 % of admission of the weaker section in private school. Thus for the first time the government authority responsible for delivering educational services become accountable to an expert neutral agency set up by the government for protecting the rights of children. This, in the medium and long-term will have a major impact in ensuring educational provision and quality.

Conclusion and Recommendations

In fine, it might be stated that the RTE Act ensures quality education for each child up to class VIII. Another objective of the Act is to reduce non-attendees and dropouts in the age group of 6–14 years, so that every child goes to school. Therefore, there is a need to open more schools in the rural areas, recruit more teachers, arrange special training for them for acting as motivating teachers, ensuring uninterrupted midday meals, free uniforms and text books should be provided on regular basis. Teachers who are trained in the traditional system of teaching have to make a paradigm shift to meet the new responsibilities and methods of teaching. This requires capacity building, without which the dropouts and non-attendees will now become non-learners within the school and thus will be worse off. This capacity building calls for teachers with new approaches to teaching and learning, more emphatic to the needs of individual children, more capable of interacting with the parents and committed to the goal of developing the potential and livelihood opportunities of all the children—especially the non performing children.

However, the extreme diversity in the background of students and their background has to be managed by new paradigms of the teaching learning processes with links to vocational options, requires the effective use of the principles of psychology. For instance after the admission of students a psychological test for aptitude and interest could be administered. The syllabus of the teacher training institutes (TTIs) must incorporate material on the psychology of children who dropout and/or non-attendees as well as children who create problems in the classroom during and after teaching. The TTIs must incorporate knowledge of psychology and practice in these areas. At the level of recruitment, teachers may be given a teacher aptitude test before they take the entrance examination for TTI admissions and only those who have the aptitude for teaching may be admitted to TTI. Apart from the know-how of differential styles of teaching to suit the needs of children, it is necessary to make them proficient also in evaluation, identification of learning obstacles and in motivation, behavior and guidance of children as well as in interacting with parents. Finally support from the parents of the children and community is essential for effective implementation of RTE Act.

References

Dash, M., & Khan, F. (2001). Impact of guided k-learning on the cognitive performance of low and high achievers. *Psychological Studies, 46*(1–2), 14–20.

DES Publication (2006). *School matters. The report of the task force on student behavior in second level schools*. SESS.ie/documents-and-publications/otherdes.

Doran, J. (2011). *Inclusive education framework*. NCSE: Bangor University, USA.

Govindaraju, R., & Venkatesan, S. (2010). A study on school dropouts in rural settings. *Journal of Psychology, 1*(1), 47–53.

Mukunda, K. V. (2009). *What did you ask at school today?—A handbook of child learning*. Noida, UP: Harper Collins Publishers.

National Sample Survey Organization (NSSR) Report. (2009–2010). 66th Round.

NCERT. (2005). *National curriculum framework (2005)*. New Delhi: NCERT.

NUEPA. (2012a). *Education for all: Status and trends*. New Delhi: NUEPA.

NUEPA. (2012b). *Elementary education in India progress towards UEE*. New Delhi: NUEPA.

Pratham. (2010). *Annual status of education report (rural)*, January 15, New Delhi.

Ricconuni, P., J., Loujeania, W. B., Antonis, K. & Dalun, Z. (2012). Cognitive behavioral interventions: An effective approach to help students with disabilities stay in school. Effective interventions in dropout prevention: A practice brief for educators.

Sajjad, H., Iqbal, M., Siddiqui, M. A. et al., (2012). Socio economic determinants of primary school dropouts: Evidence from south east Delhi, India. *European Journal of Social Sciences, 30*(3), 391–399.

SPDD. (2012). School dropouts in Cambodia, India, Tajikistan and Timor-Leste. School dropout prevention Pilot Program. Creative.

Uma, R. R. (2011). Reasons for rising school dropout rates of rural girls in India—An analysis using soft computing approach. *International Journal of Current Research, 3*(9), 140–143.

Part III
Rights of Vulnerable Children

Chapter 12
Child Rights in the Context of HIV/AIDS

Seema Sahay, Archana Verma, Suhas Shewale and Murugesan Periyasamy

Introduction

The Convention on the Rights of the Child of 1989 (United Nations 1989) defines precisely the term "child":

> [...] a child is any human being below the age of eighteen years unless, under the law applicable to the child, majority is attained earlier

The League of Nations adopted the Geneva Declaration of the Rights of the Child (1924), which enunciated the child's right to receive the requirements for normal development, the right of the hungry child to be fed, the right of the sick child to receive health care, the right of the backward child to be reclaimed, the right of orphans to shelter, and the right to protection from exploitation (League-of-Nations 1924). The Convention on Rights of the Child was adopted on November 20, 1989 by General Assembly Resolution 44/25. Almost all countries except United States and Somalia ratified this convention. In 1974, the Government of India adopted a National Policy for Children, declaring the nation's children as 'supremely important assets' but children are still vulnerable. Being minors, they do not have a voice in the adult world and needs for their voices to be heard is generally not considered by the adults. India gave accession to Convention on Rights of the Child on December 11, 1992 with the following declaration:

S. Sahay (✉) · A. Verma · S. Shewale · M. Periyasamy
Socio Behavioural Research (SBR),
National AIDS Research Institute (an ICMR Institute), Pune, India
e-mail: ssahay@nariindia.org; seemasahay@yahoo.com; ssahay@icmr.org.in

S. Deb (ed.), *Child Safety, Welfare and Well-being*,
DOI 10.1007/978-81-322-2425-9_12

> "While fully subscribing to the objectives and purposes of the Convention, realizing that certain of the rights of child, namely those pertaining to the economic, social, and cultural rights can only be progressively implemented in the developing countries, subject to the extent of available resources and within the framework of international co-operation; recognizing that the child has to be protected from exploitation of all forms including economic exploitation; noting that for several reasons children of different ages do work in India; having prescribed minimum wages for employment in hazardous occupations and in certain other areas; having made regulatory provisions regarding hours and conditions of employment; and being aware that it is not practical immediately to prescribe minimum wages for admission to each and every area of employment in India-the Government of India undertakes to take measures to progressively implement the provisions of Article 32, particularly paragraph 2(a), in accordance with its national legislation and relevant international instruments to which it is a State Party."

All children can be rendered vulnerable by the particular circumstances of their lives, especially (a) children who are themselves HIV infected; (b) children who are affected by the epidemic because of the loss of a parental caregivers; and (c) children who are most prone to be infected or affected (United Nations 2003).

One fundamental issue in the human life cycle is about one's rights. A child, however, is devoid of one important right: 'right to be born'. This is a complex problem and philosophers, policy makers, physicians, social scientists and activists have not come up with an answer. A child born to HIV infected parent and carrying infection is again a question about his/ her right. Very limited literature is available on 'responsible parenthood'. With pandemic AIDS, world has witnessed human rights issues pertaining to reproductive health of women, health of vulnerable populations, and rights of high risk groups. Rights of HIV infected children is the missing component from this bunch of 'rights'. Salisbury aptly expresses this problem, "the secrecy and stigma that still surround HIV and AIDS make it difficult for HIV affected children and youth to benefit as fully as they might from policies and programs that provide more generic types of care and assistance (Salisbury 2000)".

Under international law, children have two types of human rights:

(1) Fundamental rights of adults
(2) Special human rights that are necessary to protect them during their minority years such as the right to life, the right to a name, the right to express views in matters concerning the child, the right to freedom of thought, conscience and religion, the right to health care, the right to protection from economic and sexual exploitation and the right to education.

The International Convention on the Rights of the Child in the year 1989, for the first time legally recognizes fundamental rights of a child. The purpose of the United Nations Convention on the Rights of the Child (UNCRC) is to outline the basic human rights that should be afforded to children. The UNCRC covers the cultural, social, economic and political rights of children and is guided in interpretation and implementation by four principles:

- Non-discrimination
- The best interest of the child
- The maximum survival of the child, development of the child
- Consideration of children's opinion in matters that affect them

The UNCRC consists of 41 articles which define children's rights to life, to survival, freedom of expression and belief and to protection from exploitation. The practical relevance of the CRC for children's health and well-being, and particularly for public health, is not understood. UNCRC is among the most potent tools available to respond to and increase the significance of pediatrics to contemporary disparities and determinants of child health outcomes. There are four broad classifications of these rights. These four categories cover all civil, political, social, economic and cultural rights of every child:

- **Right to Survival**: A child's right to survival begins before a child is born. According to Government of India, a child's life begins after twenty weeks of conception. Hence the right to survival is inclusive of the child rights: to be born or not to be born, right to life, right to minimum standards of food, shelter and clothing, to be able to benefit from appropriate healthcare, and the right to live with dignity.
- **Right to Protection**: A child has the right to be protected from neglect, exploitation, and abuse at home, and or elsewhere.
- **Right to Participation**: A child has a right to participate in any decision making that involves him/ her directly or indirectly. There are varying degrees of participation as per the age and maturity of the child.
- **Right to Development**: Child has the right to all forms of development: emotional, mental, and physical. Emotional development is fulfilled by proper care and love of a support system, mental development through education and learning, and physical development through recreation, play, and nutrition.

HIV Infected Children

While alluding to the rights of the children, an even more complex situation arises because of HIV epidemic. As per UNAIDS (2012) estimates, 3.3 million children under the age of 15 are living with HIV, and 210,000 died of AIDS. The new infections occurred in 260,000 children under the age of 15. Currently, UNICEF reports estimated 220,000 children infected by HIV/AIDS in India (UNICEF 2014). With the increased availability of pediatric ART, more children born with HIV survive into adolescence and adulthood (Edmonds et al. 2011; Palladino et al. 2009; Sahay 2013). The focus of treatment has thereby changed from management of a severe debilitating disease to more long-term care with challenges such as maintaining treatment success, management of chronic co-morbidities, supporting adherence to life-long therapy, prevention of HIV drug resistance and finally transitioning children from pediatric program to adult HIV program (Haubrich et al. 1999; Volberding and Deeks 2010; Wood et al. 2004). Considering the socio-behavioral nature of the disease, growing to be adolescent with HIV has various developmental issues that add to the complexity of the adolescence. HIV presents an example of the way in which the UNCRC helps shift attention from a biomedical approach to another perspective towards social, cultural, and economic determinants of risk and survival. If the protection of human rights is seen as a societal precondition for human well-being, then the promotion and protection of these rights is enmeshed with promoting children's protection from HIV.

Scope

This chapter deals with the needs of HIV infected children, adolescents, and young adults. The ensuing discourse focuses on the impact that HIV makes on this young population. It also discusses needs and rights issue taking examples from literature. Some of the real life examples are reported from a qualitative study that explored the issues of HIV infected children and adolescents. Human rights relevant to HIV/AIDS identified in UDHR (Universal Declaration of Human Rights) treaties include the right to non-discrimination and equality, to health, to liberty and security of the person, to privacy, to seek, receive and impart information, to marry and found a family, to work, and the right to freedom of movement, association and expression. All these rights have particular importance in the context of HIV/AIDS and would imply that no person can be discriminated against on the basis of one's HIV status.

Key Findings

In studies conducted in India and Africa, adolescents wanted greater access to HIV, reproductive and sexual health education, information on how to protect themselves, privacy and confidentiality in service sites, and better control over disclosure of their HIV status to others (Mburu et al. 2013; Sahay et al. 2013). The HIV infected children not only suffer from the infection, but the family and parental care is also limited. The social nature of the disease renders the family 'self conscious', sometimes hyper vigilant and over protective, leading to restrained childhood among children who might be infected. The affected children shoulder many responsibilities of the adult and therefore child headed households emerge. The socio-psychological outcomes for children are multiple viz. discontinuation of education; having parents who have infection and may not be able to work can lead children to engage in child labor, and many children lose their parents and siblings. Overall effect is 'debilitating social status' and exploited childhood resulting into adolescent and young adults with 'fragile and vulnerable' mental health and of course physical health.

Disclosure: Debating on Rights Issue

Denying older children information about their HIV status violates the child's right to information and privacy, and the child's right to voluntary, confidential HIV counseling and testing. It also compromises the child's ability to participate in his or her own medical care, an important part of the right to health. Older children and adolescents are reaching a level of physical and emotional development that can lead to sexual activity and sexual transmission risks.

Generally, laws assume that parents act in the best interests of the child. The law might thus support a parent's decision regarding disclosure. But the law recognizes that in certain circumstances, and for various reasons, parents may not act in their child's best interest. According to the principle of *parens patriae*, protection of the child's welfare outweighs the parents' right to refuse medical treatment for the child. However, whether parents have a right to refuse disclosure of diagnosis to a child, is unclear. Children have the right to health information under the Convention on the Rights of the Child. If children are not told about their status but are mature enough to understand and appreciate it, their right to health and information may have been violated. In India, there are no guidelines available for disclosure of HIV status to minors. Sometimes organizational rules are followed and children step into the 'adult' world unprepared. Orphanages are allowed to keep only minors and hence girls after 17 years of age are turned out. Plight of such minors in the 'big world' is be wildering as seen in the excerpt from a focus group discussion below:

> Till 17 years the girl was permitted to stay in the hostel, up to 18 years to a boy, this has to be cancelled should be abolished by Government. A girl is thrown out after 17 years and today also a hostel has thrown a girl outside. After all she is on medicines, ART antiretroviral therapy-medicines for HIV. But till she became 17 years of age what that institute has taught her? Only and only to consume medicines…In the end when we enquired the girl, then she responded that she had relations with her friend, and then we discussed with them about everything, they asked us what is HIV? …But up to 17 years of girl's age also she was not taught… But the organization by rule and Child Welfare Committee (CWC) rules, had thrown her out of the hostel. [FGD of NGO representatives]

Even the uninfected adolescents of today who are aware of their rights, feel strongly about the rights of their HIV infected counterparts. To them, knowing one's status is his or her right. An adolescent talks about it eloquently about the right of both infected and uninfected adolescents in the following interview:

> ##Facilitator## THEN ACCORDING TO YOU IF A CHILD IS INFECTED THEN, WHETHER WE HAVE TO TELL ABOUT HIS OR HER HIV STATUS TO HIM OR HER OR NOT?
> ##PQO-I-PD-22## I think they should be informed about what is in him.
> ## Facilitator ## AND WHY?
> ##PQO-I-PD-22## Because it is their fundamental right. We should know that it's not like if it was something which could not affect them. They should know about it in order for them to prepare themselves. May be like not at very mature stage but little earlier… Because they would be responsible, so I guess it should be told because, first because it is fundamental right and second even for the well-being of others surrounding them.

Here, the adolescent talks about an important issue of preparing the HIV infected child for prevention of secondary transmission. He is showing acceptance for his infected peer but feels strongly for his right and right of uninfected ones who should not acquire HIV inadvertently because the infected adolescent was unaware of the infection.

The principles of human rights, as stated in the Convention on the Rights of the Child about what are the ideal characteristics of the person making disclosure regarding HIV status to the child (3), provide guidance: The choice must be made in the best interests of the child.

Stigma and Discrimination

AIDS-related stigma and discrimination refers to prejudice, negative attitudes, abuse and maltreatment directed at people living with HIV/AIDS at home, in their local community, in schools or at health care facilities. Disclosure also entails a critical repercussion of stigma. Stigma contributes to children's psychosocial problems independent of their orphan status and other key demographic factors. Disclosure/stigma are associated with child's psychosocial well-being (e.g., self-esteem, positive future expectation, hopes for future, and perceived control over the future).

> ##PQO-I-AUD-28## They behave with them normal prior to HIV infection but when they come to know that he has got AIDS then all say that if he has got this then we can also get it. If he shows ignorance then we can also get that [/infection/], so they start to ignore him; so close friends also start to behave wrongly that time.
> ##FC## THEY START TO IGNORE AND THEN START TO BEHAVE WRONGLY MEANS WHAT? HOW?
> ##PQO-I-AUD-28## They don't allow to come near, don't let him touch them, they don't go with him, and don't talk properly with him etc.

The consequences of stigma and discrimination are wide-ranging: being shunned by family, peers and the wider community, poor treatment in healthcare and education settings, an erosion of rights, psychological damage, and a negative effect on the success of HIV testing and treatment. The right to be treated equally is part of the United Nations Convention on the Rights of the Child.

Exploitation

Orphans of parents who have died from AIDS are particularly vulnerable and many survive in child-headed households. Many of them turn to crime, drugs, or to the streets in order to survive. Affected children experience an early end to their childhood since they are required to become heads of households, drop out of school, work, raise younger siblings and care for sick parents and other ill family members. With relatives, they become unpaid willing workers as we hear a very young HIV infected orphan girl living with her relatives speak:

> ##PQM-I-AD-31## Because, what happens, my aunt she has small children so leaving her small children to ....I make very big contribution means, do such, so much of the work that I become light and feel like weightless [/too much of work makes her feel faint/] means now, today such situation is at home that without me not a single work is done. On everybody lips from morning to till I go to sleep. It is = Suman* = would, = Suman = do this? = Suman = do that. = Suman = did this? = Suman = did that, = Suman = water, = Suman = tea and what not...
>
> Routine means, it is busy this much, since getting up in the morning, now where we live is a ground floor, are four rooms, two bedrooms, one kitchen, one hall. And this much, 12 people live. Means that sweeping, cleaning all rooms, keep clean etc. then to help all in work, if anyone say something do that, this only is my routine, to see all at college, parlor then eat and sleep, this is the routine.[1]

The right of a child -NOT TO BE EXPLOITED- ! Furthermore, they experience greater poverty as a result of the loss due to sickness of other wage earners in the family. These losses affect all of the children in a household and, where infection rates are high, affect entire communities. With no adequate care and support, children experience losses in health, nutrition, education, affection, security, and protection. They suffer emotionally from rejection, discrimination, fear, loneliness, and depression.

Discontinuation of Education

The first thing that happens to an infected or affected child is the break in the education. Either the parents are too sick, impoverished and thus they are unable to continue with child's education or the child is stressed/ sick and discontinues education. An HIV infected adolescent tells:

> ## PQM-I-AD-26##: He [/his father/] was not working. He became very sick over here. Then father made a phone call to us. He said to my mother that, now I don't have guarantee of my health, so you can take our son, daughter and go there [/village/]. And my school was left at that year. Mother has been told that she has too [/HIV/].

[1]Fictitious name

Right to Recreation and Good Life

Our study also showed a strict social control upon girl child who was perinatally infected:

> ## PQM-I-AD-26## "Then… Then… I am thinking on it, the girls will say to me, your father does not allow you for the Dandiya [/a folk dance form/], how can you go outside? I get disturbed over there.
> Suman laments (##PQM-I-AD-31##), "One thing is always in my mind, that I was also having right to live one beautiful life, like that I am living but one black spot is there, that I have HIV. Have AIDS that should rest be in my life…I feel this. It was also my right to live healthy life. But because of my father that life is not possible. That was my right and that I lost.

Our study showed the positive support of uninfected adolescents who seem to be aware that most of the infected adolescents are the 'hapless' victims of situation. They did not seem to stigmatize their infected counterparts making us remind about the innocence of young mind. The situation reminds of the verse from Henry Vaughn's couplet (Vaughan 1621–1695).

> Happy those early days! when I
> Shined in my angel infancy.
> Before I understood this place
> Appointed for my second race

Marriage and sexual partnerships are the issues that are emerging as matter of concern for infected, affected and uninfected adolescents

> Why can't I marry like normal child? Why don't I have boyfriend or girl friend?
> Sir, since I am now 18 years old, I will start going out, so if I get married, then will it be ok?

The HIV infected adolescent forces the civil societies to understand the needs of the adolescent which is his/ her right as a human being. The situation entitles for bringing in structural changes with in-depth perceptions of social norms pertaining to the institution of marriage in the society.

PMTCT Program as Right of the Child

Article 17 of the United Nations Convention on the Rights of the Child (3) states that every child should have, "access to information and material from a diversity of national and international sources, especially those aimed at the promotion of his or her social, spiritual, and moral well-being and physical and mental health". The transmission of HIV from an HIV-positive mother to her child during pregnancy, labor, delivery, or breastfeeding is called mother-to-child transmission. In the absence of any interventions, transmission rates range from 15 to 45 % but this rate can be reduced to levels below 5 % with effective interventions. Prevention of Mother-to-Child HIV Transmission (PMTCT) is a critical, cost-effective, healthcare intervention. PMTCT should be considered a priority in terms of humanitarian principles and human rights, since it will protect children born to HIV-positive mothers from undue suffering and death. This is also in accordance with the obligation of the State Parties to the Convention on the Rights of the Child to "recognize that every child has the inherent right to life" and to "ensure to the maximum extent possible the survival and development of the child" (Article 6). In addition, the uninfected infants would not need a 'cost' for the life long care and treatment. Preventing pediatric cases is less costly than caring for children with HIV/AIDS, especially if Highly Active Antiretroviral Therapy (HAART) is used (WHO 2004). If children are to be protected from HIV, the expansion of PMTCT programs must be complemented by increased provision of pediatric treatment. This is expensive, yet there are humanitarian, equity, and children's rights arguments to justify the prioritization of treating HIV-infected children (Tolle et al. 2013). PMTCT program respects the right of the child to survival, development, and health. In India, approximately 49,000 women living with HIV become pregnant and deliver each year. While the government of India has made progress increasing the availability of Prevention of Mother-to-Child Transmission of HIV (PMTCT) services, only about one quarter of pregnant women received an HIV test in 2010, and about one-in-five that were found positive for HIV received interventions to prevent vertical transmission of HIV (Madhivanan et al. 2014).

Discussion

The HIV epidemic has not only been straining resources but it has created newer issues of children's rights to survival, development, and protection. As suggested by Jones, the universal discourses on the concepts of risk and rights may be an inadequate basis for addressing the health and social needs of especially marginalized children and that targeted social action to tackle the processes of marginalization is also needed (Jones 2009).

Our study indicates three prominent rights areas in the context of HIV among children and adolescents:

(1) Abandoned/ orphaned: Major issue is that of 'Right to inheritance'
(2) Vulnerability: HIV infected children/ adolescents become vulnerable at the family level. Most of the time, either the parents are sick or dead and the 'Right to education' gets undermined immediately. This is a leading problem when the household becomes child headed household or children get exploited by the persons who have given them refuge.
(3) Attitude: The attitude of the family changes and without any fault of the young ones, their 'Right to marry' and their Right to recreation' is emasculated. Child gets emotionally exploited but anger and strain is evident among children/ adolescents.

A review of 23 studies showed educational disadvantages among children affected by AIDS in various educational outcomes, including school enrollment and attendance, school behavior and performance, school completion, and educational attainment (Guo et al. 2012). Discontinuation of education of HIV infected and an affected child is a matter of concern. In a study conducted in China as well, stigma and discrimination puts a dent into right to education of HIV/AIDS-affected children in rural China (Qin et al. 2013). It has thus been observed that HIV undermines a child's possibilities for exercising the rights to education, health and autonomy, as guaranteed in international treaties such as the Convention on the Rights of the Child.

It is important to build the capacities of parents and guardians. The inheritance of children who have lost their parents should be addressed. Access to education must be guaranteed to these children as education would also reduce their vulnerability.

At the programmatic level, challenge is the failure to involve young people living with HIV (YPHIV) in the planning, designing, implementation, and evaluation of programs aimed at meeting their needs including sexual and reproductive health. Research shows that young people prefer services that are offered by their peers and also those that revolve around their ideologies (Baryamutuma and Baingana 2011).

Policies aiming at protecting and fulfilling the rights of men and women living with HIV to parenthood should thus be comprehensive enough to address the continuum of care from pregnancy to infant and child care, to provide means of integrating sexual and reproductive health interventions with HIV/AIDS care and to mitigate AIDS-related stigma and discrimination. In India, PMTCT is a successful program but it focuses on mother and child as dyad and the father is excluded. Focusing on the couple, the individual or the set of adults who are responsible for raising child, rather than seeing only the woman or the infant as the unit of care, can be an innovative programmatic advance toward meeting the parenthood rights and needs of people living with or affected by HIV.

Some areas of concern are the discrimination faced by orphaned children of HIV/AIDS parents, lack of funding or utilization of funds in giving treatments, unsafe health care practices, and lack of attention to HIV/AIDS amongst children in health policy. Child affected by AIDS needs medical treatment, counseling, support from extended families, and other non-institutional care, and help with medical care for parents so as not to create debt and need for engaging child in labor. Labor exploitation remains hidden at foster families and homes. As part of an attempt to help children living with HIV/AIDS, UNICEF in collaboration with national organizations and the Government of India, have put children on the agenda of the National AIDS Control Plan 9. The aim is to prevent parent to child transmission of the disease, and provide care and medical treatment to children infected with HIV/AIDS.

Disclosure of HIV diagnosis to children is the unmet need in this whole scenario. No guidelines are available for disclosure to children but disclosure has emerged emphatically as right of the children. There is growing evidence of the benefits of disclosure and with the increasing population of children and adolescents on ART, the disclosure of HIV diagnosis is kept on hold until older childhood and beyond (Wiener et al. 2007). One guideline for children up to 12 years has recently been introduced by WHO (2011), but feasibility in cultural settings need to be tested cautiously. Sexually active children, most often older adolescents, who know their HIV status can choose to use protection during sex and other risky activities. When sexually active people do not know about their status, they are at risk of spreading HIV. The American Academy of Pediatrics stressed that a "conspiracy of silence" may isolate children from potential sources of support and undermine trust between adults and children. Health workers in Kenya have found that disclosure before adolescence is preferable, as adolescents often react badly to disclosure.

Children have the right to age-appropriate information about their HIV status. Governments around the world need to create sound policies on supportive ways to disclose HIV status to children and adolescents as more children worldwide are tested for HIV and have access to antiretroviral treatment (ART). Policy makers need to be acutely aware of the questions and nuances involved pertaining to HIV disclosure. Tensions arise if the child is psychologically and cognitively, but not legally old enough to be told. The staff may then arguably, from a purely ethical perspective, be supported in disclosing, but legally be unable to disclose. Hence, policy makers could consider broadening the concept of emancipated or mature minor so that clinicians can discuss the infection with offspring, even if parents object. Considering the regional variations in India, the state laws could also become more uniform, and allow for the development of national guidelines that are more universally applicable .

Conclusion

It is well-known that failure to ensure children's rights creates opportunities for HIV infection. At the same time, HIV/AIDS creates opportunities for the violation of children's rights. Advances in the realization of children's rights, including the implementation of the United Nations Convention on the Rights of the Child (UNCRC), are necessary to stem the growth of the AIDS epidemic.

Recommendations and/or Implications

Age stratified policies and a program for adolescents and young adults is emerging gap. Policies should be drafted specifically for this vulnerable population. PMTCT program is the right of unborn child of infected mother. Expanding and strengthening PMTCT program should be considered the right of the child in HIV context. Responsible parenthood/ responsible guardianship are required to bring up HIV infected child. Male and family involvement in the PMTCT program would help bring in the required change in the responsible parenthood. Ambient environment for disclosure of HIV diagnosis to children/ adolescent is critical as with success of ART program, developmental issues of adolescence and young adults also emerge. Mainstreaming HIV infected children with their uninfected counterparts calls for far larger and broader structural interventions where communities inclusive of families and other stakeholders need to become responsible for the 'generation growing with HIV' and struggling to survive and thrive.

References

Baryamutuma, R., & Baingana, F. (2011). Sexual, reproductive health needs and rights of young people with perinatally acquired HIV in Uganda. [Review]. *African Health Sciences, 11*(2), 211–218.

Edmonds, A., Yotebieng, M., Lusiama, J., Matumona, Y., Kitetele, F., Napravnik, S., & Behets, F. (2011). The effect of highly active antiretroviral therapy on the survival of HIV-infected children in a resource-deprived setting: A cohort study. *PLoS Medicine, 8*(6), e1001044.

Guo, Y., Li, X., & Sherr, L. (2012). The impact of HIV/AIDS on children's educational outcome: A critical review of global literature. [Review]. *AIDS Care, 24*(8), 993–1012. doi:10.1080/09540121.2012.668170.

Haubrich, R. H., Little, S. J., Currier, J. S., Forthal, D. N., Kemper, C. A., Beall, G. N., … California Collaborative Treatment Group. (1999). The value of patient-reported adherence to antiretroviral therapy in predicting virologic and immunologic response. *AIDS, 13*(9), 1099–1107.

Jones, A. (2009). Social marginalization and children's rights: HIV-affected children in the Republic of Trinidad and Tobago. *Health and Social Work, 34*(4), 293–300. doi:10.1093/hsw/34.4.293.

League-of-Nations. (1924). Geneva Declaration of the Rights of the Child of 1924 adopted Sept. 26, 1924. *League of Nations Official Journal, Special Supplement, 21*.

Madhivanan, P., Krupp, K., Kulkarni, V., Kulkarni, S., Vaidya, N., Shaheen, R., & Fisher, C. (2014). HIV testing among pregnant women living with HIV in India: Are private healthcare providers routinely violating women's human rights? *BMC International Health and Human Rights, 14*(1), 7.

Mburu, G., Hodgson, I., Teltschik, A., Ram, M., Haamujompa, C., Bajpai, D., & Mutali, B. (2013). Rights-based services for adolescents living with HIV: Adolescent self-efficacy and implications for health systems in Zambia. *Reproductive health matters, 21*(41), 176–185. doi:10.1016/S0968-8080(13)41701-9.

Palladino, C., Bellón, J. M., Jarrín, I., Gurbindo, M. D., De José, M. I., Ramos, J. T., et al. (2009). Impact of highly active antiretroviral therapy (HAART) on AIDS and death in a cohort of vertically HIV type 1-infected children: 1980–2006. *AIDS Research and Human Retroviruses, 25*(11), 1091–1097. doi:10.1089/aid.2009.0070.

Qin, J., Yang, T., Kong, F., Wei, J., & Shan, X. (2013). Students and their parental attitudes toward the education of children affected by HIV/AIDS: A cross-sectional study in AIDS prevalent rural areas, China. *Australian and New Zealand Journal of Public Health, 37*(1), 52–57. doi:10.1111/1753-6405.12010.

Sahay, S. (2013). Coming of age with HIV: A need for disclosure of HIV diagnosis among Children/Adolescents. *JAID, 1*, 1–7. doi:10.1155/2013/161085.

Sahay, S., Nirmalkar, A., Sane, S., Verma, A., Reddy, S., & Mehendale, S. (2013). Correlates of sex initiation among school going adolescents in Pune, India. *Indian Journal of Pediatrics, 80*(10), 814–820. doi:10.1007/s12098-013-1025-8.

Salisbury, K. M. (2000). National and state policies influencing the care of children affected by AIDS. [Review]. *Child and Adolescent Psychiatric Clinics of North America, 9*(2), 425–449. doi:10.1007/s12098-013-1025-8.

Tolle, M. A., Phelps, B. R., Desmond, C., Sugandhi, N., Omeogu, C., Jamieson, D., … Child Survival Working Group of the Interagency Task Team on the Prevention and Treatment of HIV infection in Pregnant Women, Mothers and Children. (2013). Delivering pediatric HIV care in resource-limited settings: Cost considerations in an expanded response. *AIDS*, *27*, S179–S186. doi:10.1097/QAD.0000000000000105.

UNICEF. (2014). The children: HIV/AIDS. *Picture in India*. Retrieved November 3, 2014, from http://www.unicef.org/india/children_2358.htm.

UNAIDS. (2012). Global statistics: More than 35 million people live with HIV. http://www.unaids.org/en/media/unaids/.

United Nations (1989). *Convention on the Rights of the Child* , *1*, Chap IV, Human Rights , New York.

United Nations. (2003). *Convention on the Rights of the Child (1989). HIV/AIDS and the rights of the child.*

Vaughan, H. (1621–1695). The Retreat.

Volberding, P. A., & Deeks, S. G. (2010). Antiretroviral therapy and management of HIV infection. [Research Support, N.I.H., Extramural Review]. *Lancet, 376*(9734), 49–62. doi:10.1016/S0140-6736(10)60676-9.

WHO. (2004). *Strategic framework for the prevention of HIV infection in infants in Europe*. Copenhagen.

WHO. (2011). *Guideline on HIV disclosure counselling for children up to 12 years of age*.

Wiener, L. S., Battles, H. B., & Wood, L. V. (2007). A longitudinal study of adolescents with perinatally or transfusion acquired HIV infection: sexual knowledge, risk reduction self-efficacy and sexual behavior. [Research Support, N.I.H., Intramural]. *AIDS and Behavior, 11*(3), 471–478. doi:10.1007/s10461-006-9162-y.

Wood, E., Hogg, R. S., Yip, B., Harrigan, P. R., O'Shaughnessy, M. V., & Montaner, J. S. (2004). The impact of adherence on CD4 cell count responses among HIV-infected patients. [Research Support, Non-U.S. Gov't]. *Journal of Acquired Immune Deficiency Syndromes, 35*(3), 261–268. doi:10.1097/00126334-200403010-00006.

Chapter 13
Adoption: A Source of Maltreatment and Violation of Child Rights

Nilanjana Sanyal

Introduction

A home in a socio-emotional flavor is adorned with the presence of a child. It is just not the conjugal intimacy of two adult individuals that constitutes the frame of a family structure; it is rather the etching of a place marked by the existence of a child with all his/her nuances that typifies the ambience of a family life. Children are just not the extensions of their parents in physical terms; they are the bearers of their values and the podium to reflect on the stylized parenting they receive in life. Parent–child interaction thus pays heavy toll on the future growth of a child, creating positive or negative ripples in the basic "present" life context. The precious presence of children is so heavily felt by most couples that a home without a child is felt as a groove that needs mending. The process might be going for "adoption". A child, be it any biological or an adopted one, being contextually available, is expected to fill up the empty hearts of wanting-to-be parents. The expected scenario is healthy family flow with glowing emotional bonding and felt security and warmth therein. But at times, reality poses different and difficult picture through its crude lenses. The resultant experience being the fact that it is not all the roses to have in a family through the existence of a child, the thorns are hurting at times.

DeVooght et al. (2011) showed that although children of all ages can be victims of abuse or neglect, infants and children are particularly vulnerable. Federal data on child maltreatment from the National Data System (NCANDS) show that young children are more likely than older children to be reported to child protective services (CPS) for suspected abuse or neglect, and are more likely than their older peers to be determined victims of maltreatment by CPS.

N. Sanyal (✉)
Department of Psychology, University of Calcutta, 92 A.P.C. Road, Kolkata 700009, India
e-mail: sanyal_nilanjana2004@rediffmail.com

S. Deb (ed.), *Child Safety, Welfare and Well-being*,
DOI 10.1007/978-81-322-2425-9_13

The data consistently show that child victims most frequently experience maltreatment in the form of neglect (with more than 78 % of all victims) in Federal Fiscal Year (FFY) 2009 experiencing neglect (DHHS 2010). Children aged five and younger are at an even greater risk for neglect than older children: almost 80 % of all maltreatment victims in the younger age group experienced neglect in FFY 2009, compared to two-thirds of children aged six and older. Furthermore, data on child fatalities consistently show that the youngest children (aged five and younger) are at greater risk of death as a result of abuse or neglect, with 87 % of all child maltreatment fatalities in FFY 2009. Children less than a year old comprise 46 percent of all child maltreatment fatalities.

Maltreatment of Children

The data furnish a new conceptual frame of maltreatment of children of every age through abuse or neglect, being intentional or unintentional. The Child Abuse Prevention and Treatment Act (2010) required states to develop minimum definitions of child abuse or neglect. The act states that abuse or neglect are "any recent act or failure to act on the part of a parent or caretaker, which results in death, serious physical or emotional harm, sexual abuse or exploitation or an act or failure to act which presents an imminent risk of serious harm." In addition to this federal law, some states define specific types of abuse or neglect, such as emotional abuse, medical neglect, sexual exploitation, and abandonment.

Despite persistent media headlines about extreme cases of child abuse and neglect, the public remains largely uninformed about the developmental status of children affected by this tragic problem. The immediate markers of abuse and neglect are obvious—bruise and battered bodies and in its most severe form death. However, research has shown that child abuse and neglect—collectively known as "child maltreatment"—are also associated with a broad array of less visible negative outcomes that may emerge at different stages of children's lives (Chalk et al. 2002).

Sensational stories of child abuse and neglect have become too frequent feature of news reports across the country. Research allows us to move beyond the headlines to get a better grasp of this pressing social problem. Child neglect is the most common form of child maltreatment. More than half (58 %) of the substantiated cases of child maltreatment involve child neglect. Additionally, about 36 % were victims of other forms of maltreatment, such as abandonment or threats of harm. Regarding consequences hundreds of research studies and agency reports have consistently reported negative outcomes from abuse and neglect for many children (English 1998). Taken together, this evidence suggests that abuse and neglect are associated with both short and long-term negative consequences for children's physical and mental health, cognitive skills, and educational attainments and social and behavioral development. What is not yet certain, however, is the extent to which these effects are caused by the child's experience with abuse and neglect or the presence or absence of other factors in the child's developmental experiences.

Child neglect can take many forms and can stem from a range of underlying conditions affecting families. These can include mental health issues, substance abuse disorders, issues involving domestic violence, and poverty. The federally supported Child Welfare Information Gateway, provides this definition, "neglect is frequently defined as the failure of a parent or other person with responsibility for the child to provide needed food, clothing, shelter, medical care or supervision, such that the child's safety, health and well-being are threatened with harm." (Devooght et al. 2011). Within the framework of the present article, the focus would be on mental health issues of adopted children, being the by-product of maltreatments of parents oozing out their own personality problems, expectations regarding parenthood, and total lack of identifications of biological parenthood itself. The presentation will take help of certain case studies as noted in psychotherapeutic situations.

Adoption: The Alternate Parenthood Context

Owing to physical or psychosocial problems, prospective couples really cannot manage to conceive a child yet cry for a baby in life tremendously—their only alternate way out is to adopt a baby. According to Nagera (2006), people adopt because of the following reasons:

a. Kindness to accommodate a poor or abandoned child in life;
b. Cannot conceive at all;
c. In order to save the bitter marriage, having a buffer through an adopted child;
d. Going to design a companion for an already existing child (biological or not).

Adoption first became a legal status and process for transferring parental rights from biological parents to substitute parents in 1926. Prior to that, the practice of babies and young children being cared for by extended family members or strangers probably goes back to the beginning of human time. At its inception, the legal framework for adoption was designed for the placement of babies with adoptive parents. The law was designed to ensure (Shiveman 2003):

- That adopted parents were suitable to care for a baby, and that this was not a financial transaction but a child-centered process.
- The anonymity of the birth parents, particularly the birth mother, was preserved, and the baby was given a new identity. The expectation was that post-adoption there would be no further contact between the child and its birth family. It was common practice for the adoptive child not even to be told that they had been adopted. Anonymity protected the birth mother from the shame of motherhood out of wedlock, the adopters from the embarrassment of infertility, and the child from the stigma of illegitimacy.

From Attachment Theory to Understanding Trauma of Adopted Children in Infancy by Bowlby

In his later works, Bowlby postulated the existence of '*an internal psychological organization with a number of highly specific features, which included representational models of the self and of attachment figures*' (Bowlby 2005). This concept made sense of the patterns of behavior that children were displaying not only in adoptive families but in foster homes. The template for attachment that they were displaying in the substitute families was the template that had been learned in a dysfunctional birth family. This attachment behavior or attachment strategy can be seen as adaptive in the context of pathologies parent–infant relationships. In 'normal' functional substitute families, it was mal-adaptive. Bowlby had made the link between poor mother–infant attachment relationships and the development of '*delinquent*' behavior in adolescence (Bowlby 1944). His followers had refined and developed his theory, and identified different attachment styles that children develop depending upon the quality and form of that primary attachment relationship between mother and infant (Main and Solomon 1986). These attachments styles have been defined as secure, insecure–ambivalent, avoidant, and disorganized (Howe 2005).

The work of Bessell van der Kolk (2005) and Bruce Perry (2006) helped us recognize that PTSD in childhood was really only applicable to children who by and large have had 'good enough' attachments to primary careers, but had subsequently suffered single traumas. For children who have experienced multiple traumas and who also had insecure attachment relationships, their whole development was impacted from birth through infancy by repeated 'relationship' or 'ambient' trauma. This phenomenon has subsequently been given the title of 'Developmental Trauma'.

This syndrome has been researched and defined by Child Traumatic Stress Network Task Force (2003) in the following fashion:

Developmental trauma disorder by Bessel van der Kolk in the Psychiatric Annals (2005)	
a. Exposure	Multiple or chronic exposure to one or more forms of developmentally adverse interpersonal trauma (e.g. abandonment, betrayal, physical assaults, sexual assaults, threats to bodily integrity, coercive practices, emotional abuse, witnessing violence, and death) • Subjective experience (e.g. rape, betrayal, fear, resignation, defeat, shame)
b. Triggered pattern of repeated deregulation in response to trauma cues	Affective • Somatic (e.g. physiological, motoric, medical) • Behavioral (e.g. re-enactment, cutting) • Cognitive (e.g., thinking that it is happening again, confusion, dissociation, depersonalization) • Relational (e.g., clinging, oppositional, distrustful, compliant) • Self-attribution (e.g., self-hate, blame)

Developmental trauma disorder by Bessel van der Kolk in the Psychiatric Annals (2005)	
c. Persistently altered attributions and expectancies	• Negative self-attribution • Distrust of protective caretakers • Loss of expectancy of protection by others • Loss of trust in social agencies to protect • Lack of recourse to social justice/retribution • Inevitability of future victimization
d. Functional impairment	Educational • Familial • Peer • Legal • Vocational

Grueling assessment, long waiting lists, exasperating bureaucracy, and considerable expense are some of the common stories or challenges that the prospective adoptive parents experience in the process. But there is a presumption that the day these parents finally take a child into their arms is the first day of the "happily ever after" dreams for both sides. But that really is a dream and is not realistic. Too many possible complications may come in the way in the source format being (Rehman 2003):

- Coming from the parents
- Coming from the child
- Coming from the interaction
- Coming from development

A. Coming from the parent

There is a common notion that if a child is picked up from an orphanage and put in a decent family, he/she will thrive and develop as per Archer and Burnell (2003) of the UK-based "Family Futures" which specializes in providing therapeutic services for children who have experienced early trauma. Unfortunately reality shows that love does not always conquer all. Hence in adoption situations, the "attachment issues" turn to be a primary problem among many. The older they are when placed in a family, the deeper the problem is likely to be. Consequently, it has been noted that children who receive poor early parenting have every aspect of their development being impaired or impacted to varying degrees by that early traumatic experience. It has been shown that their brains develop differently from those who are encouraged to develop a secure, loving attachment to a principal career—usually their mother (Monahon 1993; Archer and Burnell 2003). It is not just that they find it difficult to form secure attachment to their parents; they also have problems with problem-solving and cognitive processing and also with sensory motor development. Unless adoptive parents know about the issues and receive appropriate professional help where necessary, they are parenting on "faulty foundations", says Archer and Burnell (2003). The problems are just not there in the initial stage of settling in a family, in adoption, long-term issues can re-emerge at various later life stages, particularly in adolescence.

A. Coming from the Parents

In parenthood, most parents draw on their experiences of being parented when raising a family. But adopted children may need different forms of parenting to help with feelings that biological children of their age would not have. They need a parent to help them to make a transition from babyhood to autonomous child of middle childhood; otherwise regressive modes have deep patches in their behavioral mode. Usually children with attachment issues can become overtly self-assured and pseudo-independent or they become frustrated and intolerant, often quite aggressive, or they are very compliant and quiet. None of these coping strategies that the child has developed works in the long run and "re-parenting" is needed to make up for what that child has missed. Additionally, it has been found that human-to-human touch releases oxytocin, a feel-good hormone and it is a process that happens all the time between biological parents and babies. In adoption, if by any chance, the dearth is noted in the context, relevant fearful experiences regarding touch takes place in the child's mind. The touch seems to be the essential element in bonding with people with pleasure (Archer and Burnell 2003).

A typical emotional inadequacy is evident in most adoptive parents. They are found to be slow in looking for help for the child or for their relationship; because they may not want to admit that they are having difficulties. Faced with a child who would just not stop crying or tantruming, adoptive parents can feel a huge sense of shame. They seem not to have the visceral confidence that they know their child, and the experience can be quite harrowing. The behavior they are dealing with in their children includes extreme mood swings, aggression, and poor performance at school, low self-esteem and sometimes stealing and self-harming behavior. In fact, prospective adoptive parents need to know that it is not going to be an easy task for them. Their resilience would need to stand firm to confront the demand.

B. Coming from the Child

Children come into new families with pathological ways of relating and they at times pathologies the new family. As per the situation, it is not the parents who are a risk factor; it is the child who may be the risk factor. They endanger the marriage, endanger the mental health of parents and possibly the potentiality of the child could not be utilized in the desired ways in the family owing to his/her own constitutional factors like low intelligence, impulsivity, poor psychiatric history.

C. Coming from the Interaction

Most frequently adopted children are found to have poor identification with their parents. A constant search, even in fantasy for own parents, prevent them from having a healthy bond with the adoptive ones. They become verbally abusive, retaliate at every juncture of advice, and have displaced rage on them from the non-available biological parents. Adopted girls in a reactive mode become promiscuous and conceive illegitimate children. Boys become vandals, abuse drugs, remain asocial and can be quite destructive to adoptive parent's property.

D. Coming from the Development

Adopted children have two sets of parents, biological and adoptive. They can denigrate and idealize them at will. Because of this, the mechanism of splitting is highly facilitated in them with negative consequences for development (Freud 1909). Similarly their oedipal orientations suffer injury for the same reason. The splitting in them turns two sets of parents into four sets:

- A denigrated bad set of biological parents;
- An idealized set of biological parents;
- A good idealized set of adoptive parents;
- A bad denigrated set of adoptive parents.

They feel frustrated in any way and react negatively. Navigating a balanced developmental chart and a welfare system for them then becomes a major challenge. The theoretical roots of analysis of such a situation can be schematized as follows (Fig. 13.1):

For such children, the denigrated bad set of biological parents as well as the possibility of denigrated bad set of adoptive parents can be neutralized and erased from the socio-emotional system if the above conceived conditions are adopted and general needs of the child are normally met. Clinical cases are revealing the fact that such frames of development chart are mostly not there in the adoptive parents' mind and hence the woes of numerous variety speaks for it in different pathologies.

The Hand-On Scenario of Adopted Children: Excerpts from a Few Psychotherapeutic Case Studies

1. Riyance, a 4 year old, very frail child has been brought to the clinic with following complaints;

   - The child is restless and has difficulty in going off to sleep;
   - He needs to be bribed to make him follow any instructions;
   - He eats very fast, has frequent outbursts of temper tantrums, especially with the mother;
   - Likes to draw father's attention, but fails;
   - Gets very aggressive at times.

The background history reveals that he was from a starved mother, who just after giving his birth, died of malnutrition. The father abandoned the child instantly. Through a home, he had been placed into a well-to-do family with a professor father and a working mother. The mother being beautiful was too narcissistic and did think that her beauty would be spoiled in conceiving a child. The husband seem to be reluctant in close bonding with the wife but cooperated with her in adopting the child and in looking after the household chores. The child seemed to be a victim of maltreatment. A helping assistant was hired to look after the child in the day time, but the mother did try her best to take care of him. In the process she developed a peculiar guilt thinking that she is not up to the expected level of being his mother, maybe she is depriving him of the quality of love that his natural mother could have

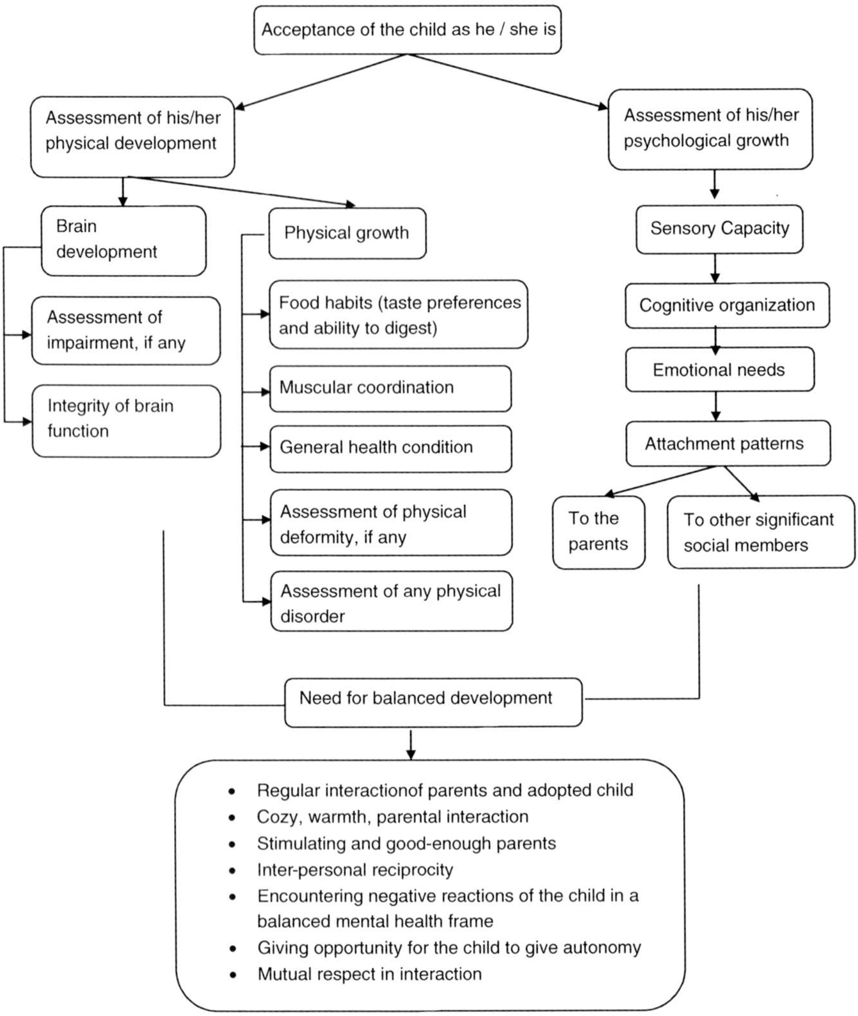

Fig. 13.1 Schematic representation showing the requisite conditions for balanced personality development of adopted children

given him. She was always worried about his food and was constantly offering him food to compensate for whatever may be his deprivation with her. While trying to help the child in any habit formation, she always felt shaky, thinking that she might be coxing him to do it. The father attended him physically at times, but very rarely attended him psychologically. Their inadequate, inconsistent, and irresponsible parenting was no doubt inking the maltreatment issue for their child.

2. Shaon, a girl of 7 years was brought to psychotherapy for her attention deficit in studies, stubbornness, non-compliant attitude to family members, dislike toward studies and going to school, constant T.V. watching habit, lying, and

extreme regressive speech. The family backdrop revealed her adoptive mother was approaching 40 years of age; father's age was 44 years. Both of them were graduates. The father worked in a private company, the mother was the home maker. The mother was brought in an extended family with a widow mother-in-law and a spinster sister, elder to her husband. The husband had strong inclinations toward them and all three of them used to criticize her for almost everything. The couple life was at stake; they constantly fought with each other. Both the members revealed an obsessive-compulsive personality pattern with extreme rigidity in their self-opinionated ways in life. They could not conceive in natural way and hence opted for adoption. Shaon was conceived as a bridge between them but very soon they started fighting over their care-giving roles. The child was the victim of family conflicts, clashes, even parents fighting physically, abusing each other in high pitches, and not being allowed by the mother to spend time with the grandmother or aunt. Ultimately the couple got separated from the mother-in-law and sister-in-law and started their home in a new locality with the daughter. She was sent to school. But they found her to be absent-minded and not at all interested in studies. She was keen on watching T.V. even at the cost of receiving thrashings from the parents. To the therapist she seemed to be a bright girl who used all her potentialities in manipulating a situation or condition to fulfill her instant pleasure-seeking habit format. Her defense was that of having regressive speech, but she seems to be aware of the minute details of the situation. On her second day of visit, feeling quite assured with the therapist, she opened her mind, saying, "I don't like my parents, they fight a lot between them, beat me up regularly, force me to obey them always and take out their own anger on me. I can't study, I watch T.V. to forget all my miseries. Can I be sent somewhere else? I like to be away from these two human beings." Her emotional plight is an instance of maltreatment.

3. A 6 year old boy, Rohit, has been brought into the clinic with concentration problem, mother-teasing and extreme demanding nature. He was an adopted son of a reputed medical practitioner and a homemaker mother. Unfolding his mind he gradually revealed the fact that he feels something amiss in the family. He always wanted to see the mother in stripped-off condition in order to see how he was born out of her. He had some confusion regarding father too that he found to be unrealistically possessive and protective about him. At the age of 6, he had been given two tutors to teach him, he was showered with gifts and toys from the father at regular basis. Mother was restrictive a bit for which she was constantly abused by the father. His little mind put a query in front—"Is there anything unnatural regarding my birth? I do not feel comfortable here." Taking the child much away from normal developmental course is another angle of maltreatment meted out to them at times.

4. A 9 year old Shreya had the problems of poor academic grade, problem of enuresis, nail biting, unusual hankering for money and electronic gadgets, a special lesbian friendship with a girl of 2 years older than her. She was the adopted

daughter of an affluent business father and was a student of a very posh school in Kolkata. She was described as an internet addict and was in a habit of constantly using her mobile for text messaging. Therapeutic interviewing was difficult with her initially. Gradually she narrated her plight saying her mother was extremely prying type and complained about her to the father that resulted even in shoe-beating for her. She had been criticized by both of them for not being beautiful in looks, good in studies and in terms of not being obedient. Her friend seemed to offer her the emotional cushion which she was not ready to part with. The discourse with the parents revealed their mentality, saying, "She is not the type we wanted to have. Neither can we accept her, nor can we abandon her. Even her body features seem repulsive to us." Barring details, isn't it good enough to conceptualize what maltreatment means?

5. 3 and 1/2 year old Reshma came with her mother to the clinic. The child was having seizure-disorder and was usually hyperactive. The home maker mother of an engineer husband found it very difficult to accept the child with her problem. She said, "To me, the child seems to be a problem, an emotional burden, a time consumer, a robber in terms of my free life. I just want her to get removed to someone else or die." The father's version was that the child was brought to fill up the void of his wife in terms of time and emotions. The contrast between the dreamt child and the child in reality, painted the canvas of maltreatment for her.

The Mental Frame of Maltreating Parents: A Few Salient Points

In the mental frame of maltreating parents, especially the mother, certain noteworthy psychological points seem to be:

- Infertile mothers' design and expectations at times do not match the reality situation—they instantly become reactive in terms of open irritation and rejection.
- Motherhood or parentage is a heavy task, carrying out which, successfully can bring enormous joy and fulfillment. But the process needs a lot of resilience and patience to bear the common hazards of developmental tasks. One needs to be totally mentally prepared to combat any errands there.
- Children are not decorative elements in life. Life follows unfolding of growth in hazardous sequential stages, one need to offer balanced "holding" there.
- Children are not your canvas to put your designs on it. They are living beings having their potentialities as well as vulnerabilities to grow in a stylized manner.
- If children are required to follow their parents, parents need to be the stable role models.
- Psychoanalytically mothers or caregivers are called "containers" in life. In order to contain (the child) in a container (mother or parent), the container must be clean to assure its quality preservation.

- Mother's/father's infertility may be the outcome of wrong parenting received and hence poor identification with the roles. Before opting for adoption, one needs to rectify the situation through self correcting therapeutic processes.
- Being parent is difficult, accepting the challenge and confronting it needs maturity to carve progression in life. Maltreating a child is a wrapping on the defects of the parents. One needs to acknowledge it.

Indicators for Child Maltreatment

Traditional indicators for child maltreatment prevention programs raise thorny ethical, methodological, and empirical issues and have significant validity problems. To inform the design of maltreatment prevention program evaluation, it is recommended that there should be a combination of indicators that measure risk and protective factors for child maltreatment along four dimensions:

- Parenting capacity
- Substance use
- Financial solvency and
- Family conflict.

In addition, Centre for Study of Social Policy (CSSP) indicators in two other areas: child well-being and home and community. Indicators of child well-being should address the domains of physical health, education and cognitive development, and social and emotional well-being. From among several dimensions of home and community factors, indicators include domain of home safety and social connectedness (Ross and Vandinere 2009) (Chart 13.1).

There are many reasons why reliable and valid indicators of child maltreatment do not exist. Maltreating a child can result in civil or criminal actions that have severe repercussions for parents and children. In addition, parents labeled as abusive or neglectful of their children bear a heavy social stigma. These qualities undermine direct observation aimed at detecting maltreatment—parents can be expected to avoid maltreating their children in the presence of researcher or therapist. In adoptive family situation, two most important factors that need consideration are:

Domain	Concept Measured
Child well-being	• Health • Education and cognitive development • Social and emotional well-being
Home and community factors	• Home safety • Social connectedness
Child maltreatment	• Parenting capacity • Substance use • Financial solvency • Family conflict

Chart 13.1 Domains and concepts for assessment of child development prevention programs

Parenting Capacity

This has many dimensions, including parenting skills, parenting knowledge of child development, and parent mental health. Strong parenting capacity can be a protective factor against maltreatment, while weak parenting capacity can be a risk factor. Some parents, especially young parents or parents going for adoption may not have had the opportunity to practice parenting skills or learn about child development. This appears especially true when parents have not experienced modeling of appropriate parenting behavior (Shiveman 2003). Mental health problems can also hamper parenting capacity, resulting in an increased risk of child maltreatment (Barth 2003). Parenting knowledge of child development is a protective factor for child maltreatment—and a lack of knowledge is a risk factor that can contribute to parenting practices that are not developmentally appropriate.

Three approaches to using indicators of parenting capacity in evaluating child maltreatment prevention programs include measuring the existence of screening and service access, directly observing parenting and parent self-reports.

Family Conflict and Discipline Practices

Nurturing parenting is a protective factor for child maltreatment. The use of non-violent and non-aggressive methods for resolving conflicts between partners and for disciplining children, for example, are protective factors. Conversely, aggressive methods for resolving conflicts, including threatening and abusive language as well as physical confrontation and punishment, are risk factors. Because witnessing violence between parents or a parent and a significant other is traumatic for children, it can be considered child maltreatment even when children are not physically harmed (Putnam 2001).

The selection of specific indicators and how they are operationalized may vary across evaluations, depending partly on available resources. Though challenging, rigorous assessment of maltreatment prevention programs are critically important. In the complex matrix of family problems from multidimensional sources, placing increasing stresses on families and threatening the resources available to support the family in terms of financial as well as socio-emotional, it is particularly important to invest in effective programs to deal with child maltreatment.

Thus, the vulnerability of infants and young children to abuse or neglect and the significant toll of maltreatment on the very young child underscore the critical importance of early and effective interventions that support and strengthen their families and ensure that these children are protected and nurtured. At the same time, reduction in the incidence of abuse or neglect among these very young children holds the promise of substantial Government savings, befitting children and families as well as society as a whole. The selection of specific indicators and how they are operationalized may vary across evaluations, depending partly on available resources. Though challenging, rigorous assessment of maltreatment prevention programs are critically important. In the complex matrix of family problems from multidimensional sources, placing increasing stresses on families and threatening the resources available to support the family in terms of financial as well as socio-emotional, it is particularly important to invest in effective programs to deal with child maltreatment.

In fact India has been a major supporter of child's rights and CRC but still it has not been able to achieve or eradicate child-related basic issues. Consistent efforts are needed in right direction. Securing child rights is not the matter to be dealt at the policy level, people has to be mobilized to this cause. The role of psychologists stands very high there.

Child Right Violation

Violation of the rights of children represents a common occurrence in many parts of the world. These violations take the form of torture, cruel, inhuman or degrading treatment, excessive work and labor, sexual abuse, and slavery. The Universal Declaration of Human Rights (UDHR 1945) contains important provisions for children, although emphasis is upon protection and non-discrimination rather granting specific, independent rights to a child as a person. Article 25(2) of the Declaration provides that motherhood and childhood are entitled to special care and assistance. All children, whether born in or out of wedlock, shall enjoy the same social protection.

As far as children's rights as a distinct category of human rights is concerned, the real impetus was provided with the adoption of the United Nations General Assembly Declaration on the Rights of the Child in 1959. The Convention came into force in September, 1994. It is the most valuable treaty in the armory of human rights law with which to protect and defend the rights of children the world over. The basic thrust of the Convention is that the child has independent rights and the primary focus of the Convention is to operate in, "the best interests of the child." According to Van Bueren (1999), the Convention is essentially about what she terms as the "four Ps". These are:

- The participation of children in decisions affecting their own destiny;
- The protection of the children against discrimination, destiny, and all forms of neglect and exploitation;
- The prevention of harm to children, and;
- The provisions of assistance for basic needs.

While accepting the realities of parental influences and rights and duties of the wider family, the Article is nevertheless reticent in dealing with situations where the interests, directions and guidance of parents are not "appropriate" or "consistent" with the evolving capabilities of the child. To bring out the best in each child, the Rights of a child to be protected against all forms of abuse and violence are as follows:

- The right to special care if disabled;
- The right to adequate nutrition and care;
- The right to learn to be useful member of society and to develop individual activities;
- The right to be brought up in a spirit of peace;
- The right to a name and nationality;
- The right to affection, love, and understanding
- The right to be among the first to receive relief in times of disaster;
- The right to protection against all forms of neglect, cruelty, and exploitation;
- The right to free education and to full opportunity for play and recreation;
- The right to enjoy these rights regardless of race, color, gender, national, or social origin.

Thus keeping in mind the common rights of children in any set up and considering the scenario of various possible maltreatments meted out on them at times, certain alternate emotional moves on the part of parents are required to have a frame for common reference.

Conclusion and Recommendations

In any context, everyone must ensure child's welfare and respect his innocence and integrity. Life may pose problems of various kinds, adults may not always be equipped with all the good qualities of taking life responsibilities, situations may provoke one's senses to operate in negative directions, come what may, one should remember and recognize the fact that children are dependent, yet respectable future agents, whose complete development should be the goal of our life, irrespective of specific life conditions that render children's status of a specific kind. Life will be full of efforts and understanding there, practices would be of positive quality, the automatic resultant effect would be child welfare and protection, rather than abuse, neglect and desertion. Children with health content will really adorn families, curving the future niche of being good parents to other children, be it natural or of adoption.

Solution-Oriented Emotional Moves of Adoptive Parents: Helping a Child to Settle

Advice for parents returning home with an adopted child includes:

- Keep the house hassle-free and physically quiet;
- Limit the number of toys and equipment available to the child to enroot him in the family realistically. Too much stimulation can cause overwhelming reaction;

- Seek support from other parents who have older adopted children, to get a sense of what things are going to be like;
- Expect that the child is going to need a lot of time settling at night;
- Try to get as much information as possible from the care home as the child's typical habits like eating, sleeping etc.
- It is better if one of the parents is available on a one-to-one basis for the child for at least a couple of years, after coming into the home.
- One should remain prepared for temper tantrums as they are the single media of expressing anxiety;
- Be prepared for the child's physical rejection of parents through pushing the parent away. Time and consistent support alters the situation.
- Professionally monitor child's development with experts on the subject;
- Use remedial techniques like psychotherapy, counseling, parental guidance when things do not move smoothly;
- Provide on-going supportive and preventive services such as parents group, marriage counseling etc.

Apart from the offered solution orientations to adoptive parents, certain policy-based approaches need to be followed to combat maltreatment effect on adopted children.

- Possible adoptive parents must go through rigorous psychotherapeutic interviews to open up their emotional files behind the desires for adoption;
- Personality profiles of such parents needs to be mapped out with projective techniques;
- They need to be counseled to heal up their emotional patches before finally taking the decision of adoption;
- Data need to be collected regarding the couples' socio-emotional basic reaction patterns;
- Follow-up interventions in the family after adoption are required to verify the comfort level of the adopted child.

Summarily, the prospective parents must be mentally prepared to accommodate the child in their lives and be equipped enough to deal with the hazards of the normal developmental course to see a bright future of their own family profile.

References

Archer, C. & Burnell, A. (Eds.) (2003). *Trauma, attachment and family permanence: Fear can stop you loving*. London: Jessica Kingsley Publishers.

Barth, R. (2003). Outcomes after child welfare services. *Children and Youth Services Review, 22*(9/10), 763–787.

Bessell Van der Kolk, A. (2005). Family futures neuro-sequential approach to the assessment and treatment of traumatized children. In A. Burnell & J. Vaughan (Eds.), *Neuro-Physiological Psychotherapy* (NPP). www.familyfutures.co.uk/wp-content/uploads/…/family-futures-rationale.

Bowlby, J. (1944). Forty-four juvenile thieves: Their characters and home life. *International Journal of Psycho-Analysis 25*, 19–52, 107–127.

Bowlby, J. (2005). *A secure base*. US: Routledge.

Bruce, P. (2006). Family futures neuro-sequential approach to the assessment and treatment of traumatized children. In A. Burnell & J. Vaughan (Eds.), *Neuro-physiological psychotherapy* (NPP). www.familyfutures.co.uk/wp-content/uploads/.../family-futures-rationale.

Chalk, R., Gibbons, A., & Scampa, H.J. (2002). The multiple dimensions of child abuse and neglects: New insights into an old problem. *Child Trend Research Brief.* www.childtrend.org.May.

Child Abuse Prevention and Treatment Act. (2010). www.acf.hhs.gov/programs/cb/resource/capta2010.

Child Traumatic Stress Network Task Force. (2003). Family futures neuro-sequential approach to the assessment and treatment of traumatized children. In A. Burnell & J. Vaughan (Eds.), *Neuro-physiological psychotherapy* (NPP). www.familyfutures.co.uk/wp-content/uploads/.../family-futures-rationale.

Devooght, K., McCoy-Roth, M., & Freundlich, M. (2011). Young and vulnerable: Children five and under experience high maltreatment rates. *Early Childhood Highlights, 2.*

DHHS. (2010). www.dhhs.tas.gov.au/about_the_department/.../annual_reports.

English, D. J. (1998). The extent and consequences of child maltreatment. The future of children: Protecting children from abuse and neglect, 8(1), 39–53. In N. B. Guterman (2001). Stopping child maltreatment before it starts: Emerging horizons in early home visitation services. Thousand Oaks: Sage.

Freud, S. (1909). Analysis of a phobia of a five year old boy. Harmondsworth: Pelican Freud Library.

Howe, D. (2005). *Child abuse and neglect: Attachment, development and intervention.* Basingstoke: Palgrave Macmillan.

Main, M. & Solomon, J. (1986). Discovery of an insecure disorganized/disoriented attachment pattern: procedures, findings and implications for classification of behavior. In: M. W. Yogman & T. B. Brazelton (Eds.), *Affective development in infancy.* Norrwood: Ablex.

Monahon, C. (1993). *Children and trauma: A guide for parents and professionals.* San Francisco: Jossey-Bass.

Nagera, H. (2006). *On adoption: Problems, successes and psychiatric consequences.* Sydney: Lecture delivered at Tampa Bay Psychoanalytic Institute, University of South Florida.

Putnam, R. (2001). *Bowlby alone: The collapse and revival of American community.* New York: Simon and Schuster.

Rehman, J. (2003). *International human rights law: A practical approach.* England: Pearson Education.

Ross, T. & Vandivere, S. (2009). Indicators for child maltreatment prevention program. *Child Trends.* www.childtrenddatabank.org.

Shiveman, J. (2003). *Critical issues in child welfare.* New York: Columbia University Press.

UDHR. (1945). Article 25 (2). Motherhood and childhood are entitled to special care and assistance. All children, whether born in/out of wedlock shall enjoy the same social prestige.

Van Bueren, G. (1999). Combating child poverty-human rights approaches. *HRQ 21*, 680.

Chapter 14
Child Labor: An Indian Scenario

N.K. Chadha and Vandana Gambhir Chopra

Introduction

Child labor is a global phenomenon and a harsh reality of contemporary times. The prevalence of child labor is one of the most important problems confronting the world at large, especially developing countries such as India. Child labor is done by any working child who is under the age specified by law. The word, "work" means full-time commercial work to sustain self or add to the family income. Every non-school going child irrespective of whether the child is engaged in wage or non-wage work or whether he or she is working for the family of others, employed in hazardous or non-hazardous occupations, employed on a day wage or on a contract basis is a child labor. Generally, any child who is employed in activities to feed self and family is being subjected to "child labor."

Child labor that is prescribed under international law falls into three categories:

- Labor performed by a child who is below the minimum age for performing that type of labor;
- Labor that jeopardizes the moral, mental, or physical well-being of a child (hazardous work); and
- The unconditional worst forms of child labor, which include slavery, trafficking, debt bondage, and other forms of forced labor, forced recruitment for use in armed conflict, prostitution, pornography, and other illicit activities.

Children are said to be the future of a nation. But no matter, how rapidly a country is developing, if the large majority of its child population is working as

N.K. Chadha (✉) · V.G. Chopra
Department of Psychology, University of Delhi, Delhi, India
e-mail: nkc_du@yahoo.co.uk

S. Deb (ed.), *Child Safety, Welfare and Well-being*,
DOI 10.1007/978-81-322-2425-9_14

bread earner for their family, it is an indication of sorry state of social equilibrium. Childhood has been considered as the most important period of life. During this period, molding and shaping of the child takes place and the behavior, conduct, and sentiments are developed. Children are the blooming flowers of the garden of society and valuable asset of a nation. They constitute a hidden treasure of potential development of a growing nation. Unfortunately, the life of most of the children is lost in poverty, destitution, malnutrition, and poor and unhygienic conditions.

Rights of Children

In 1992, India ratified the United Nations Convention on Rights of the Child (1992). The Charter of Child Rights (CRC) is built on the principle that "ALL children are born with fundamental freedom and ALL human beings have some inherent rights." The essential message is equality of opportunity. Girls should be given the same opportunities as boys. ALL children should have the same rights and should be given the same opportunity to enjoy an adequate standard of living.

The Charter confers the following basic rights on all children across the world:

- The right to survival—to life, health, nutrition, name, and nationality
- The right to development—to education, care, leisure, and recreation
- The right to protection—from exploitation, abuse, and neglect
- The right to participation—to expression, information, thought, and religion

Indian Scenario of Child Labor

India is one of the largest democratic countries in the world. India has declared the right to education as a fundamental right in the Constitution, but nonetheless the country faces a huge problem of child labor. According to the UN Study, about 150 million children of age group 5–14 are working in various industries in India. They are found working in road-side restaurants, tea stalls and shops, at construction sites, and in factories. Girls suffer labor exploitation to such a degree that millions of girls die before they reach the age of 15. They are paid low wages (Rs 20 per day) and many live in shops or work places where they are subjected to various forms of exploitation. Often these children experience physical, mental, and sexual abuse by the employers.

Mafia gangs bring children for "Begging" in urban cities. A child beggar aged between five and ten collects the maximum. With a burn scar or decapitation they can earn more. As they grow older their earnings decrease. As a consequence they graduate to be big-time traders involved in drug peddling, pick pocketing, robbery, and prostitution. A child beggar will only be paid 10 % of his earnings of Rs 300–500 a day. If he fails to meet the target fixed by the contractor he is punished brutally. The girls by the time they reach 13 years switch over to prostitution.

Bonded labor, the worst form of child labor, is also quite common in many rural areas of India. The poor parents need money for various purposes like agricultural works and other family needs and children work in order to pay off a debt. The creditors-cum-employers offer these "loans" to poor parents in an effort to secure the labor of a child, which is always cheaper than bondage. The parents, for their part, accept the loans. The arrangements between parents and contracting agents are usually informal and unwritten. The time period required to pay off such a loan will not be determined. This is a kind of slavery that mostly appears in underdeveloped and lower caste people. The children who were bonded to work cannot escape bondage because of the fear of losing their livelihood on one hand and unequal power relationships between the child workers and the creditors-cum-employers on the other.

Such inhuman acts affect millions of children across the length and breadth of the country and impinge on their future. The various problems arising in the countries' economic, political, and social condition is one of the major reasons for growth of this problem. Though the major cause of child labor in India is, like in many other countries, poverty, other causes include overpopulation, illiteracy, and lack of awareness. Due to poverty, children are sent to work to support their families. The effect of the caste system which prevailed in the country even before independence is also another reason for the problem. Only the upper caste Indians had an access to education, whereas the lower caste people remained poor and uneducated.

While the popular perception of child labor is strongly negative, it remains unclear from a theoretical perspective to what extent child labor is harmful. Child labor deprives a child from having a proper childhood. It is a hazard to a child's mental, physical, social, educational, emotional, and spiritual development. He suffers physical and mental torture. Millions of children do extremely hazardous work in harmful conditions, risking their health, education, personal and social development, and even their lives at risk. In extremely dangerous places, they work full time for excessive working hours. They are subjected to psychological, verbal, physical, and sexual abuse. Unable to escape from the poverty cycle, they work and spend their lives in the streets in bad conditions. They face an adulthood of unemployment and illiteracy.

The serious consequences that child labor brings stay with the individual and with society for far longer than the years of childhood. The problem creates and perpetuates poverty. It condemns the child to a life of unskilled, badly paid work. Ultimately this leads to child labor with each generation of poor children undercutting wages. Involved in child labor, young workers not only face dangerous working conditions but also long-term physical, intellectual, and emotional stress. They become mentally and emotionally mature too fast which is a dangerous sign.

Prevalence and Statistics

- Eleven percent of the workforce in India is estimated to belong to child labor. One in every 10 workers in India is a child (CIF 2011).
- If we allocate a tenth of India's GDP to this share we can see India's Child Labor has a stake in India's GDP (CIF 2011).
- According to a UNICEF report (2009), India has the largest number of child laborers under the age of 14 in the world.
- Nearly 85 % of child laborers in India are hard-to-reach, invisible and excluded, as they work largely in the unorganized sector, both rural and urban, within the family or in household-based units Census 2001 and 2011.

The statements documented above demonstrate the prevalence of child labor in India. The Decennial Census, the National Sample Survey Organization (NSSO), and the National Family Health Survey (NFHS) are the three main authorized sources of records on child employment. Obtaining accurate data on child labor in India remains a significant challenge. States routinely under-report the number of working children, and others simply do not conduct the surveys needed to properly identify such children (Upadhyaya 2005). However, whatever is the actual number, there is general agreement that India is home to the largest number of child laborers in the world.

Census 2001 and 2011 Data on Child Labor

The Census found an increase in the number of child laborers from 11.28 million in 1991 to 12.66 million in 2001 and 21.39 million in 2011.

The 2001 census threw up the figures that children under 18 accounted for almost 43 % of India's population of about 450 million. There were 12.6 million working children in India—6.8 million boys and 5.8 million girls.

However, an analysis of working children, as per Census 2011, in the age group of 5–14 years revealed a total of 4353247 number of working children in India. The highest percentage of working children was from states—Uttar Pradesh (896301), Maharashtra (496916), Bihar (451590), Andhra Pradesh (404851), Rajasthan (252338), and Madhya Pradesh (286310). These six states together accounted for more than 50 % population of working children in India.

NSSO Estimate of Child Labor (2004–2005)

The survey conducted by National Sample Survey Organization (NSSO) in (2004–2005) had reported the estimated number of working children as 90.75 lakh.

As per (2004–2005) NSSO data, out of 9.07 million child laborers, 12.16 million were in rural areas. Rural children age 5–14 years (12.9 %) is more likely to be engaged in work than their urban counterparts (8.6 %). This indicates that child labor in India is overwhelmingly rural. About 90 %of the working children are concentrated in the rural areas.

Child labor in India has also been analyzed on caste-wise break-up of society. NSSO data reveals that the children among lower castes are more vulnerable to labor-related exploitation in the country. The NSSO data (2004–2005) shows that the children among scheduled tribes are twice likely to be engaged in child labor activities than the 'others' essentially drawn from upper castes. Overall trend shows that child labor is more prevalent in SC, ST, and OBC categories than the other castes.

The data analysis of child Workforce Participation Rates (WPR) as per religious categories shows that minority religious communities are more vulnerable to exploitation when compared to their counterparts belonging to Hindu groups and others. Unit level records of NSSO (2004–2005) shows 2.48 % WPR of Hindus, 3.47 % of Muslims, and 1.63 % belonging to other groups. The difference is due to a long-term neglect and discrimination of minority groups in academic opportunities and job markets.

According to NSSO data (2004–2005), 66 % of child workers are engaged in the agricultural sector (62.8 % of boys and 71.1 % of girls). This work is often seasonal in nature and may involve bonded labor as part of debt repayments to moneylenders. The data also show that there is a significant increase in self-employment of children where they are involved in petty businesses like selling eatables, collection and selling of fuel wood, etc. Nearly 3.543 million children in the 5–14 age groups are employed in the non-agricultural sector, of which 1.219 million are working in hazardous occupations—Pan, Bidi, and Cigarettes (21 %), Construction (17 %), Domestic workers (15 %), and Spinning and weaving (11 %). Agriculture, manufacturing, and household are the sectors in which girl's out-number boys.

NSSO 66th Round of Survey on Child Labor (2009–2010)

The count of child laborers as documented in NSSO survey (2009–2010) is 49.84 lakh. The figures indicate a decline in the extent of the problem of child labor in the country with respect to the NSSO estimate of (2004–2005). However, many researchers have attributed the decline in the number of working children according to the definition of child labor appears magnified than the statistics given in the reports.

As per the 66th round of survey (2009–2010), NSSO estimate of child labor in major Indian states had shown a different percentage share with Uttarakhand and West Bengal contributing to 35.62 and 11.07 % share of child labor in age group 5–14. Highest percentages of working children were also reported from states—Gujarat (7.9 %), Maharashtra (5.23 %), and Rajasthan (8.14 %).

NFHS-3 Data on Child Labor (2005, 2006)

As per the NFHS-3 (2005, 2006), nearly 11.8 % children age 5–14 years works either for their own household or for somebody else. The very young children (age 5–7 years), both boys and girls, are mainly doing unpaid work for someone who is not a member of their household. The older boys age 12–14 are mainly engaged in paid work or family work, whereas girls in this age group are involved mainly in household chores or family work.

A number of particular urban centers are known to contain high concentrations of child labor in particular industries. Some of these include carpet weaving in Bhadohi, Gem polishing in Jaipur, lock making in Aligarh, glassware in Firozabad and firecrackers in Sivakasi. According to field based accounts, child labor in these sectors is often exploitative, typically involving long hours, low wages, and poor working conditions.

Gender-Specific Effects of Child Labor

Recently, *the case of a 13 year-old maid who worked for a Delhi Doctor couple in Dwarka describes a life kin to slavery. Her uncle sold her to a job placement agency, which sold her to the couple. The girl was paid nothing. She said the couple barely fed her and beat her if her work did not meet expectations. She said they used closed-circuit cameras to make certain she did not take extra food. She was rescued when the firefighters found her locked inside the apartment as the couple had gone on vacation to Thailand.*

The issue of gender is now universally regarded as a vital component in addressing child labor. Although girls are exposed to many similar types of labor as boys, they often endure additional hardships and are more susceptible to exploitation, sometimes as a result of their society's view of the role women and girls should play. A constellation of legal and practical difficulties, poverty, and parental/societal attitudes in support of girl child laborers have played a key role in this. A common concern is that girl child laborers tend to be hidden, with large numbers sexually exploited for commercial purposes and involved in domestic work. In such situations, the potential for physical and sexual abuse is magnified.

Female children work in large numbers and for long hours in and outside the household, but their labor is unacknowledged or under-represented in formal labor statistics. The female child helps the family to survive by spending her time and in this process she misses out education, good nutrition, and future employment avenues that may be remunerative. Case studies about the children in employment reflect the pathetic plight of these children, particularly girls who suffer much more than boys and are stained by neglects, discrimination, lack of opportunities, and limited life options.

Female children are exploited unmercifully in many industries. The predominance of female laborers is reflected in the findings of various studies conducted in the garment industry in India, match, fireworks, and beedi industries in Tamil Nadu or in the bangle industry in Firozabad. The findings reveal that 50–80 % of them lost their childhood, struggling between her work place and domestic chores at home.

Another fact which is of particular concern is that a large proportion of the girls are involved in some of the worst forms of child labor, namely commercial sexual exploitation. In 2005, the National Human Rights Commission (NHRC) estimated that almost half of the children trafficked within India are between the ages of 11 and 14 years; they are subjected to physical and sexual abuse and kept in conditions similar to slavery and bondage (NHRC Action Research Study 2005). Debt bondage is one of many strategies used by exploiters to keep children in constant servitude. Girls are forced to serve an average of seven 'clients' per day and have no say in the choice of the customer or the use of contraceptives. Interviews with the trafficked girls showed severe impacts on their health, with 32.3 % of respondents suffering from diseases such as HIV/AIDS, sexually transmitted infections (STIs), and other gynecological problems.

The crux of the problem of the female child is that she is caught in a situation, in which she cannot change, which is predetermined, pre-cast, and pre-destined.

Industries in Which Child Labor Is Majorly Found in India

Children in India are engaged in the worst forms of child labor. Children work in agriculture producing crops such as rice and hybrid seeds. Children who work in agriculture carry heavy loads and apply harmful pesticides. Working long hours and under severe hardships on the fields, they are exposed to the hazards of working with modern machinery and chemicals.

Children also work in dangerous occupations like glass making, mining, construction, carpet weaving, zari making, fireworks, sandstone quarrying, breaking stones, polishing gems, and others as listed under the Child Labor Act. Many children manufacture goods in the informal economy, increasingly in home-based production. Making matches, bricks, carpets, locks, glass bangles, fireworks, bidis (cigarettes), incense sticks (agarbatti), footwear, garments, hand-loomed silk, leather, brassware, and other metal goods are various other kinds of hazardous occupation in which Indian children are engaged. In addition to working long hours in cramped spaces under poor lighting and inadequate ventilation, children in such occupations are exposed to harmful chemicals and dangerous machinery and tools. The risks for these children include joint pain, headaches, hearing loss, skin infections, and respiratory problems. Children embroider (zari), who sew beads to fabric and stitch soccer balls for the domestic market usually have finger deformities.

Bonded Child Labor in the Indian Silk Industry

India is the world's second largest producer of silk, accounting for about 20 % of world production. The United States is the largest consumer of Indian silk outside of India, importing over U.S.$163 million in silk commodities from India in 2001. Germany, Italy, Japan, Spain, and Eastern Europe are also significant importers of Indian silk. However, the industry is flourishing on the blood of thousands of children employed as bonded labors in the trade. In the silk industry, children reported starting off making from nothing to around 100 rupees a month, which might eventually increase to as much as 400 or 500 rupees. However, the children may not actually receive this amount as some or all may be deducted against the loan. These salaries are far below minimum wage.

Children's Testimonies (Human Rights Watch, January 2003)

"At 4:00 a.m. I get up and do silk winding.... I only go home once a week. I sleep in the factory with two or three other children. We prepare our food there and sleep in the space between the machines. The owner provides the rice and cut it from our wages—he deducts the price. We cook the rice ourselves. We work 12 h a day with 1 h for rest. If I make a mistake—if I cut the thread—he beats me. Sometimes [the owner] uses vulgar language. Then he gives me more work." (Yeramma S., 11 year-old-bonded at around age seven for Rs 1,700 Karnataka, March 27, 2002).

"I started picking worms when I was nine and had been at an NGO-run residential school for 4 months. Most of the time, I am standing in water. I get holes in my hands because I put them in the hot water and then they get infected. I have lumpy burn scars on my hands, shins, ankles and feet. I did not like working because my hands get infected. Even if I cut my finger, I am not sent back to home. The owner puts coffee powder on it and keeps me working. I can't eat. I have to eat with a spoon." (Anesha K., 11 year-old, involved in silk reeling and twisting: Karnataka, March 29, 2002).

A large number of children also work in the street vending food shops and other goods, repairing vehicles and tires, scavenging, and rag picking. This may expose them to dangers including severe weather and criminal elements, and may lead to their involvement in traffic accidents. Children are also found working in construction and domestic service. Many work very long hours and suffer abusive treatment. Service industries that employ children include hotels, food service, and tourism. Largely invisible and silent form of child labor is domestic work in which children face higher degree of exploitation and abuse in the home of employees.

India remains a source, transit, and destination country for minors trafficked for commercial sexual exploitation and forced labor in domestic service, agriculture, and activities such as begging and making bricks. The federal police stated that an estimated 1.2 million children engage in prostitution (CNN 2009). Cases of child sex tourism continue to be reported in cities and towns with tourist attractions as well as locations with religious pilgrim centers. The majority of such children are Indians trafficked within the country. Nepali and Bangladeshi girls and Indian girls from rural areas are trafficked for commercial sexual exploitation in major urban centers such as Mumbai (Bombay), Kolkata (Calcutta), and New Delhi.

There are reports that children have been recruited to serve as soldiers by armed opposition groups in zones where armed conflict is occurring such as by the Naxalites in Chhattisgarh (UN Secretary General Report, New York 2011).

Physical Health Effects of Child Labor

There is overwhelming evidence that childhood labor comes with serious physical health problems which negatively affect the children's physical development, especially as the major part of the child laborers come from impoverished families and are nutritionally unfit to face the rigors of a hard working life. The physical damage largely depends on the job type and the number of hours worked.

Surveys indicate that more than 60 % of the 14–16 year-old child laborers work for an average of 14 h daily, which obviously causes a variety of short-term and long-term health problems. Children are mostly vulnerable because of their physical immaturity and get exposed to unsafe workplaces. Children are often required to cart heavy loads or spend hours in unnatural postures that often deform or damage their developing bodies. The long hours wear their bodies down, causing fatigue, breaking down their immune system, making them more susceptible to illness because they burn more calories faster than adults. Many children suffer from nutritional deficiencies due to the lack of proper meal breaks. This also leads the children being less resistant to disease. Children are also more prone to accidents because they are less aware of dangers and precautionary measures.

In some jobs where child labor is common, such as agriculture, children are regularly exposed, and inhale toxic chemicals. These chemicals are proven to cause malaria, tetanus, diphtheria, polio, and whooping cough in children. In the fishing industries, children dive into waters without protection to scare fish into nets. Children spending up to 12 h a day in the water, often suffer from ruptured ear drums or the side effects of decompression. Every year, dozens of children drown, or are attacked by predators.

In Mining, children work long hours without proper protections or clothing. They work in humid environments with extreme temperatures. They are exposed to dust, gases, and vapors which provoke respiratory illness and may lead to other illnesses such as silicosis, pulmonary fibrosis, asbestosis, and emphysema. Children also run the risk of hearing loss and serious injury due to large falling objects. Carrying heavy objects, such as rock, often causes damage to their developing spines and eventually to their pelvises. Children that work in automobile repair shops are regularly exposed to benzene. Inhalation of benzene may cause drowsiness, nausea, and a loss of consciousness, and exposure to benzene over long periods of time will affect the brain stem causing anemia and leukemia.

The effects of labor on a child's body are catastrophic. The children are subjected to abuse of all kinds in these industries whether it's physical, sexual, mental, or emotional. Girls in particular are often abused more than the boys. Nearly all child laborers (90 %) are affected by physical pain during working hours or afterwards. These children get little to no childhood so that they can help support their families and will have the physical downfalls their whole lives. What makes the situation worse is that most of the child laborers do not get the required treatment with regard to their health problems.

Impact of Child Labor on Mental Health

The physical and social consequences of child labor are deliberated by researchers; however, mental health area has not been explored so much. Studies are lacking especially in Indian scenario regarding impact of child labor on mental health. In this section, psychological effects and mental health of child abuse due to child labor are reviewed.

Children engaged in various forms of work suffer from serious mental and psychological problems. Children engaged as employees often do not get access to primary needs such as food, shelter, and clothing, which are important components of their growth and development. To grow up and develop normally, they need to be properly nurtured and should not be deprived of any of the essentials of normal upbringing as this could seriously affect them psychologically—mostly in the long term.

Children are not in a position to take up responsibilities as adults. Such responsibilities strain them emotionally and physically, especially if they have to take care of children of their own age or perform duties meant for adults. Such children reach mental and emotional maturity at a very early age. This is highly dangerous as they start displaying pseudo adult behavior such as smoking and physical aggression.

Child labor also impedes the process of identity formation in children. Lot of factors play role in the development of identity and behavior of a child and form the basis of his social behavior. Kids, influenced by such anti-social phenomena as a child labor, do not have a sense of clear understanding of who they are, and such things as social norms and social values do not always work upon them. They are socially isolated, deprived of rest, or treated harshly and inconsistently. They do not have ability to socialize them with their peer group members. This way, it is very hard for them to find or create an identity that would be the best for them, and, most of the times, they just go by what they know and see. They are social actors, trying to cope with their situation, negotiating with parents and peers, employers and customers, and making the best of oppressive, exploitative, and difficult circumstances. Their ability to function as a normal individual in the future and be a part of the society remains bleak.

Working children are usually more concerned with their success in what they do. Many children aren't so much affected by work as developing through their work. Their self-esteem is depends on such factors. At the same time, whatever they do is hardly noticed and appreciated. This way, they are not able to build their emotional health the right way. Some repressive situations deny children the ability to make even the most basic day-to-day personal choices (e.g., where their needs and rights are not respected and/or where their day-to-day lives are strongly regulated by an employer). In contrast, some situations demand that children exercise high levels of personal responsibility, for example, working semi-autonomously in the streets. A sense of personal agency, which talks about self efficacy, internal locus of control, and positive outlook never, develops in them.

Physical, sexual or emotional abuse that results due to child labor generally leaves severe impact on the child for years. Studies and experience suggest that survivors of child abuse or deprivation suffer immediate and long-term negative effects like lack of social acceptance, varied psychological disorders (e.g., stress, anxiety, and depressive disorders), alcohol leading to frequent arrests, risks of becoming unlawfully/criminally violent, higher employment and suicide rates, more medical illnesses, or preoccupation with certain medical conditions. Children who are neglected or abused tend to grow up to be abusive, neglectful, and inadequate parents themselves. In case of sexual abuse, the child shows extreme reactions like self-mutilation, depression, suicide attempts and anorexia, sudden loss of appetite, inability to concentrate, being isolated or withdrawn, being overly knowledgeable in a sexual way, and personality changes like feeling of insecurity.

Conclusion

India has the highest number of children in the world. The country is set to be the youngest population in the world by 2020. Child labor denies the child of his basic right that is the right to education. No education' means unskilled jobs and exploitative wages. This leads to the creation of an unskilled adult labor force which causes early physical decay, economic insecurity, low quality of life, and ultimately high poverty. Thus child labor creates a vicious circle of poverty, unemployment, underemployment, and low wages. Over the years the Government of India has multiplied its efforts to address the needs and rights of exploited children. Still, the issue remains critical, challenging, and demanding stringent laws to be framed in addressing the issue. In order to eliminate the social evil of child labor there is a need for more intensive initiatives to tackle poverty and promote education opportunities to all children to help children and families in crisis. This is possible only with the co-operation of all sections of the society and the law enforcement agencies and by removing or minimizing the causes of child labor. Human endeavor in this regard will be fruitful if others make an integrated effort.

Recommendations

Much work remains to be done in order to eliminate child labor in India, and particular attention needs to be given to the risks faced by girl children. In spite of the first UPA government manifesto of a commitment of 9 % of annual Union budget for children, even as of 2013, a little more than 4 % is allocated towards children. Presently, 15,000.00 lakh have been allocated for expenditure for all the child labor schemes by GOI. In this gap between the needs of the world's largest children's population and (amongst) the world's lowest per child budgets that is allocated in India is the story of Indian Children's contribution to the GDP. Various steps taken in this direction and passing of laws have the least impact on this issue.

One of the first steps required to protect the rights of children is the revision of existing labor legislation to ensure that it is consistent with international standards, and mechanisms for ensuring enforcement of the law must be significantly enhanced. Inter-departmental coordination at the national, state, interstate, and intra-state levels is crucial in this regard. There should be effective implementations of child protective laws and necessary prosecution of child labor defaulters. Recently, the Indian Government has imposed ban on employment of children up to the age of 14, both in hazardous and non-hazardous work by amending an anti-child labor Act. The Union Cabinet approved bringing the amendment to the Child Labor (Prohibition and Regulation) Act, 1986, which also has penal provisions for non-compliance. As per the provision of the proposed law, a person found guilty of giving employment to children would be liable to a maximum three years imprisonment or fine up to a maximum of Rs 50,000. Children between 14 and 18 years will also be defined as "adolescents" in the amended Act. The amendment will also fulfill the mandate of Right to Education for free and compulsory education for children in the age group of 6–15 years.

Given the role that poverty plays in pushing children into work at early ages, there is a pressing need to address the financial insecurity of families, particularly those that are most vulnerable to child labor. In addition education must be made more accessible to children, with the quality of education significantly improved, in order to prevent education-related problems from serving as an impetus to child labor. In order to ensure the protection of children who have been engaged in child labor, binding guidelines for the rescue, repatriation, and rehabilitation of working children need to be formulated in all states. These should, inter alia, lay down clear principles for coordination of relevant actors at different levels. Finally, information collection and dissemination concerning child labor performed by children must be improved.

Focusing on grassroots strategies to mobilize communities against child labor and reintegration of child workers into their homes and schools has proven crucial to breaking the cycle of child labor. Many NGOs like CARE India, Child Rights and You, Global March against Child Labor-etc., have been working to eradicate child labor in India. A multidisciplinary approach involving specialists with medical, psychological, and socio-anthropological level is needed to curb this evil. The involvement of the religious leaders, trade unionist, and non-government organizations and to tackle the child labor by forming advisory committees on child labor on block level should be there. Only then can this malevolence of the humanity be eradicated.

References

Childline India Foundation (CIF). (2011). *Documents and reports: Child Labor: India's growth story*. http://www.childlineindia.org.in/Child-Labour-India-growth-story.html.

CNN. (2009). *Official: More than 1 M Child prostitutes in India.* cnn.com [online] May 11, 2009. Retrieved January 26, 2012, from http://articles.cnn.com/2009-11/world/india.prostitution.children_1_human-trafficking-india-prostitutes?_s=PM:WORLD.

Human Rights Watch. (2003, January). India: Small change. *Bonded Child Labor in India's Silk Industry*, *15*, 2(C).

National Family Health Survey-3. (2005, 2006). *Ministry of health and family welfare*, Govt. of India.

National Human Rights Commission; Action Research Study. (2005).

National Sample Survey Organization (NSSO). (2004–2005). *Ministry of statistics and programme implementation*, Government of India.

National Sample Survey Organization (NSSO). (2009–2010). *Ministry of statistics and programme implementation,* Government of India.

Census of India (2001). New Delhi, Government of India. http://labour.gov.in/content/division/about-child-labour.php and http://ncpcr.gov.in/view_file.php?fid=87.

Census of India (2011). New Delhi, Government of India. http://labour.gov.in/content/division/about-child-labour.php and http://ncpcr.gov.in/view_file.php?fid=87.

UN Convention on Rights of Child Report. (1992).

UNICEF. (2009). *India-the big picture*. Electronic reference. http://www.unicef.org/infobycountry/india_background.html.

Upadhyaya, H. (2005). *Monitoring child labor: Children can't read, adults can't count, India Together* (2005). Retrieved June 3, 2010, from http://www.indiatogether.org/2005/nov/chi-cagchild.htm.

United Nations Security Council. (2010). *Children and armed conflict: Report of the Secretary-General. New York*; 2011. http://www.crin.org/docs/S2011250.pdf.

Chapter 15
Rights of Children with Disability

Prerna Sharma

Introduction

Childhood is a time of opportunity and learning, in which even small positive change or development can generate long-term benefits into the future. Therefore the care a child receives when he or she is young, as well as the manner in which his or her needs are met, has a remarkable impact on the child's intelligence, personality, and social interactions through adulthood. Further, childhood is the most sensitive part of life for every human being. It is in this period of life that every individual grows up and develops, as well as becomes educated and adjusted to realities of life. The identity of the individual is formed during childhood. Human growth is often viewed in developmental stages, each one having some cardinal characteristics and so is the case with childhood. The consideration of their individual characteristic be it age, caste, class, gender, ability, or disability are of secondary significance. As everybody is equal before the Law, the rights provided under it should also be viewed in the same light.

The United Nations Convention on the Rights of the Child (UNCRC) (1989), one of the most widely ratified international instruments, gives legal expression to the notion that children have independent human rights and those rights should be at the heart of all political, economic, and social decision making (UNICEF 2001). This convention sets universal legal standards for the protection of children against discrimination, neglect, abuse, and exploitation, as well as guaranteeing them their basic human rights, including survival, development, and full participation in social, cultural, educational, and other endeavors necessary for their individual

P. Sharma (✉)
Department of Social Work, SNDT Women's University, Mumbai, India
e-mail: 9.prerna@gmail.com

S. Deb (ed.), *Child Safety, Welfare and Well-being*,
DOI 10.1007/978-81-322-2425-9_15

growth and well-being. All children are entitled to rights listed in the UNCRC, including children with disability. However, a large number of these children face discrimination, exploitation, and barriers in accessing services and entitlements in their day-to-day living. When compared with their peers without disability, they also encounter lack of equal opportunities, which impede them from attaining their innate potential.

Children with disabilities are at a point where child rights and disability rights intersect. They belong to the constituencies of children and that of the population with a disability. Both the constituencies have specific conditions and circumstances that result in situations of disentitlements and invisibility. Therefore, children with disabilities are liable to face dual as well compounded difficulties. Inevitably, the very children who need these rights the most are unable, through personal and/or social circumstances, to use them. With respect to children with disabilities the concerns are right to education, right to development, right to participation, right to be accepted as individuals in their own right with dreams, aspirations, the need to work and contribute meaningfully, to be accepted as they are and to be able to access all public places. Further, they have a unique set of experiences, challenges, issues and concerns, which are very specific to them due to their impairments. Hence, this chapter focuses on the determinants of experiences that "dis-able" the children with impairments. It draws attention to the concern about rights of children with disability in India in the context of the UNCRC.

Children with Disabilities

Children with disabilities are those children who have an impairment leading to dysfunction in any part of their lives, hampering the fulfillment of their roles and responsibilities. In the Convention on the Rights of Persons with Disabilities (UNCRPD) (2006), children with disabilities are described as including those who have long-term impairments that, in interaction with physical, social, economic, or cultural barriers, may limit their ability to participate fully in society on an equal basis with others.

Every child craves love, attention, recognition, and acceptance, however, from a very young age children with disabilities internalize negative perceptions of society undermining their innate potentialities and self-esteem. Some children with disabilities may encounter a small number of barriers which they and their families can challenge and overcome, while many others can be identified to be at high risk of social exclusion. As a society we are conditioned to viewing children with disabilities as having a range of deficits, rather than focusing on their strengths and abilities; this is a barrier in the way of fulfillment of rights of disabled children (Alkazi 2002).

It is nearly impossible to define the precise number of children living with a disability in the world because the concepts of both "impairment" and "disability" are defined differently according to cultures and contexts. India is home to millions of children living with a disability, with the Census of India (2001) reporting 2.19 crore (2.13 %) of the total population of the country are persons living with disability. Of all persons living with disability, 78 % (i.e., 1.67 % of total population of the country) are children and young adults in the 0–19 age group. Barely 50 % of children with disabilities reportedly reach adulthood, and no more than 20 % survive to cross the fourth decade of life (Census of India 2001). One in every 10 children is born with or acquires a physical, mental, or sensory disability (Government of India estimates 2001). A World Bank report (2008), states that at least one in 12 households includes a member with a disability. Additionally, more than 75 % of disabilities are preventable (Thukral 2002).

Rights of Children with Disabilities in the Context of the UNCRC (1989)

Human rights perspective in disability means viewing children with disability as subjects and not objects. It entails a shift from viewing this group of children as problems towards viewing them as holder of rights. The UNCRC, to which India acceded on December 2, 1992, provides a set of universal minimum standards of entitlement for all children. It establishes them as rights holders and insists on the recognition of children as actors in the exercise of their rights, and participants in all matters affecting them. According to UNICEF Innocenti Research Centre (2007), in spite of almost universal ratification of the UNCRC, and the social and political mobilization that led to the adoption of the UNCRPD, children with disabilities and their families continue to be confronted with daily challenges that compromise the enjoyment of their rights. Discrimination and exclusion related to disabilities occur in all countries, in all sectors of society, and across all economic, political, religious, and cultural settings.

The shift in focus from the "welfare" to the "rights" approach is considered to be significant (UNICEF 2007). The rights approach means locating problems outside the children with disabilities and addressing the manner in which various economic and social processes can and should accommodate the difference of disability. It means including children with disabilities in all social, political, and economic processes in the manner any other citizen of the country might be expected to, this process is termed as "Inclusion." The UNCRC was the first and only human rights instrument which contained a specific reference to disability (Article 2 on non-discrimination) and a separate article (Article 23) dedicated to special rights and needs of children with disabilities. It has very clearly and specifically mentioned children with disabilities with the intention of bringing these children as a constituency to be protected and accorded rights.

Article 23 of the UNCRC is about recognizing children with disabilities as full human beings. This acknowledges that children living with a disability have the right to enjoy a full and decent life, in conditions which ensure dignity, promote self-reliance, and facilitate the child's active participation in the community. Paragraphs 2 and 3 of Article 23 stress the fact that children with disabilities are entitled to special care. The emphasis is on special efforts to provide for the special care and special needs of children with disabilities.

The priority needs, however, of children with disabilities are not special, they are basic as in the case of all children; children with disabilities need food, shelter, love and affection, protection, and education like all children do in order to achieve their inherent potential. The focus of the language used in the text is on the deficiency of the child with disability and the provision of special services to fill the deficiency. It draws instant attention to the fact of disability and highlights inability of the child. It reinforces and is reinforced by the medical model of disability where disability is seen as a tragedy, and people with disabilities are treated as if they are its victims.

The social model of disability is grounded in paradigm shift from welfare to rights based. Rather than identifying disability as an individual limitation, the social model identifies society as the problem, and looks for fundamental political and cultural changes to generate solutions. According to this model, disability is not an attribute of an individual, but rather a complex collection of conditions, many of which are created by the social environment. Through this model, the collective responsibility is placed on the society to make the environmental modifications necessary for the full participation of people with disabilities in all areas of social life. The provisions in Article 23 are too limited to ensure the fulfillment and protection of the rights of children with disabilities.

Article 2 of not only requires governments to respect the equal rights of all children but also imposes active obligations on them to ensure that children are not discriminated against in exercising of any of their rights. Offering children with disabilities different or lesser education simply because of their disability is a breach of Article 2. Segregated schooling experiences in special institutions, denial of admission to regular schools, absence of educational experiences in rural areas for children with disabilities, and exclusion from playing with all children on grounds of disability are examples of discrimination that children with disabilities face every day (Human Rights Watch 2013; SPLC 2010; Curtis 2002; IPSEA 2007).

Article 3, states that in all actions concerning children, their best interests must be the primary consideration; adults frequently make decisions and take action in respect of children, ostensibly in their best interests, but are subsequently acknowledged to be on the contrary (UNICEF 1989).

As per Article 5 of the UNCRC, "it is the responsibility of parents and other caregivers to provide direction and guidance in accordance with the evolving capacities of the child." In other words, as children acquire the competence to exercise rights for themselves, they are entitled to do so and should be encouraged and supported by their parents in that. However, children in all societies have a different legal status from adults. Autonomy involves the right of an individual to self-determination, including, e.g., the right to informed consent for treatment or refusal of treatment. The UNCRPD, therefore, needed to include additional measures to ensure their realization.

Article 6 provides for the right to life, survival, and development, meaning that governments must ensure "to the maximum extent possible" the survival and development of children. This requires that children with disabilities, like children without disabilities, are provided with support, resources, and care necessary to promote the fulfillment of their potential. According to Puri (2002), children with disabilities in India are denied personal or economic security, health care, education, and basic needs necessary for their growth and development. Further, certain disabilities such as mental disability carry even greater stigma, hampering life chances, and opportunities for their growth and development.

Article 12 provides that all children have the right to express their views on all matters of concern to them and to have those views taken seriously in accordance with their age and maturity. Too often, it is the silence and invisibility of children with disabilities that contributes to the persistence of discrimination against them, both as a group and as individuals. It is only through listening directly to the experiences of children with disabilities that adults gain awareness of the extent, nature, and impact of discrimination on their lives. The attitudes of overprotection by some parents, not seriously listening to the child, the tendency of the adults to infantilize or neglect by some others leads to the views of children with disabilities not being taken into account by the significant adults around them (Taub 2006; Audit Commission for Local Authorities in England and Wales, United Kingdom 2003).

Article 13 follows from Article 12 in terms of the rights of children with disabilities to have access to information and freedom of expression as it states that the child shall have the right to freedom of expression; this right shall include freedom to seek, receive, and impart information and ideas of all kinds, either orally, in writing or in print, in the form of art, or through any other media of the child's choice. Children with disabilities are often denied their human right to communicate their views. A study conducted by Sharma (2013) on rights fulfillment of children with disabilities in Mumbai revealed that only 34 % of parents sought their children's participation in decisions affecting them.

Article 27 affirms the right of every child to a standard of living adequate for the child's physical, mental, spiritual, and social well-being. There is considerable evidence that the standard of living of families with children with disabilities falls below the necessary standard to satisfy this right (Royal College of Nursing 2011; Brewer et al. 2009). Moreover, the presence of a child with disability in a family leads to an increase in the demands on the existing resources, as there are additional medical bills to take care of or other aids or supports that need to be arranged.

Article 28 recognizes the right of children to education and to be able to access it with equal opportunities. Ninety percent of children with disabilities in developing countries do not attend school (UNESCO 2000). With respect to disability, inclusive education was perhaps the earliest issue recognized internationally as critical. This is one area where initiatives by the government of India have stressed the critical importance of universalizing education as well as covering all children, including children with disabilities. India has been a signatory to the Salamanca Declaration held in Spain on Education for All in 1992. The Persons with

Disability Act, 1995 states that children with disabilities should, as far as possible, be educated in integrated settings. In the District Primary Education Programme, launched in 1994, the district primary schools are responsible for all children, including children with disabilities.

Article 29 directs governments to ensure that education leads to the development of child's personality, talents, and mental and physical abilities to their fullest potential. The outcome of education leading to personality development is a far cry as access to quality education for children with disabilities in inclusive education settings itself is not available to majority of disabled children.

Article 31 identifies that children with disabilities have the right to take part in play and leisure activities, and to freely express themselves in cultural and artistic ways. It recognizes that resources remain tied up in segregated services rather than being used to help children with disabilities gain equal access to cultural, artistic, recreational, and leisure activities. According to Lansdown (2009), for children with disabilities the most acute sense of marginalization and social exclusion is felt in the field of play, leisure and recreational activities. The exclusion of children with disability from play and other structured forms of recreation can stifle both physical and mental growth.

Articles 32 and 34 stress on governments to ensure the protection of children from economic and sexual exploitation and abuse. Research conducted by UNICEF indicates that violence against children with disabilities occurs at around rates 1.7 times higher than for their peers without disabilities. They are more likely to be victims of violence and sexual abuse. When compared with their peers without disabilities, children with disabilities encounter lack of equal opportunities, which impedes them from attaining their innate potential. Negative societal attitudes also exposes children with disabilities to greater risk of violence, abuse, and exploitation (UNICEF EAPR 2011). Research has revealed that children with disabilities more than other children are targets for sexual abuse because they lack the full capacity to flee the site of violence, defend themselves or seek justice (Smith and Harrell 2013; Stalker and McArthur 2012; Edelson 2010). Often sexual abuse of children with disability happens because of the widespread assumption that children with disabilities are asexual and hence unlikely to attract sexual attraction (Andrews 2011; Rogers 2005). They are also to be found working and/or living on the streets.

The UNCRC has resulted in other significant areas of children's rights being brought to the attention of the world community. Since its adoption in 1989, issues such as sexual exploitation of children, child labor, children in armed conflict, violence against children have been widely acknowledged as human rights issues demanding action. However, to date, no comparable interest has focused on the experiences of children with disabilities. According to Lansdown (2001), they remain largely invisible, hidden within families or institutions, and vulnerable to neglect of their economic, social, cultural, civil, and political rights. Some children have multiple disabilities and are often the most neglected and vulnerable children.

On 13 December 2006, the United Nations General Assembly adopted a new UNCRPD as well as an Optional Protocol on the Rights of Persons with Disabilities. India signed the Convention on 30th March 2007 and it was ratified on 1st October 2007. The Convention includes specific provisions for children with disabilities referring to the respect for the evolving capacities of children and to their right to preserve their identities. It provides them with the same rights and freedoms as all children, with particular reference to the rights to be protected from exploitation, violence and abuse; to express their views on all issues which affect them (Article 7) and to access to justice.

Factors Leading to Disabling Experiences

Lansdown (2002) reports that despite the explicit inclusion of disability as grounds for protection against discrimination in the UNCRC, and the provisions of Article 23, which specifically addresses the situation of children with disabilities, the reality for children with children with disabilities remains largely unchanged in most countries of the world. Children with disabilities can face further physical, attitudinal, policy, and practice-based barriers to full social participation, which may impact on their long-term aspirations and opportunities. Tuli (2002) argues that the pervasive tendency to underestimate the potential of children with disability leads to lack of recognition of their rights and hence their fulfillment.

UNICEF Innocenti Research Centre (2007) has found that children with disabilities constantly face barriers to the enjoyment of their basic human rights and to their inclusion in society. Their abilities are overlooked, their capacities are underestimated and their needs are given a low priority. Marta Santos Pais (2011), the special representative of the UN Secretary General on violence against children states that life of children with disabilities is surrounded by stigma, discrimination, cultural prejudices and invisibility as well as heightened risk of neglect, violence, injury, and exploitation. She further states that children with disabilities are still viewed as curse, shame for the family, and misfortune for the community. These factors are further discussed below.

Societal Attitudes

Disability brings with it many limitations. Physical limitations are those which can be worked with and worked around, but which limit nonetheless. Over and above the restrictions on mobility, there are other limitations in the area of choices and opportunities, which stem from political, economic, and attitudinal sources that are avoidable, and compound the original problems caused by physical disability. These limitations are societal attitudes, policies, and programs, as well as the resistance to accept, to include people with disabilities in mainstream society, which turn disabilities into handicap.

In most parts of India, irrespective of state, region, or religion the disgrace of giving birth to a child with a disability is unanimous. Despite modern, human rights attitudes, the idea that a child with a disability is the result of anger of Gods, or ancestors, and the embodiment of sin in the family is widely prevalent. Endless research shows that parents of children with disabilities feel guilty and sometimes take the blame for the impairment on themselves (Rangaswami 1995; Olkin 1999; Marshak et al. 1999; Austin 2000; Kumar and Akhtar 2001; Gupta and Singhal 2004; Seligman and Darling 2007). In India, disability is still viewed in terms of a "tragedy" with a "better dead than disabled" approach, the idea being that it is not possible for children with disabilities to be happy or enjoy a good quality of life. Cultural beliefs about disability play an important role in determining the way in which the family perceives disability and the kind of measures it takes for prevention, treatment, and rehabilitation (Sen 1988). There is also a very strong belief in the metaphysical causation in India. One such instance is the belief in the theory of karma, which is often invoked to explain major life events, including the occurrence of disability. It has also been shown that people tend to accept their own disability as something which has resulted from their past karma or due to God's will and thus often show low motivation to overcome the limitations (Berry and Dalal 1996; Alur 2003). A belief, in stark contrast, it is the duty of the "non-disabled" to give away food, money, and clothes in charity to those with disabilities, as a religious responsibility to attain mocha, the ultimate liberation (Ghai 2000).

Families, communities, and the medical profession often do not help parents to alleviate their guilt. Their attitude to the children and parents, in fact, makes the situation worse leading to stigma and social isolation. This stigma and guilt result in segregation of the child with a disability. So engrained is the prejudice that even the mother of a child with a disability faces humiliation and indignity (Thukral 2002). These stigmatizing social attitudes have developed due to a wide psychological gulf of exclusion existing between those with disabilities and those who are able-bodied. It is recognized and acknowledged by the UNCRPD, which formally records that it is not "disability" that hinders full and effective participation of people with disabilities in society, but rather "attitudinal and environmental barriers" in that society. Such barriers and stigmatization underscore the imperative of keeping rights clearly articulated and eventually becoming entrenched in policy and legislative frameworks.

Stigma and Discrimination

Children with disabilities suffer from discrimination based on society's prejudice and ignorance which prevents their integration and full participation in the community. In addition, they often do not enjoy the same opportunities as other children because of the lack of access to essential service leading to their segregation and deprivation from rights entitlements. Stigma leads to children with disabilities often being condemned to social isolation, loneliness, lack of friend-ships, denial of a voice, and denial of opportunities to participate within society. Barnes (1991) states that type of discrimination encountered by children with disabilities are not just a question of individual prejudice but are institutionalized in the very fabric of our society. Institutional discrimination is a complex form of discrimination that operates throughout society. Institutional discrimination is evident when the policies and activities of all types of modern organizations result in irregularity between children with disabilities and children without disabilities.

Abuse

Often prevailing attitudes perceive the life of a child with a disability as being of less worth, less importance, and of less potential than other lives (Thukral 2002). Therefore, children with disabilities are more vulnerable to all forms of abuse be it mental, physical or sexual in all settings, including the family, schools, private and public institutions, and community at large. In the home and in institutions, children with disabilities are often subjected to mental and physical violence and sexual abuse as well as being particularly vulnerable to neglect and negligent treatment since they often present an extra physical and financial burden on the family (International Disability Alliance (IDA) 2010). School bullying is a particular form of violence that children are exposed to and very often, this form of abuse targets children with disabilities. The main reasons for their particular vulnerability include their inability to hear, move, dress, toilet, and bathe independently, increasing their vulnerability to intrusive personal care or abuse; those who have communication or intellectual impairments, may be ignored, disbelieved, or misunderstood even when they report abuse (Eastgate 2011; Pownall et al. 2011).

Parents or others taking care of the child may be under considerable pressure or stress because of physical, financial, and emotional issues in caring for their child, with studies indicating that those under stress may be more likely to commit abuse. Dalal and Pande (1999) investigated cultural beliefs and attitudes of a rural Indian community toward physical disability. The results revealed fatalistic attitudes and external dependence in families with children with disabilities.

Legislation and Lack of Actionable Policies

Recognizing the needs of people with disabilities, the Directive Principles of State Policy laid down in the Constitution of India, the obligation of the government to provide assistance for children with disabilities. The National Policy for Children, 1974, has acknowledged the need of, and made provisions for, special treatment, education, and rehabilitation of children with disabilities. Similarly the National Policy on Education, 1986 has made provisions for mainstream education of children with disability in regular, mainstream schools. The UNCRC and the World Summit on Children 1990 have influenced, to some extent, India's policy of children. This led to the formulation of a National Plan of Action for Children in

1992, which calls for government departments, community and society at large for greater participation for the welfare and development of children with disabilities. Provisions to integrate children with disabilities in mainstream education system have been made in District Primary Education Program since 1998. The National Plan of Action for Children (2005) has recognized children with disabilities as a special category to be provided with special conditions for their development.

The National Trust Act aims to enable and empower persons with disabilities (mental retardation, cerebral palsy, autism and multiple disabilities) to live as independently and as fully as possible. The Persons with Disabilities (Equal Opportunities, Protection of Rights and Full Participation) Act, 1995, assures free and appropriate education to all children with disabilities up to the age of eighteen. The Act can hardly be termed a rights-based legislation. This Act holds the State responsible for the education of all persons with disabilities until the age of eighteen, and stipulates 3 % reservation for them in government educational institutions or institutions supported by the government. Government schools are bound by law to provide admission to students with disabilities and the law also stipulates that all public buildings, including educational institutions, be made accessible to everyone.

In the 17 years since the Persons with Disability (Equal Opportunities, Protection of Rights and Full Participation) Act (1995) came into being, it has met with very little success even in matters as basic as ensuring a barrier-free environment and generating employment (Mehta et al. 2012). Very few organizations have been penalized for not providing barrier-free environments. In fact, this basic requirement is seen more as a voluntary gesture, and if an organization provides a ramp it's touted as a praiseworthy achievement. No one considers the fact that, according to the Persons with Disability Act (1995), the provision is mandatory by law.

There are several instances where children with disabilities are excluded or even barred from availing the facilities provided even under government run schemes or programs. A case in point is highlighted through a research undertaken by Alur (2003) on Integrated Child Development Scheme (ICDS), run by the government of India, for children from 0 to 6 years and their mothers. She found that children with disabilities were as a matter of routine excluded from availing the benefits through ICDS offered to rest of the children. Due to ill-defined policy objectives during the policy formulation stage, policy remains silent on the issue, not clarifying that "all" includes children with disabilities as well. Implementation strategies for the inclusion of these children therefore are not worked out, which leads to non-inclusion of children with disabilities from the program. Alur (2003) further states policy has been too long silent and ambivalent, with a tacit understanding among policy makers, that children with disabilities are not to be brought into the services of the ICDS due to the difficulties this inclusion may cause. Codes of practice, putting policy into action can only be done if a decision to include this group of children is taken and the resource allocation is made.

Gender

Female children with disabilities are more likely not to survive, to be abandoned, discriminated against, excluded from education, deemed un-marriageable and excluded from motherhood and general participation in their society. There is an over-representation of male children with disabilities in education (Sharma 2007, 2013), both in special and mainstream schools. Due to differential gender-based role expectations, education is not considered a priority for female children with disabilities. Dropout rates for female children with disabilities are higher than for male children with disabilities.

Poverty

Disability is both a cause and a consequence of poverty (Sen 2000). Majority of the world's population of people with disabilities live in low-income countries and experience social and economic disadvantages and denial of rights. It is an established fact that families with members with disabilities are frequently the poorest and most marginalized. Poverty becomes one of the most serious barriers to accessing rights entitlements of children with disabilities. Singh agrees that children with disabilities are subject to multiple deprivations as they are generally from the low socio-economic groups and have limited or no awareness of their rights and entitlements. Food deprivation due to poverty has a direct negative bearing on the physical and mental development of children and even starvation deaths (Schoufour et al. 2013; Milteer et al. 2012). Nutritional deficiency disorders like vitamin A blindness, anemia, and goiter are common among poor children leading to disabilities (Rahman et al. 2013).

Tuli (2002) states that a majority of children with disabilities are from rural and low-income homes, where immunization coverage is poor, malnutrition is widespread and maternal health is severely undermined by frequent childbirth. Injuries resulting from accidents are often not attended to in time, causing irreversible damage and disability in children. Family poverty may be more likely, and this is particularly the case where more than one family member is a person with a disability, if there are significant care (or child care) costs, and/or parents are unable to work in paid employment.

Rogers and Hogan (2003) found that parents of children with disabilities experience increasing financial difficulties resulting from the needs for special equipment, special medical care, and special programs that are appropriate for each child and also families which include a child with a disability are more likely to slide down the economic scale. This may be for a number of reasons including, parental inability to access employment (e.g., due to unavailability of appropriate and affordable childcare); difficulties due to employers' failure to recognize parental responsibilities for children with special needs; impairment, and disability related costs; lack of information on, access to entitlements, and adequacy of benefits available for children with disabilities (Rogers and Hogan 2003).

Barriers in Education

Education is a medium through which the futures of children are molded. India's education system, on the whole, is designed for children without disabilities, as are most other services in the country. For children with disabilities, an attempt has been made to set up a parallel system of education by way of "special schools". Although special schools do play a role in rehabilitation, they also keep children with disabilities away from the mainstream, and the mainstream away from children with disabilities. In fact these institutions have helped push children with disabilities to the periphery where they grow up in a markedly different atmosphere compared to "normal" children.

If children are educated differently, the differential treatment is ingrained in them making their future integration into mainstream society almost impossible. The Government has provided legislative intent through the Inclusive Education Act, which makes it mandatory to include children with all kinds of disabilities. If one were to go only by the laws and policies regarding inclusion formulated in this country, there is ample reason to be optimistic. Since the 1970s, various Central Government schemes—especially those for Universalization of Elementary Education—have been advocating the inclusion of children with disabilities into the mainstream educational system. These include:

- The Integrated Education for Disabled Children Scheme, launched in 1974, to admit children with disabilities in regular schools;
- The District Primary Education Program, 1985, which acknowledges the fact that universalization of education is possible only if it includes children with disabilities;
- The National Policy on Education, 1986, which promotes the integration of children with mild disabilities into the mainstream;
- The Project Integrated Education for the Disabled, launched in 1987, which encourages all schools in a neighborhood to enroll children with disabilities;
- The Persons with Disabilities (Equal Opportunities, Protection of Rights and Full Participation) Act, 1995, which recommends making changes in assessment and curriculum, and removing architectural barriers, to support inclusion. It also recommends providing free books and uniform for children with disabilities;
- The National Trust for the Welfare of Persons with Autism, Cerebral Retardation and Multiple Disability, 1999, which recommends promotion of inclusive education;
- The Sarva Shiksha Abhiyan (SSA 2000), which pledges that the "SSA will ensure that every child with special needs, irrespective of the kind, category and degree of disability, is provided education in an appropriate environment";
- The Amendment to the Constitution in 2001, to make education a fundamental right for those in the 6–14 age group, which covers children with disabilities;
- The draft National Policy for Persons with Disabilities, which has a section on education, stating, "There is a need for mainstreaming of the persons with disabilities in the general education system through inclusive education". It also mentions that children "learn best in the company of their peers".

Till date, however, there has been no move towards the inclusive concept or equal opportunities for education provided to children with disabilities. According to the National Sample Survey Organization (2002), report on "Disabled Persons in India", states that 55 % persons with disabilities were illiterate; a very large and unacceptable percentage. Children with disabilities are 4–5 times less likely to be enrolled in school and if they remain in school, they rarely progress beyond primary levels. The main barriers they face to access school include: lack of specialized teachers for both physically and mentally challenged children, absence of teacher training programs, absence of disabled-friendly infrastructure, including ramps, special chairs, and toilet facilities, as well as the mockery of adults and other children. The World Bank Report (2007), states that children with disabilities are five times more likely to be out of school than scheduled caste or scheduled tribe (SC/ST) children, and if they stay in school they rarely progress beyond the primary level, leading ultimately to lower employment and incomes.

A study conducted by the National Centre for Promotion of Employment for Disabled People disclosed shocking facts of educational discrimination against those with disabilities. A survey of 89 mainstream schools across the country found that a mere 0.5 % of the total number of students were those with disabilities, although the Persons with Disabilities Act (1995) recommends a reservation of 3 % seats in institutions funded by the government. Eighteen of the schools surveyed acknowledged that they did not admit students with disabilities. Twenty percent of the schools polled were not aware of the 1995 Disability Act at all.

In 2007, 12 years after The Persons with Disability Act (1995) was passed, a group of young volunteers for CRY (Child Rights and You) and Sruti Disability Rights Centre conducted a study in Kolkata to discover the gap between policy and ground reality on the issue of inclusive education. In an attempt to cover various aspects of inclusive education, the group sought an appointment with 65 schools in the city, of which only 30, including 16 government schools and 14 private schools, responded positively. Shockingly, the study revealed that 50 % of government schools and 36 % of private schools were not aware of the 3 % reservation for children with disabilities. According to the study, students with disabilities comprised only 0.16 % of government school students; private schools had a slightly higher percentage of 0.31 %. The study also showed that 0 % of the 65 schools in Kolkata that were visited had a ramp or any form of infrastructural facility for supporting education of children with disabilities within their buildings and environment (Sengupta 2008).

The recent introduction and adoption of the Right to Education Act, 2009, has advocated the right of children to free and compulsory education up to the age of 14 years. The Act incorporates a section on disadvantaged children, which also includes children with disabilities. While the Act mentions the inclusion of children with disabilities in the educational system, it does not provide mechanisms for implementation. According to a study conducted by Save the Children (2009), a tandem has developed between an acute lack of services for children with disabilities, attitudinal blocks of the larger society, lack of information among parents as well as service providers, and the missing convergence between various agencies.

In a paper analyzing the situation of inclusive education facilities, Sharma (2009) identifies that legislation in favor of inclusion has also been supported by circulars issued by various state and central boards of education, such as the Central Board of Secondary Education (CBSE) and the Indian School Certificate Examinations (ICSE). The circulars list various concessions that children with disabilities can avail of. In a circular issued in May 2005, the CBSE states that children with disabilities should have "barrier-free access to all educational facilities," and that students with dyslexia can study one language instead of two and any four of the subjects such as mathematics, science, social science, music and painting, among others (Mukherji 2010a). The ICSE provides extra time to students with disabilities to complete exams, as well as scribes, if required. The children can also choose from a number of subjects such as yoga and physical training (Mukherji 2010b). Several state governments have similar policies for their boards, for instance, the Maharashtra board gives students with disabilities extra time during tests, provision for scribes, concessions while learning mathematics, and the option of studying one language less than what is otherwise mandatory.

The high number of policies in support of inclusion, unfortunately, is in no way indicative of the current situation in the country since these have not been followed through to implementation. A glaring example of segregation in education is the existence of mainstream education for children without disabilities under the Ministry of Human Resource Development, and education for those with disabilities comes under the Ministry of Social Justice and Empowerment. This dichotomy in responsibility for education of children with disabilities and those without disabilities is the beginning point in discrimination in education of the two categories of children.

Protection of Rights of Children with Disability

The rights-based approach views children as citizens, entitled to all that has been promised to them under the constitution of India and the UNCRC. They are not to be viewed as objects of sympathy, benevolence, or charity. Applying the rights-based approach to children means putting children at the center, recognizing them as rights-holders and social actors.

All children, especially children with disabilities, have a right to be protected by law from all forms of physical or mental violence, injury or abuse, neglect or negligent treatment, maltreatment, or exploitation. Such protection should cover the relationship of the child with his or her parents, legal guardians, or any other person who has the responsibility for the care of child. The UNCRC establishes duty bearers for guaranteeing children the enjoyment of their rights. The duty bearers are the state (Articles 2.2, 3.2, and 37), parents, legal guardians, and individuals responsible for children (Article 3.2); and institutions, facilities and services for the care and protection of the child (Article 3.2). These are duty bearers in immediate vicinity of children, on who is the onus of meeting all the needs children with disabilities totally dependent on them. Parents play a dual role in the life of child with a disability. One as mentioned above as duty bearers to make provisions for their child's growth and development and the other as advocates seeking from the rest of the duty bearers (i.e., institutions, NGOs and the government at the local, state and central level) services and provisions required by their children with disabilities, both as other children and the special requirements on account of their disabilities to bring them at par with children without disabilities.

Since children are dependent on their parents, they are the most important people for the former's successful growth, development, and learning. Parents are the best advocates for their children since they are most closely associated with them. They also have the maximum amount of knowledge regarding their children; knowledge that may not be available to others. Parents' knowledge is the basis for their action towards seeking services and securing entitlements for their children. The source of parents' knowledge is their perceptions and experiences with respect to disability of their child. Parental perceptions ultimately lead to awareness of rights entitlements of their children and it is expected that parents fulfill their responsibilities, which build a foundation leading to fulfillment of entitlements of their children.

Another set of duty bearers are the government, at central and state level as well as the machinery at level of local governance, responsible for provisions of services and opportunities for the children. The government has established the National Commission for protection of Child Rights and is also setting up Commission for Rights of the Child at state level. The commission is responsible for formulating policies for state governments to adopt and put into practice, monitor, and evaluate.

It is imperative for any legislation for persons with disabilities to impose obligations on governments to ensure that children with disabilities are equally protected. Most of the measures in place presently are largely inaccessible to children with disabilities (Huq et al. 2013; Kashyap et al. 2012). The Persons with Disability Act, 1995 does not touched upon the issue of protection of children with disabilities from any kind of violence, as it looks into providing measures for education and vocational training of children with disabilities and training of personnel working in the disability sector. Even the Juvenile Justice Act, 2000, does not provide for accessible complaint mechanisms for children with disabilities. Thus the legislation should guarantee protection from any kind of abuse or economic exploitation and from any work that is likely to be harmful to their development or to interfere with their education, in any way. There is a need for prohibition of violence in all settings, including the home, family, schools, institutions, and the juvenile justice systems. The respective state governments must ensure that institutions providing care for children with disabilities are staffed with specially trained personnel who have been properly screened, according to appropriate standards, regularly monitored and evaluated.

The government has set up a National Coordination Group on the Rights of the Child for implementation of child rights in the country, and has instituted a Chair on the theme of Protection of Child Rights as part of the 10 Rajiv Gandhi Chairs in Contemporary Studies in central and state universities. These mechanisms, however, are not functional.

There is a need to ensure that all children with disabilities have an easy access to courts and legal representation, and the lawyers as well as judges should be trained in dealing with children with disabilities. There should be a provision of age appropriate facilities, i.e., access to sign language, access to information in accessible and age-appropriate forms, physical access to the courts, sufficient time made available to ensure the child fully understands the court procedures, video-taped interviews, and forms of questioning that promote children's understanding and capacity to express themselves (Lansdown 2009).

Analysis of government reports to the Committee on the Rights of the Child reveals that mostly the only issues ever addressed by governments in respect of children with disabilities relates to education and social welfare, and other rights which include right to participate, to play, to information, to freedom from violence, to an adequate standard of living, and indeed, the right to life are rarely addressed (Lansdown 2005). The lack of any policy or program for children with disabilities in India depicts that the situation is same in India as well. It is imperative that any new legislation pays attention to children with disabilities in imposing obligations on governments to ensure that they are afforded equal respect for their rights.

Another scenario which needs immediate attention is that large majorities of the adults, who have decision making responsibility, implementation authority, monitoring jobs, and child rights and child development responsibility, are ignorant about rights of children in general and rights of children with disabilities in particular. Children are dependent on adults for their basic needs and fulfillment of rights the lack of knowledge and information on human rights of children among the parents and significant adults affects policies and practical day-to-day lives of children with disabilities. The problem of adult illiteracy with respect to children's rights is extensive, complex, and in urgent need of urgent resolution.

Conclusion and Recommendations

Rights of children are matters of individual entitlements and their fulfillment depends upon social conditions and conducive environment. Children's survival, development, and active participation are crucial to the progress of any society and it makes good sense to invest in the growth and development of children. Only the recognition of children as individuals with rights can pave the way for future action. In the absence of this, all efforts will be sporadic, addressing only some symptoms and not the root cause of the problems that affect the children of this country.

All rights become meaningless if the circumstances in which children live make their realization impossible, as it happens most frequently with children with disabilities. It is important to recognize that all children, including children with disabilities, have within themselves a potential for their own development, however this can only be realized in an environment where their optimal capacities can thrive. There is an urgent need to provide children with disabilities access to opportunities equally with other children and individuals with disabilities such that they can achieve their potential and become contributing citizens of the nation. An environment where children with disabilities are protected and nurtured needs to be established. Unless specific requirements for children with disabilities are recognized in ways which enable them to be included and to have equal access to the things their peers without disabilities take for granted, then they will continue to be denied access to their human rights.

Disability and those with disabilities have to be integrated into everyday life. Segregation in special schools and institutions must be minimized; the issue of disability must consciously move beyond issues of special education and medical rehabilitation, and be mainstreamed into other discourses such as the economy, polity, entertainment, sports, fashion, and lifestyle. The language of special needs and vulnerable groups has to be replaced with less stigmatizing and more empowering terms like human rights and specific needs. Families have to be helped to overcome feelings of shame at having a child with a disability. Most important of all, children with disabilities have to be helped to acquire a positive sense of self, self-confidence, and self-respect. Only when these are achieved will there be total inclusion and empowerment.

References

Alkazi, R. (2002). *Not less, just different: Children with mental impairment, in seen, but not heard: India's marginalized, neglected and vulnerable children*. New Delhi: Voluntary Health Association of India.

Alur, M. (2003). *Invisible children: A study of policy exclusion*. New Delhi: Viva Books Private Limited.

Andrews, E. E. (2011, May 20). Pregnancy with a physical disability: One psychologist's journey, *Spotlight on Disability Newsletter*, American Psychological Association.

Audit Commission for Local Authorities in England and Wales (United Kingdom). (2003). *Services for disabled children A review of services for disabled children and their families*. Retrieved February 25, 2014, from http://www.audit-commission.gov.uk/SiteCollectionDocuments/AuditCommissionReports/NationalStudies/Disabled-report.pdf.

Austin, J. F. (2000). The role of parents as advocates for the transition rights of their disabled youth. *Disability Studies Quarterly, 20*(4), 75–83.

Berry, J., & Dalal, A. K. (1996). *Disability attitudes, beliefs and behaviors: A preliminary report on an international project in community based rehabilitation*. Unpublished Manuscript, ICACBR, Kingston, Canada: Queen's University.

Barnes, C. (1991). *Disabled people in Britain and discrimination: A case for anti discrimination legislation*. London: C Hurst & Co Publishers Ltd.

Brewer, M., O'Dea, C., Paull, G., & Sibieta, L. (2009). *The living standards of families with children reporting low incomes*. London, UK: Department for Work and Pensions (DWP). Retrieved June 7, 2014, from http://lx.iriss.org.uk/sites/default/files/resources/rrep577.pdf.

Census of India: Census Data Online (2001). *Office of the Registrar General & Census Commissioner, India*, Ministry of Home Affairs, Government of India. Retrieved July 9, 2014. http://www.censusindia.gov.in

Curtis, P. (2002, December 9). *Disabled pupils face discrimination at school*. The Guardian. http://theguardian.com.

Dalal, A. K., & Pande, N. (1999). Cultural beliefs and family care of the children with disability. *Psychology & Developing Societies, 11*(1), 55–75. doi:10.1177/097133369901100103.

Eastgate, G. (2011). Sex and intellectual disability: Dealing with sexual health issues. *Australian Family Physician, 40*(4), 188.

Edelson, M. G. (2010). Sexual abuse of children with autism: Factors that increase risk and interfere with recognition of abuse. *Disability Studies Quarterly, 30*(1).

Ghai, A. (2000). Towards understanding disability. *Psychological Studies, 45*, 145–149.

Gupta, A., & Singhal, N. (2004). Positive perceptions in parents of children with disabilities. *Asia Pacific Disability Rehabilitation Journal, 15*(1), 22–35.

Human Rights Watch. (2013, July 15). *China: End Discrimination, Exclusion of Children with Disabilities*. Retrieved May 12, 2014, from http://www.hrw.org/news/2013/07/15/china-end-discrimination-exclusion-children-disabilities.

Huq, N. L., Edmonds, T. J., Baker, S. M., Busjia, L., Devine, A., Fotis, K., & Keeffe, J. E. (2013). The rapid assessment of disability–informing the development of an instrument to measure the effectiveness of disability inclusive development through a qualitative study in Bangladesh. *Disability, CBR & Inclusive Development, 24*(3), 37–60. doi:10.5463/dcid.v24i3.174.

International Disability Alliance (IDA). (2010). *IDA submission to the committee on economic, social and cultural rights day of general discussion on sexual and reproductive health rights 15 November 2010*. Retrieved June 27, 2014, from www.internationaldisabilityalliance.org.

IPSEA. (2007). *School discriminated against disabled child by excluding him from swimming, club and school trip*. Retrieved June 17, 2014, from http://ipsea.org.uk/News/News-archive/School-discriminated-against-disabled-child-by-excluding-him-from-swimming-club-and-school-trip.aspx.

Kashyap, K., Thunga, R., Rao, A. K., & Balamurali, N. P. (2012). Trends of utilization of government disability benefits among chronic mentally ill. *Indian Journal Of Psychiatry, 54*(1), 54. doi:10.4103/0019-5545.94648.

Kumar, I., & Akhtar, S. (2001). Rate of anxiety in mothers of mentally retarded children. *Indian Journal of Psychiatry, 43*, 27.

Lansdown, G. (2001, September). It is our world too: A report on the lives of disabled children, for the UN general assembly special session on children. *Disability awareness in action*, New York. Retrieved February 22, 2014, from www.daa.org.uk/uploads/pdf/It%20is%20Our%20World%20Too!.pdf.

Lansdown, G. (2002). *Disabled children in South Africa: Progress in implementing the convention on the rights of the child, the international disability and human rights network*. Retrieved June 12, 2014, from http://daa.org.uk.

Lansdown, G. (2005). Children's welfare and children's rights. In H. Hendrick (Ed.) *Child welfare and social policy: An essential reader*, The Policy Press.

Lansdown, G. (2009). *See Me, Hear Me, A guide to using the UN convention on the rights of persons with disabilities to promote the rights of children*. UK: The Save the Children Fund. Retrieved June 15, 2014, from www.crin.org/docs/See_me_hear_final.pdf.

Marshak, L. E., Seligman, M., & Prezant, F. (1999). *Disability and the family life cycle: Recognizing and treating developmental challenges*. New York: Basic Books.

Marta Santos Pais (2011). *Promoting Rights of Children with Disabilities*. Retrieved July 4, 2015. http://un.org/disabilities/documents/events/17june2011_marta_santos_pais.pdf.

Mehta, K., Garware, M. V., & Deshpande, S. (2012). Identifying and implementing social infrastructure for social inclusion of people with disabilities in India. *Aweshkar Research Journal, 13*(1), 10–22.

Milteer, R. M., Ginsburg, K. R., Mulligan, D. A., Ameenuddin, N., Brown, A., Christakis, D. A., & Swanson, W. S. (2012). The importance of play in promoting healthy child development and maintaining strong parent-child bond: focus on children in poverty. *Pediatrics, 129*(1), e204–e213. doi:10.1542/peds.2011-2953.

Mukherji, A. (2010a, February 4). *Tough to integrate special students in 'normal' schools*. The Times of India, Mumbai Edition, (p. 6).

Mukherji, A. (2010b, February 4). *CBSE policy on special kids is proactive*. The Times of India, Mumbai Edition, (p. 6).

National Sample Survey Organization. (2002). *Disabled persons in India: NSS 58th round, ministry of statistics and programme implementation*, Government of India. Retrieved November 31, 2011, from http://mospi.nic.in/rept%20_%20pubn/485_final.pdf.

Olkin, R. (1999). *What psychotherapists should know about disability*. New York: Guilford Publications.

Pownall, J. D., Jahoda, A., Hastings, R., & Kerr, L. (2011). Sexual understanding and development of young people with intellectual disabilities: Mothers' perspectives of within-family context. *American Journal on Intellectual and Developmental Disabilities, 116*(3), 205–219. doi:10.1352/1944-7558-116.3.205.

Puri, M. (2002). *The disabled child, children in globalizing India: challenging our conscience*. In Enakshi Ganguly Thukral, (Ed.) New Delhi: HAQ Center for Child Rights.

Rangaswami, K. (1995). Parental attitude towards mentally retarded children. *Indian Journal of Clinical Psychology, 22*, 20–23.

Rahman, A. S., Sarker, S. A., Ahmed, T., Islam, R., Wahed, M. A., & Sack, D. A. (2013). Relationship of intestinal parasites, H. pylori infection with anemia or iron status among school age children in rural Bangladesh. *Journal of Gastroenterology and Hepatology Research, 2*(9). doi:10.6051/j.issn.2224-3992.2013.02.333.

Rogers, M. L., & Hogan, D. P. (2003). Family life with children with disabilities: The key role of rehabilitation. *Journal of Marriage and Family, 65*(4), 818–833. doi:10.1111/j.1741-3737.2003.00818.x.

Rogers, J. (2005). *The disabled woman's guide to pregnancy and birth*. New York: Demos Publishing.

Royal College of Nursing (2011, 2011). *Health care service standards in caring for neonates, children and young people*. London: Royal College of Nursing. Retrieved June 20, 2014, from hhtp://www.rcn.org.uk.

SSA. (2009). *Department of School Education and Literacy*, Ministry of Human Resource Development, Government of India. Retrieved July 4, 2015. http://ssa.nic.in

Schoufour, J. D., Mitnitski, A., Rockwood, K., Evenhuis, H. M., & Echteld, M. A. (2013). Development of a frailty index for older people with intellectual disabilities: Results from the HA-ID study. *Research in Developmental Disabilities, 34*(5), 1541–1555. doi:10.1016/j.ridd.2013.01.029.

Seligman, M., & Darling, R. B. (2007). *Ordinary families, special children: A systems approach to childhood disability*. New York: Guilford Books.

Sen, A. (1988). *Psychosocial integration of the handicapped*. New Delhi: Mittal Publications.

Sen, A (2000). A Decade of Human Development, Journal of Human Development, Vol. 1, No. 1.

Sengupta, S. (2008). *Out of sight out of mind, info change news and features*. Retrieved September 18, 2010, from http://infochangeindia.org/200706156475/Agenda/Child-Rights-In-India/.

Sharma, P. (2007). *'Rights of children with disability', presented at the National Seminar on child rights, organized by Dept of social work*. New Delhi: Jamia Millia Islamia University.

Sharma, P. (2009). *Inclusive education: A right of children with disability. Perspectives in social work*, 24, 3, Mumbai: College of Social Work, Nirmala Niketan.

Sharma, P. (2013). Rights Entitlements of Children with Disability: Study of Parents Awareness in India, Mumbai, International Journal of Arts and Sciences, 6(3), CD-ROM ISSN 1944-6934.

Smith, N., & Harrell, S. (2013, March). *Sexual abuse of children with disabilities: A national snapshot*. New York: Vera Institute of Justice. Retrieved June 12, 2014, from http://www.vera.org/sites/default/files/resources/downloads/sexual-abuse-of-children-with-disabilities-national-snapshot-v3.pdf.

SPLC. (2010, July 28).*Children with Disabilities Face Discrimination in New Orleans Schools*. Retrieved June 18, 2014, from http://www.splcenter.org/get-informed/news/splc-complaint-children-with-disabilities-face-discrimination-in-new-orleans-schoo.

Stalker, K., & McArthur, K. (2012). Child abuse, child protection and disabled children: a review of recent research. *Child Abuse Review, 21*(1), 24–40. doi:10.1002/car.1154.

Taub, D. J. (2006). Understanding the concerns of parents of students with disabilities: Challenges and roles for school counselors. *Professional School Counseling, 10*(1), 52–57.

Thukral, E. G. (2002). *Children in globalizing India: Challenging our conscience*. New Delhi: HAQ Centre for Child rights.

Tuli, U. (2002*). Breaking barriers: Physically challenged children in seen but not heard: India's marginalized, neglected and vulnerable children*. Voluntary Health Association of India.

UNCRPD. (2006). Retrieved July 4, 2015, from http://www.un.org/disabilities.

UNICEF Innocenti Research Centre. (2007). http://www.unicef-irc.org/publications/pdf/rc7_eng.pdf.

UNICEF. (2001). *Pocket guide for a rights based approach to programming for children, application in South Asia*. Kathmandu: UNICEF Regional Office for South Asia.

UNICEF. (2007). *Promoting the rights of children with disabilities*, Innocenti Digest No. 13. Florence, Italy: UNICEF Innocenti Research Centre. Retrieved June 17, 2014, from www.unicef-irc.org/publications/pdf/digest.

UNICRC. (1989). *Convention on the rights of the child*. Retrieved June 23, 2013, from http://www.ohchr.org/en/professionalinterest/pages/crc.aspx.

UNICEF East Asia and Pacific Region. (2011). *Fight against marginalization of disabled children*. Retrieved June 23, 2013, from http://www.unicef.org/eapro/media_16363.html.

UNESCO. (2000). *Educational for all 2000 assessment, statistical document*. World Education Forum. Paris: UNESCO.

World Bank. (2007). *People with disabilities in India: From commitments to outcomes*. Retrieved June 23, 2013, from http://worldbank.org.in.

World Bank Report. (2008). *Website on data and statistics on disability at*. Retrieved July 1, 2015, http://www.worldbank.org.disability

Chapter 16
Prevention of Abandonment of Children with Special Needs Through Community-Based Programs and Intervention

Chitra Shah

Introduction

There is no clear idea about the total number of children with special needs, nationally and internationally. Different estimations indicate different figures. For example, according to the WHO estimation, 10 % of the world's population suffers from some form of disability (WHO 1989). Further WHO 2011 estimation indicates that about a billion children, i.e., 15 % of the world's population was estimated to be living with disability (WHO 2011).

On the contrary, the percentage of disabled population in India was reported to be much lower compared to global disabled population, i.e., 2 % (NSSO 2003; Census of India 2001). However, one community-based survey in India disclosed the prevalence of all types of disability as 6.3 %. Mental disability was found to be the most common type of disability (36.7 %) in India, as revealed by the study (Ganesh et al. 2008).

NSSO study (2003) further disclosed that about 8.4 and 6.1 % of the total estimated households in rural and urban India, respectively, reported to have at least one disabled person. The number of disabled persons in India was estimated to be 18.49 million during July to December, 2002. They formed about 1.8 % of the total population. About 10.63 % of the disabled persons suffered from more than one type of disability. Among the different types of disabilities, the prevalence of locomotor disability was highest in India—it was 1046 in the rural and 901 in the urban per 100,000 persons. This was followed by visual disability and hearing disability. So far as education of disabled person is concerned, the current enrolment

C. Shah (✉)
Satya Special School, Pondicherry, India
e-mail: chitra69shah@yahoo.in

S. Deb (ed.), *Child Safety, Welfare and Well-being*,
DOI 10.1007/978-81-322-2425-9_16

ratio per 1000 disabled persons of age 5–18 years in the ordinary school was higher in the rural than in the urban—475 and 444, respectively, for the two sectors. About 11 % of disabled persons of age 5–18 years were enrolled in the special schools in the urban as compared to even less than 1 % in the rural. Regarding employment NSSO data indicates that about 26 % of the disabled persons were employed. The proportion of employed among the mentally retarded was the lowest at 6 %.

Although India has a very extensive legislation regarding Children with Special Needs (CWSNs), the ground reality is still very difficult for disabled children. The presence in the family of a CWSN is perceived as a disgrace, often as the result of the anger of gods, or ancestors or even the embodiment of sin in the family. Parents of mentally disabled children also feel guilt and sometimes take on themselves the blame for the impairment.

Abuse Experienced by Children with Disability and Services

Children with disabilities are more vulnerable to neglect, abuse, and maltreatment, as reported by a number of studies. For example, Hibbard and Desch (2007) remarked that children with disabilities are recognized as a population that is also at risk of neglect and maltreatment, i.e., deprivation from education, health facilities, and rehabilitation services, especially in rural and semi-urban areas. Female children face greater violence, withstanding physical and sexual abuses. Hershkowitz et al. (2007) found that children with disabilities CWDs were more likely to be abused by parent figures and to experience physical abuse resulting in body injury or serious sexual offenses, including those involving penetration, repeated abuse, use of force, and threats. Higher levels of disability were associated with increased risk of sexual abuse. Kyam (2005) compared the prevalence of childhood sexual abuse among visually impaired children and cited children in Norway. Visually impaired women and men aged 18–65 who lost their sight before age 18 reported sexual abuse.

In a retrospective study covering among 43 in-patients with intellectual disability Balogh et al. (2001) found that 14 % intellectually disabled people experienced abuse or abusive behavior. In 13 cases sexual abuse was identified after admission. About half of the victims had been abused by a member of their close or extended family. Most cases (62 %) were adolescents.

In an exploratory study Lightfoot and LaLiberte (2006) examined the delivery of child protection services by country child protection agencies involving cases with a family member with a disability. Only 6.7 % of respondents reported their agency had a written policy related to serving persons with a disability. Barriers behind delivering child protection services to the children with disabilities varied from rural to urban areas. The most important barrier was lack of resources, followed by lack of knowledge regarding disabilities, systems conflicts, and rural issues, such as lack of providers and lack of transportation. The lack of standardization in providing services indicates a need for more attention to issues regarding disability within child protection, including more training for workers, the development of models of collaborative case management and the removal of systemic barriers.

Local Situation in Puducherry, India

The services offered in Puducherry are not adequate for the population's needs. Actors within the field of disabilities (special schools, NGOs, parents' and teachers' associations, governmental initiatives, etc.) do not interact and do not coordinate their actions. This leads to an ineffective system which places Puducherry U.T. back by 10 years compared with other Indian States.

General Context

Mentally challenged or "intellectual disability, is defined as significantly sub average general intellectual functioning, existing concurrently with defects in adaptive behavior manifested during the development period, which is taken up to 18 years, and based on the Intellectual Quotient. It can be classified as mild, moderate, severe and profound. Mental challenge is also a source of stress to the family of an individual with this disorder. From identification through treatment or education, families struggle with questions about causes and prognosis, as well as guilt, a sense of loss, and disillusionment about the future."

In most parts of India, irrespective of state, region, or religion the disgrace of giving birth to a mentally disabled child is unanimous. Families, communities, and the medical profession often do not help to alleviate this guilt by their attitude to the baby and to the parents, calling the child a "vegetable," "useless," or "a burden." Inevitably this stigma and guilt result in isolation or segregation of the mentally disabled child.

Consequently, children with disabilities are among the most marginalized sections of society in India.

According to the report "People with disabilities in India: from commitments to outcomes" published by the World Bank (2007), there is growing evidence that people with disabilities comprise between 4 and 8 % of the Indian population (around 40–90 million individuals). This includes persons with visual, hearing, speech, locomotor, and mental disabilities. In this general framework,

The National Plan of Action for Children (2005) recognizes the actual limitations existing in the system, and the need to urgently reach the next goals:

- To ensure inclusion and effective access to education, health, vocational training along with specialized rehabilitation services to disabled children;
- To ensure the right to development as well as a recognition of special needs and of care and protection to children with disabilities who are vulnerable, such as, children with severe multiple disabilities, children with mental illnesses, severe mental impairment, children with disabilities from poor families, girl children, etc.

The World Bank's report "Dying for Change" explored the views of around 60,000 people who were defined as poor. The report highlighted the problems these poor people had in accessing appropriate and affordable health care. The problems they spoke of are common to all over India:

- Cost of treatment and care (including costs of transport and loss of wages during treatment)
- Low quality of health services available
- Staff shortages and absenteeism
- Lack of drugs and equipment
- Difficulties in accessing and understanding information.
- Another problem that poor people commonly talk about is the rudeness and lack of respect shown to them by health workers.

Most of the mentally challenged children suffer from physical deformities in addition to their mental disability; they are in need of regular therapy to help overcome their gross motor difficulties. At present, the Puducherry Government health care system does not have the necessary facilities and the private facilities are beyond the reach of these children from economically poor families.

Context Analysis and Justification

The main problems to address are:

(i) **A Social Stigma and a Lack of Awareness about Mental Disability**

As already explained, being born or having a child affected by disability is often perceived as a God's punishment for some kind of past sins, a shame to bear. The incidence of CWSNs' on the total of the abandoned children has constantly increased in the last 10 years and for the majority of them it is not possible to find an adoptive family and they are doomed to a (very short) life in institution.

(ii) The Children with Disabilities Have No Access to Health, Rehabilitation, and Educational Services

For instance, children with impairments may be hidden away at home, they are more likely than their peers not to go to school, to receive less food and generally be neglected, which makes it even harder for them to develop their potentialities and find an employment when they grow up.

According to a CIAI's (Centro Italiano Aiuti all'infanzia) and Satya Special School's study report (2009–2010), in Puducherry U.T., a population of 8,000 disabled children has been estimated. Of them, around 1,700 are mentally challenged and only 1 % is receiving adequate health, rehabilitation, and education services. The number of rehabilitation facilities available in Puducherry is inadequate, and the qualification is insufficient. In the rural areas they are almost inexistent. For a population of more than 250,000 persons there are only two clinical psychologists, one small prosthetics workshop, one neurosurgeon, five special educators of which only one is trained in handling mentally challenged children and there is no occupational therapist. The existing private facilities are beyond the reach of the poor or the rural areas inhabitants.

The education for "children with mild disabilities" remains very low, due to the lack of capacities of the government to give specific trainings to the teachers, and the need of special "bridge courses", extracurricular activities, transport, and structural facilities, etc., to facilitate the integration of these children in normal schools.

The situation of children under severe disabilities' education in special schools is still worse. There are about 24 special schools in Puducherry T.U., most of them running without special teachers.

(iii) Lack of Vocational Training and Employability Opportunities for People with Disabilities

In Puducherry, there is only one government-run Vocational Training Centre for Challenged Children, but only mild and moderate mentally challenged children (1 % of the seats in the centre) can attend the trainings because of limited capacity of the centre. The Government of India has reserved 3 % of vacancies for people with disabilities in Government establishments. The categories of handicapped persons that benefit by this scheme are the blind, the deaf and the orthopedically handicapped with 1 % reservation for each category. The mentally challenged have been left out from the provisions of the act. This leaves a sizeable population in the employable age of 18–25 years marginalized away from mainstream society.

(iv) Lack of trained Human resource professional to work with Children with Special Needs in Pondicherry

The law-established ratio of one teacher for every seven mentally challenged children is definitely not attained in Puducherry, with only 15 qualified special educators for 24 special schools. The main reason for the qualified human resources' lack is because a certified training course for special teachers does not exist in

Puducherry. The nearest available program is in Chennai, where the higher costs of training, boarding, and lodging make it unattractive for Puducherry aspirants.

Satya Special School has started a 2-year Diploma in Special Education with specialization in Mental Retardation, but the result of this effort will be noticed only in 1 year when the first students finish the program.

(v) **Lack of Coordination among Actors in the Field of Disabilities**

- A preliminary research conducted in governmental centers, special schools, and institutes in Puducherry, showed that:
- Among CWSNs' parents there is no networking in order to share information and practices and so be able to better help their children
- Special schools, fearing competitors or for lack of professionalism, do not share information among them;
- Special schools are concentrated in urban areas, where duplication of services is abundant and rural areas are uncovered;
- There are no associations entirely led by PWD that can fight and advocate for their rights in first person.

Generally speaking, the disability sector's actors lack of coordination, a lot of small schools competing on the same territory with the same services and there being neither common vision nor common action to find optimized common solutions to common problems.

Ideally facilities like maternity clinics responsible for child birth, the child specialist or pediatrician who does the first assessment of the new born child, early intervention clinics or special schools, therapist must have a network where any child identified with special needs is immediately referred for therapy or early intervention as the case may be. Unfortunately, in India parents are neglecting the crucial developmental years (0–3 years), due to fear of social acceptance: parents rely more on "God men" and "quacks" for quick and easy ways of changing their 'karma' or past sins. In some cases, even the medical practitioners, understanding the desperation shown by parents in "curing" their child's condition rather than "rehabilitating" them to live with their condition, promise miracles through unnecessary medical interventions like scanning, various tests, expensive medicines, etc. Traditional alternative medical treatments like Ayurveda, Unani, or herbal medicines also promise cure for mental disability. The situation gets further complicated as therapy facilities are too expensive even for the middle income group.

Even among parents of children with special needs, there is no networking to share best practices of aiding these children. Special schools working with children with special needs for fear of competition and unprofessionalism do not share information either. Also since most of the schools are charity driven rather than dignity driven, they work more toward creating sympathy about the child's condition rather than actual rehabilitation. Concentration of special schools in urban areas and duplication of services is also a major cause of concern. In Puducherry, the added vacuum created due to lack of community-based rehabilitation initiatives is also a major cause of concern as facilities are beyond the reach of children in the semi urban and rural areas.

Initially as parents are keen on curing the child's condition, when all their efforts have failed by running from one specialist who promises cure to a "quack" who promises a miracle to happen on full moon days to a therapist who can provide quick results eventually having exhausted all their financial capabilities, as a last option with almost no hope and only as relief in caring for the child for a few hours in a day, approach special schools. In some cases due to lack of awareness and since the child has lost its important years of development, parents reconcile to a fact that there is no future for their children and do not even make the effort of getting the child to attend any special school. In some cases medical intervention is also stopped. For example: when Satya organized a dental checkup for the children—even children as old as 15 years had never been assessed or treated by a dentist bringing to light the fact that children with special needs are deprived on a social, medical and emotional level—they lead second class citizen lives. It is only ironical that some Indian cities boast of the state of the art clinics but less than human facilities for children with special needs.

The plight of the child with special needs is heart wrenching as in most cases the parents are being cheated in the name of cure by medical professionals, "quacks," "godmen," and "therapists." This happens only due to the monetary benefits each of the stakeholders have in curing the child. By the end of the initial years in attempting to cure the child what special schools are mostly left with are dejected parents having no interest in the child; wanting to shift their responsibility of even caring for the child to either day care centers or institutionalizing them. Though awareness creation is the answer, a major hurdle is the lack of coordinated rehabilitation efforts by Government, NGO's and professionals involved in working with children with special needs. Lack of coordination has left facilities in Puducherry lagging behind by 2 decades with established NGOs in the major metros, doing some unique and wonderful work.

Negative contributing factors include over crowded government medical facilities in Puducherry and a lack of specialized therapy services and qualified staff to attend the mentally and multiply challenged children. In addition, existing private facilities are beyond the reach of the economically poor.

In the Territorial Union of Puducherry, Satya estimated that the disabled children population is almost 8000 and only 1 % is receiving adequate heath, rehabilitation and education services. Puducherry is the fourth state in India in the ranking of "proportion of disables not seeking any treatment" (in 2002 almost the 90 % of CWSN had not being attended) and the main health constraints remain the demand and the supply of services:

- At an individual level Satya observed the lack of awareness, and/or physical and financial ability to demand or access to the existing governmental schemes, and the general problems in health delivery for all.
- At Puducherry UT and national level, Satya find out the low priority to disability in an already overburdened health system.

The number of rehabilitation staff available in Puducherry is inadequate, and the qualification is insufficient overall in the case of therapies for multi mentally challenged children. As examples we can mention that in Puducherry for a population of more than 250,000 persons there is only two clinical psychologists, one prosthetics small workshop (one almost one trained personnel is required to meet the needs of 1000 people, as per WHO's guidelines), cero occupational therapist, one neurosurgeon, five special educators of which only one is trained in handling mentally retarded children, etc.

In Puducherry, and in the villages around, not only the health and school facilities are insufficient, but there is also lack of studies and knowledge about what is the reality of mentally challenged children in rural areas.

Lack of Training and Education of Challenged Children in Puducherry

In a country like India where education levels even among the normal children are not flattering, it is not entirely unexpected that disabled children stand at an even greater disadvantage. After Indian Independence, an important turning point was the National Policy on Education (1986). This policy, for the first time, included a section on disabilities (Section 4.9). Briefly it includes:

- Inclusive education possibilities for children with mild disabilities in regular schools;
- Provision for the training and education of children with severe disabilities in special schools;
- Vocational training as being a part of the education for the disabled.

For instance, children with impairments may be hidden away at home; they are more likely than their peers not to go to school, to receive less food and to generally be neglected, which makes it even harder for them to find employment when they grow up:

- The education for "children with mild disabilities" remains very low, due to the lack of capacities of the government to give specific trainings to the teachers, and the need of special "bridge courses," extracurricular activities, transport and structural facilities, etc., to facilitate the integration of these children in normal schools.
- The situation of education of children with severe disabilities in special schools is still worst, and in Puducherry there is only one governmental special school for visually impaired (blind) children; added to this, is the lack of proper vocational training facilities in Puducherry to increase employability of the children.
- Lack of Vocational Training Centre for disabled children is a big challenge for addressing their need. The issue requires special attention of the Ministry of Social Justice and Empowerment, Government of India.

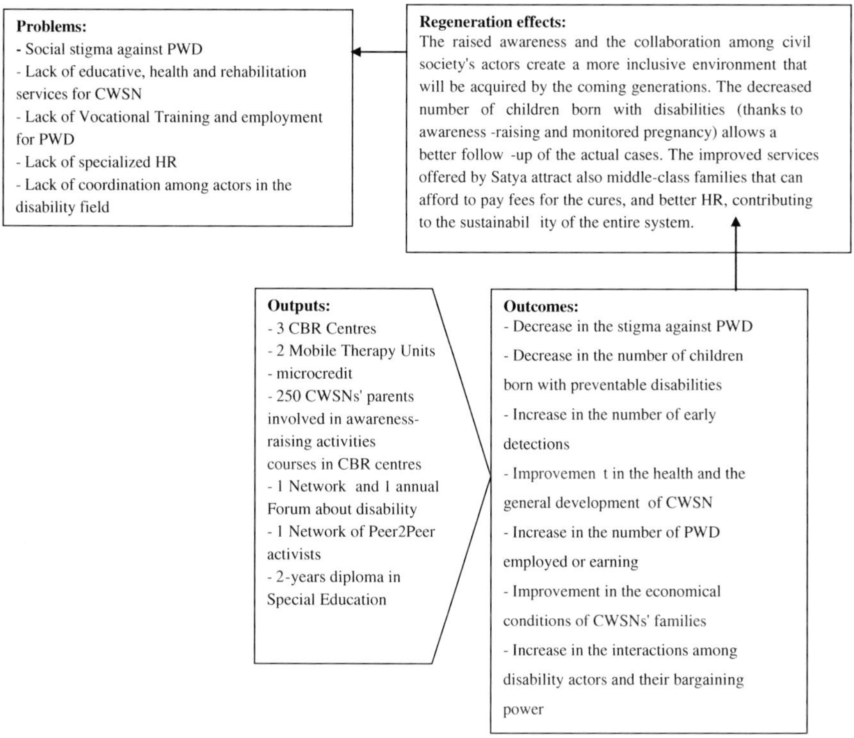

Fig. 16.1 Logical Chain of Interventions, Shah Chitra, 2009

The mentally challenged have been left out from the provisions of the act. This leaves a sizeable population in the employable age of 18–25 years marginalized and away from the mainstream of society.

Concerning the overall logic of intervention, the following logic chain has been adopted (Fig. 16.1):

Relevance of the Project

The main legislative text about disability in India is the Rights of Persons with Disabilities Bill of 2011. The overall goal of the present project is to improve the quality of life of mentally disabled children and their families in Puducherry Territorial Union. It is perfect in compliance with the above mentioned text's principles and aims.

Generally speaking, the Bill states in its preamble that "Citizens with Disability are an essential part of human diversity [and that they] have a right:

- To integrity, dignity and respect with full participation and inclusion;
- To live a life free of shame, ridicule, or any form of disempowerment and stereotyping;
- To be entitled on an equal basis with others to all civil-political and socio-economic rights guaranteed by international and national law."

And it specifies, immediately after, that one of the "salient features of the legislation [is] to recognize the special vulnerabilities of children with disabilities and ensure that they are treated on an equal basis with other children."

In the inner sections of the text, a variety of specific rights' protection is discussed. In details, for the present proposal the relevant ones are (quoting the Rights of Persons with Disabilities Bill of 2011):

Section 68. (1) The appropriate governments [...] shall carry out sensitization and awareness-raising among care-givers, service-users and the general public as regards the human rights, dignity, autonomy and needs of persons with disabilities. [...]

Section 70. (1) The appropriate governments [...] shall formulate habilitation plans for children with disabilities with strategies for ensuring that it starts as early as possible;

These plans shall inter alia provide for:

a. Appropriate support and guidance to parents of infants and young children with disabilities to enable them to perform their parenting responsibilities; [...]
b. Provision of social skills and social networking between children with disabilities; other children; extended family, and larger community; [...]
c. disseminate information on nature of disabilities and the plan of habilitation to the community generally; and to community workers, doctors, and teachers particularly.

Section 88. The appropriate governments [...] shall:

a. undertake the development of human resource so that both inclusive and specialized services are made available to persons with disabilities;
b. orients, sensitizes and trains existing personnel and creates curricula which is disability sensitive;
c. make provision for adequate numbers of professionals in such manner that such personnel are available in appropriate ratios to provide services for persons across all disabilities at the central, state, local, and Panchayat level; [...]
d. Initiating capacity building programs, including training in independent living and community relationships for families, members of community, and other stakeholders and care providers on care giving and support;
e. Ensuring independence training for persons with disabilities to build community relationships on mutual contribution and respect.

The present project operates on all these areas of intervention (awareness-raising, capacity building/rehabilitation, and human resources) through:

- Strengthen the rights advocacy campaign, focusing on networking and leaders training not only with the CWSN families but also within the communities;
- Creation of a Peer 2 Peer network of disable youth and adults that act as field agent of sensitization and spreading of best practices;
- Strengthen the autonomy and the caring capacities of CWSNs' families, through the microcredit program.

Since the 2011 Bill states that "the appropriate government shall be entrusted with the welfare of persons with disabilities," and that these institutions do not always have the resources nor the capacity to implement such tasks, the action of NGOs or private institutions becomes of primary importance to fill the gap between laws and the ground reality. The lawmakers are aware of the fact that well to be aware of the "The National Policy recognizes the NGO sector as a very important institutional mechanism to provide affordable services to complement the endeavors of the Government." The intervention of NGOs such CIAI and SSS is not only legitimate but has to be indeed encouraged. The added value of years of successful experiences in the field of disabilities must be capitalized and the effort toward a more inclusive society supported.

Stakeholders

CWSNs Families

They are mostly low-income families, sometimes single mothers, living in rural or semi-urban areas. They do not have the knowledge or the skills to care about their children in an appropriate way. In order to stay at home to look after the disabled child, they sometimes lose important work opportunities, worsening their already fragile economic conditions. They will take an active part in their children's education, acquiring important knowledge about disability, being involved in the definition of the rehabilitation plan and becoming, adequately instructed co-therapists. They will start networking and sharing information and best practices with the other CWSNs' parents. Thanks to the microcredit program, they will improve their family's living conditions.

Disabled Youth and Adults

They are excluded from all forms of participation in economic, civil, and social life. They stand the risk of abandonment even in late age. They will be Peer to Peer educators and they will start to autonomously advocate for their rights.

Actors in the Field of Disabilities (Schools, Parents' Associations, PWDS' Associations, Governmental Institutions and Agencies, NGOS)

They work in the same field, with different methodologies and results, but they are not coordinated and they do not share their problems and achievements among them. They will start networking, sharing their success and problems and having a space for discussion and confrontation. They will increase their bargaining power toward the institutions.

Social Welfare Department, Government of Puducherry U.T.

India's legislation concerning disability is very comprehensive and versatile, but is rarely enforced. Puducherry welfare department is no exception: things can be moved only by connections, there is not a shared vision and mission with the civil society. This stakeholder can be an obstacle to the project, if it decides to persist in its lax policy, or on the contrary be an agent of the change if it decides to support and facilitate the networking and rights advocacy activities.

Beneficiaries

The project's direct beneficiaries are:

- *175 Children with Special Needs*, from 0 to 18 years old, described as individuals who require assistance for disabilities that may be medical, mental, psychological, educational and/or vocational, living in the rural and semi-urban villages of Villainur, Thirukkanur, Pudupakkam, Thirubuvanai, Madagadipet, Puducherry city, and its surroundings. They will benefit from a wide range of activities concerning health, education, and rehabilitation. Thanks to Satya Special School services, they will better their health, increase their independence and develop new skills;
- *350 CWSNs' parents* living in the rural and semi-urban villages of Villainur, Thirukkanur, Pudupakkam, Thirubuvanai, Madagadipet, Puducherry city, and its surroundings. They will benefit from the assistance and education given to their children. Freed from the time-consuming attentions required by the disable children, they will have more time to spend in other activities. For example, they will have the opportunity to obtain a loan from the microcredit program and they will be involved in awareness-raising sessions and networking with other CWSNs' parents;

- *100 youth and adults living with disabilities*, in the rural and semi-urban villages of Villainur, Thirukkanur, Pudupakkam, Thirubuvanai, Madagadipet, Puducherry city, and its surroundings. They will benefit from the leadership trainings and the Peer2Peer network organized in the framework of the rights advocacy activities, they will become an active part of their community's civic life and they will be able to autonomously advocate for their rights. They will have the opportunity to learn an income generating activity and becoming an earning members of their families through the Vocational Trainings provided by Satya Special School;
- *1000 stakeholders-community members*, parents, authorities, teachers, community-based, and nongovernmental organizations' members, living in the rural and semi-urban villages of Villainur, Thirukkanur, Pudupakkam, Thirubuvanai, Madagadipet, Puducherry city, and its surroundings. They will benefit from information and best practices' sharing that will start with the disability actors' network's creation. Through the networking, they will be able to find common solutions for their issues and to lobby with an increased bargaining power toward institutions.

The project final beneficiaries are:

- *The disabled population in Puducherry*: 25.857 persons—as per Census 2001. A part from the general data, the lack of proper statistics, studies, and surveys about the different disabilities is a common deficiency in studies and surveys in India. No more specific data are thus available in this respect. They will benefit from the increased rehabilitation and education services available in the Puducherry District thanks to Satya Special School Centres. They will benefit from the increased networking and advocacy capacities of the associations and institutions part of the network animated by Satya;
- *The total population of Puducherry District*: 735.332 persons—as per Census 2001. They will benefit from the more inclusive environment they are living in and from the increased networking and advocacy skills of some civil society's members.

Community-Based Rehabilitation (CBR)

The general concept about CBR is that it is a quick, cheap episodic distribution of some appliances for physically disabled people living in a rural area. Many government as well as non government agencies with all good intentions to rehabilitate disabled people resort to quick fix solutions with no long lasting impact on the community. Rehabilitation, considered as functional restoration, can be achieved only by empowering the disabled as well by enriching their community. Rehabilitation, which is based in the community, thus acquires a deeper meaning. It amounts to development of the community as a whole, empowering the disabled persons to achieve their complete potential, enabling them to integrate into the fabric of the community and make decisions for themselves. This would also involve dealing with both physical and architectural barriers within the community.

CBR has seven different components

i. Creation of a positive attitude toward people with disabilities
ii. Provision of rehabilitation services
iii. Provision of education and training opportunities
iv. Creation of micro and macro income—generation opportunities
v. Provision of long-term care facilities
vi. Prevention of causes of disabilities
vii. Monitoring and Evaluation.

Satya's CBR Strategy

Due to the lack of rehabilitation facilities in rural villages, a child /adult with a special need remains as someone who is a burden and a monetary liability for the family. Satya's CBR project aims at changing this scenario wherein the isolated person/child with disability becomes a contributor to the family, thereby earning community's acceptance.

The first step in the CBR program is to make the person with disabilities capable of being independent and managing his daily activities. This is done through specialized need-based training which is identified by a formal assessment of the PWD. In addition to the training, depending on the type and extent of disability, along with the necessary therapy sessions the PWD is provided with aids and appliances that help in increasing mobility. Depending on the age of the PWD either through special education or vocational training or both, the PWDs competencies are improved. With the help of micro credits or employment the PWD from being a liability becomes a contributor to the family. While this process is taking shape, both the members of the immediate family and the community is initially acting as an observer. As the change in the PWD is remarkable, observers start to interact and take keen interest in the CBR programs. They are then involved in the CBR programs as Village counselors who spread awareness and help in bringing together the community—in simple words they become SATYA's spokesperson in the village. This increases community participation and social inclusion of the PWD becomes a reality (Fig. 16.2).

We at Satya feel that the above strategy would help in long-term sustainability of the program as the community will ensure CWSN born in the years to come are not isolated.

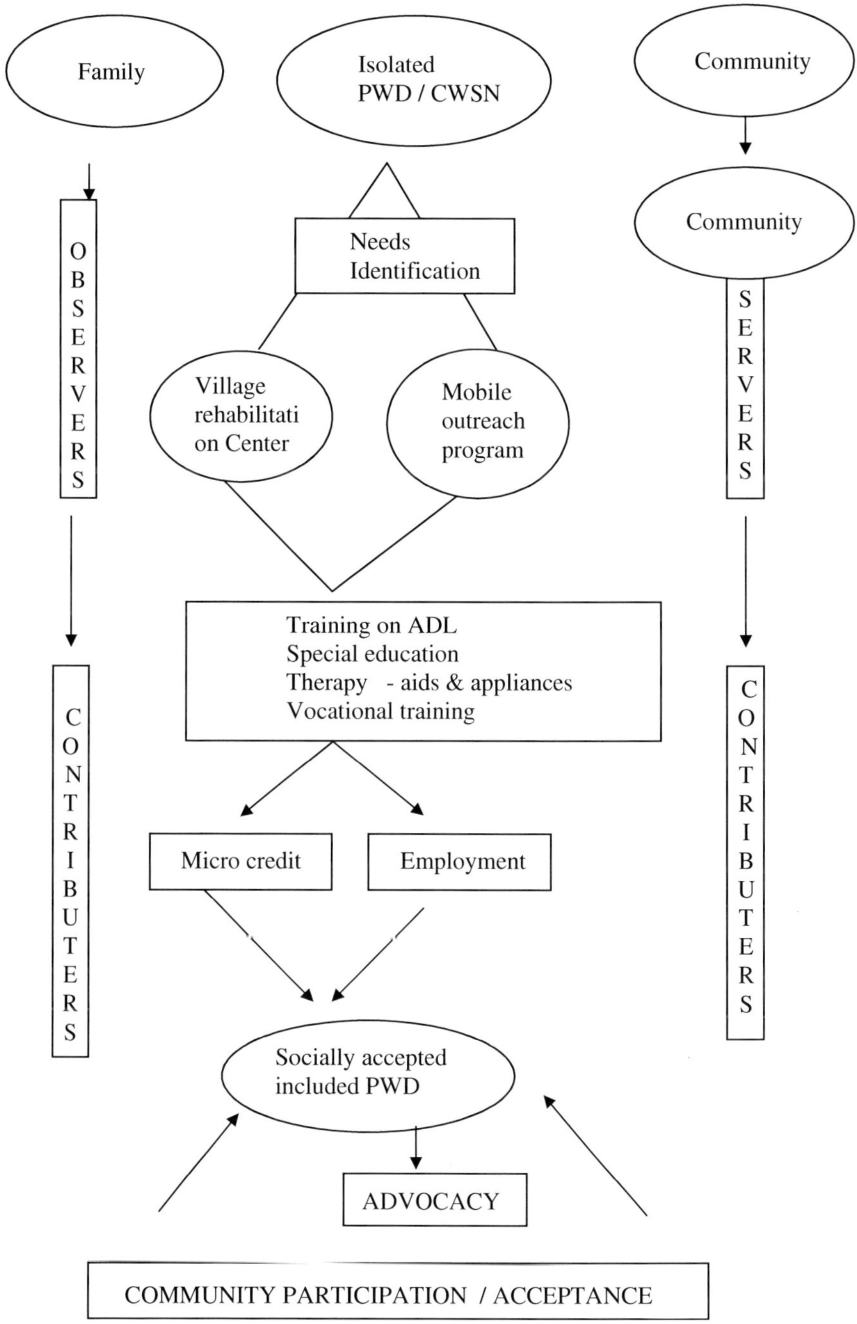

Fig. 16.2 Flowchart of Stakeholder Participation, Shah Chitra, 2009

Success Story

Name: Meeramoideen
Village: Ariyur

The birth of a male child Meera Moideen brought cheer to Abbas and Madinabee. With meager earnings from the cycle repair shop that the father runs, the family was looking forward to the birth of the second child. The happiness, however, was short-lived when the parents realized that Moideen had developmental delays and lacked neck control. Fearing for the child's well-being the family was completely stressed and started visiting a number of medical doctors and also experimented with various alternative medicines. With medical intervention having failed, the parents visited all religious places and performed many rituals in turn spending a lot of money that they had to borrow for interest from others. With no satisfactory results, they accepted their child's condition and left him uncared and unattended in a corner of their home. The lack of any movement or therapy meant that Moideen's limbs started to tighten and contracture started to develop (Fig. 16.3).

Satya's community workers identified him during a scheduled village survey. After initial hesitation the parents agreed to send him to the Village Rehabilitation Center for assessment and intervention. Moideen was a challenge to the staff and therapist as he was dependent on others for his daily activities, he needed to be fed, since his limbs were stiff he could not walk or stand and had to be carried around, he also had fluency disorder and hence could not communicate properly.

A multidisciplinary program including physiotherapy, speech therapy, occupational therapy, activities of daily living and special education was planned and followed. Quarterly assessments were also done to keep track of his improvement. After a year and half of intervention, Moideen today is able to sit without support and stand with support. His eating skills have improved and are independent. He communicates with others; he likes to sing and is also able to recite poetry. The family is now relieved and happy to see the progress he has made. They are hopeful of more improvement in his condition in the months to come.

Name: Pavitra

Pavitra was diagnosed with multiple disabilities when she was 2 years. Initially the family was shocked and being a girl child rejected her and her mother. Even

Fig. 16.3 Moideen after receiving rehabilitation services from Satya

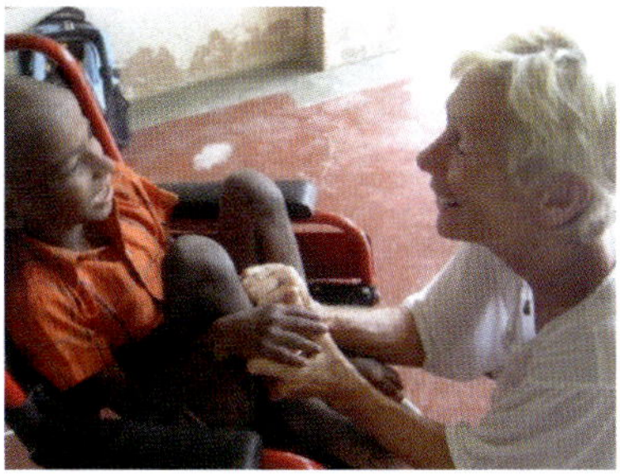

Fig. 16.4 Kandasamy, now a part of Satya

her brother did not want to take responsibility of the child; she was left on the streets. A kind-hearted family agreed to give the mother a house maid's job and some space in their house for them to stay. As the day to day survival was itself an issue, the mother did not have the time or resources to take Pavitra to even a doctor for fever or a common cold. Physiotherapist or allied rehabilitation services was unmanagable. When Satya's Mobile Unit identified her, Pavitra was 8 years old. The mother could not believe her ears when she was informed that Satya's Mobile Unit will provide her physiotherapy and also train the mother in some basic techniques that can help her in taking care of her daughter. With good cooperation from both Pavitra and her mother, today she is able to move her limbs a little. She also has been provided with a wheel chair that has increased her mobility. For the first time she even visited the village temple and went around the village fair. The MTU team has given her a hope to be less dependent on her mother and bring some happiness into this otherwise forgotten life.

Name: Kandasamy

Hailing from a poor family of 5, Kandasamy's father is the sole bread winner and works as a daily laborer. Due to Kandasamy's condition, his mother could not take up any job. Lack of awareness and the necessary financial resources, led to the child being left unattended. His inability to move meant that he was dependent on others for his daily activities. Satya's center came to his family as a blessing. The center has now provided him with a wheel chair with which he not only attends the day care but the other children push him around the village lanes—a sight he had never seen in his life. While the physiotherapist works on his limbs, the speech therapist teaches him to say a few words. The whole village is watching the progress he is making and now begins to show keen interest in Satya's work in their village (Fig. 16.4).

Conclusion

Working for over 10 years in the urban and rural areas of Pondicherry (India), it is evident that any successful sustainable rehabilitation model must not only cater to the needs of the child but also ensure participation of the immediate family, community, and the society in general. Sensitization of various stake holders, government officials, law makers, etc. also plays a major role in removing stereotyping of CWSNs. Prevention of abandonment of Children with Special needs can only be achieved through interventions at various levels : from the individual family to the neighborhood and the society.

Challenges

There are a number of challenges in delivering effective services at the community level. Social stigma is one of the barriers which prevent people to come forward for the need-based support services. Lack of trained professionals compared to the need of services required for the beneficiaries, need-based materials, lack of financial support for expenses related to logistics, and lack of coordination between the Government and NGOs are other challenges which hinder the quality of services at the community level.

Admitting children with multiple or severe disabilities in the educational institutions and ensuring barrier free infrastructure is also another challenge especially in the rural set ups. It is important to bring the children with disabilities into mainstream society after providing them need-based support services.

Recommendations

- There is an urgent need for advocacy with the authority of social welfare department for mainstreaming and strengthening the systems and support services.
- NGOs in collaboration with the Social Welfare Department should take up periodic skill development training programs for capacity building of the health care providers and Program Managers through.
- It is also urgently needed to increase public awareness through electronic media for understanding the disability issue from right perspective.
- NGOs and government institutes should emphasize on documentation system and systematic research which will in turn help in designing effective intervention program and for providing need-based quality support services (Kumar et al. 2012).

Let all join hands in making this world a better place for CWSNs.
Our Commitment to CWSNs:

WE WILL NOT CHANGE YOU FOR THE WORLD
BUT
WE WILL CHANGE THE WORLD FOR YOU

References

Census of India. (2001). Data on disability. Office of the Registrar General and Census Commissioner, India. Retrieved 9 August, 2004, from http://www.censusindia.net/disabilioty/disability_mapgallery.html.

CIAI Centro Italiano per l'AdozioneInternazionale (Italian Center for Inter-Country Adoptions) and Satya Special School Study Report on Disability in Puducherry. (2009–2010).

Balogh, R., Bretherton, K., Whibley, S., Berney, T., Graham, S., Richold, P., et al. (2001). Sexual abuse in children and adolescents with intellectual disability. *Journal of Intellectual Disability Research, 45*(3), 194–201.

Ganesh, K. S., Das, A., & Shashi, J. S. (2008). Epidemiology of disability in a rural community of Karnataka. *Indian Journal of Public Health, 52*, 125–129.

Hibbard, R. A., & Desch, L. W. (2007). Maltreatment of children with disabilities. *Pediatrics, 119*(5), 1018–1025. doi:10.1542/peds.2007-0565.

Hershkowitz, I., Lamb, M. E., & Horowitz, D. (2007). Victimization of children with disabilities. *American Journal of Orthopsychiatry, 77*(4), 629–635. doi:10.1037/0002-9432.77.4.629.

Kumar, G. S., Roy, G., & Kar, S. S. (2012). Disability and rehabilitation services in India: Issues and challenges. *Disability and Rehabilitation Services, 1*(1), 69–73. doi:10.4103/2249-4863.94458.

Kyam, M. H. (2005). Experiences of childhood sexual abuse among visually impaired adults in Norway: Prevalence and characteristics. *Journal of Visual Impairment & Blindness, 99*(1), 5–14.

Lightfoot, E. B., & LaLiberte, T. L. (2006). Approaches to child protection case management for cases involving people with disabilities. *Child Abuse and Neglect, 30*(4), 381–391. doi:10.1016/j.chiabu.2005.10.013.

National Sample Survey Organization (58th Round, July–December 2002). (2003). A report on disabled persons. New Delhi: Department of Statistics, Government of India.

The World Health Organization. (1989). Training in the community for people with disabilities. Geneva: WHO.

The World Health Organization. (2011). World report on disability. Geneva; WHO.

The World Bank Report, Human Development Unit, South Asian Region. (2007, May). People with disabilities in India: From commitments to outcomes.

The National Plan of Action for Children, Government of India. (2005).

The National Policy on Education, Government of India. (1986).

The Right of Persons with Disabilities Bill. (2011).

Chapter 17
Psycho-Social Support for Protection of Children in Disasters

Subhasis Bhadra

Introduction

With the development and growth at high speed in the twenty first century, the danger and humanitarian challenges are also increasing considerably at every space of life. The vulnerability to disasters is increasing day by day, and the intensity of the problem is becoming deeper and exhaustive. With the threat of climate change the numbers of natural disasters have increased in last few decades and in India too. The political unrest all over the world also has created considerable human-made disaster through multiple incidents of conflict, war, and refugee situations. The issues of vulnerability also differ according to the nature of the disaster. The factors of vulnerability are typically connected with the social system and capacity of the system to deal with the threats. Disaster as a threatening situation destroys the social support systems that usually exist to maintain the tranquility of a social structure. Thus, the vulnerability increases for the groups and the destroyed social support system fail to ensure adequate protective mechanisms for these vulnerable groups. While there is debate that every society may not have adequate concern for protection even in a normal situation, the vulnerable groups are exploited in a systematic default, but the situation becomes worrisome and out of control after a disaster. This disorder and disorganization due to disaster is well defined by WHO 1991 that states "it as a severe disruption of ecological and psycho social which greatly exceeds the coping capacity of the affected community." For the purpose of social intervention practice, Bhadra 2006 defined disaster as "physically, psychosocially, ecologically devastating event of such a nature

S. Bhadra (✉)
Department of Social Work, Gautam Buddha University,
Greater Noida, Uttar Pradesh, India
e-mail: bhadrasubhasis@gmail.com

S. Deb (ed.), *Child Safety, Welfare and Well-being*,
DOI 10.1007/978-81-322-2425-9_17

which exceeds the coping capacity…. It demands external help to rejuvenate the life by facilitating the psychosocial resources of the survivors to reduce the stress of various life events immediately as well as in long term at individual, family, and community levels." Reduction of stress is connected with the reduction of vulnerabilities among the survivors of disaster. The disaster increase the vulnerability of the marginalized sections of the society and reduction of vulnerability could only be activated through enhancing protective mechanisms and supporting atmosphere to normalize the life and build normalcy at faster rate.

There are number of survivors in any disaster situation and the vulnerability of the survivors differs based on some important determining factors dealing with gender, age profile, disabilities, cultural practices, local belief system, government policies, program, and ultimately capacity of the vulnerable groups to deal with the limitations and challenges. Children are often described as the most vulnerable groups of the society and specifically in the disaster situation (Sekar and Bhadra 2003; Sekar et al. 2005b; Bhadra and Jadav 2003; Dyer and Bhadra 2013, p. 195). The reasons of multiple complicated vulnerabilities of the children and adolescent in the disaster need to be understood in the background of the impact of the disaster to examine the importance and implementation of the various psychosocial support interventions and protection for the children in the critical difficult circumstance like disaster.

Tender Age and Developmental Risk Among the Children in Disaster

Tendering age needs special care and protection for flourishing in a healthy manner in future. Childhood as a tender age is a period of growth and development to lay the foundation for a healthy life. The atmosphere and upbringing at childhood and adolescent stage is crucial for development into a well-adjusted adult. At each stage of development there are certain tasks which the child must get opportunities to master for healthy, emotional, and personality development. Relevant and continuous interactions with caregivers, as well as their environment, enable children to master these tasks and move on to the next phase of development. The development theories by Erick Erikson (Morgan et al. 1997, pp. 472–474) highlighted the important role environmental factors play within the normal development of the child, adolescent and how lack of opportunities to adequately master the developmental tasks can lead to dysfunctional behavior.

Disaster leads to multiple developmental risks for the children and adolescents as the destroyed environment and facilities fail to give the required caring atmosphere. Care and support in the childhood is most essential task of the primary socializing agents for the development of the child to be well-adjusted in the society. These primary socializing agents facilitates developmental atmosphere by cultivating cultural values, norms, practices, daily routine, and ensure social control, the disaster alters the tranquility and systematic arrangements of this developmental order.

Destruction of the Nurturing Atmosphere

Children in difficult circumstances suffer from the harshness of the environment and surroundings that puts them in multiple developmental risks. Disaster is characterized by destruction of the nurturing atmosphere and puts the children in a harsh reality. In such a situation the children and adolescents finds themselves in a most unprecedented condition and feel alien to the situation. A disaster disrupts the process of interaction the child has with his/her environment. It leads to a displaced lifestyle wherein the familiar environment (home, school, peers, etc.,) is lost. Loss of familiarity from the known caring atmosphere causes a severe distress among the children and adolescent that they are most incapable to handle and thus shows multiple stress reactions (Sekar et al. 2005a). The nurturing atmosphere is essential requirement for learning and developing a socially desired behavior and for the protection of the children from the abuses and difficulties like struggle for food, stay, physical abuse, exploitation, etc. (Dyer and Bhadra 2013, p. 183). Thus, disaster is a situation that cripples the capacity of the institutions and social systems that suppose to ensure care and protection.

Inability of the Family and Care Givers to Provide Adequate Support

The family is the primary caregiver for the children. During disaster and in post disaster situation the destroyed social structure causes a serious disabling impact on the families to perform the regular activities. The family routine gets altered and family resources usually shrink or destroy. Families may lose their livelihood assets, regular income and become dependent on external support for daily requirements. External help is also needed to rebuild their life and to start normal life as a family unit. If the assistance is inadequate or the response and support is delayed in the situation, this may also be worsening. In such a situation the parents and other adult family members find it difficult to provide adequate supportive and caring atmosphere to the children. Immediately after the disaster, it is difficult to ensure adequate food, health care, accommodation in a safe and secured environment and in long term it may continue as multifold problems. These inadequacies of support care and protected environment leads to living in cramp unhygienic camps or temporary shelters. Such a camp or settler obviously lacks the basic amenities and the children are devoid of their basic rights for days, months, and years together based on the response strategy in the country in a particular disaster.

Traumatic Experiences Due to Disaster

Disaster is connected with various traumatic experiences that are related to personal loss, injury, multiple deaths, and loss of normal living atmosphere. The children also witness and experience exploitation, violence, torture, and struggle for basic facilities. These experiences are not an issue of daily life that the child ever experienced in such magnitude prior to the specific disaster experience and thus termed as traumatic experiences of disaster. The loss leads to stress, psychosocial disability, and traumatic experience for the child survivors of the disaster. As an impact of these traumatic experiences the children exhibit multiple stress reactions that include body discomfort, psychological reaction (i.e., nightmare, crying spell, anxiety, depression, etc.) behavior reactions, relational problems, scholastic decline, etc. Thus the disaster experiences become severely disabling at the tender age and these unhealed traumas may cause severe detrimental impact on the development of the children.

Destruction of Educational Set-up

Education is the basic rights of children. Lacks of educational facilities lead to high disengagement among the children and causes child abuse. In a situation of disaster the children out of school and educational environment become victim of the chaotic situation and subjected to experience and witness problems around them characterized by anger, frustration, fighting, and untoward behavior of adults. Many a time it is also seen that the children are used for different assisting job not appropriate for the age.

> "Education is not only a right, but in situations of emergencies, chronic crises and early reconstruction, it provides physical, psychosocial, and cognitive protection which can be both life-saving and life-sustaining. Education sustains life by offering safe spaces for learning, as well as the ability to identify and provide support for affected individuals—particularly children and adolescents." (The Inter-Agency Network for Education in Emergencies (INEE) 2004, p. 5) Educational set-up is not just for the purpose of teaching lessons for the children; rather it is part of their identity and a formal mechanism of facilitating the growth and personality. The children learn group norms, desired expected behavior, get affectionate peer relations, and also gets guided, protected, safe atmosphere from the teacher. Educational set-up is meant to provide a protective and safe environment, and destruction of this formal set-up accounts for a large vacuum in the life of the children.

Subsidiary Impacts of Disaster on Child and Adolescent Survivors

The impacts of disaster described previously highlight other arising problems connected to the situation of a disaster and can be called as fallout of the disaster due to inadequate policies, program and insufficient rehabilitation measures to ensure protections are care. These issues are often referred as the second wave of disasters. IASC-MHPSS (2007) specially mentioned humanitarian aid related problems. In the post disaster period lack of appropriate measures and policies cause severe humanitarian crisis which are threat to the well-being of the survivors.

Sense of Insecurity

In the post disaster period, due to lack of basic amities and fear of reoccurrence of the disaster and presence of threat in the surrounding areas cause a wider sense of insecurity among the children and adolescents. Children fail to get any reassurance about the situation that prevails and the fear of the disaster is being exhibited in various psychosomatic, behavioral stress reactions. The feeling of security is derived by the children from the atmosphere that they live-in. Conducive atmosphere, regular routine, living with the caregiver, having interaction with peer-groups, well-accustomed with the surrounding (e.g., play ground, prayer hall, school, roads, places to hang around on regular basis) generate the sense of security and adjustment. Familiar environments is a key factor for having a sense of security which is lost after the disaster for a long as long as the factors of providing a secured environment is being evolved through rehabilitation, normalization, and establishing predictable pattern of positive interactive atmosphere. Lack of security makes the children vulnerable to abuse and exploitation in a disaster and post disaster situation.

Threat to the Sense of Well-Being

A psychological sense of well-being is a pre-requisite for health development for the children and adolescents. The environment has as essential considerations and contribution in giving a sense of well being. As it is seen in different disaster that attachments are affected within caregivers relationships. The affected surrounding area of disaster can cause distress and disaffection multiplied with the continued unorganized pattern of daily living. Being dependent on the common kitchen, living in camps the family seize to function as a cohesive family unit that provided the sense of well-being for a child or adolescent. If these situation in post disaster period continues for long the developmental problems and stress among the children goes higher that may even jeopardize their future.

Struggle for Survival

Disaster relief, rehabilitation is important humanitarian concern that is not just essential to support rather it is important human rights consideration for the survivors to get the support in the time of distress. Effective relief distribution, quick rehabilitation program reduces the struggle for the survival as normal, regular pattern of interaction can be established and strengthen. An unattended disaster or a disaster receives less attention cause more problems for the survivors. Though at times a disaster gets quick response for relief, but get much less attention during rehabilitation increases the difficulties in long term. The struggle is much higher for the marginalized survivors of disaster who may belong to a far-off place, women, disabled, the survivors belonging to lower caste and category. Thus, the social status of the survivors and their capacity to control the aid mechanism, the government system, the response of civil society are combined to contribute toward the struggle for survival. In such a situation, the children and adolescents become obvious party to the situation.

Issues of Child Protection as the Worse Victim of Disaster: Indian Context

India has witnessed multiple disasters within this century with some large natural and human-made disasters of the history. Namely, the natural disaster like, Orissa Super Cyclone (1999), Gujarat Earthquake (2001), Indian Ocean Tsunami (2004), Kashmir Earthquake (2005), repeated severe floods in north and north-east India, and the recent disaster in called as Himalayan Tsunami (2013) in Uttarakhand showed the nature's fury and increased vulnerability of the people across the different zones of India. Similarly, there were number of human-made disaster that showed the frazil nature of social structure in different parts of India that always imposed a higher order challenge for disaster interventions and humanitarian response. The human-made disasters namely, the Gujarat riots (2002), Mumbai serial train Blast (2006), Mumbai terrorist attack, continuous Kashmir unrest, riots in Orissa (2008), recent incident of riots in Assam and many other such incidents of increased vulnerability of human-made disaster poses a real threat to the tranquility of the disaster-affected zones in particular and the nation in general. A detail analysis of impact of these different disasters in India showed some specific points of vulnerability of the children and adolescents that are close connected to the child protection concerns and requirements.

Considering the various impacts of disasters on the children, it can be said that any disaster is connected with the issues of protection. Disasters impose security threats, challenge in daily living, witnessing or experiencing violence, shutdown of educational facilities, loosing family members, and ultimately it shrinks the opportunities of living a free life for the children and adolescents. In all these disasters, the specific child protection issues that aroused were complex and critical and some of these issues are described here. The protection issues of the children are connected with four basic dimensions of human rights.

(a) Rights related to physical security and integrity:

1. Sexual assault of the children and adolescents.
2. Physical assault and violence.
3. Deliberate harm to the children, forced labor, and displacement.
4. Harm to psychological integrity and dignity.

(b) Rights related to basic necessities of life:

1. Inadequate food, clean water, sanitation health care.
2. Inadequate shelter, lack of privacy (specifically for adolescent girls), breakup of family.
3. Problem of reproductive health care (specifically for adolescent girls).

(c) Rights related to other economic, social, and cultural protection needs

1. Denial of the right to education or delay in right to education.
2. Relocation to areas where there are no opportunity for schooling and other facilities.
3. Discriminatory practice against children, adolescents, and children with disability (Differently abled).
4. Children adolescents lose of rights of property of their parents/ancestors.

(d) Rights related to other civil and political protection needs:

1. Separation from family members.
2. Denial of freedom of expression, speech, association, and religion.
3. Loss of certificates, personal documents.
4. Arbitrary restrictions on freedom of movement, including punitive curfews or roadblocks that prevent access to school, play ground.

Guidelines in Disaster for Child Protection

The international guidelines for disaster intervention in schools and community have included both psychological and physical health aspects or recovery and holistic wellbeing for development. The International declaration of child rights is a premier document to establish the importance of child rights. In General Assembly Resolution 1386 (XIV) of 20 November 1959, the general assembly expressed profound concern about the "that the situation of children in many parts of the world remains critical as a result of inadequate social conditions, natural disasters, armed conflicts, exploitation, illiteracy, hunger and disability, and convinced that urgent and effective national and international action is called for

(Steven 2003). The sphere project (The Sphere Project 2011, p. 25) is one of the most important documents to uphold and advocate the minimum stands in disaster response mentioned the protection to ensure human dignity and commitment to humanitarian charter. "The Humanitarian Charter provides the ethical and legal backdrop to the Protection Principles and the Core Standards and minimum standards that follow in the Handbook (i.e., Sphere Handbook)" (The Sphere Project 2011, p. 20). The concerns for protection give rise to four basic Protection Principles that inform all humanitarian action according to the Sphere Handbook:

1. Avoid exposing people to further harm as a result of your actions.
2. Ensure people's access to impartial assistance—in proportion to need and without discrimination.
3. Protect people from physical and psychological harm arising from violence and coercion.
4. Assist people to claim their rights, access available remedies, and recover from the effects of abuse.

The Child Protection Working Group (2012) meticulously designed The Minimum Standards for Child Protection in Humanitarian Action (Child Protection Working Group (CPWG) 2012) that broadly categorized the standard responses in humanitarian action under four headings. These are as following:

(a) Standards to ensure a quality child protection response, that deals with coordination with major actors in the field; appropriate trained human resources for working with children, facilitating adequate communication, advocacy and dealing with media; developing adequate program cycle for management; standard information management, and ensuring child protection monitoring. These standards are to ensure a child protection oriented view for each of the work that that humanitarian agencies and Government do in a situation of emergency.
(b) Standards to address the child protection needs focused on various risk that the children and adolescents face after a disaster. These standards included protection form danger and injuries, physical violence and other harmful practice, sexual violence, psychosocial distress and mental disorders, protection of the children associated with armed force or armed groups, child labor, and the unaccompanied, separated children. The last standard of this section has specified the need of ensuring justice for the children as a vital component of humanitarian action.
(c) Standards to develop adequate child protection strategies recommended developing case management, community-based programming, developing child friendly spaces, and protecting excluded children.
(d) Standards to mainstream child protection in humanitarian sections are wider description that targeted the different sectors of intervention which has clear implication to strengthen and maintain child protection standards. These sectors are focusing on economic recovery of the disaster survivors, reestablishing educational system, health system, facilitating adequate nutrition, water, sanitation, and hygiene practice. Children protection is also connected with adequate shelter, camp management, and distribution of the relief items.

INEE (The Inter-Agency Network for Education in Emergencies (INEE) 2004) and IASC-guidelines on Mental Health and Psychosocial Support in emergency settings (2007) also highlight the protection principles for humanitarian action. These includes guidelines and documents detailing protection mechanisms, psychological, physical health interventions, protection of the children in disaster, facilitating hygienic practices, promoting life skills education, working with community, participatory approach in educational intervention, development of policies and guidelines for the country, etc. The unique features which are noted in these documents, as follows;

- Formal and informal education: Both formal and informal education has been promoted for the children and adolescents. Hence, educational involvement is considered as a need of the community to enhance protection and psychosocial support. After a disaster, informal educational set-up is most suitable option to facilitate normalcy. Though restarting the formal education may be time consuming, the informal education should be initiated as early as possible. In this process involving larger number of local community leaders, volunteer, and teachers are encouraged.
  For the disaster-affected communities different pattern of progressive educational strategies to be adapted. This may be ranged from various recreational activities, sports, games, cultural activities, simple creative expressive activities (Drawing, drama, storytelling etc.), and catch-up courses to deal with studies, alternative classes, and vocational skill classes for youths. These patterns of engagements would help to bring the child and adolescent to develop a routine in the most unorganized state of affairs and also protect the children being misused or abused.
- Community-based program: School is the integral part of disaster interventions and always it should be done in adequate coordination with the local community. Hence the program become part of the community recovery and connectivity of intervention between the schools, communities, and familiars are consolidated. This specifically focused about participation of the parents and other community leaders in school intervention with the students, teachers, and others involved in the regular school activities.
  It is essential to develop the school committee and also community-based child protection committee to monitor and protect the vulnerable children. Equally, the parents need support to ensure adequate care for the children. Community engagement, mobilization, and developing social support mechanism that ensure community control over the recovery process are essential strategies for strengthening the community-based protection for the children in disaster.
- Accessibility of learning: This focused on accessibility of education for all that deals with ensuring no discrimination and creating opportunities for all. The marginalized groups to be included and ensured that the traditional discrimination of the society is not promoted. Accessibility of physical space and availability of services within the vicinity of shelter or housing, creating safe, and stimulating atmosphere is being highlighted.

To facilitate accessibility in MHPSS guidelines (Inter Agency Standing Committee (IASC) (2007) it is being recommended to rapidly organize safe spaces where children can play and participate in structured, supportive activities and where children and adults can receive or mobilize psychosocial support. Within the facility including life skills training and provision of information about the emergency and other education support that build confidence and strengthen resiliency to be adapted and practiced.

- The skill building of educators: Educators are the key personnel for intervention in schools. Developmental program in the schools or a disaster response is dependent on the knowledge, skills, and capacities of the educators. Giving recognition to the educators and ensuring required skills through capacity building sessions, follow-up, and culturally appropriate materials are very crucial. Therefore, involving the teachers in various training module on psychosocial support, hygiene promotion, nutritional supplement, safe school protocol should be considered.

  Teachers or educational staffs are the key in facilitating a protective environment and sense of well being among the children. Thus preparing and encouraging educators to support learners' psychosocial well-being, helping them, e.g., to deal constructively with learners' issues such as anger, fear and grief, to cope with their own situation is a crucial need and service requirements after the disaster. The teachers should also be trained to make referrals for severely affected learners. This supportive atmosphere keeps the children within a secured environment.
- Creating safe and secure learning environment: Creating safe and supportive education through formal or non-formal systems of education has been prioritized in any disaster intervention. Safety of the children is an important concern which deals with structural and non-structural safety from internal and external factors related to disasters (threat, possibility or reoccurrence, etc.), health and nutritional safety as well as creating a cultural of safety and prevention of disaster/crisis among the school community.

  Thus, the guidelines focused on developing both physically and emotionally safe environment. Physical environment is most important determinant for the children to have a healthy pattern of living with availability safe drinking water, mead-day meal, free of possibilities of diseases, like water-borne, vector-borne, and air-borne diseases. Equally, the structural safety, and safety from any violent attacks are vital. These safety aspects are also connected with the safety at home and the safety in the area the students travel to come to the school. Developing skills of the teachers, strengthening and reviving the facilities in schools, awareness generation, and community action are combine efforts toward the commitment of ensuring safe and secure learning environment.
- Health promotion and disease prevention: In the school promoting health and facilitating hygienic environment is crucial for recovery of the survivors. Post disaster situations as well as prevailing condition are very important to be considered for reducing the health risk and problems of the target population and children. The Sphere project (2011) has minute details of each of the factors under this category to be considered for the water, sanitation, nutrition, and health promotion of the pupil.

WHO (2003) defines a health-promoting school as "one that constantly strengthens its capacity as a healthy setting for living, learning, and working" (WHO 2003, p. 4). WHO (2005) also published a manual that titled "The Physical School Environment, As essential Component of Health—Promoting School." The American Academy of Pediatrics defines a "healthful school environment" as "one that protects students and staff against immediate injury or disease and promotes prevention activities and attitudes against known risk factors that might lead to future disease or disability" (American Academy of Pediatrics 1993). These documents mentioned about provision of safe and sufficient water, sanitation, and shelter form the elements of basic necessities for a healthy physical learning environment. Equally protections from biological, physical, and chemical risks are important to maintain safety and security of the children and adolescents.

- Educational Policies: In any country an effective educational policy should be promoted and organized that the children could be educated by maintain quality and effective development in a consistent manner throughout the developmental age. The educational policy should have clear mention of providing education to children and adolescents of different age group, capacity building of the educators, maintain and developing the educational facilities, facilitating easy accessibility of education for all, etc. Many a time lack of education policy in the country cause lack of resources in the educational system and also this sector become a low priority area. Inadequate priority on education make the children out of safety and protection network especially during post disaster situation.
- Psychosocial Interventions: These guidelines dealing with disaster situation have very high emphasis on the mental health care and resiliency building among the students. Facilitating normalization, establishing routine life, strengthening disaster preparedness, reducing traumatic experiences, are the goals of psychosocial support interventions in disaster (Herrman 2012). The Sphere Handbook (2011) has considered psychosocial support activities and school intervention under each of its sectoral domain that deals with health, water sanitation, food security, shelter, etc.

  Psychosocial considerations in Child protection: Rapidly organize safe spaces where children can play and participate in structured, supportive activities and where children and adults can receive or mobilize psychosocial support; provide sports that promote non-violent conflict resolution; organize youth clubs that promote joint problem-solving and life skills; organize social support for parents, especially mothers of very young children; ensure that community-based child protection committees monitor and respond to risks and support highly vulnerable children; support parents and community members to better support and care for their children. Remember to give children control and power over the decisions that affect them. Also keep them regularly informed of events, or even non-events such as 'we have not found your parents yet, we looked here and here'. This is often forgotten and is an enormous source of distress (Inter-Agency Standing Committee (IASC) Global Cluster Working Group and IASC Reference Group for Mental Health and Psychosocial Support in Emergency Settings 2010, p. 10).

These guidelines depicted a wider frame to work in the education system immediately after a disaster or as part of long-term rehabilitation. In practice adapting and following each of these guidelines require a strong commitment of the local government, humanitarian actors, and flow of resources. Though the government of India does have any special guidelines for protection of children in India, but the existing policy and law regarding the protection child are having equal importance and implementation requirements during the disaster too. The National Commission for Protection of Child Rights (NCPCR) was set up in March 2007 under the Commission for Protection of Child Rights Act, 2005, which is essential act and policy implementation authority for child protection in disasters in India.

The Psychosocial Support and Mental Health Services (PSS-MHS) guidelines (Government of India 2009) have mentioned protection is important in the event of disaster and especially for the children. The guideline mentioned "provision of special care will be made for children, especially who have lost their parents and siblings" (Government of India 2009, p. 42) and "the rights of the children among survivors as well as the international convention stipulations for this vulnerable group shall be taken into consideration. Child Trafficking and violence against children need to be tackled". (p. 52). Psycho-social first aid is recommended as one of the most essential service provisions for normalization and protection of further emotional harm of the children in the post disaster periods through non-formal schooling, group engagement activities and play therapy.

Psychosocial Support for Children in Disaster

Considering the international/national guidelines the psychosocial interventions in a school should be designed and implemented. In order to promote psychosocial support and protection for the school children, school intervention program was developed and implemented by the Red Cross in Kanyakumari District of Tamil Nadu, after the Indian Ocean Tsunami. The school intervention program was designed strategically and sustainability components were build-in within the program. For this intervention the objectives were three folded, first, developing resiliency among the children affected by tsunami through various psychosocial support activities; second, facilitating physical health and well-being of the children; and third, creating culture of safety through safe school practices. Based on these objectives the program activities were developed.

(a) Building resiliency among the children and adolescents through creative expressive activities.
(b) Developing participatory model for working in the school for designing, planning, implementing, and evaluating the program.
(c) Capacity building of the teachers and other members of school community to ensure rebuilding and rehabilitation focusing on child protection and welfare.
(d) Organizing activities toward creating "sense of place" among the children in the school, developing "child friendly" atmosphere and culture of safety.

Important Concepts for School Interventions

Before going into the details of the school intervention some important concepts are discussed here that are relevant for further explanation about the intervention strategies in the schools.

Psychosocial Support: IASC-MHPSS (Inter Agency Standing Committee (IASC) 2007, p. 1) guidelines defined psychosocial support as "any type of local or outside support that aims to protect or promote psychosocial well-being and/or prevent or treat mental disorder." The most accepted definition for the development practices can be "psychosocial care as a broad range of community-based interventions that promote the restoration of social cohesion and infrastructure, as well as the independence and dignity of individuals and groups. Psychosocial care fosters resilience in survivors and the community, and serves to prevent pathological developments and further social dislocation" (Aarts 2001). Psychosocial refers to the dynamic relationship between the psychological and social dimension of a person, where the one influences the other. The psychological dimension includes the internal, emotional and thought processes, feelings, and reactions. The social dimension includes relationships, family and community networks, social values, and cultural practices. Psychosocial support refers to the actions that address both the psychological and social needs of individuals (Hansen 2008). Considering this definition the broad range of activities which need be carried out include working with the individual, groups, families, social institutions, and in community at large. Numbers of psychosocial activities were conducted through the school interventions. Psychosocial interventions are most crucial to prevent further damage and to ensure well-being of the disaster-affected children for strengthening the protective atmosphere (Des Marais et al. 2012, pp. 347–49).

Resiliency: "Resiliency is the capacity to transform oneself in positive way after a difficult event" (Annan et al. 2003). In other wards resiliency is increased or enhanced ability to cope with difficult situations. Children and adolescents learn and adopt coping mechanisms from the environment they live in. It is very important that they receive an environment which is supportive for appropriate growth and development. Through psychosocial interventions resiliency building is fostered by engaging the children in activities that encourage to expressive their views, overcome stress reactions, develop abilities to deal with challenges, encourage group participation, and strengthen social networks and relationships. From the very first day the resiliency building activities were started in the relief camps and in the schools subsequently.

Creative Expressive Activities: Children cannot express themselves with words so well. Adolescents are hesitant to talk about their thoughts as many social norms and restrictions are imposed on them. There are some methods and activities by which the children can express their feelings, emotions, views, and opinion. These methods of expression are called as creative expressive methods and activities are conducted by using drawing, story-telling, creative writing, clay modeling, school drama, skit, etc. (Bhadra 2012, p. 221). Play or games as a form of physical activity also help a lot to express their ideas, learn social norms, and develop new thoughts.

Child Friendly Space: Various international documents (UNICEF 2012; The Sphere Project 2011) explained child friendly space as one of the physical space within the living area of the survivors or in the school to mitigate emotional and psychological impact of disaster on the children by practicing the activities that provide a caring, protective, safe, and normalizing environment. Child friendly approach allows the children to express their views and also allow the children to participate in making a better environment for themselves (Dyer and Bhadra 2013, p. 189). Child friendly approach is characterized by five main points which were ensured through the projects implementation in the Tsunami affected schools in Kanyakumari District (IFRC 2009). (a) The school environment should be actively designed to ensure that the children feel free from any threat and hazards from the immediate environment. (b) Recovery program should be participatory; specifically involvement of parents, local leaders, and eminent personalities would ensure an effective planning, implementation of the school activities and projects. (c) The children in the school have chance to develop skills through various experiential learning facilitated by the teachers. (d) The educational system ensures equal opportunities of the marginalized group and the children who have faced the direct impact of disaster. The children having problem in the home due to poverty or any other reasons are also taken care adequately to support their educational needs. Similarly, the weak students should get the options of additional learning space. (e) The physical health is an integral part of growth and development of the children. Child-friendly school ensures adequate sanitation facilities, hygiene promotional activities, consider the nutritional requirements of the children and adequate preventive and promotional health interventions.

Sense of Place: With various loss and damage the specific problem which the disaster survivors face is the loss of "sense of place." The sense of place (Fullilove 1996) deals with identity, familiarity and attachments with the place, environment, and neighbors. A change due to disaster disrupts this equilibrium of the society, predictable daily routine activities, and feelings of safety. In the rehabilitation process, developing sense of place among children is vital for their growth. McMillan and Chavis (1986) propose that "sense of community" is composed of four elements, (1) membership, (2) influence, (3) integration and fulfillment of needs, and (4) shared emotional connections. This concept is being used for the development of the school atmosphere after a disaster. Membership means a sense of identity, belonging and working together for a common purpose and goal by the school community and specifically for the children. Influence reflects that the members have equal opportunities of participation in the activities in schools and could influence the planning, decision making or implementation process for their own well-being. The group norms are followed and shared responsibilities facilitate cohesive atmosphere. Integration and fulfillment of needs refer to integrated approach with multiple activities with common goal orientation. Shared emotional connections consider the common identity, familiarity among the community people who are living in the same place, have common cultural orientation, language, pattern of living and many other factors like, shared history, common experiences, and even the presence of a spiritual bond (Holms et al. 2003). The school interventions were designed in the Tsunami-affected schools to ensure development of "sense of place" among the children.

Safe School: The concept of safe school has been used in different aspect of safety like, safety from crisis, events of disaster, gender-based violence, psychological, physical abuse, free from threats or dangers, etc. Within United Nations Decade of Education for Sustainable Development (2005–2014) UNESCO (2005), it is emphasized that education for disaster reduction should be part of the curriculum and disaster reduction begins at school. Safe school program ensures the culture of protection and safety among the students and teachers by understanding the hazards and risk within the school and immediate environment and utilizing the resources to mitigate the same. Hence, safe school program is an important component for developing the safety aspect of schools. As part of the program the students and teachers join together, assess the school's risk and resources, develop safe school protocol and practice the same on regular basis thus ensure that the school is capable of dealing with the hazards. The regular practice and update ensures the practice of safety rules based on the hazards that the school children may face (UN/ISDR 2007; Satapathy and Yoshida 2007).

Intervention in Kanyakumari Tsunami Affected School

Immediately after Tsunami in the relief camp the volunteers started working with the children to facilitate care and support. Within few days, the local NGOs of the area were contacted and also the Government systems or support mechanisms (i.e., government school, integrated child development scheme centers "Anganwadi," village health care system) were identified. Subsequently capacity building for psychosocial support was conducted for the NGO and Government staffs who were directly working with the survivors in the relief camps and temporary shelters. The NGO staffs were mainly the field workers, coordinator for the program, the community level volunteers, self-help group members, or other community leaders. From the Government sector mainly the school teachers, health workers and "*anganwadi*" (Pre-school teachers) were trained. This group of trained workers continued psychosocial support activity with the affected children through regular meetings, sessions with parents and through close interaction with the children by using multiple creative expressive activities. This engagement helped the children to deal with their traumatic experiences and develop confidence. These activities also protected the affected children from any kind of further psychological harm and abuse while the nurturing and protective environment was completely destroyed in the Tsunami-affected areas (NIMHANS and WHO 2006; WHO 2006; NIMHANS 2007).

As the formal school started recovery program focused on these schools in a designed manner to implement various concepts of international guidelines (like, safe school, and child friendly space) in a structured fashion. An outline of the school recovery program is presented here that was developed by American Red

Cross-India Delegation team with Indian Red Cross local branch in Tsunami affected areas of Kanyakumari District (IFRC 2008; Bhadra and Pratheepa 2009). The main features of this program were:

1. Primary assessment of the school by involving the teachers, students, and parents.
2. Development of proposal for facilitating the school recovery.
3. Administrative clearance from Education Department of Government to work in the schools.
4. Training of the teachers by focusing on the three main issues that includes, facilitating the concept and approach of child-friendly space, developing sense of place in the schools and safe school protocol.
5. Developing the school committee by involving the teachers, parents, and student representative to facilitate a community school interaction and to ensure holistic recovery of the children.
6. Conducting joint assessment by the students, teachers, and parents and developing the three-dimensional school map to understand the situation and the possibilities of making changes.
7. Designing various protection activities toward health, psychosocial, safe-school interventions, and events that will encourage the children to participate and gain resiliency to deal with future challenges.

The school recovery program was a series of continuous activities that ensured creating child friendly space, developing sense of place and safe school program. In this process capacity building of the teachers, to provide adequate knowledge and skills to work with the children was a vital step. The training was conducted in two phases. In the first phase, the module of training focused on psychosocial interventions and health promotion. The psychosocial components included working with children by using different mediums, developing positive habits, positive coping skills among the students, facilitating study habits, etc. Heath interventions included promoting health and hygiene practice, providing first aid, awareness about prevention of various communicable diseases, nutritional support etc. In the second phase the teachers were specifically trained on "safe school" intervention that focused on identifying the risk, hazards and developing response strategies as part of disaster preparedness. Following the training program the teachers with the project staffs through community interaction developed the school committee that could design the interventions according to the need of the children and community perspective. The parents, village leaders, traditional leaders became most crucial member in the school committee and facilitated this process of school intervention. They were also provided with various reading materials and had meeting to explain the school recovery program. The committees took active role in mobilizing local resources to strengthen the activities in the schools. In the classroom teachers started conducting various psychosocial support activities with specific goal to reduce fear, to talk about the issues, changes after Tsunami over time, developing positive attitude toward studies, etc. To facilitate these activities the teachers were supported with materials (like, Note books, color box, pencils, color papers, etc.) and activity manuals. These manuals were produced for the primary, middle, and high school students with different activities and corresponding goals. Some of the activities were spread over 3–4 classes and also can be repeated from time to time to generate, discussion, and review the progress over time.

In the activity manuals, for psychosocial support the activities were "build the strength of group," "support your family," "help your friend," "develop and achieve your dream," "study well," "develop concentration and motivation," etc. All these sessions were designed to conduct in group with the students based on experiential learning and participatory methodology. The sessions were written as guiding tool for teachers, as they could follow step by step. Each session was having clear aim, objectives, and process to be followed, with a broad outcome and session follow-up steps for the same. Similarly, there were sessions on the health and hygiene promotion that deal with topics like, "fool hygiene techniques," "hand washing practice," "drinking water solution," "water/air/vector born disease and prevention," "first aid", etc. (Singh and Mini 2009). These sessions were also focused on specific learning points and skill orientation for the student to strengthen the behavioral pattern for adapting healthy practices.

All the schools implemented the safe school program. In the second phase of the training the teachers were trained on disaster preparedness and safe-school module. Further in the schools the teachers developed the safe-school practice. As part of this module each school developed the school map to identify the specific risks and resources in the schools. This assessment is called as "hazard, vulnerability, and capacity assessment" and further the students were trained on the preparedness aspects of identifies risks of Tsunami, cyclone, high tide, incidence of fire and road accidents. On each of these risks the students and teachers were engaged to identify the strategies for safety and thus mock drills were conducted regularly. Each school developed their disaster safety plans and displayed the same for everyone's understanding and knowledge. The schools were provided with the basic disaster safety tools like, megaphone, rope, blanket, sand buckets for fire safety, water pipes, etc. according to the safe school protocol developed by them.

Protective Environmental Framework

Protecting the civilians and specially the child and other vulnerable groups during war and national disaster is a prime concern of United National and various international bodies. Boothby and Ager (2010) explained "Protective Environment Framework" that was developed as a basis to identify the key areas, where actions can be taken to increase the protection available to children (Landgren 2005). This framework is designed to promote children's wellbeing with recommended eight actions points, which together can reduce harm toward the children or develop a "shield" around children, but necessarily not eliminating all the risks and vulnerabilities. The belief is that the implementation of this framework will reduce the impact of the disaster and develop better active protective mechanisms and strategies for the children. These action points include, (a) government commitment and capacity; (b) legislation and enforcement; (c) culture and customs; (d) open discussion; (e) children's life skills, knowledge, and participation; (f) capacity of families and communities; (g) essential services; and (h) monitoring, reporting, and oversight. Bizzarri (2012) criticized that despite significant development of knowledge and theoretical understanding the protection of the vulnerable groups in disaster is far from being practiced in disaster management. There is considerable inconsistency in the application of the different international law for the protection of the marginalized sections and lack of disaggregated data about different vulnerable groups is a major challenge to ensure enough protective mechanism for the vulnerable groups. The model explained in the Tsunami rehabilitation of Kanyakumari district has all these characters as explained, but this is also crucial to ensure sustainability of this framework in a very active mode to ensure child protection in normal situation and in disaster specifically.

Conclusion

Child protection in disaster is a matter of long-term commitment and practice for the humanitarian sector and also for the government mechanisms of a nation to ensure well-being. Psychosocial support program is crucial for strengthening and implementing child protection work in an effective and efficient manner through participatory practice in the community and schools. Child protection is an essential mandate of United Nations for all time but during disaster this becomes a crucial issue with increased factors of vulnerability and erosion of social support and traditional protective mechanism of society (i.e., family, neighborhood, school etc.). Thus, disasters increase the vulnerability of the children and expose the children to a situation of higher risk that they are unable to comprehend and control. Disaster interventions at every stage (i.e., rescue, relief, rehabilitation, recovery, preparedness) needs considerable focus on building mechanisms for child protection.

References

Aarts, P. G. (2001). *Guidelines for programmes: Psychosocial and mental health care assistance in post disasters and conflict areas.* Netherlands Institute for Care and Welfare. Utrecht: The Netherlands: International Centre.

American Academy of Pediatrics. (1993). *Committee on school health: School health policy and practice* (5th Edition ed.). Washington: American Academy of Pediatric.

Annan, J., Castelli, L., Devreux, A., & Locatelli, E. (2003). *Training manual for teachers, AVSI.* Edinburgh: AVSI. Retrieved January 9, 2005, from http://www.forcedmigration.org/psychosocial/papers/WiderPapers/Teachers%20manual.pdf.

Bhadra, S. (2006). *Impact of disaster and life events among the survivors of disasters.* Bangalore: NIMHANS (National Institute of Mental Health and Neuro Sciences).

Bhadra, S. (2012). Psychosocial support for the children affected by communal violence in Gujarat, India. *International Journal of Applied Psychoanalytic Studies, 9*(3), 212–232. doi:10.1002/aps.1327.

Bhadra, S., & Jadav, B. (2003). Child and adolescent survivors of riots in Gujarat. *Psychosocial Support for the people living in the conflict affect areas, in reference to Gujarat* (p. 15). Ahmedabad: Gujarat Harmony Project.

Bhadra, S., & Pratheepa, C. M. (2009, November 8, 9). *Strengthening communities and recovery through psychosocial support.* Retrieved June 26, 2013, from National Institute of Disaster Management: 2nd India Disaster Management Congress: http://nidm.gov.in/idmc2/PDF/Presentations/Psycho_Social/Pres3.pdf.

Bizzarri, M. (2012). Protection of vulnerable groups in natural and man-made disasters. In A. d. Guttry, M. Gestri, & G. Venturini (Eds.) *International disaster response law* (pp. 381–414). The Hague: T. M. C. Asser Press.

Boothby, N., & Ager, A. (2010). Promoting a protective environment for children affected by disaster and war. In J. Garbarino & G. Sigman (Eds.), *A child's right to a healthy environment: The Loyola University Symposium on the human rights of children* (pp. 105–121). New York: Springer.

Child Protection Working Group (CPWG). (2012). *Minimum standards for child protection in humanitarian action.* Retrieved February 25, 2014, from www.unicef.org: http://www.unicef.org/iran/Minimum_standards_for_child_protection_in_humanitarian_action.pdf.

Des Marais, E., Bhadra, S., & Dyer, A. (2012). In the wake of Japan's Triple Disaster: Building capacity through international collaboration. *Advances in SOCIAL WORK, 13*(2), 340–357.

Dyer, A. R., & Bhadra, S. (2013). Global disaster, war conflict and complex emergencies: Caring for special population. In E. Sorel (Ed.), *In 21st century global mental health* (pp. 171–209). Washington: Jones and Bartett Learning.

Fullilove, M. T. (1996). Psychiatric implications of displacement: Contributions from the psychology of place. *American Journal of Psychiatry, 153*(12), 1516–1523.

Government of India. (2009, December). *National disaster management guidelines, psychosocial support and mental health services in disasters.* New Delhi: A Publication of National Disaster Management Authority, Government of India.

Hansen, P. (2008). *Psychosocial interventions—A handbook.* In W. Agen (Ed.) Copenhagen: International Federation Reference Centre, for Psychosocial Support.

Herrman, H. (2012, April). Promoting mental health and resilience after a disaster. *Journal of Experimental & Clinical Medicine, 4*(2), 82–87. doi:10.1016/j.jecm.2012.01.003.

Holms, G. E., Patterson, J. R., & Stalling, J. E. (2003). Sense of place: Issues in counseling and development. *Journal of Humanities, Education and Development, 42*(Fall). doi:10.1002/j.2164-490X.2003.tb00009.x.

IFRC. (2008, July 21). *Federation-wide tsunami semi-annual report 2004–2008: India appeal No. 28/2004.* http://reliefweb.int/report/india/federation-wide-tsunami-semi-annual-report-2004-2008-india-appeal-no-282004.

IFRC. (2009). *Report 2004–2009: Federation-wide tsunami 5 Year progress report.* Geneva: International Federation of Red Cross and Red Crescent Societies. Retrieved June 26, 2013, from http://reliefweb.int/sites/reliefweb.int/files/resources/3DA9790D55FAE3364925768C00203B11-Full_Report.pdf.

Inter Agency Standing Committee (IASC). (2007). *Guidelines on mental health and psychosocial support in emergency settings (MHPSS).* Geneva: IASC.

Inter-Agency Standing Committee (IASC) Global cluster working group and IASC reference group for mental health and psychosocial support in emergency settings. (2010). *Mental health and psychosocial support in humanitarian emergencies: What should protection programme managers know.* Geneva: Inter-Agency Standing Committee (IASC).

Landgren, K. (2005). The protective environment: Development support for child protection. *Human Rights Quarterly, 27*(1), 214–248.

Mcmillan, D. W., & Chavis, D. M. (1986). Sense of community: A definition and theory. *American Journal of Community Psychology, 14*(1), 6–23.

Morgan, C. T., King, R. A., Weisz, J. R., & Schopler, J. (1997). *Introduction to psychology*. New Delhi: Tata McGraw-Hill Publishing Company Limited.

NIMHANS. (2007). Conference on psychosocial care and mental health services in disasters. *Summary report and recommendations of the national conference on psychosocial care and mental health services in disasters* (pp. 1–46). Bangalore: NIMHANS.

NIMHANS and WHO. (2006). Psycho social support in disaster: Proceedings and recommendations of NIMHANS-WHO India workshop. *Psycho social support in disaster* (pp. 1–12). Bangalore: NIMHANS and WHO India Country Office.

Satapathy, S., & Yoshida, M. (2007). Sri Lanka: Integrating disaster risk reduction into education through teacher training curricula building teachers' DRR capacity across borders. *UN/ISDR, Towards a Culture of Prevention: Disaster Risk Reduction Begins at School-Good Practices and Lessons Learned* (pp. 33–36). Geneva: International Strategy for Disaster Reduction.

Sekar, K., & Bhadra, S. (2003). Gujarat riot impact of event on children. *Workshop on issues and challenges in psychosocial care for persons living in conflict situation: experience from Gujarat riots. 8th and 9th February,* (pp. 31–40). Ahmedabad: NIMHANS; Bangalore; GHP Care India.

Sekar, K., Bhadra, S., Jayakumar, C., Aravindraj, E., Henry, G., & Kumar, K. K. (2005a). *Facilitation manual for trainers of trainees in natural disaster*. Bangalore: NIMHANS and Care India.

Sekar, K., Biswas, G., Bhadra, S., Jayakumar, C., & Kumar, K. K. (2005b). *Tsunami disaster: Psychosocial care for children; Information Manual-3*. Bangalore: NIMHANS-CARE-India.

Singh, N., & Mini, J. (2009, November 8, 9). *Important of community health assessment through community based approach in post disaster period*. National Institute of Disaster Management, 2nd India Disaster Management Congress. Retrieved June 26, 2013, from http://nidm.gov.in/idmc2/PDF/Presentations/PHE/Pres3.pdf.

Steven, T. W. (2003). *Declaration of the rights of the child*. Retrieved August 26, 2013, from www.unicef.org: http://www.unicef.org/lac/spbarbados/Legal/global/General/declaration_child1959.pdf.

The Inter-Agency Network for Education in Emergencies (INEE). (2004). *Minimum standards for education in emergencies, chronic crises and early*. London: INEE Network.

The Sphere project. (2011). *Humanitarian charter and minimum standards in humanitarian response*. United Kingdom: The Sphere Project.

UN, ISDR. (2007). *Towards a Culture of prevention:disaster risk reduction begins at school-good practices and lessons learned*. Geneva: International Strategy for Disaster Reduction.

UNESCO. (2005). *UN decade of education for sustainable development, 2005–2014*. Paris: UNESCO—Education for Sustainable Development. Retrieved September 14, 2014, from http://unesdoc.unesco.org/images/0014/001416/141629E.pdf.

UNICEF. (2012, May 25). *Child friendly schools*. Retrieved August 27, 2013, from www.unicef.org: http://www.unicef.org/lifeskills/index_7260.html.

WHO. (1991). *Psychosocial consequences of disasters: Prevention and management*. Geneva: World Health Organization.

WHO. (2003). *Information series on school health document: The physical school environment: an essential component of a health-promoting school*. Geneva: World Health Organization.

WHO. (2005). *The physical school environment, as essential component of health—promoting school*. Geneva: World Health Organization.

WHO. (2006). *Psychosocial support for tsunami affected populations in India*. New Delhi: Non Communicable Diseases and Mental Health Cluster, WHO Country Office, India.

Chapter 18
Education for Vulnerable Children: Innovative Experiments in Urban India

Neela Dabir, K. Anuradha and Raji Satyamurthy

Introduction

The Indian Government passed the Right to Education (RTE) Act in 2009, which came into effect from April 2010. India became one of the 135 countries to make education a fundamental right of children. The Ministry of Human Resource Development released a status report in 2011 stating that 8.1 million children in the age group 6–14 remain without education creating a shortage of 508,000 teachers countrywide. A shadow report by the RTE Forum highlights several key legal commitments of the RTE Act that are falling behind schedule. Many experts feel that the RTE Act (2009) has more wrongs than rights (Khalik 2012). Rather than concentrating on the criticisms received related to the implementation of the Act, it will be fruitful to explore some of the innovative experiments in the field that have a potential for scaling up. The RTE implementation is to be done using the SSA framework. Within this framework, there is emphasis on giving priority to the education of girls and special groups like street children, children of migratory workers, the disabled, and other children affected. These children require a lot more effort to go through the entire process of education, from enrollment to retention. There cannot be a uniform strategy that can be applied to all the special

N. Dabir (✉)
Tata Institute of Social Sciences, Mumbai, India
e-mail: neela.dabir@gmail.com

K. Anuradha
Rainbow Homes, Rainbow Homes Foundation India, Hyderabad, India

R. Satyamurthy
ECC Campaign, Door Step School, Pune, India

S. Deb (ed.), *Child Safety, Welfare and Well-being*,
DOI 10.1007/978-81-322-2425-9_18

categories of children. Multiple strategies by different civil society groups along with the government machinery will be valuable when achieving the goals of RTE.

This paper aims to highlight two innovative experiments for the education of marginalized children: the first for the girls living on the street by Rainbow Homes and the other for the children of the construction workers by the Door Step School. While Rainbow Homes offers a residential care model, the Door Step School involves multiple stakeholders to facilitate the education of the children of migrant laborers, especially on construction sites. Both Rainbow Homes and the Door Step School have initiated their interventions much before the RTE. The organizations aim to achieve the 4As in education through their projects by making education acceptable, available, accessible, and adaptable to children who are otherwise likely to be excluded from the formal education system.

The article includes the findings of two studies involving the Rainbow Homes and the Door Step School. The study of the Rainbow Homes was completed in August 2011, and the report on the Every Child Counts Campaign by the Door Step School, in January 2013. A brief sketch of these two organizations, their objectives and other details of the program implementation would unfold how these interventions are innovative and cost effective.

Rainbow Homes

The term street children in general are now replaced by street connected children. Meincke (2011) has termed them as *street connected children*, who can be understood as "children, for whom the street has become a central reference point, playing a significant role in their everyday lives and identities." Benitez and Hiddleston (2011) explain how this definition is more inclusive by emphasizing "connections" in the terms *street-connected child* or *child with street connections*. The guiding philosophy of the Rainbow Home aims to provide underprivileged and vulnerable street connected girls' access to education. Rainbow Homes believes in the right of accessibility to education in the formal schooling system to all girls regardless of their socio-economical background. One of the key points in educating these children connected with streets includes unlearning of mistrust on adults, aggressive behavior and abusive language adapted for survival, habituated recognition, and appreciation by the adults in their lives for undignified acts such as stealing, rag-picking, and begging. The new education should drive out the premature adult with all its accompanying traumas from the child's body by bringing in a regularized and healthy regime, with new appreciative indicators, and unconditional love and care. This shift in education of vulnerable girls is the model Rainbow Homes intends to bring in practice. They aim to mainstream street connected girls in education and provide long-term substitute care in a secure, open, enabling environment with opportunities to enhance skills necessary for goal setting, practical support to achieve stability for independent living. In doing so, the girls become self-fulfilling and socially connected individuals. Thus, they combine the concepts of RTE with the Right to Protection.

Objectives

The objectives of the Rainbow Homes study were to:

- Assess the merits and demerits of the various intervention methods, strategies, and programs for street connected girls.
- Provide in-depth insights on the implementation of successful large scale interventions and strategies for street connected girls.
- Suggest standards of care for street connected girls residing in the Rainbow Homes.

Research Design and Data Collection

The study was primarily qualitative and looked at the child and organizations related information through the secondary sources of data. Data were collected through in-depth interviews with management, staff, and children of the homes. In addition, focus groups discussions were conducted to understand major policy issues and their impact on the children and the lessons learnt in the process.

Sampling

At the time of the study the Rainbow Homes were operational in three cities, namely, Kolkata, Hyderabad, and Delhi through 18 homes. Two homes in each city were selected and as these homes were in different phases of evolution, represented a mix of well evolved and are newly set up homes. One non-residential intervention was studied in order to appraise the Rainbow Homes interventions alongside other interventions for street children in the same cities and to understand and explore good practices that could be incorporated within the Rainbow Home model.

The Rainbow Homes Perspective

The underlying belief of Rainbow Homes is each street connected girl has the capacity to emerge on her own merit if she is provided a healthy environment by placing her in a residential set up within formal schools. The initiative intends to improve the living conditions and the future possibilities of vulnerable and street connected girls living in India through all round development and education. Based on the belief that vulnerable and street connected girls can be mainstreamed into regular academic schools, Partnership Foundation has opened residential setups for vulnerable street connected girls in existing schools. In collaboration with the Government, NGOs and the corporate sector, the girls stay at these homes during the academic sessions and may return to their families during holidays and vacations.

The concept was developed by Sr. Cyril Mooney of the Loretto Congregation at Kolkata in a small way in 1979. She was also the Principal of the school run by the congregation. The project has now grown into 30 Homes in five cities providing predominant mainstream education and shelter to approximately 2000 vulnerable and street connected girls with support from the Partnership Foundation. Partnership Foundation was founded in 2002 by a group of people with a background in business in Netherlands on a 100 % volunteer basis. The foundation's administration rests on committed and engaged volunteers, people with a background in business, thus positioning the direct costs of the foundation to only 2.5 % of income. Partnership Foundation intends to support 50 rainbow homes reaching out to 10,000 street connected girls and escort them to adulthood through these homes.

The Rainbow Homes are promoted through corporate contribution. Each corporate entity is responsible for one home and provides the needed resources at the rate of 500 € per girl per annum, a low cost intervention given that no additional resources are required for putting in place a infrastructure to set up Rainbow Homes. The Rainbow Homes function as midway homes for the girl children on the streets. The existing school building is demarcated for use by the Rainbow children. With minimal redesign, the buildings are equipped to house a kitchen, showers, toilets, and lockers. This is cost effective as there is no infrastructural cost; it incurs only a fraction of the expense of building a home. Some of the resources of the school are made available to the Rainbow Home after school hours and the school environment provides the ethos for the education of the girls.

The "former street connected girl" is provided shelter, education (in regular schools with general population children) and training, clothing (school uniforms), healthy nutrition, and medical care. Children are provided age appropriate or level appropriate extra tutorials from school students or through volunteers from the regular schools. The focus is on de-stigmatizing these children of their "street" background, mainstreaming the children into regular schools and preparing the children to compete on an equal platform with the general population children.

The local NGO or school becomes the implementing partner for the initiative and develops the Home on the guidelines provided. The manual, "management and organization of Rainbow Homes," provides the direction for the essential program and reporting requirements that the NGO partners need to comply with. The approach is based on the premise that it is the girl who makes the decision to live within the premises of the Rainbow Home. Hence, the gates of the home are open; girls are not forced into the Home by adults and they are allowed to leave when they wish to do so. When a girl runs away or leaves of her own accord and returns, she is received with love and care and no questions are asked. Staff members are not allowed to use violence against the girls. Girls are brought up with love, care, and affection where they can grow as individuals who can decide for themselves. The Rainbow Home has demonstrated a model on the principles of equitable education, a model accepted by Sarva Shiksha Abhiyan.

Highlights of the Findings

- The Rainbow Home concept has contributed to demonstrable changes in the lives of girls "of the streets" and "on the streets" by mainstreaming them into regular schools and providing them shelter within residential care systems. Family should be the first choice for care; however, when family is not an option that scores high on weighted desirability, residential care should be available for girls. Rainbow Homes have provided a mid-way option where children do not necessarily break away from their families, but continue to stay within the schools during the academic period.
- The Rainbow Homes provide girls with basic material, emotional, and educational support. Rainbow Home girls are provided nutritious meals three times a day and snacks once a day (in some homes, twice a day). Medical care, nutrition, and better hygiene practices that the children receive at the Rainbow Homes help in improving their health. Children also receive clothing and other essentials mobilized through donations and direct procurement, reducing the burden of care on the parents.
- The children's sense of happiness is related to the nurturing they receive. The warmth and care that the girls receive from the caretakers help them to evolve with emotional stability against the background realities of their life circumstances. The Rainbow Homes have an open door concept, which stems from the premise that the girls have a right to decide for themselves. The principle of child participation is central to the process. There is also an element of guided decision making that opens those dimensions which the child may not understand.
- RTE is the unique selling point of the Rainbow Homes. The model has put in processes and systems to ensure that girls have access to mainstreamed schooling. Through the bridge school education, they try admit the girls in age appropriate class/level of the mainstream school education.
- The major advantage of the residential set-up is the ability of the girls to distance themselves partially from their harsh realities and be focused on the education process. The Rainbow Homes has helped girls to unwind themselves from the day-to-day concerns that their families witness and focus on academic achievement.
- Older girls from the school spend 2 hours a week with the Rainbow Girls and help them in studies and other activities. This helps in sensitization of the girls from privileged backgrounds to the social realities of the marginalized sections of society.
- The mothers of the Rainbow Girls are referred to other NGOs for participation in self-help groups or vocational training. This helps some of the families to improve their income.
- Girls from well established Rainbow Homes have shown considerable success in completing 10 years of education and entering collegiate education, a resource that could put a girl on an equal footing or even above her peers from

the same neighborhood. A few of these girls have entered into the competitive market for employment, which is in itself an achievement that can be considered as a move toward life independent of charity.

- By making care personalized through the management of residential set ups by NGOs, the Rainbow Homes are making a considerable effort toward a personalized humanitarian approach to reduce the disadvantages of long-term institutionalization.
- Those girls, who can exit, have an option of reintegration within their families. Those who require long-term support are provided additional help through Rainbow Flats and other assistance.
- One of the older Rainbow Homes has evolved to broad-based outreach and strengthening linkages and networks for girls once they are discharged from the Home or those who are considered for care within their own homes or neighborhoods. Follow up of girls even after being discharged from Rainbow Homes for long periods after integration has ensured maintaining stability for the girls' post reintegration.

It can be seen that the Rainbow Homes is a viable model that could be considered part of the RTE Act as well as the Integrated Child Protection Scheme. It provides a meaningful partnership model for bringing the most vulnerable and the street connected girls into the fold of education and mainstream society.

Challenges

The major challenges in scaling up of the project are issues related to identifying motivated partners, schools as well as NGOs to run the project. Minimal numbers of private schools are ready to host the Rainbow Homes on their premises. There is a major resistance from private schools to admit Rainbow Homes girls in these schools for education and one needs to work on the same. The standards of care have to be maintained alongside ensuring community participation for running the residential care facility that ensures safety and security of the girls under care. The project also needs to evolve strategies for networking with other NGOs for improving the family situations so as to take care of the girls when they leave the Rainbow Home. Networking is also needed for many other facilities such as medical care, counseling, and special education for girls with learning difficulties and vocational training for grown up girls. They have recently started a Rainbow Academy to take care of the training of the caretakers in these Homes.

Expected Outcomes

Girls in residential care emerge as individuals in their own right who can as empowered individuals contribute effectively to their own progress well as to that of their family and society (Dabir et al. 2011, p. 116).

Current Status of the Project

Today there are 30 Rainbow Homes in seven cities, caring for 2560 girls. The management has taken measures to improve the Standards of care, quality of education, alignment with the provisions of child protection as per the Juvenile Justice Act (2000 and its amendments in 2006), facilities for skill training of the older girls and local fund raising mechanisms to ensure sustainability of the project in the long run.

Every Child Counts Campaign, the Door Step School

In January 2012, Door Step School launched a citizens' campaign to enroll in school all 6–7-year-old children in the city of Pune by June 2012. The campaign is called Every Child Counts Campaign (ECCC). The campaign was conceived as a Citizens' Campaign and was designed accordingly.

This campaign envisaged partnership from all angles—people, government, media, students and whoever was interested. It was important to document the process from the beginning and develop a replicable model for ensuring the enrollment of every child in school. The whole activity was therefore treated as action research, and it was documented thoroughly and analyzed objectively.

Objectives of the Research

To document the following aspects of the "Every Child Counts—Pune Citizens' Campaign."

- Total enrollment of children in the age of group 6–8 years by June 2012 in the Pune Municipal Corporation (PMC) area with a focus on street children, children from unauthorized slums and children from migrant labor camps.
- Monitoring of the enrolled children for the first academic semester (till September end) to ensure attendance for continuity and to prevent school drop outs.
- Developing project methodology based on the experience for future replication, to launch such projects/initiatives elsewhere.

Methodology

a. A core group was initiated and more organizations and volunteers joined as the campaign unfolded. A blog was created for volunteer registration, http://everychildcounts-pune.blogspot.com.

b. The core group mobilized all the necessary resources and information using the following strategies:
    1. Use of technology such as Google Maps for collecting school related information, for instance, location, current capacity, and so on.
    2. Use of media for creating awareness among citizens.
    3. Partnering with government agencies like child help-line, ICDS, PMC officials, Pune Police, PMC Education Department for reaching out to all children eligible for enrollment in PMC schools.

c. Partnering with the corporate sector, educational institutions like universities and colleges for voluntary technical support and field work.
d. Identification of children (age group 6–8 by 2012) who were out of school by volunteers/citizens.
e. Actual enrollment of children by volunteers/citizens.
f. Collecting basic data for every enrolled child.
g. Monitoring of every enrolled child for one term.

    - First follow up after 2 weeks from the date of enrollment of the child and thereafter at a monthly interval.
    - In case of non-attendance, counseling of parents, and teacher.
    - to get the child back to school.

h. Follow-up data were collected focusing on

    - Reasons for not attending school.
    - Number of times hand holding was required for retention.

The Door Step School Perspective

The Door Step School was established in 1988. The organization built its program to address three major problems: non-enrollment, wastage, and stagnation. The Door Step School provides education and support to the children of pavement dwellers, slum dwellers, construction site families, and many other underprivileged families. Many of these children are not enrolled in school and have limited access to books and an environment to study. Additionally, many children drop out of school to work or care for younger children. With neither support nor resources at home, some children suffer from very low learning levels. The project is trying to bridge this gap by bringing education to the "Door Step" of these underprivileged children.

This concept was developed by Prof. Rajani Paranjpe, a social work educator and researcher, who started the project in a small way through the students' field work in Nirmala Niketan, College of Social Work, Mumbai. The Door Step School was established in Mumbai in 1988 and extended to Pune in 1992. It has impacted the lives of over 5,00,000 children since its inception. At any given point in time, the project reaches out to more than 50,000 children through various programs.

The Pune project concentrates on the children of construction workers and children in Municipal schools through its Project Foundation and Project Grow with Books. Project Foundation now covers 147 construction sites under the Direct Education program. Children of construction site laborers do not go to school for various reasons. The Door Step School sets up temporary education facilities with the help of the builders at the construction site. Over 39,000 children have gained literacy in the last 5 years through this program.

"School on Wheels": Specially fitted buses are deployed to reach children when there are delays in setting up schools at sites or when sites are small or remote. These buses then become "Schools on Wheels" and reach out to more than 500 of school children annually.

The Project, Grow with Books, is implemented in 145 Municipal schools in Pune. The Door Step School works with Municipal Schools to conduct 90 min reading classes per week in the primary schools. The goal of this program is to enhance the reading capabilities of the children and to improve their overall educational performance. Nearly 145,000 children have benefited through these programs over the last 5 years.

Recently they have launched a campaign titled, "Every Child Counts—Citizens' Campaign" in Pune to reach out to all the children on the construction sites aged 6–7 years and enroll them in school. This paper highlights the experiences of this campaign.

Every Child Counts—Citizens' Campaign by the Door Step School

The Door Step School launched a campaign in January 2012 to enroll all 6–7-year-old children in the city of Pune into schools by June 2012. The campaign called, "Every Child Counts—Citizen's Campaign" envisaged involving a large number of citizens to participate in the Goal of Universal Elementary Education. The first phase of the campaign concluded in December 2012. The TISS team documented the whole process of the campaign during this period. The following are the highlights of this initiative:

The seeds of this campaign were sown at the World Innovation Summit for Education (WISE)—held in Doha, Qatar, from November 3–5, 2011 where the Door Step School was invited to participate. At the summit, Former British Prime Minister Gordon Brown gave a passionate speech calling for global support for the UN Millennium Goal of primary education for all children by 2015. It was highlighted that the pace of progress across the world was insufficient to ensure that, by 2015, all girls and boys complete a full course of primary schooling. To achieve the goal by the target date, all children at the official entry age for primary schooling would have had to be attending classes by 2009.

This was reinforced by Door Step School's own experience of following the RTE Act and its implementation in India, and in the state of Maharashtra in particular. While the roadmap for RTE exists, systematic steps to achieve this goal starting with "Mapping to Facilitate Children's Access in Neighbourhood Schools" is slow to be implemented. Measures to include children from marginalized groups, for instance, children of migrant laborers and provisions to address the inability to attend full-time school are still not in place. To compound the issue, the government has stopped support to all official programs and those run by NGOs that addressed "out-of-school" children through non-formal teaching methods.

Goal of the Campaign

Every 6-year-old child in Pune should be enrolled in a municipal corporation school by June-2012. Looking at the potential volume of children to be enrolled, this has to be a citizens' campaign.

Scope of the Campaign

1. Address 6–7-year-old children
2. Focus on Construction sites/Brick Kilns/Street Children and Unauthorized Slums
3. Focus on Children who are never enrolled
4. Focus on Government Schools for enrollment
5. Follow up after enrollment for one term.

Campaign Process

The campaign process has three main components

1. Appeal to citizens
2. Mapping and survey of children and schools
3. School Enrollment.

Before launching the citywide campaign, a pilot project was initiated in one site having 87 locations of construction sites and slums. The experiences in the pilot helped in designing the main campaign.

ECC Campaign Strategy—January to June 2012

- Most of these out-of-school children are from migrant families.
- Immediate admissions are required for these children.
- During the schools' summer vacation, it is likely that we lose track of these children identified through surveys. Hence, it is needed to hold a camp for these children during the summer. This can prepare them for admission into schools.
- Once corporation schools reopen in June 2012, these children will start attending regular school.

ECC Campaign Strategy—June to September 2012

- Admission of all children to the nearest Schools.
- Two-week Camp to "welcome first timers to school" at as many schools as possible.
- Arrange for transport for the children to attend school regularly (necessary interventions with schools/SSA).
- Create parent awareness to take ownership of transport and ensure that children attend school regularly.
- Engage volunteers for follow up on the children to ensure that they have the required support.
- Survey and admissions at new construction sites in August and September.

The ECC campaign envisaged partnership from all groups: citizens, government, media, students and whoever was interested. The Campaign team approached NGOs, corporate offices, social groups, educational institutes, government offices, and builders for creating awareness on the RTE and also for enlisting their support for making the campaign successful. NGOs, social groups, corporate offices, institutes, the media, builders, the Government and citizen volunteers partnered with the campaign team for various purposes such as media publicity, field surveys, mobilizing volunteers, fundraising, documentation support, making a list of slums, list of builders, and so on. Campaign promotion was done through online channels (Blog, Face book, E-mail, Twitter etc.) to reach out to maximum number of individuals.
Blog: http://everychildcounts-pune.blogspot.com
E-mail: everychildcounts.pune@gmail.com
Twitter: http://twitter.com/eccpune
Facebook: http://on.fb.me/eccpune.

Highlights of the School Enrollment Program

- From April to June 2012, all 76 Wards of the PMC under 34 Geographic Areas were surveyed by Partner Volunteer Groups, Individual Volunteers, NGOs, and field staff. A total of 716 sites were surveyed and a total of 2680 children aged 6–7 years were located in 468 sites (65 %).
- It was observed that 48 % of the sites were with one or two children who were 6–7 years old and most likely to migrate.
- Nearly 61 % of the children were engaged through NGOs, Camps, Builder Appointed Teachers and Community Environment in authorized slums and therefore likely to be admitted.
- Around 39 % of the children were from 341 small Construction Sites.
- Neighborhood Schools in all PMC Areas were mapped and 41 PMC Schools and 6 Zilla Parishad (ZP) Schools were identified for admission.
- Admissions were required to be done by Every Child Counts (1370) as well as by Partner NGOs (1310).

Table 18.1 School admission summary

ECC admission summary-31st Oct 2012	
6–7 yr old children identified by Survey up to 20th May 2012	**2680**
Sites where NGOs work	1310
Sites where no NGOs work	1370
Children enrolled from 15th June to 31st Oct 2012 (at sites where no NGO works)	**788**
6–7-yr-old children enrolled	570
4–6-yr-old children enrolled in pre-primary classes	51
Older children enrolled (3rd std and above)	167
Follow up	**788**
No of children attending school	562
No of children not attending school	214
Follow up to be done	12
Transport support for children attending school	**562**
By ECC campaign initially, then by School	67
ECC campaign	69
Partner NGOs	139
Arranged by parents	44
By school initially and then discontinued	20
Children go by walk or are escorted by parents	223
Children enrolled from 15th June to 31st Aug 2012 (at sites where NGOs work)	
Door step school	439
Other NGOs	To be determined

Source Dabir and Satyamurthy (2012). Process document report of ECC Campaign

- School capacity assessment was done for the 41 PMC Schools It was observed that 44 % of the schools (18/41) had a Capacity Shortfall—10 Schools with a Capacity Shortfall of more than 80 children (2 Classrooms), and 2 Schools with a Capacity Shortfall of more than 160 children. Transport Requirement Assessment for 458 Construction sites and 10 Community Slums revealed that transport is required at 82 % of the sites and for 84 % of the children. A large number of sites (89 %) are 2–4 km away from the nearest school.

The ECC team was successful in enrolling 730 Children from 162 sites to nearby schools. School orientation camps of 15 day duration were held in 18 schools for Standard I Children (first time school goers). In some cases, it was evident that there was increased parental awareness and there were a few admissions by parents themselves!

Table 18.1 indicates the school admission summary.

Identifying the importance of documenting the process from the beginning and developing a replicable model for ensuring the enrollment of every child in school, the whole activity was undertaken as an Action Research Project, to be documented thoroughly and analyzed objectively. The campaign has been successful in reaching out to some of the marginalized children, enrolling them in schools, and convincing their parents about the need for education.

Challenges

However, several challenges were faced during the process, which need to be attended to in order to achieve the goal of total enrollment.

- **Participation of Citizens:** The goal of taking every child in Pune to school can be achieved only by involving local citizen volunteers from all sections of the city. From identifying out-of-school children to making their admissions in nearest schools to ensuring their regular attendance—all activities need strong local support. The campaign has been seeking support from all citizens—students, professionals, housewives, senior citizens, NGO representatives, media, and government officials—to make this happen. The biggest challenge has remained to be able to reach out to more citizens with the concept of localized volunteering.
- **Identifying Out-of-School Children:** The other challenge is to find out the number of children who should be, but are not in schools across Pune. Since most of these children are from migrant labor families, it is difficult to assume the inclusion of all children in one particular area at any given point of time. While ongoing survey activity ensures reach out to some extent, a strong and simple reporting mechanism is highly sought after, wherein any citizen can at least report sighting of an out-of-school child across Pune city. ECC has been working on developing such tools for better reach. Early efforts to gather data from Pulse

polio campaigns and builders are just beginning to show results and there is need to establish consistent mechanisms to mine this data for locating children.

- **Parent Awareness:** It has been observed that children, whose parents are willing to send them to school, are regular in attending classes, while those who are irregular may have indifferent parents or those who are afraid. Convincing parents to enroll their children in school and not to let them grow sans education is one of the biggest challenges ECC has been facing. A strong parent awareness drive is required to counsel and convince parents about the importance of education for their child, be it a boy or a girl. This also involves gaining their trust by supporting them in overcoming barriers of schooling.
- **Availability and Capacity of Government Schools:** The RTE Act insists upon the availability of a government school within the reach of every child. Although the city area has enough number of schools within walking distance, there is a scarcity of schools in newly developing areas, especially on the outskirts of the city. ECC has begun a dialogue with the concerned authorities to gear up for total enrollment and this need to be taken to conclusion.
- **School Transport Facility:** The target age group of the ECC campaign is 6–8 years, at which age children cannot commute to and from school on their own. Some means of transport is required for long-distance schools, while escorting is required for short-distance schools, since both parents are working as laborers during the day time. At present, neither the school nor PMC provides any kind of transport facility. The challenge is to arrange funds as well as vehicles to transport children from migrant labor families to school.
- **Addressing Migrant Children:** The migrant nature of the work of construction laborers continues to pose challenges to schools and NGOs working for the enrollment of children. It is proposed to carry out a survey of Contractors in the city to establish mechanisms to trace migrant children and parents.

The Project Status After the Research Period

The Campaign team has decided to continue the project beyond December 2012 and has defined a revised plan of action to address the above challenges and to accomplish the planned project goals.

Campaign Focus 2012

The key focus during the second year was to address the barriers to enrollment that were identified in year 1.

- **Involving Parents in Children's Education:** To address this key barrier a special intervention Program called "Parent's Participation in Children's Education" was launched in 2 areas of Pune with high density of migrant

Table 18.2 Number of children benefitted

Year	2012	2013
Sites surveyed	800+	800+
Children enrolled	1354	1717
Children in target age group	750	950
Parents counseled	600	1615
School transport arranged	290	1900[a]

population. The program's focus was to create awareness among parents on the value of education, the ease of access to education under RTE act, the process of enrolling children and ensuring regular attendance of children, once enrolled. 674 children were mainstreamed and enrolled and 1254 parents counseled under this program.

- **Increasing Citizen Participation:** The campaign team designed and implemented a special website where any citizen can report about out-of-school children found in the city. The website "Report children" was launched in February 2013. This website has had limited success with volunteers reporting construction sites and children. A larger effort and resources were required to evangelize the website and make it usable to agencies like education department to retain. However, with increased citizen awareness, the volunteer groups took ownership of the issues facing migrant children. Many groups initiated fund raising activities. One private school donated the use of their school buses for transporting children to municipal schools.
- **Scaling the program beyond PMC limits:** With volunteer mobilization, groups of volunteers were able to own new areas in Pimpri Chinchwad and carry out survey and enrollment activities on their own with the help of the Volunteer kit provided.
- **Government support:** With the regular meetings with the Department of Education, PMC, the Every Child Counts team was successful in obtaining financial support for "School Transport" for all children attending mainstream schools during the year 2013–14. This was a significant step as it eliminated one of the key barriers to enrollment and regular attendance. A total of 1902 children benefited from this through the year, including children enrolled in 2012 (Table 18.2).

Global Recognition: The Every Child Counts program was selected for presentation under the "Innovative programs" category at the World Literacy Summit in Oxford in April 2014 (http://worldliteracysummit.org/) (2014).

Year 3: 2014–2015: Scaling up the Program

Encouraged by the positive outcomes and foreseeing the need to scale this program beyond PMC, Door Step School mobilized local Companies to support this campaign in their areas. The Campaign was extended to reach children in Pimpri Chinchwad and Areas surrounding Pune known to have high density of construction activity and migrant settlements.

Table 18.3 Number of children enrolled in mainstream schools

2014–2015—Phase II	
Sites surveyed	2205
Children enrolled	2973
Children in target age group (Balwadi, 1st/2nd std)	1903
Schools enrolled in	204
School transport arranged	985
2014-Phase 1	
Sites surveyed	1589
Children enrolled	1660
Children in target age group (Bal, 1st/2nd)	1056
Schools enrolled in	147
School transport arranged	614

The parent participation program continued into its second year, enrolling children and counseling parents.

A total of 1660 children have been enrolled in mainstream schools between June and March 2015 (Table 18.3).

It is very encouraging to see that both the projects are not only continuing the important interventions but expanding the scope of work and are able to reach out to more number in the successive years.

Let us now look at these initiatives using the 4A framework developed by the former UN Special Rapporteur on the RTE, Katarina Tomasevski.

The Circle of Right to Education

The circle illustrates the operational definition of each of the "**As**" that need to be in place if we are to ensure the RTE for every child. Even in urban areas there are many children who are still not enrolled. Reaching out to them is the major challenge (Fig. 18.1).

One can see that both the projects take care of most of the aspects of the 4A framework that fit into their framework of operations.

Interventions in Education are usually assessed on the basis of teaching-learning innovations, sustaining the motivation of the students and finally documenting evidence of Children's improved learning. However, interventions like Rainbow Homes and Door Step School's Every Child Counts—Citizens' Campaign address the 4-As in education by making education Acceptable, Available, Accessible, and Adaptable to vulnerable children such as street connected girls and children of migrant construction workers, who are completely "excluded" from the education system in our county, despite the RTE Act. The process of education begins with "inclusion" of the children through a process of mobilizing government, communities, funding partners, citizen volunteers and virtually all key players to

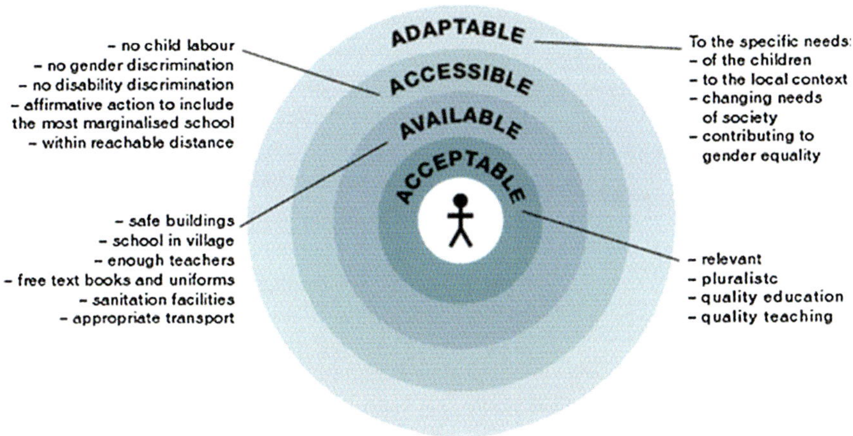

Fig. 18.1 *Source* Education and the 4 as, http://www.right-to-education.org/node/226

acknowledge the large number of children who continue to be denied the benefits of teaching-learning. In Rainbow Home project the child is temporarily shifted out of the vulnerable environment and given a chance to experience the childhood in a conducive atmosphere. A lot of relearning happens with an assurance of acceptance and unconditional love. Under the Every Child Counts, a special program for motivating parents, Parents' Participation in Children's education has been implemented, which has shown impact on the parents involvement in Schools as well as children's regular attendance, thereby enhancing the chances of children continuing in schools and attaining the desired learning in mainstream schools. The critical issues leading to success here are the innovations in approaches used to reach out to these children who have multiple hurdles to get access to mainstream education by looking at the issue in a holistic manner. The approach to involve multiple stakeholders has also helped in making the programs effective.

Conclusion and Recommendations

The common thread between these two projects is the fact that they work toward the realization of the RTE of marginalized children, who are most likely to remain outside the formal education system. It can be seen that the Rainbow Home project and the ECC citizen's campaign provide two different models for reaching out to the children of vulnerable populations and demonstrate how their RTE can be ensured. They also help us to understand the problems in the process. Both the projects envisage active involvement of different partners/stakeholders from society to achieve the goals of RTE. The standards of education facilities needed to achieve the 4As are far from desired and therefore we need to duplicate such programs that try to overcome the challenges and make education accessible to these groups of marginalized children.

The Government needs to take cognizance of such efforts and provide all the necessary support in terms of finances, infrastructure, and policy level changes. If all the out of school children are mobilized for enrollment, there is a major gap between the availability of school infrastructure and the demand.

Since the number of out of school children in India is still very large, all sections of society need to have a commitment to participate in initiatives that help in ensuring RTE for all. To a certain extent, the ECC citizen's campaign in Pune has achieved the objective of sensitizing a large number of people in different fields to the cause of RTE of children in urban areas. The Rainbow Home program has made a difference in the lives of several girls and prevented the multiple disadvantages that girls face by virtue of being "on" and "of" the street. A well-conceptualized and implemented program within quality parameters can facilitate the plan of expansion and provide for lessons for other partners to emulate (Dabir et al. 2011, p. 126).

References

Benitez, T.S., & Hiddleston, T. (2011). *Research paper on the promotion and protection of the rights of children working and/or living on the street: OHCHR 2011 Global Study*. Geneva: OHCHR.

Dabir, N., Rego, A., & Kapadia, K. (2011). *Rainbow homes-sunbursts in the lives of vulnerable girls*. Mumbai: Tata Institute of Social Sciences.

Dabir, N., & Satyamurthy, R. (2012). *Process document report of ECC campaign*. Mumbai: Tata Institute of Social Sciences.

Education Rights Circle Diagram-Education and the 4 As. Retrieved December 3, 2012 from http://www.right-to-education.org/node/226.

Khalik, A. (2012). An education act with more wrongs than rights, The Hindu, July 27, 2012. Retrieved November 10, 2014 from http://www.thehindu.com/opinion/op-ed/an-education-act-with-more-wrongs-than-rights/article3687858.ece.

Meincke, A. L. (2011). *Children's voices paper: "Nothing about us, without us"*. London: Consortium for Street Children.

The Rights of Children to Free and Compulsory Education Act, 2000 (or Right to Education Act 2009).

The Juvenile Justice (Care and Protection of Children) Act, 2000 (amended in 2006, India).

World Literacy Summit in Oxford (April 2014). (http://worldliteracysummit.org/).

Part IV
Protective Measures

Chapter 19
Protecting Children: Building Effective Systems

Jenny Gray

Introduction

> No violence against children is justifiable; all violence against children is preventable (Pinheiro 2006, p. 5).

Child maltreatment is not a new phenomenon. In 1962, over 50 years ago, Drs. Henry Kempe and Brandt Steele published their seminal paper, *The Battered Child Syndrome*, which ignited debate internationally about child protection and highlighted the importance of professionals working together when responding to maltreated children. Their efforts, along with those of their contemporaries, to prevent and treat victims of child abuse and neglect continue to this day.

Despite child maltreatment being known about and responded to for decades, we still do not have reliable data on its prevalence. Data on physical violence compiled for the UN Secretary General's Study on Violence against Children (2006) estimated that between 500 and 1.5 billion children experience violence annually. A recent UNICEF report (2012) on children living in an urban world has estimated that crime and violence affects hundreds of millions of these children. This demonstrates that much progress is still required across the world to implement fully the Convention on the Rights of the Child (CRC) adopted in 1989.

There is increasing international and national awareness of the scale and societal costs of child maltreatment and a growing consensus on the types of violence which constitute child maltreatment (Dubowitz 2012). We have, however, yet to reach what Henry Kempe described as the sixth stage of community recognition of

J. Gray (✉)
International Society for the Prevention of Child Abuse and Neglect,
Aurora, CO, USA
e-mail: jennyagray@ntlworld.com

S. Deb (ed.), *Child Safety, Welfare and Well-being*,
DOI 10.1007/978-81-322-2425-9_19

child maltreatment—where each child is wanted, loved and well for, sheltered, fed and receives first class preventative and curative services and health care (Kempe 1976). The challenge for all nations and societies is still to develop effective systems which both prevent maltreatment and protect those children who have been abused or neglected. This paper focuses on the key elements of an effective system which will support implementation of the UNCRC and in particular Article 19, the Right of the child to freedom from all forms of violence.

The UN Convention on the Rights of the Child, Article 19

The UNCRC sets out internationally agreed obligations on state parties to assure the rights of children are respected. Article 19 refers specifically to all forms of violence, which are elaborated in the recent *General comment no 13 (2011): The right of the child to freedom from all forms violence*. Paragraphs 17–31 of this General Comment describe an extensive number of specific forms of violence including corporal punishment and violence through information and communication technologies as well as the more well understood forms such as physical and sexual abuse and neglect.

UN Convention on the Rights of the Child, Article 19

1. State parties shall take all appropriate legislative, administrative, social, and educational measures to protect the child from all forms of physical or mental violence, injury or abuse, neglect or negligent treatment, maltreatment or exploitation, including sexual abuse, while in the care of parent(s), legal guardian(s), or any other person who has the care of the child.
2. Such protective measures should, as appropriate, include effective procedures for the establishment of social programs to provide necessary support for the child and for those who have care of the child, as well as for other forms of prevention and for identification, reporting, referral, investigation, treatment, and follow up of instances of child maltreatment described heretofore, and, as appropriate for judicial involvement.

The *General Comment No 13: The Right of the Child to Freedom from All Forms of Violence* was adopted by the UN Committee on the Rights of the Child in February, 2011. It aims to assist implementation of Article 19 by providing “clear interpretations, greater detail and supportive guidance” to all those working with and for children. The General Comment No 13 is particularly directed at governments which have ratified the Convention on the Rights of the Child (CRC), other stakeholders such as professionals, international and national non-government agencies and advocates, including children and young people (Bennett et al. 2012).

The document takes a child rights approach to care giving and protection, broadening the traditional narrow emphasis on protecting the child from loss of life and immediate harm to also securing optimal outcomes for the child's well-being and development through into adulthood. It provides a conceptual framework which emphasizes that "child protection must begin with proactive primary prevention" of all forms of violence as well as explicitly prohibiting them (Bennett et al. 2012).

Taking a child rights approach is not new in the field of child protection. Dr. C. Henry Kempe, the founder of International Society for the Prevention of Child Abuse and Neglect (ISPCAN), took this approach. Indeed this was a key area for discussion at his first international meeting held in Bellagio, Italy in 1975, to exchange information on child abuse. This discourse predated the UNCRC, which Henry Kempe actively supported, by 14 years.

Legislative Framework

Within each country it is critical that there are national laws to protect children from all forms of violence and associated protocols and guidelines in place. The latter can set out clearly not only what the law says in relation to child protection but also explain what the policy intentions were in passing the legislation. They can be updated from time to time to ensure their underlying evidence base is current. These tools can help support the implementation of legislation as we know that in some countries although the law is sound, it is not implemented or only partially followed, e.g., depending on the availability of resources.

In England and Wales, the Children Act 1989 is the key legislation regarding the welfare of children. Section 17 of this Act places a duty on local authorities[1] to safeguard and promote the welfare of children in need in their local area: in addition, Section 27 places a duty on education and health bodies to co-operate with the local authority in carrying out its responsibilities. In complementary legislation, the Children Act 2004, Section 11 places a duty on key organizations and senior managers to ensure their functions are undertaken having regard to the need to safeguard and promote the welfare of children. The organizations named in the legislation are all those which have a statutory responsibility for providing direct services to children and families—the police, health, probation, prison service, institutions working with young offenders, and local authority social services. Critically the primary legislation provides a duty "to safeguard and promote the welfare of children." It thus encompasses statutory responsibilities on agencies to prevent children from being harmed, to protect them from recurring harm and to provide services which focus on securing the best possible outcomes for them.

[1]There are 152 local authorities in England.

More detailed guidelines for professionals, such as in *Working Together to Safeguard Children* (HM Government 2010), assist organizations and professionals to implement the law in consistent and evidence-based ways.

Working Together to Prevent and Treat Child Maltreatment

As the founder of the ISPCAN in 1977, Henry Kempe firmly believed that different professions needed to work together if communities were going to be able to effectively prevent and respond to maltreated children. This way of working also applies to state parties. Experience has shown that the more that a government is committed to securing the optimal well-being of the nation's children across all its relevant Ministries, the more likely it is to achieve good outcomes for them.

In any civilized society everyone has a responsibility to:

- Protect children from harm;
- Respond to all forms of violence;
- Promote children's well-being; and
- Ensure the right of each child to be free from all forms of violence.

This means taking responsibility for children's well-being and safety within every strata of society—from the government having a Minister/Ministerial Department with specific responsibility for the protection of the nation's children, to senior managers in public/state bodies and all those who are delivering services to children and families having public accountability for children's well-being, through to individual members of each local community believing they too must take action to prevent violence to children.

Process for Developing Collaborative Arrangements

Effective professional working will be supported by having common child protection policies in place across the different partner organizations. This results in professionals from different disciplines being expected to follow the same overarching processes when managing an individual case. Importantly from an individual child and family's perspective, this means that they are experiencing a coherent service response from all professionals with whom they are in contact. This is particularly important in the field of child maltreatment because different approaches to responding to a child where there are concerns about maltreatment, or professionals acting in conflict with each other about how to respond, can result in a loss of professional focus on the child's well-being and safety. Written agreements or protocols between all the different professional parties may also support effective working together. This could be in relation to a particular area of work, such as sharing information about a child and family, where different professionals may work to different codes of practice or to the overall process. Having one document where the principles have been agreed by key stakeholders and senior professionals will also reduce the need for time being wasted debating conflicting views about how to manage an individual abuse or neglect case.

In establishing a starting point for inter-sectorial collaboration on responding to child maltreatment, it is important to start where the land is most fertile. This can be from the ground up or government down or ideally both. Leaders taking forward this type of development should identify influential stakeholders within the key organizations (state and NGO) and those who have expertise in child protection. These key people can form the basis of a "Working Group" or a number of working groups with specific tasks. It is also important to identify which organization (s) are able to provide the administrative support for these working groups as good quality minutes and efficient organization of meetings are also crucial to the delivery of such a project.

In considering who should be involved, consideration should be given to being inclusive of all stakeholders—those from small as well as large organizations and those with relatively small parts to play in the protection of children as well as those that have a key role such as in child protective or children's health services. Successful implementation of new policies and ways of working will depend not only on the commitment of all those working with children and families and but also on those working with adults who are caregivers for children.

In some countries the legislation may be sound but consideration may need to be given to amending it to provide additional powers or underpin new ways of working. In other countries the legislation may be outdated or piece meal having developed over time and require new legislation to be developed and enacted. The working group should be well placed to consider the legislation. Here, the involvement of government officials will be invaluable in providing guidance on what might be possible and the best way of framing requests to politicians for change. International documents such as the UNCRC and the General Comment 13 will provide the underpinning principles for incorporation into new or amended laws. As in all our work, research and practice experience should also inform these developments.

Having decided on a working group's objectives, it can play a number of different roles such as:

- Leading the development of guidance, protocols, policies (local and/or national levels);
- Training staff across sectors—multi-disciplinary where possible;
- Supporting new/different evidence-based ways of working; and
- Monitoring and evaluating changes.

Developing Guidelines or Protocols

There is general agreement (see paragraphs 48–53 of the General Comment 13) across all countries that any child protection guidelines or protocols should include the following common components:

- A referral/reporting system to the services that have statutory responsibility for protecting children, e.g., child protective or social services;
- Agreement on how to undertake rapid multi-disciplinary assessments of the nature and level of any harm being or likely to be suffered by the child;
- Legal provisions for emergency protection (i.e., Rescue) of children;
- Agreement on how to undertake multi-disciplinary assessments of a child and family's long-term needs;
- Services provided by different organizations to meet the identified needs of children and their families; and
- Multi-disciplinary follow up and evaluation of the adequateness of the interventions in a child and family's life.

This framework should be consistent with the legislative framework within which work with children and families takes place and any other national or standard setting guidance as well as the UNCRC. The process of obtaining agreement on the above areas will require careful discussion and debate across all the key professional groups that will be involved in implementing the framework. These groups could include, e.g., social workers, police, doctors, nurses, teachers, staff working with pre-school children and ideally those working with parents who have problems relating to drug and alcohol misuse, mental ill health, learning disabilities and domestic violence. The involvement of professionals working with adults who have parenting responsibilities is very important as we know that these types of parental problems are commonly identified in child protection cases (Cleaver et al. 2011). It should also involve all sectors of the community, most importantly including the meaningful participation of children (Article 12 of the UNCRC 1989).

This collaborative effort to develop child protection guidelines or protocols will not only draw on professionals' knowledge and experience in the field of child maltreatment but also facilitate their buy into the final document. This means that they in turn will support its implementation within their own organization or setting. It also enables all professionals to understand the policy intentions of these documents which support their successful implementation. Where local organizations and professionals work well together, such a framework provides the glue that binds these different people and groups together.

Some countries have had these inter-agency processes in place for many years. For example, in England the first known inter-departmental communication from the government exhorting agencies to work together was issued in 1950. For others these may be relatively new, e.g., in Serbia and Georgia.

Effective Inter-sectorial Collaboration

Effective collaboration between agencies and professionals is essential in order to effectively prevent maltreatment and protect children from harm. This shared professional commitment to working together across different sectors may take some time to generate. Regular meetings between and within organizations or sectors regarding common issues or projects can be a very important way of people getting to know each other and feeling sufficiently trusting to be able to discuss new approaches to working together or to debate controversial or sensitive issues, e.g., corporal punishment or forced marriages. Raising such topical subjects in a neutral environment can be a more productive method of considering new ways of working and responding to children who are being subjected to harmful practices than when discussing a very difficult case.

The support of professional organizations can also play an important role in developing these relationships as evidenced by the Department of Applied Psychology, Pondicherry University in association with Sri Balaji Vidyapeeth University, Puducherry hosting an International Conference on *Protection of Child Rights: Issues and Challenges*, in Puducherry in 2013. In England an example is provided by the General Medical Council which developed guidance, *Protecting children and young people: The responsibilities of all doctors* (2012), aimed at supporting all doctors working with adults and children irrespective of whether it is the child or the adult who is their patient. It clearly states that "in sharing concerns about possible abuse or neglect, doctors must remember that they work within a wider team of professionals, all of whom have a responsibility to keep children safe from abuse."

Multi-disciplinary, Multi-agency Training

Whilst individual professionals have a responsibility to make sure they are trained to recognize and respond to maltreatment, their employing institutions also have a role, both in ensuring their staff are trained to know what to do if they suspect abuse or neglect (single agency training) and in enabling them to take part in multi-agency, multidisciplinary training.

Working together across professionals and organizations can be very challenging especially when there are differences in values and beliefs about how best to work with cases of child abuse and neglect. It is, however, extremely rewarding when it goes well and the joint efforts of professionals support good outcomes for children. This collaboration can be facilitated by many different factors. Multi-disciplinary training, especially those events which involve the professionals who work together on a daily basis, not only teaches people what they need to do when they are concerned about a child's safety and well-being, but it also enables them to meet colleagues and understand better what they do and how they work. It is this face to face contact, knowing who you are talking to and understanding each others' roles and responsibilities which builds up a sense of trust between professionals and enables them to share information and work together effectively in often very stressful circumstances.

Although there is a strong belief in the value of inter-disciplinary training, surprisingly there is little available research to demonstrate whether it is indeed effective. To redress this deficit in England, Carpenter et al. (2010) looked at the outcomes from multi-disciplinary training which had been commissioned by Local Safeguarding Children Boards.[2] The researchers found that inter-agency training is highly effective in helping professionals understand their respective roles and responsibilities, the procedures of each agency and in developing a shared understanding of assessment and decision-making practices. Furthermore, the opportunity to learn together is greatly valued: participants report increased confidence in working with colleagues from other agencies and greater mutual respect.

Developing Multi-disciplinary Training Resources

The development of multi-disciplinary training resources can be a very cost effective way of supporting this training by providing those who lead it with quality materials. In England, the implementation of government policy has been supported by national training materials. Two examples are: *The Developing World of the Child* (2008) intended to support the development of professional knowledge about normal child development and *Childhood Neglect: Improving Outcomes for Children* (2012) which focuses on identifying, responding to and intervening in child neglect cases. These materials were commissioned by the government and developed by multi-disciplinary teams of professionals drawing on the most up to date research and knowledge from the field. The materials were piloted and reviewed prior to their completion, thereby involving an even larger group of professionals in their development and again giving greater assurance about their evidence base and relevance to practice.

At an international level, ISPCAN leads a major multi-disciplinary International Training Program (ITPI), made possible by funding from the OAK Foundation. It has developed curricula in relation to medical, mental health and inter-disciplinary working which are available to members and can be used to support local training. ISPCAN focuses on inter-disciplinary, inter-sectorial training and promotes concepts of effective working together, sharing of information and professional collaboration on individual cases. ITPI training has been undertaken

[2]These are bodies set up by Local Authorities under the Children Act 2004. The purpose is to coordinate and ensures the effectiveness of member agencies in safeguarding and promoting the welfare of children. Membership consists of senior representatives from all organizations that work with children and families, including adults.

in Asia—India, Philippines, Thailand; Africa—Congo, South Africa, Kenya; South America—Brazil, Columbia; and Eastern Europe—Estonia, Russia, Georgia. In the Philippines, a resource centre has also become established to support local teams and work across the region. This successful model is now being rolled out in Argentina and South Africa through the *Program de Capacitación Internacional de ISPCAN* (PROCAPI) in Patagonia and Childline South Africa, respectively. An important consequence of these initiatives has been the subsequent development of local child protection teams and further work undertaken at a strategic level to prevent and intervene in cases of child maltreatment.

Data Collection and Evaluation Systems

As was noted at the beginning of this paper we have not yet implemented systems which enable us to know how many children are being maltreated. We do, however, know that these numbers are greater than those reflected in official statistics. For example, a recent UK study by Radford et al. (2011) found that 11 times more young people reported being maltreated than were known to statutory children's social care services.

A number of countries are developing or refining their national child protection data systems (for further information, see Gray and Bowen 2010) and in a recent ISPCAN survey some 54 % (of 68 respondents) reported maintaining an official count of child maltreatment cases (Dubowitz 2012). ISPCAN continues to support these developments through its child protection data collection working group in recognition of the importance of having robust systems for collecting data and just as importantly of using these data for strategic planning. Its website (http://www.ispcan.org) has resources to assist professionals who are developing their own data collection system and the ISPCAN Child Abuse Screening Tool (ICAST) instruments (available in a number of languages) which can be administered to populations of older children, young adults and parents/caregivers to examine the occurrence and types of violence against children.

As well as having systems for knowing how many children are being maltreated, it is also important to be continually evaluating if the current systems and ways of working are effective. Again we know more about what professionals do than how effective their work is. This is particularly so when it comes to preventive programs which by their very nature make it challenging to measure the impact they have on improving outcomes for children.

In England, an overview of a major safeguarding children research initiative was published in 2011 (Davies and Ward 2011). It summarizes the findings from 15 individual studies which were commissioned by the government to support the development of a stronger evidence base in the following three areas:

- Identification and initial response to neglect;
- Effective interventions after abuse or its likelihood have been identified;
- Effective inter-agency and inter-disciplinary working to safeguard children.

Each of these areas was selected as it was considered to be significant in the statutory inquiry into the violent death of Victoria Climbie at the hand of her caregivers (Cm 5730 2003). The findings are being used currently to inform improvements in policy and practice. Their use provides an example of action that can be taken using a program of research to improve outcomes for children.

From Protection to Prevention

Although we know that "programs that prevent occurrence of abuse are likely to be more effective than those that address its consequences" (Davies and Ward 2011). Actioning prevention programs can be low on the national priority list. There may be because, e.g., there is a more pressing need to do something about the children who are being abused or neglected today and/or due to resourcing constraints. There is evidence of the importance of prevention becoming a higher priority in some countries and in a recent ISPCAN survey (Dubowitz 2012), of 63 respondents, the four most common prevention strategies used were prosecution of child abuse offenders (96 %), advocacy for children's rights (95 %), professional training (90 %), and media campaigns to raise public awareness (89 %). However, some of the strategies were not considered to be effective. For example, prosecuting child abuse offenders was reported to be effective by just over a third of respondents (38 %) in contrast to the other three areas. The picture was brighter in other areas, with professional training, advocacy, and media campaigns being reported to be successful by 60, 56 and 63 % of respondents, respectively.

The majority of respondents to the ISPCAN study also reported four other strategies being available: improving or increasing local services (73 %), universal health care and access to preventive medical care (85 %), improving living conditions (89 %), and increasing individual responsibilities for child protection (60 %). However, it was also reported that these first three strategies appeared to be more widely used in countries within the Oceania and European Regions and were more commonly reported by high and middle income rather than low income countries.

In addition less than half the respondents reported the following services as being used in their countries: home-based services and support for at risk families, risk assessments to target families at high risk for child maltreatment and universal home visitation programs for new parents. Here, low and middle income countries reported these strategies are being used less often than high income ones. Interestingly less than a third thought they had been effective. This is despite evidence that the "most effective targeted programs to prevent maltreatment and neglect are home visiting schemes and multi-component schemes" (Davies and Ward 2011). Programs such as the Triple P-Positive Parenting Program (Prinz et al. 2009), Nurse Family Partnership programs (Barnes et al. 2009; Olds et al. 1994, 2002, 2004) and the Webster-Stratton Incredible Years program (Hutchings et al. 2009; Webster-Stratton and Reid 2010) have all had positive evaluations.

It is clear that key challenges remain in not only resourcing preventative work but also in commissioning those services where there is strong evidence of their effectiveness in improving outcomes for children and in training staff to use these approaches competently within their own local setting. Finally there is a need to continue to evaluate preventive approaches and programs in a wide variety of contexts to ensure they can transfer successfully across different cultures, races, languages, and legal jurisdictions.

Conclusion and Recommendations

When we look back over 50 years it is easy to wonder if anything has improved to prevent children suffering harm but there is some cause to be optimistic. Our understanding of the impact of different forms of abuse and neglect has increased dramatically and will continue to do so with the combination of advances in neuro-science and knowledge from practice with children and families. We are using this knowledge to improve services and systems both to protect children and prevent them from violence.

Regular international and national conferences such as this one in Puducherry provide professionals with up to date information on key research and international and national policy developments, as well as support the exchange of information and ideas about new practices.

Leading change is always potentially challenging. This is no less so in the field of child maltreatment where it may be difficult to get communities and politicians to recognize that abuse and neglect is occurring and recurring. The value of collaborative working—at all levels—is not always recognized as being cost effective and supporting good outcomes for children. Here research findings can assist as can the testimonies of children and families who have been helped by professionals working together.

Supporting agencies and staff to work together is an ongoing process, not just a one off and it is crucial for those controlling budgets to recognize its value, even in a difficult fiscal climate. One aspect of being cost effective is ensuring that the services provided are the most effective for the nature of problems being addressed. This may require professionals to move to different ways of working and to stop doing some of their preferred but ineffectual practices. It also requires senior managers and others to move beyond the process indicators of success traditionally used by the sector to those defined by measuring improved outcomes for the child and the protection of their rights.

As Professor Margaret Lynch, a past President of ISPCAN, is keen to point out: effective multi-agency working is "all about building bridges," i.e., ones that join up in the middle and are safe to travel across. We owe it to the children and families we are working with to work effectively with our colleagues and offer the best possible services to prevent maltreatment and to protect children from suffering harm.

References

Barnes, J., Ball, M., Meadows, P., Belsky, J. & the FNP Implementation Research Team (2009). Nurse-family partnership program, second year sites implementation in England. The infancy period. London: Department for Children, Schools and Families and the Department of Health.

Bennett, S., Hart, S., & Wernham, M. (2012). The UN convention on the rights of the child general comment 13: Towards enlightenment and progress for global child protection. In H. Dubowitz (Ed.), *World perspectives on child abuse* (10th ed., pp. 120–123). ISPCAN: Denver.

Carpenter, J., Patsios, D., Szilassy, E., & Hackett, S. (2010). Outcomes of inter-agency training to safeguard children. Research Report DCSF-RR209. London: Department for Children Schools and Families. Retrieved November 30, 2012, from https://www.education.gov.uk/publications/eOrderingDownload/DCSF-RR209.pdf.

Cleaver, H., Unell, I., & Aldgate, J. (2011). Children's needs—parenting capacity. child abuse: Parental mental illness, learning disability, substance misuse, and domestic violence (2nd ed.). London: The Stationery Office. Retrieved November 22, 2011, from https://www.education.gov.uk/publications/eOrderingDownload/Childrens%20Needs%20Parenting%20Capacity.pdf.

Cm 5730. (2003). The victoria climbie inquiry: Report of an inquiry by Lord Laming. London: The Stationery Office.

Davies, C., & Ward, H. (2011). Safeguarding Children across Services: Messages from Research on Identifying and Responding to Child Maltreatment. London: Jessica Kingsley Publishers. Retrieved November 22, 2012, from https://www.education.gov.uk/publications/eOrderingDownload/DFE-RR164.pdf .

Department for Education. (2012). Childhood neglect: Improving outcomes for children. Retrieved November 22, 2012, from http://www.education.gov.uk/childrenandyoungpeople/safeguardingchildren/childhoodneglect/b00209825/training-resources-on-childhood-neglect.

Dubowitz, H. (Ed.). (2012). *World perspectives on child abuse* (10th ed.). ISPCAN: Denver.

General Medical Council. (2012). *Protecting children and young people: The responsibilities of all doctors*. London: General Medical Council.

Gray, J., & Bowen, S. (Eds.). (2010). *World perspectives on child abuse* (Ninth ed.). ISPCAN: Denver.

HM Government. (2010). Working together to safeguard children. London: Department for Children Schools and Families. Retrieved November 30, 2012, from https://www.education.gov.uk/publications/eOrderingDownload/00305-2010DOM-EN.PDF.

Hutchings, J., Bywater, T., Williams, M. E., Shakespeare, M. K., & Whitaker, C. (2009). *Evidence for the extended school aged incredible year's parent program with parents of high-risk 8–16 year olds*. Bangor: School of Psychology, Bangor University.

Kempe, C. H. (1976). Approaches to preventing child abuse: The health visitors concept. *American Journal of Diseases of Children, 130*(9), 941–947. doi:10.1001/archpedi.1976.02120100031005.

Kempe, H., & Steele, B. F. (1962). The battered child syndrome. *Journal of the American Medical Association, 181*, 17–24.

Olds, D., Henderson, C. R., Robert Cole Jr., J. E., Kitzman, H., Luckey, D., Pettitt, L. et al. (2004). Long-term effects of nurse home visitation on children's criminal and antisocial behavior: 15-year follow-up of a randomized controlled trial. *Early Intervention: The essential readings*, 280, 238–255.

Olds, D. L., Henderson, C. R., & Kitzman, H. (1994). Does prenatal and infancy nurse home visitation have enduring effects on qualities of parental care giving and child health at 25–50 months of life? *Pediatrics, 93*, 89–98.

Olds, D. L., Robinson, J., O'Brien, R., Luckey, D. W., Pettitt, L. M., Henderson, C. R., & Talmi, A. (2002). Home visiting by paraprofessionals and by nurses: a randomized, controlled trial. *Pediatrics, 110*(3), 486–496. doi:10.1542/peds.110.3.486).

Pinheiro, P.S. (2006). Report of the Independent expert for the United Nations study on violence against children. New York, NY: United Nations (UN) General Assembly.

Prinz, R. J., Sanders, M. R., Shapiro, C. J., Whitaker, D. J., & Lutzker, J. R. (2009). Population–based prevention of child maltreatment: The US Triple P system population trial. *Prevention Science, 10*(1), 1–12. doi:10.1007/s11121-009-0123-3.

Radford, L., Corral, S., Bradley, C., Fisher, H., Bassett, C., Howat, N., & Collinshaw, S. (2011). Child Abuse and Neglect in the UK Today. NSPCC. http://www.nspcc.org.uk/Inform/research/ findings/child_abuse_neglect_research_PDF_wdf84181.pdf [9 July 2012].

UNICEF. (2012). The State of the World's Children: Children in an Urban World. UNICEF, New York. Retrieved November 22, 2012, from http://www.unicef.org/pubications/index_61789.hmtl.

United Nations Committee on the Rights of the Child. (2011). General Comment No 13: The right of the child to freedom from all forms of violence. Retrieved November 22, 2012, from http://www2.ohchr.org/english/bodies/crc/comments.htm.

Webster-Stratton, C., & Reid, J. (2010). Adapting the incredible years, and evidence-based parenting program, for families involved in the child welfare system. *Journal of Children's Services, 5*(1), 25–42. doi:10.5042/jcs.2010.0115.

Chapter 20
Child Protection in Child Custody Cases: Issues and Concerns

Stefanie Platt, Juhayna Ajami, Nicole Kluemper, Robert Geffner, Morgan Shaw and Alexandra Assalley

Introduction

Child Abuse in Custody Cases

Given the often intense, contentious nature of litigation that surrounds child custody cases, many presume that there are high rates of child abuse allegations between potential custodial parties in these cases. Further, when abuse allegations are involved in child custody cases, people often question whether they are a strategic ploy by parental parties. How often are these allegations made? How often are these allegations valid when gaining custody can be seen as a motive for the allegation? In informal surveys conducted by one of the authors in presentations and conferences for mental health professionals, child custody evaluators, child protection services workers, attorneys, law enforcement, and judges during the past several years, the overwhelming response is that there are child abuse allegations in most child custody cases, and that a majority of them are false.

However, Thoennes and Tjaden (1990) examined these questions using information from formal surveys and interviews with legal and mental health professionals, as well as empirical data from 12 domestic relations courts throughout the United States. Following analysis of these data, Thoennes and Tjaden concluded that only a small proportion (less than 2 %) of contested custody and visitation

S. Platt (✉) · J. Ajami · N. Kluemper · R. Geffner · M. Shaw · A. Assalley
Institute on Violence, Abuse & Trauma, Alliant International University, San Diego, CA, USA
e-mail: stefaniebplatt@gmail.com

R. Geffner
e-mail: bgeffner@pacbell.net

S. Deb (ed.), *Child Safety, Welfare and Well-being*,
DOI 10.1007/978-81-322-2425-9_20

cases involved child sexual abuse (CSA) allegations. Moreover, from a sample of 169 cases, Thoennes and Tjaden found that fathers were accused in 51 % of all cases, but allegations were also made against mothers, mothers' new partners, and extended family members. Similar studies concerning child abuse were then conducted in other countries as well over the next 10 years or so, and none found that the percentage of abuse allegations exceeded a rate of 20 % (Brown et al. 2000; Hume 1995). No study has found that there are a high percentage of child abuse allegations in divorce cases. Thus, the perception that child abuse allegations are rampant in divorce cases is a myth.

When there is an allegation of child abuse, there is often little medical evidence and a lack of independent corroboration from other sources, increasing the difficulty in substantiating allegations of abuse, specifically of CSA (Neoh and Mellor 2009). Moreover, allegations of child abuse involving children under 4 years old are especially difficult to assess due to the child's cognitive limitations and the difficulty verbalizing allegations. Due to these limitations, outcries and disclosures are often made to protective parents by their children (Hewit 1999). Despite this limitation in a child's ability to make a disclosure, true CSA reports may still be interpreted as a weapon in the parent's separation conflict and dismissed outright or ignored when such allegations are made in a child custody case (Bala and Shuman 2000; Myers 1993; Neoh and Mellor 2009).

False Allegations of Child Abuse

When allegations of child physical or sexual abuse are made, either through disclosure by a child, suspicions from parents, observations of professionals or others in contact with the child, an assessment of the probability of the allegations being true and the future risk to the child is needed (Faller 2007b; Neoh and Mellor 2009). However, there is also a widespread misperception that there is a high incidence of intentionally false allegations of child abuse made by parents, specifically mothers, in the context of parental separation and divorce in order to gain a tactical advantage or to seek revenge on their ex-spouses. Trocme and Bala (2005) suggest that confusion defining false allegations is a key source of misunderstanding in the debate about false allegations. Specifically, it is important to distinguish allegations that are false from those where abuse cannot be substantiated but remains suspected, and from those which are misperceived or misinterpreted. Trocme and Bala (2005) note that because many jurisdictions and studies do not distinguish between suspected, unsubstantiated, and intentionally false allegations, confusion in interpretation of investigation statistics is probable. It should be noted that "false" allegations are defined as those in which a person makes an allegation of abuse when s/he knows it did not happen. When a person believes that abuse occurred due to misinterpreting or misperceiving an observation, statement, or behavior, then that should be labeled as such and differentiated from those intentionally false ones.

Rates of unsubstantiated abuse reported by child welfare services range from 30 to 70 % in the United States. Further, 60 % of investigations tracked in the United States reported by the third National Incidence Study were unsubstantiated. Trocme and Bala (2005) suggest that most unsubstantiated investigations are the result of well-intentioned reports triggered by a suspicious injury, concerning behavior, or a misunderstood story, rather than an intentionally fabricated allegation. These are different, as noted above, from false allegations. However, too often many people and the media then use the term "false" to lump together and describe all for these categories.

Despite many unsubstantiated abuse reports being well intended, common misconceptions exist about false allegations being intentionally produced by parents and children alike in divorce cases. Children, specifically, have been a key focus of studies on the probability and ability to coach a child. Studies examining children's eyewitness accounts and the susceptibility of children to suggestion from adults have concluded that children, especially children under the age of five, are vulnerable to certain types of suggestion (Neoh and Mellor 2009). They conclude, however, that children are mostly accurate in oral accounts of their experiences (Ceci and Bruck 1993). Further, Seidl (1992) postulated that it is very difficult to make young children stick to a repetition of a false or programmed story because it is difficult for them to fabricate elaborate allegations on their own, especially if they have no cognitive or experiential knowledge of the events or behaviors. Moreover, most research on abuse reports is based on studies with compelling medical evidence, audiovisual evidence, or other independent indicators of abuse occurring without a child's disclosure (Faller 2007a). Numerous studies of this kind suggest that false negatives occur at statistically significant and much higher rates than false positives in reports of abuse (Faller 2007a). Subsequently, research suggests that children are more likely to refrain from reporting actual abuse than to fabricate stories of abuse. However, this often seems to be ignored in child custody cases.

Evidence of whether children can be programmed or coerced into false allegations of abuse is rather scarce due to ethical limitations in conducting such research. Studies related to the prevalence of false allegations of abuse, however, are not. For instance, as noted above, Thoennes and Tjaden (1990) found that only a small percent (less than 2 %) of 6,100 Family Court cases actually involved reports of child sexual abuse. Further, Thoennes and Tjaden (1990) noted that half of these reports of child sexual abuse in divorces cases in the United States were confirmed to be true, one third were confirmed to be untrue (including false as well as misinterpreted), and the rest were unclear. They found that age of the victim, frequency of the alleged abuse, prior abuse reports, and the amount of time elapsing between filing for divorce and the emergence of the allegation were all associated with the perceived validity of the abuse report.

Likewise, Jones and Seig (1988) many years ago investigated 20 cases of child sexual abuse allegations in custody cases and found most these allegations to be reliable. Specifically, these researchers found 70 % of these cases to be true, 20 %

to be false allegations, and the rest of the cases to be unsubstantiated due to lack of evidence. Similarly, Faller (1991) found that only 15–25 % of the 136 cases she researched contained false allegations, while the majority of cases substantiated allegations of abuse. Further, the US Department of Health and Human Services, Administration on Children (2003) reported that less than 1 % of investigated cases in five states in the United States in 2002 were found to have intentionally falsified reports of abuse. Specific to false allegations involved in child custody disputes, studies have concluded that rates of intentionally false allegations range from 4 to 15 % (Bala and Shuman 2000; Brown et al. 1998; Faller 1991; Faller and DeVoe 1995; Thoennes 1988).

Of allegations that were determined to be intentionally false, Jones and McGraw (1987) found that 6 % of allegations were made by parents and 2 % of these allegations were made by children. Years later, Oates et al. (2000) replicated Jones and McGraw's study, finding that 2.5 % of false accounts were by children and that less than 1 % of cases involved adult-child collaborative false allegations, such as coaching. Although there are many theories of why false allegations may also be more likely at the time of parental separation, it appears that children make relatively few false disclosures. Subsequently, such allegations, despite concerns about malicious motivations in custody cases, should be taken very seriously and should be attended to in the same investigative fashion as allegations outside of the Family Court since the research has been clear that allegations of child abuse in divorce cases are not rampant, and no more likely to be false than in any other situation. A key issue here, then, is the suggestibility of children to make an allegation of abuse.

Suggestibility

Some question the ability of young children to report accurately on their traumatic experiences (i.e., Ceci and Bruck 1993; London et al. 2005) and imply that suggestibility plays a major role in our inability to extract true and accurate information (Poole and Lindsay 2001). Lyon (1999) came up with the term "the new wave" to describe said individuals because in the history of this debate, this cohort represents a new wave of disbelievers of the idea that children can accurately report past events. Studies have shown that children as young as 3 years old can provide useful and factually accurate information regarding traumatic experiences such as abuse (Leander et al. 2007), intrusive medical procedures (Melinder and Gilstrap 2009), and having witnessed the murder of a loved one (McWilliams et al. 2013). Other research has focused on ways forensic interviewers can reduce suggestion and, therefore, reduce the potential for suggestibility by implementing specific interview protocols (Cronch et al. 2006; Crossman et al. 2002; Lamb et al. 2003; London 2001; Saywitz et al. 2010). Still others suggest that certain mental exercises prior to the interview can increase recall (Drohan-Jennings et al. 2010).

New wave researchers tend to harbor a debate regarding the relative importance of social versus cognitive factors that underlie suggestibility (Bruck and Melnyk 2004). Some hypothesize that suggestibility is the result of a desire to comply on the part of the child respondent, while others see suggestibility as the inability to recall correctly as a result of cognitive limitations (Bruck and Melnyk 2004). In terms of the former, studies have shown that children can accurately reject false suggestions (Drohan-Jennings et al. 2010). This weakens the position that compliance drives so-called "false reporting." Moreover, the new wave fails to recognize that children are actually motivated not to report occurrences of sexual abuse. Lawson and Chaffin (1992) found that 57 % of children who had been abused and diagnosed with a sexually transmitted disease (STD), failed to report the abuse which allowed for the transmission of said STD. Children may be disinclined to report such experiences due to shame, embarrassment, fear of retribution, or a sense of loyalty to the abuser.

With regard to the idea that suggestibility is a cognitive weakness, new wave researchers have hypothesized that trauma experiences are in and of themselves enough to cause such a cognitive weakness. Some from this camp go so far as to hypothesize that such a weakness is biological, and that such children are more prone to report traumatic experiences because they are more prone to fantasy and, therefore, more dissociative (Giesbrecht et al. 2007, 2008; Merckelbach and Muris 2001; Merckelbach et al. 2007). With regard to the latter, known as the fantasy model of dissociation, recent research has not supported the idea that individuals are inherently fantasy prone and thus more suggestible (Kluemper and Dalenberg in press). In fact, recent research does not support the idea that suggestibility, dissociation, or being prone to fantasy are in any way correlated with reported trauma experiences (Chae et al. 2011; Kluemper and Dalenberg in press; Leander et al. 2007).

Bruck and Melnyk (2004) go on to state that demographic variables, gender, traditional tests of memory, executive functioning, social engagement, self-concept/self-efficacy, emotional state, IQ, and children's behavioral symptoms all failed to significantly correlate with suggestibility overall. This in no way discounts the research that suggests that young children can be relied upon to provide accurate reporting in the right set of circumstances. In several studies, the child's memory for the specific event (as opposed to memory in general) was negatively correlated with suggestibility for the same event (March and Howe 1995; Marche 1999; Pezdek and Roe 1995).

Bruck and Melnyk (2004) also found that increased language skills correlated negatively with suggestibility in a total of four studies (three conducted in English and one in German). How does this finding impact our ability to trust the accuracy of the reports of very young children? Perhaps looking at the problem from a different perspective would help. Ahern et al. (2011) conducted research in which they attempted to assess the ability of children of increasing age to intentionally deceive. This research concluded that before the age of 3½, participants were unable to maintain false claims across questions. By 3½, the majority of normally developing children are becoming increasingly verbal. As stated previously, studies have shown that children as young as three can provide accurate reports of known (laboratory controlled) events (Leander et al. 2007), and they can be relied upon to provide details in non-laboratory setting as well.

A significant amount of research has been conducted regarding the optimal circumstances under which a child's recall is most accurate (i.e., Saywitz et al. 2010; Verkampt and Ginet 2010). For example, Bright-Paul and Jarrold (2012) found that, not surprisingly, repetition of misinformation regarding an event following that event increases suggestibility for that event. Some hypothesize that the way in which suggestibility is measured impacts the outcome (Roma et al. 2011). Melinder and Gilstrap (2009) suggest that the nature of the relationship between the child and the interviewer is key. Still others suggest mentally preparing the child by having them recall details about the environment in which the abuse took place (Drohan-Jennings et al. 2010) or implementing a verbal labeling procedure (Kulkofsky 2010) in which children are taught about the elements of complete accounts of past events reduces suggestibility. Finally, there is significant research regarding the format of the questions to utilize when questioning a child to avoid leading them (i.e., open-ended vs. forced choice, multiple choice, true/false; Faller and Everson 2012; Rocha et al. 2013).

Typically, new wave researchers conduct studies in which they attempt to implant false memories of some common events or situations, while those attempting to show the reliability of children's testimony tend to look more at true events and the ability to recall in the face of various types of questioning. When one considers the real world effects of type I versus type II error in this situation, it seems clear to some that the safety of the child is of the utmost importance. New wave researchers, on the other hand, feel the opposite: that even one falsely accused parent is unacceptable compared to an abused child who is not identified (Herman 2009). Both positions have some merit, although the safety of the child does seem to be paramount in this instance.

In the end, there is a science behind the currently accepted format for interviewing children (Saywitz et al. 2010). It involves setting up an age-appropriate, private environment in which to conduct the interview, age-appropriate explanation of the purpose of the interview, and use of general open-ended and non-leading questions. The interviewer must also provide a supportive and non-threatening atmosphere, while matching the demands of the interview to the child's stage of development (Saywitz et al. 2010). When appropriate interview protocols are utilized, children can be relied upon to provide accurate accounts of past experiences (see below for more discussion of forensic interviewing models and appropriate evaluation techniques).

"Parental Alienation Syndrome" (PAS/PAD)

Coined by Richard Gardner in 1988, Parental Alienation Syndrome (PAS) has been a term most commonly used in high conflict divorce and child custody cases when there are allegations of child abuse (Gardner 1992). The general concept of PAS is that a child will have a strong alignment with one parent while rejecting a relationship with the other parent without "legitimate justification" (Bernet 2010; Gardner 1992). In these cases, a child reportedly refuses contact with the rejected parent and harbors "irrational anxiety and/or hostility" toward him/her (Bernet 2010). Controversial since its inception, its proponents have spawned different versions of it over the past two decades, including more recently Parental Alienation Disorder (PAD) and Parental Alienation Relational Problem (Bernet 2010). Due to a lack of any empirical and peer-reviewed research, PAS/PAD has been discredited by a wide portion of mental health professionals (Geffner et al. 2009a, b; Walker and Shapiro 2010; Zorza 2009) and almost all professional organizations. It was also excluded from the most recent version of the Diagnostic and Statistical Manual of Mental Disorders (DSMV) (American Psychiatric Association 2013; Faller 2010). Despite the lack of evidence supporting it, PAS continues to be used in family courts around the world, and the assumptions behind it have influenced child protective services (Geffner et al. 2009a, b). In order to ensure the safety and well-being of parents and children, it is essential for the various parties involved in such cases to develop a thorough understanding of the dynamics involved in parental rejection.

What Is PAS/PAD?

In an effort to include it in the DSM-V, proponents of parental alienation have created four proposed diagnostic criteria for PAD (Bernet 2010). This is interesting in that the theory and foundation of such a supposed disorder was created two decades after it was formulated, with no research support. What is also interesting is that much of the ideas behind PAS/PAD are circular (i.e., since the allegation of abuse is not believed, then it much be false, and since it must be false, someone had to program or coach the child to make up the allegation, and they must be alienated from the accused parent, and the person who has supposedly the most to gain is the parent who supports the child, which therefore means that parent suffers from PAS/PAD). For good recent reviews of the lack of research, theory, and the issues with PAS/PAD, see Meier (2009) and Pepiton et al. (2012).

Parental Alienation Versus Rejection Due to Abuse

An excellent article over a decade ago defined and pointed out the important differences among alienation, abuse, rejection, estrangement, and alignment (Kelly and Johnston 2001). When evaluators and/or the court suspect the presence of parental alienation, it is important to consider the various factors that could lead to a child rejecting his/her parent. Drozd and Olesen (2004) describe several of these factors, including normal developmental variation, poor parenting, and abuse. Knowledge about the dynamics of physical, emotional, and sexual abuse is particularly essential in cases where abuse is alleged, as not all abused children exhibit the same characteristics. For instance, while some may try to avoid contact with the abusive parent, others maintain a strong attachment to him/her. An evaluator must understand these dynamics in order to avoid the mistake of ruling out abuse in favor of parental alienation. In addition, evaluators must be aware of the emotional effects of domestic violence on children (Geffner et al. 2009a, b). A child could feel anger toward and reject his/her parent due to observing domestic violence in the home, even if the child is not a direct target of the abuse (Walker and Shapiro 2010). Furthermore, a child could align with one parent over another due to feeling anger about the separation and/or divorce (Walker and Shapiro 2010). Finally, it is essential to note that there is little to no evidence regarding a parent's ability or the techniques to use to program or alienate his/her child against the other parent (Geffner et al. 2009a, b). A clear understanding of these various dynamics is essential in order to ensure that evaluators and court officials do not dismiss a child's outcries due to misconceptions about parental rejection due to abuse and protective parenting versus parental alienation.

Alienation Versus Protective Parenting

One of the major criticisms of PAS is its poor consideration of the role of domestic violence and child abuse in children's behavior. Behavior that is typically indicative of abuse is instead considered to be further proof of alienation. Additionally, the child's rejection is attributed to the preferred parent's behaviors, which reportedly cause the child to develop a false belief that the rejected parent is somehow dangerous or bad (Bernet 2010). These behaviors include speaking ill of the rejected parent in front of the child and complaints to child protection and law enforcement agencies with allegations about the rejected parent (Bernet 2010).

Claims of parental alienation are particularly common in situations where fathers have been abusive toward their children and accuse mothers of alienating the children against them (Walker and Shapiro 2010). In these cases, mothers typically report their child's outcries of abuse to the authorities and, under Child Protective Services' (CPS) guidance, may remove the children from the home or make recommendations for restricted access to the child for the accused parent. The mothers in the above situations are often referred to as protective parents, as they are responsible for ensuring their child's safety (there are also protective fathers when the situation is reversed). If the protective parent does not fulfill this duty, CPS will likely remove the child from her/his care for "failure to protect." Protective parents often find themselves in a bind. If they try to protect their child by removing him/her from the home and limiting contact with the abuser, they could be accused of alienating the child from the abusive parent. If they continue to allow contact with the abusive parent, however, they could risk having their child re-victimized and ultimately removed from their care due to a failure to protect him/her.

CPS, law enforcement, and/or mental health professionals often become involved in these cases in order to evaluate the child's allegations of abuse and recommend a custody arrangement that best ensures the child's safety. Proponents of PAS, however, state that in addition to protective parents, mental health and child protection workers have the ability to help alienate a child against his/her parent (Bernet 2010). Although one of the diagnostic criterions for PAD is that the diagnosis should not be assigned in cases where the rejection is "justified" and abuse or neglect have occurred, the above statement undermines those who are responsible for determining the veracity of abuse allegations. By instilling a sense of doubt regarding these workers' evaluations and recommendations, proponents of parental alienation ensure that the rejection of a parent is never "justified," even in circumstances where allegations of abuse are substantiated.

In cases where the court finds that parental alienation has occurred, proponents of PAS/PAD recommend increased contact with the rejected parent as an intervention strategy (Walker and Shapiro 2010). A misinformed judge and/or evaluator could place a child at risk of re-victimization if this occurs. In some cases, judges have also been known to award custody to the rejected parent and restrict access between the child and protective parent. This is particularly alarming in cases of abuse, as survivors of trauma need to feel a sense of safety in order to heal (Walker and Shapiro 2010). In these situations, children would likely develop Post Traumatic Stress Disorder (PTSD) or other symptomatology due to their continued exposure to the "traumatic trigger" without the presence of a source of support or safety (Walker and Shapiro 2010). The entire series of recommendations by proponents of PAS/PAD ignore decades of research and theory in child development, attachment, and separation trauma. In summary, serious and often dangerous repercussions can arise from the use of PAS/PAD in child custody cases. Therefore, it is extremely essential that a thorough and exhaustive evaluation of the child and parents' behaviors be completed in order to determine the true cause of parental rejection, not unsupported labels and syndromes.

Appropriate Protocols for Evaluating Child Abuse

Child maltreatment is something that happens far more frequently than one may think. According to ChildHelp.org, a foundation that was created in order to prevent and treat child abuse, every year there are more than 3 million child abuse reports made within the United States alone (http://www.childhelp.org). As such, it is important that mental health clinicians be appropriately trained in conducting child abuse evaluations. While there has not yet been a "standardized" structure for conducting child abuse evaluations, there have been models that are "suggested" as being the standard in which one should conduct an evaluation.

First and foremost, there are important concepts to keep in mind when doing a child abuse evaluation. For instances, there is only so much an evaluator can ascertain when he or she has not witnessed the abuse. Additionally, it is rather rare that victims of CSA sustain physical injuries as a result of their experienced abuse. Unfortunately, this often complicates things, as without physical evidence (including the presence of sexually transmitted infections, semen, and vaginal or anal abrasions); it is often difficult for one to substantiate abuse. This, however, does not mean that abuse did not occur. In fact, due to the rarity of the presence of physical or medical evidence (in a major study, over 90 % of the cases of confirmed CSA did not have such evidence; Heger et al. 2002), it is even more important for those conducting forensic evaluations to utilize appropriate interviewing techniques in order to try and determine the likelihood of the child having been victimized.

According to Faller (2007b), there are six ways in which one can determine the likelihood that child abuse occurred. Those six ways consist of the following: (1) the child having the ability to verbally or behaviorally describe sexual behavior; (2) the child being able to provide detail as to the framework in which the abuse occurred; (3) the child's affect while describing the abuse; (4) the presence of medical or physical evidence that corroborates with the child's disclosure; (5) a confession from the accused perpetrator; and (6) collateral statements from those whom have witnessed the abuse.

Assessment Models

Comprehensive Forensic Evaluation Models

Keeping all of the above in mind, it is important to discuss the child abuse investigation protocols that are available. In addition to the six investigative techniques mentioned above, one investigative tool that is available is called CHIC. According to Everson and Faller (2012), CHIC stands for "comprehensive, hypothesis-testing, idiographic, corroborative" and is a comprehensive forensic evaluation model (CFE) that is used with CSA allegations.

Within the *Comprehensive* phase of the interview, there is a focus on obtaining information from several different sources (Everson and Faller 2012). It is important to gather all of the following: agency records, medical examinations, interviews with all parent figures and caregivers, collateral interviews, interviews with the alleged abuser, and behavior ratings as completed by adults who know the child. Everson and Faller also argue that this phase of the evaluation is strengthened when combined with a multidisciplinary team approach that can include investigations by CPS as well as law enforcement personnel (see also APSAC 2012; Faller 2007a).

The *hypothesis-testing* stage is a phase that is designed to help the evaluator examine other possible explanations for the alleged abuse. This phase allows for the evaluator to take the information available and determine what is the best possible explanation for all of the information presented. According to the literature, when conducting hypothesis-testing, it is important to be "case-specific" (Everson and Faller 2012), as it is from this testing that one determines which assessments to utilize.

Idiographic assessment is thought of as an accompaniment to hypothesis-testing. The notion behind idiographic assessment is that all cases are unique; as such, they need to be treated this way. By approaching the case in this manner, the evaluator will be able to not only examine key components of the case, but better piece together what may have happened. The idiographic approach creates a situation in which the evaluator can take the information provided and test the proposed hypotheses in an attempt to determine which scenario most likely occurred.

The final component of the CHIC approach is the *corroborative* phase. It is during this stage in which the evaluator seeks out "independent verification" for the case (Everson and Faller 2012). Often times such verification can come in the form of documentation, independent witnesses, and/or information from non-involved individuals. The strength of the corroborative information is positively correlated with the emphasis given on the specific evidence that is being supported (Everson and Faller 2012). The key in the last two phases is that each case is handled individually without assumptions being made, and that full investigations and assessments of the likelihood of child abuse are conducted, and whether this is a child custody case is not relevant.

Assessment of Parent–Child Interaction

Additionally, when evaluating for the possibility of child abuse, it is also important that the evaluator assess the parent–child interactions (National Crime Victims Research and Treatment Center 2003; Faller 2007b). According to the literature, it is important for the evaluator to not only examine the relationship between the alleged offender and victim, but also the alleged protective parent and victim (National Crime Victims Research and Treatment Center 2003; Saunders and Meinig 2001). This suggests that the evaluator examines attachment style, as well as "communication, affectional connection, styles of conflict management, discipline practices, and levels of trust" (National Crime Victims Research and Treatment Center 2003, p. 26).

Utilizing a Forensic Interview

When trying to determine whether the child may have been a victim of abuse, Faller (2007a) indicates that it is important to assess the child to determine if he or she has verbal statements or physical behaviors (indicative of sexuality or sexualized behavior—see below) that are considered to be beyond what is considered to be within age appropriate development. A forensic interview would provide the setting in which these behaviors or statements could be explored further. Heiman (1992) argues that the more specific details that a child can provide, the higher the likelihood that the child has been a victim of abuse. According to Heiman, there is a strong agreement among professionals regarding the relationship between explicit details and the increased likelihood of having experienced abuse.

While it was previously mentioned that there is no universal standard for conducting the evaluation, many agencies, like those of Child Advocacy Centers (CAC), have created minimum standards that are required in order for the interviewer to be credentialed in forensic interviewing. In fact the National Association of Certified Child Forensic Interviewers (NACCFI) has developed such standards in order to ensure "fidelity to practice, evidence of practice competency and evidence of the applicant having good moral character" (NACCFI 2014, p. 4). In addition, Saywitz et al. (2011) suggested a method for interviewing children that has been included in the American Professional Society on the Abuse of Children's (APSAC) (2011) handbook. A forensic interview is a key part of the evaluation.

Based upon the available empirical evidence, it is suggested that a forensic interview consist of the following components: (1) rapport development, (2) narrative practice, (3) introducing the topic of abuse, (4) avoiding concepts that confuse children, (5) instructions to children, (6) phrasing of questions, (7) evidence-based strategies for eliciting details, and (8) multiple interviews (APSAC 2012; Saywitz et al. 2011). It is important for the interviewer to be cognizant of his or her environment, demeanor, and the child's level of comfort, as well as even subtle suggestibility (Saywitz et al. 2011). Moreover, there has been a debate within the field as to how structured one should make the interview. Forensic interviews can range from completely unstructured, in which the child is left to run the interview, to that of highly structured, in which the entire interview is scripted out. The preferred semi-structured or structured formats allow for the interviewer to utilize a "phased approach" in which the evaluator helps the child prepare for the interview, gather information, and then close the interview (Saywitz et al. 2011).

During the preparation phase, the interviewer introduces him or herself, develops rapport with the client, has the child promise to tell the truth or ensure they understand the concept of truth, practice narratives, and receive instructions. It is also important to keep in mind that children respond to adults' demeanor. If the child thinks that he or she is answering incorrectly because the interviewer asks the same question repeatedly, or is in some type of trouble, there is a higher likelihood that the child will not disclose or will recant any previous disclosure. Additionally, it is important for the interviewer to encourage the child to be as verbal as possible, and for the interviewer to instruct the child that it is okay for him or her to say he or she does not know an answer or does not understand the question being asked as this provides the child a sense of control and assists with clarification. When working with children, it is important that the language that is being utilized is age appropriate.

When additional information is needed, the interviewer should utilize mostly "Wh" questions consisting of what, where, when, why, who, and how, in order to prompt the child to provide details that may not have been provided through free recall (Hershkowitz and Terner 2007; LaRooy et al. 2009; Saywitz et al. 2011).

Evidence-Based Models of Forensic Interviews

There are some major models of forensic interviewing that are widely accepted in the field of child abuse, and then various hybrids of these that are currently in use. These models include: The National Institute of Child Health and Human Development (NICHD) model (Lamb et al. 2003, 2007) and its recent modified version (Brown et al. 2013), the National Child Advocacy Centers (NCAC) model (National Children's Advocacy Center 2011), the Corner house/Finding Words RATAC (Rapport, Anatomy identification, Touch inquiry, Abuse scenario, and Closure) model (Anderson et al. 2009), and the recent RADAR (Recognizing Abuse Disclosure types And Responding) model protocol (Everson et al. 2014). These vary in rigidity of structure in questioning the child, the time spent in rapport building, the order of the questioning and engagement of the child, the flexibility on the types of questions asked, the use of demonstration aids such as anatomically detailed drawings or dolls, and the time spent in the interview. For a discussion of the comparison of the various models, see Toth (2011). Unfortunately, what appears to be happening in too many child custody cases where there are child abuse allegations is that a standard professional forensic or other interview of the child following one of these models does not occur because of the preset biases and assumptions noted above.

Impact of Multiple Forensic Interviews

Currently, there is a debate within the field regarding whether multiple interviews could be either beneficial or detrimental to the child (Faller 2007b; Tishelman and Geffner 2010). Another myth often promoted in the media and to many in the CPS field is that only one forensic interview can be conducted with a child to determine the likelihood of abuse. This was derived from a misinterpretation of the Ceci and Bruck (1995) research about the effect of repeated interviews. What was not realized is that their research focused on repeated interviews of a child that were coercive, manipulative, misleading and often reinforced by a trusted person. It is now much more widely recognized in the child abuse field that to ascertain whether the child was likely abused, especially younger children, extended interview sessions may be needed (Faller 2007b). When this occurs, the likelihood of false negatives decreases significantly while not increasing false positives (Faller 2007b; Lyon 1999; Poole and White 1991, 1993, 1995). This may be even more relevant for a child custody case where several issues are involved within the family situation. For a discussion of extended forensic interviews, see Faller et al. (2010) and Tishelman and Geffner (2010).

Sensitivity Versus Specificity in Child Abuse Evaluations

The field of forensic child abuse evaluations is one that is tremendously challenging and frequently debated. Due to the controversial topic of these evaluations, the issue of managing sensitivity versus specificity in these assessments is incredibly important, especially in child custody cases. Ensuring that innocent men and women are not being found guilty of child abuse when none has taken place (i.e., specificity), while also making certain that children are not being overlooked when abuse is occurring (i.e., sensitivity) is a difficult challenge, but one of high importance. Child abuse evaluations are typically conducted without the availability of concrete evidence, such as medical or photographic evidence, or eyewitnesses as mentioned above. Evaluators must often rely on the diagnostic validity of a number of potential indicators to increase the accuracy and likelihood of correct identification.

There are researchers who believe that an emphasis on specificity has long dominated the field of forensic assessment of child abuse and they are now promoting a realignment of perspectives within the field (Everson and Faller 2012; Faller and Everson 2012). While much of the literature is specific to CSA evaluations, many of the same principles and concepts can be applied to physical, emotional, and verbal abuse as well. Due to the serious and controversial nature of this debate, further consideration of this topic is merited. The concept of sensitivity, as it relates to child abuse, refers to the correct identification of true victims of abuse, or a true positive. Specificity, on the other hand, refers to the correct identification of those individuals who have not been abused, or a true negative. While a perfect predictor would be described as 100 % sensitive (i.e., identifying all children who had been abused as abuse victims) and 100 % specific (i.e., identifying all children who had not been abused as non-abused), in reality, for any test or procedure, there is typically a trade-off between the measures.

In the book, *the evaluation of child sexual abuse allegations: A comprehensive guide to assessment and testimony* (Kuehnle and Connell 2009), Herman distinguishes between "hard" and "soft" evidence in CSA evaluations. He considers "hard" evidence to be anything that definitively proves or disproves the occurrence of sexual abuse in a child abuse assessment, such as photographic or DNA evidence or a perpetrator confession. "Soft" evidence, in his view, would then include anything that requires substantial professional judgment, such as a child's own disclosure, school reports of behavior changes, or a teacher or therapist's description of a child's sexual acting out behaviors. Since "hard" evidence is not frequently found in cases of CSA assessments, evaluators must often rely on the analysis of "soft", or psychosocial, evidence (Everson and Faller 2012). However, Herman condemned the use of "soft" evidence in the determination of sexual abuse, arguing that the use of such evidence has been empirically shown to be unreliable. In response, there have been several points of contention within the research concerning Herman's standpoint on this issue (Everson and Faller 2012; Myers 2012).

First, there is disagreement over the dichotomy that Herman has drawn between "hard" and "soft" evidence of sexual abuse. He cited no authority as to where these definitions came from and did not indicate why he suggests that "hard" evidence helps in the search for truth, but "soft" evidence does not (Myers 2012). Similarly, it is unclear why he equated a child's verbal description or disclosure of abuse with "soft" evidence, but a perpetrator's confession with "hard" evidence. While it is true that it can be difficult to evaluate the truthfulness of a child's statement, the same can be said for adults, and Herman already described a perpetrator's confession as "hard" evidence. Many researchers contend that children's statements, particularly when acquired through an appropriate forensic interview as discussed above, are critical elements to a good forensic child abuse evaluation. These researchers vehemently disagree with Herman's belief that they hold no probative value other than in the search for actual "hard" evidence (Everson and Faller 2012; Myers 2012).

The diagnostic utility of children's disclosures of abuse is a specific topic that has been debated within the literature. It is also important to be able to discriminate between the true positive rate and the false positive rate, as they are often viewed as inverses of each other, which is incorrect. They are calculated based on different groups of children; the true positive rate is calculated based on children who have been abused, while the false positive rate is based on children who have not been abused (Lyon et al. 2012). Confusion over these terms can also lead to what is considered by many as the inverse fallacy (Kaye and Koehler 1991). It has been argued that some researchers have been dismissing the use of relevant evidence, such as a child's disclosure, by committing the inverse fallacy (Lyon et al. 2012).

There is also substantial disagreement in the literature over the reliability, validity, and accuracy of professional judgments about child abuse when these are derived from psychosocial evidence, in general (Faust et al. 2009; Herman 2009). While several studies have examined the psychometric properties of professional judgment in CSA assessments, e.g., (Horner et al. 1993; Jackson and Nuttall 1993), much of the research that Herman based his conclusions on focused primarily on reliability. Reliability is defined as the level of agreement between evaluators who are examining the same evidence (Everson and Faller 2012). To assess for validity and accuracy in research studies examining CSA, one must actually have knowledge about the truth of the abuse allegation. Much of the research that Herman cited used fictional case vignettes without a "true" abuse event, and because of this, he had to deduce the validity and accuracy in the studies, which has been discussed by others as not accurate (Everson and Faller 2012).

While some researchers claim that psychosocial information and evidence does not have the greatest diagnostic utility, others have concluded that acquiring this type of evidence can substantially increase the accuracy of correct identification. This sensitivity versus specificity and the use of "hard" evidence has even broadened to include the issues of sexuality knowledge beyond the developmental level of the child or sexualized behavior by children. Years of research studies by Friedrich et al. (2001) has clearly established normal versus unusual sexual behavior according to age and gender of the child. Certain behaviors that frequently occurred with sexually abused children in order to differentiate them from more typical developmental behaviors were then described in his *Child Sexual Behavior Inventory* (Friedrich 1997) as only being likely if the child was sexually abused or exposed to explicit sexuality. Even though Herman and others indicate this type of evidence is not to be included, it is clear that the use of such research is accepted in the field of CSA (e.g., Everson and Faller 2012) and should therefore be utilized in child custody evaluations (Geffner et al. 2009a). While there will continue to be contested issues in the field of child abuse evaluations, the continued expansion of the research should work toward guiding practice and appropriately informing debate, and these same techniques should then be applied to child custody and child protection cases as well.

Conclusion and Recommendations

As can be seen in this chapter, there has been a myth about the overabundance of allegations of child abuse in child custody cases, and the misperception that a large majority of such allegations are false. The research has never supported either of these assumptions, but they have been widely promoted. The consequence of these misperceptions and myths is that standardized, professional, objective, and neutral evaluations of these allegations do not occur as often as they should by mental health professionals, child custody evaluators, or CPS workers. Thus, even more cases are then labeled as false allegations, sometimes even before an investigation has been conducted, and then this is reified by a poor evaluation.

It is tragic for the children in these cases in which abuse has occurred because they become multiply re-victimized and traumatized: first from the abuse itself, second from the lack of validation and belief by the people who are supposed to evaluate and protect them, third by being taken away, sometimes abruptly without warning, from the protective parent who has been the primary caretaker, fourth by being awarded into the care of the person they accused of abuse, and finally by sometimes not even being allowed to see the protective parent and primary caretaker. In most of these cases, the circular reasoning that leads to these misguided actions is focused on such discredited ideas as PAS/PAD, or its offshoots. Even if these words or terms are not used specifically, the procedures and recommendations are almost exactly what were originally promoted and self-published by Gardner over two decades ago (Gardner 1992).

It is important that all evaluators, courts, law enforcement, CPS workers, and others involved in child custody cases be trained carefully in child abuse dynamics and its research, appropriate techniques and the accepted procedures in evaluations and interviewing before dealing with such cases. It is time to discard myths and assumptions in such cases that often produce invalid conclusions and can lead to re-victimization of child abuse victims. Perhaps then we can avoid the major traumatic adverse effects of such situations, and reduce the long-term consequences for the victims of child abuse in child custody cases.

References

Ahern, E. C., Lyon, T. D., & Quas, J. A. (2011). Young children's emerging ability to make false statements. *Developmental Psychology, 47*, 61–66.

American Professional Society on Abuse of Children (APSAC). (2011). *The APSAC handbook on child maltreatment* (3rd ed.). Thousand Oaks, CA: Sage Publications Inc.

American Professional Society on the Abuse of Children (APSAC). (2012). *Practice guidelines: Forensic interviewing in cases of suspected child abuse.* http://www.apsac.org.

American Psychiatric Association. (2013). *Diagnostic and statistical manual of mental disorders: DSM-5* (5th ed.). Washington, D.C.: Author.

Anderson, J., Ellefson, J., Lashley, J., & Miller, A. L. (2009). Cornerhouse forensic interview protocol: RATAC. *The Thomas M. Cooley Journal of Practical and Clinical Law, 12*, 193–331.

Bala, N., & Shuman, J. (2000). Allegations of sexual abuse when parents have separated. *Allegations of child abuse in the context of parental separation: A discussion paper.* Department of Justice Canada, Research Report, 2001-FCY-4E.

Bernet, W. (2010). *Parental alienation, DSM-5, and ICD-11.* Springfield: Charles C Thomas Publisher.

Bright-Paul, A., & Jarrold, C. (2012). Children's eyewitness memory: Repeating post event misinformation reduces the distinctiveness of a witnessed event. *Memory, 20*(8), 818–835. doi:10.1080/09658211.2012.708345.

Brown, D. A., Lamb, M. E., Lewis, C. N., Pipe, M.-E., Orbach, Y., & Wolfman, M. (2013). Evaluating the NICHD Investigative Interview Protocol: A laboratory study. *Journal of Experimental Psychology: Applied, 19*, 367–382.

Brown, T., Frederico, M., Hewitt, L., & Sheehan, R. (1998). Problems and solutions in the management of child abuse allegations in custody and access disputes in the family court. *Family and Conciliation Courts Review, 36*(4), 431–443.

Brown, T., Frederico, M., Hewitt, L., & Sheehan, R. (2000). Revealing the existence of child abuse in the context of marital breakdown and custody and access disputes. *Child Abuse and Neglect, 24*(6), 849–859.

Bruck, M., & Melnyk, L. (2004). Individual differences in children's suggestibility: A review and synthesis. *Applied Cognitive Psychology, 18*, 947–996. doi:10.1002/acp.1783.

Ceci, S. J., & Bruck, M. (1993). Suggestibility of the child witness: A historical review and synthesis. *Psychological Bulletin, 113*(3), 403.

Ceci, S. J., & Bruck, M. (1995). *Jeopardy in the courtroom: A scientific analysis of children's testimony*. Washington, DC: American Psychological Association.

Chae, Y., Goodman, G. S., Eisen, M. L., & Qin, J. (2011). Event memory and suggestibility in abused and neglected children: Trauma-related psychopathology and cognitive functioning. *Journal of Experimental Child Psychology, 110*(4), 520–538. doi:10.1016/j.jecp.2011.05.006.

Childhelp.org. (1959–2014). National child abuse statistics. http://www.childhelp.org/pages/statistics.

Cronch, L. E., Viljoen, J. L., & Hansen, D. J. (2006). Forensic interviewing in child sexual abuse cases: Current techniques and future directions. *Aggression and Violent Behavior, 11*, 195–207.

Crossman, A., Powell, M., Principe, G., & Ceci, S. (2002). Child testimony in custody cases: A review. *Journal of Forensic Psychology Practice, 2*(1), 1–32.

Drohan-Jennings, D. M., Roberts, K. P., & Powell, M. B. (2010). Mental context reinstatement increases resistance to false suggestions after children have experienced a repeated event. *Psychiatry, Psychology and Law, 17*(4), 594–606. doi:10.1080/13218711003739110.

Drozd, L. M., & Olesen, N. W. (2004). Is it abuse, alienation and/or estrangement? A decision tree. *Journal of Child Custody, 1*(3), 65–106.

Everson, M. D., & Faller, K. (2012). Base rates, multiple indicators, and comprehensive forensic evaluations: Why sexualized behavior still counts in assessments of child sexual abuse allegations. *Journal of Child Sexual Abuse, 21*(1), 45–71. doi:10.1080/10538712.2012.642470.

Everson, M., Ragsdale, C., & Snider, S. (2014). *RADAR forensic interview protocol.* Unpublished manuscript available from author: Mark_Everson@med.unc.edu.
Faller, K. C. (1991). Possible explanations for child sexual abuse allegations in divorce. *American Journal of Orthopsychiatry, 61*, 86–91.
Faller, K. (2007a). Coaching children about sexual abuse: A pilot study of professionals' perceptions. *Child Abuse and Neglect, 31*, 947–959.
Faller, K. C. (2007b). *Interviewing children about sexual abuse: Controversies and best practice*. New York, NY: Oxford University Press Inc.
Faller, K. C. (2010). APSAC responds to inclusion of PAS/PAD information in diagnostic and statistical manual of mental disorders. *The APSAC Advisor, 22*(2&3), 20–23.
Faller, K. C., Cordisco Steele, L., & Nelson-Gardell, D. (2010). Allegations of sexual abuse of a child: What to do when a single forensic interview isn't enough. *Journal of Child Sexual Abuse, 19*(5), 572–589.
Faller, K., & DeVoe, E. (1995). Allegations of sexual abuse in divorce. *Journal of Child Sexual Abuse, 8*(2), 1–23.
Faller, K., & Everson, M. D. (2012). Contested issues in the evaluation of child sexual abuse allegations: Why consensus on best practice remains elusive. *Journal of Child Sexual Abuse, 21*(1), 3–18. doi:10.1080/10538712.2012.642944.
Faust, D., Bridges, A. J., & Ahern, D. C. (2009). Methods for the identification of sexually abused children: Issues and needed features for abuse indicators. In K. Kuehnle & M. Connell (Eds.), *The evaluation of child sexual abuse allegations: A comprehensive guide to assessment and testimony* (pp. 3–19). Hoboken, NJ US: Wiley.
Friedrich, W. N. (1997). *Child sexual behavior inventory: Professional manual*. Lutz, FL: Psychological Assessment Resources Inc.
Friedrich, W. N., Fisher, J. L., Dittner, C., Acton, R., Berliner, L., Butler, J., & Wright, J. (2001). Child sexual behavior inventory: Normative, psychiatric, and sexual abuse comparisons. *Child Maltreatment, 6*(1), 37–49. doi:10.1177/1077559501006001004.
Gardner, R. (1992). *The parental alienation syndrome: A guide for mental health and legal professionals*. Cresskill, NJ: Creative Therapeutics.
Geffner, R., Conradi, L., Geis, K., & Aranda, M. B. (2009a). Conducting child custody evaluations in the context of family violence allegations: Practical techniques and suggestions for ethical practice. *Journal of Child Custody, 6*, 189–218.
Geffner, R., Griffin, D. A., & Lewis, J, I. I. I. (Eds.). (2009b). *Children exposed to violence: Current issues, interventions and research*. Philadelphia, PA: Taylor & Francis Publishers.
Giesbrecht, T., Lynn, S. J., Lilienfeld, S. O., & Merckelback, H. (2008). Cognitive processes in dissociation: An analysis of core theoretical assumptions. *Psychological Bulletin, 134*, 617–647.
Giesbrecht, T., Merckelbach, H., & Geraerts, E. (2007). The dissociative experiences taxon is related to fantasy proneness. *Journal of Nervous and Mental Diseases, 195*(9), 769–772.
Heger, A., Ticson, L., Velasquez, O., & Bernier, R. (2002). Children referred for possible sexual abuse: Medical findings in 2384 children. *Child Abuse and Neglect, 26*(6/7), 645–659.
Heiman, M. L. (1992). *Annotation:* Putting the pieces together: Validating allegations of child sexual abuse. *Journal of Child Psychology, 311*, 317.
Herman, S. (2009). Forensic child sexual abuse evaluations: Accuracy, ethics, and admissibility. In K. Kuehnle & M. Connell (Eds.), *The evaluation of child sexual abuse allegations: A comprehensive guide to assessment and testimony* (pp. 247–266). Hoboken, NJ US: Wiley.
Hershkowitz, I., & Terner, A. (2007). The effects of repeated interviewing on children's forensic statements of sexual abuse. *Applied Cognitive Psychology, 18*, 263–281.
Hewitt, S. K. (1999). *Assessing allegations of sexual abuse in preschool children: Understanding small voices*. London: Sage.
Horner, T. M., Guyer, M. J., & Kalter, N. M. (1993). The biases of child sexual abuse experts: Believing is seeing. *Bulletin of the American Academy of Psychiatry and the Law, 21*(3), 281–292.

Hume, M. (1995). *Study of child sexual abuse allegations within the Family Court of Australia*. Paper presented at Enhancing Access to Justice: Family Court of Australia Second National conference, Sydney, Australia.
Jackson, H., & Nuttall, R. (1993). Clinician responses to sexual abuse allegations. *Child Abuse and Neglect, 17*(1), 127–143. doi:10.1016/0145-2134(93)90013-U.
Jones, D. P. H., & McGraw, J. M. (1987). Reliable and fictitious accounts of sexual abuse to children. *Journal of Interpersonal Violence, 2*(1), 27–45.
Jones, D. P. H., & Seig, A. (1988). Child sexual abuse allegations in custody or visitation disputes: A report of 20 cases. In E. B. Nicholson & J. Bulkley (Eds.), *Sexual abuse allegations in custody and visitation cases* (pp. 22–36). Washington, DC: American Bar Association.
Kaye, D. H., & Koehler, J. J. (1991). Can jurors understand probabilistic evidence? *Journal of the Royal Statistical Society A, 154*, 75–81.
Kelly, J., & Johnston, J. (Eds.). (2001). The alienated child: A reformulation (special issue). *Family Court Review, 39*(3).
Kluemper, N., & Dalenberg, C. (in press). Is the dissociative adult suggestible? A test of the trauma and fantasy models of dissociation. *Journal of Trauma and Dissociation*.
Kuehnle, K., & Connell, M. (2009). *The evaluation of child sexual abuse allegations: A comprehensive guide to assessment and testimony*. Hoboken, NJ US: Wiley.
Kulkofsky, S. (2010). The effects of verbal labels and vocabulary skill on memory and suggestibility. *Journal of Applied Developmental Psychology, 31*(6), 460–466. doi:10.1016/j.appdev.2010.09.002.
Lamb, M., Orbach, Y., Hershkowitz, I., Esplin, P., & Horowitz, D. (2007). A structured forensic interview protocol improves the quality and informativeness of investigative interviews with children: A review of research using the NICHD Investigative Interview Protocol. *Child Abuse and Neglect, 31*, 1201–1231.
Lamb, M. E., Sternberg, K. J., Orbach, Y., Esplin, P. W., Stewart, H., & Mitchell, S. (2003). Age differences in young children's responses to open-ended invitations in the course of forensic interviews. *Journal of Consulting and Clinical Psychology, 71*, 926–934.
LaRooy, D., Lamb, M. E., & Pipe, M. E. (2009). Repeated interviewing: A critical evaluation of the risks and potential benefits. In K. Kuehnle & M. Connell (Eds.), *The evaluation of child sexual abuse allegations* (pp. 327–361). NJ: Wiley.
Lawson, L., & Chaffin, M. (1992). False negatives in sexual abuse disclosure interviews: Incidence and influence of caretaker's belief in abuse in cases of accidental abuse discovery by diagnosis of STD. *Journal of Interpersonal Violence, 7*, 532–537.
Leander, L., Christianson, S. Å., & Granhag, P. (2007). A sexual abuse case study: Children's memories and reports. *Psychiatry, Psychology & Law, 14*(1), 120–129. doi:10.1375/pplt.14.1.120.
London, K. (2001). Investigative interviews of children: A review of psychological research and implications for police practices. *Police Quarterly, 4*, 123–144.
London, K., Bruck, M., Ceci, S. J., & Shuman, D. (2005). Children's disclosure of sexual abuse: What does the research tell us about the ways that children tell? *Psychology, Public Policy, & the Law, 11*, 194–226.
Lyon, D. (1999). The new wave in children's suggestibility research: A critique. *Cornell Law Review*. http://www.falseallegations.com/new-wave-in-childrens-suggestibility.htm.
Lyon, T. D., Ahern, E. C., & Scurich, N. (2012). Interviewing children versus tossing coins: Accurately assessing the diagnosticity of children's disclosures of abuse. *Journal of Child Sexual Abuse, 21*(1), 19–44. doi:10.1080/10538712.2012.642468.
March, T. A., & Howe, M. L. (1995). Preschoolers report misinformation despite accurate memory. *Developmental Psychology, 31*, 554–567.
Marche, T. A. (1999). Memory strength affects reporting of misinformation. *Journal of Experimental Child Psychology, 73*, 45–71.
McWilliams, K., Narr, R., Goodman, G. S., Ruiz, S., & Mendoza, M. (2013). Children's memory for their mother's murder: Accuracy, suggestibility, and resistance to suggestion. *Memory, 21*(5), 591–598. doi:10.1080/09658211.2013.763983.

Meier, J. S. (2009). A historical perspective on parental alienation syndrome and parental alienation. *Journal of Child Custody, 6*, 232–257.

Melinder, A., & Gilstrap, L. L. (2009). The relationships between child and forensic interviewer behaviors and individual differences in interviews about a medical examination. *European Journal of Developmental Psychology, 6*(3), 365–395.

Merckelbach, H., & Muris, P. (2001). The causal link between self-reported trauma and dissociation: A critical review. *Behavior Research and Therapy, 39*, 245–254.

Merckelbach, H., Zeles, G., van Bergen, S., & Giesbrecht, T. (2007). Trait dissociation and commission errors in memory reports of emotional events. *American Journal of Psychology, 120*(1), 1–14.

Myers, J. B. (1993). Expert testimony regarding child sexual abuse. *Child Abuse and Neglect, 17*, 175–185.

Myers, J. B. (2012). "Nobody's perfect"—Partial disagreement with Herman, Faust, Bridges, and Ahern. *Journal of Child Sexual Abuse, 21*(2), 203–209. doi:10.1080/10538712.2012.661691.

National Association of Certified Child Forensic Interviewers. (2014). *The applicants' handbook: Qualifications, regulations, standards and definitions*. http://www.naccfi.com/Applicants%20Handbook%202014%20%20FEB%202.pdf.

National Children's Advocacy Center (NCAC). (2011). National Children's Advocacy Center Forensic Interview Structure. Author. Retrieved October 19, 2012, from http://www.nationalcac.org/professionals/images/stories/pdfs/fi%20structure.pdf.

National Crime Victims Research and Treatment Center, Center for Sexual Assault and Traumatic Stress. (2003). *Child physical and sexual abuse: Guidelines for treatment*. https://www.musc.edu/vawprevention/general/saunders.pdf.

Neoh, J., & Mellor, D. (2009). Professional issues related to allegations and assessment of child sexual abuse in the context of family court litigation. *Psychiatry, Psychology, and Law, 16*(2), 303–321.

Oates, R. K., Jones, D. P. H., Denson, A., Sirotnak, A., Gary, N., & Krugman, R. (2000). Erroneous concerns about child sexual abuse. *Child Abuse and Neglect, 24*(1), 149–157.

Pepiton, B. M., Alvis, L. J., Allen, K., & Logid, G. (2012). Is parental alienation disorder a valid concept? Not according to scientific evidence. A review of parental alienation, DSM-5 and ICD-11 by William Bernet. *Journal of Child Sexual Abuse, 21*, 244–253.

Pezdek, K., & Roe, C. (1995). The effect of memory trace strength on suggestibility. *Journal of Experimental Child Psychology, 60*, 116–128.

Poole, D. A., & Lindsay, D. S. (2001). Children's eyewitness reports after exposure to misinformation from parents. *Journal of Experimental Psychology: Applied, 7*, 27–50.

Poole, D. A., & White, L. (1991). Effects of question repetition on the eyewitness testimony of children and adults. *Developmental Psychology, 27*, 975–986.

Poole, D. A., & White, L. (1993). Two years later: Effects of question repetition on the eyewitness testimony of children and adults. *Developmental Psychology, 29*, 844–853.

Poole, D. A., & White, L. (1995). Tell me again and again: Stabilities and change in the repeated testimonies of children and adults. In M. Zaragoza, J. Graham, G. Hall, R. Hirschman, & Y. Ben-Porath (Eds.), *Memory and testimony in the child witness* (pp. 24–40). Newbury Park, CA: Sage Publications.

Rocha, E. M., Marche, T. A., & Briere, J. L. (2013). The effect of forced-choice questions on children's suggestibility: A comparison of multiple-choice and yes/no questions. *Canadian Journal of Behavioral Science, 45*(1), 1–11. doi:10.1037/a0028507.

Roma, P., Sabatello, U., Verrastro, G., & Ferracuti, S. (2011). Comparison between Gudjonsson Suggestibility Scale 2 (GSS2) and Bonn Test of Statement Suggestibility (BTSS) in measuring children's interrogative suggestibility. *Personality and Individual Differences, 51*(4), 488–491. doi:10.1016/j.paid.2011.05.003.

Saunders, B. E., & Meinig, M. B. (2001). *Family resolution therapy in cases of child abuse*. Charleston, SC: Authors.

Saywitz, K., Camparo, L. B., & Romanoff, A. (2010). Interviewing children in custody cases: Implications of research and policy for practice. *Behavioral Sciences and the Law, 28*(4), 542–562. doi:10.1002/bsl.945.

Saywitz, K. J., Lyon, T. D., & Goodman, G. S. (2011). Interviewing children. In J. E. B. Myers (Ed.), *The APSAC handbook on child maltreatment* (3rd ed., pp. 337–360). Newbury Park, CA: Sage.

Seidl, T. (1992). Special interviewing techniques. In S. Ludwig & A. E. Kornberg (Eds.), *Child abuse: A medical reference* (2nd ed., pp. 279–294). New York: Churchill Livingston.

Thoennes, N. (1988). *Sexual abuse allegations. Report of a study funded by the US Department of Health and Human Services.* Washington, DC: National Center on Child Abuse and Neglect.

Thoennes, N., & Tjaden, P. J. (1990). The extent, nature, and validity of sexual abuse allegations in custody/divorce disputes. *Child Abuse and Neglect, 151*, 153–154.

Tishelman, A. C., & Geffner, R. (2010). Forensic, cultural and systems issues in child sexual abuse cases—Part 1: Forensic evaluations and disclosures. *Journal of Child Sexual Abuse, 19*(5), 485–490.

Toth, P. (2011). Comparing the NICHD and RATAC child forensic interview approaches: Do the differences matter? *The Link: Official Newsletter of ISPCAN, 20 (1),* 1, 4–6.

Trocme, N., & Bala, N. (2005). False allegations of abuse and neglect when parents separate. *Child Abuse and Neglect, 29*, 1333–1345.

US Department of Health and Human Services, Administration on Children. (2003). *You and families: Child maltreatment, 2002* (pp. 16–17, Table 2–5). Washington, DC: US Government Printing Office, 2003.

Verkampt, F., & Ginet, M. (2010). Variations of the cognitive interview: Which one is the most effective in enhancing children's testimonies? *Applied Cognitive Psychology, 24*(9), 1279–1296. doi:10.1002/acp.1631.

Walker, L. E., & Shapiro, D. L. (2010). Parental alienation disorder: Why label children with a mental diagnosis? *Journal of Child Custody, 7*, 266–286.

Zorza, J. (2009). On navigating custody and visitation evaluations in cases with domestic violence: A judge's guide. *Journal of Child Custody, 6*, 258–286.

Chapter 21
Developing Countries and the Potential of Mandatory Reporting Laws to Identify Severe Child Abuse and Neglect

Ben Mathews

Introduction

Child abuse and neglect affects many children worldwide, with severe and lifelong consequences. All societies face ethical, economic and practical challenges in determining how to respond to child maltreatment, how to prevent it, and which types of child maltreatment to prioritize. The four classical forms of child abuse—physical abuse, sexual abuse, emotional abuse, and neglect—are often grouped together as if they are homogenous. Yet, different forms of abuse have different characteristics. There are also particular types of maltreatment that may present as significant problems in some societies but not others, such as child trafficking, child sexual exploitation, unlawful child labor, and female genital cutting. This heterogeneity of maltreatment, and the jurisdiction-specific contexts and priorities that may exist, are important to recognize when considering what legal and policy frameworks may be most useful and feasible to detect and respond to cases of child maltreatment, both in Western nations and in developing economies. Severe physical battering of an infant, and sexual abuse, e.g., are very different to mild poverty-related neglect of a child who lives in an otherwise loving family. This heterogeneity across and even within types of maltreatment, together with the cultural, social and economic conditions present in a particular society, suggests that some legal and policy responses will suit one form of maltreatment better than others.

This chapter will first consider some of the key characteristics of different types of child abuse and neglect, and will outline the nature and justifiability of mandatory reporting laws, which are one of the key legal responses made to child abuse

B. Mathews (✉)
Faculty of Law, Queensland University of Technology, Brisbane, Australia
e-mail: b.mathews@qut.edu.au

S. Deb (ed.), *Child Safety, Welfare and Well-being*,
DOI 10.1007/978-81-322-2425-9_21

and neglect in many nations. Mandatory reporting laws have been created in many jurisdictions in different forms, as a way of identifying cases of severe maltreatment which are likely to otherwise remain hidden, so that the child's victimization can cease, health rehabilitation and other support can be delivered, and where necessary perpetrators can be held accountable (Mathews and Kenny 2008; Mathews and Bross 2008; Mathews 2012; Drake and Jonson-Reid 2007). The issue of whether such a strategy may be useful for child protection in developing countries with emerging economies is an important one. "Developing country" is an arbitrary term used by various institutions for convenience to describe a nation which has a lower living standard, industrial base, and human development index (HDI) compared to other countries (World Bank 2012; United Nations Development Program 2013). In the context of developing countries, the chapter will then address two questions: first, might some forms of maltreatment more suited to this legal response to child maltreatment than others? Second, what options may be considered by developing countries, taking into account children's needs, cultural conditions and practices, economic imperatives, and the different levels of preparedness to implement child protection strategies?

Key Characteristics of Different Types of Child Abuse and Neglect

Different Types of Abuse and Neglect

Since this chapter deals with child maltreatment across cultures, it must first be observed that different cultural practices in child-rearing must be considered (Korbin 1977, 1979; Finkelhor and Korbin 1988). Some practices specific to some cultures would be seen by others as maltreatment, and vice versa; accordingly there is no comprehensive all-encompassing model of what practices can be defined as abusive or neglectful. Later in this chapter, further remarks will be made about cultural differences.

Nevertheless, there are some areas of common ground which can be adopted for the purposes of this discussion. Using the basis of a previous model (Mathews and Bross 2014), I will use the following general definitions of discrete abuse types, which draw on those proposed by leading scholars and which are generally consistent with rights and obligations in criminal law and civil law[1]:

- *Physical abuse* includes acts of physical assault by parents or caregivers which result in death or serious physical harm, or which present an imminent risk of doing so; it excludes lawful corporal punishment;

[1]There may still be some examples of conduct around the margins of these definitions which are seen as acceptable in some cultures, but I propose these as general definitions for the purpose of this discussion.

- *Sexual abuse* includes acts not only of penetrative abuse, but also acts of masturbation, oral sex, fondling, voyeurism, exposure to sexual acts, exposure to or involvement in pornography and other forms of commercial sexual exploitation, all of which are acts done to sexually gratify the abuser; it is usually inflicted by an adult, but is often and can be inflicted by another, usually older child, where the victim is not developmentally capable of understanding the acts or is not able to provide true consent (World Health Organization 2006);
- *Psychological or emotional abuse* exists when the relationship between the parent or caregiver and the child is characterized by pervasive or persistent acts or omissions which result in serious emotional harm or present an imminent risk of doing so (Glaser 2002, 2011)[2];
- *Neglect* is constituted by omissions by parents or caregivers to provide the basic necessities of life such as food, shelter, clothing, supervision, and medical care, which result in serious harm or present an imminent risk of doing so (Dubowitz 2000).

Each definition includes a qualification of "severity" or "seriousness." Not all manifestations of harm are "abuse" or "neglect." In the case of sexual abuse, all sexual abuse is seen as seen as having such seriousness as to merit some kind of response. For the other three types, the abuse or neglect must have already been of sufficient severity to cause serious harm, or to involve acts which have already been committed which may not yet have caused such harm but present an imminent risk or likelihood of causing such harm. These definitions aim to non-exhaustively mark the terrain within which social policy responses and sometimes legal responses are legitimately and clearly warranted.

The Consequences and Costs of Serious Child Abuse and Neglect

There is heterogeneity across and within types of maltreatment, and in their consequences for individuals. Neglect, e.g., has several subspecies: medical, nutritional, emotional, educational, and supervisory. All these can have different extents: an infant who is not provided with necessary vaccinations when these are available will be exposed to a different level of risk than a 7-year-old who is left alone at home for a day. Different kinds of maltreatment are more likely to present

[2]According to Glaser's (2011) typology, there are five categories of such harmful acts and omissions: first: emotional unavailability, unresponsiveness and neglect; second: interacting with the child with hostility, blame, denigration, rejection, or scapegoating; third: developmentally inappropriate or inconsistent interactions with the child; fourth: failure to recognize or acknowledge the child's individuality and the psychological boundary between the parent and the child, and fifth: failure to promote the child's socialization within the child's context, by either active mis-socialization or corruption; isolating the child; or by failing to provide adequate stimulation and opportunities for learning.

different kinds of consequences for the child; and even within types, and even where the acts are the same kind, duration and chronicity, not all individuals will experience the same type or extent of all kinds of physical, social, and behavioral consequences (Putnam 2003; Widom 2014).

However, there is broad acceptance of the variety of severe consequences and the size of the costs of child maltreatment. The youngest children are most often victimized, apart from sexual abuse (United States Department of Health and Human Services 2009). The adverse physical and mental health, behavioral, educational, social, and economic consequences of respective kinds of serious abuse and neglect, are often extremely substantial (Gilbert et al. 2009; Paolucci et al. 2001). Studies have identified these consequences, especially in relation to physical abuse (see e.g., Gershoff 2002; Landsford et al. 2002), sexual abuse (see e.g., Chen et al. 2010; Paolucci et al. 2001; Putnam 2003), and neglect (Perry 2002). Fewer studies have explored the effects of emotional abuse but there is still convincing evidence of its adverse effects (Egeland 2009; Stoltenborgh et al. 2012). The economic costs to survivors, families, and communities are vast (Fang et al. 2012; Fromm 2001). Overall, in addition to fatalities, prominent common effects, which in many cases compromise development and which persist through the lifespan, include: failure to thrive; impaired brain development; impaired social, emotional, and behavioral development; reduced reading ability and perceptual reasoning; depression; anxiety; post-traumatic stress disorder; low self-image; physical injuries; alcohol and drug use; aggression; delinquency; long-term deficits in educational achievement; and adverse effects on employment and economic status. All these consequences also affect the child's dignity and capacity to develop fully and functionally as a human being; their core capabilities are compromised (Nussbaum 2011).

The Nature and Justifiability of Mandatory Reporting Laws

Mandatory reporting laws were first created to respond to the problem presented by the fact that severe child maltreatment is a largely hidden phenomenon. It occurs within the family sphere, and apart from sexual abuse, it is most frequently inflicted on infants who are pre-verbal and young children, who cannot resist, represent themselves, resolve the situation or disclose the experience (Mathews 2012). For a range of reasons, sexual abuse is also typically undisclosed by the child and the perpetrator (Paine and Hansen 2002). Neonates, infants, and very young children are most vulnerable to fatality and serious harm from severe abuse and neglect. In the definitive article which exposed physical abuse and doctors' failure to respond appropriately to it, Kempe et al. (1962) stated that severe physical abuse was mostly inflicted on children aged under 3 years of age. Overall, children rarely disclose their own suffering, and because the acts are severe and often constitute criminal conduct, those who inflict the abuse or neglect are also unlikely to reveal it to authorities or agencies which can help the child (Mathews 2012). Disclosure by children of their maltreatment will be even less frequent in societies which have not yet developed a culture of child protection and in which other societal features silence children and girls in particular (Shalhoub-Kevorkian 1999).

A mandatory reporting law is a specific kind of legislative enactment which imposes a duty on a specified group or groups of persons outside the family to report suspected cases of designated types of child maltreatment to child welfare agencies. These designated persons are usually members of occupational groups who frequently encounter children in the course of their work: typical examples are doctors, nurses, teachers, and police. The underlying concept is to impose a requirement on designated people who are well-placed to detect cases of severe child abuse and neglect to report known and suspected cases to the attention of government welfare agencies, so that measures can be taken to ensure the child is safe, that the maltreatment stops, that rehabilitation can be provided, and that the needs of the child and the family can be identified and supported. By employing the expertise and concern of persons outside the family who encounter the child, the hidden nature of child maltreatment can be overcome. The laws are accompanied by training mechanisms, because reporters need to know the scope of their duty, the indicators of child abuse and neglect, what they should and should not report, how to make a useful report, and to whom they must report. Child welfare agencies are equipped with staff to receive reports and assess them, and where necessary to investigate them and determine the appropriate course of action as set out in child protection legislation. Generally, the least intrusive course of action is preferred, but where necessary, cases of severe maltreatment where a child cannot be protected within the home may result in more formal action including court orders which may extend to removal of the child from the family home for the child's protection. Such removal to foster care or kinship care is often only temporary before being returned to the family home, but in some cases it may be necessary to be of a more extended duration, and sometimes may result in permanent placement with other careers.[3]

Because of its hidden nature, the first primary objective of these laws is to identify cases of serious child abuse and neglect. For example, if in the course of their work a doctor or a police officer or a teacher encounters a 3-year-old child who has suffered severe intentional physical injury, or injuries suggesting sexual abuse, or severe neglect, the legal obligation requires the professional to report their knowledge or reasonable suspicion that the child has been abused and has suffered harm to a government child welfare agency so that the agency can assess the child's situation to determine what protective and supportive actions need to be taken. The legislation provides the reporter with protections: their identity as the

---

[3]The cost component of out-of-home care (foster care, kinship care, and other forms, e.g., residential care) is by far the greatest economic burden for child protection systems.

reporter is confidential, and they cannot be liable in any civil, criminal, or administrative proceeding for any consequences of the report (Mathews and Kenny 2008). It should be noted that reporters are not expected to always be correct; it is often not easy to detect child abuse because the indicators of abuse can mimic other health conditions or accidental injury (Mathews and Bross 2014). There is a range of evidence indicating that implementation of these laws with their associated mechanisms will identify substantially more cases of child maltreatment, although there will also be an element of systems burden which depends on the nature and scope of the laws and the efficacy of their implementation (Mathews 2012, 2014; Mathews and Bross 2008; Drake and Jonson-Reid 2007).

The laws can be designed to be broad or narrow. There are two major dimensions in which the laws differ across jurisdictions (both between countries, and within countries): first, which types of abuse and neglect must be reported; second, which persons have to report. Hence, there is a spectrum of mandatory reporting laws. At one extreme, a law might require reports only of sexual abuse, and limit the reporter groups to teachers, doctors, nurses, midwives, and police. Or, like the first reporting laws, it might only require doctors to report serious physical abuse. At the other extreme, a jurisdiction might design its law more broadly, requiring reports of all four forms of child abuse and neglect, and perhaps even others such as situations of a child being exposed to domestic violence; and there may be a broader range of reporter groups.

Many Western jurisdictions now have relatively broad laws, requiring a range of occupational groups to report a number of types of child maltreatment. However, it is important to note that these laws are generally not designed to require reports of any and all manifestations of harm or "maltreatment"; rather, for the most part they are directed at serious forms of harm and maltreatment of children (Mathews and Kenny 2008; Mathews 2012). Some jurisdictions, though, do have a more preventative orientation and so have a lower threshold for the activation of the reporting duty; these jurisdictions would need to devote a higher level of resourcing to receive and respond to the corresponding higher number of reports. In all cases, systemic problems can arise where laws are poorly drafted, and reporters are not appropriately prepared to comply with the duty (Mathews 2012). It is known that differential reporting practice accompanies different maltreatment types. For example, neglect and emotional abuse, and exposure to domestic violence, are far more frequently reported than are sexual abuse and physical abuse (Mathews 2012).

Mandatory reporting laws can be seen as one part of an overall public health response to child protection which should include primary prevention at the population level, secondary prevention of high-risk subsets of the population, and tertiary responses to identify and assist those who have already endured severe maltreatment. Being primarily concerned with identifying cases of maltreatment that have already occurred, the laws are an aspect of tertiary response (Turnock 2009; Gostin 2008). However, in their capacity to also identify cases of maltreatment before they have occurred, they are also a measure of secondary response.

A number of circumstances must be created to enable this legal response to be implemented successfully (Mathews 2012; Mathews and Bross 2014). While mandatory reporting legislation of its nature tends to use some concepts which are not concrete, such as "suspects on reasonable grounds", the legislation must be drafted well to avoid ambiguity and vagueness. Reporter training programs must be high quality, delivered to all reporters, and delivered repeatedly. Positive working relationships between child welfare agencies and reporters must be maintained. Intake and response agencies must be adequately resourced by sufficient numbers of well-trained staff. Data systems must be well-maintained to enable monitoring of effectiveness and identification of problems so that solutions can be designed and implemented. All these aspects of the strategy clearly require substantial economic investment and personnel and expertise. To avoid overreach, the scope of any mandatory reporting law (e.g., its application to which types of maltreatment, and applying to which groups of reporters) should be congruent with the realistic capacity and ambition of the jurisdiction's child welfare system (Mathews 2012). A jurisdiction which is considering this strategy may have to make hard choices, at least in the short-term, about its scope.

In the Context of Developing Countries, Might Some Forms of Maltreatment be More Suited to this Legal Response than Others?

Jurisdictions continue to explore the use of mandatory reporting laws and to implement them in various forms. Saudi Arabia recently introduced the laws (Al Eissa and Almuneef 2010) and Ireland has legislation currently being debated. Yet, even in the context of those countries' child protection systems which use mandatory reporting laws as one element of their approach, not all forms of maltreatment are always included within the ambit of mandatory reporting laws. Some jurisdictions do not require reports of neglect, for example. Others enable reports of neglect to be made to welfare agencies rather than child protection authorities. Others require reports of neglect, but not of neglect caused only by poverty. Some jurisdictions do not require reports of emotional abuse; some have suggested that more formal immediate child protection responses may not be appropriate for emotional abuse, due to its particular characteristics which distinguish it from other maltreatment types (Glaser and Prior 1997) and others have also questioned the use of formal child protection processes for this form of maltreatment (Melton and Davidson 1987). These parameters do not necessarily mean that these jurisdictions do not take seriously these forms of maltreatment; it may simply mean that other strategies are preferred to deal with these kinds of adversity, or that other forms of maltreatment are deemed to have priority.

Developing Countries

It is all the more likely that in developing countries, a variety of conditions mean that some forms of maltreatment may be more suitable targets of a mandatory reporting law than others. In general, the term "developing country" is a shorthand term which is inevitably arbitrary and used for convenience to describe a nation which has a lower living standard, industrial base, and human development index (HDI) compared to other countries. The term is generally derived from an assessment of a country's GDP per capita and is implicitly related to an economic standard of living. Different institutions have slightly different calculation methods. For example, the World Bank (2012) classifies countries into four income groups: low income, lower middle income, upper middle income, and high income. The World Bank classifies all low-income and middle-income countries as developing countries. Moving beyond a pure economic measure, the United Nations Development Program and its *Human Development Report* (2013) gauges human development progress using life expectancy, schooling, and per capita income (gross domestic product); or, as concisely described, it is a "composite index measuring average achievement in three basic dimensions of human development—a long and healthy life, knowledge and a decent standard of living" (p. 151). On these dimensions, an overall HDI score is calculated, and four categories of nations' overall development are devised: very high; high; medium; and low. The UN also reports on gender inequality, on measures of inequality in achievements between women and men in three dimensions: reproductive health, empowerment, and the labor market.

By its nature, a developing country will normally possess less favorable economic conditions. It is likely to have competing priorities, many of which may be thought to be even more urgent than child welfare. There may also be cultural practices toward children which circumscribe any approach to particular forms of maltreatment, especially neglect. The nature of societal attitudes, and sometimes religious attitudes, may also preclude an approach using a mandatory reporting law; for example, a society which generally endorses corporal punishment may not be suited to implementation of mandatory reporting of all kinds of physical abuse, although a reporting law can be specified as only applying to certain types of conduct, and other methods of response may also be chosen, such as public education efforts.[4] As well, a society may have a low level of overall preparedness

[4]Corporal punishment is still often seen as a natural incident of parental authority. Yet, despite being customary for thousands of years, dozens of countries have prohibited it in the last 30 years, influenced by evidence of its detrimental effects on physical and mental health (Gershoff 2002), its association with more severe abuse (Zolotor et al. 2008) and the impact of recognizing children's rights to personal inviolability. By 2011, 29 nations had prohibited corporal punishment in all forms, and many more had prohibited it within defined contexts such as schools and institutions (Durrant and Smith 2011). By October 2012, 33 nations prohibited corporal punishment (Global Initiative to End All Corporal Punishment of Children 2012). While debate continues, many have concluded that such prohibitions, with supportive educational measures, have influenced positive changes in attitudes and behavior (Naylor and Saunders 2012; Janson et al. 2011; Bussman 2011).

to deal with various types of child maltreatment both individually and in combination. Before proceeding, it should be noted again that there are various methods which a society can choose to respond to various forms of child maltreatment and maltreatment as a whole. Mandatory reporting laws are only one option, which as we have seen, constitute a primarily tertiary form of response. A country may be experiencing such difficult social and economic conditions that no form or only an extremely limited form of mandatory reporting law may be currently viable.

Cultural Difference and Fundamental Norms

Cultural child-rearing practices differ widely across human societies. Some practices which would be seen in most Western nations as maltreatment may not be in other societies; similarly, some non-Western societies would see some Western practices as maltreatment (Korbin 1977, 1979 1980). Accordingly, it is difficult and perhaps impossible to arrive at a comprehensive model of child maltreatment that applies universally. However, it is nevertheless still possible to identify some classes of maltreatment that at a universal level are and should be seen as unacceptable. The variation in humanity's cultural norms and practices does not restrict discussion or policy to a completely relativistic acceptance of any and all behavior (Finkelhor and Korbin 1988; Korbin 1979), which would preclude social, legal, and policy approaches to responding to child maltreatment. That is, in this context it is not acceptable to adopt a posture of *normative moral relativism* which would hold that different cultural standards both exist *and* preclude any and all claims that some customs are unacceptable. In contrast, a posture of *moral universalism* acknowledges and accepts that different standards exist, but maintains that we can still assert that some standards are more justifiable than others, and proceed on this basis at the policy level.

Such an endeavor is essentially the same kind of task undertaken at a general level by international human rights instruments. The *United Nations Convention on the Rights of the Child* 1989 contains a range of children's rights. Most specifically in this context, Article 19 obliges States parties to take all appropriate legislative, administrative, social, and educational measures to protect children from all forms of abuse and exploitation while in the care of parents and caregivers. Somewhat more specifically, there are also rights to life (Article 6), a minimum standard of health especially in early childhood (Article 24), and to freedom from economic exploitation and hazardous labor (Article 32). More specifically still, there are other rights which relate to abuse and neglect: the right to an education, including free primary education (Article 28) (mirrored by the United Nations Millennium Development Goal 2 of achieving universal primary education); freedom from sexual abuse and exploitation (Article 34); and freedom from sale and traffic (Article 35).

Despite cultural variance, within the context of child maltreatment there appear to be some classes of conduct that are universally condemned, or are so close to being universally condemned, that they form absolute standards of unacceptable behavior. These fundamental norms include:

- Child sexual abuse and exploitation;
- Child trafficking;
- Severe physical abuse; and
- Severe neglect.

Scholars have also noted types and manifestations of child abuse and neglect that occur internationally and within which there are subspecies which can form the basis for international action (Finkelhor and Korbin 1988). As long ago as 1988, Finkelhor and Korbin recommended that three forms of child abuse should be the immediate focus of international action: parental child battering, sexual abuse and selective neglect (i.e., neglect based on discrimination related to gender, disability, or birth order) (p. 16). A cogent case can therefore be made for a systematic response in all societies to some specific forms of child maltreatment.

Context-Specific Priorities: An Example of India

Internationally, problems of child maltreatment are widespread. Emotional abuse affects an estimated 36 % of all children, while being even more prevalent in some societies (Stoltenborgh et al. 2012). Sexual abuse is also widespread globally, affecting an estimated 11 % of all children, and again being more widespread in some societies than others (Stoltenborgh et al. 2011). However, it appears to be less widespread in some nations; China, e.g., appears to have a lower than normal prevalence (Ji et al. 2013; Finkelhor et al. 2013).

Some societies will have particular areas of concern. The Indian context is a useful illustrative example. The United Nations (2013) ranked India at 136 in human development and 132 in gender inequality. Its health index reported 42.5 % of children aged under 5 being moderately or severely underweight, a prevalence exceeded by only two other nations (p. 168). Around three in ten (28 %) children are born with low birth weight (UNICEF 2008). In 2008, 1.8 million children under 5 died, including 1 million in the first month of life; undernutrition caused between one third and one half of all these deaths (Black et al. 2010). Of all children under age 5, almost half are stunted and 43 % are underweight (International Institute for Population Sciences and Macro International 2007). The state of children's nutrition in India—which is not strictly a matter of parental neglect, but which is more related to poverty—is a national emergency, and one which could legitimately be argued to take priority over, or at least alongside, any other imperative.

Yet there are other significant issues. Child abuse and neglect are serious problems, influenced by factors including poverty, over-population, lack of education, cultural beliefs and practices, gender bias, and patriarchy. A national study revealed widespread maltreatment (Ministry of Women and Child Development,

GOI, 2007): 69 % of children reported being physically abused (p. 44); 53 % reported having been sexually abused; 48 % reported emotional abuse (p. 106). Runyan et al. (2010) found substantial levels of harsh physical discipline (almost 20 %) including striking the child with an object (over 40 %).

Child labor in India is extremely prevalent. A national study found a substantial incidence of overworked children, with over 50 % of children classed as "children at work" working 7 days per week (Ministry of Women and Child Development 2007, p. 58). Indian children work in various industries, and especially in agriculture. Dangerous working conditions are rife, including exposure to chemicals, lack of protective clothing, lack of water, physical and verbal abuse, and deprivation of the opportunity to attend school (Physicians for Human Rights Child Rights Group 2003). An estimated 15 million children alone work in debt bondage, an illegal practice of paying off family debt.

Child trafficking is also a significant problem in India. Estimates suggest that human trafficking involves over 20 million people worldwide, with approximately 26 % of these being children: a figure of 5.5 million (International Labor Office 2012). Child trafficking involves the recruitment, transport, and transfer of children, through abduction, deception or force, for exploitative purposes. Trafficking of children for commercial and sexual purposes is highly lucrative, and is known to be a serious problem in South Asian and East Asian countries (Deb 2006; International Labor Organization 2005). Trafficking in India is usually conducted through outright abduction and sale, or by false offers of marriages and jobs, which entice desperate individuals seeking marriage, enhanced employment prospects, and a higher standard of living (Kempadoo et al. 2005). Parents sell their children, mostly daughters, who are trafficked to cities or across borders. Once relocated, the children work as laborers, domestic servants, or in commercial industry, and many become involved in prostitution.

In addition, the rate of children's school attendance is low, despite being compulsory (Deb and Mathews 2012). National data indicate that only 73 % of children attend school to the end of primary school (UNICEF 2008); and only 62 % of the population aged over 15 years are literate (United Nations 2013, p. 172). Child marriage is also extremely common despite being illegal (Deb and Mathews 2012; Raj et al. 2009), severely restricting girls' and women's life chances.

Some of these phenomena are not hidden, and are not the traditional forms of child abuse and neglect. Some, such as labor, may be argued by some to be essential for children's livelihoods and those of their families, and responses may require fundamental structural, economic, and attitudinal change. Yet, some of these phenomena are exactly those which inspired the first reporting laws; and others such as trafficking and child marriage are also serious issues which demand attention. When considering methods of responding to such issues, especially those which are clandestine, India and other nations may consider whether a form of mandatory reporting may assist to identify hidden cases and also help to influence culture change about what standards of conduct are acceptable.

What Options May be Considered by Developing Countries, Taking into Account Children's Needs, Cultural Conditions and Practices, Economic Imperatives, and the Different Levels of Preparedness to Implement Child Protection Strategies?

Each nation will have its own jurisdiction-specific conditions, concerns, and hierarchy of priorities. Acknowledging this, while they recommended priority action internationally in three specific fields—parental child battering, sexual abuse, and selective neglect—Finkelhor and Korbin (1988) also suggested that individual nations should develop their own focuses and plans of action. This strategy can accommodate the unique set of cultural and societal conditions, economic resources, and human infrastructure characterizing each society. It would be driven from the ground up and would have a higher chance of being sustainable, as well as avoiding or diminishing the problems inherent to a set of priorities imposed in a "top-down" manner by an external authority. Similarly, Mikton et al. (2013) noted that countries have different levels of preparedness to implement child maltreatment prevention programs, due to the extent to which they possess features including (1) professionals with the required skills, knowledge and expertise to implement programs; (2) institutions to train these professionals; and (3) funding, infrastructure and equipment.

In addition, the attitudes held by adults about what is acceptable conduct toward children are a crucial feature of society which influences behavior and the success of child protection initiatives. Efforts to identify and improve attitudes may be just as necessary as other legal and systemic reforms. For example, Dunne et al. (2008) noted the mismatch between the maltreatment of children in Chinese societies and adults' perceptions regarding the acceptability of violence inflicted toward children. Deb et al. (2013) found a widespread belief among Indian parents and teachers that children should not possess rights (although some particular rights were unanimously approved), and a very low level of awareness of the existence of children's rights as enshrined in legislation.

Accordingly, a particular nation may choose to focus first on a smaller selection of priorities, or in some cases it may be even one particular issue that receives priority attention in the first instance. A focused "small-target" approach could be adopted especially if economic resources are extremely limited; for example, in nations where the population endures dire conditions such as food shortages, low life expectancy, or civil conflict. Hence, in such conditions, a chosen priority could be sexual abuse generally, trafficking for commercial or sexual exploitation, child marriage, child soldiers, gender-based infanticide, neonatal health, or primary schooling. Depending on the priority and the nature of the problem addressed, especially whether it is a clandestine problem or not, mandatory reporting (with associated educational campaigns, reporter training, systemic capacity-building and the like) may assist to uncover cases and change cultural attitudes toward the practice.

Such a pragmatic approach would not mean that other grave problems and injustices were accepted or endorsed; nor would it mean that government was resigned to those other problems always existing. Rather, it may mean accepting that in the short-term, a concerted and thorough approach to one severe problem or a small number of them is all that can feasibly be accommodated such that it has a realistic chance of success; whereas if an inadequately resourced effort to confront a wider set of problems was attempted, all these may be hopelessly compromised and doomed to failure. Such challenges face public administrations daily. However, less leeway in this respect can reasonably be granted to wealthier countries. On Nussbaum's view (2011), it is the State's responsibility to ensure the individual's core capabilities are protected and nurtured, and it is their task to ensure that sufficient resources from the public purse are devoted to such tasks.

What can motivate societies to make greater efforts to identify and respond to severe child maltreatment? To prosper, nations require inclusive political and economic institutions and conditions ensuring security and opportunity for its citizens (Acemoglu and Robinson 2012). It may be that some forms of responses to children's maltreatment or deprivation may be seen by developing countries as being important and indeed essential for its economic development and social fabric, as well as being a principled approach to children's and human rights. India's newly elected Prime Minister Narendra Modi recently called for a development of the nation's intellectual capital if the nation is to be competitive (Bagchi 2014). Nobel Prize winning researchers in development economics have advocated for investment in human capital from the perspective that an educated workforce is more productive and efficient (Schultz 1971). A nation cannot flourish if its children are not properly educated generally, and if the education of girls in particular is marginalized. Equally, national development and prosperity is compromised if children's health and security and life chances are jeopardized through maltreatment. Efforts to identify severe child maltreatment and to rehabilitate children and provide them with adequate life chances represent a part of a much broader concern to ensure a society is inclusive at political, humanitarian, and economic levels, and can prosper and grow.

References

Acemoglu, D., & Robinson, J. (2012). *Why nations fail: The origins of power, prosperity and poverty*. London: Profile.

Al Eissa, M., & Almuneef, M. (2010). Child abuse and neglect in Saudi Arabia: Journey of recognition to implementation of national prevention strategies. *Child Abuse and Neglect, 34*(1), 28–33. doi:10.1016/j.chiabu.2009.08.011.

Bagchi, I. (2014). Narendra Modi gives mantra to take on China. *The Times of India*. Retrieved June 9, 2014, from http://timesofindia.indiatimes.com/India/Narendra-Modi-gives-mantra-to-take-on-China/articleshow/36265685.cms.

Black, R. E., Cousens, S., Johnson, H. L., Lawn, J. E., Rudan, I., Bassani, D. G., … Child Health Epidemiology Reference Group of WHO and UNICEF. (2010). Global, regional, and national causes of child mortality in 2008: A systematic analysis. *The Lancet, 375*(9730), 1969–1987. doi:10.1016/S0140-6736(10)60549-1.

Chen, L. P., Murad, M. H., Paras, M. L., Colbenson, K. M., Sattler, A. L., Goranson, E. N., et al. (2010, July). Sexual abuse and lifetime diagnosis of psychiatric disorders: systematic review and meta-analysis. In: *Mayo Clinic Proceedings* (Vol. 85, No. 7, pp. 618–629). Elsevier. doi: 10.4065/mcp.2009.0583.

Deb, S. (2006). *Children in agony*. New Delhi: Concept Publishing Company.

Deb, S., & Mathews, B. (2012). Children's rights in India: Parents' and teachers' attitudes, knowledge and perceptions. *The International Journal of Children's Rights, 20*(2), 241–264. doi:10.1163/157181811X616022.

Deb, S., Gireesan, A., Kumar, A., Roy, A. & Sun, J. (2013). *Attitudes, knowledge and perceptions towards child rights among parents, teachers and community members across five cities in India*. Paper presented in the International Conference on Protection of Child Rights: Issues and Challenges, held during January 18–20, 2013, Puducherry, India.

Drake, B., & Jonson-Reid, M. (2007). A response to Melton based on the best available data. *Child Abuse and Neglect, 31*, 343–360. doi:10.1016/j.chiabu.2006.08.009.

Dubowitz, H. (2000). What is child neglect? In H. Dubowitz & D. DePanfilis (Eds.), *The handbook for child protection* (p. 2000). Thousand Oaks, CA: Sage.

Dunne, M., Chen, J., & Choo, W. (2008). The evolving evidence base for child protection in Chinese societies. *Asia-Pacific Journal of Public Health, 20*(4), 267–276. doi:10.1177/1010539508325047.

Durrant, J., & Smith, A. (Eds.). (2011). *Global pathways to abolishing physical punishment: Realizing children's rights*. New York: Routledge.

Egeland, B. (2009). Taking stock: Childhood emotional maltreatment and developmental psychopathology. *Child Abuse and Neglect, 33*, 22. doi:10.1016/j.chiabu.2008.12.004.

Fang, X., Brown, D., Florence, C., & Mercy, J. (2012). The economic burden of child maltreatment in the United States and implications for prevention. *Child Abuse and Neglect, 36*, 156–165. doi:10.1016/j.chiabu.2011.10.006.

Finkelhor, D., & Korbin, J. (1988). Child abuse as an international issue. *Child Abuse and Neglect, 12*, 3–23. doi:10.1016/0145-2134(88)90003-8.

Finkelhor, D., Ji, K., Mikton, C., & Dunne, M. (2013). Explaining lower rates of sexual abuse in China. *Child Abuse and Neglect, 37*(2013), 852–860. doi:10.1016/j.chiabu.2013.07.006.

Fromm, S. (2001). Total estimated cost of child abuse and neglect in the United States: Statistical evidence. Prevent Child Abuse America. Retrieved October 22, 2007, from http://www.preventchildabuse.org/site/DocServer/cost_analysis.pdf?docID=144.

Gershoff, E. (2002). Corporal punishment by parents and associated child behaviors and experiences. *Psychological Bulletin, 128*, 539. doi:10.1037//0033-2909.128.4.539.

Gilbert, R., Widom, C. S., Browne, K., Fergusson, D., Webb, E., & Janson, S. (2009). Burden and consequences of child maltreatment in high-income countries. *The Lancet, 373*(9657), 68–81. doi:10.1016/S0140-6736(08)61706-7.

Glaser, D. (2002). Emotional abuse and neglect (psychological maltreatment): A conceptual framework. *Child Abuse and Neglect, 26*, 697–714. doi:10.1016/S0145-2134(02)00342-3.

Glaser, D. (2011). How to deal with emotional abuse and neglect—Further development of a conceptual framework (FRAMEA). *Child Abuse and Neglect, 35*, 866–875. doi:10.1016/j.chiabu.2011.05.013.

Glaser, D., & Prior, V. (1997). Is the term child protection applicable to emotional abuse? *Child Abuse Review, 6*, 315–329. doi:10.1002/(SICI)1099-0852(199712)6:5<315:AID-CAR361>3.0.CO;2-A.

Global Initiative to End All Corporal Punishment of Children. (2012). Prohibiting all corporal punishment of children: Progress and delay. http://www.crin.org/docs/Progress%20and%20delay%20leaflet%20October%202012%20EN%20singles.pdf.

Gostin, L. (2008). *Public health law: Power, duty, restraint* (2nd ed.). Berkeley CA: University of California Press.

International Institute for Population Sciences and Macro International. (2007). *National Family Health Survey (NFHS-3): 2005-06: India*. Mumbai: International Institute for Population Sciences and Macro International.

International Labor Office, Special Action Programme to Combat Forced Labor (SAP-FL). (2012). *ILO global estimate of forced labor: results and methodology*. Geneva: ILO.
International Labor Organization. (2005). *A global alliance against forced labor*. Geneva: International Labor Organization.
Janson, S., Langberg, B., & Svensson, B. (2011). A 30-year Ban on physical punishment. In: J. Durrant & A. Smith (2011) (Eds.). *Global pathways to abolishing physical punishment: Realizing children's rights* (pp. 241–255). Routledge, New York.
Ji, K., Finkelhor, D., & Dunne, M. (2013). Child sexual abuse in China: A meta-analysis of 27 studies. *Child Abuse and Neglect, 37*(9), 613–622. doi:10.1016/j.chiabu.2013.03.008.
Kempadoo, K., Sanghera, J., & Pattanaik, B. (Eds.). (2005). *Trafficking and prostitution reconsidered: New perspectives on migration, sex work, and human rights*. Boulder, CO: Paradigm.
Kempe, C. H., Silverman, F., Steele, B., Droegemueller, W., & Silver, H. (1962). The Battered-child syndrome. *Journal of the American Medical Association, 181*, 17–24.
Korbin, J. (1977). Anthropological contributions to the study of child abuse. *Child Abuse and Neglect, 1*, 7–24.
Korbin, J. (1979). A cross-cultural perspective on the role of community in child abuse and neglect. *Child Abuse and Neglect, 3*, 9–18.
Korbin, J. (1980). The cultural context of child abuse and neglect. *Child Abuse and Neglect, 4*, 3–13. doi:10.1016/0145-2134(80)90028-9.
Lansford, J. E., Dodge, K. A., Pettit, G. S., Bates, J. E., Crozier, J., & Kaplow, J. (2002). A 12 year prospective study of the long-term effects of early child physical maltreatment. *Archives of Pediatric and Adolescent Medicine, 156*, 824–830.
Mathews, B. (2012). Exploring the contested role of mandatory reporting laws in the identification of severe child abuse and neglect. In M. Freeman (Ed.), *Current legal issues* (Vol. 14, pp. 302–338)., Law and childhood studies Oxford: Oxford University Press.
Mathews, B. (2014).The nature and development over time of mandatory reporting laws. In: B. Mathews, D. Bross (Eds.) (2014, in press). *Mandatory reporting laws and the identification of severe child abuse and neglect*. Dordrecht: Springer.
Mathews, B., & Bross, D. (2008). Mandated reporting is still a policy with reason: Empirical evidence and philosophical grounds. *Child Abuse and Neglect, 32*, 511–516. doi:10.1016/j.chiabu.2007.06.010.
Mathews, B., & Bross, D. (2014). Using law to identify, manage and prevent child maltreatment. In J. Korbin & R. Krugman (Eds.), *Handbook of child maltreatment* (pp. 477–502). Dordrecht: Springer Scientific.
Mathews, B., & Kenny, M. (2008). Mandatory reporting legislation in the USA, Canada and Australia. A cross-jurisdictional review of key features, differences and issues. *Child Maltreatment, 13*(1), 50–63. doi:10.1177/1077559507310613.
Melton, G., & Davidson, H. (1987). Child protection and society: When should the state intervene? *American Psychologist, 42*, 172–175.
Mikton, C., Power, M., Raleva, M., Makoae, M., Al Eissa, M., Cheah, I., & Almuneef, M. (2013). The assessment of the readiness of five countries to implement child maltreatment prevention programs on a large scale. *Child Abuse and Neglect, 37*, 1237–1251. doi:10.1016/j.chiabu.2013.07.009.
Ministry of Women and Child Development. (2007). *Study on child abuse: India 2007*. New Delhi, Government of India. Retrieved September 22, 2011, from http://wcd.nic.in/childabuse.pdf.
Naylor, B., & Saunders, B. (2012). Parental discipline, criminal laws, and responsive regulation. In M. Freeman (Ed.), *Current legal issues* (Vol. 14, pp. 506–529)., Law and childhood studies Oxford: Oxford University Press.
Nussbaum, M. (2011). *Creating capabilities*. Cambridge MA: Harvard University Press.
Paine, M., & Hansen, D. (2002). Factors influencing children to self-disclose sexual abuse. *Clinical Psychology Review, 22*, 271–295. doi:10.1016/S0272-7358(01)00091-5.

Paolucci, E., Genuis, M., & Violato, C. (2001). A meta-analysis of the published research on the effects of child sexual abuse. *The Journal of Psychology Interdisciplinary and Applied, 135*, 17–36. doi:10.1080/00223980109603677.
Perry, B. (2002). Childhood experience and the expression of genetic potential: What childhood neglect tells us about nature and nurture? *Brain and Mind, 3*(1), 79–100.
Physicians for Human Rights Child Rights Group. (2003). Child labor in India: A health and human rights perspective. *The Lancet Extreme Medicine, 362*, 32–33. doi:10.1016/S0140-6736(03)15067-2.
Putnam, F. (2003). Ten-year research update review: Child sexual abuse. *Journal of the American Academy of Child and Adolescent Psychiatry, 42*, 269–278. doi:10.1097/00004583-200303000-00006.
Raj, A., Saggurti, N., Balaiah, D., & Silverman, J. G. (2009). Prevalence of child marriage and its effect on fertility and fertility-control outcomes of young women in India: A cross-sectional, observational study. *Lancet, 373*, 1883–1889. doi:10.1016/S0140-6736(09)60246-4.
Runyan, D. K., Shankar, V., Hassan, F., Hunter, W. M., Jain, D., Paula, C. S., et al. (2010). International variations in harsh child discipline. *Pediatrics, 126*(3), e701–e711, e708–e709. doi:10.1542/peds.2008-2374.
Schultz, T. (1971). *Investment in human capital: The role of education and of research*. New York: Free Press.
Shalhoub-Kevorkian, N. (1999). The politics of disclosing female sexual abuse: A case study of Palestinian society. *Child Abuse and Neglect, 23*(12), 1275–1293. doi:10.1016/S0145-2134(99)00104-0.
Stoltenborgh, M., van Ijzendoorn, M., Euser, E., & Bakermans-Kranenburg, M. (2011). A global perspective on child sexual abuse: Meta-analysis of prevalence around the world. *Child Maltreatment, 16*(2), 79–101. doi:10.1177/1077559511403920.
Stoltenborgh, M., Bakermans-Kranenburg, M., Alink, L., & van Ijzendoorn, M. (2012). The universality of childhood emotional abuse: A meta-analysis of worldwide prevalence. *Journal of Aggression, Maltreatment and Trauma, 21*, 870–890. doi:10.1080/10926771.2012.708014.
Turnock, B. (2009). *Public health: What it is and how it works* (4th ed.). Sudbury MA: Jones and Bartlett.
UNICEF. (2008). *India: Maternal, newborn and child survival*. Retrieved September 22, 2011, from http://www.childinfo.org/profiles.html.
United Nations Development Programme. (2013). *Human development report 2013*. Retrieved June 9, 2014, from http://hdr.undp.org/en/statistics/hdi.
United States Department of Health and Human Services Report. (2009). *Child maltreatment 2007*. Washington, DC: US Government Printing Office
Widom, C. (2014). Long-term consequences of child maltreatment. In J. Korbin & R. Krugman (Eds.), *Handbook of child maltreatment* (pp. 225–250). Dordrecht: Springer Scientific.
World Bank. (2012). *How we Classify Countries*. Retrieved June 9, 2014, from http://data.worldbank.org/about/country-classifications.
World Health Organization. (2006). *Preventing child maltreatment: A guide to taking action and generating evidence*. Geneva: World Health Organization and International Society for Prevention of Child Abuse and Neglect.
Zolotor, A. J., Theodore, A. D., Chang, J. J., Berkoff, M. C., & Runyan, D. K. (2008). Speak softly—and forget the stick: Corporal punishment and child physical abuse. *American Journal of Preventive Medicine, 35*(4), 364–369. doi:10.1016/j.amepre.2008.06.031.

Chapter 22
The Power of the Butterflies-Hearing the Children's Story: A Case-Based Discussion

Sue Foley, Jenny Rose and Liana Lowenstein

Introduction

It is essential that children really have a voice in therapeutic, forensic, and legal contexts. It is equally important that clinicians and investigators are able to hear the story of the child's experience. It is essential that children are seen as significant individuals, whose experience is respected and perspective validated. In particular, children need the opportunity to talk about what might be currently troubling them about their functioning and memories. The use of purely verbal and question and answer talking processes are rarely adequate. This paper has been developed from a case-based presentation and discussion given by Sue Foley at the Delhi conference in 2011. The presentation relies on the use of tools developed by Liana Lowenstein and the approaches used by Sue Foley and Jenny Rose in their work with children and families affected by trauma.

This article outlines a de-identified case situation, and describes tools and techniques that formed a creative approach to hearing from the children. Liana Lowenstein's work, tools and strategies will be referenced in this article as resources in this area (Lowenstein 1999a, 1999b, 2006). Liana is a play therapist, child psychotherapist, and social worker who has developed creative therapeutic techniques to engage children and families. Playfulness in therapeutic contexts is recognized as a helpful way of interacting about serious and worrying experiences (Hughes 2007). Whilst cognitive approaches have developed pre-eminence in the

S. Foley (✉) · J. Rose
The Children's Hospital at Westmead, Westmead, NSW, Australia
e-mail: sue.foley@health.nsw.gov.au

L. Lowenstein
Child Psychotherapist in Private Practice, Toronto, Canada

S. Deb (ed.), *Child Safety, Welfare and Well-being*,
DOI 10.1007/978-81-322-2425-9_22

psychological literature, the social work authors of this article all recognize creative, play-based techniques as effective and developmentally appropriate ways to gather information, process feelings, thoughts, and beliefs and assist in the child's healing process.

Children's Participation

Sometimes children who have experienced assault or maltreatment are primarily seen as sources of "evidence" for legal processes. The opportunity to communicate must be helpful for them as well as valid for legal and case management processes. Telling the story must not be an experience of being re-traumatized.

Children must be given the opportunity to tell their story in a safe, therapeutic way that does not re-traumatize them and may facilitate the development of a coherent memory. Story telling must take place in a safe, engaging, and developmentally appropriate context. The telling of the story with associated emotions allows integration of the feelings and a realistic and holistic account of the child's past and current experiences. The Stones cards are one of many therapeutic tools available to clinicians. These are developed by Innovative Resources (Innovative Resources). These cards can be sorted so that ten or more cards with feelings are shown to the child who is asked to pick the ones that are relevant to their experience. The feelings can then be named and discussed. For example, the child (and therapist) may both describe a time that they last felt this way. The Stones picture-based card have no writing on them, making them suitable for use with children from diverse cultural backgrounds and a range of developmental stages.

The children from this case situation had not had the opportunity to openly talk about their experiences or specify the associated feelings, such as "scary" or "frightened" or "angry". Importantly they had not been assisted in telling their parents how those experiences continued to adversely impact on them 3 years after the events had occurred. The opportunity to tell their story is sometimes a form of exposure and can be a way of meaning making and healing for the child.

Engagement is the first step in hearing from children. An important adverse effect of trauma is hypersensitivity and hyper-arousal or anxiety. The beginning of contact with a new or unfamiliar person has the potential to be distressing to children. Hyper sensitivity to criticism, and hyper arousal or emotional distress can influence the child's emotional functioning in interview. A playful or creative approach may be able to assist in reducing the associated physiological arousal when children are being interviewed.

Playful processes offer the opportunity of engaging with children at their developmental level and gaining understanding of the child's perceptions, their inner world and their representation of their feelings. The playful process can increase the child's sense of strength and capacity; it can offer opportunity to become familiar with their counselor or caseworker; playfulness can reduce cognitive barriers, triggers, and the threat that remembering past events creates.

Theory and Tools

Trauma treatment theorists contribute wisdom, skills, and tools that can be used by practitioners. The work of family therapist, Dr. Hughes (2007), Lowenstein (1999a, 1999b, 2006), and Malchiodi and Perry (2008) influenced the work undertaken in this case story. Other therapy such as Trauma Focused Cognitive Behavioral Therapy also lends itself to playful approaches (Cavett 2012; Scheeringa et al. 2011).

The events that affected the children in this case took place some 3 years before this assessment. Their father had decided that he was the primary victim and that he should be able to care for the children. The mother had formulated that the incident in which she had stabbed the father was a defensive situation and that she had been assaulted regularly by the father. The police records showed that there was a history of assaults in the home, to which the police had responded. There were also validated records of substance abuse (alcohol and marijuana) by each of the parents. There were concerns reported that the children had suffered from emotional abuse, neglect of physical needs and health needs and were living an itinerant lifestyle.

The three children were reported to be each suffering from significant post-trauma symptoms. These included sleep walking, anxiety, intrusive memories, and behavioral problems. Specifically, Paige age 5 (girl) was reported to have significant aggressive behavior problems, Peter age 7 (boy) was noted to have learning and behavior problems and Kerry age 9 (girl)—presented as pseudo mature, and having serious anxiety issues, including regular sleep walking. The children were noted by their careers to be aggressive toward each other. They had been in a stable foster family for 3 years. The children were ambivalent about their parents.

The Task

The main referral tasks in this assessment were to:

- Evaluate the current impact of past trauma
- Understand the meaning and value of the children's current relationships, including their family of origin, their extended family, the current foster carers and each other.
- Evaluate the possible impact on each of the children, of restoration to someone in their family.
- identify the children's views on the above
- evaluate current safety
- identify parental understanding of the children's needs
- identify what the children would need to assist them in the healing process.

From a therapeutic, systemic point of view, a very important task was to assist the parents to understand the needs of the children. The assessment process needed to not just address the parameters of the legal system. Importantly this was an opportunity to address the relationship and systemic needs of the children.

The use of creative tools and games can be a way of expediting this assessment process. The professional conducting the assessment was going to be an independent assessor, not engaged in an ongoing process. In this instance the assessment with the children and their parents took place over a period of 5 hours including the sessions with the parents.

The Process

In summary, the assessment process included meeting with the children together and individually at their foster home. After this session, a further session with each parent, at an office, took place 3 days later. A meeting had previously taken place with the parents without the children on an earlier occasion. After introducing me and talking with the careers briefly, the children together did the following activities and then individually spoke about what they had written or indicated in the activity sheet.

The tools used included *Butterflies in My Stomach* (Lowenstein 1999a, p. 9); *People in My World* (Lowenstein 2006, p. 42) and *Stones Have Feelings Too* cards (Innovative Resources). The Stones cards allow exploration of the feelings and were used with the whole family after the initial assessment.

Liana Lowenstein, the third author of this article advises as follows: "*Butterflies in My Stomach* is an engaging and concrete tool to assess the child's presenting problems. The practitioner introduces the activity by pointing out that everyone has problems and worries, and this can feel like having Butterflies in Your Stomach".

The child is provided with paper butterflies and asked to write his or her worries each on a separate butterfly. The purpose of the intervention is to normalize that everyone has worries, to assess the child's worries (and presenting problems) and to facilitate open communication of salient issues. The older two children appeared to readily understand this idea. It took a little longer to explain to Paige, the 5 year-old child.

Several days later, the Butterflies activity facilitated the children's communication with each of their parents about their current emotional and mental state. The clinician (the first author) assisted them to talk about these issues using the completed activity sheet. The parents became very emotional when they heard from the children about their memories and their distress. This was the first time there had been a discussion between the children and their parents about what they had experienced, what they remembered of this and how they currently felt about the past events and their current memories.

The engaging and concrete nature of the Butterflies activity helped the children to tell their parents about their worries. Through this activity, the children communicated that they were worried about whether their Mum would hurt them or someone else again. They were worried that Dad would not keep his promises. They were worried about their symptoms—sleep walking, crying, and angry behavior. They were worried about resources such as toys, games, and activities that they had at the foster home but may not have at the home of either parent or their grandparents.

People in my world (Lowenstein 2006, pp. 45–46) evaluated the children's perception of family and community relationships. The activity identified important supportive people and also identified people who were creating stress, including a foster carer relative who was identified as always angry.

The tool looks like a world globe and is acceptable to both boys and girls. Stickers and stamps helped to increase the appeal of this activity and it became a discovery journey for the children as they chatted about various people in their world and activities they had enjoyed with them. It also allowed them to put their relationships into context, including family members, teachers, foster careers, and friends. The child is asked to label the world globe with significant people in their world, and then directed to use stickers and symbols to identify how they feel toward these people. For example: "Put happy face stickers on the people in your world who feel happy. Put an X on people who did something mean or bad. Put star stickers on people who help you." The clinician then asks exploratory questions to gather additional assessment information, such as: "I see you put an X on your mum. What did she do that was mean or bad?" and "You put a star sticker on your foster mum. In what ways does she help you?"

Safety

Any assessment tool must do no more harm and so continually monitoring verbal and non-verbal expression of emotion, ideas, and stated concerns is the responsibility of the clinician. In this instance there was some information identified which needed to be evaluated further in order to enhance the children's current wellbeing. That is, that a member of the foster family was often angry with the children.

The *People in my World* process also allowed the beginnings of a discussion about closeness and distance, grief, and celebration. These issues are essential to ensuring that children living in out of home care are well supported in maintaining helpful relationships. Their primary attachment relationships have usually been interrupted and it is unlikely that they will be adequately repaired. It is also unlikely that good enough attachments will be made with professional foster carer that need to make multiple relationships with children that are not necessarily focused on each individual child. This tool allows the child to tell the story of their relationships and to begin to share where the gaps may be in the support and connections available to them. The effect of this approach was some healing for the children and improved understanding of the children's experience for the parent.

Discussion

Drawing and writing, cards, and games are familiar and normal activities for most children. The clinician's comfort and confidence with these activities will ensure that the children will experience comfort and calmness. It is very important that the creative processes recognize both the strengths and difficulties experienced by the child and are relevant to their situation. The process was positive and the children were heard. Their story was understood. The parents said that this was the first time they understood the long-term impact of the children's exposure to violence and neglect. The uniqueness of the children's experience was identified and contributed to an in-depth assessment-based case plan. The dynamic of the assessment process was playful, accepting, curious and empathic (2. Hughes).

Assessments that are intentionally child-focused are more likely to elicit the authentic voice of the child. In many child protection matters, the therapeutic process of engagement of the child in telling their story to a clinician and also telling their story to a prepared and mindful parent will have immediate and long-term benefit to the children and their current and future relationships. Playfulness allows tolerance of anxiety and challenges resistance and avoidance. Using metaphors and symbols, such as butterflies, allows potentially frightening or uncomfortable feelings to be tolerated and increases the likelihood of a new narrative being created, helping to reduce emotional and psychological symptoms of the trauma.

Conclusion

There are many ways of engaging with children and this chapter demonstrates the use of various playful approaches, in particular two of Liana Lowenstein's tools. The use of tools in this case example ensured that the assessment could be undertaken efficiently. They also provided a communication tool that allowed the story of the children's past and current experiences to be heard by the parents.

The assessment activities were helpful tools to facilitate the development of a sound treatment plan which incorporated elements such as the children's current perceptions of potential danger or fear; ideas about who are safe and comfortable people in their lives, and what the children would like to have happen. Some children are never asked this question.

It is essential that all assessments are respectful and articulate the children's needs and circumstance in the voice of the child. Assessments, like the one described above, one have a significant therapeutic benefit to the individual child and to their family members, both their birth families and their foster carer.

References

Cavett, A. M. (2012). *Playful trauma focused cognitive behavioral therapy with traumatized children*. Retrieved from http://www.lianalowenstein.com/cavett.pdf.

Hughes, D. (2007). *Attachment-focused family therapy*. New York: Norton, Innovative resources, stoneshave feelings too. http://www.innovativeresources.org/default.asp?cmd=Product&productid=44299.

Lowenstein, L. (1999a). *Creative interventions to assess children and families*. www.LianaLowenstein.com.

Lowenstein, L. (1999b). *Creative interventions for troubled children and youth*. Toronto: Champion Press.

Lowenstein, L. (2006). *Creative interventions for bereaved children*. Toronto: Champion Press.

Malchiodi, C., & Perry, B. (2008). *Creative interventions with traumatized children*. New York: Guildford Press.

Scheeringa, M. S., Weems, C. F., Cohen, J. A., Amaya-Jackson, L., & Guthrie, D. (2011). Trauma-focused cognitive-behavioural therapy for posttraumatic stress disorder in three-through 6 year-old children: a randomized clinical trial. *Journal of Child Psychology and Psychiatry, 52*(8), 853–860. doi:10.1111/j.1469-7610.2010.02354.x.

Chapter 23
Child Sexual Abuse in Brazil: Awareness, Legal Aspects and Examples of Prevention Strategies

Lucia C.A. Williams and Sabrina M. D'Affonseca

Introduction

Child sexual abuse is a traumatic event with well-documented immediate and long-term effects, such as problems in individual physical health, mental health, and school functioning, as well as problems in social interactions and community life. Unfortunately, child sexual abuse is a widespread phenomenon, with comparable prevalence rates among internationally studied countries ranging from 7 to 36 % for females, and 3–29 % for males (Finkelhor 1994).

A recent meta-analysis of the prevalence of CSA involving 65 studies covering 22 countries (Brazil not included) showed that 7.9 % of men, and 19.7 % of women had suffered some form of sexual abuse prior to the age of 18 (Pereda et al. 2009). These authors call attention to the fact that even the lowest prevalence rates include a large number of victims that need to be taken into account, confirming the seriousness of the problem. Stoltenborgh et al. (2011) also conducted a meta-analysis encompassing 217 studies, published between 1980 and 2008, on the prevalence and incidence of child sexual abuse across all continents, indicating a global rate of 11.8 % (18 % of girls; 7.6 % of boys). The lack of epidemiological comparison studies involving Brazil in the above studies is not coincidental, as the country has yet to conduct population studies covering prevalence rates of child sexual abuse.

The objectives of this chapter are: (a) to present a brief overview of legal aspects pertaining to CSA in Brazil; (b) to describe cases widely reported in the national media which helped increase awareness of stakeholders; and (c) to give examples of preventive intervention strategies to curb this serious problem in the country.

L.C.A. Williams (✉) · S.M. D'Affonseca
Laprev – the Laboratory of Violence Analysis and Prevention,
Universidade Federal de São Carlos, São Carlos, Brazil
e-mail: williams@ufscar.br

S. Deb (ed.), *Child Safety, Welfare and Well-being*,
DOI 10.1007/978-81-322-2425-9_23

Brazil's Legislation on CSA

To understand and address the problem of CSA in Brazil, one must first mention Brazilian laws against sexual offenses. Brazil is a federal republic, composed of 26 states, and the federal state of Brasilia, the capital. Brazilian laws are regulated federally, and not by state; therefore, the country has a uniform legislation covering its wide territory. Sexual abuse is covered under the Brazilian Criminal Code under Title VI - Crimes against Sexual Dignity in two chapters: I—Crimes against Sexual Freedom, and II—Crimes against Vulnerable Persons (Gomide, 2012). The Criminal Code was altered in 2009, (Law no. 12.015, Brasil 2009), the first change since 1940 to include several articles that typify sexual abuse. The most important one is Article 213, dealing with rape, which is defined by the law as "to embarrass someone through violence or serious threat to body penetration or to practice or allow other sexual acts," with the detention penalty of 6–10 years, which is increased to 8–12 years if the rape results in serious physical harm or if the victim is under 18 or older than 14, and to 12–30 years if the rape results in death.

Article 218 deals with the Corruption of Minors, defined by law as "to induce someone younger than 14 to satisfy another person's lust," with a detention penalty of 2–5 years. Article 218-A concerns sexual acts in front of children; and article 218-B deals with "favoring prostitution or other types of sexual exploitation of vulnerable persons." In addition to the Criminal Code, the Child and Adolescent Act (*Estatuto da Criança e do Adolescente—ECA*) was revised to incorporate several types of child sexual abuse, including child pornography.

Although Brazil has not conducted prevalence CSA studies to inform practice and public policies, the country has been concerned and actively involved in establishing a network of protection services to address child maltreatment, and child sexual abuse in particular. The most striking example is the nation's efforts to pass pertinent laws in terms of child protection. Brazil's Constitutional Article 227 (Brazil 1988) was approved with the support of 1.5 million signatures from a popular initiative led by activists, intellectuals, and religious leaders, giving rise to a movement called *Children, a National Priority*. The article reads, in part:

> It is the family's duty, society's, and the State's to ensure that children and adolescents have as an absolute priority the right to life, to health, food, education, leisure, professional training, culture, dignity, respect, freedom, family and community life, in addition to rendering them safe from all types of negligence, discrimination, exploitation,violence, cruelty, and oppression (Brazil 1988).

Subsequently, Brazil's Child and Adolescent Act, implemented in 1990, and inspired by the Convention of the Rights of the Child (CRC), is considered a progressive regulation in child protection, requiring mandatory reporting of child abuse by professionals who serve or have direct contact with children. A Child Protection Service (CPS) was created and regulated in the Child and Adolescent Act, designated as the agency responsible for monitoring and assuring the rights of children. Every municipality with 100 000 inhabitants must have its CPS office, whose members are elected by the community for a 3 year term.

Media Attention to CSA

Although there is no scientific knowledge of the scope of CSA in Brazil, professionals working with children agree that it is a serious and widespread health problem requiring immediate attention by the government, policy makers, and society as a whole. A review of notorious sexual abuse cases reported by Brazilian media illustrates clearly the need for CSA prevention in the country.

The readiness to consider this problem is illustrated by the fact that Brazil has a national day, May 18, to fight child sexual abuse and sexual exploitation proposed by Federal Representative Rita Camata, and instituted by federal law (no. 9.970) in the year 2000. The initiative sprang from a group of over 80 agencies in 1998 at the first Brazilian meeting in Salvador, State of Bahia of ECPACT (End Child Prostitution, Child Pornography, and Trafficking of Children for Sexual Purposes). The date, May 18, was chosen to mark the day Aracelli Crespo, an 8 year-old girl from the State of Espírito Santo, was brutally raped and murdered after being abducted in 1973. The murder suspects were two youths with a history of drug abuse, but who came from influential families, and whose conviction on plentiful evidence in 1980 was nullified. The two were acquitted at a second trial in 1991.

José Louzeiro's 1976 book on the Aracelli case (Louzeiro 2013), described how 14 possible witnesses suffered suspicious deaths, and the author himself was threatened while doing his research for the book. Although, fortunately, murder following sexual violence is rare in Brazil, the case is considered emblematic of the difficulties encountered when prosecuting CSA.

Another significant and notorious case of sexual abuse was featured in the media in 1994, when a private school in Sao Paulo, *Escola Base*, was closed after allegations were made against six different adults, including a teacher and the school's owner, of child sexual abuse of 4 and 5 year olds. The allegations had some similarities with those presented at the McMartin trial in California (Pezdek et al. 2004), and were later to be judged unfounded. The accused were able to successfully manage to charge important stakeholders of the Brazilian press for biased coverage. While the *Escola Base* case is often mentioned in Brazilian discourse to stress ethical coverage by the press, it has unfortunately given the general public, lawyers, and politicians the incorrect notion that most sexual abuse allegations are false.

Brazilian public opinion was horrified in 2007, with a case involving a 15 year-old girl who was placed in a jail cell amongst men in the city of Abaetetuba, State of Para, in the Amazon region. She was sexually abused by different inmates in all but two of the 27 days that she was incarcerated. The notoriety of this case was exacerbated when the media revealed that judge Clarice Maria de Andrade had authorized the police chief to place the girl in an adult male cell, as the girl had a history of thefts handled by the same judge. This incident not only calls attention to the serious violation of human rights, and of the Child and Adolescent Act by officers of the law, but also to the disparities of protection services in remote parts of the country.

In 2008, Joana Maranhão, a 20 year-old international award-winning swimmer disclosed publicly that she had been sexually abused as a child by her swimming coach. This provoked, as a consequence, the altering of Brazilian law, in 2012, to accept delayed allegation of previous CSA cases which in the past would have been prescribed. The so-called *Joana Maranhão Law* (no. 12.650) is an advance for Brazilian children in terms of CSA prevention, as well as bringing awareness of the problem of CSA concerning coaches in sports.

More recently, in 2012, there was public outcry, including reprimanding remarks from the United Nations, when the media reported that Brazilian Supreme Court Judge Maria Theresa de Assis Maura considered non-guilty a male adult who had sex with three 12 year-old girls prior to Brazil's current legislation on sexual crimes, with the argument that the girls were "prostitutes". The case was subsequently reviewed and the man found guilty.

In May, 2012 Brazilian TV star Xuxa cried and disclosed on public television that she had been sexually victimized as a child by three different adults (her father's friend, her grandmother's fiancé, and a teacher) and that she had kept the abuse secret to family members. The Human Rights Secretary communicated that, as a consequence of the actress's disclosure, they had to train more staff to work for the Children's Helpline (*Disque 100*), as the average number of calls jumped 30 % —from the daily average of 80 thousand calls to 285,051 in the following 2 days.

The six examples above help to assess the impact CSA has in the country, showing that Brazil is still learning how to implement effective prevention strategies, such as the training of its key professionals as recommended by ISPCAN (International Society for the Prevention of Child Abuse & Neglect). However, there is a growing awareness about the harmful consequences of CSA in the country, and the Brazilian media have been instrumental in this regard.

Preventive Intervention Strategies and Challenges

The Child and Adolescent Act has allowed for a diverse creation of services to attend victims. Health professionals are required to send documentation of child abuse cases to the Ministry of Health. Unfortunately, specialized treatment to offenders is still rare in Brazil (Williams 2012). The Ministry of Social Services (*Ministério do Desenvolvimento Social*) created Project Sentinel in 2002 to help victimized children (Castanha 2006), and this project was instituted in each municipality. Project Sentinel has since been expanded to incorporate all forms of child maltreatment in the local municipal centers called CREAS (*Centro de Referência Especializado de Assistência Social* (Specialized Referral Center of Social Assistance).

Brazil's Ministry of Education developed an ambitious and countrywide project called *Escola que Protege* (*School which Protects*), in 2004, (Henriques et al. 2007), which was initially aimed at training teachers on child sexual abuse, and was later expanded to incorporate other forms of child maltreatment and school violence, as well as to train professionals other than educators. This project particularly targets municipalities located along child sexual exploitation routes which are routinely mapped by the government (Secretary of Human Rights), with the help of the police, the International Labour Organization, and Childhood Brazil.

The latter is the Brazilian branch of *World Childhood Foundation* (WCF), founded by Queen Silvia of Sweden who gives Brazil special attention due to the fact that she has a Brazilian mother. Along with *Save the Children*, WCF illustrates the important role NGOs have in child abuse prevention in Brazil, with valuable initiatives (see Marques 2009), such as the prevention of child sexual exploitation associated with tourism, by partnering with tourist businesses, as hotels, and teaching truck drivers as prevention agents.

Brazil's Secretary of Human Rights has had, since 2003, a free of charge helpline (*Disque 100*) to report child sexual abuse, which also may be accessed by the internet (www.disque100.gov.br). The country has had, since 2000, a *National Plan to Face Child Sexual Abuse,* and has given an example of international leadership when hosting the *Third World Congress Against Sexual Exploitation of Children and Adolescents,* organized by ECPACT International, in 2008, when the *Rio de Janeiro Declaration and Call for Action to Prevent and Stop Sexual Exploitation of Children and Adolescents* was written.

In spite of all these efforts, Child Protection Services in Brazil are short-funded, professionals still need specialized training, services for victims and offenders are scarce, CSA cases are under-reported, and reporting is done manually without a computerized general registrar or database. In addition, child abuse offenses have a disturbingly low conviction rate (Williams 2009): the child has to take part in repetitive interviews with different professionals, which is inadequate as it re-traumatizes the victim, as well as contaminates evidence, and the child is seldom requested to testify in court, or, when this occurs, the testimony is often conducted in an inadequate or unsafe way.

A research group involving professors and graduate students from ANPEPP (National Association of Research and Graduate Studies in Psychology) working in different Universities throughout Brazil in violent prevention is currently collecting data on CSA prevalence in Brazil. The group includes researchers from the Amazon region to the Southern State which borders Argentina, and has published a book on CSA prevention (Williams and Habigzang, 2014). This research group has developed a questionnaire to gather epidemiological data on CSA prevalence. Data have started to be collected initially with University students, to later be expanded to other populations segments. This data will help us have a better understand about CSA in Brazil and design efficient prevention programs.

Brazilian psychologists have also developed evidence based therapeutic interventions for sexually abused children using a cognitive-behavioral model (see for example Habigzang et al. 2013). The Laboratory of Violence Analysis and Prevention (Laprev) (www.ufscar.br/laprev), has also several examples of successful CSA prevention efforts (Williams et al. 2009). These efforts range from doing research to better understand the phenomenon in the Brazilian population (as in Padovani and Williams 2010) to assessing intervention efforts to teach child abuse prevention to health professionals (Bannwart and Williams 2012) and teachers (Brino and Williams 2006).

Recently Brazil's National School of Magistrates Training and Development (ENFAM) offered its first course on CSA to judges. This online multidisciplinary course was very well received and over 200 judges from all areas of the country took part of this first initiative. Among jurists involved in teaching such course there were one social worker, one physician and one psychologist. Finally, Brazil has recently initiated efforts to validate the NICHD (National Institute of Child Health and Human Development) protocol (Lamb et al. 2008), the well-researched structured protocol to interview children suspected of child sexual abuse victimization (http://nichdprotocol.com/nichdbrazil.pdf). Preliminary results of training in the use of the NICHD Protocol with 15 Brazilian forensic professionals (psychologists and social workers) involved in CSA cases from different municipalities showed significant changes in the interviewing of children: professionals increased the number of open-ended questions, and gathered more relevant information about details involved in the CSA cases (Hackbarth & Williams, submitted) when using the NICHD Protocol compared to when not using this method.

Conclusions

Although Brazil has not had yet solid epidemiological research to estimate the prevalence of CSA to inform practice, professional experience has been confirming the high prevalence shown in most countries. The media has been instrumental in raising awareness about CSA's impact, giving visibility to a once unspoken phenomenon. Preventive interventions in education, health, and forensic areas are present in the country. Many challenges still remain and will take a well-coordinated effort from many segments of society.

David Finkelhor (Finkelhor 2011; Finkelhor and Jones 2006), has been analyzing the declining trends of CSA in the US, Canada and some European countries (among other types of child maltreatment), a phenomenon which is associated with different variables involving prevention measures. The impression one has from Brazil is that we have to have solid data on CSA rates to observe a subsequent raise (motivated by awareness and improvement of the protection system), followed by a much needed future decline.

References

Bannwart, T.H. & Williams, L.C.A. (2012). Increasing awareness of Brazilian Family Health Team Professionals on reporting child abuse: A case study. In: A. Muela (ed.). *Child Abuse and Neglect—A Multidimensional Approach.* (pp. 117–136). Rijeka, Croácia: InTech.

Brasil (1988). Constituição da República Federativa do Brasil [Constitution of the Federative Republic of Brazil]. Brasília: Senado Federal.

Brasil (1990). Lei Federal nº 8.069, de 13 de julho de 1990 [Federal Law No. 8069 of 13 July 1990]. Brasília, DF.

Brasil (2009). Lei nº 12.015, de 7 de agosto de 2009 [By-Law No. 12 015, August 7 2009]. Brasília, DF.

Brino, R.F. E. & Williams, L.C.A. (2006). Brazilian teachers as agents to prevent child sexual abuse: An intervention assessment. In D. Daro (2006). *World Perspectives on Child Abuse.* (pp.75–78). (7a ed.). Chicago: ISPCAN—International Society for Prevention of Child Abuse and Neglect.

Castanha, N. (2006). Plano Nacional de Enfrentamento da Violência Sexual Infanto-Juvenil: Uma política em movimento. [National Plan to Curb Child Sexual Violence: A changing policy]. 2003–2005 Report. http://www.sedh.gov.br/clientes/sedh/sedh/spdca/publicacoes/.arquivos/.spdca/plano_naparte1.pdf (March 29, 2013).

Finkelhor, D. (1994). The international epidemiology of child sexual abuse. *Child Abuse and Neglect, 18*(5), 409–417. doi:10.1016/j.chiabu.2008.07.007.

Finkelhor, D. (2011). Prevalence of child victimization, abuse, crime, and violence exposure. In J. W. White, M. P. Koss, & A. E. Kazdin (Eds.), *Violence against women and children: Mapping the terrain* (pp. 9–29). Washington, D.C.: American Psychological Association.

Finlkelhor, D., & Jones, L. (2006). Why have child maltreatment and child victimization declined? *Journal of Social Issues, 62*(4), 685–716.

Gomide, P.I.C. (2012). A legislação brasileira sobre ofensas sexuais. [Brazilian legislation on sexual offenses]. In: L.C.A., Williams. *Pedofilia: Identificar e prevenir. [Pedophilia: How to identify and prevent].* (pp. 87-96). São Paulo: Editora Brasiliense.

Habigzang, L. F., Damásio, B. F., & Koller, S. H. (2013). Impact evaluation of a cognitive behavioral group model in Brazilian sexualized abused girls. *Journal of Child Sexual Abuse, 22*(2), 173–190. doi:10.1080/10538712.2013.737445.

Hackbarth, C & Williams, L.C.A. (submitted). Avaliação de capacitação do protocolo NICHD em duas cidades brasileiras. [Evaluation of the NICHD protocol training in two Brazilian municipalities].

Henriques, R., Fialho, L. & Chamusca, A. (Orgs.). (2007). Proteger para Educar: A escola articulada com as redes de proteção de crianças e adolescentes. [Protect to educate: The school articulated with child protection networks]. Caderno SECAD, 5. Brasília: Ministério da Educação. http://portaldoprofessor.mec.gov.br/storage/materiais/0000015504.pdf, March 29, 2013.

Lamb, M. E., Hershkowitz, I. Y., Orbach, W. & Esplin. (2008). *Tell me what happened: structured investigative interviews of child victims and witnesses.* Wiley Series in Psychology of Crime, Policing and Law. Chichester, UK and Hoboken, NJ: Wiley Blackwell.

Louzeiro, J. (2013). *Aracelli, meu Amor.* [Aracelli, my Love]. São Paulo: Editora Prumo.

Marques, M. (2009). O papel do Instituto WCF-Brazil (*World Childhoold Foundation*) no combate e prevenção da violência sexual: Relato de experiências bem sucedidas no Brasil. [WCF's role in curbing and preventing sexual violence: Reporting successful experiences in Brazil]. Em L.C.A. Williams & E.A. C. Araújo (Orgs.). (pp.193-202). *Prevenção de Abuso Sexual Infantil: Um enfoque interdisciplinar.* [Child sexual abuse prevention: Aninterdisciplinary approach). Curitiba: Editora Juruá.

Padovani, R.C. & Williams, L.C.A. (2010). Family violence history and poverty among psychiatric patients in Brazil. In: G.M. Lovisi, J.J. Mari & E.S. Valencia (Orgs.). *The psychological impact of living under violence and poverty I n Brazil.* (pp.9-103). New York: Nova Science Publishers.

Pereda, N., Guilera, G., Forns, M., & Gómez-Benito, J. (2009). The prevalence of child sexual abuse in community and students samples: A meta-analysis. *Clinical Psychology Review, 29*, 328–338. doi:10.1016/j.cpr.2009.02.007.

Pezdek, K., Morrow, A., Goodman, G., Quas, J. A., Saywitz, K. J., Bidrose, S., & Brodie, M. (2004). Detection deception in children: Event familiarity affects criterion-based content analysis ratings. *Journal of Applied Psychology, 89*(1), 119–126. doi:10.1037/0021-9010.89.1.119.

Stoltenborgh, M., Ijzendoorn, M., Euser, E., & Bakermans-Kranenburg, M. (2011). A Global perspective on child sexual abuse: Meta-Analysis of prevalence around the world. *Child Maltreatment, 16*(2), 79–101. doi:10.1177/1077559511403920.

Williams, L. C.A. (2012). *Pedofilia: Identificar e prevenir*. [Pedophilia: How to identify and preventing].São Paulo: Editora Brasiliense.

Williams, L.C.A. (2009). Introdução ao estudo do abuso sexual infantil e análise do fenômeno no Município de São Carlos. [Introduction to Child Sexual Abuse and analysis of the phenomenon in the city of São Carlos].Em L.C.A. Williams & E.A. C. Araújo (Orgs.).(pp.21-40). *Prevenção de Abuso Sexual Infantil: Um enfoque interdisciplinar*. [Child sexual abuse prevention: Na interdisciplinary approach). Curitiba: Editora Juruá.

Williams, L.C.A. & Habigzang, L.F. (2014). *Crianças e adolescentes vítimas de violência: Prevenção, avaliação e intervenção*. [Children vitimized by violence: Prevention, assessment and intervention]. Curitiba: Juruá.

Williams, L. C. A., Padovani, R. C., & Brino, R. F. (2009). *Empowering families to face domestic violence*. São Carlos: EDUFSCar/PAHO.

Chapter 24
Child Protection: Many Milestones on an Estranged Path

Bharti Ali

Abbreviations

CRC	Convention on the Rights of the Child
CWC	Child Welfare Committees to be set up under the Juvenile Justice (Care and Protection of Children) Act, 2000 for care, protection, treatment, and rehabilitation of children in need of care and protection
DCPU	District Child Protection Unit
GDP	Gross Domestic Product
ICDS	Integrated Child Development Services
ICPS	Integrated Child Protection Scheme
IMR	Infant Mortality Rate
JJB	Juvenile Justice Boards to be set up under Juvenile Justice (Care and Protection of Children) Act, 2000 for disposition of cases involving children in conflict with the law and their care, protection, treatment, and rehabilitation
MMR	Maternal Mortality Rate
PC&PNDT	Pre-conception and Pre-natal Diagnostic Techniques (Prohibition of Sex Selection) Act
POCSO Act	Protection of Children from Sexual Offences Act
PNDT Act	Pre-natal Diagnostic Techniques (Regulation and Prevention of Misuse) Act
SCPS	State Child Protection Societies

B. Ali (✉)
HAQ: Centre for Child Rights, New Delhi, India
e-mail: bharti@haqcrc.org; info@haqcrc.org

S. Deb (ed.), *Child Safety, Welfare and Well-being*,
DOI 10.1007/978-81-322-2425-9_24

SJPU Special Juvenile Police Units to be set up under Juvenile Justice (Care and Protection of Children) Act, 2000 for dealing with all matters involving children in need of care and protection (including victims of crimes) and children in conflict with the law

Introduction

Children are equal citizens of a country. However, they are more vulnerable than adults, and unable to vote and express their voice. Hence, they are affected more than any other age group by action or inaction of the Government.

Independent India gave itself a strong Constitution that mandates fulfilment of basic human rights of all people of the country, including children. Hence, the reality of children and their situations is disturbing on many counts, calling for urgent and serious attention.

Changing Socio-Economic Context and Developments in the Field of Child Rights and Child Protection

Since the 1990s, a period of global economic turmoil has impacted the economic policies and social reality of many countries. India witnessed a paradigm shift in economic policies; promoting free markets as the most effective way to achieve the greatest public good for society and individuals.[1] As financial capital gained importance over all sectors the common man was relegated to the oblivion.[2] Consequently child well-being was not prioritized; there were conflicts of interest between two sets of legal persons, the children on the one hand and the corporations on the other. The interests of the corporations were promoted and those of children neglected.[3] A Gross Domestic Product (GDP) growth rate reaching 8–9 % in 2007–2008, widened the gap between the rich and the poor. In all this, children remained vulnerable to exploitation and abuse, falling out of the social security and protective jurisdiction (Tables 24.1 and 24.2).

---

[1]HAQ: Centre for Child Rights and Terre des hommes (Germany) (2011). Introduction to Twenty Years of CRC—A Balance Sheet by CJ George, Regional Coordinator, South Asia, terre des hommes Germany. In *Twenty Years of CRC—A Balance Sheet, Volume I, II and III*. p. x. New Delhi. CRC20BS Collective publication.

[2]Ibid. p. x.

[3]Ibid. p. x.

Data from the Home Ministry show that 2,891 children below 14 years, including 1,345 girls and 1,546 boys, ended their lives in 2013.[4] There has been a 1094.4 % increase in cases of abetment to suicide of children between the year 2000 and 2013, 732.7 % increase in cases of "procuration of minors for immoral purposes" and 294.7 % increase in child rape. Over 3861 % increase in kidnapping of children during this period calls for serious attention.[5] While greater reporting is one of the reasons for such visible increase, on the whole, large numbers of children are becoming victims of crimes. Besides dowry and customary beliefs that have perpetuated child marriages, lack of protection of girls has today become a common excuse for parents to marry off their daughters at an early age. There has been further deterioration in the sex-ratio of children in 0–6 age group from 927 in 2001 to 919 in 2011.[6] In 2001, sex ratio in the age group 10–19 years was 882, lower than the sex ratio of 927 in the 0–6 years' age group. It was 902 for younger adolescents aged 10–14 years and 858 for older adolescents aged 15–19 years.[7] While the 2011 figures for adolescent sex-ratio are yet to become public, there is a grim situation in which a large number of adolescent girls die to due to child birth, human trafficking or as victims of honor killings.

Comparatively the rate of conviction has gone down by 16.3 % points between 2001 and 2013.[8] Clearly, there is a need for better investigation and trial procedures, reduction in delays in trials, and most importantly in creating child-friendly laws and judicial system to help children fight for justice.

Not only have crimes against children increased over the years, even crimes by children have witnessed a spurt with a 44.4 % increase in juvenile crimes between 2001 and 2013 and an 23.8 % increase in number of juveniles apprehended.[9] Given further change in the juvenile justice law post 2007, apprehension of juveniles should reduce as the law does not require apprehension in all cases involving petty and non-serious offences. However, a high rate of apprehension of juveniles suggests that either the law is not being followed or children are committing

---

[4]National Crime Records Bureau, Ministry of Home Affairs, Government of India, All India Deaths and Suicides (2013). Available at: http://ncrb.gov.in/adsi2013/table-2.5.pdf.

[5]Data is computed from crime statistics provided in the Crime in India publications of the National Crime Records Bureau, Ministry of Home Affairs, Government of India, available at: http://ncrb.gov.in/.

[6]Census of India 2001 and 2011.

[7]HAQ: Centre for Child Rights and Terre des hommes (Germany) (2011). Introduction to Twenty Years of CRC—A Balance Sheet by CJ George, Regional Coordinator, South Asia, terre des hommes Germany. In *Twenty Years of CRC—A Balance Sheet, Volume III*. p. 8. New Delhi. CRC20BS Collective publication.

[8]National Crime Records Bureau, Ministry of Home Affairs, Government of India, Crime in India 2001 and 2013.

[9]Statistics looked at are for the period 2001 onwards as the juvenile justice law was amended in the year 2000 to include boys up to the age of 18 years. The source remains the Crime in India Publications of the National Crime Records Bureau.

Table 24.1 Nature of Crime Experienced by the Children during 1999–2013

Crime Head	Year														
	1999	2000	2001	2002	2003	2004	2005	2006	2007	2008	2009	2010	2011	2012	2013
Kidnapping & Abduction	791	711	2845	2322	2571	3196	3518	5102	6377	7650	8945	10670	15284	18266	28167
Exposure & Abandonment	593	660	678	644	722	715	933	909	923	864	857	725	700	821	930
Procuration of minor girls	172	147	138	124	171	205	145	231	253	225	237	679	862	809	1224
Buying of girls for prostitution	5	53	6	9	24	21	28	35	40	30	32	78	27	15	6
Selling of girls for prostitution	13	15	8	5	36	19	50	123	69	49	57	130	113	108	100
Child Marriage Restraint Act	58	92	85	113	63	93	122	99	96	104	3	60	113	169	222
Child Rape	3153	3132	2113	2532	2949	3542	4026	4721	5045	5446	5368	5484	7112	8541	12363
Importation of girls	1	64	114	76	46	89	149	67	61	67	48	36	80	59	31
Infanticide	87	104	133	115	103	102	108	126	134	140	63	100	63	81	82
Feticide	61	91	55	84	57	86	86	125	96	73	123	111	132	210	221
Murder	NA	NA	1042	1073	1212	1304	1327	1450	1377	1296	1488	1408	1451	1597	1739
Total	4934	5069	7217	7097	7954	9372	10492	12988	14471	15944	17221	19481	25937	30676	45085

NA stands for 'Not Available'
Source Crime in India Publications (1999–2013), National Crime Records Bureau, Ministry of Home Affairs, Govt. of India

Table 24.2 Purpose of Child Kidnapping, Abduction, and Trafficking (2003–2013)

Purpose of kidnapping, abduction and trafficking	2003	2004	2005	2006	2007	2008	2009	2010	2011	2012	2013
Adoption	21	15	41	23	36	34	44	37	62	46	111
Begging	6	20	19	24	13	17	30	34	45	29	44
Illicit Intercourse	383	414	501	676	649	825	765	749	1373	1113	2910
Marriage	1369	1593	1693	2621	3224	4003	4177	5193	8409	10572	14242
Prostitution	58	101	117	148	130	130	165	93	137	143	60
Selling body Parts	0	1	3	1	0	0	0	0	0	0	0
Unlawful activity	109	92	58	30	84	138	219	160	222	270	382
Slavery	6	16	4	15	35	32	49	26	24	5	19
Sale	13	13	9	11	12	14	39	51	166	54	49
Total	1965	2265	2445	3549	4183	5193	5488	6343	10438	12232	17817

Source Crime in India Publications, National Crime Records Bureau

serious and heinous offences that warrant apprehension. Both these situations ought to raise an alarm, as children in conflict with the law are also victims of their circumstances requiring equal attention.

As more families and children are visibly falling out of the protective net, child protection must become an area of concern for both civil society and policy makers and planners. Developments in the area of child protection need to be assessed.

Some Milestones

A separate Ministry for Women and Child Development was established in 2006 to cater to children's needs. Children's rights today are met through 49 special and local laws. In addition there are 78 legal provisions in the Indian Penal Code (IPC), the Code of Criminal Procedure (CrPC) and the Indian Evidence Act to deal with crimes against children, 9 policy documents impacting children's lives, many goals and targets set out under Five Year plans and the National Plan of Action for Children, 2005. Similarly, there are also 98 central government's budgeted programs and schemes for children from 14 different Ministries, a National Commission for Protection of Child Rights and 25 State Commissions.[10]

For the first time in the history of planned development in India, the Eighth Five Year Plan, (1992–1997) had a separate section on child development in its chapter on social welfare, focusing on "child survival, protection, and development." The Eighth Plan recognized the "girl child" as an important target group and the need to fight against prevailing gender discrimination. It also recognized the need to address child abuse and juvenile justice.[11]

The Ninth Five Year Plan, 1997–2002 reaffirmed its priority for the development of early childhood through inter-ministerial strategies as an investment in the country's human resource development. Major areas of child development such as health, nutrition, and education remained the key focus.[12]

The Tenth Five Year Plan, 2002–2007 set certain targets for monitoring women and child development, including

- all children in school by 2003;
- all children to complete 5 years of schooling by 2007;

[10]HAQ: Centre for Child Rights. Update on Twenty Years of CRC—General Measures of Implementation. In *Twenty Years of CRC—A Balance Sheet, Volume I, II and III*. p. 24. New Delhi. CRC 20 BS Collective Publication.

[11]HAQ: Centre for Child Rights and terre des hommes (Germany). Twenty Years of CRC—General Measures of Implementation. In *Twenty Years of CRC—A Balance Sheet, Volume I, II and III*. p. 24. New Delhi. CRC 20 BS Collective Publication.

[12]Ibid. p. 25.0.

- reduction in gender gaps in literacy and wage rates by at least 50 % by 2007;
- reduction in the IMR to 45 per 1000 live births by 2007 and 28 by 2012; and
- Reduction in MMR to 2 per 1000 live births by 2007 and to 1 per 1000 live births by 2012.

The other objectives of the Tenth Plan included addressing the decline in the child sex ratio, and universalization of the Integrated Child Development Services (ICDS) scheme. It recognized heterogeneity within groups, acknowledged multiple discriminations and suggested pilot interventions to resolve problems.[13] The mantra for achieving the targets was convergence between all sectors, ministries, departments, and schemes.

For the first time in the history of planned development in India, the Eleventh Five Year Plan, 2007–2012 had a section called "Child Rights" within a chapter titled "Towards Women's Agency and Child Rights". There was a paradigm shift in the Plan's approach to children: it strove to create a protective environment that will ensure every child's right to survival, participation and development. It recognized the need for investing in preventive aspects of protection, i.e., strengthening families to ensure that children do not fall out of the social security and protective net.[14] It launched the Centrally Sponsored Integrated Child Protection Scheme (ICPS) as a flagship program to achieve these goals. The need for convergence between ministries and states was reiterated, calling for a review of policies, programs, services, laws, budgets, and procedures to be laid down by every ministry/department to examine how it can incorporate and integrate better development and protection of children.

The ICPS was conceived as a comprehensive child protection scheme bringing all existing schemes for protection of children in difficult circumstances under one umbrella such as the program for dealing with juvenile maladjustment, the program for street children, adoptions through Shishu Grehas and Childline. Indeed strengthening families to protect children and establishing a child tracking system were the additional and most significant components of ICPS.

For years, the focus of child protection planning remained confined to dealing with post-harm situations through laws, programs, and schemes. On prevention, nothing moved beyond awareness generation programs. ICPS thus brought the most welcome change by focusing on "building a protective environment for children," thereby enhancing the preventive aspect of child protection.

Along with efforts made at strengthening the programmatic framework, the last 20 years have witnessed significant and crucial reform in laws protecting children and their human rights.

---

[13]Ibid. p. 25.

[14]Ibid. p. 25.

Legal Reform

- Right to Education for the 6–14 year-old children became a Fundamental Right. The Right of Children to Free and Compulsory Education Act was enacted in 2009.
- For the first time, early childhood care and development found space in the Constitution as a Directive Principle of State Policy, to give children a safe place while their parents toiled for a living.
- The PNDT Act was amended to become PC & PNDT Act, laying down provisions to cover pre-conception sex selection and providing for better monitoring and action against the erring persons.
- The Infant Milk Substitutes, Feeding Bottles and Infant Foods (Regulation of Production, Supply, and Distribution) Act of 1992, was also amended to ban advertisement of baby food and provide for punishments in case of violation.
- Additions were made to the list of hazardous occupations and sectors banning child labor, particularly the 10 October 2006 notification banning child labor in the domestic sector and dhabas and eateries. And a further amendment to the law is on the anvil, which will prohibit all forms of child labor up to the age of 14 years as well as child labor in the 14–18 in hazardous occupations and processes, while regulating child labor in the 14–18 age categories in non-hazardous sectors.
- A new Juvenile Justice Act was put in place in 2000 and further amended in 2006 as an attempt to bring it in conformity with the international law and principles of diversion and restorative justice, and best interest of the child.
- The Commission for the Protection of Child Rights Act was enacted in 2005 to set up children's commissions at the centre and in the states.
- The earlier child marriage law was replaced with the Prohibition of Child Marriages Act in 2006, shifting from mere restraint to prohibition of child marriages and providing greater punishments.
- The State of Goa framed a comprehensive law for children called the Goa Children's Act, 2003
- The Information Technology Act in 2008 was also amended to address the use of children for pornography and their abuse in print and digital form.
- Several amendments took place in the criminal legislation, particularly the Code of Criminal Procedure and the Indian Evidence Act to provide protection for victims of rape in the course of investigation, medical examination, and trial.
- The Protection of Children from Sexual Offences Act, 2012 and the rules made there under are the most recent steps to deal with all forms of child sexual abuse and provide for stringent measures, making it mandatory for all to report sexual offences against children.
- Several laws for persons with disability came into existence between 1992 and 1995—The Rehabilitation Council of India Act, 1992, The Persons with Disabilities (Equal Opportunities, Protection of Rights and Full Participation) Act, 1995, and The National Trust for Welfare of Persons with Autism, Cerebral Palsy, Mental Retardation and Multiple Disabilities Act, 1999.

Role of Judiciary on Child Rights' Issues

Some progressive orders and judgements invoking the CRC and upholding children's rights in certain key areas include the following:

- Guardianship—recognizing "mother" too as a natural guardian;
- Right to education—monitoring implementation of the constitutional guarantee and addressing violations brought to the notice of the courts;
- Right to food and adequate nutrition—court order requiring universalization of ICDS and monitoring implementation of the food programs;
- Judgments providing for and establishing guidelines for protection of victims of child sexual abuse and witness assistance;
- Juvenile justice—courts have been monitoring implementation and requiring child protection system to be put in place.
- Constitutional validity of the Juvenile Justice (Care and Protection of Children) Act, 2000, as amended in 2006 has been upheld by a three-judge Bench of the Supreme Court of India recently despite a populist campaign against the law after the gang rape incident in Delhi on 12 December 2012 involving a minor.

Challenges

Is ICPS the Vehicle to Ensure Effective Implementation of All Child Protection Laws?

Unfortunately, the juvenile justice legislation is seen as the answer to all child protection issues and ICPS as the vehicle for implementing the juvenile justice law.

Almost 10 years later, the scheme is still in its nascent stage, yet to fully set up the implementation mechanism and have a functional system and structures in place. While the states report that they have set up Child Welfare Committees (CWCs),[15] Juvenile Justice Boards (JJBs)[16] and Special Juvenile Police Units (SJPUs)[17] in all districts, the website of the Ministry of Women and Child Development does not support this. According to the website, 20 states, the Union Territory of Chandigarh and the National Capital Territory of Delhi have 463 CWCs as against 512 districts (Table 24.3).

[15]CWC—Child Welfare Committees to be set up under the Juvenile Justice (Care and Protection of Children) Act, 2000 for care, protection, treatment and rehabilitation of children in need of care and protection.

[16]JJB—Juvenile Justice Boards to be set up under Juvenile Justice (Care and Protection of Children) Act, 2000 for disposition of cases involving children in conflict with the law and their care, protection, treatment and rehabilitation.

[17]SJPU—Special Juvenile Police Units to be set up under Juvenile Justice (Care and Protection of Children) Act, 2000 for dealing with all matters involving children in need of care and protection (including victims of crimes) and children in conflict with the law.

Table 24.3 State-wise number of child welfare committee's

S. No.	States	No. of Districts	No. of CWCs
1	Andhra Pradesh	23	23
2	Assam	27	27
3	Bihar	38	28
4	Chandigarh	1	1
5	Delhi	11	6
6	Gujarat	26	25
7	Haryana	21	9
8	Himachal Pradesh	12	12
9	Karnataka	30	30
10	Kerala	14	14
11	Madhya Pradesh	50	48
12	Maharashtra	35	35
13	Manipur	9	9
14	Meghalaya	7	7
15	Nagaland	11	11
16	Odisha	30	30
17	Rajasthan	33	33
18	Sikkim	4	4
19	Tamil Nadu	32	20
20	Tripura	4	4
21	Uttar Pradesh	75	69
22	West Bengal	19	18
Total		512	463

Yet another source from the Ministry gives a different set of figures. A report of the Ministry of Women and Child Development (Twelfth Five Year Plan) suggests that the numbers of statutory bodies to be established for child protection under the ICPS has increased since the scheme was launched in 2009. The Child Welfare Committees (CWCs) and Juvenile Justice Boards (JJBs) are reported to have doubled from 240 before introduction of the Integrated Child Protection Scheme (ICPS) to 548. Similarly, there are reportedly 561 JJBs as against 211 before introduction of the scheme. 660 Special Juvenile Police units (SJPUs) are also stated to have been set up. Further, 21 State Child Protection Societies (SCPS) and District Child Protection Units (DCPU) in 14 States, are also reported to have been established under the Scheme.[18] More recent and reliable data on CWCs and JJBs is available in the 264th report of the Parliamentary Standing Committee on Human Resource Development that reviewed the proposed Juvenile Justice Bill,

[18]HAQ: Centre for Child Rights and terre des hommes (Germany). Twenty Years of CRC—General Measures of Implementation. In *Twenty Years of CRC—A Balance Sheet, Volume III*. PP. 19–20. New Delhi. CRC 20 BS Collective Publication.

2014. According to this report, in a total of 660 districts in the country, there are 626 CWCs and 612 JJBs.

Amidst discrepancies in the figures regarding structures and juvenile justice system, the functionality of these bodies has come under severe question. Poor selection of staff, lack of personnel such as dedicated police officers to deal solely with child matters, welfare officers and probation officers, and necessary training are some of the serious gaps in the system.

Laws such as the Protection of Children from Sexual Offences (POCSO) Act 2012, calls for more mechanisms and a larger number of personnel such as support persons for children, translators and interpreters, counselors, special courts, etc. to deal with such cases. None of this can be met through ICPS as it has no budget for implementation of the POCSO Act.

Laws relating to child marriage, child trafficking and child labor either fall under different sections of the Ministry of Women and Child Development or under a completely different Ministry and none of these division/section is deal with child protection.

Investing in Child Protection Remains a Shameful Story

Unfortunately, investment in the area of child protection has remained a challenge. An analysis of the budget for children carried out by HAQ: Centre for Child Rights over the last decade reveals continuous neglect to child protection when it comes to backing law, policy and program commitments with financial commitment. Both in the overall budget of the Central Government and within the Central Government's budget for children, the share of child protection has remained the lowest and has increased only marginally in the last decade.

In financial year 2000–2001, share of child protection in the central government's budget was 0.01 %, increasing to 0.06 % in 2011–2012. On the other hand, within the limited budget for all child rights programs and schemes of the central government, the share of child protection schemes has increased only by 0.2 % points, from 1.07 % in 2000–2001 to 1.27 % in 2011–2012. Interestingly, while protection gets the least allocation in the Union Budget as compared to other child specific sectors, it also has highest budget under spending.[19]

The Ministry of Women and Child Development had made a request for Rs. 5300 Crores for ICPS in the Eleventh Five Year Plan i.e. an average of Rs. 1060 Crores per year, which was reduced to 186.40 Crores in the first year of the plan period, going up to Rs. 400 Crores only in the last year of the Eleventh Five Year

[19]HAQ: Centre for Child Rights and terre des homes (Germany). Twenty Years of CRC—General Measures of Implementation. In *Twenty Years of CRC—A Balance Sheet, Volume III*. p. 300. New Delhi. CRC 20 BS Collective Publication.

Plan.[20] Much of this was attributed to the lack of formalized agreements between the Centre and the states to implement the scheme. However, in the very first year of the Twelfth Five Year Plan (2012–2013), the budget estimates showed an 18 % decline over 2011–2012 in the share of child protection within the Centre's overall budget for children.

The Approach paper to the Twelfth Plan unfortunately did not even mention child protection as an area of concern, the focus being on health, nutrition and education. ICPS did not figure in the list of flagship programs and schemes of Government of India in the approach paper. This was despite a clear focus of the plan on "inclusive growth" and given the fact that the scheme requires more funds as almost all state governments have signed MOUs with the Central Ministry to implement it. Finally, after series of consultations, consolidation and enrichment of ICPS found a place in the Twelfth Plan document.

For the innumerable child protection laws existing today there are no financial commitments to ensure their implementation. Despite repeated demand from the civil society to back all laws with a financial memorandum, no heed is being paid to it. HAQ: Centre for Child Rights has drawn attention of the Planning Commission of India as well as other relevant authorities to make it mandatory for all Ministries/Departments to include a specific "budget for children" in their annual budgets so as to ensure the coordination and convergence required for implementation of various laws, polices, and programs.

Solutions are available, but children have not been given the priority when it comes to financial planning and investment. Child protection today demands far more attention than ever before. However, considering the decline in GDP and economic growth, the commitment to 'build a protective environment' for children is likely to result in a major set-back.

Greater and deliberate reliance on private public partnerships in the field of child protection reflects a shift in the government fulfilling its responsibilities and obligations toward children. State governments openly cite inability to run child protection services as a reason for inviting "Expressions of Interest" from civil society actors and the corporate sector.

For the corporate sector, it is a favorable opportunity which provides legally a viable option to deal with profits and taxes. Nonetheless, many states welcome such contribution as they have not been able to fulfil their obligations due to poor governance and inadequate efforts to protect child protection. Ethically, on the other hand, there are activists questioning the role of the corporate sector when the mining lobby and other industrial houses displace several families, rendering women and children vulnerable to all forms of exploitation and abuse, or tourism is promoted at the cost of child sexual abuse, or for that matter aggressive promotion of infant milk substitutes replaces breast feeding practices in a significant way.

At the same time, governments have been passing on critical child care services to NGOs and other charitable organisations expecting them to provide quality

[20]HAQ: Centre for Child Rights, *Mr. Finance Minister, what have you got for me this year? Budget for Children (BfC) in the Union Budget* 2012–2013. p. 4. New Delhi.

service at very low costs. For example, what the government invests in running an institutional care service for children in need of care and protection is far greater than what government gives to NGOs for providing the same service by way of grant-in-aid. The logic is that charities receive donations and grants from private agencies to provide quality care.

As is evident, simple administrative measures and lack of a political will have resulted in total failure in dealing with this issue.

Way Forward

The voice which resonates the "political will" to protect children has to be more strong and integrated than before to find an appropriate place in all the electoral manifestoes of various political parties. Unless "All rights for All children" becomes an indicator for national development, protection of children and the national economy will remain in peril.

References

HAQ: Centre for Child Rights. B-1/2 Malviya Nagar, Ground Floor, New Delhi – 110017, Tel: +91-11-26677412/26673599, Fax: +91-11-26674688, E-mail: bharti@haqcrc.org/info@haqcrc.org, Website: www.haqcrc.org.

HAQ: Centre for Child Rights and Terre des hommes (Germany). (2011). Introduction to Twenty Years of CRC—A balance sheet by CJ George, Regional Coordinator, South Asia, terre des hommes Germany. In *Twenty Years of CRC—A Balance Sheet, Volume I, II and III*. New Delhi. CRC20BS Collective publication.

HAQ: Centre for Child Rights. (2012–2013). *Mr. Finance Minister, what have you got for me this year? Budget for Children (BfC) in the Union Budget 2012–2013* (p. 4). New Delhi.

Ministry of Women and Child Development, Government of India. www.mwcd.nic.in.

National Crime Records Bureau, Ministry of Home Affairs, Government of India. Crime in India Publications. (1999–2013).

National Crime Records Bureau, Ministry of Home Affairs, Government of India, All India Deaths and Suicides. (2013). http://ncrb.gov.in/adsi2013/table-2.5.pdf.

Office of the Registrar General and Census Commissioner of India. Government of India. Census 2001 and 2011.

Chapter 25
A Multidisciplinary Approach to Child Protection for Sexual Abuse in India: The Law

Lina Acca Mathew

Introduction: The Ideology Governing Child Rights Against Sexual Abuse in India

The Government of India ratified the Convention on the Rights of the Child on 12 November 1992. Thereby India committed to follow a principle of child sensitivity within the legal and policy level framework. The need to address offences against children came to the forefront during discussions relating to the commission of the Study on Child Abuse: India 2007, which identified widespread abuse of children in the country. The consultations, which were initiated in 2005, led to the conclusion that there was a need for legislation on child abuse. Consultations in 2009 with NGOs (Non-Government Organizations), legal experts, child rights activists, and concerned government officers revealed that, instead of a general legislation covering all offences against children, focus should be on a Bill for Sexual Offences against children. It was felt that the relevant sections of IPC (Indian Penal Code), CrPC (Criminal Procedure Code), Evidence Act, and other laws could be amended concurrently to ensure that children were not victimized further and justice was rendered in a time-bound manner. It was further felt that the Draft Bill on Sexual Offences against children should be expanded to cover pornography and to provide for more child-friendly procedures. Later in the second stage, the Juvenile Justice Act, 2000, would be expanded to include other offences against children, which were not addressed in any other law. The system of child protection as laid down in legislations, requires collaborative and coordinated efforts of various stakeholders for effective implementation of the child protection framework in India.

L.A. Mathew (✉)
Government Law College, Ernakulam, Kerala 682011, India
e-mail: linamathew@gmail.com

S. Deb (ed.), *Child Safety, Welfare and Well-being*,
DOI 10.1007/978-81-322-2425-9_25

International Obligations

India is signatory to a host of International Covenants and Instruments focusing on child protection. The following are the international documents which guarantee certain rights to children in India:

UN Standard Minimum Rules for the Administration of Juvenile Justice (The Beijing Rules), 1985, which endeavors to provide a stabilizing environment to a juvenile and a juvenile in conflict with the law so as to reduce and reform delinquent behavior.

United Nations Convention on the Rights of the Child, 1989—a convention which states that in all actions concerning children, whether undertaken by public or private social welfare institutions, courts of law, administrative authorities, or legislative bodies, the best interests of the child shall be a primary consideration. In addition, appropriate legislative, administrative, social, and educational measures are to be taken to protect the child from all forms of physical or mental violence, injury or abuse, neglect or negligent treatment, maltreatment or exploitation, including sexual abuse, while in the care of parent(s), legal guardian(s), or any other person who has the care of the child. India acceded to the UNCRC on 11th January 1993.[1]

UN Guidelines for the Administration of Juvenile Delinquency 1990 (the Riyadh Guidelines), UN Rules for the Protection of Juveniles Deprived of their Liberty 1990 (JDLs or Havana Rules), and UN Standard Minimum Rules for Non-custodial Measures 1990 (The Tokyo Rules) are other guidelines to reform juveniles from delinquent behavior. These guidelines concern counteracting the detrimental effects of all types of detention, fostering integration in society, and promoting the use of non-custodial measures in punishment, as well as minimum safeguards for person(s) subject to alternative punishment to imprisonment.

Stockholm Declaration and Agenda for Action, 1996: The Agenda for action agreed upon by 119 countries including India were the setting targets for reducing children vulnerable to exploitation at the local/national level, developing implementation, and monitoring mechanisms in cooperation with civil society to reduce the vulnerability. This was achieved by creating a database of at-risk children at the local/national level, and close cooperation and coordination with the government and non-government sectors to monitor and evaluate the measures against sexual exploitation of children.

Optional protocol to the convention on the rights of the child on the sale of children, child prostitution, and child pornography 2000 mandates international obligations to pass specific laws against child pornography "punishable by appropriate penalties that take into account their grave nature" as well as enable

---

[1]Office of the United Nations High Commissioner for Human Rights (2006). "Status of Ratifications of the Principal International Human Rights Treaties As of 16 June 2006" at 6 http://www2.ohchr.org/english/bodies/docs/RatificationStatus.pdf (accessed on 31/05/2013 at 11:54).

extradition, mutual assistance in investigation, and seizure of property. The protocol expresses grave concern over the problems of child sexual exploitation—international traffic in children, sale of children, sex tourism, and online child pornography. Furthermore, it is stated that member states of the United Nations were "concerned about the growing availability of child pornography on the Internet and other evolving technologies…" India ratified this instrument on 16th September 2005.[2]

Optional Protocol on the Involvement of Children in Armed Conflict 2000 requires governments to ensure that children under the age of 18 are not recruited compulsorily into their armed forces, and requires governments to do everything feasible to ensure that members of their armed forces who are under 18 years of age do not take part in hostilities. India ratified this instrument on 30th December 2005.[3]

The Yokohama Global Commitment 2001: The commitment was to develop national agendas and strategies or plans of action for implementation of measures to address the root causes which lead to sexual exploitation, for closer networking with stakeholders and enforcement agencies to combat sexual exploitation. Furthermore, to ensure adequate resource allocation, to take adequate measures to address negative aspects of new technologies, to stress the importance of family and strengthen social protection of children, and to commit to cooperation and protection at levels to eliminate all forms of sexual exploitation.

SAARC Convention on Prevention and Combating Trafficking in Women and Children for Prostitution 2002 emphasizes that trafficking women and children for the purpose of prostitution is a violation of basic human rights.

SAARC Convention on Regional Arrangements on the Promotion of Child Welfare in South Asia 2002 recognizes survival, protection, development and participatory rights of the child, and promotes solidarity, cooperation, and collective action between SAARC countries in the area of child rights.

UN Convention on the Rights of Persons with Disabilities 2006 intends to protect the rights and dignity of persons with disabilities. Parties to the convention are required to promote, protect, and ensure the full enjoyment of human rights by persons with disabilities including such children, and ensure that they enjoy full equality under the law. India ratified the Convention on 1st October 2007.[4]

The Rio de Janeiro Declaration and Call for Action to Prevent and Stop Sexual Exploitation of Children and Adolescents 2008 provides a blueprint for governments, inter-governmental and non-governmental organizations, human rights institutions, ombudspersons, the private sector, law enforcement and legal

---

[2] *Id.*

[3] *Id.*

[4] National Human Rights Commission India (2012). *A Handbook on International Human Rights Conventions* at 168 http://nhrc.nic.in/Documents/Publications/A_Handbook_on_International_HR_Conventions.pdf (accessed on 31/5/2013 at 13:07).

community, religious leaders, parliamentarians, researchers and academics, civil society, and children and adolescents. This declaration seeks to call such bodies and persons to prevent, prohibit, and stop sexual exploitation of children and adolescents and to provide the necessary support to children who have fallen victim to abusers. Non-commercial sexual exploitation in the family, child marriage, sexual exploitation of child domestic laborers, the commercial sex industry, child pornography, and sexual exploitation of children in cyberspace were examined.

Indian Constitutional Provisions

The Indian Constitution guarantees certain values to all its citizens, which aim to protect the dignity of the individual and create conditions in which every human can develop to the fullest potential. The Indian Constitution imposes negative obligations on the State not to encroach on individual liberty in its various dimensions. The following rights are relevant to child protection:

Article 14: The State shall not deny to any person equality before the law or the equal protection of the laws within the territory of India;

Article 15: The State shall not discriminate against any citizen on grounds only of religion, race, caste, sex, place of birth, or any of them;

Article 15(3): Nothing in this article shall prevent the State from making any special provision for women and children;

Article 19(1) (a): All citizens shall have the right (a) to freedom of speech and expression;

Article 21: Protection of life and personal liberty-no person shall be deprived of his life or personal liberty except according to the procedure established by law;

Article 21A: Free and compulsory education for all children of the age of 6 to 14 years;

Article 23: Prohibition of traffic in human beings and forced labor-(1) Traffic in human beings and beggars and other similar forms of forced labor are prohibited and any contravention of this provision shall be an offence punishable in accordance with law;

Article 24: Prohibition of employment of children in factories, etc.,—No child below the age of 14 years shall be employed to work in any factory or mine or engaged in any other hazardous employment;

Article 39: The state shall, in particular, direct its policy toward securing: (e) that the health and strength of workers, men and women, and the tender age of children are not abused and that citizens are not forced by economic necessity to enter vocations unsuited to their age or strength; (f) that children are given opportunities and facilities to develop in a healthy manner and in conditions of freedom and dignity and that childhood and youth are protected against exploitation and against moral and material abandonment.

National Legislations on Child Rights

There are various national legislations for protection of children in India like The Indian Penal Code, 1860, Guardian and Wards Act, 1890, Hindu Adoption and Maintenance Act, 1956, Probation of Offenders Act, 1958, Orphanages and Other Charitable Homes (Supervision and Control) Act, 1960, Bonded Labor System (Abolition) Act, 1976, Immoral Traffic Prevention Act, 1986, Prevention of Illicit Traffic in Narcotic Drugs and Psychotropic Substances Act, 1987, Pre-natal Diagnostic Techniques (Regulation and Prevention of Misuse) Act, 1994, Persons with Disabilities (Equal Protection of Rights and Full Participation) Act, 2000, The Information Technology Act, 2000, Juvenile Justice (Care and Protection of Children) Act, 2000, Commission for Protection of the Rights of the Child Act, 2005, Prohibition of Child Marriage Act 2006, The Juvenile Justice (Care and Protection of Children) Rules, 2007, The Protection of Children from Sexual Offences Act, 2012, The Protection of Children from Sexual Offences Rules, 2012. In addition to these national instruments, there exists the Goa Children's Act 2003, a law applicable only to the State of Goa, which guarantees children's rights in Goa.

The first legislation catering to children was the Apprentice Act, 1850, which provided vocational training to children in the age group of 10–18 in order to provide opportunities for convicted children for rehabilitation. The Reformatory Schools Act 1987 amended the law relating to reformatory schools. It also made provisions for male offenders below the age of fifteen. The Indian Jail Committee (1919–1920) stressed the importance of a fair trial and fair treatment of children in conflict with law. This Committee's recommendations paved way for the enactment of the Children Act in Madras in 1920.[5] The Bengal Act 1922 and the Bombay Act 1924 followed the 1920 Madras Act.

The Children Act 1960 was a Central enactment passed post-Independence. It aimed to provide for the care, protection, maintenance, welfare, training, education and rehabilitation of neglected or delinquent children and for the trial of delinquent children in the Union territories. Cases involving neglected children were to be handled by separate Child Welfare Boards. Both neglected and delinquent children were to be advised by a probation officer. Cases involving delinquent children were to be handled by separate Children's Courts.[6] Certain amendments were made to the Children's Act 1960 in the year 1978. However, this enactment was confined to the Union Territories of India alone.

While uniform legislation regarding juvenile justice for the whole country was needed, it was not legally possible to pursue the matter at the Union level as the subject matter of such legislation fell in the State List of the Constitution. However, such changes were later possible with India becoming signatory to the UN Standard Minimum Rules for the Administration of Juvenile Justice in 1985.

---

[5]Pinho, E. (2011). Juvenile Justice Act; A reformative step for children in Conflict with Law. http://www.scanindia.in/blog/tag/juvenile-justice-act-2000/.

[6]Representing Children Worldwide. (2005). India. http://www.law.yale.edu/rcw/rcw/jurisdictions/assc/india/frontpage.htm#_edn5.

In order to bring the operations of the juvenile justice system in the country, in conformity with its international obligations, the Parliament exercised its power under Article 253[7] and passed the Juvenile Justice Act 1986, authorizing the establishment of separate Juvenile Welfare Boards for neglected children nationally.

After the Convention on the Rights of Child of 1989 was ratified by India, the Central Government repealed the 1986 Juvenile Justice Act and passed a new Act known as the Juvenile Justice (Care and Protection) Act (2000) with a view to incorporate the principles of the UNCRC and further streamline the judicial system for children.

The Juvenile Justice (Care and Protection of Children) Act 2000 (*JJA*) and the Juvenile Justice (Care and Protection of Children) Rules 2007 (*JJ* Rules)

The *JJA* consolidates two issues, namely the law relating to children in conflict with law, and children in need of care and protection. It stresses a child-friendly approach with a focus on the best interests of children. Children in conflict with law are to be tried by the Juvenile Justice Board (also known as JJB) under Section 4, which consists of a Metropolitan Magistrate or Judicial Magistrate of the First Class, and two social workers of whom at least one shall be a woman. Section 29 of the Act lays down the legal procedure for protecting a child victim of sexual abuse through the mechanism of a Child Welfare Committee (called the CWC in short). The CWC consists of a Chairperson and four other members, of which one shall be a woman and the other an expert on matters concerning children. However, this committee does not have any member of the judiciary. The constitution of a Child Protection Unit (called CPU) for the State and for every district, in order to ensure the implementation of this Act, is a highlight of the 2006 Amendment to the *JJA* 2000. Rule 81 of the *JJ* Rules 2007 elaborates on the functions of the District Child Protection Unit. It shall ensure the implementation of the infrastructure of JJBs, CWCs, Special Juvenile Police Units and homes in each district, identifications of families at risk and children in need of care and protection, creating district-specific databases to monitor trends and patterns, setting up of District, Block, and Village level Child Protection Committees for effective implementation of programs and carrying out coordination with governmental and other agencies for effective child protection. The creation of the Special Juvenile Police Unit (SJPU) for police officers to coordinate and to upgrade the police treatment of the juveniles and the children by virtue of

[7]Article 253: Legislation for giving effect to international agreements, Notwithstanding anything in the foregoing provisions of this chapter, Parliament has power to make any law for the whole or any part of the territory of India for implementing any treaty, agreement or convention with any other country or countries or any decision made at any international conference, association or other body.

Section 63 is another special feature of this legislation. Rule 84 of the *JJ* Rules deals with the setting up of the SJPU. There can be SJPUs at city and district levels. The SJPU at the District level shall consist of a juvenile or child welfare officer of the rank of police inspector and two paid social workers having experience of working in the field of child welfare, of which one shall be a woman. The District Child Protection Unit of the State Government shall provide services of its two social workers to the Special Juvenile Police Unit for discharging their duties. The SJPU at district level shall coordinate and function as a watch-dog for providing legal protection against all kinds of cruelty, abuse and exploitation of children or juveniles. The superintendent of police in a district shall head the SJPU and shall oversee its functioning from time to time. A nodal officer from police, not less than the rank of Inspector General of Police, shall be designated in each state to coordinate and upgrade the role of police on all issues pertaining to care and protection of children or juveniles under the Act. Any police officer found guilty, after due inquiry, of torturing a child, mentally or physically, shall be liable to be removed from service, besides being prosecuted for the offence.

This Act provides for punishment of adult offenders who have treated a child with cruelty, or given the child intoxicating liquor, narcotic drug or psychotropic substance or exploited a child employee. Under Section 21, the law also provides penalty for disclosure of identity of a child in need of care and protection and a child in conflict with law by the media. The principles of best interests of the child, non-stigmatizing semantics and principles embodied in the UN Convention on the Rights of the Child have been incorporated into these enactments.

The machinery for trial of adult offenders of children was not covered by the *JJA*. Offences committed by adults against children, follow ordinary courts of the land, governed by the Criminal Procedure Code of 1973. Formerly, the general rules of evidence were applicable uniformly to all. However, with the advent of the historical case of *Sakshi* versus *Union of India*,[8] a separate child-friendly procedure came into existence in the ordinary courts. Here, the Supreme Court lay down that the following specifications are to be kept into consideration by all courts in the Union of India during the trial of a case of child sexual abuse, namely:

(1) The provisions of sub-Section (2) of Section 327, *CrPC*, in addition to the offences mentioned in the sub-section, shall also apply in inquiry or trial of offences under Sections 354 and 377, *IPC*. (2) In holding trial of child sex abuse or rape: (i) a screen or some such arrangements may be made where the victim or witness (who may be equally vulnerable like the victim) does not see the body or face of the accused; (ii) the questions put in cross-examination on behalf of the accused, in so far as they relate directly to the incident, should be given in writing to the Presiding Officer of the Court who may ask questions put to the victim or witness in a language which is clear and is not embarrassing; (iii) the victim of child abuse or rape, while giving testimony in Court, should be allowed sufficient breaks as and when required.

[8]AIR 2004 SC 3566.

Thus, through this judgment the Supreme Court attempted to incorporate the principles of non-stigmatizing semantics, the dignity and worth of the child, innocence of the child, safety and positive measures, equality and non-discrimination, privacy and confidentiality, best interest of the child, etc., as enshrined in the UNCRC, into the Indian court procedure.

Goa Children's Act, 2003 (*GCA*): In the meantime, the State of Goa felt the need to draft a separate law for itself on the issue of child protection against adult abuse, incorporating child-friendly practices in tune with the UNCRC. For the first time in Indian statutory legislation, the term "child abuse" was used and sexual offences defined in this legislation.[9,10] Section 8 criminalizes "child abuse" punishment for sexual assault, grave sexual assault and incest.[11] Soliciting children for purposes of commercial exploitation is prohibited, which includes hosting websites, taking suggestively or obscene photographs, etc.[12] Any person who exploits a child for commercial sexual exploitation shall be liable to pay a penalty which

[9]Section 2 (m) of *GCA*: "Child abuse" refers to the maltreatment, whether habitual or not, of the child which includes any of the following: (i) psychological and physical abuse, neglect, cruelty, sexual abuse and emotional maltreatment; (ii) any act by deeds or words which debases, degrades or demeans the intrinsic worth and dignity of a child as a human being; (iii) unreasonable deprivation of his basic needs for survival such as food and shelter; or failure to immediately give medical treatment to an injured child resulting in serious impairment of his growth and development or in his permanent incapacity or death.

[10]Section 2 (y) of *GCA*: Sexual offences' for the purposes of awarding appropriate punitive action means and includes,

(i) "Grave Sexual Assault" which covers different types of intercourse: vaginal, oral, anal, use of objects, forcing minors to have sex with each other, deliberately causing injury to the sexual organs, making children pose for pornographic photos or films;
(ii) Sexual Assault which covers sexual touching with the use of any body part or object, voyeurism, exhibitionism, showing pornographic pictures or films to minors, making children watch others engaged in sexual activity, issuing of threats to sexually abuse a minor, verbally abusing a minor using vulgar and obscene language;
(iii) Incest which is the commission of a sexual offence by an adult on a child who is a relative or is related by ties of adoption.

[11]Section 8(2) of *GCA*: Whosoever commits any sexual assault as defined under this Act, shall be punished with imprisonment of either description for a term that may extend to 3 years and shall also be liable to fine of Rs. 1,00,000. Whoever commits any Grave Sexual Assault shall be punished with imprisonment of either description for a term that shall not be less than 7 years but which may extend to 10 years and shall also be liable to a fine of Rs. 2,00,000. Whoever commits incest shall be punished with imprisonment of either description for a term of 1 year plus fine of Rs. 1,00,000.

[12]Section 8(12) of *GCA*: Any form of soliciting or publicizing, or making children available to any adult or even other children for purposes of commercial exploitation is prohibited. This includes hosting websites, taking suggestive or obscene photographs, providing materials, soliciting customers, guiding tourists and other clients, appointing touts, using agents, or any other form which may lead to abuse of a child.

may extend to Rs. 1,00,000 and simple imprisonment of 1 year. This will be in addition to any penalty or punishment that may be enforced under any other Act in force. Developers of photographs or films, as well as airport authorities, border police, railway police, traffic police have to report sexual/obscene depictions of children, suspected cases of trafficking of children, etc. The preparation of a Child Code by the Goa Police, provision for Child Friendly Police Stations, prohibition of children below 14 years arriving unaccompanied inside any cyber café are other prevention and protection measures envisaged by the *GCA*.. *GCA* establishes a Children's Court for the purpose of prosecution of adult offenders. This court has the powers of a District (civil) and Sessions (criminal) Court. *GCA* defines "child" as any person who under 18 years of age. Principles that are in the best interests of the child and non-stigmatizing semantics have been adopted by *GCA*. *GCA* lays down fair procedure for children like presumption of age of innocence; privacy and confidentiality, shifting of burden of proof upon the accused; child-friendly cross-examination, in-camera trial, reduced delays in procedure, etc.

The Protection of Children from Sexual Offences Act, 2012, (*POCSOA*): It defines various forms of sexual offences including Penetrative Sexual Assault,[13] Sexual Assault,[14] Sexual Harassment,[15] and Use of child for pornographic

[13]This has been defined as Penetration by penis (to any extent) of any person or Insertion (to any extent) of any object or part of the body of any person or Manipulation of any part of the body of a child so as to cause penetration, into vagina, mouth, urethra or anus of the child or making the child to do so with such person or any other person or Application of such person's mouth to the penis, vagina, anus, urethra of the child or making the child to do so to such person or any other person. This offence is punishable by imprisonment of either description from 7 years to life and fine (Sections 3–4).

[14]Whoever, with sexual intent, touches the vagina, penis, anus, or breast of the child or makes the child touch the vagina, penis, anus, or breast of such person or any other person, or does any other act with sexual intent which involves physical contact without penetration, is said to commit sexual assault. The punishment for sexual assault is imprisonment from 3 to 5 years and fine (Sections 7–8).

[15]Whoever, with sexual intent utters any word or makes any sound or makes any gesture or exhibits any object or part of body with the intention that such word or sound shall be heard or such gesture or object or part of body shall be seen by the child, makes a child exhibit his body/any part, shows any object to a child in any form or media for pornographic purposes, repeatedly or constantly follows or watches or contacts a child either directly or through electronic, digital, or any other means, threatens to use in any form of media, a real or fabricated depiction through electronic, film or digital or any other mode, of any part of the body of the child or the involvement of the child in a sexual act, entices a child for pornographic purposes or gives gratification therefore, shall have committed the offence of sexual harassment. The punishment shall be imprisonment up to 3 years and fine (Sections 11–12).

purposes[16] etc. For the first time in a national legislation, reporting of the offences was made mandatory. Any person (including the child), who has apprehension that an offence under the *POCSOA* is likely to be committed or has knowledge that such an offence has been committed, shall provide such information to (a) the Special Juvenile Police Unit or (b) the local police. The report shall be recorded in writing and ascribed an entry number; be read over to the informant and be entered in a book kept by Police Unit. The SJPU/local police are to make immediate arrangement to give him such care and protection (admitting child to shelter home or nearest police station) within 24 h, after recording reasons in writing. Within 24 h, the SJPU/local police has to report the matter to CWC and Special Court or Sessions Court.

The statement shall be recorded at the residence of the child or place of his choice and as far as possible by a woman police officer not below rank of sub-inspector. When the statement of child is recorded, it shall be in presence of his parents or any person of child's trust. This shall be done when the police officer is not in uniform. The police officer is to ensure that the child does not come into contact with accused while examination is taking place. No child is to be detained in police station at night. The police officer is to ensure that child is protected from public media. The Magistrate shall record the statement of the child in the presence of his parents or any person of child's trust. The Advocate of the accused shall not be present while recording the statement of the child. A copy of the

[16]Whoever, uses a child in any form of media (including programme or advertisement telecast by television channels or internet or any other electronic form or printed form, whether or not such programme or advertisement is intended for personal use or for distribution), for the purposes of sexual gratification, which includes—representation of the sexual organs of a child; usage of a child engaged in real or simulated sexual acts (with or without penetration); the indecent or obscene representation of a child, shall be guilty of the offence of using a child for pornographic purposes. An explanation is appended to the relevant section regarding the expression "use a child." This expression shall include involving a child though any medium like print, electronic, computer or any other technology for preparation, production, offering, transmitting, publishing, facilitation, and distribution of the pornographic material. Punishments are many and varied. For mere usage of a child for pornographic purposes, the punishment is imprisonment of either description up to 5 years and fine. In the event of subsequent conviction, punishment shall be imprisonment of either description up to 7 years and fine.

If a person uses the child for pornographic purposes, he shall be guilty of penetrative sexual assault. He shall be liable for not less than 10 years imprisonment of either description to life imprisonment and fine. If a person uses the child for pornographic purposes commits an offence of aggravated penetrative sexual assault, the punishment is imprisonment for life and fine.

If any person using a child for pornographic purposes commits an offence of sexual assault, the punishment shall be imprisonment of either description for a term which is not less than 6 years imprisonment up to 8 years and fine.

If any person using the child for pornographic purposes commits an offence of aggravated sexual assault, the punishment shall be not less than 8 years imprisonment up to 10 years and fine.

If any person commits the offence abetment of any offence under the *POCSOA*, the punishment shall be as provided for the actual commission of the offence. If any person attempts to commit an offence under the *POCSOA*, punishment is imprisonment for a term up to one half of the imprisonment for life or one half of the longest term of imprisonment provided for that offence or with fine or with both (Sections 13–15).

final report of the police is to be given to the child and his parents/representative. Whenever possible, the statement of child shall also be recorded by the Magistrate and the police officer by audio-video electronic means.

Even though FIR or complaints are not registered offences under this Act, medical examination is also to be conducted. For a girl victim, medical examination is to be conducted by a lady doctor only. The medical examination is to be conducted in presence of a parent of the child/other person of the child's trust. In case a parent or other person of trust is not present, the medical examination is to be conducted in the presence of a woman nominated by the head of the institution.

The presumption of culpable mental state is upon the accused. Hence the burden of proof is on the accused to prove that he had no such intention. A Court of Sessions is to be the Special Court in order to conduct speedy trial. The evidence of the child is to be recorded within 30 days of the Special Court taking cognizance and the reasons for delay to be recorded. The trial is to be completed within 1 year.

A post of Special Public Prosecutor has been created. The Special Public Prosecutor and Advocate for the accused is to put questions for chief, cross and re-examinations to the Judge, who shall ask the child. A child-friendly atmosphere is to be created by allowing a family member, friend, relative or any person of the child's trust, to be present. The child shall not be repeatedly called to testify in the court; he/she shall be given frequent breaks, there shall be no aggressive questioning or character assassination, non-disclosure of identity of child during investigation and trial including identity of family, school, relatives, neighborhood, etc. Video conferencing can be used for recording the child's statement or by utilizing single visibility mirrors or curtains or any other devices. The trial must be in camera.

The Legal Services Authority is to provide a lawyer for the indigent. Subject to rules, the State Government shall prepare guidelines for the use of non-governmental organizations, professionals and experts or persons having knowledge of psychology, social work, physical health, mental health, and child development to be associated with the pre-trial and trial stage to assist the Child. The National Commission for Protection of Child Rights (NCPCR) and the respective State Commissions (SCPCR) shall monitor the implementation of this Act.

The Criminal Law Amendment Act 2013 brought about extensive changes to the Indian Penal Code, 1860. The old laws relating to sexual offences against women have been considerably changed. It raises the age of consent for sexual activity for a woman from sixteen to eighteen. However, vestiges of the past still remain as the amended Indian Penal Code still upholds that sexual intercourse by a man with his wife above 15 years of age is an exception to rape. As a result, sexual intercourse with a wife above 15 years of age and below 18 years of age will not amount to rape under the IPC. But the *POCSOA* (2012) conflicts with this, as it penalizes sexual activity among or with all children below the age of eighteen. This is a matter of debate, given the existing Prohibition of Child Marriage Act, 2006 which was enacted for the lofty purpose of rendering child marriages voidable at the option of the under-age party to such marriage.

The Child Witness Court Room

An interesting development is India's first Child Witness Court Room (CWCR), designed specifically to protect and insulate children appearing in courts against the usual rigors associated with a courtroom. This was set up at New Delhi's Karkardooma Court Complex in September 2012, even before the *POCSOA* came into force. The model court room resembles a "child-friendly play area" with brightly colored walls, toys, a small pantry and a one-way mirror where the child will not be able to see the accused. The child has a different entrance to the sixth floor court room. In order to make the child feel more at ease and not get intimidated under the normal court set-up, the dais of the judge is made much lower. The child (witness/victim) is allowed to interact with the court in two ways. One is through video conferencing which is connected to the courtroom and which enables the judge and the accused to see and hear the child. In the second arrangement, the child friendly court room is fitted with a one-way mirror. Here the accused sits in an adjacent room and is able to see the victim through the mirror, while the child witness/victim will be seated in front of the judge, on a couch, with his attendant. The accused can see the examination of the witness and be a part of the fair trial using the one-way glass.

In September 2014, the second vulnerable witness deposition complex for kids was set up at Saket District Court in New Delhi. In the Saket Court complex, the vulnerable witness is escorted to the court by a facilitator in a vehicle. The vehicle is provided by the court administration to build rapport and make the witness comfortable. The witness enters the court complex through a separate entry away from the public glare. The facility has been developed in such a manner that while in the court complex including during recording of evidence, the accused and witness are never face to face.

The Role of NGOs Laid Down in Legislations

The Juvenile Justice (Care and Protection of Children) Rules, 2007 have outlined the role of NGOs as follows:

Rule 55 states that every institution in charge of providing services to juveniles under the JJA shall have a Management Committee for the management of the institution and will monitor the progress of every juvenile and child. A representative of voluntary organizations providing professional and technical services like education, vocational training, psychosocial care, mental health intervention, and legal aid may be invited as special invitee to the Management Committee meetings.

Rule 56 states that the Officer in Charge of every institution shall set up Children's Committees and shall as far as possible; seek assistance from local voluntary organizations or child participation experts for the setting up and functioning of the Children's Committees.

Rules 80 and 81 state that in setting up a State Child Protection Unit and District Child Protection Unit for implementation of the *JJA* and supervision of the agencies and institutions under the Act, it shall network and coordinate with civil society organizations working in the same field.

Rule 84 states that Special Juvenile Police Units shall particularly seek assistance from voluntary organizations recognized as protection agencies by the State Government for the purpose of assisting the SJPUs and local police stations. Assisting at the time of apprehension, in preparation of necessary reports, for taking charge of juveniles until production and at the time of production before the JJB are essential steps.

Rule 87 states that among the various duties of the Probation Officer or Child Welfare Officer or case worker, there is a duty to establish linkages with voluntary workers and organizations in order to facilitate the rehabilitation and social reintegration of juveniles and to ensure the necessary follow-up.

Rule 94 states that the State Government shall constitute a Selection Committee for 5 years in order to make a panel of names for appointment to the JJB or CWC; there shall be two representatives from a reputed NGO working in the area of child welfare.

The Role of NGOs under the *POCSOA* and its Rules is as follows:

Section 39 of the *POCSOA* states that the State Government shall prepare guidelines for use of NGOs, professionals and experts or persons having knowledge of psychology, social work, physical health, mental health and child development to be associated with the pre-trial stage and trial stage to assist the child. As mentioned earlier, Section 44 of POCSOA states the role of NCPCR and SCPCR. Rule 9 of the *POCSO* Rules states that the NCPCR and SCPCR shall be in charge of monitoring the formation of guidelines under Section 39 of the Act and monitoring the application of these guidelines. This means that from the time a child comes into contact with the justice delivery system, a social worker can actively engage with police to bring the child to the Child Welfare Committee and ensuring support from the CWC to the child.

Conclusion and Recommendations for a Multidisciplinary Approach

It can be understood that no longer can civil society organizations be excluded from governance. The challenge lies in coordinating the various functionaries under the *JJA* and *POCSOA*. Guidelines should be framed regarding how NGOs and civil society groups can help in pre-trial and trial stage assistance, as per Section 39 of the *POCSOA*.

One way could be thc preparation of a panel of trained doctors, police personnel, psychologists, social workers, and lawyers by the District Child Protection Unit for each gram Sabha, corporation or municipality to assist the concerned

Special Courts, JJB, CWC, and SJPUs in each locality. The services of the State and National Legal Services Authority should be utilized under Section 40 of the *POCSOA*.

Every child who has reported abuse should be examined by concerned personnel from this panel. Interview before the concerned police officer should be videotaped as per Section 26(4) of *POCSOA*. Medical examination should be conducted as per provisions in Section 27 of *POCSOA*. Translator or interpreter or special educator facilities for the concerned police officer should made available as per Sections 26(2) and (3) of *POCSOA*.

Accredited non-governmental/civil society organizations can be put in charge of coordinating the panel of experts for contacting the child, so that the child's victimization by the legal system is minimized.

Rule 64 of the *JJ* Rules, 2007 states that (1) the Central Government or the State Government shall monitor and evaluate the implementation of the *JJA* annually. This is achieved by reviewing matters concerning establishment of JJB or CWC or SJPU where required, functioning of JJB or CWC or SJPU, functioning of institutions and staff, functioning of adoption agencies, child friendly administration of juvenile justice and any other matter concerning effective implementation of the Act in the State (2). The social audit shall be carried out with the help and support of organizations working in the field of mental health, child care and protection and autonomous bodies like the National Institute of Public Cooperation and Child Development, ICCW, Child Welfare, Child line India Foundation, Central and State level Social Welfare Boards, Schools of Social Work, and School of Law.

In order for the social audit to work, the process would require a full time professional team to oversee, as well as strong initiative and significant resources contributed by those conducting the audit. Additional rules will have to be framed by each state government regarding how to conduct the social audit. Accredited NGOs can go a long way in helping the state in this.

An issue which has remained unaddressed regarding child protection is the unavailability of accurate and updated statistical data and unavailability of official statistical reports nationally and regionally. Rules for each state have to make provision whereby accredited civil society organizations can be used to compile data on child sexual abuse cases, to be coordinated at the State level by the SCPCR.

References

Pinho, E. (2011). Juvenile Justice Act; A reformative step for children in Conflict with Law. http://www.scanindia.in/blog/tag/juvenile-justice-act-2000/.

Representing Children Worldwide. (2005). India. http://www.law.yale.edu/rcw/rcw/jurisdictions/assc/india/frontpage.htm#_edn5.

Chapter 26
Child Protection: The Grassroots Issues and Challenges

Mala Bhandari

Introduction

India is home to almost 19 % of the world's children. It is the second most populous country in the world with a population of nearly 1.21 billion. Of the total population of the country, children in age up to 18 years represent 39 %; this amount to around 472 million according to the census data of 2011 (Government of India, Ministry of Home Affairs 2011). However, looking at the state of our children convey that millions of our children are condemned to stumble right from the start. The first 6 years of life, and especially the first two, are integral years for gaining much-needed nutrients, establishing good health and developing learning abilities. If not achieved, it is a burden that is very difficult to overcome in later years (Dreze et al. 2007).

Child Protection: Issues and Concerns

It is evident that children are vulnerable to all kinds of abuse and exploitation with statistics on the status of world's children showing high incidence of abuse, violence, and neglect. Child Protection in very simple words refers to protecting children from physical, emotional, sexual abuse, or neglect. UNICEF refers to the term child protection as to prevent and respond to violence, exploitation, and abuse against children including commercial sexual exploitation trafficking, child

M. Bhandari (✉)
Social and Development Research and Action Group, Noida, Uttar Pradesh, India
e-mail: mail@sadrag.org

S. Deb (ed.), *Child Safety, Welfare and Well-being*,
DOI 10.1007/978-81-322-2425-9_26

labor, and harmful traditional practices such as female genital mutilation/cutting and child marriage.

Article 19 of the Convention on the Rights of the Child commits State parties to

> take all appropriate legislative, administrative, social, and educational measures to protect the child from all forms of physical or mental violence, injury or abuse, neglect or negligent treatment, maltreatment or exploitation, including sexual abuse, while in the care of parent(s), legal guardian(s) or any other person who has the care of the child.

Additionally, Article 32 recognizes children's right to be protected from economic exploitation and hazardous work, Article 34 targets sexual exploitation and Article 35, trafficking.

Child Protection is about protecting children from, or against, any perceived or real danger or risk to their life, their personhood, and childhood. It is about reducing their vulnerability to any kind of harm and protecting them in harmful situations. It is about ensuring that no child falls out of the social security and safety net and, those who do, receive necessary care, protection, and support to bring it back into the safety net. While protection is a right of every child, some children are more vulnerable than others are and need special attention. The Government recognizes these children as "children in difficult circumstances," characterized by their specific social, economic, and geo-political situations. In addition to providing a safe environment for these children, it is imperative to ensure that all other children also remain protected. Child protection is integrally linked to every other right of the child. Failure to ensure children's right to protection adversely affects all other rights of the child. Thus, the Millennium Development Goals (MDGs) cannot be achieved unless child protection is an integral part of programs, strategies, and plans for their achievement. Failure to protect children from issues such as violence in schools, child labor, harmful traditional practices, child marriage, child abuse, the absence of parental care, and commercial sexual exploitation among others, means failure in fulfilling both the Constitutional and International commitments toward children (O'Kane et al. 2006).

Child Protection Issues in India

In India, child protection issues need prime attention, especially as a child goes missing every 8 min, according to data from the National Crime Records Bureau. Almost 40 % of those children have not been found. The situation is so grave that even the political leadership acknowledged in the Upper House of Parliament that almost 60,000 children went missing in the year 2011 from a total of 28 states and union territories. Of these more than 22,000 are yet to be located (Shah 2012).

Peculiar to India are the issues related to lack of concern for children and their neglect at multiple levels that may range from their immediate environment within the family, neighborhood, community, and the society at large. There is ample evidence that children suffer due to general apathy of adults, as a result of which they are made to suffer on following accounts:

(i) **Child Labor**: Child labor is work that children, aged less than 18 years, are forced to do in return for meager or no payments. Young childhoods, unaware and uncared, can be seen working in hazardous occupations anywhere and everywhere. Deprived of childhood, their physical, mental, emotional, and social development is hampered and access to school is largely unattainable. There are 1.26 crore working children in the age group of 5–14, out of which approximately 12 lakh children are working in the hazardous occupations/processes which are covered under the Child Labor (Prohibition and Regulation) Act 1986, i.e., 18 occupations and 65 processes (INDUS 2007).

(ii) **Child Marriage**: Child marriage is when a child is married before they reach legal age, 18 years for girls and 21 years for boys, and is widespread in India. Factors that contribute to child marriage include gender norms and expectations, traditional practices around marriage, safety concerns and family honor, poverty, limited education, livelihood opportunities, and weak implementation of the law against child marriage. Patriarchal values, in particular, play a significant role in child marriage, with girls being considered as "property" moving from the father's to the groom's household and their role as homemakers is the only future conceived for girls by their family.

(iii) **Child Trafficking**: Child trafficking is a harsh reality found in both developed and developing nations, it is one of the hardest crimes to track and investigate. According to UNICEF (Unicef 2012), a child victim of trafficking is "any person under 18 who is recruited, transported, transferred, harbored or received for the purpose of exploitation, either within or outside a country." Trafficked children are used for prostitution, forced into marriage, illegally adopted, used as cheap or unpaid labor, used for sport, and organ harvesting. Trafficking exposes children to violence, abuse, neglect, and exploitation. The latest figures estimate that 1.2 million children are trafficked worldwide every year (The Childline India Foundation, MWCD, Government of India.

(iv) **Children without Parental Care**: Children sometimes lose their first line of protection, their parents. There are multiple reasons for separation, including abduction, trafficking, migration, living on the street, being displaced, or recruited by armed forces; living in alternative care due to health issues, educational reasons, household violence, poverty, death of parents, or stigma (O'Kane et al. 2006).

(v) **Sexual Violence against Children**: Sexual violence against children occurs in the form of abuse, harassment, rape or sexual exploitation in prostitution, or pornography. There are instances where children are sexually abused within their homes, schools, market places or places of tourist interest (UNICEF 2006).

(vi) **Conflict with Law**: Children in conflict with the law refers to any person below the age of 18 who has come in contact with the justice system as a result of committing a crime or being suspected of committing a crime. Apart from the above types of violence in the life of children, there are issues of health, education, malnutrition, and stunted growth, drug abuse that often find their way in case of those who live on streets and are left to fend for themselves. Missing children is another major issue of concern (The Childline India Foundation).

Existing Child Protection Mechanisms

The Constitution of India recognizes the vulnerable position of children and their right to protection. Article 15 of the Constitution guarantees special attention to children through necessary and special laws and policies that safeguard their rights. The Right to equality, protection of life and personal liberty and the right against exploitation is enshrined in Articles 14, 15, 16, 17, 21, 23, and 24.

The Indian Government has framed a robust mechanism for child protection aligned provisions made under the National Policy for Children, 1974 and 2013, Juvenile Justice (Care and Protection of Children) Act, 2000, National Charter for Children, 2003, and National Plan of Action for Children, 2005. An Integrated Child Protection Scheme was introduced in 2009–10 by the Government to bring several existing child protection programs under one umbrella, with improved norms and cardinal principles of "protection of child rights" and the "best interest of the child" (Government of India, Ministry of women and Child Development 2003).

i. **Juvenile Justice for Children**: Any child below 18 years, if found in conflict with law, is provided support and care in state sponsored homes. The Government provides all the infrastructure and required facilities for the proper care and rehabilitation of such a child.
ii. **An Integrated Program for Street Children**: Children who do not have parental care, support, home, or family ties are provided shelter and care under this program. The non-governmental organizations are supported to run 24 h shelters and provide food, clothing, shelter, non-formal education, recreation, counseling, and guidance and referral services for children.
iii. **Childline**: Childline is a 24/7 emergency phone outreach service for children in need of care and protection linking them to emergency and long-term care and rehabilitation services. The service can be accessed by a child in difficulty or an adult on his or her behalf, by dialing 1098.
iv. **Scheme for Assistance to Homes for Children**: This scheme promotes In-Country Adoption for care and protection of orphans/abandoned/destitute infants and children up to 6 years.
v. **Scheme for Working Children**: This scheme provides bridging education and vocational training, medicine, food, recreation to children who are working as domestic labor, in roadside dhabas (eateries) and mechanic shops.

vi. **Rajiv Gandhi National Creche Scheme**: This scheme provides comprehensive day-care services including facilities like food, shelter, medical, and recreation to children up to the age of six, with working mothers.
vii. **Project to combat the trafficking of women and children**: This scheme is for providing care and protection to trafficked and sexually abused women and children in source and destination areas. The components of the scheme includes new-working with law enforcing agencies, rescue operations, temporary shelter, legal service, and repatriation to hometown.
viii. **National Child Labor Project (NCLP)**: Under the scheme, Special Schools and Rehabilitation Centers are opened to provide non-formal education, vocational training, and rehabilitate the child laborers.
ix. **Central Adoption Resource Agency (CARA)**: This is to promote in-country adoption and regular inter-country adoption. CARA also helps both Indian and foreign agencies in adoption of Indian children to function in a regulated framework, thus, exploitation do not take place.

The present paper reviews the child protection mechanism in district, Gautum Budh Nagar in the state of Uttar Pradesh. The data has been collected from Childline working in the district since 2013.

Childline the Important Innovation for Child Protection

Childline concept is a brainchild of Jeroo Billimoria, who was professor in Tata Institute of Social Sciences (TISS), Mumbai as she used to respond to the needs of the distressed children on the street in personal and professional capacity. In June 1996 as part of the departmental work of Family and Child Welfare Department, TISS childline was initiated and it walked a long way to become a nationwide network for helping children in distress. Ministry of Social Justice and Empowerment, Government on India agreed to fund Childline at national level and in 1999, it become operational. As of March 2014 childline is operational in 291 cities/districts in 31 States and UTs through its network of 540 partner organizations across India (Childline India 2015). In order to create a protective environment for children in all parts of the country, ICPS envisages the expansion of the CHILDLINE service to all districts/cities by 2015. The vision of childline is "a child-friendly nation that guarantees the rights and protection of all children." The four important C's that child line operates are catalyzed, collaborate, connect, and communicate.

Taking this concept of childline that considered child protection is the central theme Ms. Jeroo Billimoria extended the idea of similar service in other countries by using their own resources. In 2003 International Consultation was held in Amsterdam, Netherlands, and the event was attended by 49 child helpline from around the globe. In this event officially the Child Helpline International was launched. Presently, in 149 countries this helpline is existing and emerged as a strong global network for child protection (Child Helpline International 2014).

Child Protection Mechanism in District Gautam Budh Nagar

Uttar Pradesh is one of the highly populated states in northern India. As per the India Human Rights Report, 2007, the state has rampant incidence of child rights violations. Child labor in brassware, carpet, and bangle industries continue to exploit children despite a ban. The sexual abuse of children occurs even in the state sponsored institution child homes that have been built for the care and protection of children. A total of 53,224 cases of crime against children were reported in 2013 as compared to 38,172 cases in 2012 as per the National Crime Record Bureau. The state of Uttar Pradesh accounts for as high incidence of crime committed against children (16.9 %). The other states next in order were Madhya Pradesh (14.2 %), Delhi (12.4 %), and Maharashtra (11 %) (Government of India, Ministry of Home Affairs 2013). The extent of various types of crime and violence against children occurring in India as well as Uttar Pradesh has been represented in the Table 26.1.

District Gautam Budh Nagar is situated in the west of Uttar Pradesh. It was formed in 1997 by carving out the portions of Ghaziabad and Bulandshahar. The district is divided into three Tehsils named as Sadar, Daadri, and Jewar, which are divided into Development Blocks. While Dankaur is the development block in the Sadar Tehsil, Bisrakh, and Dadri are the development blocks in the Daadri Tehsil; Jewar is the development block in the Jewar tehsil.

Gautam Budh Nagar is a developing district, moving on the path of rapid industrialization. Large number of manufacturing units and industries attract a lot of migrants who come here in search of employment, with many settling here for good. The total population of the district is 1,105,290 with more males than females. A major section of the total population comprises the migrant population particularly in the twin cities of Noida and Greater Noida. They occupy the villages situated within the peri-urban localities, which were carved out of the rural

Table 26.1 Incidence of crimes committed against children

Name of crime	Total (All-India)	Uttar Pradesh
• Infanticide (Sec. 315 IPC)	82	10
• Murder (Sec. 302 IPC)	1739	492
• Rape (Sec. 376 IPC)	12363	1381
• Kidnapping and abduction	28167	6002
• Foeticide	221	17
• Abetment to suicide	215	–
• Exposure and abandonment	930	–
• Procuration of minor girl	1224	–
• Buying of girls for prostitution	6	–
• Selling of girls for prostitution	100	–+

Source National Crime Record Bureau (Government of India, Ministry of Home Affairs 2013)

villages. These spaces are, however, reeling under the basic facilities. The local dominant community people have built tiny rooms, one upon the other and rent them out at an exorbitant rate to migrants, who live in these dwellings with their families.

The contribution of labor and skill by migrant population to the overall development and prosperity of the district cannot be underestimated in lesser terms. However, in their struggle for food and nutrition, the most neglected are their children, who do not attend school and are left behind in their shabby single room tenements when parents are away to work. In the absence of any common space in and around their localities, and lack of community support, these children are very likely to fall prey to abuse from sources within their immediate environment. There are ample numbers of cases where children are abused, killed, and dumped. The Nithari serial abuse and killings of children that occurred during the year 2006, reminds us of this gruesome reality.

To address the issues of child protection in the district, in 2011 Childline India Foundation initiated a 24 h help line under the Integrated Child Protection Scheme, Ministry of Women and Child Development, Government of India.

CHILDLINE 1098 Service works for children in distress, especially children in need of care and protection so as to rescue them from abuse, provide shelter to them, medical services, counseling, repatriation, and rehabilitation.

Childline works in a selected district through a structured network of institutions such as non-governmental organizations, academic institutes, corporate sector, and the allied systems. Working on Partnership Model, each partner has specific role and responsibilities based on the premise of collective action for providing care and protection to children. The Childline India Foundation initiates the following structure in a district:

- **Childline Advisory Board (CAB)**: Comprises of senior level functionaries from the allied systems, NGOs, concerned individuals, media, etc. It is the policy making body for Childline at the city level and it periodically undertakes reviews of Childline.
- **The Collaborative Organization**: A 24 h service for children that responds to calls on 1098, provides emergency intervention, and links children to services for ultimate rehabilitation, conduct awareness, and outreach programs.
- **The Support Organization**: Responds to calls referred by the collaborative organization, conducts awareness, and outreach programs.
- **Resource Organizations**: Act as referral centers for Childline. They also participate in outreach and awareness programs for Childline.

In addition, The Childline India Foundation operates through "partner organizations"—a range of large, medium, and small child rights agencies. These agencies run the full Childline services in designated areas with resources provided by The Childline India Foundation.

The Existing Structure for Child Protection at District Level

In district Gautum Budh Nagar, U.P., issues of Child protection are addressed through following functional arms and services:

1. Childline—24 h Help-line for children in distress
2. District Child Welfare Committee (CWC) comprising the President and two other members
3. Juvenile Justice Board that has been formed under the Juvenile Justice (Care and Protection of Children) Act 2000 (amended in 2006).
4. District Protection Officer who oversees the CWC and Juvenile Justice Board
5. Special Juvenile Police Unit that began in June, 2012
6. District Labor Department that implements the Child Labor (Prohibition and Regulation), Act 1986 for the rescue and rehabilitation of the child labor.

Childline working in the district has the following operational structure:

1. **Collaborative Organization**: A non-governmental organization operates in the designated area of Noida City. It works 24 h with a team of dedicated members. They receive complaints, conduct awareness programs, and coordinate and support the Sub-centers working in other parts of the district.
2. **Sub-centre**: A non-governmental organization has been entrusted the geographical location of Greater Noida and Dadri. They attend to complaints of violence and child rights violation in the given area with the help of five dedicated members. They conduct awareness programs and handle individual cases with support from the other Sub-centre, collaborative organization, and other stakeholders.
3. **Sub-centre**: A non-governmental organization has been assigned the geographical area of Dhankaur. They attend to complaints of violence and child rights violation in the given area with the help of five dedicated members. They conduct awareness programmers and handle individual cases with support from the other Sub-centre and the collaborative organization.

The three arms of Childline work together for addressing the child rights issues in the district. They report cases of violation to the district Child Welfare Committee and act as per their official order. There is a District Child Protection Committee which has members from various government departments, police, Childline, and other non-governmental organizations working on concerned issues.

From the inception of Childline services in the district in April 2011 through until December 2013, a total of 908 cases of child rights violation have been received and attended. These cases are of various kinds such as children in need of shelter, medical help, counseling and rehabilitation for sexual abuse, rescue from labor, etc.

Table 26.2 suggests that incidence of child rights violation has been on a constant increase over the last 3 years. The increasing trend may also indicate that presence of Childline in the district which has resulted into reporting and visibility of child rights violation cases. The local newspapers in English and Hindi do not hesitate to report cases of child rights violation. However, there are a few issues of concern that need an urgent attention at policy as well as implementation levels:

- **Gap between Childline and Government Departments**: The convergence among the various government departments is severely lacking. There is no communication among the departments of health, education, social welfare, and labor and as a result, the child rights violation cases remain in isolation. The district protection officer deals with cases for state support but there is yet to be seen any success. The Childline has approached the department of child protection, social welfare, and other associated departments, but has never succeeded in getting support from any. In such a scenario, there remain very limited options for institutional support and rehabilitation of victims of violence.
- **Police of Their Own Will**: Police are the major stakeholders within child protection framework. Police works closely with Childline; the later remains dependent on the former. The police presence is required at each stage of child protection such as rescue from abuse, registering the FIR, locating the child's parents, repatriation and getting the child to a safe and secured place. However, often unprecedented delays occur due to unavailability of police personnel when required.
- **Lack of Information on Schemes for Support to Children**: The district administration does not divulge details on government schemes and programs that can provide relief to children in need. Childline refers critical cases for support by the district authorities, but despite repeated follow-ups, no outcome emerges
- **Lack of Political Will**: The political will is conspicuous by its absence on issues of child rights in the district. The elected representatives of people have never spoken about child rights and there has not been a single official statement on the subject.

Table 26.2 Number of child rights violation in recent years

SI no.	Period	Number of cases
1.	April 2011–December 2011	139
2.	January 2012–December 2012	342
3.	January 2013–December 2013	427
	Total	908

Source Collaborative organization, District Gautum Budh Nagar

- **Lack of coordination between Childline and NCPCR**: The National Apex Body on child rights, NCPCR works independent of Childline that works in the district. The cases of child rights violation remain compartmentalized with either of the organizations despite having common goals and objectives otherwise.
- **Lack of Rights Approach**: Children are considered meek and voiceless with no rights and entitlements of their own. It is the charity approach that works more than the rights approach. There is a serious lack of efforts to get victimized children their Constitutional dues and entitlements by the government as well as civil society at large.
- **An Isolated District Child Protection Committee (DCPC)**: DCPC works with a strict bureaucratic approach. The meetings occur more as a compulsory requirement rather than as a conscious effort to address child rights issues. Meetings are conducted under the supervision of district's Chief Development Officer as a routine affair. No action-based follow ups are done.
- **Lack of Institutional Structures**: There is no government sponsored Child Home in the district. A few such homes are run by charitable organizations and non-governmental organizations. As a result, the children in need for temporary shelter are moved from one Home to another. The concerned civic authorities for Noida and Greater Noida remain, by and large, unconcerned.

The child protection issues that are handled by childline and the coordinating agencies in Gautam Budh Nagar District are explained in the five case stories. These case stories gave a specific learning and understanding about the vulnerability of the children and child protection scenario in India. All the case stories explained the specific vulnerabilities of the children and how the children were provided with safety and security through childline initiatives.

A Few Case Studies

- **Case I: Home for a Toddler**: A new born baby girl was deserted by her mother immediately after birth in Yatharth Hospital, a private hospital in Greater Noida. She was only 4 days old and had nobody to take care of her. The hospital tried to find her mother but they could not. The hospital informed the police at Kasna police station. The police in turn reported to the District Protection Officer who contacted the Childline Sub-centre in Greater Noida. The Childline team went to Kasna Police Station, took the baby to district government hospital where she was kept till the district Child Welfare Committee was informed. The Childline team members looked after the baby in hospital to ensure her security. The Child Welfare Committee issued the order for the baby to be taken to Government *Shishu Grah*, Mathura for a permanent home. The Childline, Greater Noida contacted a local non-governmental organization to sponsor the transfer of the baby to Mathura in a private cab. The entire process of taking care of the baby to getting her to a Child Home was facilitated by Greater Noida Childline Sub-centre.

- **Case II: An Innocent Childhood Rescued From Abuse**: Raju, a 7 year-old boy was a member of an underprivileged family. He used to work as a domestic helper in order to be able to study in school. While working in a house, he was brutally beaten up by the owner of the house. With no one around to save him from beatings, Raju kept tolerating it; however, the neighbors somehow came to know about this abuse. They knew someone in the press and the case was highlighted through the local newspaper, Amar Ujjala. The team members of Greater Noida Sub-centre read the news and found the details. They reached the particular house and spoke to Raju. However, Raju's brother refused to follow the procedure and offered no support. He did not allow the team members to present Raju before the district Child Welfare Committee. He said that he would take Raju with him to their native village and he would complete the school exams there. The team members did not force Raju and his brother to pursue it further. In this case, the labor department could not be involved due to a strict resistance from Raju's brother. However, through Childline's presence and pursuance, an innocent child could be saved from continued physical abuse.
- **Case III: A Lost Child Restored to Her Family**: Renu, 8 years, lived in Greater Noida. She attended a neighborhood government school. The distance between her home and school was around 1 km. She commuted alone since her parents left for work early and returned home late in the night. However, 1 day, Renu lost her way while she went to some other area with her friends to a village fest. That day her parents happened to return home early and did not find Renu at home. They looked around but could not find her. In the meantime, Renu wandered around looking for her house and was found by the police personnel at Dadri and she was brought to police station. They contacted Childline and the team members reached Dadri police station and spoke to Renu. Renu said that she had forgotten the way to her house, so the Childline team brought her to a charitable child home in Noida. The police managed to locate Renu's parents in 2–3 days. She was presented before Child Welfare Committee who ordered to hand over Renu to her parents. This is a case where police extended its support, acted promptly, Childline took care of the child and thus an innocent life could be saved from being permanently lost.
- **Case IV: Providing Shelter to Child without a Family**: Beenu, 6 years, was found wandering around at Dadri railway station. The railway police contacted Childline whose members arrived at the location and met Beenu. Beenu could hardly tell where he had come from and where his home was. He was therefore sent to a charitable child home in Noida until his parents could be traced. The police could not trace his parents, even after a fortnight. The Child Welfare Committee ordered for Beenu to be sent to a permanent shelter to Government child home in Lucknow. The Childline team ensured that Beenu was safely enrolled at Lucknow child home. There are many such cases where parents cannot be located and children become "homeless." The state provides permanent

home to children in such cases. Childline facilitated the entire process. In the absence of a child home in the district, children are taken far to other districts.
- **Case V: Child Labor with Deterrence**: Ram, 12 years, lived in Dadri. There was a financial crisis at his home. Seeing his family's condition, he set out to work to earn a living. He started working in a small sweet shop at NTPC road. A civil society member called Childline to convey that a small child was working at a shop. The Childline team reached the shop and spoke to Ram, who was initially reluctant to talk. So the team members spoke to the shop owner but he too did not say much. The Childline team visited the shop a second and a third time, but Ram could not be seen there. The shop owner said that Ram was his relative and he had gone back to his village after the festival Rakshabandan. Childline acts as a deterrent in many cases of child labor. Repeated follow ups and counseling deter the employer not to keep a child for work.

The case of this baby girl (case story-I) explains the vulnerabilities of the girl child in India that is not new but explains how authorities become helpless in the hospital while they did not have all required information in case of an emergency. While this case showed a well coordinated effort by the agencies to ensure safety, but it critically reflected that the rejection of the girl child in a highly industrialized urbanized locality is equally a concern for child protection. A place with a floating migrant population may have higher vulnerabilities for the children than a very traditional social structure where community linkages and support systems are strong.

Abandoning the unwanted child is not an uncommon event in India or in other developed countries too. The new born children have been abandoned in public places or in dustbin have been reported by different news media. Considering this tendency few charitable organizations also used the mechanism where anyone can leave a newborn child in designated secured box (baby hatch) and thus, the organization accept the child, without raising any questioning about the person who abandon a child. In this case safe recovery of the unwanted children is the main focus, therefore an important step for protection of the children. This is also an important step to prevent female feticides and the mothers to be safe from social stigmatization due to an unwanted pregnancy. In different countries the law dealing with unwanted new born babies leaving in baby-hatch is called as "Safe Heaven law" or "Baby Moses Law" (FindLaw 2015). In India, in 1994, a baby-hatch was set up in the State of Tamilnadu. In India yet, there is no law to deal with the concept of baby-hatch. The concept is also being debated as per the UN Convention of rights of the children that highlight the rights to know his/her own identity (Mohanty 2012).

Abusing child domestic help by so called well-off section of the society is rather a very serious concern about degradation of moral social values and this matter needs a serious focus as these incidents should be called as white collar crime. A family chooses to have a residential domestic help also has an obligation to ensure basic safety security of the person. In India the job of domestic help is widely an unorganized sector. Such incident of abuse of the domestic help largely go unnoticed or not-reported. Usually, neighbors do not want to get indulged in the domestic issues of other families and such child domestic help continue to leave in such situation. Specifically, not using child domestic help should be focused as in most the cases, such children live in deprived, helpless, and caged situation looking into wealth around them and they have no access to those facilities which other children (the children of the employer) has.

Poverty is a root cause of child labor. Unfortunately the poor parents or guardian send their children for working as domestic help (or any other form of child labor) to ensure food security and safety for their young wards as they fail to fulfill the needs of their children in family. Thus, the child labor reunited with the family (as in case of case story-II) does not really ensure safety and security of the child in his own family. Such situation of reunion with the biological family of origin needs a close monitoring and support further that the child again do not become a victim as biological family often consider these "home returned children" as a financial burden. This matter needs lot more exploration as child protection is an issue extreme closely connected with poverty.

Often the family members use the children from their extended family as child labor and thus make the social situation even more complex to handle and ensure safety, protection for the child. As in case story-V, the employer of the child labor just sends the child back to the family as childline staffs intervened and it is expected that he (shop owner) would not appoint any child labor further. But, still use of child labor in hotels, shops, tea stalls are very common all over India and children are being pushed to do such job as they live in an impoverished condition in their family. These children face multiple harsh exploitative conditions that also contribute toward development of delinquent behavior in future and thus they continue to live in a vulnerable and threatening social situation (Jamshed and Bhadra 2015).

Poor working parents often leave behind their children with a pretension that the child would be able to maintain himself/herself. Keeping a little elder child with responsibility of looking after younger children is also not uncommon. But in any case children are often left to fend for themselves. Thus, these children become vulnerable to get lost, abused, neglected, and injured that goes unnoticed and unattended. Though in case story-III the little girl was fortune enough but, the huge numbers of children who get lost every year usually have a similar story. These incidents also focus about the need of educating the primary school children about the vulnerabilities that they could face and incidents of crisis that are common. The children need to be given knowledge and skill to handle them in a situation of crisis and a Life Skills Education (LSE) intervention in school should be strongly advocated through training of teachers (Bhadra 2011). Child protection is an issue for all, parents, teachers, neighbors and cannot be counted upon with only law and agencies.

Providing safe shelter to the lost and abandoned children is a crucial need to ensure a circle of child protection for the vulnerable children. There is a serious dearth of this facility as per the need of the hour. Equally, a safety standards and close monitoring of these homes need to be ensured as many of these sheltered children come with multiple traumatic experiences and needs care, protection to rejuvenate their life to normalcy.

Conclusion

Child protection issues need to be addressed through an integrated approach whereby, a consolidated package of services and facilities should be collectively mobilized to provide a child his or her Constitutional Right for a safe and healthy childhood. The protective legislation and Constitutional rights need to be brought alive if the intention is to ensure a healthy and happy childhood in India. In a scenario where child protection mechanisms are in place, all it needs is to interlink its various arms such as Juvenile Justice Board, Child Welfare Committee, Childline and the police for an effective conversion of policy into action. Unless the missing institutional and functional linkages are addressed, issues of Child Protection would remain as evasive as we find them now. Similarly, the child protection issues need a considerable academic focus and continuous research, data assessing and monitoring to understand the changes in the long term. What happened to the children send back to an impoverished family, or how is the future secured for the children in the government home, how the child labor can become a professional in future and such issues need a strong academic exercise from the university departments of Social work, Psychology, Sociology, and allied disciplines.

Its only when the entire mechanism works in unison that we can achieve the mission of providing protection to each child. There is ample evidence to support that government programs implemented with political will have a higher chance to succeed. Therefore, for an overall success, a strong political leadership needs to emerge to provide a direction and monitor the implementation of child protection norms particularly at the grassroots.

Note: The Childline India Foundation has been set up by the Ministry of Women and Child Development, GOI, to facilitate child protection services through 24 h phone service. The Childline India Foundation is an organization that provides the Childline services in India. The two terms, The Childline India Foundation and Childline have therefore been used interchangeably in the Paper.

Acknowledgments I express my sincere gratitude to Dr. Subhasis Bhadra for his invaluable inputs in preparing the chapter.

References

Bhadra, S. (2011). *Life skills for children and adolescents: Teacher trainees' perception*. Saarbucken: LAP LAMBERT Academic Publishing.

Child Helpline International. (2014). *The CHI concept was the initiative of child helplines themselves*. Retrieved March 26, 2015, from http://www.childhelplineinternational.org/about/our-story/.

Childline India. (2015). *Childline 1098 services*. Retrieved March 25, 2015, from http://www.childlineindia.org.in/1098/1098.htm.

Drèze, J., Khera, R., & Narayanan, S. (2007). The state of India's children. *Indian Journal of Human Development*, 32–46.

FindLaw. *Safe heaven law.* Retrieved March 23, 2015, from http://family.findlaw.com/adoption/safe-haven-laws.html.

Government of India, Ministry of Home Affairs. (2011). *Primary census data highlights—India.* Retrieved March 13, 2015, from http://www.censusindia.gov.in/2011census/PCA/PCA_Highlights/pca_highlights_india.html.

Government of India, Ministry of Home Affairs. (2013, December). National crime records bureau*: Crime against children.* Retrieved March 27, 2015, from http://ncrb.gov.in/CD-CII2013/Chapters/6-Crime%20against%20Children.pdf.

Government of India, Ministry of women and Child Development. (2003, January 9). *The integrated child protection scheme (ICPS).* Retrieved March 29, 2015, from http://www.childlineindia.org.in/cp-cr-downloads/icps.pdf.

INDUS. (2007). *Child labour facts and figures: An analysis of census 200* . Report on Child labour. Geneva: International Labour Organization.

Jamshed, M., & Subhasis, B. (2015). *The condition of the child labour that contribute for development of delinquent behaviour.* Unpublished MSW dissertation, Greater Noida: Department of Social Work, Gautam Buddha University.

Mohanty, R.I. (2012, May 25). *Trash bin babies: India's female infanticide crisis.* Retrieved March 2015, from http://www.theatlantic.com/international/archive/2012/05/trash-bin-babies-indias-female-infanticide-crisis/257672/.

O'Kane, C., Claudia, M., Raluca, V. S., & Evelyn, W. (2006). *Child rights situation analysis.* Rights-based situational analysis of children without parental care and at risk of losing their parental care: Global literature scan. Brigittenauer Lände: SOS-Kinderdorf International.

Shah, S. (2012). *India's missing children, by the numbers.* (2012, October 16). Retrieved March 21, 2015, from http://blogs.wsj.com/indiarealtime/2012/10/16/indias-missing-children-by-the-numbers/.

Unicef. (2006). *Child protection information sheet.* The Child Protection Section, New York: Unicef.

Unicef. (2012). *Child trafficking.* Retrieved March 29, 2015, from http://www.unicef.org.au/About-Us/What-We-Do/Protection/Child-Trafficking.aspx.

Printed by Printforce, the Netherlands